# The Collected Papers of James Meade

# The Collected Papers of James Meade

Volume I
*Employment and Inflation*

Volume II
*Value, Distribution and Growth*

Volume III
*International Economics*

Volume IV
*The Cabinet Office Diary 1944–46*

# The Collected Papers of James Meade

# Volume II

*Value, Distribution and Growth*
Edited by Susan Howson

Routledge
Taylor & Francis Group

LONDON AND NEW YORK

First published by Unwin Hyman Ltd in 1988

This edition published by Routledge in 2005
2 Park Square, Milton Park, Abingdon, Oxon, OX14 4RN

Simultaneously published in the USA and Canada
by Routledge
711 Third Avenue, New York, NY 10017

*Routledge is an imprint of the Taylor & Francis Group, an informa business*

Typeset in Times by Keystroke, Jacaranda Lodge, Wolverhampton

*British Library Cataloguing in Publication Data*
A catalogue record for this book is available from the British Library

ISBN 0–415–35049–2 (set)
ISBN 0–415–35051–4 (volume II)

**Publisher's Note**
The publisher has gone to great lengths to ensure the quality of this reprint,
but points out that some imperfections in the original may be apparent.

# The Collected Papers of James Meade

*Volume II:* Value, Distribution and Growth

*Edited by*

SUSAN HOWSON

*University of Toronto*

London
UNWIN HYMAN
Boston    Sydney    Wellington

# Contents

# Editorial Preface

This is the second of three volumes of an edition of Professor Meade's papers. As with the first volume (*The Collected Papers of James Meade, Vol. I: Employment and Inflation*, 1988), it includes both previously published papers and hitherto unpublished memoranda written during Meade's period of government service, 1940–7, in the Economic Section of the Cabinet Offices, of which he was Director 1946–7.

Over five decades Professor Meade has written and published on a wide range of topics in economic theory and policy. The selection of his published and unpublished papers included in this edition has been organised in five broad categories corresponding to the five parts of his *An Introduction to Economic Analysis and Policy* (Oxford: Clarendon Press, 1936; second edition, London: Oxford University Press, 1937). These he called Unemployment; Competition and Monopoly; The Distribution of Income; The Supply of the Primary Factors of Production; and International Problems. Volumes I and III are devoted to the first and last, respectively, of these categories. This volume contains items in the second, third and fourth groups, which I have called here Price Theory and Policy; Distribution; and Growth and Development.

There are fewer previously unpublished memoranda than in Volume I since the major part of Meade's work in the Economic Section was concerned with employment policy and the post-war international economic order. This volume does, however, include not only official memoranda written solely by Meade but also an example of collaborative work, on 'The Socialisation of Industries', undertaken under Meade's directorship. (Meade formally took over from the previous Director, Lionel Robbins, in January 1946 but he had been appointed in November 1944 to succeed Robbins at the end of the Second World War.) Of the remaining papers in this volume the first was written while Meade was Fellow and Lecturer in Economics at Hertford College, Oxford (1931–7), the rest after he returned to academic life in 1947, first as Professor of Commerce with special reference to International Trade at the London School of Economics (1947–57), subsequently Professor of Political Economy in the University of Cambridge (1957–67). (For further biographical details the reader is referred to Meade's own account of his life published in Volume I, pp. 1–5.)

Inevitably some papers cover more than one of the five categories. In this volume the Economic Section paper, 'The Post-war Treatment of the National Debt', discusses several policy issues besides questions of distribution. It is included here (in Part II) because its centrepiece is an analysis of the case for a capital levy after the war.

The published papers selected for this edition are generally major articles in major academic journals, and essays, lectures or pamphlets presenting Meade's policy proposals or analyses of their effects. The unpublished papers have been selected mainly from the Meade Papers in the British Library of Political and Economic Science, which include copies of forty-five papers that he chose to take with him when he left government service in 1947, supplemented by research in the Public Record Ofice and other archives. The origins and reasons for inclusion of the individual documents are indicated in the introductory notes, which precede each paper and include information on the sources of the papers. Apart from the correction of minor inconsistencies of spelling and obvious typographical errors and the completion or correction of bibliographical references, the papers appear as they were originally typed or printed.

I am grateful to the Controller of Her Majesty's Stationery Office for permission to reproduce Crown Copyright material, to the editors of the *Review of Economic Studies*, *The Economic Journal*, *Economica*, *Oxford Economic Papers* and the *Political Quarterly* for permission to reprint articles from their journals, to the British Academy and Manchester University Press for permission to republish lectures given by Meade, and to the Trustees of the Public Policy Centre for permission to reproduce his pamphlet on 'Different Forms of Share Economy'. I also wish to thank Professor Meade, Dr Angela Raspin of the British Library of Political and Economic Science, Dr Stephen Bird of the Labour Party, the Warden and Fellows of Nuffield College, Oxford, and the Humanities and Social Sciences Committee of the Research Board of the University of Toronto for their generous assistance with the research for this volume.

Susan Howson
*March 1987*

PART I

# Price Theory and Policy

# 1

# Notes on the Elasticity of Substitution

*The first two issues of the* Review of Economic Studies *contained a series of notes on the concept of the elasticity of substitution by Paul Sweezy, Abba Lerner, Richard Kahn, J. R. Hicks, Lorie Tarshis and James Meade. Meade's two contributions, reprinted below, appeared as notes III and IV in the second issue* (Review of Economic Studies, *vol. 1, 1933–34, pp. 149–153).*

## The Elasticity of Substitution and the Incidence of an Imperial Inhabited House Duty

In discussing the theory of a tax on Inhabited Houses and its incidence upon the occupier, the building owner and the ground-landlord, it has always been clear that one of the important factors which must be considered is the degree to which land can be substituted for building in providing the commodity 'house-room'. It may be of interest to readers of the *Review of Economic Studies* to see how the idea of elasticity of substitution, which we owe to Mr Hicks and Mrs Robinson, and which was discussed in the last number of the Review, can help one in solving this problem.

If we suppose that the demand for land and buildings is a case of pure joint demand, or in other words that land and building must be used in a given fixed proportion to provide 'house-room', so that the elasticity of substitution of these two factors is zero, we may make certain qualitative statements about the incidence of the tax. The incidence will fall the more on the consumer, the less is the elasticity of demand and the greater the elasticity of supply of 'house-room', i.e. the greater the elasticities of supply of buildings and of land. The elasticity of supply of buildings in the long run depends upon the technical conditions in the building industry, and the elasticity of supply of land depends upon the degree to which it is profitable to transfer land to uses other than house building, when its rent in this occupation falls. The incidence of that part of the tax which falls on the producers will fall the more on builders and the less on landlords the less elastic is the supply of buildings and the more elastic is the supply of land. So far the propositions are simple and familiar. There are, however, certain interesting limiting cases. If the elasticity of supply of one of the factors, e.g. of land, is zero, the tax will not fall at all on builders or occupiers, but entirely on landlords; for the same amount of land is always forthcoming and therefore, since the proportions in which land and buildings are used is fixed, the same amount of buildings and of house-room will be forthcoming, so that the supply price of buildings and the demand price of house-room will remain unchanged. If the elasticity of supply of land and of building is the same, the proportionate fall in the cost price of buildings and of land will be the same, and so the incidence of the tax on producers will fall equally upon builders and landlords;[1] and, moreover, the elasticity of supply of house-room will be equal to the elasticity of supply of either of the factors. If the elasticity of supply of one of the factors (e.g. of buildings) is infinite, no part of the incidence will be upon builders; the incidence will fall upon the occupiers and the landlords. It will fall rather upon the occupiers than upon landlords the less the elasticity of demand of occupiers, the greater the elasticity of supply of land and the smaller the proportion of the total costs of house-room which goes to landlords, since the smaller is this proportion the greater is the elasticity of supply of house-room in the case we are examining.

But suppose that there is some elasticity of substitution between buildings and land in the provision of house-room. What difference does this make to the limiting cases examined above? If the elasticity of supply of building is equal to the elasticity of supply of land, this elasticity of substitution has no effect upon the result. For if, when the demand for house-room falls, the supply of building and of land decrease in the same proportion, their prices will fall by an equal proportion; and since their prices fall in this way there will be no incentive to change the proportion of buildings to land in the provision of house-room, whatever may be their elasticity of substitution. If, however, the elasticities of supply of the two factors are different, the greater the elasticity of substitution, the less will be the disadvantage to the factor in inelastic supply and the advantage to the factor in elastic supply, since the first factor, whose price falls more, will be substituted for the second factor, whose price falls less. Thus the greater the elasticity of substitution, the less in fact will the price of factors in inelastic supply fall and the more will the price of factors in elastic supply fall. If we now take the limiting case in which land is in perfectly inelastic supply, there will be some incidence on builders, since as the price of land falls, land will be substituted for buildings.

These conclusions can be accurately stated in quantitative terms:

Let $L$ = amount of land,     $l$ = price of land,

$$\lambda = \text{elasticity of supply of land} = \frac{l}{L} \cdot \frac{dL}{dl}$$

---

[1] In this case the fall in the total reward of land will be greater than the fall in the total reward of buildings, if the proportion of total costs which goes to the payment of land is > ½. But throughout this note I measure the incidence as between builders and landlords by the ratio between the proportionate fall in the price of buildings and the proportionate fall in the price of land.

$B$ = amount of building, $b$ = price of building,

$$\beta = \text{elasticity of supply of building} = \frac{b}{B} \cdot \frac{dB}{db}$$

Let $\sigma$ = elasticity of substitution.

If we assume perfect competition and the absence of economies of large-scale production then the value of the marginal product of a factor must be equal to its price:

$$\therefore \sigma = \frac{l/b}{L/B} \cdot \frac{d(L/B)}{d(l/b)} = \frac{\dfrac{dL}{L} - \dfrac{dB}{B}}{\dfrac{dl}{l} - \dfrac{db}{b}}$$

$$= \frac{\lambda \dfrac{dl}{l} - \beta \dfrac{db}{b}}{\dfrac{dl}{l} - \dfrac{db}{b}}$$

$$\therefore \frac{b}{l} \cdot \frac{dl}{db} = \frac{\beta - \sigma}{\lambda - \sigma}$$

$\sigma$ is always negative, i.e. an increase in the proportion between $L$ and $B$ is always accompanied by a decrease in the proportion between the marginal products of $L$ and $B$. It follows, therefore, that $(\beta - \sigma)/(\lambda - \sigma)$ is always $+ve$. $(b/l).(dl/db)$ is the ratio between the proportionate fall in the price of land and the proportionate fall in the price of buildings. If $\sigma = 0$, i.e. if we are dealing with a case of pure joint demand, it follows that the incidence of the tax as between the factors of production is in inverse proportion to their elasticities of supply. If $\beta = 0$ and $\sigma = 0$, there is no incidence on land. If $-\sigma$ is $> 0$, then the ratio between the fall in the price of land and the fall in the price of buildings will be nearer to unity than is the inverse ratio between their elasticities of supply, and as $\sigma$ becomes numerically larger the advantage of being in elastic supply and the disadvantage of being in inelastic supply is seen to diminish.

We have seen, then, that $(\beta - \sigma)/(\lambda - \sigma)$ measures the incidence as between landowners and builders of that part of the tax which falls on the producers. We have now to determine the incidence of the tax as between occupiers and producers. It is a familiar proposition that if a tax is put on a commodity, the ratio between proportionate rise in price to the consumer and the proportionate fall in price to the producer equals $\eta/e$ where $\eta$ is the elasticity of supply and $e$ the elasticity of demand. We have, therefore, to express $\eta$ in terms of $\lambda$, $\beta$ and $\sigma$.

Let $x$ = output of house-room = $F(L, B)$,

$c$ = price of $x$ to the producer,

and $q = \dfrac{lL}{bB} = \dfrac{\text{income of landlords}}{\text{income of builders}}$

$$\text{Now } dx = \frac{\partial x}{\partial B} \cdot dB + \frac{\partial x}{\partial L} dL \qquad\qquad (i)$$

and since we are assuming that, if $L$ and $B$ increase in the same proportion, $x$ will also increase in this proportion:

$$x = \frac{\partial x}{\partial B} B + \frac{\partial x}{\partial L} L . \qquad\qquad (ii)$$

In competition the price of a factor is equal to its marginal product $\times$ the price of the product, and therefore

$$\frac{\partial x}{\partial B} c = b, \text{ and } \frac{\partial x}{\partial L} c = l . \qquad\qquad (iii)$$

From (i) and (iii) it follows that $cdx = bdB + ldL$ .
From (ii) and (iii) it follows that $cx = bB + lL$ .
This equation is true for all values of $x$, and it follows that

$$cdx + xdc = bdB + Bdb + ldL + Ldl$$

so that $xdc = Bdb + Ldl$ .

$$\text{But } \eta = \frac{cdx}{xdc} = \frac{bdB + ldL}{Bdb + Ldl} = \frac{\beta Bdb + \lambda Ldl}{Bdb + Ldl} \cdot \frac{Bdb}{Ldl} = \frac{\eta - \beta}{\lambda - \eta} .$$

$$\text{But } q = \frac{lL}{Bb} \text{ and } \frac{ldb}{bdl} = \frac{\lambda - \sigma}{\beta - \sigma}$$

$$\therefore \frac{\lambda - \sigma}{\beta - \sigma} = q \frac{\lambda - \eta,}{\eta - \beta,} \text{ or } \eta = \frac{q\lambda(\beta - \sigma) + \beta(\lambda - \sigma)}{q(\beta - \sigma) + \lambda - \sigma} .$$

From these equations we may draw certain conclusions:[2]

(1) If $\sigma = 0$, i.e. if we are dealing with a case of joint demand,

$$\eta = \beta\lambda \, \frac{1 + q}{\lambda + q\beta}$$

---

[2] I have not concerned myself in this note with the possibility of $\beta$ or $\lambda$ being negative, but Mr Kahn, who had arrived independently at the same formula for $\eta$ as myself, had pointed out to me the strange result that if $\beta = \sigma$, $\eta = \beta = \sigma$ .

(2) If $\lambda = \beta$, $\eta = \lambda = \beta$.

(3) Since $\dfrac{\lambda - \sigma}{\beta - \sigma}$ is +ve and equal to $q\,\dfrac{\lambda - \eta}{\eta - \beta}$ it follows that if $\lambda \neq \beta$,

  $\eta$ lies between $\lambda$ and $\beta$.

(4) If $\sigma = -\infty$, $\eta = \dfrac{q\lambda + \beta}{1 + q}$.

(5) If $\lambda = 0$, $\eta = \dfrac{\beta\sigma}{\sigma - q\,(\beta - \sigma)}$.

(6) If $\beta = \infty$, $\eta = \lambda + \dfrac{\lambda - \sigma}{q}$. [3]

Finally the incidence of the tax as between occupiers and producers $=$

$$\frac{1}{e} \cdot \frac{q\lambda(\beta - \sigma) + \beta\,(\lambda - \sigma)}{q\,(\beta - \sigma) + \lambda - \sigma}.$$

## The Elasticity of Substitution and the Elasticity of Demand for One Factor of Production

In this note I wish to examine the effect of a reduction in price of one factor of production upon the demand for that factor, and also upon the demand for a second factor with which it is used. As in the previous note, it is assumed that there are only two factors of production, that there is perfect competition, and that there are no economies of large-scale production. The notation is the same as that employed in the previous note.

$$\sigma = \frac{\dfrac{dL}{L} - \dfrac{dB}{B}}{\dfrac{dl}{l} - \dfrac{db}{b}}.$$

$e$, the elasticity of demand for the product, $= \dfrac{ldL + bdB}{Ldl + Bdb}$.

$$q = \frac{lL}{bB}$$

$\lambda$ = the elasticity of supply of $L$
$\beta$ = the elasticity of demand for $B$.

[3] This is the same as Mrs Robinson's formula on page 123, footnote 2, of her *Economics of Imperfect Competition* (London: Macmillan, 1933)

From the equation for $\sigma$ we have

$$\frac{dl}{l} \cdot \frac{b}{db} = \frac{\sigma - \beta}{\sigma - \lambda} \qquad\qquad \text{(i)}$$

and from the equation for $e$

$$-\frac{dl}{l} \cdot \frac{b}{db} = \frac{1}{q} \cdot \frac{\beta - e}{e - \lambda}. \qquad\qquad \text{(ii)}$$

It follows that $\dfrac{\sigma - \beta}{\sigma - \lambda} = \dfrac{1}{q} \cdot \dfrac{\beta - e}{e - \lambda}$ or $\beta = \dfrac{\sigma q(e - \lambda) + e(\sigma - \lambda)}{q(e - \lambda) + \sigma - \lambda}$.[4]

If $L$ is in perfectly elastic supply to the industry in question, $\lambda = \infty$, and in this case $\beta = (\sigma q + e)/(1 + q)$.

If we eliminate $\beta$ from equations (i) and (ii) we have

$$\frac{dl}{l} \cdot \frac{b}{db} = \frac{\sigma - e}{q(e - \lambda) + \sigma - \lambda}$$

and multiplying both sides by $\lambda$ it follows that

$$\frac{b}{L} \cdot \frac{dL}{db} = \frac{\lambda(\sigma - e)}{q(e - \lambda) + \sigma - \lambda}.$$

This expression shows the elasticity of demand for $L$ in terms of the price of $B$. Since $\sigma$ and $e$ are negative and $\lambda$ positive, it follows that this expression is $+ve$, i.e. a fall in the price of $B$ will decrease the demand for $L$, if $e$ is numerically $< \sigma$, while it is $-ve$ if $e$ is numerically $> \sigma$.[5] If $L$ is in perfectly elastic supply, this expression becomes $(e - \sigma)/(1 + q)$, so that if half the income goes to $L$ and half to $B$ the elasticity of demand for $L$ in terms of the price of $B$ would be equal to half the difference between the elasticity of demand for the product and the elasticity of substitution.

---

[4] This is the same as Dr Hicks' formula for $\lambda$ on page 244 of his *Theory of Wages* (London: Macmillan, 1932). The only advantage I would claim for my proof is that it is simpler for the inexpert mathematician.

[5] This is the result which Mrs Robinson proves by a different method, on page 258, footnote 2, of her *Economics of Imperfect Competition*.

# 2

# Government Intervention in the Post-War Economy

*The Economic Section of the War Cabinet Offices commenced work on post-war employment policy early in 1941 (see Volume I, pp. 171–183). Later that year Meade suggested that this should be supplemented by consideration of other post-war economic problems that might require state intervention. The paper reprinted below was written in April 1942; Meade's later work in the Economic Section on the issues of 'socialisation' raised there is reflected in the three following papers. (Public Record Office T230/34 and 14; Meade Papers 3/2).*

## Government Intervention in the Post-war Economy

1   This note is confined to the problem of government intervention in the post-war 'normal' peace-time economy, and it neglects entirely the special reasons, which will no doubt exist during a longish period of transition from war to peace, for the continuation, adaptation or institution of particular governmental controls. The problems raised by the special conditions of the transition will, no doubt, be the most urgent immediately after the war. Nevertheless it seems worth while starting to think about the longer-term problems; for it is difficult to consider the problems of transition at all reasonably, unless one knows whither one wishes to go as well as whence one has come.

2   It has always seemed clear to me that there are four main economic objectives, the attainment of which requires a greater or less degree of public control over the economic system:

(i)   The attainment of a higher and more stable level of employment and of general trade activity.

(ii)  The attainment of a more equitable distribution of income than would otherwise be achieved.

(iii) The attainment of a closer correspondence between private and social interests in particular lines of production. (This objective is concerned primarily with the control of monopolies or of mono-polistic conditions, which constitute the main cause of divergence between private and social interests in various branches of economic activity. There are, however, a number of other such divergences (e.g. smoke pollution) which are not necessarily associated with monopolistic conditions.

(iv)   The attainment of a greater degree of international economic harmony and efficiency in conditions in which national states intervene in economic affairs for the above reasons (i), (ii) and (iii).

3   The following paragraphs attempt to outline very briefly the main forms of state intervention which appear to me to be desirable in the post-war world (in the long run and after the immediate period of transition) for the attainment of the above objectives. These paragraphs are written on the assumptions (i) that there is general agreement that we shall need some controls in the post-war world to achieve these objectives and to eliminate the corresponding economic evils from which we suffered in the pre-war world, but (ii) that there is also agreement on the need to maintain the maximum amount of individual liberty of action, that is compatible with a reasonably just and efficient economic system. In my own view this does not necessarily mean that state intervention should be reduced to the barest minimum, but rather that the *forms* of intervention should be such as to achieve their objectives with the minimum interference with the freedom of individual choice as to what each individual should purchase and what work he or she should do. (For example, a socialised or state-controlled industrial system should rely rather upon a pricing system to indicate how much of each product should be produced and upon the offer of appropriate relative wages to attract more or less labour to particular occupations than upon the fixation of fixed quotas of production and upon the conscription of labour).

## 4   The Prevention of Unemployment

As we have already given considerable attention to this problem I will merely enumerate the main forms of control which we are, I think, agreed in believing to be appropriate:

(i)    Control over the total supply of money and the rate of interest.
(ii)   The timing of planning of public works and of all forms of investment which are already under, or can readily be brought under, the control of the public authorities. (This consideration provides one argument in favour of the control of, or socialisation of, industries which make large demands for more capital equipment).
(iii)  The planning and timing of taxation and of state expenditure in such a way as to maintain and stabilise the general money demand for goods and services. (I personally would add here the need for a direct state regulation of the spendable incomes of consumers).
(iv)   The possibility that it will be necessary to maintain some form of control over prices and wage-rates in order to prevent a high level of money demand for goods and for labour in peace-time from leading to a vicious spiral of inflation.

## 5   Regulation of International Economic Relations

We have also given a good deal of attention to this problem. It is clear that
the main controls in this field ought to be international or supra-national
rather than national, if international economic relations are to be truly
harmonious and efficient. On the assumption that we can hope for the
necessary degree of international co-operation the following seem to me
to be the main international controls or regulations at which we should
aim:

(i)    An international monetary arrangement which (a) would measure
       the lack of balance in each country's payments vis-à-vis the rest of
       the world and (b) would put as much of the strain of adjustment
       upon the countries with favourable, as upon those with unfavour-
       able, balances.
(ii)   An international arrangement for the capital development of
       undeveloped regions, directly or indirectly financed from the
       favourable balances of payments of those countries with favourable
       balances.
(iii)  An international commission to co-ordinate the internal anti-
       depression policies of the various national states.
(iv)   An international system of commodity controls, acting for the
       stabilisation of their prices and for the gradual adjustment of such
       prices to an 'equilibrium' level rather than through the quantitative
       control of production, exports or imports.
(v)    An international commercial charter outlining which forms of
       behaviour were permissible and which were not permissible in
       national commercial policies. (Such a charter would presumably be
       based upon two principles: (i) permitting more protective devices
       to countries with unfavourable balances than to those with favour-
       able balances and (ii) completely outlawing certain of the worst
       forms of protective or discriminatory devices).


## 6   The Attainment of a more Equitable Distribution of Income

Although we have not yet given much time to any direct discussion of this
issue, I imagine that we should not find it difficult to agree upon the main
forms of intervention that are appropriate for this purpose:

(i)    Progressive and high direct taxation on incomes and property
       (including – in my opinion – a heavy and highly progressive capital
       levy).
(ii)   Development of the social services (in particular of family allow-
       ances, of a free and equal educational system and of a free and
       extensive national medical service).

The three greatest causes at present of inequities in the distribution of
incomes are probably (a) inequalities of educational opportunity, (b)
inequalities of family needs, and – greatest of all – (c) inequalities in the

ownership of property. (a) and (b) should be removed by appropriate extensions of the social services. (c) should be removed by high and progressive taxation on income and – in particular – on property, the proceeds of which might be used in part for the redemption of national debt, for the purchase of property which it was desired on other grounds to socialise, or for investment in other forms of property.

7   There is one form of control which should *not* be used (except very sparingly) for the equalisation of the distribution of incomes. Any attempt to obtain a really significant redistribution of incomes through pushing up money wage-rates would lead to very grave difficulties and dangers. In the first place, it would be likely very seriously to prejudice the success of policies for the prevention of unemployment. For rapidly rising wage-rates in the absence of simultaneous price increases will remove the incentive for giving employment; and if prices rise simultaneously, the workers are no better off but there is a danger of an inflationary spiral. Secondly, a piecemeal pushing up of wages in particular industries is liable to restrict the opportunities for employment in the best-paid occupations and may thus react very unfairly on labour employed in other occupations or industries. For these reasons it is most desirable that any interventions for the redistribution of income should take forms (e.g. progressive taxation, changes in the ownership of property, extension of social services, etc.) which do not interfere with the use of wage-rates as the economic regulating price of labour.

8   This does not, however, imply that there should be no state regulation of wages at all. The imposition of *minimum* wage-rates may be desirable in many cases to prevent 'exploitation' of labour by monopolistic employers. The imposition of *maximum* wage-rates may be desirable to prevent monopolistic wage-earners in certain industries from preventing the proper development of employment in those industries and to prevent a high general demand for labour from leading to the danger of an inflationary vicious spiral.

## 9   *The Removal of Divergences between Private and Social Interests in Particular Lines of Production*

It is this group of problems which raises in its most direct form the question of the relations between the state and industry. For this purpose it appears to me to be convenient to distinguish between three main forms of economic or industrial organisation – (i) that of atomistic competition, (ii) that of socialised or socially controlled industry, and (iii) that of syndicalist or corporative organisation. I think that we may agree that pure atomistic competition – *where it is possible* – and socialisation or social control of industry both have much to recommend them, while the syndicalist or 'self-governing' industry is to be avoided like the poison.

10   A 'self-governing' industry or occupational organisation is almost bound to indulge in anti-social activities of a restrictive character; for the

sectional interest is invariably to be found in the restriction of output and the raising of prices against the rest of the community. Such restrictive action by private monopolies leads to three great evils: it means that a smaller proportion of the community's resources are applied to the monopolised articles than is necessary to achieve the best satisfaction of consumers' demands; it may, if it becomes widespread, severely intensify the problem of expanding general production in order to reduce unemployment; and it is very likely to lead to a less desirable distribution of the national income (both as between profits on the one hand and wages on the other and also as between the well-organised and ill-organised workers). Such restrictive monopolies were without doubt growing at an alarming rate before the war, often with the expressed or tacit encouragement of the state. Many war-time developments (e.g. the fact that the war-time controls are in many cases run by the interests affected) threaten to increase these dangers unless these private monopolies are either broken up or else are turned into truly social controls in which those whose interests are directly affected have no power whatsoever. The success of our post-war economic reconstruction depends upon the removal of these particular restrictive forces.

11   In many cases it may be economically possible to restore atomistic competition; and I personally would go so far as to say that this is economically the best policy to pursue *wherever it is technically possible to restore market conditions approximating to those of perfect competition.* For we may agree that this would effectively remove the dangerous restrictive forces and the possibility of the misuse of the powers of sectional interests. I can see only two serious economic arguments against this course. (i) It may be desirable to socialise an industry which, although it would function properly in competitive conditions, has such importance from the point of view of its demand for capital equipment that its control may be necessary for the control of the total volume of investment activity. But such cases are probably in fact rare, and it may moreover be possible to control to some extent the investment activity of an otherwise freely competitive industry. (ii) It may in the end be desirable that the state should own property, even if it is invested in industries which are technically capable of free competition, in order that the state may obtain their income from property.[1] But we are so far away from this position (which would be reached only after the state had not only redeemed the whole of the national debt but had also bought up all property in industries which were not technically capable of perfect competition) that we need not at this moment face the issue. It is, however, perhaps worth while observing that there would be nothing to prevent the state from owning property and hiring it out to the highest bidder among competitive users.

[1] I cannot avoid this opportunity of letting my bee out of my bonnet by declaring that, in my opinion, in a community which was not over-populated the state would *have* to own *all* property in order to make the pricing system work properly (cf. Part IV of my *An Introduction to Economic Analysis and Policy,* Oxford: Clarendon Press, 1936).

12   It is important to realise that the restoration of competitive conditions does not necessarily mean a purely negative action on the part of the state in removing those conditions which favour monopoly. Undoubtedly much of this would be involved. But the encouragement of competitive conditions involves also much action of a positive character. For example, state measures which improve the mobility of labour between regions and between occupations will make conditions approximate more closely to those of perfect competition in the hire of labour. Any action which improved the knowledge of consumers about the real qualities of alternative products would have the same effect.

13   But there are a large number of industries in which (a) there is no close substitute for the product and (b) the efficient scale of operations of a single firm is so large in relation to the market demand that there is not room for a large number of competitors in each market. In these cases there are *bound* to be monopolies or monopolistic conditions.[2] In really important cases of this kind I personally would favour complete social ownership and control. Over a much wider field there is probably a case for the fixation of maximum (not, as is so usual, minimum) product prices; and it seems to me that the suggestion of a general price commission with the power to fix maximum prices is a very fruitful one for a community in which we hope that a high level of demand will be followed by increased production and employment rather than by higher prices. But in any case, in order to preserve the liberal nature of the economy, it is desirable to operate on prices rather than on quantities, and to use socialisation or social control to make the price system work rather than to plan for the production and distribution of rigidly pre-determined quantities of various products.

14   Apart from the cases of monopolistic conditions, there are undoubtedly certain cases in the most competitive conditions in which private and social interests may diverge. For example, the location of a factory may have certain disadvantageous effects upon the surrounding countryside, the costs of which are not automatically borne by the owner of the factory. In such cases we should all no doubt agree that certain forms of state intervention were desirable.

15   *Summary of paragraphs 9–14*

  (i) The economic powers of trade associations, occupational bodies and of all private monopolies should be restricted as much as possible.
 (ii) As free competition as possible should be restored in those industries in which an approximation to perfect competition is technically possible.

---

[2] I must let my bee buzz once more by saying that, in my opinion, unless the community is over-populated these conditions are bound to exist over the greater part of the field of industry (cf. Part IV of my *Economic Analysis and Policy*).

(iii) The encouragement of such competitive conditions involves a certain amount of positive state action (such as the organisation of a mobile labour market).

(iv) It should, however, be recognised that in a large number of cases conditions approximating to those of perfect competition are technically impossible. In these cases social ownership and management or social control are desirable in order to prevent restrictive action and to make the price system operate properly.

(v) Controls should operate on prices rather than on quantities and purely restrictive controls (e.g. maximum production quotas, restrictions on new investment, the fixation of minimum commodity prices) should be avoided.

# 3

# Price and Output Policy of State Enterprise: A Symposium

*By J. E. Meade and J. M. Fleming, from* The Economic Journal, *vol. 54 (December 1944), pp. 321–339. This famous set of articles originated as Economic Section discussion papers in January 1944, Meade's original memorandum being prompted by Lionel Robbins' note of dissent on 'Restrictive Developments in Industry' to the January 1944 report of the official Steering Committee on Post-war Employment. According to Meade it was Keynes' idea to publish the papers in the* Economic Journal, *of which he was editor (Public Record Office T230/16 and CAB87/7; Meade Diary, 16 December 1944).*

I

1   In order to achieve that use of the community's resources which is both the most efficient and the most in conformity with consumers' wishes, they should be distributed among the various uses in such a way that the value of the marginal product of a given factor is the same in every occupation. In so far as the reward paid to any factor is the same in every occupation, this rule means that the value of the marginal product of a factor should, in every occupation, bear a constant ratio to the price of that factor.

2   The principle that the value of the marginal product of a factor should be equal to the price of that factor is a special case of this general rule; but it is a special case which, for labour at least, has a great deal to commend it. If labour is paid everywhere a reward which is not merely in a constant ratio to, but actually equal to, the value of its marginal product, two additional advantages may be achieved:

(i)   A larger proportion of the total national income will accrue to labour than if labour is paid everywhere a wage lower, by a constant proportion, than the value of its marginal product. This will probably serve to improve the distribution of the national income.

(ii)   Labour has the choice between earning more income or enjoying more leisure. The more nearly the reward for an additional unit of work approaches the value of the marginal product of labour, the greater – it may be presumed – will be the welfare achieved by means of a proper balance between work and leisure.[1]

3   How can the principle of equality between the value of the marginal product of a factor and its price best be achieved? Where competition is technically possible, by vigorous and unimpeded competition.[2] Much might be done by the state to promote such competition by removing legal enactments which positively promote monopolisation, by reform of the patent law and of company law with this end in view, and by the outlawing of certain forms of business practices which are primarily designed to restrict competition. But there are many cases where monopoly is inevitable. When the scale of production necessary to take advantage of technical economies is large in relation to the market to be served, 'trust-busting' must either be ineffective or lead to technical inefficiency. The outstanding examples of such cases are, of course, the public utilities. Where a community needs only one gasworks, or electricity station, or railway network, monopoly must obviously exist. In these cases, socialisation in one form or another, of the industries concerned, is the only radical cure to ensure that they are run in such a way as to equate marginal costs to prices of the product produced (or the prices of the factors of production to the value of their marginal products) rather than to make a profit.

## II

4   Recent work by economists[3] has served to make it clear on what principles the output and use factors by the managers of a socialised plant should be determined:

(i)   Output should be increased so long as the price of the product exceeds the marginal (not the average) cost of production.

(ii)   One factor should be substituted for another so long as that quantity of the factor taken on, which is required to replace the production of a unit of the factor released, has a lower market price than the unit price of the factor released.

(iii)   Rules (i) and (ii) can sometimes most conveniently be stated as above, and sometimes most conveniently combined into the single rule that each factor should be taken on in greater quantity so long as the value of its marginal product is greater than its market price.

(iv)   Thus, as a practical set of rules for the operation of a particular firm, it may be best often to state (*a*) that more should be produced with a given plant and equipment, so long as the price of the

[1] See Chapter II of Part IV of the American edition (edited by C. J. Hitch) of my *An Introduction to Economic Analysis and Policy* (New York: Oxford University Press, 1938).

[2] With, of course, certain measures of state regulation to deal with divergences between private and social net products of a kind that are compatible with perfect competition.

[3] See, in particular, Oskar Lange, *On the Economic Theory of Socialism* (Minneapolis: University of Minnesota Press, 1938).

product exceeds the marginal prime cost of production, and (b) that a greater amount of fixed capital should be invested so long as the annual interest on the capital plus the annual cost of repair, depreciation, etc., is less than the price of any additional output expected from the investment plus the price of any existing prime factors which it is expected to save, minus the price of any additional prime factors which it is expected to take on as a result of the investment.

(iv)  It is taken for granted, of course, that maximum efficiency will be an objective throughout, in the sense that the maximum amount technically possible will always be produced from any given collection of factors of production.

5   The fundamental difficulty of supervising state production is to determine whether managers of state plants are behaving efficiently, (a) technically in getting the maximum output from any given collection of factors of production, and (b) economically in combining factors in such proportions and producing output in such amount that the value of the marginal product is in each case brought as near as possible to the market price of the factor. *Ex hypothesi* – since the aim is equality between prices and marginal costs, and not between prices and average costs – the amount of profit or loss made is irrelevant.

6   In those cases in which there are a large number of plants under different managers, producing the same product,[4] it may be possible, by collecting data from every plant for every period, to construct production functions expressing output as a function of the collection of factors used. Any manager who was exceptionally inefficient or exceptionally efficient technically would then probably stand out, since his output would not correspond to that derived from the production function based on average experience. Moreover, by working out from the production function partial derivatives of output in respect of each factor for different amounts and combinations of factors employed, some basis might be obtained for checking the marginal product of different factors in different plants. It is difficult to suggest any comparable procedure where only one or two plants exist; but, in such cases, it is doubtful whether the profit motive under private monopoly deals adequately with the problem.

7   It is, however, worth pointing out one advantage which state production will have over private production in this respect. The task of the manager of a state plant is in two respects simpler than that of a manager of a private plant; for the object of the former is to equate the price of the product to the cost of the marginal factors involved in its

---

[4] It might, at first sight, appear inconsistent with the argument to assume that there could be a large number of socialised plants producing the same product, since the argument for socialisation rests upon the necessity of monopoly for technical reasons. There is, however, no contradiction. Because of the costs of transport of the product, there may need to be local monopolies; but the conditions of production in the various localities may be sufficiently similar to make comparisons of costs, etc., useful. Thus, for example, cost and output data might be compared for a large number of local gasworks.

production, while that of the latter is to equate the marginal revenue derived from the product with the marginal cost of its production. The state manager need not consider the market questions – how much his extra sales will depress the price of his product and how much his extra purchase of factors will raise their prices; the private manager has to consider both these market questions in addition to all the other questions which the state manager must take into account. Thus:

(i) both managers must consider their technical efficiency, i.e. methods of producing the maximum amount from any given collection of factors;

(ii) both managers must consider the marginal productivity of the various factors, i.e. the additional output to be obtained from the use of an additional unit of the factor;

(iii) the state manager's job is then done, since he has now only to compare the market price of this additional output with the market price of the additional factors; but

(iv) the private manager must proceed next to consider the marginal revenue to be derived from the sale of the additional product, which depends upon the effect which his additional sales will have in depressing the market; and

(v) he must also consider the effect which his additional purchase of the factor may have in hardening the market against him, before he is ready to compare marginal revenue with marginal cost.


## III

8    The rules mentioned in the preceding paragraphs would probably serve adequately to cover all the main problems except that of a large new investment either for the production of a completely new product, or for the production of an old product in a new area (e.g. a new electrical generating plant), or – possibly – for a very large new investment increasing very substantially the total output of an existing product. In such cases, however, we cannot make the 'atomistic' assumption that we have to deal only with changes at the margin where (i) the effect upon the total output of the product in question is not appreciable, and (ii) the effect upon the total amount of factors left for employment in any other particular alternative occupation is not appreciable. The former condition would justify the assumption that the price of the product measures the addition to utility due to its production, and the latter the assumption that the price of the factor concerned measures the loss of utility due to the contraction of output in the industries from which it is withdrawn.

9    In the exceptional cases, however, one cannot afford to neglect the consumers' surplus involved in the additional product. In order to evaluate the gain to consumers of the additional product, one needs to integrate the area under the relevant range of the demand curve for the product in question. This needs to be compared with the value to

consumers of the output which is sacrificed in the alternative occupations open to the factors involved. If these factors can be abstracted at the margin from a number of different alternative uses, it will be sufficient to compare the area under the demand curve in the new industry with the price of the factors involved. If, however, it involves the abstraction of the factors in a lump, on a substantial scale, from some other particular industry, it becomes necessary to compare the area under the demand curve in the new industry with the area under the relevant range of the demand curve in the industry or industries from which the factors are to be abstracted.

10    Unfortunately, all this must remain a matter of considerable numerical imprecision. While the rules for determining relatively small variations in output may be made sufficiently precise to use as actual working rules, the decision whether or not to make a large new investment must be based upon rules which, though logically watertight, are of extreme difficulty to apply accurately in practice. One thing, however, is clear. The issue does not depend upon whether the new plant has a prospect of making a profit or avoiding a loss. In other words, it has nothing to do with the question whether at any output of the new plant the consumers will offer a price which covers the average cost of production. It depends, on the contrary, upon whether the total area under the consumers' demand curve in the new plant does or does not exceed the total areas under the relevant portions of the demand curves for the various goods, from the production of which the necessary factors of production are to be abstracted.

## IV

11    These rules for the operation of socialised industries are by now more or less generally accepted by technical economists. But certain results of these rules are less familiar. Their budgetary implications are most striking. The principle is to socialise just those industries in which considerable economies of large-scale production may be enjoyed (i.e. precisely those industries in which the marginal cost is below the average cost) and to operate these industries in such a way that the price charged for the product is equal to its marginal cost (i.e. in such a way that a loss is made). This involves doing away with the principle of 'charging what the traffic will bear' in the operation of the railways or in the sale of electric current, and charging only the marginal cost of the provision of these services. The previous owners having presumably been fully compensated will receive interest on capital now operated in such a way that a considerable loss is made upon it.

12    Nor is it possible to take comfort in the belief that these losses will necessarily be exceptional. I have argued at length elsewhere[5] that if a community's population is of the size which maximises income per head, the value of the marginal product of labour over the whole range of

[5] See Chapter II of Part IV of my *Introduction to Economic Analysis and Policy.*

industries and occupations will be equal to the average product of labour, and in this case the payment of a wage equal to the marginal product of labour would absorb the whole of the national income. In terms of our present problem, this would mean that the actual losses made in the socialised 'increasing returns' industries, due to charging a price for the product no greater than its marginal cost of production, would just be covered by what profits were still made in socialised industries where 'increasing returns' were less marked or in competitive industries in which 'increasing returns' did not play an appreciable part and in which a full return on land and capital was accordingly still being earned.

13　The rules for operating socialised industries *may* thus involve losses commensurate with the total income earned on property in other sectors of the economy.[6] To raise taxation on a scale which will cover defence, social security and the normal expenses of government as well as the losses to be contemplated in socialised industries would involve 'announcement' effects which even the most sanguine might hesitate to neglect. Even if the necessary funds could be raised by, for example, a proportionate income tax, the rate of tax might well be high enough seriously to interfere with the achievement of the best balance between work and leisure, to which reference has been made in paragraph 2 (ii) above.

14　The socialisation of 'increasing returns' industries is, for these reasons, best accompanied by some measure of public ownership of property. A capital levy, or similar measure, which transfers property to state ownership, permits either the cancellation of debt (whether or not it has occurred in the past purchase of socialised industries) or state investment of funds in privately operated concerns. In the former case, it removes a current interest charge from the state's expenditure, and in the latter it provides for the state a current income without the unfavourable announcement effects of high rates of taxation. In a community which starts with a large national debt, such a principle can, in fact, be carried a long way before it raises any problems associated with state ownership of privately operated capital. But in such a community *state operation* of 'increasing returns' industries may, through the excessive charge which it would impose on the tax revenue, do more harm than good unless it is accompanied by some extension of the principle of *state ownership* of property.

## V

15　There are two incidental advantages to be derived from the socialisation of 'increasing returns' industries and their operation on the above mentioned principles.

---

[6] This has not always been fully realised by writers on this subject. Thus, Lange (*op. cit.,* pp. 74–75, 84) discusses the way in which the income earned in socialised industries may be distributed among consumers or used for corporate savings without recognising that, far from any net profit being realised, the net losses made in socialised industries might even absorb all the profits made in competitive industries, where he allows (*op. cit.,* pp. 120 and 125) private enterprise and private property to continue.

16    First, it would open up a large new range for capital investment, and this, in an economy otherwise threatened with large-scale unemployment, might appreciably aid in the maintenance of economic activity. In a socialised plant new investment will be undertaken so long as the price of the additional output (and not the marginal revenue derived from it) represents a return on the cost of the investment greater than the ruling rate of interest. Moreover, in determining whether an entirely new plant should be set up, criteria should be observed (as is argued in paragraphs 8–10 above) which, in many cases, will justify the investment, although a loss is bound to be realised on it. For both these reasons, the application of the current principles of pricing to socialised industries should justify much economically productive capital investment which private enterprise could never undertake.

17    Secondly, these principles of pricing in socialised industries involve a shift of income from profits to wages – a shift which, in the case of an optimum population, would involve the distribution of the whole national income in wages. Such a shift will be brought about by bringing down to the marginal cost of production the prices charged for the products of the socialised industries, without reducing money wages at the same time. Such a shift of income from profits to wages would probably lead to a more equal distribution as between persons.

J. E. Meade

## COMMENT

1    Mr Meade's statement of the principles which should govern the price and output policy of a state-controlled enterprise, though possibly a little over-simplified, is not, I think, open to serious objection. Indeed, one only wishes that they commanded a wider measure of understanding and acceptance outside the narrow ranks of the economists. Where I differ from him, however, is in attaching greater importance to the administrative, and less to the financial difficulties involved in applying these principles.

2    In paragraph 4 of his article, Mr Meade formulates acceptably the conditions for 'optimising' inputs and outputs where the associated variations of input and/or output can be made very small by comparison with the total turnover in the factor and product markets concerned.[1] Where, however, by reason of the indivisibility of the units of input or output, relatively large associated variations of input and/or output have

---

[1] Even in these cases the principles have to be applied with certain commonsense modifications to maintain a measure of price stability. A strict application would lead to an intolerable fluctuation of prices. For example, unless one were a season-ticket holder, one might not know how much one had to pay for one's ticket in a train or tram until one got to the station! It is worth while, in order to facilitate the planning of expenditure by one's customers, to introduce some stability into selling prices, even at the cost of maintaining them a little above the optimal level, and even at the cost of a little surplus capacity. Similarly, it is better to pay wages which are slightly too low than wages which fluctuate like a fever chart.

to be considered, one can no longer determine optimal behaviour by simply comparing marginal rates of substitution with relative prices.

3   For example, if the problem is to determine whether or not a public undertaking should expand output by an amount which is significantly large in relation either to product- or to factor-markets, it will be impossible to apply the criterion that the marginal cost must not exceed product price i.e. that the factor cost per unit of additional output must not exceed the unit price of the product relative to the unit price of the factors. If the managers of the undertaking apply this criterion in terms of the prices existing prior to the contemplated expansion of output, they will be unduly predisposed to expand output. If they calculate in terms of the less favourable prices expected to exist after the contemplated change, they will be unduly biassed against expansion. The right course is to value the increment of output at the price expected to prevail after the change *plus* the surplus accruing from the fall in product prices to consumers of the increment of output; and to value the increment of factor cost at the factor prices prevailing after the change *less* the surplus accruing from the rise in factor prices to the owners of the additional factors required to produce the increment of output.

4   In paragraphs 8–10, Mr Meade gives some attention to this case, but he neglects the producers' surpluses (which may often be more important than the consumers' surpluses), and he greatly exaggerates the exceptional character of the circumstances in which such surpluses would have to be taken into account. He says that the ordinary 'marginal' rules would 'probably serve adequately to cover all the main problems except that of a large new investment either for the production of a completely new product, or for the production of an old product in a new area (e.g. a new electric generator plant) or – possibly – for a very large new investment increasing very substantially the total output of an existing product'. This is surely wrong. Almost every enterprise socialised on the grounds advocated by Mr Meade will find the ordinary rules inapplicable to certain of its large inputs. The question of socialisation in order to secure proper pricing and output policy will only arise in cases where the size of the optimal plant in relation to markets is such that there is a significant difference between profit at optimal output and that same profit *plus all consumers' and producers' surpluses*. It is only because there is such a significant difference that there is an opportunity of making monopoly profits by restricting output, and that the enterprise or industry cannot be left in private hands. Therefore, in all such cases, the question of setting up a new plant, or even of substantially extending an old plant, will necessitate taking account of such surpluses.

II

5   Having agreed – for Mr Meade would probably not dispute the foregoing propositions – on the abstract criteria of price- and output-policy appropriate to a public enterprise, let us consider some of the practical difficulties and implications, beginning with those to which Mr

Meade attaches the greatest importance – viz., the budgetary implications. It is clear that if enterprises which have previously been run on monopolistic lines, with a view to making the maximal profit, are taken over by public authorities and run on the lines advocated by Mr Meade, the profit earned will diminish, and, if full compensation has been paid to the previous owners, the difference will have to be met from the public purse. This will happen whether increasing, constant, or diminishing returns prevail in the undertakings in question.

6   Mr Meade, however, seems to regard it as a circumstance particularly unpropitious from the financial point of view that undertakings socialised in order to secure optimal behaviour will, as he asserts, operate under conditions of increasing returns (in the sense of diminishing factor cost per unit of output). I doubt whether this assertion is either true or relevant.

7   Socialisation, of the type Mr Meade is considering, comes into question only when it is impossible to secure genuine competition between units of optimal size. This will occur when the production units are so large, relative to the product and factor markets concerned, that it would be impossible, by trust-busting, etc., to create a sufficient number of firms to secure competition without making production units too small. Under such conditions it will probably be the case that to set up, and operate in optimal fashion a single additional plant, will so depress product prices and enhance factor prices as substantially to reduce the profit earned by the additional plant below the level which it would have attained if prices had been unaffected. We saw, in paragraphs 3 and 4, that in such circumstances it may be right to build an additional plant if the profit at 'previous' prices is substantially in excess of the capital cost, even if profit at 'subsequent' prices fails to cover the cost. In this case, the additional plant (and all similar plants in the same industry) will work under conditions of increasing returns or diminishing average cost.[2] But is not another outcome equally possible? It may be right to *refrain* from building an additional plant if the prospective profit at 'subsequent' prices is substantially below the capital cost, even though prospective profit at 'previous' prices somewhat exceeds the capital cost. In this case the remaining plants in the industry, of a type similar to the additional plant which is just not worth while building, will work under conditions of diminishing returns, and will therefore make large profits. *Prima facie,* therefore, in the absence of precise knowledge regarding the demand and cost conditions in the actual industries and undertakings ripe for socialisation, it appears just as likely that socialised undertakings will work under diminishing as under increasing returns. On the average, therefore, they will probably make much the same rate of profits (abstracting from considerations of risk, etc.) as prevails in the competitive sector of private industry, where, of course, constant returns is the rule.

[2]     Profit < capital cost
∴ revenue < total cost
∴ product price < average cost
∴ marginal cost < average cost
∴ average cost is declining.

8  Even if Mr Meade were justified in assuming that his socialised undertakings would operate under increasing returns, the bearing of this on the financial problem of socialisation would be at best very indirect. It is true that in such circumstances the undertakings would have to be run at a loss (in the sense of failing to cover their capital cost, failing to make a normal profit). What matters, however, in the present context is not the level of profits after socialisation, but the decline in profits as compared with the previous level. This, however, is affected not by the slope of the *average* cost curve, but by the slope of the *marginal* cost curve over the range of output extending between monopoly output and optimal output. It can be shown that the more negatively inclined the marginal cost curve over this range of output the greater will be the disparity between monopoly profits and optimal profits.[3] I would not, of course, deny that there is a certain correlation between the slope of the *marginal* cost curve between monopoly and optimal output and the slope of the *average* cost curve at optimal output, and that if one were assured that, in socialised undertakings, average cost at optimal output was always declining, one would expect the disparity between monopoly profit and optimal profit to be greater than if increasing average cost had been the rule. But the connection is indirect and uncertain. In any event, there is, as we have seen, no particular reason to expect the average cost curve in socialised undertakings to be falling rather than rising, nor is there any particular reason why the slope of the marginal cost curve in such undertakings should as a rule be less positive than in other undertakings.

[3] Take the case where the demand curve is linear, and the supply curve of the factors is infinitely elastic.
Then, if $R$ = revenue,

$O$ = output,

$C$ = cost (at constant factor prices),

$X$ = the loss involved in moving from the maximal profit position to the optimal position,

$a, b, \alpha, \beta, S$, are constants,

and if the values of the variables at the maximal profit position, and the optimal position, are indicated by suffixes $m$ and $o$ respectively;

Let $\qquad\qquad R = aO - bO^2$.

Then marginal revenue $= dR/dO = a - 2bO$ and product price $= R/O = a - bO$.

Let $\qquad\qquad C = S + \alpha(O - O_m) + \beta(O - O_m)^2$ where $O$ is not $< O_m$.

Then marginal cost $= dC/dO = \alpha + 2\beta(O - O_m)$.

At the maximal profit position,

$$\frac{dR_m}{dO_m} = \frac{dCm}{dO_m}$$

$$\therefore\ O_m = \frac{a - \alpha}{2b}$$

At the optimal position,

$$\frac{R_o}{O_o} = \frac{dC_o}{dO_o}$$

$$\therefore\ O_o = \frac{a - \alpha + 2\beta O_m}{b + 2\beta}.$$

9   Whatever bearing the shape of the cost curves may have on the magnitude of the disparity between monopoly profits and optimum profits, it is indisputable that some disparity will exist, and will constitute a burden on the Exchequer. The seriousness of a financial burden of this sort consists in the adverse effects on productive incentives and on the distribution of income to which it may give rise. What these effects are will depend on how the money to meet the deficit is raised. In the present case it appears likely that if the most appropriate method of financing the loss arising out of socialisation is followed, the effect will be to annul some, but not all, of the benefits which, as Mr Meade explains in paragraphs 1 to 4 of his article, would otherwise result from the policy of socialisation.

10   Suppose, first, that the loss is financed out of a tax levied on the product of the socialised undertakings. The effect in this case is entirely to annul the benefits of socialisation. The undertaking on being socialised will be run at the same output as formerly; what was previously a disparity between price and marginal cost will now be called a tax, and what was formerly monopoly profit will accrue to the Exchequer as the proceeds of the tax and will be used to pay compensation to the former owners of the loss of their monopoly revenue.

11   Suppose next, that the tax, instead of being levied on the produce of the socialised undertakings, is levied *ad valorem* on output generally. The effect of this change will be to restore one of the most important – in fact *the* most important – of the benefits for which the socialisation was undertaken, in that it will correct the mal-distribution of resources as between the different branches of industry which resulted from the inequality in the ratio of marginal cost to price in the different branches. The other benefits, however, which it was expected that socialisation

Substituting for $a - \alpha$

$$O_0 = \frac{2O_m(b + \beta)}{b + 2\beta}.$$

(Since $O_0 - O_m = bO_m/(b + 2\beta)$ = a quantity which is positive for positive values of $O_m$ it is legitimate to determine optimal output with the aid of a cost equation applicable only to outputs in excess of $O_m$.)

Now the loss involved in moving from the maximal profit position to the optimal position $= X$

$$= R_m - R_0 - C_m + C_0$$
$$= aO_m - bO_m{}^2 - aO_0 + bO_0{}^2 + \alpha(O_0 - O_m) + \beta(O_0 - O_m)^2$$
$$= \frac{(a - \alpha)^2 (b + \beta)}{4(b + 2\beta)^2}.$$

Now, suppose that $\beta$ varies ($O_m$ of course remaining constant). When $\beta = \infty$, $X$ = zero. As $\beta$ falls, $X$ rises, until, as $\beta \to -\frac{1}{2}b$, $X \to \infty$. ($\beta$ can never fall below $-\frac{1}{2}b$.) In words, the loss involved in moving from the maximal profit position to the optimal position varies inversely with the slope of the marginal cost curve for outputs exceeding monopoly output.

Similarly, it can be shown that, when the supply curve of a factor is linear, the demand curve of the product infinitely elastic, and the supply curves of any other factors also infinitely elastic, the loss involved in moving from the maximal profit position to the optimal position varies directly with the slope of the marginal product curve for inputs exceeding monopsony input.

would bring – the increase in the proportion of national income accruing to labour, the raising of the incentive to work to its appropriate level – will be annulled, for the reason that, on the average of all industries, the gap between marginal cost and price will remain as great as ever.

12    There are many other ways in which the loss could be financed, by an increased income tax, or death duty, by a tax on capital, by a reduction in public expenditure, etc. This is not the place to enquire into their relative merits or demerits in respect of effect on income distribution, on incentive to invest, on propensity to consume, on incentive to work etc. One general observation can, however, be made on each and every one of them regarded as an alternative to a general indirect tax. If it is right, after the socialisation, to finance the losses resulting from the socialisation by method $x$ rather than by a general indirect tax, it would have been right before the socialisation to raise money by method $x$ in order to finance a general subsidy on output. The only benefit, therefore, which is properly attributable to the socialisation is that of an improved inter-industrial distribution of resources. Any other benefits which may accrue from the fact that the socialisation is financed by some other way than by a general indirect tax, could have been obtained by appropriate fiscal measures, without the socialisation.

13    It might perhaps be surmised that a similar objection could be advanced against the sole remaining virtue which, in paragraph 11 above, is still attributed to socialisation – viz., that it enables the mal-distribution of resources between different industries to be corrected. Could not the same result be equally well achieved without socialisation by a combination of a subsidy on goods produced under monopolistic conditions and a tax on goods produced under competitive conditions? The answer is that once the monopolistic industries have been socialised and are being managed according to correct principles, it becomes possible to reduce the 'tax' formerly imposed on their products by the monopolist owners and increase the tax on products produced by private enterprise under competitive conditions, without untoward effects on the distribution of income. Whereas a policy of subsidising goods produced by private monopolies and taxing other goods would have the effect of expanding the share of monopoly profits in the national income. In addition, of course, it would provide a very undesirable incentive to adopt monopolistic practices.

14    It follows from what had been said in the foregoing paragraphs that Mr Meade is mistaken in believing that socialisation, with its concomitant increase in taxation, provides any additional argument for the state's taking heroic steps to reduce its indebtedness or acquire property. No doubt it would be very gratifying if the state could painlessly acquire a property income which could then be used to relieve taxation. But this cannot be done except by achieving a budget surplus, which is never a painless procedure. If a large surplus is aimed at, such as would probably be required in order to offset the capitalised value of the losses involved in socialising a substantial sector of industry, it could probably only be achieved by resort to a capital tax or levy. But such a levy, particularly if it is expected to be repeated at irregular intervals, has many

unfortunate effects on incentive and the distribution of income. In order to decide whether it is worth while, it is necessary to balance the marginal disadvantages of a levy on capital now against the marginal advantages of the permanent reduction in general taxation which would thereby be made possible. Now, a combination of socialisation of the type under discussion *plus* a general indirect tax on output has, as we have seen, no net effects on incentive or income distribution, favourable or unfavourable, except that of removing barriers to an optimum inter-industrial distribution of resources. The marginal disadvantages of a capital levy are in no wise diminished, nor are the marginal disadvantages of current taxation in any way increased. The desirability of socialisation to eliminate monopoly has therefore no bearing on the case for or against a capital levy, or (more generally) for or against budgeting for a surplus.

### III

15     While I am less impressed than Mr Meade by the financial difficulties involved in the application of criteria of optimal production and pricing by public undertakings, I am more impressed than he is by the difficulty of securing efficient management under these conditions. In the first place, I do not agree that, given good-will, the task of a manager of a state plant run on the optimal principles is significantly simpler than that of the manager of a private plant or of a state plant run on the lines of a private monopoly. Mr Meade says that the state manager, unlike the private manager, is dispensed from considering how much extra output would depress the price of his product and raise the price of his factors. But this is only true if the state manager sets out to find his optimal position by a process of random trial and error. If he tries to cut short this process – and since, in reality, the optimal position is always changing, he ought to try to cut it short – he must guess how much a given expansion of output will affect product and factor prices, since he has to equate marginal factor cost with the ratio of product to factor prices. Much the same is true of the private manager. He can find the output corresponding to maximum profit by trial and error, but if he wishes to cut short the process, he must guess at the relationship between output and prices. Whatever may be the relative difficulty of the problems confronting state and private managers in deciding on the scale of operation of existing plants, it is clear, from what has been said in paragraph 4 above, that when it comes to deciding whether or not to set up an additional plant there is nothing to choose between the difficulties confronting state and private enterprise respectively.

16     Secondly, and more important, the application of the principles of optimisation will make it more difficult to weed out the inefficient managers than it is when the enterprises are run for profit. Admittedly, it is just as difficult for an outsider to estimate the precise efficiency of the management in the one case as in the other. But in the latter case the level of profits is at any rate a rough-and-ready index of managerial efficiency, whereas in the former case it is no guide at all. This for two reasons. A

lowering of the cost curve, reflecting technical efficiency of management, will raise monopoly profits by much more than profits at optimal output. The latter, indeed, may not be affected at all. In the second place, the manager of a plant which purports to be run on optimal lines can easily cover up any shortfall of profits due to his technical inefficiency by slightly restricting output.

17 Mr Meade suggests that it would be possible for someone at the centre to obtain, by means of comparative statistics, an accurate and up-to-date idea of the technical production functions of the various plants in a socialised industry. If this were possible, it would certainly facilitate the task of weeding out inefficient managers. But, of course, the same methods of control would be applicable to a socialised industry run for profit, so that the relative advantage of running such an industry on the maximal profit principle rather than the optimal principle, in respect of the elimination of inefficient managers, though it would be reduced to vanishing point, would, at any rate, not be reversed.[4] In most cases, however, these methods of central control by statistics would prove themselves to be unsatisfactory. It is just because different plants have different production functions ('special circumstances') which cannot be fully comprehended at the centre, that it is necessary for private combines (and will probably be necessary for socialised industries) to devolve a good deal of initiative on the managers of individual plants.

18 More serious than the difficulty of weeding out inefficient managers is that of providing managers, so long as they are maintained in their functions with an adequate incentive to effort and efficiency. Where the enterprise is run for profit, such an incentive can be provided partly by the fear of being replaced and partly by making managerial remuneration vary with profits of the firm. Now the first incentive will, as we have seen, apply somewhat less effectively to the manager of an enterprise run on the optimal principles than to the manager of one run for profit. In any case, dismissal is a drastic and exceptional remedy for inefficiency. The lack of gentler but more persistent and finely modulated pressure in the direction of efficient management is, therefore, a serious drawback.

19 What is the upshot of the argument? We have found that the socialisation of monopolistic or oligopolistic undertakings, accompanied by compensation, and followed by the application of the accepted criteria of optimal output and price policy, will result in an improvement in the inter-industrial distribution of resources, but it is also likely to result in a lower technical efficiency of production in the industries directly affected than could have been attained had the undertakings been run for profit. From this two consequences follow: (1) Where there is a choice between securing the application of the desired criteria by direct instructions to the managers or by the restoration of competitive conditions, the latter policy should have a measure of preference even at the cost of *some* reduction in the unit of management below the optimal size. This implies giving a measure of preference to 'trust-busting' and other anti-restrictionist

---

[4] Mr Meade's point may count as an argument for the superior efficiency of public over private enterprise as such, when both are conducted according to the same principles. But this is a question with which we are (happily) not concerned here.

measures over socialisation as a means of coping with monopoly, unless there is reason to believe public enterprise more efficient than private, even where an industry is competitive. (Incidently, if anti-monopoly measures of the trust-busting type can be carried through without the payment of compensation to the monopolists, additional advantages arise, particularly an improvement in the incentive to work). (2) Even where the restoration of competition is impossible, industries should be managed in accordance with the principles of optimal production only in cases where the avoidance of monopolistic restriction of output with a given technique is more important than the preservation of the maximum incentive to maintain technical efficiency and progress.

J. M. FLEMING

## REJOINDER

1    Mr Fleming doubts whether the assertion that financial losses will be made in socialised industries is either true or relevant. As to its truth, he argues that the average cost in socialised industries is just as likely to be rising as falling. His argument is based upon considerations of the discontinuity of cost curves of which I had failed to take account. There is, however, still, in my opinion, a presumption that decreasing costs will be more frequent than rising costs. A large number of cases probably exist (e.g. transport, public utilities, and industries where the cost of transport of the product from one local market to another is high) where there is room only for a single plant in a local market. In these cases, decreasing costs alone will operate up to the optimum output of such a single plant. Between this output and the output of many plants of optimum size – in spite of intermediate ups and downs at the points at which new plant is introduced – there will be no net change in average cost, unless there are economies of large-scale production external to the individual plant. Over this range, there is no net rise or fall in average cost, while up to this point there will be only falling costs. As Mr Fleming has pointed out to me, this is not conclusive proof that falling costs (and losses) are more probable than rising costs (and profits) at the points of intersection of the demand curve and the marginal cost curve. But to me, at least, it suggests a strong probability that on further examination this will be found to be the case.
2    The probability of decreasing costs is reinforced if allowance is made – as it should be made – for economies of large-scale production external to the individual plant. In this case, the average cost of the optimum output from a plant of optimum size will be lower when there is a large number of such plants than when there is only one. This is a second reason for expecting socialised industries to be operating under decreasing rather than increasing costs.
3    As Mr Fleming himself points out, even when plants are operating under increasing average cost, optimal profits will be less than monopoly profits, so that even in these cases the financial problem exists if full

compensation has been paid to the owners when the industry was socialised.

4  As to the relevance of the financial consideration, Mr Fleming points out that my argument for the state ownership of property was not properly grounded. Without the further extension of state ownership of property, the financing of losses in socialised industries will not necessarily worsen the distribution of income and the incentive to work, since such losses could be financed by indirect taxation without any net adverse effects in these respects. State ownership of property should rather be regarded as a means (which could be adopted independently of the socialisation of 'increasing returns' industries) for positively improving the distribution of income and the incentive to work. Mr Fleming's criticism is correct; but I remain unrepentant in my conclusion, since I am prepared to kill more than one bird with a single stone. The socialisation of 'increasing returns' industries can improve the inter-industrial distribution of resources without further state ownership of property; but the full improvements which it might also bring to the distribution of income and the incentive to work cannot, I still maintain, be enjoyed without such extension of state ownership.

5  Finally, in paragraph 15 of his comment, Mr Fleming has overlooked the central point which it was my intention to make. Given that state managers and private enterprise managers both know (i) the prices of the factors, (ii) the prices of the products, and (iii) the marginal physical products of the factors, then the state manager will, and the private enterprise manager will not, know whether more or less of any factor should be employed. True, the state manager will not yet know how much more or less to employ, but – unlike the private enterprise manager – he will at least know in which direction he should move.

J. E. MEADE

# 4

# Mr Lerner on *The Economics of Control*

*This review article, of Abba P. Lerner's* The Economics of Control: Principles of Welfare Economics *(New York: The Macmillan Company, 1944), was, Keynes told Meade, the longest review ever to have appeared in the* Economic Journal (The Economic Journal, *vol. 55 (April 1945), pp. 47–69; Meade Diary, 27 April 1945).*

I

From Adam Smith to the 1930s professional economists, in this country at least, believed in competition and the virtues of allowing the pricing mechanism to bring about the most economic use of resources. The development of the 'economic calculus' was the basic purpose of economic study. During the 1930s and more recently a different strand of economic thought has developed. The imperfections and inadequacies of the competitive system and of the pricing mechanism (which were always recognised to a greater or lesser extent by economists) have been so emphasised by some recent writers that the whole idea of an economic calculus has been abandoned by them. Consumers' irrationalities and ignorance of what is good for them; wastes due to imperfections in competitive markets; external economies and diseconomies which necessitate a divergence between the private and social interest; the evils of unemployment; the difficulty of improving the distribution of income without interfering with the price system – the realisation of all these phenomena has led some people to the view that the price mechanism is a snare and a delusion and that the quantitative planning of production and consumption by the state provides the answer to our economic discontents.

This development of thought has already, in its turn, provoked some reaction. Professor Hayek, in *The Road to Serfdom* [London: Routledge, 1944], leads a counter-revolution, the main purpose of which is twofold: first, to reassert the usefulness of the competitive price mechanism; and, secondly, to assert the arbitrariness of all acts of centralised planning and to establish the danger to freedom of accepting anything but the impersonal conclusion of the competitive market. Thus, the stage is set for a battle royal between Planning and *Laissez-faire*.

There is, however, a third school of thought, ably represented by Mr A. P. Lerner's recent book. Mr Lerner believes passionately in the principles of the economic calculus, in the use of the price mechanism, in the avoidance of arbitrary centralised planning, and in freedom of choice for consumers and workers; but he does not believe in unqualified *laissez-faire*. He preaches the 'controlled economy', by which he means an economic system in which the price mechanism is made to work, at the dictation of the free choice of the individual consumer, in such a way as to attract factors of production to the uses in which the valuation set by consumers on their marginal product is highest. In many cases, according to Mr Lerner, this can best be achieved by competition; in other cases it is necessary to institute socialist production to achieve this end of equating prices to marginal costs. The 'controlled economy' is the economy in which controls are introduced of a kind and on a scale necessary to achieve just this object of making the price system work, and from which all other regulations are removed.

Mr Lerner himself was for many years an advocate of an extensively socialised economy, run expressly on these impersonal principles of economic pricing.[1] In his present book, while he still advocates socialisation where competition will be imperfect, he has swung markedly towards a more extensive use of the competitive mechanism. But, fundamentally, he remains consistent: to him the important question is not so much the means (whether socialism or *laissez-faire*) as the end of so using the pricing system as to achieve the most economic satisfaction of the freely expressed desires of the consumer.

In Mr Lerner's opinion, the weapons of state intervention for the controlled economy are various. A system of monetary and fiscal policy should be adopted to ensure that there is a sufficiently high demand throughout the economy to give full employment without inflation. Such a policy will involve intervention by the state in taxation and spending (so as to affect the total demand for goods and services) and in borrowing and lending (so as to affect the rate of interest at which money can be borrowed for new capital development) (cf. Chapter 24, on 'functional finance').

In Mr Lerner's system the state should also intervene to ensure a more equal distribution of income, both through a progressive income tax (pp. 234–240) and also through the payment on an egalitarian principle of any 'social dividend' which it may be necessary for the state to pay out in order to maintain consumers' purchasing power in the interests of the maintenance of full employment (p. 267). Mr Lerner argues on familiar lines that the total satisfaction achieved from any given income will be maximised if that income is so divided among individuals that its marginal utility is the same for everyone; but he adds an interesting and elegant proof of the proposition that (on the assumption that the marginal utility of income declines in the case of each individual) the maximisation of *probable* total satisfaction is attained by an equal division of income, even although we cannot directly compare the satisfactions of different individuals (pp. 29–32).

---

[1] A type of non-arbitrary socialism, the feasibility of which Professor Hayek dismisses in a footnote (p. 30) of his *The Road to Serfdom*.

In order to ensure the best use of resources it is necessary to bring it about that prices are equal to marginal costs in all lines of production. This, says Mr Lerner, can be done in either of two ways: by promoting competition where perfect competition is technically possible, since in such circumstances the search for private profit will itself automatically result in the equating of marginal costs to prices; or by the socialisation of industry and its decentralised operation by managers who are under instructions to obey The Rule (p. 64) that they must take on each factor up to the point at which its price is equal to the value of its marginal product.

Mr Lerner definitely prefers the competitive to the socialist solution, where perfect competition is technically possible, on two grounds: first, because the competitive solution automatically provides just the correct incentive for the owners and managers to act efficiently and economically; and, secondly, because 'alternatives to government employment are a safeguard of the freedom of the individual' (pp. 83–85). Above all, competitive speculation (i.e. speculation carried on in conditions in which the speculator cannot by his own individual action affect the buying or selling prices of the commodity in which he is speculating) should be positively encouraged, since by transferring resources from less valued to more valued uses it confers an unequivocal benefit on the community (pp. 69–71).

Competitive conditions can, according to Mr Lerner, in many cases be preserved by the device of government 'counterspeculation'. That is to say, the state can deny to individual buyers and sellers the power of affecting prices, and thus exercising a monopolistic influence, if it is willing itself to enter the market and to buy and sell freely at the price which it considers to be the competitive price (pp. 55–56).

There are, however, serious difficulties connected with this idea of government 'counterspeculation'. If, for one reason or another, private producers are in a position to restrict output and to hold prices above the competitive level, how can the government prevent this merely by expressing its willingness to sell *ad lib.* at the lower competitive price? Will it not itself have to buy at the higher monopoly price in order to sell at the lower competitive price? And, in this case, will not the demand for the product exceed the supply which the government can obtain for resale to the consumers?

Perhaps the answer to this conundrum lies in Mr Lerner's later statement that the state should, in certain circumstances, itself undertake production in competition with private enterprise (pp. 85–87). This would, no doubt, be a means of ensuring that sufficient supplies were forthcoming at the competitive price; but in this case it would be the state production rather than the 'counterspeculation' which would hold the monopoly in check.

In any case, where there are important economies of large-scale production, 'counterspeculation' alone, as Mr Lerner points out, will not suffice to preserve the results of 'perfect competition'. In these cases monopoly may be inevitable, and the sale of the product at a price equal to its marginal cost may involve the continuation of production at a loss

(p. 179). Here, socialisation is the remedy proposed by Mr Lerner. For example, the public utilities (which, in the absence of a clear recognition of the simple rule that prices should be equated to marginal costs regardless of the effect upon total profitability, are the subject of 'unending regulations') should be socialised and run according to The Rule (p. 181).

Such socialisation – undertaken solely in order to make the pricing system work, and based upon decentralised control of socialised industries by managers who would have simply to obey The Rule (p. 64) equating prices with marginal costs – is, of course, something quite different from centralised quantitative planning and control over the economy. For such a system Mr Lerner, on the grounds that it would make impossible any rational use of prices and costs as the means of allocating resources to their most economic use, has nothing but contempt. 'Any attempt to run the economy from a central office must result in utter confusion, although it can all be adjusted satisfactorily with the proper use of the price mechanism' (p. 170).

Mr Lerner maintains that the 'controlled' economy would involve less state regulation than the 'uncontrolled' economy, since this system would involve sweeping away many 'partial and haphazard' regulations which did not promote (to say nothing of those which actually hindered) the competitive or socialist process of equating prices with marginal costs (pp. 2–4). His programme is thus one of freeing the competitive process from a host of regulations; extending the socialisation of industry (on the principle of decentralised management) where monopoly was inevitable; maintaining a mixed system of state and private enterprise; using the device of government 'counterspeculation' to preserve, wherever possible, competitive markets; and employing the fiscal and monetary functions of the state both to achieve a more equal distribution of income and to maintain aggregate demand at a level sufficient to maintain employment without inflation.

In exposition of this type of economic policy, Mr Lerner has written a brilliant book, full of stimulating ideas and presenting in a fresh and elegant manner the main principles of welfare economics. But it is also a queer book. Mr Lerner delights in dressing up even the most familiar principles in provocative and sometimes unnecessarily unrealistic disguises; there are strange omissions from, and strange inconsistencies within, this closely packed analysis of welfare principles; and Mr Lerner, who in some of the passages of his book seems to be explaining familiar first principles at great length to the untutored schoolboy, on the next page engages in complexities and niceties of the most advanced analysis which only those with years of training in the traditions of the modern school of English-speaking economists will be able to understand. But it is always easy (though never profitable) to reproach a pioneer for failing to display a perfect sense of proportion. If the remaining paragraphs of this review are devoted mainly to an examination of some of the more surprising omissions, inconsistencies and oddities in Mr Lerner's book, this is not meant to imply that the reviewer has anything but the most profound respect for Mr Lerner's achievement.

II

The conclusions of welfare economists, such as Mr Lerner, depend on the correctness of the basic assumption that the choice of the individual consumer should determine the use of economic resources. The doctrine of Consumers' Sovereignty is the crux of the problem.[2] If this doctrine is accepted, it is difficult to see how the general principles of 'marginalism' developed by the welfare economists can be challenged. If this doctrine is rejected, then much of the type of economic analysis deployed in Mr Lerner's book becomes irrelevant.[3]

The 'marginal' principles of the welfare economists would follow at once if it were right to assume that each consumer represented a separate island of satisfaction, the degree of which depended solely on the amounts of the various goods and services which he was at that moment consuming. In this case, total satisfaction would undoubtedly be maximised by a system which (a) so divided income among individuals as to make the marginal utility of income equal to all consumers, (b) allowed consumers to compete freely for the available supplies of consumption goods, (c) caused factors to move to the production of those commodities for which the valuation set by consumers on the factors' marginal product was highest, and (d) caused total consumers' incomes to be maintained at a level which forced no resources to remain in involuntary idleness.

Mr Lerner in effect makes just this simple assumption. Yet this assumption so clearly needs modification if it is to be made realistic, and is so central to the argument, that it is a little disconcerting to find a welfare economist of Mr Lerner's stature failing to examine it more carefully. The assumption of Consumers' Sovereignty will no longer hold good in an unqualified form, if (i) the consumer can enjoy some things most economically only by means of their joint consumption simultaneously with other consumers, (ii) the consumer's present enjoyment depends on what others are at present consuming, (iii) the consumer's present satisfaction depends in part on what he or others have been in the habit of consuming in the past, or (iv) the consumer does not know what he wants or does not know what is good for him.

(i)  *Collective Wants.* There are some goods (such as public parks, public monuments, etc.) which are normally provided in the modern community by the state collectively for all citizens. It might be possible to leave it to private citizens to use their private incomes to provide each his own little private park; but this would clearly be a wasteful form of consumption. It might be possible to leave it to private initiative to form voluntary clubs to

[2] The points gathered together in this section are familiar to most economists; but I am indebted to Mrs Robinson for suggestions about their systematic arrangement.

[3] That is to say, it would no longer be suitable to use the pricing system to decide whether the production of commodity $A$ should or should not be expanded at the expense of commodity $B$. But, having decided on other principles how much of $A$, $B$, $C$, $D$, etc., should be produced, it would still be appropriate to use the pricing system to determine by what means these commodities could be produced most economically. For it is only if the ratio between the marginal products of factors $X$ and $Y$ are the same in all lines of production ($A$, $B$, $C$, $D$) that it is impossible to produce more $A$ without producing less $B$, $C$, or $D$.

provide out of the incomes of the members a rather larger park than any one member could himself provide; but once the park was there, it would probably be uneconomic to exclude non-members from its use. It might be possible for the state to provide the park but, by charging an entrance fee instead of financing it out of taxation, to lay the burden of its cost upon those who were willing to use it at a cost. But part of the charm of a public park may, after all, be that it is a public park freely open to all; and, in any case, it would clearly be uneconomic to surround parks or monuments with large screens and to dole out the enjoyment of a sight of these public amenities only to those who were willing to pay the necessary charge for a peep. Such goods are, in fact, the extreme case of those in whose production there are 'internal economies'; once a monument is erected the marginal cost of its enjoyment is zero. Nor is the division between those goods which should be collectively consumed and those which should be privately consumed a simple one to draw. Many goods may be rather more economically consumed collectively than privately; but private consumption may help to avoid the dangers (*a*) of taxing one class of person who gets no benefit from the type of collective consumption which is undertaken to the exclusive benefit of those who do, and (*b*) of putting much too much or much too little of the community's resources into this particular type of product.

(ii) *External Economies and Diseconomies in Private Consumption.* Individual $A$'s increased consumption of commodity $X$ may increase or may decrease the satisfaction of individual $B$. When a man spends money on beautifying his house, this may give pleasure to his neighbours as well as to himself. When he wears a top-hat or displays his diamond ring, his display may cause his envious neighbours deep dissatisfaction.[4] Broadly speaking, there are external economies connected with any individual consumption which beautifies or otherwise improves conditions for others, and external diseconomies with forms of luxurious consumption which people desire only because it is the fashion, so that each consumer would feel the loss less acutely if all restricted their consumption simultaneously.

(iii) *Historical Factors.* An individual may enjoy a particular form of consumption because he is used to it, and in fact (although he may not realise it) he might not miss the commodity at all once he had got used to going without it. On the other hand, he may enjoy a commodity because it is novel, and may grow tired of it as soon as he grows used to it. These are merely special forms of the irrational element in consumption discussed in the following paragraph.

[4] Display goods may be of two kinds. Thus, although I may have my total satisfaction diminished the more people have top-hats or diamonds to display, yet an increase in others' consumption of top-hats may increase the marginal utility of a top-hat to me (since it is clearly the right thing to wear), but an increase in others' consumption of diamonds may diminish the marginal utility of diamonds to me (since they are clearly not so rare as I thought they were). Moreover, I may react differently to the display of different persons. Increased display by my neighbours may invariably cause me envious pain, but by a public figure may cause me great satisfaction.

(iv)   *Irrational Factors.* An individual may not know what is good for him, while the state does. The clearest example of this is probably to be found in the case of nutrition. The consumer may not know what foods contain what vitamins or in what vitamins his diet is deficient. In this case, clearly, unguided consumer's choice will not maximise satisfaction. But there is a less clearly defined form of irrationality in consumer's choice. He may in a more fundamental sense not really know what he wants. He has money in his pocket to spend, and all the experts in salesmanship proceed to spend money in competitive advertisement simultaneously to persuade him to consume $X$ instead of $Y$ and to consume $Y$ instead of $X$. Many consumers' preferences for many articles are based on sound and rational foundations. But it is probable that many are not; and while many of the most blatant wastes of this type of imperfect competition would be automatically removed by the principles of pricing advocated by Mr Lerner, yet the problem would still remain unsolved whether (and if so, how, and to what extent) the state should attempt to distinguish between rational and irrational consumers' preferences.

Many of these complicating factors on the side of demand may go together. Thus, suppose that each consumer wanted oranges because others had oranges to eat, because he had always eaten oranges (though he would not miss them when he got used to going without them), and because he overestimated the difficulty of obtaining the same nutrient elements in his diet from other sources. Then, in time of war, there would be much to be said for eliminating supplies of oranges altogether. Such an argument would not, of course, square with the familiar 'marginalist' argument that the way to release factors of production with the least harm to consumers would be to reduce consumption of all commodities at the margin (thus preserving consumers' surpluses on the remaining supplies) rather than to eliminate one or two objects of consumption altogether.

Mr Lerner pays little or no attention to these complicating factors on the side of demand. He makes a passing reference (pp. 21–22, 43) to the fact of irrationality in consumers' behaviour. In one passage, where he is explaining in small print the first of his six 'welfare equations' (p. 76), he uses a form of words which is compatible with an awareness of the possibility of what has been called above 'external economies or diseconomies in private consumption'; but the possibility is ignored in all that goes before or follows after. In discussing the distribution of income (pp. 33–37, 41) he discusses a number of complicating factors which affect the principle of an equal distribution of income. Some of these (such as the possibility that the satisfaction which one derives from one's income depends on how much income one has had in the past, or how much income one's neighbours have now) are similar to those mentioned above. But he does not discuss how far these factors affect the problem (even when income is ideally distributed) of allocating resources and supplies at the dictation of consumers to their various uses. Yet this is a basic, if not the basic, problem of the welfare economist.

These complicating factors may drive some extremists to abandon completely the consumers' market as a means of determining the use of resources, and to advocate the quantitative planning by the state of all forms of consumers' consumption. But, clearly, there are real differences in consumers' tastes, and it would be most wasteful to neglect these, which can show themselves adequately only in a consumers' market; and others would add that individual freedom of choice was itself an end as fundamental as economic welfare itself. There are, however, a large number of intermediate positions between unadulterated Consumers' Sovereignty in a completely free consumers' market, and complete state planning of consumption. By consumers' guidance and education, individuals may be informed what is good for them and helped to decide what they really want. Moral and psychological training might in some respects (e.g. by diminishing the envy which people feel at others' good fortune) remove external diseconomies in private consumption. Extensions of collective consumption may, in some cases, be desirable. State prohibition or quantitative planning of some forms of consumption (such as in medicines, drugs, nutrients, etc.) may be required. Taxes or bounties on other forms of consumption might be used to adjust the private to the social interest. Quite a lot of the queer sense of extremism and even of unreality which pervades much of Mr Lerner's book is due to the fact that these are problems which he has almost completely assumed away.

III

The first two-thirds of Mr Lerner's book deal with the problem of maximising satisfaction from a given amount of factors of production in a closed economy and on the assumption of full employment. The fundamental propositions and conclusions of this section are not themselves novel. The discussion is, however, carried out in an extremely stimulating manner; and these passages of the book may well become one of the set works of reference on these essential problems of welfare economics.

As has already been indicated, Mr Lerner's method is to demonstrate, first, that a free market for consumers' goods will maximise welfare from any given supply of the various products and within the framework of any given distribution of income; secondly, that an equal distribution of income will maximise the probable satisfaction to be obtained from any given income; and, thirdly, that resources will be used in the way which will maximise consumers' welfare if (either by perfect competition or by socialised production run according to The Rule) factors of production are moved from points of lower to points of higher value of their marginal products. This third proposition is elegantly examined both for fixed and for variable proportions between both factors and products.

The problems which raise the most complex issues in connection with this third proposition are those concerned with economies of large-scale production. Strangely enough, Mr Lerner nowhere discusses the problem of external economies in production, in the same way that (as has been observed above) he nowhere discusses the problem of external economies or diseconomies in consumption. External economies, it is now generally realised, may be of either of two types: first, they may be due to internal economies in another industry, when, for example, the expansion of firm $A$ increases the demand for railway transport, the development of which, as a result of economies internal to the railway, reduces the cost of transport also to firm $B$; or, secondly, external economies (or in this case, diseconomies) may arise because the conventions of accountancy are such that when one firm expands production it may not itself receive payment for the whole of the marginal product of the additional factors which it hires (or may not itself pay for all of the additional factors which it uses), as, for example, when the drainage of a particular piece of land improves (or injures) the productivity of neighbouring land.

By implication, Mr Lerner may be said to have dealt satisfactorily with the first type of external economy, when he argues that in all firms subject to increasing returns (as the result of the use of indivisible factors of production which give rise to internal economies) The Rule should be so applied as to equate the price charged for the product to the marginal and not to the average cost of production. For, if the cost of railway transport to firm $A$ and to firm $B$ is, *as a result of the application of The Rule within the railway system*, equal to the marginal cost of such transport, then there is no reason to take special measures to expand the production of firm $A$ or firm $B$ beyond the level which perfect competition between them will bring about. Each will now bear no more than the cost to society of its own additional demand for railway transport. External economies, due to internal economies within another firm, present no divergence between social and private products, provided that prices are equal to marginal costs in the firm to which the economies are internal.

But it is an unfortunate omission that Mr Lerner does not refer to the second type of external economy. There may well be perfect competition all round and yet a misuse of resources because, for example, firms are not charged for the damage which their smoke causes in the district; because they are not charged (or rewarded) for the pain (or pleasure) which the design of their building causes as a part of the surrounding landscape; or because of the many other ways in which they are not charged or paid for the various disadvantages or advantages which their actions may confer on others. These possibilities are in many cases indistinguishable from the problem, discussed earlier in this review, of external economies or diseconomies in private consumption. Thus, the effect which the design and planning of my house has in improving or worsening the amenities for my neighbours may be regarded indifferently as an external economy or diseconomy either of the production or of the consumption of my house. Here is a whole range of effects demanding state control (whether by a system of taxes and subsidies or by other means) of which Mr Lerner does not write.

On the other hand, Mr Lerner writes at length and to great effect upon the problem of indivisibilities of factors of production which are the cause of internal economies (Chapters 15 and 16). But in this connection Mr Lerner falls into an error for which I have recently myself been justly rebuked.[5] I take this opportunity of passing on the rebuke. Mr Lerner argues that, for technical reasons, factors of production may be indivisible, in the sense that one has to employ a factor for a particular purpose (if one is going to employ it at all for that purpose) in a large and indivisible lump. Such indivisibilities, if they are significant (i.e. if they are large in relation to the total market for the commodity in question), are bound to cause a monopolistic situation.

Up to this point, Mr Lerner's argument is unassailable. But he then proceeds to argue that in all such cases, if the industry is socialised and run in such a way as to equate the price of the product to its marginal cost, the price will be below the average cost, and losses will be incurred. But this is not the case. It is true that losses may be incurred in this case; but it is also true that abnormal profits may be earned. Suppose that there are two factors, $A$ and $B$, producing a given product; that factor $A$ is indivisible and fixed in amount for technical reasons; and that successive units of $B$ are applied to the indivisible factor $A$ until so much is produced that the price of the product is equal to its marginal cost in terms of $B$. Now, at given market prices for $A$[6] and $B$ there would be a certain optimum or most economical proportion in which the factors $A$ and $B$ would be employed, if the total market for the product were large enough to enable a large number of units of $A$ (instead of only one) to be employed. A huge expansion in the demand for the product would make it possible to produce with a large number of units of $A$, each served by a rather smaller (or greater) number of units of the divisible factor $B$. In this case the most economical relation between $A$ and $B$ would be found; returns to $A$ and $B$ together would be constant; average costs would equal marginal costs; and the payment of rewards to $A$ and $B$ equal to the value of their marginal products would absorb the whole of the product, no more and no less.

But suppose the market for the product to leave room for only one unit of $A$. The market may be too small to allow (on the principle of equating the price of the product to the marginal cost) the amount of $B$ to increase until the optimum ratio between $B$ and $A$ is reached; or it may be great enough to cause the ratio of $B$ to $A$ to grow beyond the optimum ratio without being large enough to justify the employment of a second unit of $A$. The payment of a reward to $B$ equal to the value of its marginal

---

[5] See symposium on 'Price and Output Policy of State Enterprise' by J. E. Meade and J. M. Fleming, [Chapter 3 above, pp. 16–31].

[6] It may, at first sight, appear meaningless to talk of the market price of $A$ because, being a single indivisible fixed factor, its value will simply depend on the actual profit which it earns; and in this case the statement in the text would merely beg the question of the most economical ratio between $A$ and $B$. But this is not so. A factor may well be indivisible in one industry, but divisible in many alternative occupations. Thus, the capital invested in the permanent way of a railway system is indivisible in the railway system; but if it were allowed to depreciate, the depreciation funds so released could be invested at the margin in a host of alternative industries in which capital could be employed in small divisible units. The market price of the indivisible unit of capital in the railway system is the price which the same resources could have obtained if they had been invested at the margin in alternative uses.

product will mean that in the first case a loss, and in the second case a profit, is made on $A$.[7]

Throughout Chapters 15 and 16 of his book Mr Lerner assumes that the first case is universally true. He argues (quite correctly) that all industries in which there are significant indivisibilities will be monopolistic; he adds (quite incorrectly) that if they are socialised and run so as to equate price to marginal cost they will necessarily be run at a loss. This contention is all the more remarkable because in the following chapter Mr Lerner, in connection with a discussion of the size of firms, pays attention to precisely the opposite case in which the ratio of the divisible to the indivisible factors is 'too great' and an abnormal profit is made in consequence. There is a strange inconsistency in this. Mr Lerner writes as if, in one pigeon-hole in his mind, there was a theory about 'too great' a ratio of indivisible to divisible factors leading to losses in socialised industries run according to The Rule, while in another pigeon-hole there was a quite separate theory about 'too great' a ratio of divisible to indivisible factors causing positive quasi-rents and affecting the size of firms. In fact, there is only one theory.

Mr Lerner is right in arguing that if there are significant indivisibilities (i.e. significant in relation to the size of the market for the product), perfect competition will be ruled out. It would, in fact, always pay a firm in perfect competition either to expand or to close down if the ratio of the divisible factor $B$ to the indivisible factor $A$ were too great or too small. In the former case the firm could always produce at a lower cost per unit by taking on more $B$ with the single unit of $A$, and in the latter by taking on two units of $A$ instead of one, but taking on rather less than twice as much $B$. Significant indivisibilities and uneconomic ratios between $A$ and $B$ are incompatible with perfect competition.

Mr Lerner is also right in arguing that where there are significant indivisibilities, the question whether another unit of the indivisible factor $A$ should be employed or not involves measuring consumers' surplus (pp. 189–198). The employment of a first unit of an indivisible input does not involve merely adding a small increment to the existing output of the product concerned, the value of which can be measured by the price which consumers are willing to pay per unit. It involves producing a large output of the product concerned instead of producing none of it; and the amount which consumers would pay rather than go without this product entirely is something quite different from the number of units produced multiplied by the price which they are willing to pay for the last unit.

Mr Lerner has written some interesting paragraphs on this problem. But here is a field, in the reviewer's opinion, in which much further work remains to be done before the pure theory (let alone the practical implications) of this matter can be considered to be adequately covered.

[7] A realistic example may help. The demand for transport on a socialised railway may be so small that the indivisible permanent way, etc. is necessarily excessive in relation to the traffic carried, and losses are made if only marginal costs are charged. But the demand might grow until there was an excessive load of traffic on the permanent way, and marginal costs were in consequence very high, and considerably in excess of average costs. Yet there might not be enough traffic to justify building a second permanent way.

The pure theory is really fairly simple when there is an indivisible factor in only one industry. But suppose that the indivisible factor in industry $X$ would also be an indivisible factor in its alternative uses in industries $Y$ or $Z$. Then it would be necessary to compare the consumers' surplus lost in $X$ with the consumers' surplus gained in $Y$ or $Z$ by transferring the indivisible factor from $X$ to $Y$ or $Z$. This may be theoretically fairly simple if products $X$, $Y$ and $Z$ are independent of each other in consumption. But what is the answer if $X$ is a close substitute for $Y$ or jointly demanded with $Z$? What do the consumers' surpluses for $X$, $Y$ and $Z$ now mean?

Or suppose that industries $X$ and $Y$ produce close substitutes (gas and electricity), and that each involves the employment of an indivisible factor, though not necessarily of the same factor in each case. Should the community produce (*a*) no gas and no electricity, (*b*) some gas but no electricity, (*c*) some electricity but no gas, or (*d*) some electricity and some gas? How are the consumers' surpluses for different amounts of the close substitutes, gas and electricity, to be measured simultaneously? It is to be hoped that Mr Lerner will set his mind to work to round off his system of thought with answers to these basic questions. There are few, if any, economists better qualified than he to discover them.

## IV

On page 3 of his book Mr Lerner writes that 'the three principal problems to be faced in a controlled economy are employment, monopoly and the distribution of income.' There is, however, a fourth and equally fundamental problem in the economics of welfare – namely, the problem of the optimum supply of the factors of production. It is a pity that Mr Lerner did not give this fourth basic problem the same consistent treatment which he affords to the others. As it is, there are certain observations on this question made in passing in the various chapters of his book; but when his views on this subject are collected together and considered as a whole, they are found to be less satisfactory than his work on the other fundamental topics; they are both inconsistent and incomplete.

It is not only that the problem of the best supply of the factors has as much formal right in logic to separate treatment as the problem of the full use of resources, the problem of the best use of resources as between different employment, and the problem of the best distribution of incomes. There are likely to be clashes between certain acts of policy which will promote one of these objectives, but react adversely on one of the others. Most of these conflicts can be resolved by one means or another; but there is likely to be a basic conflict between the problem of the best distribution of income and the problem of the best supply of the factors of production. To take an extreme example, a tax system which (in the interests of the distribution of income) was so progressive as to take 100% of income away from incomes above $X$, while it took nothing away from incomes below $X$, would clearly have adverse effects upon the amount of work and risk-bearing, to say nothing of the amount of saving, which would be undertaken. And in the case of the amount of work done, it is difficult to conceive of any solution on reasonably liberal lines of this conflict which is not, in fact, a compromise. This conflict is recognised by Mr Lerner when he writes that 'the principle of equality would have to compromise with the principle of providing such incentives as would increase the total of income available to be divided' (p. 36). But it is to be regretted that he has nowhere systematically treated this problem.

This problem of incentives is often used as one of the principal arguments in favour of the repayment of state debt or even of the accumulation of net income-bearing assets by the state, on the grounds that to the extent to which this is done it will not be necessary to raise revenue by taxation. This lessened incidence of taxation on work, risk-bearing and private savings will, it is argued, improve incentives.

Mr Lerner nowhere develops this argument. Indeed, he develops a startling argument which is its direct denial. In the first half of Chapter 24 he argues that the interest paid by the state on the internal national debt is in no sense a burden on the community – an argument which is, of course, the direct reverse of the view that it is desirable for the state to earn a net income on state-owned property. But Mr Lerner's assertion is manifestly not true. Consider two communities which are otherwise identical, but in the first of which there is no internal national debt, while in the second there is a national debt the interest on which is as great as the rest of the national income put together:

|  | Communities: | |
|  | I | II |
| Net National Income at Factor Cost | 100 | 100 |
| National Debt Interest | Nil | 100 |
| Taxable Income | 100 | 200 |
| Rate of Taxation of Taxable Income | Nil | 50% |
| Income after payment of Tax | 100 | 100 |

In community I, individuals earn 100; the state has nothing to pay out, and there is no taxation. Individuals are left with a tax-free income of 100 *on the assurance that they will lose the enjoyment of the whole of any income which they desist from earning.* In community II, individuals earn 100; they receive 100 in interest from the state; their taxable incomes are, therefore, 200, of which the state takes 100 in taxation to finance the national debt interest. Individuals are left (as in community I) with a tax-free income of 100, *but this time on the assurance that they will lose only 50% of any income which they desist from earning.* Naturally, in the second case they will work less hard, and will strike a balance between work and leisure which is more inclined to leisure than the facts of the economic situation really warrant.

Nor is Mr Lerner able to escape from the logic of this argument by pleading that the national debt interest may not matter because, on his principles of 'functional finance' (see Chapter 24), the correct course may be to continue to borrow and not to tax in order to meet the interest on the debt. Suppose that in both the communities examined above (which – it will be remembered – are assumed to be identical in all respects except the sizes of their national debts) individuals save one-sixth of their tax-free incomes; that there are no profitable outlets for investment; and that the state therefore (on the correct principles of functional finance) borrows 20 and puts this back into circulation, in the case of community I by paying a social dividend to consumers, and in the case of community II by reducing taxation below the revenue required to pay the interest on the national debt. The situation is then as follows:

|  | Communities: | |
| --- | --- | --- |
|  | I | II |
| Net National Income at Factor Cost | 100 | 100 |
| National Debt Interest | Nil | 100 |
| Social Dividend | 20 | Nil |
| Taxable Income | 120 | 200 |
| Rate of Taxation | Nil | 40% |
| Income after payment of Tax | 120 | 120 |
| Of which: (i) saved | 20 | 20 |
| (ii) spent on goods and services | 100 | 100 |

Again, individuals will in both cases have the same real spendable income; but while, in community I, an individual will keep the whole, in community II he will keep only 60% of the last units of income which he chooses to earn. Again, he will cut down the amount of work which he does in community II, though not by quite so much as he would have done in the case previously examined.

We may conclude that the existence of a national debt will have an adverse effect upon incentives, unless (on the principle of running a budget deficit just sufficient to maintain full employment but not large enough to provoke inflation) the necessary borrowing is as great as the total interest payable on the national debt. But if this is the case, the continued increase in the national debt will sooner or later bring the interest payable on it above the level of the budget deficit required to maintain employment; and at this point, in order to prevent inflation, increasing rates of taxation will be required to finance the debt interest, with consequential ill effects upon incentives.

To what extent the existence of a large internal debt is a burden to the community will depend, of course, on the degree to which high rates of taxation in themselves exert an adverse influence upon incentives to work and enterprise. On this subject Mr Lerner makes a number of observations in different passages of his book; but his position is not entirely a consistent one.

On the one hand, in certain passages he lays great stress on the principle that people should be paid rewards equal to the value of the marginal product of their effort. Thus (pp. 102–105), he examines the proposition that, in order to obtain the optimum use of resources, it is necessary only to see that prices are everywhere proportional, and not necessarily equal, to marginal costs. This solution he rejects on the grounds that this, involving as it does a divergence between the reward of labour and its marginal product, will disturb the choice between work and leisure. In another passage (p. 267) he insists that any 'social dividend' which the state may wish to pay to consumers in order to maintain demand may be distributed on any principle considered equitable, the only proviso being 'that the amount paid out to any individual should not in any way be affected by the amount of work he does'. This proviso, he argues, is necessary in order to preserve an equality between the reward of labour and the value of its marginal product 'so as to induce neither too much nor too little labour'.

On the other hand, Mr Lerner's paragraphs on the income tax (pp. 234–240) are largely designed as a defence of this form of tax; and they play down the importance of the principle (of equality between the net reward and the value of the marginal product of labour) which, in the two cases quoted immediately above, he has so much emphasised. And yet a proportional income tax has exactly the same effect as making prices proportional, instead of equal, to marginal costs. True, Mr Lerner still recognises the problem when he writes of the income tax; and, admitting that the income tax, by falling on money income but not on leisure, may upset the proper balance between work and leisure, he proposes (what must surely be one of his less practical suggestions) that one might add 'to a man's income, for income-tax purposes, that part which he was able to earn but did not because he preferred to work less than some standard amount'. He admits that, even if this were done, people would still have a bias against the high-paid (though arduous or unpleasant) tasks, but asserts that 'these deviations would not be of very great magnitude'. He hardly makes any mention of the possible evil effects upon the amount of work done of a progressive income tax, which may greatly reduce the marginal reward below the value of the marginal product of labour. He merely asserts that 'this is not of importance because the high incomes are rarely the result of work. . . In those few cases where individual effort is of importance the work is usually of a kind that is sufficiently interesting to bring about the socially desirable amount of work whatever the payment for it'.

Mr Lerner does recognise (pp. 238–239) that, theoretically, progressive taxation (on the 'heads I lose, tails you win' principle) may be inimical to business enterprise. But, in the first place, he does not recognise that a high rate of tax, as opposed to a highly progressive tax, may discourage enterprise merely by reducing the net reward that remains for undertaking any given risk.[8] And, in the second place, he again stresses the reasons for believing that, in this respect, too, the case against the income tax 'is easily exaggerated'. This may be the case. But Mr Lerner must make up his mind whether or not the principle of equality between rewards and marginal products is important; and he must apply the conclusion indifferently to taxation, the social dividend, the relation between prices and costs and all the other problems in which essentially this same analysis is at issue.

There are also a number of passages in Mr Lerner's book where he

---

[8] See J. R. Hicks, U.K. Hicks and L. Rostas, *The Taxation of War Wealth* (Oxford; Clarendon Press, 1941), p. 192.

discusses what may be called 'the optimum rate of savings'. There are some passages which suggest that the optimum supply of savings is the amount which people would be willing to save at the current rate of interest in a free market for their savings, i.e. the amount by which individuals would be willing to postpone their consumption in return for earning on this postponed consumption an amount equal to the market rate of interest.[9]

But in certain other passages Mr Lerner gives a very strange twist to this proposition (pp. 265–269). Having argued that the determination of the level of investment, and so of the proportion of its annual resources which a controlled economy will put aside for the benefit of future production, must be largely a political question, he goes on to suggest that consumers might be left free to save from their income at the current rate of interest, and that their actions in this respect could be used as a guide to determine whether, in the fully controlled economy, steps should be taken (through a change in the rate of interest) to increase or decrease total investment. The criterion which he suggests seems to be that if consumers lend more than they borrow (however small their net savings may be), then the rate of investment should be increased (however large it may already be). But surely the criterion of consumers' choice can only be used to equate the rate of consumers' saving with the rate of total national investment. There can surely be no point at all in determining whether the rate of investment should be raised or lowered by the criterion whether consumers' savings are positive or negative.

Mr Lerner does not, in this connection, refer to the criterion for the optimum rate of saving developed by F. P. Ramsey in his article in the *Economic Journal* for December 1928, on 'A Mathematical Theory of Saving', [vol. 38, pp. 543–59] nor to the reasons (such as the mortality of the human individual as compared with the practical immortality of the human community) for believing that the aggregated actions of individual savers may differ from the social optimum. Yet if Mr Lerner had studied the implications of Ramsey's conclusion that the optimum rate of saving was independent of the rate of interest, he might have seriously modified his analysis.[10]

## V

In Chapters 20–25 of his book Mr Lerner turns to the problems of Investment and Employment, his previous discussion of the principles of welfare economics being based on the assumption that all factors are fully employed.

Mr Lerner opens this section with what is probably the most stimulating and original part of his work (Chapter 20), in which he

---

[9] See, for example, the paragraph beginning at the bottom of page 344, and ending at the top of page 345.

[10] Mr Lerner does not consider the problem of the optimum population, which is also an essential problem of the optimum supply of the factors of production.

outlines a theory of interest for the economy which is in equilibrium with full employment. He argues that it is the nature of capital that productive methods which take time increase the total product available. For this reason, the resources which are released by refraining from producing 100 units of steel this year are able to produce 110 units of steel next year. Steel this year is a different commodity from steel next year; but since, in equilibrium, the cost of the factors must be equal to the value of the marginal product of those factors, it follows that the cost of 100 units of steel this year must be equal to the value of 110 units of steel next year. In other words, the price of any commodity must be falling at a rate equal to the rate of return on the postponement of its consumption.

Mr Lerner then proceeds to point out that this general decline in the price level is prevented by the device of a rate of interest on money. The rate of interest must be added to the cost of this year's factors before their cost is equated to the value of next year's product. Thus, in equilibrium, the money rate of interest plus the rate of decline in prices is equal to the rate of return on capital. What started off as a startling and paradoxical new truth turns out to be the familiar distinction between the money and the real rate of interest in a new form. Nevertheless, the method of analysis is extremely novel and stimulating.[11]

Passing from the theory of interest in a state of full employment to the theory of unemployment, Mr Lerner has much of interest to say. The reader is referred to his discussion on Keynesian lines of the mechanisms by which an uncontrolled economy corrects a position of unemployment and of the various points at which this mechanism fails to operate effectively (Chapters 22 and 23); and to his highly satisfactory discussion of the relationship between the marginal productivity of capital and the marginal efficiency of investment (graphically represented on page 336).

Unfortunately, it is not possible here to explore thoroughly all the ideas developed in this part of his book. But it may be useful to expound briefly and to comment on the main prescriptions of employment policy which Mr Lerner outlines in Chapters 21 and 24. The steps in his argument seem to be as follows:

(i)     In the controlled economy, steps should be taken (e.g. through the rate of interest) to see that investment proceeds at the correct rate from the point of view of obtaining the optimum allocation of resources for future as opposed to present uses (pp. 264–265).

(ii)    Through its taxation policy or, if necessary, through the payment of a 'social dividend' to all consumers, the state should see that this level of investment is accompanied by a level of consumption sufficient to give full employment (pp. 266–270).

(iii)   Such action may admittedly involve a continuing budget

---

[11] Unfortunately, there is no space to explain here the way in which, for a dynamic world in which relative prices are changing, Mr Lerner works out the relationship between the rate of interest and rates of productivity and of price change of the various commodities.

deficit.[12] But Mr Lerner argues that a budget deficit is innocuous, because an internal national debt is innocuous. He argues for what he calls the principles of 'functional finance', namely that the state should lend or borrow money in order to affect the rate of interest, and so the incentive to invest, and should tax or pay money out in a social dividend in order to affect consumers' incomes, and so the level of consumption. By these means the state should control the total national expenditure in such a way as to achieve full employment without inflation, regardless of the effect upon the budget deficit or the national debt, which are really matters of complete indifference.

Reasons have already been adduced above for doubting whether the size of the national debt is really in effect a matter of indifference. Some may, therefore, wish to add to Mr Lerner's objectives the balancing of the budget, or indeed some net repayment of the national debt over the average of years. There would seem to be two main ways of aiming at this objective without prejudicing the objective of full employment.

In the first place, a monetary policy which reduces the money rate of interest (or a price policy which allows for a rising level of money prices) will reduce the real rate of interest and will, thus, stimulate the level of investment. If, however, the level of investment has already been fixed at the optimum level from the point of view of the division of resources between present and future uses, this method would maintain employment and the balance of the budget at the expense of devoting too large a proportion of resources to future uses.[13]

Secondly, fiscal changes might be adopted to persuade people to spend a larger proportion of their income on consumption and to save less. Mr Lerner discusses one such type of change (p. 319) by redistributing income through heavier taxes on the rich and lower taxes on the poor, who save a smaller proportion of their income at the margin than do the rich. But, as has been suggested earlier in this review, beyond a point, progressive taxation may have a serious effect upon incentives; and it is therefore to be regretted that Mr Lerner has not also considered the possibility of taxes which, apart from their effect upon the distribution of income, might induce people to spend a larger proportion of a given income upon consumption.

---

[12] The continuation of a budget deficit for the purpose of stimulating consumption (e.g. by tax remission or the payment of a 'social dividend') would, of course, mean that investment was continually less than the amount which consumers decided to save out of their incomes. If, as has been suggested earlier in this review, there are passages in Mr Lerner's book in which he suggests that the correct level of investment corresponds with the amount which consumers freely decide to save, the continuation of a budget deficit of this kind would indicate that investment had not, in fact, been fixed at the optimum level.

[13] But if the optimum use of resources for the future is defined as that which corresponds to the free savings of consumers, there can be no conflict of principle between the balanced budget and the correct division of resources between present and future uses.

## VI

Mr Lerner concludes his book with a series of chapters on the application of his principles of welfare economics to foreign trade and to external economic relations in general. These passages (Chapters 26–29) provide an interesting exercise in the application to external relations of the principles of pricing which have been developed at length for the internal economy in the earlier chapters.

Unfortunately, this review has already reached such a length that it is impossible to discuss these chapters in detail. But they are as interesting and provocative as the rest of Mr Lerner's book, and are highly to be recommended to the reader's attention. It must suffice here to draw attention to one particular 'Lernerism'. On pages 356–362 and 382–385 Mr Lerner provides an ingenious formula for the optimum rate of tax on foreign trade which a country should impose 'if it is desired to exploit the foreigner'. The technical economist will be fascinated. The commonsensical reader will be puzzled when he realises that the formula involves taxes on exports as well as on imports, and altogether discouraged when he learns that, if the foreigner retaliates, the formula falls to the ground and all parties suffer an economic loss.

.

# 5

## The Socialisation of Industries. Memorandum by the Economic Section of the Cabinet Secretariat

*This memorandum represents the views of the Economic Section on several issues relating to nationalisation as expressed officially in November and December 1945 during the initial deliberations of the first post-war Labour Government on their nationalisation programme. Several members of the Section, most notably D. N. Chester and J. M. Fleming, worked on it; Meade wrote the first draft of the introductory paragraphs and, after 'innumerable discussions' and debate within the Section, the final version of a large part of it. (The questions of the Lord President of the Council, Herbert Morrison, to which the memorandum is a reply, had been suggested to him by Meade, and drafted in the Economic Section, in September 1945.) (Public Record Office T230/18, 19 and 106; Meade Papers 3/2; Meade Diary, 16 September, 3 and 18 November, and 2 December 1945; for the Labour Government's decisions on the issues involved see Sir Norman Chester,* The Nationalisation of British Industry 1945–51 *(London: HMSO, 1975).*

### Introduction

1   In the later paragraphs of this paper the Economic Section expresses its comments on the questions which the Lord President addressed to the departments concerned with the socialisation of various industries. It may, however, be useful, by way of introduction, to explain the general principles which the Economic Section have had in mind in framing their comments on these questions.

2   Industries may be socialised for a variety of reasons, political, strategical, social or economic. We are here concerned exclusively with the economic objectives. If full compensation is paid, the socialisation of an industry will have little or no direct effect upon the distribution of income. The principal economic effects of such a measure are, therefore, to be sought in the sphere of productive efficiency.

3   Productive efficiency is not attained merely by applying the most

up-to-date engineering, chemical or other technical methods of production to the socialised industry. It also depends upon securing a proper balance in the allocation of resources between the various plants and industries, whether publicly or privately operated. It is, therefore, a necessary part of the efficiency of any industry that, in determining the scale and methods of production, due regard should be had to the criteria of costs and prices.

4   In general, output should be produced by whichever methods are, at currently prevailing prices and costs, the cheapest, and production should continue to be expanded so long as the cost of additional output does not exceed the price which consumers are willing to pay for it. Social considerations (such as the need to moderate the speed of social adjustments which a sudden economic change might otherwise necessitate) may, of course, dictate a departure from this broad principle in particular cases.

5   It is not possible for the economist as such to say whether any particular industry is likely to be run more efficiently under private or public operation. This will depend on a great many circumstances of a political, psychological and administrative character. It is possible, however, to give certain general indications as to the characteristics which, other things being equal, tend to make an industry, from the economic standpoint, more suitable for socialisation.

6   The following are the principal considerations which arise in this connection:—

(a) *The degree to which competition prevails or can be made to prevail in the industry.* Firms working under conditions of full and free competition have at least a strong incentive to conduct their operations according to economic principles. Firms working under more or less monopolistic conditions have an incentive unduly to restrict output and to stifle enterprise. There are a number of industries in which, for technical reasons, true competition is not possible. For example, there is no room for more than one railway network to serve one region. In any single city it would, for technical reasons, be uneconomical to have a large number of independent firms supplying gas or electricity. In such industries the application of anti-restrictive measures, however strenuously adopted, are not likely to restore private competition; they are, therefore, *prima facie*, more suitable for socialisation than those where full competition obtains. Industries which, though potentially competitive, have shown a strong tendency to develop restrictive practices by the formation of cartels, price-fixing associations and the like, which could only be counteracted by state action, fall into an intermediate category.

(b) *Ratio of capital costs to current costs.* Other things being equal, highly capitalistic industries, which use a great deal of plant and equipment and relatively little labour, are more suitable for socialisation than other industries. There are a number of reasons for this:—

(i)    Industries which use a great deal of durable plant and equipment have to make a great many investment decisions, i.e. decisions affecting the more or less distant future. But the competitive market system is less efficient as an instrument for co-ordinating economic decisions affecting the more distant future than for those affecting the immediate future. The advantages of central planning by an industry as a whole are therefore greatest where investment is concerned, and industries which incur a great deal of capital outlay are relatively suitable for centralised control, whether private or public.

(ii)   The arrangements for providing capital funds to industry are subject to imperfections which it is difficult to remedy under private enterprise.

(iii)  Private investment expenditure is one of the most volatile and disturbing elements in the aggregate national expenditure on goods and services. In so far as socialisation will tend to make industrial investment more amenable to control from the point of view of general employment policy, this consideration applies specially to the socialisation of capitalistic industries.

(c) *The degree of 'senility' of an industry.* An old industry whose personnel may have become ossified and conservative, and which may therefore have tended to fall markedly behind recognised modern standards of technical efficiency, is perhaps more likely to derive immediate benefit from socialisation than a new industry which is still in the stage of experimentation and growth and which will probably have attracted to itself a more enterprising type of business man. Account would have to be taken of the fact that there may be efficient firms in an otherwise inefficient industry, and of the possibility of combating the inefficiency by regulation falling short of complete socialisation.

7    It does not follow, because an industry or service is socialised, that all competing industries should be socialised too. Competition among public enterprises, and between public and private enterprises, has some of the same virtues as competition between private firms. Without it, it may be difficult not only to maintain an adequate incentive to efficiency, but even to decide what is in fact the most economic scale and method of production. If private enterprise or competing suppliers in other countries can provide an alternative service at lower cost than the socialised industry then, in the interests of a higher standard of living, the alternative service should expand. Similarly, if the service provided by the socialised undertaking could undercut any domestic or foreign competitors it should expand at their expense. For these reasons, in deciding the scope of the concern to be socialised it is not essential to socialise every undertaking that may compete with the socialised undertaking. Competitive coastal shipping may be left to compete with a nationalised railway system. In the iron and steel industry it may even be wise to socialise certain sections of the industry which must, for technical reasons, be on a very large scale in relation to the market for their product, but to leave other sections of the industry unsocialised.

8    From a purely economic point of view there would be considerable advantages in an early Government decision and announcement which particular industries or sections of industry were to be socialised, and which were to be left to the conduct of private enterprise. Such an announcement would remove existing uncertainty from those industries not on the list for socialisation; and this would free them from doubts which are likely otherwise to impede their development. If such an announcement were accompanied by a statement that freedom from socialisation was conditional upon the avoidance of restrictive practices by industries which were left to private enterprise, and by a statement that the Government intended to take powers to prevent such restrictive practices, the result might be to encourage the unsocialised sector of industry to concentrate upon the economically cheapest methods of production and to expand output so long as the cost of the additional production was lower than the price obtainable for it.

9    This would confine the range of uncertainty to those industries which were on the list for socialisation, but had not yet been socialised. The problem of securing adequate capital development and increased technical efficiency in these industries during the interim period before socialisation is a special one to which reference is made in later paragraphs of this paper.

## (1)   On what basis and on what scale of generosity should the owners of industries which are being socialised be compensated?

1    The amount of compensation must be fair to the existing owners, if only for the bad effect which unfairness would have upon other industries on the list to be socialised. It is only in a 'once-for-all' revolution that one can afford to disregard the consequences of expropriation.

2    There is no simple rule for ascertaining the fair price for an industry. The proper price would be that arranged between a willing buyer and a willing seller under normal market conditions. The problem is how best to assess this fair market price.

3    Before considering the methods of assessing fair market value, there is a general question of principle as to what should be included in this value. The earnings of certain firms or industries may be higher by virtue of such firms having a monopoly or being protected by tariffs from foreign competition. Should a continuation of this monopoly or protection be assumed for purposes of calculating the fair price? This question arises in its most acute form when as in the case of tariff protection the higher earnings are in effect due to state intervention. The Coal Mines Act of 1930 undoubtedly increased the general prosperity of the coal industry, as did the Import Duties Act [of 1932] improve the position of the British steel industry. On the one hand it may be argued that the state

should not be asked to pay for that part of an industry's earnings which is due to Government action; in the case of unsocialised industry, it may be argued, the Government might reverse such action without the payment of compensation. On the other hand, if past investors have put their money into the industry in the legitimate expectation of the continuation of a Governmental policy, which would probably not have been reversed if the industry had not been socialised, it may be argued that it would be arbitrary not to allow for these expectations in assessing the desirable level of compensation. No doubt the theoretically fair assessment would allow for that degree of monopoly revenue or of protection which the Government would have permitted to continue if the industry had not been socialised, but in practice this must clearly be a matter of dispute.

4    The nearest approach to a normal market price would be the value set upon the share capital of the industry by free transactions on the Stock Exchange at a date or over a period prior to the nationalisation announcement. The value of the shares should reflect the market's assessment of the present and future prospects of the industry's earning power. The difficulties in the way of the use of this method are largely practical: in most industries only a small part of the total capital is in the form of shares with Stock Exchange quotations and even these shares may come on the market only at infrequent intervals and in small batches.

5    Whilst for various reasons the Stock Exchange quotations are not a completely reliable guide, they may in some cases act as an additional check on the fairness of the price, e.g. the quotations of almost all railway stocks and shares are readily obtainable. H. Campion, in his *Public and Private Property in Great Britain* [London: Oxford University Press, 1939] obtained a direct valuation of the railway companies by using Stock Exchange quotations. He obtained a figure for the railway companies as a whole (excluding the London Underground Companies and the Manchester Ship Canal) of £720–£800 million in 1932–1934 (the value of capital expenditure stated in the Annual Railway Return for 1934 was over £1,100 million).

6    In some cases the actual capital cost incurred less depreciation may be a rough guide to a fair price, though it can never be more than this for several reasons:—

(*a*)    The capital expenditure may or may not have been wisely incurred and therefore may or may not be reflected in current earnings.

(*b*)    Capital expenditure incurred in the past is no guide to future earning and a large element in the purchase price must be the weight given to the possibility of the undertaking continuing to be profitable.

(*c*)    Actual capital expenditure would take no account of changes in the price level: e.g. the cost of heavy steel plant was some 50 per cent higher in 1939 than in 1934.

7    The current cost of constructing a similar undertaking may be no

guide to its market price. The prospective earning power may be much lower by reason of a decline in the demand for the industry's products and a good deal of the existing capacity may be surplus. And where much of the plant in an industry is out of date the capital cost of reproducing that plant is clearly no guide to a possible purchase price.

8    As it will seldom prove possible to arrive at the fair price by the normal method of finding what the article would be worth if sold in a free market, it will often be best to estimate this figure by an indirect method. The market value of an asset, being a capital figure, is a compound of three elements:—

(*a*)    The prospective earning power of the asset.
(*b*)    The degree of risk involved.
(*c*)    The market rate of interest.

The last two elements are combined into a multiplier or 'number of years purchase'. The higher the market rate of interest or the risk element, the lower should be the multiplier. But (*a*) and (*b*) are closely interrelated, for the more difficult it is to reach a figure of prospective annual earning power, the more likely it is that those uncertainties will be reflected in (*b*), the degree of risk involved. Thus, where an industry has been making a steady profit of say £10 millions over a period of say 10 years, one would expect the multiplier to be higher than where the profits of the industry have fluctuated very considerably in past years.

9    A special problem will arise in the acquisition of local authority or other non-profitmaking undertakings. Some local authorities have run their undertakings at a loss either deliberately or because they could not avoid it, and in most cases the custom has been to make little or no profit. It will therefore be impossible in this case to obtain any figure of earning power from records of past net profits. In all such cases no doubt the main emphasis will have to be placed upon the original cost of the undertaking less depreciation. Sometimes, net outstanding debt is advocated as a basis, and in most cases this would be highly favourable to the socialised industry as the basis for purchase. Here again, however, it must be stressed that the basis used must bear a close relation to a reasonable estimate of the earning power of the undertakings acquired.

10    The objection to the net outstanding debt basis from the local authority point of view is that it is likely to prove unfair as between different localities. Thus, one local authority may have adopted a conservative financial policy by meeting small items of capital expenditure out of current revenue, whereas another authority may have incurred debt for such items. Some authorities may be obtaining relief in aid of local rates from their undertaking as they are entitled to do, for example, under the Electricity Supply Act, 1926: the net outstanding debt basis would leave these authorities with an added burden. Finally, in so far as the different financial policies adopted by different local

authorities are likely to be reflected in the price charged for gas or electricity in their area, they may well claim that any advantages accruing to their ratepayers as consumers should be at least safeguarded, and that the Board in fixing prices in their area should have regard to the favourable purchase price at which they acquired that part of the total undertaking. Otherwise the local authorities may argue that the advantages which should accrue to the consumers in their areas will be shared with the consumer in the Company area where the purchase price has been at a higher rate. The position of the local authority undertaking will therefore require special consideration.

11    There are two main ways in which the total purchase price for the whole industry can be ascertained. The first would be to make a separate valuation of each plant or undertaking or, in effect, to find the net maintainable revenue of each firm in the industry. The total purchase price by this method would be a summation of a series of individual purchase prices. The alternative method, which is at present generally favoured, is for a global valuation to be made of the industry as a whole and for the payment to the individual firms to be made in the same ratio as their individual valuation bears to the total sum of the individual claims. The global valuation thus acts as a ceiling price and, should the sum of the individual claims be higher, then each claim is scaled down proportionately.

12    The arguments in favour of the second method are that the same factors have to be taken into account in making each of the individual valuations, and that only in a global valuation can such factors be given their correct weight. Thus, each firm in an industry may claim that its production would be likely to expand and the valuer might find it difficult to disprove this claim, though it would be clear, taking the prospects of the industry as a whole, that one firm's output and profitability must inevitably mean lower output and possible losses for another firm.

13    The danger of the global valuation is that it may do less than justice to the efficient and profitable undertaking. Thus, where a coal-mine has shown a loss over a period and has little or no prospects of making a profit in the future, the relative position of that firm to an efficient and profit-earning pit could be maintained only if the first pit paid a sum into the pool. But it will probably prove necessary to pay the losing or inefficient pit at least a sum based on the physical valuation of its assets. As this figure will rank against the global calculation the Government's charity to the losing or inefficient firms will be at the expense of the profitable and efficient firms. The point could be met by not acquiring any firm which had consistently made a loss or which showed no prospects of earning as much as the figure they claimed for their individual purchase price. Such a firm would ultimately go out of existence, though in so far as the price it could obtain for its products covered its operating costs, it might remain in existence for some time. On the other hand, the state-acquired undertaking, being the more profitable and more efficient, should fear no competition from these losing firms.

14   Special consideration will need to be given to developments incurred after the date of the announcement of socialisation otherwise there may be a tendency to avoid development during a gap between the date of the announcement and the date of actual socialisation. This tendency will be stronger

(*a*)   if the period for measuring current earning power is a long time previous to the date of acquisition, e.g. if the period normally chosen was some time in the 1930s;

(*b*)   if the capital expenditure to be incurred is not likely to show a full yield immediately, e.g. where the plant to be installed anticipates a rising demand and is not completely justified on current demand.

15   Yet the compensation terms cannot provide for a refund on an actual cost basis of capital expenditure incurred after a stated date. Much of that expenditure may be replacement of existing capital and may be necessary in order to maintain the earning power of the undertaking. Some of the expenditure may be unwisely incurred or may be incurred at a price level which cannot be reflected in future earnings. It would, therefore, be unwise to deal specially with capital expenditure incurred after the date without having regard to its relation to the general earning position of the undertaking in the future. It may be that some special arrangement will have to be worked out whereby the compensation basis for development taking place after a stated date will be arranged as and when the necessary consent for development is granted.

16   Development by way of capital expenditure is, however, only one aspect of the problem of maintaining initiative and progressive efficiency during the interregnum between the announcement of and the date of socialisation. The surest incentive would come if it were known that too much stress would not be placed on the global sum, but that the price would be based on the summation of a series of individual valuations in which the fullest regard would be paid to the state of efficiency, plant development and maintenance of each individual undertaking.

## (2)   Should compensation be paid in cash, Government stock, fixed-interest stock secured on the industry, or partly equity stock?

1   There is no special point in paying cash, save where quite small sums are involved, so long as the payment is in the form of a saleable security. Most of the people who received cash would wish to invest it again, possibly in Government securities, and as generally it will be more convenient to the state and of little inconvenience to the owners, it is fair and proper to pay them in the form of securities.

2   The real question is whether the securities should be issued by the Board and secured on the earnings of the socialised industry with or

without a form of Treasury guarantee, or whether the owners should be paid in ordinary Government stock.

3   There are many economic reasons why it may not be desired in the future to run a socialised industry in such a way as to make a profit equal to the interest payable on the compensation money. For example, the industry before it was socialised may have been making a monopoly profit, some part of which has had to be reflected in the cost of compensation and which it is desired to eliminate after socialisation. As will be shown in the comments on Question 5 there are arguments, in certain circumstances, for so running a socialised industry that, either temporarily or permanently, it earns a profit greater or less than the normal rate of return on the capital invested in the industry.

4   The Government would clearly not be free to give general directives to the industry on price policy and similar questions which would have the effect of causing it to make an abnormal profit or loss, if the financial consequences would fall on private stockholders in the industry. For this reason, it would appear inappropriate to compensate by means of stock secured on the profits of the industry with or without Government guarantee. The proper solution would appear to be to raise the money for compensation by means of Government stock. The Government would then be free to give the Board general directives about price policy. It would then be open for the Government to make any arrangements which might be suitable in each particular case for determining the contribution to be made by the industry to the national Exchequer.

## (3)   What form of organisation should be set up to run the industry?

1   The form of organisation is largely a political and administrative question, whilst this note is primarily concerned with the economic aspects of socialisation. But the economic and administrative cannot altogether be separated, for the economic basis on which the industry is to be operated may indicate a particular form of organisation.

2   The purpose of socialisation is to ensure that the industries concerned are operated with the greatest efficiency and economy. To achieve these purposes, the form of organisation must enable the Board[1] to be chosen purely on grounds of its technical and economic ability and of its experience to run an industry of that particular kind. The members of the Board must not be representatives of particular interests, which would be liable to put the economic interest of a special group above that of the community as a whole. They must be directors and managers appointed by the Government purely on grounds of their ability.

[1] The Board form of organisation is assumed in this note. There are, of course, many alternatives: operation by a Government department directly or by an elected Authority or by a Joint Board, etc.

3   The Board must clearly have a large measure of freedom. If it is to have only limited powers and little freedom then people of ability will not be attracted. The proper management of industrial undertakings requires the right and opportunity to take risks and to have the results judged over a period. Annual detailed supervision by the Public Accounts Committee, for example, would probably be inimical to risk-taking and progressive enterprise.

4   Yet the Board cannot be completely independent of the Government. For example, at a time when the Government has decided that investment must be influenced by considerations of employment policy, it would clearly be absurd if the Government had no more control over a socialised industry in this respect than over a privately owned industry. Again, the Government must clearly be in a position to lay down the broad principles of policy on which the Board shall determine the output and price policy of the socialised undertaking.

5   It is not easy to draw a clear distinction between the form of control desirable on general economic grounds and the degree of independence which it is necessary to leave with the Board if they are to feel a sense of responsibility. The question is not wholly settled by drawing a distinction between general control and the avoidance of detailed control for too much general control would leave the Board with few major decisions of policy and might well turn them into largely an executive authority carrying out instructions from a Government department. No doubt the precise balance will be struck over a period by experiment and the use of administrative discretion within the powers given in the Act. But one thing is clear – where a Government direction or Government decision of policy affects what may be called 'commercial' principles of operation (in the sense of causing a divergence from the normal economic calculus of costs and prices), then the responsibility is upon the Government to provide a Treasury subsidy for that purpose. For example, a decision by the Government that the Development Areas should be helped by having a lower price for electricity should be followed by a Treasury subsidy. There is no economic argument for meeting this by means of a higher price for electricity sold to other users.

## (4)   Should we in certain circumstances contemplate separate organisations for different sections or regions of the industry?

1   There is much to be said in favour of dividing large national industries into sections or regions instead of placing them under one national Board. The word 'nationalisation' has tended to imply single national ownership, whereas the same result might well be achieved by having public ownership in the form of several regional Boards. It is not easy to run an industry from Whitehall, and with a strongly centralised administration there is a tendency for power to be concentrated in the hands of

those not directly concerned with the industry, but with its purely administrative and political aspects. The railways were undoubtedly suffering at one time from over centralisation, leaving the local managers too little discretion.

2  It may be that sufficient decentralisation can be obtained by giving the actual works managers large powers of discretion or by having some form of regional Board, but without giving the Boards financial autonomy. But such decentralisation is not always easy to achieve and there is a case for a statutory division of responsibility even to the extent of having regional Boards with their own statutory powers and financial autonomy as has been suggested for electricity supply.

3  Some of the industries will lend themselves to regional organisation; for example, in the case of gas supply there is no apparent technical reason why the gas supply for the North-West should be run by a Board in London. Gas undertakings are essentially single units supplying purely local areas and no gas grid is likely to do more than link up a few local undertakings. Similarly there appear no good economic reasons why the Scottish coalfield or the Durham coalfield should be managed by a Board located in London. It would obviously be quite proper to socialise them by placing them under a local Board appointed by the Government and financially self-supporting.

4  The argument sometimes used in favour of a national Board rather than a series of regional Boards is that only by this method can prices, etc., be made uniform throughout the country. In the answer to Question 5 below strong doubt is thrown upon the validity of the arguments used to favour uniform or pooled prices. Even within the structure of a national Board, it would still be possible to allow for local variations in costs and to avoid pooling. The advantage of regional Boards from this viewpoint would be that it would not be possible for the Boards to do more than pool within their area. Thus the important geographical and economic factors deciding levels of costs in different parts of the country would necessarily be reflected in price.

5  Every effort should be made to leave the managers of particular plants or areas with as much discretion and scope for initiative as possible. Initiative cannot be spoon-fed from a central Board. The Board can do the overall planning and make broad decisions of policy, but in the end the efficiency of the undertaking as a whole will depend upon the ability of the people in the regions and in charge of particular plants, and the incentive which they have to use that ability. Inter-plant or inter-area competition should be encouraged either by circulation and publication of detailed costs or even by a special bonus system.

6  We are still in an experimental stage in the organisation of socialised industries. There is therefore every reason against using one particular method and concentrating upon that. Instead, we should try

out a variety of methods. For example, if there are to be regional electricity Boards, it is not essential that they should all be appointed in the same way or have precisely the same methods of finance. It will look tidier if they are all uniform and it may be that the particular uniform decision may be absolutely right. But serious consideration should be given to varying the structure and methods of organisation so as to provide data upon which to judge the effectiveness of any particular form.

### (5)   How should prices be fixed? Should they pay regard to the regional or sectional differences within the industry? Should the aim be to make some profits, sell at average cost or, in certain circumstances, to sell below average cost?

1   The following observations on price policy in socialised industries are intended to present an ideal, applicable to conditions of comparative normality, towards which we should steadily move, rather than something to be put, in its entirety, into immediate operation. Each industry, on socialisation, will inherit a price structure and a mode of price determination which it would be unwise to abolish overnight but which can be gradually modified in the desired direction. Moreover, some of the principles advocated here are not strictly applicable to conditions of shortage and potential inflation when the pricing system is necessarily in eclipse, and some of its functions are for the time being exercised by controls of the war-time variety. But the pricing problems of the transition period will be more happily solved if the longer-term goal is kept in mind.

2   The basic function of prices is to guide production towards those goods and services which are most needed by the community, and to ensure that production is carried out by the most economical methods. This can be done by providing, in the case of unsocialised industry, an incentive to produce the most highly valued commodities and by providing to socialised industry, at any rate, a measure of what is most needed and, in some cases perhaps, also an incentive to produce it. In order to see how the pricing system may fulfil these functions in socialised industry, it is necessary briefly to consider the whole nexus of rules by which output, prices and costs in socialised industry should be determined.

3   If the pricing system is to be effective, the following five rules affecting output and prices should be observed. Of these, the two first are:—

(I)   *The prices of finished products should be so set as to bring the demand for the products into balance with the supply.*

(II)   *Similarly, the prices of the factors of production (i.e. land, labour, capital, raw materials, intermediate products, etc.) should be such as to bring the demand for each factor into balance with its supply.*

4 If price rules of this kind are observed, they will provide a coherent mechanism for allocating finished goods and services among consumers and factors of production among producers. For example, if the prices of finished products are used in this way, each individual consumer can choose to purchase what he himself most desires. If the pricing system is not used in this way, the distribution of commodities must be undertaken by a system of rationing or priority distribution, or must be left to an arbitrary first-come first-served scramble. While there may well be many special cases in which the effect of the pricing system should be modified in order to guide consumption in particular ways, there seems no overriding reason to assume that the basic principle for socialised industries should not be to set prices which equate the demand with the supply of the goods or services produced. Similarly, with the prices of factors of production. If they are set in this way, they can be used as a mechanism for ensuring that the factors are fully employed in their most productive uses. (Reference is made to this problem in the case of labour in the comments on Question 6.)

5 But rules (I) and (II) above are useful not only as providing mechanisms for the allocation of finished products and of factors of production. They are an essential condition for the further use of prices as a guide to the production by the most economical means of the things which are most needed. If the prices of finished products are set in this way, the price paid by consumers may be taken as a measure of the value to them of the last additional units of each commodity or service. Similarly, the prices of the factors of production will measure the relative scarcity to the community of the various factors of production.

6 In those conditions, the three following rules are applicable:—

(III) *The managers of production units should produce any given volume of output by the most economical methods by taking on more of one factor of production and less of another, if the cost of the former is less than the cost of the latter.*

(IV) *The managers of production plants should use any given amount of resources to produce more of one product and less of another if, on the basis of current prices, the value of the former is greater than that of the latter.*

(V) *The managers of the production units should take on more factors and produce more output so long as the cost of the additional resources required is less than the value of the additional output produced.*

7 Rule (III) means that the community's output will be produced in the economically cheapest manner; and rules (IV) and (V) mean that the community's resources will be used to produce the goods and services which are most highly valued by consumers.

8 The managers of the socialised industries might conceivably

attempt to bring about the same result without making use of a properly functioning price system. But in that case, their task will be enormously complicated, they will founder amidst uncertainties and their decisions will be more arbitrary than is inevitable. If demands are not automatically screened by the charging of a price they have to be screened by some more arbitrary system of allocation. If the alternative uses of human and material resources are not reflected in the money costs of production some central body will be responsible for the impossible task of trying to envisage all the alternative uses of resources in all the different industries and of choosing the most productive combination. In the absence of a properly functioning price system to serve as a guide, the managers of plants in socialised industries would lack criteria for the economic conduct of their enterprises and it would become necessary to transfer to the centre the responsibility for many types of decisions which could otherwise, with advantage, have been taken locally.

9    The principles of pricing outlined above are, of course, merely abstract principles. In their application to particular industries modifications are likely to be required, for example, to promote an adequate degree of price stability, to allow for the existence of unemployed labour, or to promote a measure of guidance for consumers' choice. These considerations do not, however, mean that the whole mechanism of pricing should be scrapped. They mean merely that its operation should be modified by introducing into the pricing mechanism (whether through taxes and subsidies or through variations from actual prices for accounting purposes) such allowances as are considered appropriate to meet these points.

10    On social grounds it may be desired to restrict the consumption of a particular commodity below, or to expand it beyond, the limit which would be involved if it were produced on the strict principles of pricing outlined above. Or it may be considered that the commodity is a luxury one enjoyed only by the rich, and that in the interests of a more equitable distribution of income the production of such commodities should be restricted in order to promote a larger production of essential commodities. In this case, however, it will probably be preferable to operate directly through a redistribution of income rather than by means which are designed to promote the production of one type of commodity at the expense of another.

11    If the principles of pricing outlined above suggest that it is economic to restrict the output of a particular industry, it may be wise, in the interests of employment policy, to limit the speed of the contraction. A too rapid contraction of a particular industry might lead to serious local pockets of unemployment which could not be rapidly absorbed. This would be an indication that the wage-rates in the trades and areas affected no longer genuinely reflected the supply and demand conditions for that type of labour, i.e. that rule (II) was not being strictly applied. In these cases, in order to avoid unemployment, it may be desirable to taper off

production in the industry gradually, while simultaneously special measures are being taken to facilitate the transfer of labour. This problem will be much eased if a high level of demand is being successfully maintained throughout the rest of the economic system, so that there is a high demand for labour in alternative employments. Moreover, this is not exclusively a problem of socialised industry; and special measures taken for subsidising output and for facilitating the transfer of activity from one industry to another might appropriately be applied indifferently both to private industry and to socialised industry.

12   The application of these pricing principles will require different techniques in different circumstances. Under conditions of private enterprise, the economic price is attained only when competition is so full and free that the individual firm has no control over price but accepts it as given. Only then is there no temptation to restrict production below the economic level in order to maintain or enhance price. In these circumstances, since individual producers will be unable to raise prices by restricting output, they will expand production so long as the additional costs involved are less than the current price of the additional output produced. It is in this sense that economists frequently favour free competition. But where these conditions are not present, positive action by the state is required in order to see that output is expanded so long as the additional cost is greater than the price of the additional output.

13   Under public ownership the problem of establishing an economic price can be tackled, according to the circumstances of the industry, by a variety of methods, of which the following are five important examples.

14   *Method One.* The simplest way to bring about an economic price in a socialised industry where the production unit is small in relation to the market, and where there are a large number of such units, is simply to instruct the managers of the individual plants to compete freely with each other and, subject to this, to make their profits as large as possible. Certain further instructions might be issued by the central Board for the industry, designed to avoid wasteful types of competition (e.g. excessive advertisement) or to impose standardisation of product. Decisions with respect to investment would also no doubt be subject to approval at the centre, but the local managers would have control over the volume of current output. Prices would be determined by competition and would tend to equal the additional cost incurred by producing the last units of output. Output would be at the optimum level. The profits earned by individual plants of similar character would provide some indication of the relative ability of the different managers, and if the rewards of these managers were partly based on the profits earned, they would have every incentive to adopt the most efficient methods of production. This simple type of socialist competition is, however, only applicable to industries where free competition would be technically feasible – though it might not exist in fact – under private enterprise. Such industries are not normally candidates for socialisation. The method could conceivably be

applied to coal-mining or to road haulage; but in the former case there is some doubt as to whether the most efficient unit of production may not be very large, and the system described in Method Two would appear preferable, while in the latter case there are a great many routes where the traffic is too small to permit of true competition between public concerns of optimal size.

15 *Method Two*. Wherever a socialised industry is engaged in producing a non-specialised product of sufficient durability to permit of storage, the following system of public wholesaling may prove the most suitable way of arriving at an economic price. A publicly operated marketing organisation (whether it be a completely separate organisation or a part of a single Board in charge of the industry) would be set up which would purchase the entire output of the individual plants in the socialised industry, which it would resell to the ultimate consumers. This organisation would fix the prices at which it buys and the prices at which it sells to the consumers in various regions. These prices would not fluctuate continuously. The organisation would achieve a measure of price stabilisation by accumulating or drawing on stocks, but prices would be altered from time to time in such a way as to equate demand and supply over a period for each of the various qualities and types of product in each area, and to leave a margin between buying and selling prices sufficient to cover costs of transport and selling costs. The managers of the individual plants or groups of plants would be instructed to take the price paid by the organisation as a datum and on this basis to arrange volume of output and method of production in such a way as to maximise profits. This would have the effect of expanding production so long as the cost of the additional output was below the price. The individual managers might again be given an incentive to produce the right amount by the cheapest methods, if their remuneration were in part at least dependent upon the profits which they made.

16 *Method Three*. A variant of Method Two might be applied in the case of industries the products of which are unsuitable for the holding of large stocks, or where demand is liable to fluctuate to a greater extent than can conveniently be met out of stock variations. In these cases it might be expedient to abandon the idea of a more or less fixed margin between the buying and selling prices of the public marketing organisation, and allow the selling price to vary more widely and at more frequent intervals than the buying price. This will reduce the amount of stock variation necessary to bring demand and supply into equilibrium, but it will mean that the marketing organisation will sometimes be earning substantial profits and sometimes making substantial losses.

17 *Method Four*. In socialised industries engaged in the provision of certain services (e.g. transport, gas, electricity) a completely different approach is required. Instead of leaving prices to be determined by demand and supply, the price has to be fixed in advance and the producers have to be laid under obligation to meet whatever demand may

come forward at the fixed price. Subject to this obligation, they may be encouraged to maximise profits by applying the most efficient methods of production. The prices of the various services produced will be fixed either centrally or locally, but in any case by some authority other than the management of the socialised undertaking. The prices should be fixed so as not to exceed, nor fall short of, the cost due to producing the last additional units of output, save in cases where the available plant is being worked to capacity or as near to full capacity as is compatible with safety. In this case, prices should be raised to a level calculated to restrict demand within the limits of capacity.[2] If, as is notably the case with railway transport, a variety of services of different types is provided, the relative prices charged for different services when the plant is being operated in the vicinity of full capacity should reflect the degree to which the provision of one service necessitates the exclusion of another. These criteria of pricing are by no means easy to apply, and nothing but a very rough approximation to the economic price can be expected. No matter how full the cost-accounting data supplied to the price-fixing authority, the latter, judging from a distance, can do little more than make a guess at the additional cost of producing the last units of output.

18    *Method Five.* The principal case which remains to be considered is that of an industry whose products are manufactured to order and, being more or less adapted to a specific use, are not suitable for storage or for marketing through an intermediary, as described in Methods Two or Three. This case admits of two variants: one in which the products, though somewhat specialised, are sufficiently capable of general definition to be amenable to price-fixing of the type described in Method Four, and the other in which this is not so. In the latter case, one possible course is to instruct the managers of the individual plants to quote prices for their produce based on the criterion of the additional costs involved in producing the last units of the product and, subject to this, to try to minimise costs. It will, however, be very difficult to judge the performance of the managers in these circumstances, since it will be necessary to distinguish between those managers who make profits by efficient production and those who make profits by charging unduly high prices. Alternatively, all attempts to apply the economic price in these circumstances may be abandoned and managers simply left to maximise profits without any restriction on the prices which they may charge in the hope that the incentive to cost reduction thus provided will outweigh the disadvantage of undue restriction of output.

19    The following arrangements, though often recommended, are contrary to the above criteria, and are anti-economic:—

(a)    *The pooling principle* whereby widely different prices are paid to different plants, designed to cover their respective costs of production, the entire product of the industry being sold at a price which

---

[2] The comments on Question 7 deal with the circumstances in which capacity should be expanded by new capital investment.

covers the average cost of all plants combined. The result of this system is that output is produced in high-cost plants which could be produced more cheaply by a more intensive working of low-cost plants. In the case of coal-mining, for example, if the pooling principle, as exemplified by the Coal Charges Account, is permanently retained in the industry after it has been socialised and the prices paid to the various mines continually differ by more than would be justified by transport costs this will lead to underproduction in the better mines and overproduction in the marginal mines. The pithead prices of coal should therefore be allowed to rise to a level sufficient to cover the marginal cost of all mines which have to be kept in production. This would lead to a substantial increase (at any rate, temporarily) in the price of coal, the benefit of which would, of course, accrue to the state in the form of profits. Such an increase would raise the cost of living somewhat and the general cost of production slightly. If this were believed to be undesirable it would be possible to subsidise the selling price of coal. This could be done without any additional net charge on the Exchequer because of the profits made on the production side. The net effect ought to be to secure some reduction in the price of coal as compared with the pooling system, reflecting the reduction in total costs and increased output per man resulting from the greater concentration on the better pits which would tend to result from the new price policy. In the long run, however, it would be preferable gradually to reduce the subsidisation of coal in order to remove the incentive to undue consumption of coal as compared with other things.

(b) *The postalisation principle*, a subcategory of the pooling principle, according to which the same or only a slightly greater price is charged for communication or transportation over long than over short distances in spite of the fact that the costs involved are very different. The result of this is to give an undue encouragement to long-distance, and an undue discouragement to short-distance communication or transportation. Postalisation, as a device for simplifying or standardising charges may be justified on account of the economies which it permits in the actual making and collecting of payments in types of business when the costs of collection are very important. On these grounds, and because the differences in costs are probably not great, the uniform charges of the Post Office may be justitified; but where substantial differences in cost are involved and the administrative problem of collecting charges which are closely related to costs are not too great, the principle of postalisation should be avoided.

(c) *The fixing of uniform prices 'ex-works' or as from a 'basing point'.* These are typical cartel devices adopted for purposes of restriction. The first of these devices leads to output being drawn from a nearer source which could more economically be drawn from a more distant source. The second device leads to supplies being drawn from a more distant source which could more economically be drawn from a nearer source and also favours the faulty location of consuming firms which are attracted to the 'basing point' instead of to the actual source of supply.

20    In what has been said in the preceding paragraphs no mention has been made of the possible effect of the pricing principles upon the earning power of the socialised industry. There are a number of cases in which the adoption of these principles would, in fact, result in the industry earning more or less than the service of the stock issued in compensation of the previous owners.

21    The following are examples of circumstances in which on the principles of pricing discussed above the industry would make earnings either greater or less than the interest on the compensation stock:—

(i)    If the previous owners of the capital in the industry are compensated with stock possessing a Government guarantee, they will be receiving a riskless income in place of the risky profits which they were previously earning. The Government will be bearing the risk. If the price policy adopted by the industry before socialisation were correct, the mere fact that the cost of the compensation money was lower than the risky profits previously earned should afford no argument for reducing prices and earnings.

(ii)    After socialisation, the demand for the product of a socialised industry may temporarily rise above or fall below the norm assumed for the basis of compensation. In the case of a rise in demand the most economic procedure will be to allow the price of the industry's product to rise so as to keep the demand in balance with the capacity output of the industry. In these circumstances, a larger profit than normal may properly be made. It might, in such circumstances, be very undesirable to keep the price of a product down to the level which would only just suffice to cover the interest on the compensation stock. In the case of a temporary decline in demand it would be most wasteful to raise the price of the product to a level sufficient to prevent its earnings from falling by spreading the fixed overheads on the smaller turnover. Such a rise in price would lead to a still further decline in demand and so to the dismissal of workers and the unnecessary idleness of plant. So long as the plant and equipment exist in the industry, it is to the interest of society that it should be operated, provided the operating costs are below the value of the product produced. Private competitive business would not restrict output so as to cover all overheads in a period of depression; and it would be a disagreeable result of socialisation if the effect were to make industry more, rather than less, restrictive in its reaction to a decline for its product.

(iii)    The rise or fall in the demand for an industry's product may be permanent. In the former case a relatively high level of prices and profits should be permitted to rule until there has been time to install new capacity.[3] In the latter case, so long as the existing equipment is available it would be uneconomic not to make the best use of it; prices and profits should remain relatively low until the passage of time has removed the excess capacity.

(iv)    The industry, before socialisation, may have been making a monopoly profit, some part of which has had to be reflected in the price paid in compensation to the previous owners of the industry. If a rigid rule were laid down that an industry must cover the total costs of the compensation money, this would mean that the state would be precluded from expanding the output and reducing the price of the product beyond the previous monopolistic basis.

(v)    In a number of industries, the cost of producing additional units once the plant has been constructed may well be below the average cost of production. In order to get the most economic use of the plant once it has been constructed, it may well be in the interests of society to expand production and to increase sales so long as the price offered for the additional supplies is greater than the additional cost incurred in producing those additional supplies. In such industries, the dilemma arises between covering total costs and charging a price for a product which promotes the consumption of the product in question to the socially desirable limit.

22    In the case of industries of the kind referred to at (v) above, there are certain more complicated price systems which may enable costs to be covered without raising the price charged for the last additional units of consumption above the additional cost due to producing these units. In gas and electricity, for example, it may be possible to use the two-part tariff whereby each consumer, after paying a fixed standing charge, is able to purchase additional units for his consumption at a cost no greater than the additional costs involved in producing those units. A somewhat similar, but less satisfactory, principle is that which is often applied to railway rates of 'charging what the traffic will bear'. Under this system it may be possible to cover total costs by charging high prices for those units of output which are likely to be demanded whatever the price charged for them; and this may enable low prices, no greater than the additional costs involved in producing the last units of output, to be charged for those units of output which consumers would not buy at a higher price. These price systems are never perfect. Fixed standing charges are liable uneconomically to discourage potential consumers from taking on the service; and, in fact, it is not possible to find classes of consumers to be charged a higher price than the average without in some degree uneconomically reducing their consumption.

23    But even with the adoption, where possible, of price systems such as these, there will certainly remain circumstances in which the adoption

---

[3] See the comments on Question 7 for a discussion of the principles on which capacity should be expanded through new capital investment.

of the pricing principles outlined above would involve losses in particular industries. It is also possible, though by no means certain, that the application of these pricing principles to the whole range of socialised industries would involve some net loss being made on the whole of them taken together.

24    There are certain disadvantages in a pricing system which may give rise to losses of this kind. The knowledge that there are circumstances in which an industry is not required to cover its total costs may encourage the demand for Treasury assistance to socialised industries, for the subsidisation of which there is, in fact, no real economic case. If the principle were laid down and inflexibly maintained that each industry must cover its own costs, it might be politically easier to resist such pressure. But if, for any of the reasons given in paragraph 21, this rule is not inflexibly enforced, its value disappears; and it may well be better consistently to apply the pricing principles outlined in this paper rather than to make a series of exceptions from an incorrect principle.

25    There is, however, a second point. If on the balance of all socialised industries a net loss is made, the finance for this net loss will have to be found out of increased tax revenue. And while there is real economic loss involved in deviating from the pricing principles outlined in the preceding paragraphs, there are also real economic disadvantages in high rates of taxation. But to raise the price of a particular commodity above the economic price in order to avoid a loss is itself equivalent to an indirect tax imposed upon that commodity. This issue, therefore, depends in large measures upon whether it is thought that an indirect tax on the particular commodity in question is the best available way of raising the revenue necessary to meet the loss which the industry would otherwise make.

## (6)    Should there be a single, nation-wide basis for wage-rates or should there be regional or sectional variations? Should the rate of wages be related to productivity?

1    The answer to the second of these questions will largely determine the answer to the first; in so far as productivity differs in different regions of the country or in different sections of industry, then wage-rates based on productivity will vary accordingly.

2    In the interests of economic efficiency, the essential desiderata are (i) to employ labour in those industries in which the value of labour's product is the greatest; (ii) within each industry to employ labour in those plants where the output of labour is greatest; and (iii) within each plant to employ labour on those productive methods which are most efficient and economic. The only practicable way of doing this is to ensure that, in each branch of production, wages reflect the value of the worker's specific contribution to output, and to encourage the movement and transfer

of labour to the most remunerative jobs. If wages are unrelated to productivity, manpower may well be wasted in the production of less valuable commodities or in the production of commodities by less efficient methods.

3   If wages are not related to productivity, an important incentive to the worker to change his job may be weakened. Socialised industries will be subject to changes in size as the technical and economic environment changes, equally with non-socialised industries. If this kind of change, essential to economic progress, is not to be impeded, then new and developing parts of the economic system should be able to attract workers by higher wages, related to their higher productivity relatively to other parts of the system which should decline in importance. The present situation, when certain industries whose products are urgently needed but which have relatively low wage levels and consequently suffer from an acute shortage of manpower, is in various ways abnormal and transitory.

4   If industrial stagnation and the consequent adverse effects upon the standard of living of the community is to be avoided, the only conceivable alternative is to continue a rigid system of labour control, and to direct the movement of individual workers from the less productive to the more productive employments, even though this did not mean a movement to positions of higher earnings. Even if this were politically feasible, great technical difficulties would be involved in measuring, in the absence of differences in wage-rates, the relative productiveness of different employments.

5   If it be agreed that wage-rates in general should be related to productivity, there arises the further question how far the wage of the individual worker should vary with his productivity, i.e. whether time or piece rates are preferable. The answer to this question must depend to some extent on the particular circumstances of each industry, or each trade within an industry. But, in general, the more direct the relationship, the more likely is a high degree of efficiency and productivity to be achieved. A bonus to the individual worker for efficiency is likely to be a more effective incentive than a bonus to the plant or to the industry as a whole.

6   Regional and sectional variations would follow from wage-rates related to productivity – unless, of course, an attempt were to be made to assess some sort of average productivity for the whole industry. This, however, would destroy much of the *raison d'être* of relating wages to productivity, since adjustments within an industry are as important as those between industries. At present, even where wage-rates are negotiated nationally, allowance is usually made for regional and sectional differences. The degree to which these differences arise will depend upon the varying circumstances of each industry.

7   The question arises as to the mechanism by which wages might be brought into relation with productivity. It is presumably to be accepted that socialisation of a number of industries does not involve radical change in the wage structure of the country, that two essential features of the present (or rather pre-war) situation – wage determination through the familiar mechanisms of collective bargaining, wage boards, etc., and freedom of workers to move from one occupation to another, with the corresponding freedom of employers, including the state, to engage and discharge workers – will be maintained.

8   If the price and output policies of socialised industries are determined on methods of the kind suggested in the comments on Question 5 above, the various units in the socialised industries will take on more labour so long as the wage cost of the labour taken on is less than the price received from the sale of its product. This means that in the fixation of wages by collective bargaining, by wage boards or by similar mechanisms, due regard must be paid to the relation between the supply and demand for labour in the different industries, occupations and regions, wage-rates being adjusted upwards where there was an unsatisfied demand and, if necessary, downwards where the demand was persistently below the supply. If this is done, wage-rates will automatically be adjusted to take account of variations in productivity.

9   This principle should not, of course, be carried to an extreme. In particular, it should not be held to rule out the fixation of national minima. The objective of a national minimum wage in an industry is, of course, to ensure that no worker falls below a given standard and to prevent exploitation. Provided that the minimum does not exceed the contribution of the worker to the value of the product, these objectives can be achieved without imposing on an industry an undesirably rigid wage structure.

10   A most important reason for adopting some system which will have the effect of relating wage-rates to productivity is to avoid the vicious spiral of inflation which would result from a persistent tendency for wage-rates to rise out of relation to increased productivity. If the state does adopt a successful policy for expanding and maintaining the general level of national demand at a height adequate to maintain 'full employment', the danger of such wage inflation may be serious unless, in the socialised industries, the state can set the example of a system which relates wages to productivity.

## (7)   What arrangements should be made for the planning and timing of new investment in the industry?

1   The principles which should determine the investment programme of socialised industries are fundamentally the same as the pricing principles for current output, set forth in the comments on Question 5. That is to

say, investment in any industry, whether it take the form of installing new plant or replacing old, or of improving land, should be carried to the point beyond which the value of any additional output which it would produce, *plus* the value of any net saving in current costs, would fail to cover the cost of the investment itself.

2    For example, whether or not an investment programme for the electrification of part of the railway system should be undertaken can be determined on the principles of pricing to which reference is made in the comments on Question 5. An attempt can be made to see whether a given traffic could be carried at a lower total cost after electrification than before. For this purpose an estimate would have to be made of the savings in the operating expenses of the railways due to the electrification scheme, and this would have to be compared with an estimate of the additional capital costs (including interest) involved by the new installation. In order to ensure that the best use of the community's resources is made the new capital installation must be one for which the new capital costs are less than the old operating costs which it economises. The natural enthusiasm of the engineers for the most up-to-date technical discovery must not be allowed to overrule these economic considerations.

3    In other cases the main purpose of an investment project may be to increase the total output rather than to save labour costs or other operating expenses. In this case an estimate must be made of the value to consumers of the additional product which would be produced and this must be compared with the additional costs incurred in respect of the new capital equipment. The estimation of the value to consumers of the additional product is bound to be a matter of some uncertainty. If the additional product is likely to be large in relation to the existing output, it will not be sufficient to value it at the present current prices; it will be necessary to make an allowance for the reduction in price which will be necessary in order to sell the greater output. The real value to consumers of the additional output will be something between its value at the price ruling before, and its value at the price ruling after, the additional output is being produced. Whatever criterion is adopted for determining the investment programme, it will always be a matter of considerable uncertainty to decide whether or not a programme of investment in long-lasting capital equipment is economically justifiable, just because future conditions are uncertain; and in the case of large-scale capital projects, this general uncertainty is still further increased by the need to make an estimate of the effect which the additional output will have upon the selling price of the product.

4    The formulation of investment programmes in each socialised industry will have to rest upon estimates of investment for individual plants prepared in the first instance by the individual managers of each plant, which they will have to justify on the above principles. But the actual determination of the industry's investment programme and the

approval at any rate of all substantial individual projects must rest with the central Board responsible to the Government for the conduct of the industry. This is so for a number of reasons. In the first place (assuming that compensation is paid for taking over the socialised industries in the form of issue of new Government stock) the finance for new investment will in some way or another have to be raised by the Treasury and provided to the industry through the central Board responsible for that industry. Thus the finance of investment in each particular plant will have to be canalised through the central Board for the industry. In the second place, by centralising the individual investment plans with the central Board, it is possible to remove some part of the uncertainty that is involved in investment. In a competitive industry one particular producer normally has little or no knowledge of the investment intentions of his competitors. For this reason the total investment undertaken by the industry as a whole may well be on too large or too small a scale simply because each competitor is underestimating or overestimating what the rest of the producers in the industry have in mind to spend on capital development. A centralised investment programme would enable the manager of each individual plant to consider his individual investment plan in full knowledge of what the total economic development in the industry is likely to be.

5    Given such an investment programme, planned to cover a term of years with the first year or two in detail, the actual time for introducing particular improvements into a socialised industry, year by year, should be a matter between the Government and the industry, as part of the Government's employment policy. The socialisation of some industries can materially assist the Government's achievement of a stable volume of investment as part of its task of maintaining aggregate national expenditure.

6    First, there will be the advantage to the Government's economic intelligence service in that, for the plans of a number of separate producers, details of which may be difficult to obtain, there will be substituted a single national programme for the industry agreed with the Government. Secondly, within the range of the industry's overall programme, timing of investment should be much more readily controllable by the Government and can be made an additional instrument in the Government's hands for offsetting changes elsewhere which have proved impossible to control. For this purpose, it will be necessary that the details of the industry's investment programme should have as much flexibility as possible.

## (8)   On what principles should the import and export trade of the commodities concerned be conducted?

1    The fact that an industry has been brought under public ownership makes no very fundamental difference to the policies which it is

appropriate to preserve with respect either to the export of the produce of the industry or to the import of foreign goods competing with that produce. It will probably be right to maintain after nationalisation the same degree of protection or the same degree of competition with foreign supplies which was appropriate before nationalisation.

2    After an industry has been nationalised there may be considerable pressure to give it increased protection. The department responsible for the industry may tend to put more emphasis on the prosperity and size of the industry than on the provision of the product from the cheapest source, whether imported or home-produced; the financial problem of ensuring that the industry earns sufficient to meet the cost of the compensation money issued when it was taken over may afford a further pressure for its protection; and there may be increased political pressure to ensure that the state takes action on behalf of the workers in the industry to prevent any contraction of employing power in the industry. But if real standards of living are to be advanced throughout the community it will be essential to ensure that proper regard is paid to the problem of obtaining supplies in the cheapest manner.

3    To the broad principle set forth above, viz., that the arguments for different commercial policies are little affected by the nationalisation of individual industries, it is, however, necessary to make a number of qualifications.

4    Certain arguments for protection are somewhat weakened by the nationalisation of the protected industry. For example, the protection given to iron and steel in the past was partly advocated on the grounds that it was necessary to ensure an adequate level of profits to the industry in order that the capital necessary for modernisation might be forthcoming. The argument was that if 'reasonable' profits were not earned on existing capital, new capital would not be forthcoming even for investment projects which in themselves were profitable and economically desirable. If, however, the iron and steel industry, or part of it, is nationalised, capital can be made available to it for such purposes in adequate volume, so that there is no need on this account to maintain profits artificially.

5    Similarly, the case for stabilising – as well as restricting – imports by such quantitative import controls as quotas is somewhat weakened by nationalisation. The nationalised industry, with its large financial resources, should be better able to stabilise its own production and employment in the face of unstable market conditions than would a collection of private firms.

6    Before the war certain sections of the iron and steel industry took advantage of the tariff protection against imported steel to practise a policy of dumping and discrimination in the export trade. That is, they sold goods in foreign markets at a lower price than they could have sold

them in the home market; moreover, they sold cheaper to some foreign countries than to others. If these sections of the industry were national-ised, the continuance of this policy would become both more difficult and less justifiable. It would be more difficult because dumping by state action is normally regarded by other countries as a more heinous offence than dumping by private firms. It would be more likely to meet with retaliatory action in the form of anti-dumping duties. It would be liable to fall within and be prohibited by the provisions of a multilateral commercial agreement or limited by bilateral commercial agreements. The practice would also become less justifiable. When dumping is practised by private firms it is not usually the case that exports are being produced below the cost of production, but rather that prices charged in the home market are above the cost of production. Nationalised industries would presumably abandon such restrictive practices in the home market and any economic justification for selling in the foreign market cheaper than in the home market would thereby be removed.

7  Though nationalisation has comparatively little bearing on the case for or against different commercial policies, it may have an important bearing on the appropriate *form* under which international trade should be controlled or carried on. This point arises mainly in connection with the exportation of the produce of nationalised industries and the importation of raw materials required by such industries. The creation of a single seller, in the former case, or a single buyer, in the latter case, in place of a number of private sellers or buyers, clearly tends to reduce the usefulness of private merchants or other intermediaries. Merchants are most required where buyers and sellers are numerous. Of course, the purchasers of the exports of our nationalised industries may still be numerous, and private trade may still have a useful rôle to play, but the effect of nationalisation should be to increase the relative advantage of a system of organising foreign trade which permits a more direct contact with foreign customers. This might be done by setting up a publicly operated export organisation either as a branch of the nationalised industry or closely associated with it. In considering the above, however, it has to be borne in mind

(*a*)  that public enterprise in the conduct of foreign trade suffers from a serious disadvantage to which public enterprise in the conduct of domestic industry or trade is not exposed in that by making trade more 'political' it tends to multiply possible points of diplomatic friction and to introduce new bones of contention into international relations; and

(*b*)  that the fact that foreign trade is publicly operated does not invalidate the norms of international behaviour in the commercial sphere, i.e. the need to avoid undue discrimination, dumping, or other aspects of economic nationalism.

# 6

## Degrees of Competitive Speculation

*From the* Review of Economic Studies, *vol. 17 (1949–50), pp. 159–167. Meade described the origin of this paper:*

'This note is a by-product of work which I am doing under the auspices of the Royal Institute of International Affairs on *The Theory of International Economic Policy* [*Vol. 1: The Balance of Payments* (London: Oxford University Press, 1951)]. In order to deal with the influence of speculation in the foreign exchange market it was necessary to analyse speculative forces on these lines. The analysis is in many respects merely an elaboration of the ideas on speculation put forward by A. P. Lerner in his *Economics of Control* [New York: The Macmillan Company, 1944]. The argument in this note and the proofs in the Appendix owe their present form to Professor A. Henderson and Mr Lomax, of Manchester University. I had attempted to establish my propositions by a geometric treatment which Professor Henderson pointed out to me to be unconvincing. I owe the more rigorous proofs to his intervention, aided by Mr Lomax's mathematics.'

The purpose of this note is to consider certain effects of competitive speculation. By 'competitive' speculation as opposed to 'monopolistic' speculation we mean speculation in a market in which the individual speculator is himself unable to affect the price of the commodity in which he deals by expanding or contracting the scale of his own operations. The competitive speculator who, for example, buys up a commodity this year for resale at a profit next year, does not, of course, expect the price of that commodity to remain constant. Indeed, the whole point of his operation is that he expects to be able to resell next year at a higher price than that which he pays this year. But he does not believe that his purchases this year will raise this year's price or that his sales next year will lower next year's price.

We exclude, therefore, from our consideration, all 'monopolistic' speculative deals. A 'monopolistic' speculator may attempt, by buying up the whole of this year's supply of a commodity, to sell a small part of the supply this year at a very inflated price, and thereby to make a gross profit this year which will more than cover any losses caused on the rest of his holding when he ultimately comes to dispose of it.

In what follows we shall speak of four states of competitive speculation, which we shall call 'perfect', 'perverse', 'deficient' and 'excessive' competitive speculation respectively.

By 'perfect competitive speculation' we mean speculation in a competitive market in which the individual speculators correctly foresee the price differentials on which they are speculating. According to the carrying costs of the commodity and the degree of (correctly anticipated) price change, perfect competitive speculation will lead to a given amount of purchases of the commodity in the low-price market for resale in the high-price market.

By 'perverse competitive speculation' we mean speculation in the opposite direction from that which would have occurred with 'perfect competitive speculation'. Suppose, for example, that the price of a commodity goes up now and will, in fact, fall again next year. With 'perfect competitive speculation' speculators will sell this year from their stocks, which they will replenish next year. But if as a result of a lack of correct anticipation of market changes the rise in price this year makes speculators expect a still larger rise in price next year, they will purchase this year for sale next year instead of selling this year for re-purchase next year.

By 'deficient competitive speculation' we mean a speculative movement in which speculators speculate in the same direction as they would in conditions of 'perfect competitive speculation', but speculate on a smaller scale than they would if their foresight had been perfect.

Finally, by 'excessive competitive speculation' we mean a speculative movement in the same direction as, but on a larger scale than, would have occurred in conditions of 'perfect competitive speculation'.

We wish to consider the effects of these different cases of competitive speculation from two points of view.

First, we wish to examine the effect of such speculation upon total economic welfare without, however, considering price stability itself as socially advantageous or disadvantageous.

Secondly, since for various institutional reasons in certain markets rapid upward and downward movements of prices may themselves be a cause of dislocation and friction, we wish to consider the effect of each of these degrees of competitive speculation upon the stability of the price of the commodity concerned.

We shall proceed to consider the following simplified problem:

(1) We confine ourselves to speculation in a single commodity which makes up a small part of the community's total production and consumption so that, in Marshall's terminology, the marginal utility of money may be considered to be unaffected by changes in the supply and demand conditions for this commodity.

(2) We confine ourselves to a consideration of only two markets in this commodity, which markets we will call the market of period 0 and the market of period 1. The supply and/or demand conditions change between period 0 and period 1 so that, in the absence of a speculative carry-over of extra stocks from period 0 to period 1, the

equilibrium price for the commodity would rise between period 0 and period 1.[1]

(3)   People hold stocks of the commodity for two purposes: convenience in trading and speculation on price changes. If no price change is expected, then stocks are held up to the point at which the marginal trading convenience of holding additional stocks is equal to the marginal cost of holding additional stocks. If a price rise is expected, people will hold more than the normal stocks or, in other words, there will be a positive holding of speculative stocks. The marginal and total cost of holding no speculative stocks is zero. But as more and more speculative stocks are held the marginal cost of holding speculative stocks rises because (*a*) the marginal trading convenience of holding additional stocks falls and (*b*) the marginal cost of storage rises as the total stock held increases.[2]

(4)   We are not in this article concerned with the effect upon economic welfare of any redistribution of income which speculation may cause. We treat a loss or gain to producers, consumers, or speculators as of equal importance if it is of equal money value.

In the mathematical appendix to this note we establish the following welfare propositions:

(1)   The surplus of all classes taken together will rise consistently with every increase in the speculative carry-over of stocks so long as the carry-over is less than that required by perfect competitive speculation. At this point it will be a maximum. Thereafter it will fall consistently as the carry-over increases. This conclusion recommends itself to common sense: so long as the carry-over is below that corresponding to perfect competitive speculation the price differential in the two markets will exceed the marginal cost of carrying the stock; and the price in each market is equal to the marginal utility of consumption and the marginal cost of production in that market, so that the real cost of carrying over one more unit of stock would still be less than the excess of the marginal utility of that unit in the new market over the old market and than the excess of the marginal cost of production of that unit in the new market over the old market.

(2)   The surplus of producers and consumers taken separately from that of speculators will always be increased by an increase in speculation whether this be in a positive or negative direction, i.e. whether the carry-over be, in fact, in the correct or the perverse direction. This

---

[1] All the conclusions of this note could be applied to the case where period 0 is the market in which the higher price will occur in the absence of speculation. In this case a carry-over of speculative stocks from period 1 to period 0 (i.e. by running down normal stocks now and replacing them later) would be appropriate. See the mathematical appendix [pp. 84–9].

[2] These points are also true of an increase in a speculative carry-over from period 1 to period 0. In this case stocks are now reduced below the normal required for trading convenience. The more they are so reduced, (*a*) the higher becomes the marginal trading convenience of holding stocks, and (*b*) the lower becomes the marginal cost of storage. In other words, the more stocks are reduced (i.e. the greater the negative speculative carry-over) the higher the marginal loss through reducing them still more.

at-first-sight paradoxical conclusion also on consideration recommends itself to common sense. Speculators by buying more in period 0 will bid up the price against producers and consumers in period 0; producers will therefore produce more, so that the high price will be enjoyed by producers on an abnormally large volume of production; but consumers will consume less so that the high price will be suffered by consumers on an abnormally small volume of consumption. When the speculative stocks are sold in period 1 the opposite will occur; producers will suffer an abnormally low price but on an abnormally small volume of production, and consumers will enjoy an abnormally low price on an abnormally large volume of consumption. The more the speculators speculate, the better for the producers and consumers taken together over both years.

(3)   The surplus of the speculators taken alone will be negative for perverse speculation, will be zero for no speculation, will become positive as speculation starts to take place in the right direction, will attain its maximum at some point when speculation is still deficient (i.e. before the point of perfect competitive speculation is reached), will be positive but falling at the point of perfect competitive speculation, will be falling for all greater volumes of speculation (i.e. so long as speculation is excessive), and will become negative when speculation is sufficiently excessive.

Bearing these results in mind we can now consider the effects of perverse, deficient, and excessive speculation upon (*i*) the total surplus of consumers, producers, and speculators, and (*ii*) upon the degree of price stability, in comparison both (*a*) with no speculation, and (*b*) with perfect competitive speculation.

## (1)   Perverse Speculation

### (i)   Effect on Welfare

In this case speculators run down their stocks instead of adding to them in period 0. The total welfare is less than with perfect competitive speculation and also less than with no speculation, though the position is not, of course, so bad in comparison with the latter as in comparison with the former position.[3] If, however, we separate the interest of the speculators from that of the producers and consumers, we can say that, as compared with the position of no speculation, the producers and consumers will be better off[4] and the speculators worse off[5]; but, as compared with the position of perfect competitive speculation, the speculators will be worse off[5] and the producers and consumers will be worse or better off according as the amount of speculation in the perverse direction is smaller or greater than is necessary to balance the effect on their welfare of the correct amount of positive speculation.[4]

[3] See Proposition (*i*) on page 87.
[4] See Proposition (*ii*) on page 87.
[5] See Proposition (*iii*) on page 88.

## (ii)   Effect on Price Stability

Perverse speculation will necessarily increase the instability of prices because it will cause prices to fall in the lower-priced market and to rise in the higher-priced market.

## (2)   Deficient Speculation

### (i)   Effect on Welfare

The total welfare of society will be improved as compared with no speculation, but will not be as great as with perfect competitive speculation.[6] The welfare of the producers and consumers will be greater than with no speculation but less than with perfect competitive speculation.[7] The welfare of the speculators will be greater than with no speculation; but it may be greater or less than with perfect competitive speculation. This latter result will depend upon the scale of the deficient speculation. If it is very small in extent, then a very small surplus will be made by speculators and this may be less than the surplus made with perfect competitive speculation. But as the scale of deficient speculation rises, the speculators' surplus will rise until it reaches the same height as would be achieved in conditions of perfect competitive speculation; thereafter it will rise to a maximum and then decline till the point of perfect competitive speculation is reached. Throughout this range the surplus of the speculators will be greater with deficient than with perfect competitive speculation.[8]

### (ii)   Effects on Price Stability

Deficient speculation will improve the degree of price stability as compared with no speculation, since it will bring down the price in the higher-priced market and raise the price in the lower-priced market. But there will still remain an excess of price in the former over price in the latter market which is greater than would remain with perfect competitive speculation. Deficient speculation will, therefore, do less to stabilise prices than perfect speculation.

## (3)   Excessive Speculation

### (i)   Effect on Welfare

The total welfare of society will be less than with perfect competitive speculation; but it may be greater or less than with no speculation. If the speculation is not very excessive, the total welfare will be only just below

---

[6] See Proposition *(i)* on page 87.

[7] See Proposition *(ii)* on page 87.

[8] See Proposition *(iii)* on page 88.

its maximum point, and thus above the level corresponding to no speculation; but if the speculation is very excessive the total welfare may have fallen below that of no speculation.[9] Producers and consumers, however, will be better off with excessive speculation, both as compared with no speculation and also as compared with the position of perfect competitive speculation.[10] But speculators will always be worse off with excessive speculation than with perfect competitive speculation; and if the speculation is sufficiently excessive they will make a net loss and will be worse off than with no speculation.[11]

## (ii) Effect on Price Stability

Excessive speculation will bring down price in the higher-priced market relatively to the price in the lower-priced market so that the price margin is no longer sufficient to compensate for the marginal cost of speculation. Up to a point, therefore, excessive speculation will bring greater price stability than perfect competitive speculation; indeed, if the excess of speculation were just sufficient to bring the high price down and the low price up until they were equal, complete price stability would be achieved. Even if the speculation were more excessive than this, and $p_1$ (the price in the original high-price market) fell below $p_0$ (the price in the original low-priced market), there would be a net improvement in price stability as compared with perfect competitive speculation so long as $p_0 - p_1$ with excessive speculation did not rise above $p_1 - p_0$ with perfect competitive speculation. Beyond this point $p_0 - p_1$ with excessive speculation would be greater than $p_1 - p_0$ with perfect competitive speculation, and prices would be less stable than with perfect competitive speculation. But they would still remain more stable than with no speculation. This would be so until speculation was so excessive that $p_0 - p_1$ with excessive speculation was actually greater than $p_1 - p_0$ with no speculation. We should have reached the extremely perverse[12] kind of speculative price destabilisation where the following type of situation may have developed. What threatened to be the scarce market is so glutted by the speculators, and what threatened to be the plentiful market is so starved by the speculators that the price in the former has fallen below the original price in the latter and the price in the latter has risen above the original price in the former.

---

[9] See Proposition *(i)* on page 87.
[10] See Proposition *(ii)* on page 87.
[11] See Proposition *(iii)* on page 88.
[12] We have defined perverse speculation as a speculative movement of stocks from the market which, in the absence of speculation, would have been high-priced to the market which, in the absence of speculation, would have been low-priced. In our present example, speculation is in the correct direction but is so excessive that we have reached a different type of perversity. Speculative stocks are being carried from a market in which the price would have been low but is, in fact, high because of the excessive drawing of supplies away from that market to a market in which the price would have been high but is, in fact, low because of the glutting of that market with speculative sales.

## Mathematical Appendix

Let the demand curve for commodity $x$ change so that the demand price becomes $f_1(x)$ instead of $f_0(x)$, and let the supply curve change so that the marginal cost or supply price becomes $\varphi_1(x)$ instead of $\varphi_0(x)$.

Let the output be $x_0$ in period 0 and $x_1$ in period 1.

Let the price be $p_0$ in period 0 and $p_1$ in period 1.

Let $y$ be the speculative carry-over of supply from period 0 to period 1 ($y$ can be negative).

Competition between producers and consumers is assumed to ensure that:

$$p_0 = f_0(x_0 - y) = \varphi_0(x) \text{ and } p_1 = f_1(x_1 + y) = \varphi_1(x_1). \tag{1}$$

Let $r$ represent the money rate of interest so that all money values of period 0 must be multiplied by $(1 + r)$ in order to compare them with those of period 1. It is assumed that the rate of interest is unaffected by developments in the market for our commodity $x$.

Let $\psi(y)$ represent the marginal net cost to speculators of the speculative carry-over of stocks from period 0 to period 1 ($y$), this marginal cost excluding the purchase price of the marginal unit of stock carried ($p_0$) and the rate of interest on the purchase price of the marginal unit stock and on the marginal cost incurred in holding the stock ($[p_0 + \psi(y)]\,r$).

We must pause to consider the nature of $\psi(y)$. Stockholders, if they increase the level of their total stocks, will: (*a*) obtain greater trading advantages and conveniences from a larger operating cost, but (*b*) incur greater gross expenses of storage. The marginal net cost to them is the difference between (*b*) and (*a*). Let $z$ represent total stocks held for all purposes; let $U(z)$ represent the marginal trading convenience of holding stocks; and let $E(z)$ represent the marginal expenses of stockholding (other than the purchase price of the commodity and interest on holding the stock). Then the net marginal cost to stockholders is defined as $E(z) - U(z)$. Thus if $\bar{p}_1$ represents the price expected next year and $p_0$ the actual price this year, the total stock held ($z$) in competitive speculation will be determined by the equation:

$$E(z) - U(z) = \frac{\bar{p}_1}{1 + r} - p_0. \tag{2}$$

We define the normal trading stock $\bar{z}$ as that which would be held in competitive conditions if the price next year were expected to be the same as the price this year, which from (2) is determined by the equation:

$$E(\bar{z}) - U(\bar{z}) = p_0 \frac{-r}{1 + r}. \tag{3}$$

The speculative stock $y = z - \bar{z}$; and

$$\psi(y) = E(\bar{z} + y) - U(\bar{z} + y). \tag{4}$$

In equation (1) we have already tacitly assumed that $\bar{z}$ is constant, because we have assumed that the whole difference between current production and consumption represents a speculative carry-over and not an addition to normal trading stocks. This is not strictly correct, since, as can be seen from equation (3), the size of normal trading stocks may be affected by changes in the level of present prices, which in turn may be affected by speculation. But from equation (2) we find:

$$dz \left( \frac{dE}{dz} - \frac{dU}{dz} \right) = \frac{d\bar{p}_1}{1+r} - dp_0. \tag{5}$$

If we start from a position of equilibrium in which $p_0 = \bar{p}_1$, and then consider two developments, (a) in which $p_0$ remains equal to $\bar{p}_1$ but both prices rise by 10 per cent, and (b) in which $p_0$ rises by 5 per cent but $\bar{p}_1$ by 15 per cent, we obtain from equation (5):

$$\frac{dz_a}{dz_b} = \frac{-2r}{2-r}$$

when $dz_a$ is the increase in stock which will occur in situation (a) and $dz_b$ the increase in stock which will occur in situation (b). If $r = 4$ per cent $dz_a/dz_b = -8/196$ or if $r = 2$ per cent $dz_a/dz_b = -4/198$. This serves to show how small will be the effect on stocks of changes in the absolute price level as compared with the effect of changes in the relation between present and expected future prices, provided that the rate of interest is reasonably low. We shall, therefore, assume that changes in $\bar{z}$ are negligible for our purposes.

From (3) and (4) we can then deduce that:

$$\psi(0) = p_0 \frac{-r}{1+r} \text{ and } \frac{d\psi(y)}{dz} > 0 \text{ because } \frac{dE}{dz} \text{ is } +ve \text{ and } \frac{dU}{dz} - ve.$$

It now follows that Consumers' Surplus (which we will call $C$) =

$$\int_0^{x_0 - y} f_0(x)dx - p_0(x_0 - y) + \frac{1}{1+r} \left[ \int_0^{x_1 + y} f_1(x)dx - p_1(x_1 + y) \right]$$

Producers' Surplus (which we will call $P$) =

$$p_0 x_0 - \int_0^{x_0} \varphi_0(x)dx + \frac{1}{1+r} \left[ p_1 x_1 - \int_0^{x_1} \varphi_1(x)dx \right]$$

and Speculators' Surplus (which we will call $S$) =

$$y \left( \frac{p_1}{1+r} - p_0 \right) - \int_0^y \psi(y)dy.$$

Now:

$$\frac{d}{dy}\left\{\int_0^{x_0-y} f_0(x)dx\right\} = \frac{d(x_0-y)}{dy} \cdot \frac{d}{d(x_0-y)}\left\{\int_0^{x_0-y} f_0(x)dx\right\} =$$

$$\left(\frac{dx_0}{dy}-1\right)f_0(x_0-y) = \left(\frac{dx_0}{dy}-1\right)p_0.$$

Similarly:

$$\frac{d}{dy}\left\{\int_0^{x_1+y} f_1(x)dx\right\} = \left(\frac{dx_1}{dy}+1\right)p_1,$$

$$\frac{d}{dy}\left\{\int_0^{x_0} \varphi_0(x)dx\right\} = \frac{dx_0}{dy}p_0, \text{ and}$$

$$\frac{d}{dy}\left\{\int_0^{x_1} \varphi_1(x)dx\right\} = \frac{dx_1}{dy}p_1,$$

Hence:

$$\frac{d(C+P+S)}{dy} = \frac{p_1}{1+r} - p_0 - \psi(y) \tag{6}$$

$$\text{and } \frac{d^2(C+P+S)}{dy^2} = \frac{1}{1+r} \cdot \frac{dp_1}{dy} - \frac{dp_0}{dy} - \frac{d\psi(y)}{dy}. \tag{7}$$

But in conditions of perfect competitive speculation $\psi(y) + p_0 = p_1/(1+r)$ (see equations (2) and (4)), so that from (6) $d(C+P+S)/dy = 0$. This will be a point of maximum advantage provided that the expression in (7) is negative. We have already seen that $d\psi(y)/dy$ is $> 0$. Now:

$$\frac{dp_0}{dy} = \left(\frac{dx_0}{dy}-1\right)\frac{dp_0}{d(x_0-y)} = \left(\frac{dx_0}{dp_0}\cdot\frac{dp_0}{dy}-1\right)\frac{dp_0}{d(x_0-y)}$$

so that:

$$\frac{dp_0}{dy} = \frac{1}{-\dfrac{d(x_0-y)}{dp_0}+\dfrac{dx_0}{dp_0}}$$

But $d(x_0-y)/dp_0$ is $< 0$ if the demand curve in period 0 is downward sloping and $dx_0/dp_0$ is $> 0$ if the supply curve in period 0 is upward sloping. $dp_0/dy$ is, therefore, $> 0$. Similarly $dp_1/dy = [d(x_1+y)/dp_1 - dx_1/dp_1]^{-1}$ which is $< 0$ if the new demand curve is downward sloping and the new supply curve upward sloping. $1/(1 + r) \cdot dp_1/dy - dp_0/dy$ is therefore $< 0$.

It follows that the expression in (7) is always $< 0$. From this we can conclude that $C + P + S$ rises with every increase in $y$ until the point of perfect competitive speculation is reached (whether this point is reached at a positive or negative value of $y$) and thereafter falls with every increase in $y$.

Next, we can show that an increase in speculative activity, whether it take the form of increasing a positive or of increasing a negative carryover will always be to the advantage of the consumers and producers considered together separately from the speculators. Thus from the above expressions for $C$ and $P$ we find that:

$$\frac{d(C + P)}{dy} = y\left(\frac{dp_0}{dy} - \frac{dp_1}{dy}\frac{1}{1 + r}\right).$$

Now we have shown above that $dp_0/dy - dp_1/dy \cdot 1/(1 + r)$ is $> 0$. It follows that if $y$ is $+ve$ an increase in $y$ will always increase $C + P$, and if $y$ is $-ve$ a decrease in $y$ (i.e. an increase in the negative speculative stock) will always increase $C + P$.

Finally, let us consider the speculators' welfare alone. Since:

$$S = y\left(\frac{p_1}{1 + r} - p_0\right) - \int_0^y \psi(y)dy \quad \text{and}$$

$$\frac{dS}{dy} = \frac{p_1}{1 + r} - p_0 + y\left(\frac{dp_1}{dy} \cdot \frac{1}{1 + r} - \frac{dp_0}{dy}\right) - \psi(y)$$

we can establish the following propositions:

*(i) With no speculation $S$ is zero, but would become positive if speculation started in the correct direction but negative if speculation started in the perverse direction.* When $y = 0$, $S = 0$ and $dS/dy = (p_1 - p_0)/(1 + r)$ since $\psi(0) = p_0[-r/(1 + r)]$. In other words, with no speculation $S$ is zero; but $S$ will become positive with positive speculation if $p_1 - p_0 > 0$ or with negative speculation if $p_1 - p_0 < 0$, i.e. if speculation starts in the required direction. But $S$ will become negative if perverse speculation starts, i.e. if $y$ is $+ve$ when $p_1 - p_0$ is $< 0$ or $y$ is $-ve$ when $p_1 - p_0 > 0$.

*(ii) The more perverse speculation becomes, the larger become the losses of speculators.* Consider first the case where $y$ is $+ve$ but perverse. Since this is the perverse direction, it follows that $p_1/(1 + r) - p_0 - \varphi(y)$ must be $-ve$, since this expression must have been $-ve$ when $y$ was zero and the increase in $y$ will have lowered $p_1$ and raised $p_0$ and $\psi(y)$. At the same time $y[dp_1/dy \cdot 1/(1 + r) - dp_0/dy]$ will be $-ve$. Therefore $dS/dy$ is $-ve$. Therefore $S$ which starts at zero when $y$ is zero becomes a larger and larger negative quantity as perverse speculation becomes larger and

larger in the positive direction. Consider next the case where $y$ is $-ve$ but perverse. Then $p_0/(1 + r) - p_1 - \psi(y)$ which was $+ve$ when $y$ was zero will have become even greater as $-y$ increases; and $y[dp_1/dy \cdot 1/(1 + r) - dp_0/dy]$ will be $+ve$. Therefore $dS/dy$ will be $+ve$, i.e. $dS/d(-y)$ will be $-ve$; and an increase in the perversity of speculation will again cause increased losses to speculators.

*(iii)   At the point of perfect competitive speculation S will be positive but will be falling with every further increase in the (negative or positive) volume of speculation.* At the point of perfect competitive speculation $p_1/(1 + r) - p_0 = \psi(y)$, so that

$$S = y\left(\varphi(y) - \frac{\int_0^y \psi(y)dy}{y}\right).$$

But $\psi(y)$ represents the marginal and $\frac{1}{y}\int_0^y \psi(y)dy$ the average cost of speculation; and since $d\psi(y)/dy$ is $> 0$ for all values of $y$, positive or negative, the marginal cost is always rising, so that the marginal cost will be $\gtrless$ than the average cost according as $y \gtrless 0$. It follows that $S$ will be $+ve$ for all perfectly competitive values of $y$. In other words, the 'business' of speculation being subject to increasing costs will afford some 'producers' surplus' to speculators. In these conditions $dS/dy = y[dp_1/dy \cdot 1/(1 + r) - dp_0/dy]$ and this is $\lessgtr 0$ according as $y \gtrless 0$. In other words, $S$ will be falling with every increase in the size of the carry-over, whether positive or negative.

*(iv)   When speculation is excessive a further increase in speculation will always cause a fall in S.* There are two possible cases: $y$ is $+ve$ and $p_1/(1 + r) - p_0 - \psi(y) < 0$, or $y$ is $-ve$ and $p_1/(1 + r) - p_0 - \psi(y) > 0$. As is argued in *(ii)* above, in the former case $dS/dy$ and in the latter case $dS/d(-y)$ will be $< 0$.

*(v)   When speculation becomes sufficiently excessive in either direction S will become negative.* When speculation is on a sufficiently large scale in either direction $y[p_1/(1 + r) - p_0]$ becomes $-ve$, because if $y$ is sufficiently great $p_1/(1 + r)$ can be lowered and $p_0$ raised so as to make $p_1/(1 + r) < p_0$. Conversely, with $-y$ sufficiently great $p_1/(1 + r)$ can be raised above $p_0$. Moreover, the term $-y[p_1/(1 + r) - p_0]$ will increase without limits as $y$ or $-y$ increases, because $p_1/(1 + r) - p_0$ will always decrease as $y$ increases and increase as $-y$ increases. The term $\int_0^y \psi(y)dy$ is $+ve$ for all $-ve$ values of $y$, since $\psi(0)$ is $-ve$ and $d\psi(y)/dy$ is $> 0$. It follows that if $-y$ is sufficiently great $S$ must be $-ve$. But the term $\int_0^y \psi(y)dy$ will be negative for certain small $+ve$ values of $y$, since $\psi(0)$ is $-ve$. But since $d\psi(y)/dy$ is always $> 0$, and $\psi(y)$ will

eventually be $+ve$ when the marginal trading convenience of additional stocks has fallen below the marginal expenses of such stocks, $\int_0^y \psi(y)dy$ cannot fall below a certain lower negative limit. It follows that if $y$ is sufficiently great $S$ will again become $-ve$.

# 7

# External Economies and Diseconomies in a Competitive Situation

*From* The Economic Journal, *vol. 62 (March 1952), pp. 54–67.* *According to Meade,*

'This note has arisen, out of a consideration of the problems of the economic development of underdeveloped territories, in the preparation of Volume II of my *Theory of International Economic Policy* [*Trade and Welfare* (London: Oxford University Press, 1955)] for the Royal Institute of International Affairs.'

## I  The Scope of the Paper

The purpose of this note is to distinguish between certain types of external economies and diseconomies which are connected with marginal adjustments in purely competitive situations. We shall not be dealing with divergences between private and social interests due to monopolistic or monopsonistic situations, nor with any of the problems which arise from indivisibilities such as the lumpiness of investment in particular forms, nor with any questions about large structural changes such as whether a particular industry should exist at all or not. We shall be concerned only with small adjustments to existing competitive situations.

## II  The Competitive Situation with No External Economies or Diseconomies

Let us consider two industries. These 'industries' may or may not in fact produce identically the same product and so in reality constitute a single industry. That is immaterial to our general theory. But we assume that within each 'industry' there are a large number of independent competing firms, so that to each individual entrepreneur the price of the product and of the factors is given. In the absence of any external economies or diseconomies, each entrepreneur will hire each factor up to the point at which the additional product of the factor multiplied by its price is equal to the price of the factor. Moreover, there will be constant returns to scale. If every factor in either of our two industries were increased by

10%, including the number of entrepreneurs, then the product also would be increased by 10%.

Let us write $x_1$ and $x_2$ for the products of industry 1 and industry 2 respectively. We assume that there are two factors, $l$ and $c$, or labour and capital, employed in both industries, so that $l_1 + l_2 = l$ and $c_1 + c_2 = c$. We will write $\bar{x}_1, \bar{l}_1, \bar{c}_1$, etc., for the market prices of the products and factors; and $X_1 = x_1\bar{x}_1, L_1 = l_1\bar{l}_1, C_1 = c_1\bar{c}_1$, etc., for the total value of the output of $x_1$ or for the total income earned by $l_1$, etc. Finally, we shall write $\check{L}_1, \check{C}_1$, etc., for the amounts which the factors would have to be paid if they received the value of their marginal social net products. In our model capital is always the hiring factor, and its reward is, therefore, always equal in each industry to the total output of that industry minus the wages paid to labour in that industry, so that $C_1 = X_1 - L_1$ and $C_2 = X_2 - L_2$.

In the case in which there are no divergences between private and social net products we can write

$$\left. \begin{array}{l} x_1 = H_1(l_1, c_1) \\[2mm] x_2 = H_2(l_2, c_2) \end{array} \right\} \tag{1}$$

where $H_1$ and $H_2$ are homogeneous functions of the first degree, expressing the fact that there are constant returns to scale in both industries. Now

$$x_1 = \frac{\partial x_1}{\partial l_1} l_1 + \frac{\partial x_1}{\partial c_1} c_1$$

or

$$1 = \frac{l_1}{x_1} \frac{\partial x_1}{\partial l_1} + \frac{c_1}{x_1} \cdot \frac{\partial x_1}{\partial c_1}.$$

We shall write $\varepsilon_{l_1}^{x_1}$ for $l_1 / x_1 \cdot \partial x_1 / \partial l_1$ and so on, so that we have

$$\varepsilon_{l_1}^{x_1} + \varepsilon_{c_1}^{x_1} = \varepsilon_{l_2}^{x_2} + \varepsilon_{c_2}^{x_2} = 1. \tag{2}$$

These expressions describe the fact that if, for example, a 10% increase in labour alone causes a 3% increase in output, then a 10% increase in capital alone must cause a 7% increase in output, because a 10% increase in both factors will cause a 10% increase in output.

In this situation $l_1$ will be paid a money wage $(L_1)$ equal to $(\partial x_1 / \partial l_1) l_1 \bar{x}_1$ or $\varepsilon_{l_1}^{x_1} X_1$, and this will also be equal to the value of its marginal social net product. Capital in industry 1 will receive $X_1 - L_1$ which from equation (2) equals $\varepsilon_{c_1}^{x_1} X_1$, which is also equal to the value of capital's marginal social net product, so that in this case we have

$$L_1 = \check{L}_1 = \varepsilon_{l_1}^{x_1} X_1 \qquad\qquad L_2 = \check{L}_2 = \varepsilon_{l_2}^{x_2} X_2$$

$$C_1 = \check{C}_1 = \varepsilon_{c_1}^{x_1} X_1 \qquad\qquad C_2 = \check{C}_2 = \varepsilon_{l_2}^{x_2} X_2$$

Moreover, since $\varepsilon_{l_1}^{x_1} = L_1 / X_1$, we can measure $\varepsilon_{l_1}^{x_1}$ from the proportion of the total product in industry, which goes to labour. And similarly for the measurement of $\varepsilon_{c_1}^{x_1}$, $\varepsilon_{l_2}^{x_2}$ and $\varepsilon_{c_2}^{x_2}$.

## III   Two Types of External Economy and Diseconomy

Such is the simplest competitive model. We intend now to consider cases where what is done in one industry reacts upon the conditions of production in the other industry in some way other than through the possible effect upon the prices of the product or of the factors in that other industry. All such reactions we shall describe as constituting external economies or diseconomies, because the individual entrepreneur in the first industry will take account of the effect of his actions only upon what happens inside the first industry (the internal effect), but will leave out of account the effect of his actions upon the output of the second industry, in which it may improve production (an external economy) or diminish production (an external diseconomy).

But the purpose of this note is to distinguish between two types of such external economies or diseconomies. The first type we shall call 'unpaid factors of production', and the second the 'creation of atmosphere'. The essential difference between these two types of external economy or diseconomy is that in the first case there are still constant returns to scale for society as a whole, though not for the individual industry, whereas in the second case there are still constant returns to scale for each individual industry but not for society as a whole.

## IV   Unpaid Factors

Suppose that in a given region there is a certain amount of apple-growing and a certain amount of bee-keeping and that the bees feed on the apple-blossom. If the apple-farmers apply 10% more labour, land and capital to apple-farming they will increase the output of apples by 10%; but they will also provide more food for the bees. On the other hand, the bee-keepers will not increase the output of honey by 10% by increasing the amount of land, labour and capital applied to bee-keeping by 10% unless at the same time the apple-farmers also increase their output and so the food of the bees by 10%. Thus there are constant returns to scale for both industries taken together: if the amount of labour and of capital employed both in apple-farming and bee-keeping are doubled, the output of both apples and honey will be doubled. But if the amount of labour and capital are doubled in bee-keeping alone, the output of honey will be less than doubled; whereas, if the amounts of labour and capital in apple-farming are doubled, the output of apples will be doubled and, in addition, some contribution will be made to the output of honey.

We call this a case of an unpaid factor, because the situation is due simply and solely to the fact that the apple-farmer cannot charge the bee-keeper for the bees' food, which the former produces for the latter. If social-accounting institutions were such that this charge could be made, then every factor would, as in other competitive situations, earn the value of its marginal social net product. But as it is, the apple-farmer provides to the bee-keeper some of his factors free of charge. The apple-farmer is paid less than the value of his marginal social net product, and the bee-keeper receives more than the value of his marginal social net product.

This situation is shown if industry 1 represents bee-keeping and industry 2 apple-farming and if we replace equations (1) and (2) with

$$x_1 = H_1(l_1, c_1, x_2)$$
$$x_2 = H_2(l_2, c_2)$$

so that $\quad \varepsilon_{l_1}^{x_1} + \varepsilon_{c_1}^{x_1} + \varepsilon_{x_2}^{x_1} = \varepsilon_{l_2}^{x_2} + \varepsilon_{c_2}^{x_2} = 1 \qquad (4)$

In this case $l_1$ will be paid the value of its marginal social net product, and we have $L_1 = \bar{L}_1 = \varepsilon_{l_1}^{x_1} X_1$. $c_1$ will be paid $X_1 - L_1$ or $\varepsilon_{c_1}^{x_1} X_1 + \varepsilon_{x_2}^{x_1} X_2$; but $\varepsilon_{c_1}^{x_1} X_1$ is the value of $c_1$'s marginal social net product, so that we have $C_1 = \bar{C}_1 + \varepsilon_{x_2}^{x_1} X_1$. In other words, $c_1$ will have to have its earnings taxed at an *ad valorem* rate of $(X_1/C_1)\varepsilon_{x_2}^{x_1}$ in order to be paid a net reward equal to the value of its marginal social net product.

But, on the other hand, $l_2$ and $c_2$ will be paid just so much less than the value of their marginal social net products.

$$\bar{L}_2 = l_2\left(\bar{x}_2 \frac{\partial x_2}{\partial l_2} + \bar{x}_1 \frac{\partial x_1}{\partial x_2} \cdot \frac{\partial x_2}{\partial l_2}\right)$$

$$= \varepsilon_{l_2}^{x_2} X_2\left(1 + \frac{X_1}{X_2} \varepsilon_{x_2}^{x_1}\right)$$

But $l_2$ will receive only $\varepsilon_{l_2}^{x_2} X_2$, so that $\bar{L}_2 = L_2(1 + (X_1/X_2)\varepsilon_{x_2}^{x_1})$ and the wages of labour in apple-farming will need to be subsidised at an *ad valorem* rate of $(X_1/X_2)\varepsilon_{x_2}^{x_1}$ in order to equate rewards to the value of the factor's marginal social net product. Similarly, $\bar{C}_2 = C_2(1 + (X_1/X_2)\varepsilon_{x_2}^{x_1})$, and the same *ad valorem* rate of subsidy should be paid to the earnings of capital in apple-farming. Since $C_2 + L_2 = X_2$, the total tax revenue of $X_1\varepsilon_{x_2}^{x_1}$ raised on $C_1$ will be equal to the two subsidies of $C_2(X_1/X_2)\varepsilon_{x_2}^{x_1}$ and $L_2(X_1/X_2)\varepsilon_{x_2}^{x_1}$.[1] In order to discover the appropriate rates of tax and subsidy, the essential factor which will need to be estimated is $\varepsilon_{x_2}^{x_1}$, the percentage effect on the output of honey which a 1% increase in the output of apples would exercise.

Now the relationship which we have just examined might be a reciprocal one. While the apples may provide the food of the bees, the

---

[1] In this case it would, of course, have exactly the same effect if the subsidy were paid not on the wages of labour and profits of capital in apple-farming but at the same *ad valorem* rate on the value of the apple-output, $X_2$.

bees may fertilise the apples.[2] Once again we may have constant returns to scale for society as a whole: a 10% increase in all factors in both industries would cause a 10% increase in the output of both products. In this case instead of equations (4) we should have

$$
\left.\begin{aligned}
x_1 &= H_1(l_1, c_1, x_2) \\[6pt]
x_2 &= H_2(l_2, c_2, x_1) \\[6pt]
\varepsilon_{l_1}^{x_1} + \varepsilon_{c_1}^{x_1} + \varepsilon_{x_2}^{x_1} &= \varepsilon_{l_2}^{x_2} + \varepsilon_{c_2}^{x_2} + \varepsilon_{x_1}^{x_2} = 1
\end{aligned}\right\} \tag{5}
$$

By a process similar to that adopted in the previous case we can obtain formulae to show what subsidies and taxes must be imposed in order to equate each factor's income in each industry to the value of its marginal social net product.

We can obtain the actual rewards of the factors in exactly the same way as in the previous example. Labour in industry 1 will obtain a wage equal to the value of its marginal private net product or $\bar{x}_1(\partial x_1/\partial l_1)$, so that $L_1 = \varepsilon_{l_1}^{x_1} X_1$. Capital in industry 1 will receive the remainder, or $X_1 - L_1$, so that from equations (5) $C_1 = X_1(\varepsilon_{c_1}^{x_1} + \varepsilon_{x_2}^{x_1})$. Similarly, $L_2 = \varepsilon_{l_2}^{x_2} X_2$ and $C_2 = X_2(\varepsilon_{c_2}^{x_2} + \varepsilon_{x_1}^{x_2})$.

To obtain expressions for the value of each factor's marginal social net product we have now to allow for the repercussions of each industry upon the other. Thus the value of the marginal social net product of labour in apple-farming includes not only the increased output of apples directly produced but also the increased output of honey caused by this increase in apple-output plus the further increase in apple-output due to this increase in honey-output plus the still further increase in honey-output due to this increase in apple-output and so on in an infinite progression. The final result can be obtained in the following manner. Differentiating the main equations in equations (5), we have

$$
dx_1 = \frac{\partial x_1}{\partial l_1} dl_1 + \frac{\partial x_1}{\partial c_1} dc_1 + \frac{\partial x_1}{\partial x_2} dx_2
$$

$$
dx_2 = \frac{\partial x_2}{\partial l_2} dl_2 + \frac{\partial x_2}{\partial c_2} dc_2 + \frac{\partial x_2}{\partial x_1} dx_1
$$

If we keep $c_1$, $l_2$ and $c_2$ constant ($dc_1 = dl_2 = dc_2 = 0$) but allow $l_1$ to vary ($dl_1 \neq 0$), $dx_1$ and $dx_2$ will give the marginal social net products of $l_1$ in the two commodities. We obtain

---

[2] If the bees had a bad effect upon the apples, then we should have an external diseconomy, which may be regarded as an unpaid negative factor of production. The bee-keepers, in addition to getting the bee-food free of charge, are also not charged for some damage which they do to the apple-farmers. In what follows $\varepsilon_{x_1}^{x_2}$ would be $< 0$, so that $\varepsilon_{l_2}^{x_2} + \varepsilon_{c_2}^{x_2} > 1$.

$$\frac{dx_1}{dl_1} = \frac{\dfrac{\partial x_1}{\partial l_1}}{1 - \dfrac{\partial x_1}{\partial x_2} \cdot \dfrac{\partial x_2}{\partial x_1}} \quad \text{and} \quad \frac{dx_2}{dl_1} = \frac{\dfrac{\partial x_2}{\partial x_1} \cdot \dfrac{\partial x_1}{\partial l_1}}{1 - \dfrac{\partial x_1}{\partial x_2} \cdot \dfrac{\partial x_2}{\partial x_1}}$$

But

$$\bar{L}_1 = l_1 \bar{x}_1 \frac{dx_1}{dl_1} + l_1 \bar{x}_2 \frac{dx_2}{dl_1}$$

$$= l_1 \frac{\partial x_1}{\partial l_1} \frac{\bar{x}_1 + \bar{x}_2 \dfrac{\partial x_2}{\partial x_1}}{1 - \dfrac{\partial x_1}{\partial x_2} \cdot \dfrac{\partial x_2}{\partial x_1}}$$

$$= L_1 \frac{1 + \dfrac{X_2}{X_1} \cdot \varepsilon_{x_1}^{x_2}}{1 - \varepsilon_{x_2}^{x_1} \varepsilon_{x_1}^{x_2}}$$

Similarly, we get the following expressions for the values of the marginal social net products of the other factors.

$$\bar{L}_2 = L_2 \frac{1 + \dfrac{X_1}{X_2} \varepsilon_{x_2}^{x_1}}{1 - \varepsilon_{x_2}^{x_1} \varepsilon_{x_1}^{x_2}}$$

$$\bar{C}_1 = \varepsilon_{c_1}^{x_1} X_1 \frac{1 + \dfrac{X_2}{X_1} \varepsilon_{x_1}^{x_2}}{1 - \varepsilon_{x_2}^{x_1} \varepsilon_{x_1}^{x_2}} = (C_1 - \varepsilon_{x_2}^{x_1} X_1) \frac{1 + \dfrac{X_2}{X_1} \varepsilon_{x_1}^{x_2}}{1 - \varepsilon_{x_2}^{x_1} \varepsilon_{x_1}^{x_2}}$$

$$\bar{C}_2 = (C_2 - \varepsilon_{x_1}^{x_1} X_2) \frac{1 + \dfrac{X_1}{X_2} \varepsilon_{x_2}^{x_1}}{1 - \varepsilon_{x_2}^{x_1} \varepsilon_{x_1}^{x_2}}$$

On these expressions we can make the following three comments:

First, remembering that $L_1 + C_1 = X_1$ and $L_2 + C_2 = X_2$, we can see from the above expressions that $\bar{L}_1 + \bar{L}_2 + \bar{C}_1 + \bar{C}_2 = X_1 + X_2$. In other words, if the factors were all paid rewards equal to the value of their marginal social net products, this would absorb the whole of the product, neither more nor less. This is due, of course, to the essential constant-returns nature of the production functions at equations (5), from which it can be seen that if $l_1$, $l_2$, $c_1$ and $c_2$ were to increase by 10%, then the production conditions would be satisfied if both outputs also increased by 10%. In other words, we are still dealing with a pure unpaid-factor case; there is no adding-up problem for society; every factor can be given a reward equal to the value of its marginal social net product if the revenue from the taxes levied on those which ought to be taxed is used to subsidise the earnings of those which ought to be subsidised.

Secondly, $\check{L}_1$, $\check{L}_2$, $\check{C}_1$ and $\check{C}_2$ are all seen to be positive finite quantities, provided that $\varepsilon_{x_2}^{x_1}\varepsilon_{x_1}^{x_2} < 1$. From the last of equations (5) it can be seen that $\varepsilon_{x_2}^{x_1}$ and $\varepsilon_{x_1}^{x_2}$ are both $< 1$; it requires a 10% increase of land, labour and apple-blossom to increase the output of honey by 10%, so that a 10% increase in the supply of apple-blossom alone will increase the output of honey by less than 10%. But $\varepsilon_{x_2}^{x_1}$ and $\varepsilon_{x_1}^{x_2}$ are both positive, since we are dealing with external economies and not diseconomies. It follows, therefore, that $0 < \varepsilon_{x_2}^{x_1}\varepsilon_{x_1}^{x_2} < 1$, so that $\check{L}_1$, $\check{L}_2$, $\check{C}_1$ and $\check{C}_2$ are all positive finite quantities. It is because $\varepsilon_{x_2}^{x_1}$ and $\varepsilon_{x_1}^{x_2}$ are both positive fractions that the infinite progression of an increase in apple-output causing an increase in honey-output, causing an increase in apple-output and so on, adds up only to a finite sum. For example, if both $\varepsilon_{x_2}^{x_1}$ and $\varepsilon_{x_1}^{x_2}$ are one-half, a 10% increase in apple-output causes a 5% increase in honey-output, but this 5% increase in honey-output causes only a 2½% increase in apple-output; which causes only a 1¼% increase in honey-output and so on in a diminishing geometric progression.

Thirdly, from the above expressions for $L_1$ and $\check{L}_1$, we obtain

$$\frac{\check{L}_1 - L_1}{L_1} = \frac{\dfrac{X_2}{X_1}\varepsilon_{x_1}^{x_2} + \varepsilon_{x_2}^{x_1}\varepsilon_{x_1}^{x_2}}{1 - \varepsilon_{x_1}^{x_2}\varepsilon_{x_2}^{x_1}}$$

which shows the *ad valorem* rate of subsidy which must be paid to $l_1$ to bring its earnings up to the value of its marginal social net product. We can obtain a similar expression for the rates of tax levyable upon $C_1$.

$$\frac{C_1 - \check{C}_1}{C_1} = \frac{\varepsilon_{x_2}^{x_1}\dfrac{X_1}{C_1} - \dfrac{X_2}{X_1}\varepsilon_{x_1}^{x_2} + \dfrac{X_2 - C_1}{C_1}\varepsilon_{x_2}^{x_1}\varepsilon_{x_1}^{x_2}}{1 - \varepsilon_{x_2}^{x_1}\varepsilon_{x_1}^{x_2}}.$$

Corresponding expressions for $(\check{L}_2 - L_2)/L_2$ and $(C_2 - \check{C}_2)/C_2$ can be obtained by interchanging the subscripts 1 and 2. It can be seen from adding $C_1 - \check{C}_1$ and $C_2 - \check{C}_2$ that there will be a positive tax revenue raised from capital as a whole. But either $C_1 - \check{C}_1$ or $C_2 - \check{C}_2$ might be negative, i.e. a subsidy might be payable on the earnings of capital in one of the two industries as well as upon the earnings of labour in both of the industries. For example, $C_2 - \check{C}_2$ would be $< 0$ if $\varepsilon_{x_2}^{x_1}$ were very large relatively to $\varepsilon_{x_1}^{x_2}$. This would mean, for example, that the production of honey (industry 1) did very little to help the production of apples (industry 2), while the production of apples did much to help the production of bees. Capitalists in apple-farming should be subsidised because the unpaid benefits which they confer upon the bee-keepers more than outweigh the unpaid benefits which they receive from labour and capital employed in bee-keeping. Indeed, all the results obtained from equations (4) can be obtained from the expressions derived from equations (5) by writing $\varepsilon_{x_1}^{x_2} = 0$.

## V   The Creation of Atmosphere

A distinction must be drawn between a 'factor of production' and a physical or social 'atmosphere' affecting production. We may take the rainfall in a district as a typical example of atmosphere. The rainfall may be deficient in the sense that a higher rainfall would increase the farmers' output, but nevertheless what rainfall there is will be available to all farms in the district regardless of their number. Thus if in the district in question the amount of land, labour and capital devoted to, say, wheat-farming were to be increased by 10%, the output of wheat would also be increased by 10% even if the rainfall were to remain constant. This is quite different from the case of a factor of production for which no payment is made; in our previous example, a 10% increase in the output of apples (and so in the supply of apple-blossom) would be necessary, in addition to a 10% increase in the amount of land, labour and capital devoted to bee-keeping, if the output of honey is to be increased by 10%. In these examples, rainfall is an 'atmosphere' for wheat-farming; but the output of apples is an 'unpaid factor of production' for bee-keeping.

The distinction should now be clear. Both a factor of production and an atmosphere are conditions which affect the output of a certain industry. But the atmosphere is a fixed condition of production which remains unchanged for all producers in the industry in question without anyone else doing anything about it, however large or small – within limits – is the scale of operations of the industry. On the other hand, the factor of production is an aid to production which is fixed in amount, and which is therefore available on a smaller scale to each producer in the industry if the number of producers increases, unless someone does something to increase the total supply of the factor.

The external economies which we have examined in the last section are concerned with factors of production for which the individual producer pays nothing. We must turn now to external economies and diseconomies which are due to the fact that the activities of one group of producers may provide an atmosphere which is favourable or unfavourable to the activities of another group of producers. For example, suppose that afforestation schemes in one locality increase the rainfall in that district and that this is favourable to the production of wheat in that district. In this case the production of timber creates an atmosphere favourable to the production of wheat.

In these cases there is an adding-up problem for society as a whole. There may be constant returns to the factors of production employed in either industry alone. That is to say, a 10% increase in the amounts of land, labour and capital employed in producing wheat might, in any given atmosphere, result in a 10% increase in the output of wheat. And a 10% increase in the amount of land, labour and capital employed in producing timber might, apart from its effect in changing the atmosphere for wheat-farmers, cause a 10% increase in the output of timber. It follows that a 10% increase in the amount of land, labour and capital employed both in the timber industry and in wheat-farming will increase the output of timber by 10% and the output of wheat by more than 10% (because of the improvement in the atmosphere for wheat producers). To society as a whole there are now increasing returns to scale; to pay every factor a reward equal to the value of its marginal social net product will account for more than the total output of the two industries; revenue will have to be raised from outside sources by general taxation if subsidies are to be paid on a scale to bring every factor's reward up to the value of its marginal social net product.

We can express this sort of situation by the following equations:

$$x_1 = H_1(l_1, c_1)A_1(x_2)$$

$$x_2 = H_2(l_2, c_2)$$

where once more

$$\varepsilon_{l_1}^{x_1} + \varepsilon_{c_1}^{x_1} = \varepsilon_{l_2}^{x_2} + \varepsilon_{c_2}^{x_2} = 1. \, ^3$$

$$\tag{6}$$

$x_2 = H_2(l_2, c_2)$ is the ordinary competitive constant-returns production function for the timber industry. There is the same type of production function for the wheat industry; but in this case the output due to the use of labour and land $(H_1[c_1, l_1])$ is subject to an atmosphere $(A_1)$. If the atmosphere is favourable then $H_1(l_1, c_1)$ is multiplied up by a large factor to give the actual output $(x_1)$. In the case which we are examining, the atmosphere for the wheat industry $(A_1)$ is made to depend upon the output of the timber industry $(A_1 = A_1[x_2])$.

The atmosphere factor $(A_1)$ is thus subject to the following conditions. $A_1(0) = 1$, i.e. we define our terms in such a way that $H_1(l_1, c_1)$ is equal to what the output of wheat would be if there were no timber output. $A_1$ is always $> 0$, i.e. there cannot be so powerful an external diseconomy that the output of the industry affected becomes negative. When $A_1(x_2) > 1$, then there is an average external economy, i.e. the output of wheat is greater than it would have been had there been a zero output of timber instead of a positive output $(x_2)$; and similarly, when $A_1(x_2) < 1$, there is an average external diseconomy. When $A_1'(x_2)$ is $> 0$, then there is a marginal external economy, i.e. the output of wheat would be improved by a further increase in the output of timber; and when $A_1'(x_2)$ is $< 0$, there is a marginal external diseconomy.

The actual rewards of the factors of production are easily seen to be $L_1 = \varepsilon_{l_1}^{x_1}X_1$, $C_1 = X_1 - L_1 = \varepsilon_{c_1}^{x_1}X_1$, $L_2 = \varepsilon_{l_2}^{x_2}X_2$ and $C_2 = X_2 - L_2 = \varepsilon_{c_2}^{x_2}X_2$. In the case of the factors employed in wheat-farming (industry 1) there will be no divergence between the reward paid and the value of the marginal social net product; and $L_1 = \check{L}_1$ and $C_1 = \check{C}_1$.

---

[3] Since $l_1 \, \partial H_1 / \partial l_1 = l_1 / H_1 A_1 \cdot (A_1 \partial H_1 / \partial l_1) H_1 = l_1 / x_1 \cdot (\partial x_1 / \partial l_1) H_1 = \varepsilon_{l_1}^{x_1} H_1$, we have $H_1 = \varepsilon_{l_1}^{x_1} H_1 + \varepsilon_{c_1}^{x_1} H_1$, so that $1 = \varepsilon_{l_1}^{x_1} + \varepsilon_{c_1}^{x_1}$.

But the rewards actually paid to the factors of production in the timber industry (industry 2) will be lower than the value of their marginal social net products because they will not be paid for the favourable atmosphere which they create for wheat farmers. Thus

$$\bar{L}_2 = \varepsilon_{l_2}^{x_2} X_2 + l_2 \bar{x}_1 \frac{\partial x_1}{\partial x_2} \cdot \frac{\partial x_2}{\partial l_2}$$

$$= L_2 \left( 1 + \frac{X_1}{X_2} \cdot \varepsilon_{x_2}^{x_1} \right)$$

where $\varepsilon_{x_2}^{x_1} = x_2/x_1 \cdot \partial x_1 / \partial x_2$ or $x_2 / A_1 \cdot \partial A_1 / \partial x_2$, the percentage increase in the output of wheat which would be brought about by a 1% increase in the output of timber through the improvement in the atmosphere for wheat production. And similarly, it can be shown that $\bar{C}_2 = C[1 + (X_1/X_2) \varepsilon_{x_2}^{x_1}]$. In other words, the earnings of both $l_2$ and $c_2$ or, alternatively, the price of the product $x_2$ must be subsidised from general revenue at the *ad valorem* rate of $(X_1/X_2) \varepsilon_{x_2}^{x_1}$ if all factors are to receive rewards equal to the value of their marginal social net products.

As in the case of unpaid factors, these reactions of one industry upon the other may be reciprocal. Industry 1 may create a favourable or un-favourable atmosphere for industry 2, as well as industry 2 for industry 1. In this case we have

$$\left. \begin{array}{c} x_1 = H_1(l_1, c_1) A_1(x_2) \\[2mm] x_2 = H_2(l_2, c_2) A_2(x_1) \\[4mm] \varepsilon_{l_1}^{x_1} + \varepsilon_{c_1}^{x_1} = \varepsilon_{l_2}^{x_2} + \varepsilon_{c_2}^{x_2} = 1. \end{array} \right\} \quad (7)$$

where

Here again $L_1 = \varepsilon_{l_1}^{x_1} X_1$, $C_1 = X_1 - L_1 = \varepsilon_{c_1}^{x_1} X_1$, $L_2 = \varepsilon_{l_2}^{x_2} X_2$ and $C_2 = X_2 - L_2 = \varepsilon_{c_2}^{x_2} X_2$.

But when we come to consider the marginal social net product, we have to take into account the infinite chain of action and reaction of the one industry upon the other, as in the case of apple-growing and bee-keeping examined above. The marginal social net product of $l_1$, for example, is obtained by differentiating the first two of equations (7), keeping $l_2$, $c_1$ and $c_2$ all constant. We obtain

$$\frac{dx_1}{dl_1} = \frac{\varepsilon_{l_1}^{x_1} \cdot \dfrac{x_1}{l_1}}{1 - \varepsilon_{x_2}^{x_1} \varepsilon_{x_1}^{x_2}} \quad \text{and} \quad \frac{dx_2}{dl_1} = \frac{\varepsilon_{l_1}^{x_1} \varepsilon_{x_1}^{x_2} \cdot \dfrac{x_2}{l_1}}{1 - \varepsilon_{x_2}^{x_1} \varepsilon_{x_1}^{x_2}} \cdot$$

Now

$$\bar{L}_1 = l_1 \bar{x}_1 \frac{dx_1}{dl_1} + l_1 \bar{x}_2 \frac{dx_2}{dl_1} ,$$

so that
$$\frac{\bar{L}_1}{L_1} = \frac{1 + \dfrac{X_2}{X_1}\varepsilon_{x_1}^{x_2}}{1 - \varepsilon_{x_2}^{x_1}\varepsilon_{x_1}^{x_2}}.$$

Similarly, we can show that $C_1/C_1 = \bar{L}_1/L$ and that

$$\frac{\bar{L}_2}{L_2} = \frac{\bar{C}_2}{C_2} = \frac{1 + \dfrac{X_1}{X_2}\varepsilon_{x_2}^{x_1}}{1 - \varepsilon_{x_2}^{x_1}\varepsilon_{x_1}^{x_2}}.$$

In other words, in order that each factor should obtain a reward equal to the value of its marginal social net product both labour and capital in industry 1, or alternatively, the price of the product of industry 1, should be subsidised at the *ad valorem* rate of $\varepsilon_{x_1}^{x_2}(X_2/X_1 + \varepsilon_{x_2}^{x_1})/(1 - \varepsilon_{x_2}^{x_1}\varepsilon_{x_1}^{x_2})$; and similarly, in industry 2 a rate of subsidy of $\varepsilon_{x_2}^{x_1}(X_1/X_2 + \varepsilon_{x_1}^{x_2})/(1 - \varepsilon_{x_2}^{x_1}\varepsilon_{x_1}^{x_2})$ should be paid.

So far throughout this note we have assumed that in all external economies or diseconomies, whether of the unpaid-factor or of the atmosphere-creating kind, it is the *output* of one industry which affects production in the other. But this is, of course, not necessarily the case. It may be the employment of one *factor* in one industry which confers an indirect benefit or the reverse upon producers in the other industry.[4] Moreover, in the case in which atmosphere is created, the output of industry 2 may create an atmosphere for industry 1 which increases the efficiency of a particular *factor* in industry 1 rather than the general level of *output*.[5] Or the employment of a particular *factor* in industry 2 might create conditions which improved the efficiency of a particular factor in industry 1.[6] And any combination of these indirect effects of industry 2 upon industry 1 might be combined with any other combination of such effects of industry 1 on industry 2. Clearly, we cannot consider in detail all the very many possibilities.

But consider the following particular case:

$$\left.\begin{array}{l} x_1 = H_1(\lambda_1, c_1) \\ x_2 = H_2(\lambda_2, c_2) \\ \lambda_1 = l_1 A(l) \\ \lambda_2 = l_2 A(l) \\ l = l_1 + l_2 \end{array}\right\} \tag{8}$$

where $l_1$ = the number of workers employed in industry 1 and $\lambda_1$ = the equivalent number of workers of an efficiency which an individual worker would have if the total labour force were very small ($l \rightarrow 0$, so that $A \rightarrow 1$).

---

[4] In this case we should have equations of the type of $x_1 = H_1(l_1, c_1, l_2)$ in the case of unpaid factors, and of the type of $x_1 = H_1(l_1, c_1)A_1(l_2)$ in the case of atmosphere-creation.
[5] In this case the equations would be of the type $x_1 = H_1\{l_1 A_1(x_2), c_1\}$.
[6] For example, $x_1 = H_1\{l_1 A_1(c_2), c_1\}$.

This is the case where the total labour force in the two industries ($l$) affects the general efficiency of labour. We may suppose that, up to a certain point, a growth in the absolute size of the labour force employed in these two industries causes a general atmosphere favourable to the efficiency of labour by enabling workers to communicate to each other a certain know-how about, and interest in, the mechanical processes which are common to the two industries.

Now the individual employer in any one firm in either industry will regard $A$ as being unaffected by his own actions, because the indirect effect which an increase in the number of workers employed by him alone will have upon the general efficiency of his own labour will be a negligible quantity. He will go on taking on labour of any given level of efficiency until the wage paid to a unit of labour is equal to the price paid for its marginal product at that level of efficiency. In other words,

$$L_1 = \lambda_1 \bar{x}_1 \frac{\partial x_1}{\partial \lambda_1} = \varepsilon_{\lambda_1}^{x_1} X_1 \, .$$

The reward paid to $c_1$ will be $C_1 = X_1 - L_1 = \varepsilon_{c_1}^{x_1} X_1$.
Similarly, $L_2 = \varepsilon_{\lambda_2}^{x_2} X_2$ and $C_2 = \varepsilon_{c_2}^{x_2} X_2$.

In this case $\bar{C}_1 = \varepsilon_{c_1}^{x_1} X_1$ and $\bar{C}_2 = \varepsilon_{c_2}^{x_2} X_2$ because there are no external economies or diseconomies involved in decisions to apply more capital in either industry, so that $C_1 = \bar{C}_1$ and $C_2 = \bar{C}_2$.

But in evaluating the value of the marginal social net product of labour we have to take into account the effect which the employment of more labour by one particular employer may have upon the efficiency of labour for all other employers in industry 1 and for all other employers in industry 2. The value of the marginal social net product exceeds the wage which will be offered for it by these two sums, so that

$$\bar{L}_1 = L_1 + l_1 \bar{x}_1 \frac{\partial x_1}{\partial \lambda_1} \cdot \frac{\partial \lambda_1}{\partial l} \cdot \frac{\partial l}{\partial l_1} + l_1 \bar{x}_2 \frac{\partial x_2}{\partial \lambda_2} \cdot \frac{\partial \lambda_2}{\partial l} \cdot \frac{\partial l}{\partial l_1} \, .$$

Since $\partial l / \partial l_1 = 1$, $\partial \lambda_1 / \partial l = \lambda_1 / A \cdot \partial A / \partial l$, and $\partial \lambda_2 / \partial l = \lambda_2 / A \cdot \partial A / \partial l$, we have $\bar{L}_1 = L_1 + (L_1 + L_2)(l_1/l)\varepsilon_l^A$, where $\varepsilon_l^A = l/A \cdot dA/dl$. Similarly, $\bar{L}_2 = L_2 + (L_1 + L_2)(l_2/l)\varepsilon_l^A$. Now if the wage-rate is the same in both industries so that $l_1/l = L_1/(L_1 + L_2)$ and $l_2/l = L_2/(L_1 + L_2)$, we have $\bar{L}_1/L_1 = \bar{L}_2/L_2 = 1 + \varepsilon_l^A$. The employment of labour in both industries must be subsidised at the *ad valorem* rate of $\varepsilon_l^A$, if rewards are to be raised to the value of marginal social net products.

## VI Conclusion

It is not claimed that this division of external economies and diseconomies into unpaid factors and the creation of atmosphere is logically complete. External economies exist whenever we have production functions of the form

$$x_1 = F_1(l_1, c_1, l_2, c_2, x_2)$$

$$x_2 = F_2(l_2, c_2, l_1, c_1, x_1)$$

where $F_1$ and $F_2$ are not necessarily homogeneous of the first degree. But it is claimed that it may clarify thought on different types of external economy and diseconomy to distinguish thus between: (1) those cases in which there are constant returns for society, but not necessarily constant returns in each industry to the factors which each industry employs and pays for, and (2) those cases in which there are constant returns in each industry to those factors which it controls and pays for, but in which there are not constant returns for the two industries taken together, the scale of operations being important in the one industry because of the atmosphere which it creates for the other. One of the most important conclusions to be drawn is that in the case of type (1) – the unpaid-factor case – there is no adding-up problem for society as a whole; in order to pay every factor a reward equal to the value of its marginal social net product some factors must be taxed and others subsidised, and the revenue from the appropriate taxes will just finance the expenditure upon the appropriate subsidies. But in the case of the creation of atmosphere (type 2)) the subsidies (or taxes) required to promote (or discourage) the creation of favourable (or unfavourable) atmosphere are net additions to (or subtractions from) society's general fiscal burden. But, in fact, of course, external economies or diseconomies may not fall into either of these precise divisions and may contain features of both of them.

# 8

# Little's *Critique of Welfare Economics*

*This review of the second edition of I. M. D. Little,* A Critique of
Welfare Economics *(London: Oxford University Press, 1957) appeared
in* The Economic Journal, *vol. 69 (March 1959), pp. 124–29. It
stimulated 'Welfare Criteria: An exchange of notes', by D. H. Robertson, Meade, Little, and E. J. Mishan, in* The Economic Journal, *vol. 72
(March 1962), pp. 226–244.*

Normally a reviewer's duty is to tell the reader what the book under
review contains, and only after that is done to criticise those contents. But
in reviewing this book the normal rule does not apply; for as the result of a
series of unfortunate accidents the first edition of this famous book, which
appeared as long ago as 1950, was never reviewed in the *Economic
Journal*. It would indeed be a waste of time to offer at this late stage to any
economist who has any interest in the theory of economic welfare a brief
sketch of what Mr Little has said on the subject. The author has already
through this book established his position as one of the few outstanding
contributors to the subject, and his contribution is already incorporated
into the thought of all those who study these problems.

This book has indeed had a significant influence on economic thought.
In the first place, the present fairly widespread realisation among
economists of many basic difficulties involved in deciding whether a
community is in any meaningful sense better off economically in one
situation than another is largely due to Mr Little's work. If consumers are
not consistent in their choices, how can we say whether they are better off
in the one situation rather than the other? If the community is made up of
one set of individuals in one situation and another set in the other
situation, in what sense can we say whether the community as a whole is
better or worse off? If people's tastes and wants are affected by what
other people consume, how can one tell whether they are better off in one
situation rather than in another? If we cannot assume that all individuals
know what is good for them, how can we construct a criterion for an
increase in economic welfare in a non-authoritarian society? It has been
much less easy to neglect questions of this kind since Mr Little's book was
first published.

There is a second way in which Mr Little's work has radically changed
the atmosphere in which welfare economics are discussed. By insisting as
he did on the emotive and prescriptive nature of many judgements which

in form are innocent statements of objective fact he has significantly increased the chances that in economic discussion disputes about the values attached to certain ends will be less easily muddled up with disputes about the objective economic effects of certain acts of policy. Certainly the present reviewer is not ashamed to admit that Mr Little's book acted on him as a salutory reminder that he ought to avoid a misuse of persuasive language in making what purported to be judgements of fact and not judgements of value.

Thirdly, there is a basic element of balanced common sense in Mr Little's work which has done much to bring sanity into discussions about economic welfare. Having shown that it is impossible to use any exact and precise criterion of economic welfare except on simplifying assumptions that are certainly in many respects unrealistic, he does not rush to the conclusion that the whole analysis is a mere waste of time. For example, suppose that we can show that there would have been a very large increase in economic welfare if all consumers were consistent in their choices and if no new citizens had been born or old citizens had died between the two situations under consideration; in such conditions Mr Little is prepared to say that the representative citizen is in some meaningful sense probably better off, even though there have been some intervening shifts in tastes and some intervening births and deaths, but that we can attach importance to such a criterion only if it shows a really substantial change. This is certainly a healthy attitude; a criterion of economic welfare can be a useful pointer, but not an exact and precise measuring rod.

But the actual criterion of an increase in economic welfare which Mr Little adopts cannot, in the reviewer's opinion, be regarded as acceptable. As the choice of this criterion is the central technical economic issue in Mr Little's book, and as Mr Little has made more substantial changes in his second edition in this part of his work than in any other, the matter deserves closer attention. Let us state Mr Little's criterion in his own words (p. 275): 'an economic change is desirable if (a) it would result in a good redistribution of wealth and if (b) the potential losers could not profitably bribe the potential gainers to oppose the change.' And let us illustrate this argument by the sort of diagram which Mr Little himself uses in his book (Fig. VII on p. 104):

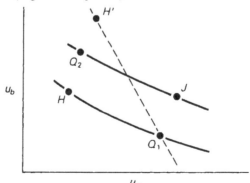

We consider a community made up of two individuals A and B, and we measure some ordinal index of A's utility along the horizontal, and of B's utility along the vertical, axis. We start at a position $Q_1$, and some change of economic circumstances or of policy moves us to the situation $Q_2$. Does the change, which has made A worse off and B better off, represent an increase or decrease in economic welfare? Let us suppose that we prefer the sort of distribution of real income between A and B which is represented by $Q_2$ to that represented by $Q_1$. Suppose, then, that starting from $Q_1$, we made a simple redistribution of income from A to B by lump-sum transfers of money income from A to B, thus moving along a line such as $Q_1H$. (Little makes it clear that we need not assume that such a purely redistributive policy is at all practicable; we use the line $Q_1H$ and the hypothetical point $H$ merely as an indirect means for comparing actual $Q_2$ with actual $Q_1$.) Now if the sort of distribution of real income represented by $Q_2$ is better than that represented by $Q_1$, then $H$ is better than $Q_1$, because $H$ is $Q_1$ modified *solely* by a straight lump-sum redistribution of purchasing power to make $Q_1$ more like $Q_2$. But $Q_2$ is better than $H$ because at $Q_2$ both A and B are better off than at $H$. *A fortiori*, therefore, $Q_2$ is better than $Q_1$. The first part (a) of Mr Little's criterion for an improvement in economic welfare is satisfied because a distribution like $Q_2$ and $H$ is better than a distribution like $Q_1$; and the second part (b) of his criterion is satisfied because the line $Q_1H$ passes to the left of $Q_2$, which means that if, starting from $Q_1$, A gave to B sufficient money income to make B as well off without the change of economic policy as B would be with the change of policy at $Q_2$, then A would be worse off than he would be at $Q_2$.

The first comment to be made on this is that Mr Little's criterion as expressed in the passage quoted above is unduly restrictive. The second part (*b*) of it should read 'and if (*b*) *either* the potential losers could not profitably bribe the potential gainers to oppose the change *or* the potential gainers could compensate the potential losers to accept the change.' Suppose that the line $Q_1H$ passes to the right of $Q_2$, as in the case of $Q_1H'$ in the diagram above; then the criterion as expressed in the passage quoted from Mr Little's book does not tell us whether the change is an improvement or not; we know only that $H'$ is better than $Q_1$ and $Q_2$. But suppose now that having reached $Q_2$ we make notional lump-sum transfers from B to A, thus moving along the line $Q_2J$ and suppose that, as drawn in the diagram above, the line $Q_2J$ passes above $Q_1$. This means that B (the gainer from the move to $Q_2$) could make a lump-sum payment to A of a kind which would leave A as well off as at $Q_1$, with B remaining better off than at $Q_1'$. We can now say that a point like $J$ is better than $Q_1$, since both A and B are better off at $J$ than at $Q_1$; and we can add that $Q_2$ is better than $J$, because $Q_2$ and $J$ differ solely in the distribution of income and the kind of distribution at $Q_2$ is better than that at $J$; therefore, *a fortiori*, $Q_2$ is better than $Q_1$.

Mr Little has in fact in the second edition of his book much improved the assumptions and analysis of this basic part of his argument. This part of his analysis is now based on the assumption that no lump-sum redistributions are going to be made so that $H$ and $J$ are purely notional reference points to help in making a comparison between the two points of actual choice $Q_1$ and $Q_2$. If we compare the table on p. 105 of his second edition with the similar table on p. 103 of his first edition we find that the analysis now tells us that the change should be made if the distribution of income is improved and *either* the Kaldor–Hicks *or* the Scitovsky criterion is satisfied, whereas formerly we were told that the change should be made only if, the distribution of income being improved, the Scitovsky criterion is satisfied. But this further enlargement of the criterion has not yet been absorbed into some other parts of Little's book.

Let us accept this enlargement of Mr Little's criterion. There appears, however, to the present reviewer to be a flaw in the whole criterion. Let us consider once more the basic argument with the aid of the diagram above. A central feature of Mr Little's analysis is the following type of argument: by a lump-sum transfer of money income we move from $Q_1$ to $H$; we prefer distributions of a kind like $Q_2$ to those of a kind like $Q_1$; therefore, $H$ is better than $Q_1$, being $Q_1$ modified solely by a lump-sum redistribution which makes it more like $Q_2$. This argument is a *non sequitur*. Let us remember that $Q_1$ is not assumed to be a point at which all the necessary marginal conditions for a Paretian optimum are satisfied. There may be all sorts of inefficiencies and divergences between marginal values and marginal costs throughout the economy. We then make a lump-sum transfer of money income from A to B. In one institutional and economic set-up we may reach $H$, if, for example, the goods which A ceases to buy are produced under conditions of increasing returns to scale and in a sector of the economy where there was a minimum of economic inefficiency, while the new goods which B buys are produced in conditions in which a limited specialised factor plays an important role, without any economies of scale, and in a sector of the economy where there are all sorts of institutional and other inefficiencies. In the opposite conditions we might move from $Q_1$ to $H'$. Whether or not there is any sense in the unqualified statement that in general one prefers distributions of the kind $Q_2$ to those of the kind $Q_1$ is not clear to the present reviewer; but it is clear to him that one might well say that one prefers $H'$ to $Q_1$ (if a lump-sum transfer from A to B would make B much better off but A only a little worse off) while one prefers $Q_1$ to $H$ (if the same lump-sum transfer would make B only slightly better off at the cost of making A much worse off). If we are going to have a notional line to help us to make a comparison between the actual points $Q_2$ and $Q_1$ we cannot use the line $Q_1H$, for the effect of a lump-sum transfer of income in fact depends upon the actual institutional and other economic conditions for production and exchange which are irrelevant to the present issue. We should have to use a line which plotted out the combinations of $u_a$ and $u_b$ between which we as priest or parliament or dictator (pp. 80–1 of Mr Little's book) or as superman (Chapter VII of Mr Little's book) or as policy-maker (as the reviewer has elsewhere expressed it) are indifferent. We cannot avoid the social welfare function which Mr Little criticises so severely in Chapter VII of his book. In crude and inaccurate language, we cannot separate the considerations of the 'distribution' and the 'size' of real income, but must weight the two together in a single one-part criterion.

Mr Little in his book (cases 2 and 6 in Table II on p. 105) already admits that there are cases in which his criterion cannot tell whether a change should be made or not. These are the cases where there is an unequivocal increase in real income (in the sense that $Q_2$ is north-east of $H$ and $J$ is north-east of $Q_1$) combined with an undesirable change in the distribution of income, or – conversely – in which there is an unequivocal reduction in real income combined with a desirable redistribution of real income. So long as a criterion is used which applies a 'distribution' test and a 'size' test separately, cases of this kind are bound to arise. And in real life they may be of the greatest importance. Thus there may well be a conflict in society between equality and incentives; less progressive taxation might well sharpen incentives so that by any reasonable measure real income increased while the distribution of income changed for (what the reviewer would regard as) the worse. The policy-maker must in such cases decide in some sense how much increase in real income is worth how much worsening of distribution. If the present criticisms of Little's criterion are accepted, this problem must in fact be faced in all, and not only in some, cases in which a policy change makes some people better off and others worse off.

If, however, we are prepared to use a social welfare function but also to be somewhat more modest in the questions which we address to it, we can make some progress towards the solution of this problem beyond the rather obvious and sterile conclusion that we must simply decide whether we prefer $Q_2$ to $Q_1$. Suppose that there are only two citizens A and B and only two goods $X$ and $Y$, $x_a$ representing the amount of $X$ consumed by A and so on. Then we can write our social-welfare function as:

$$W = \{u_a(x_a, y_a), u_b(x_b, y_b)\} .$$

Suppose, for example, that the change from $Q_1$ to $Q_2$ represents the change due to the introduction of a policy of freer trade in a country with a high uniform *ad valorem* duty on all imports. We no longer ask whether complete free trade would be better than the present position; we content ourselves with the much more modest question whether a small reduction in the rate of import duty would make things better or worse. Let $T$ be the rate of import duty. Then a small reduction in the rate of duty would improve matters if

$$\left(\frac{dW}{dT}\equiv\right)\frac{\partial W}{\partial u_a}\cdot\frac{\partial u_a}{\partial x_a}\cdot\frac{dx_a}{dT}+\frac{\partial W}{\partial u_a}\cdot\frac{\partial u_a}{\partial y_a}\cdot\frac{dy_a}{dT}$$

$$+\frac{\partial W}{\partial u_b}\cdot\frac{\partial u_b}{\partial x_b}\cdot\frac{dx_b}{dT}+\frac{\partial W}{\partial u_b}\cdot\frac{\partial u_b}{\partial y_b}\cdot\frac{dy_b}{dT} < 0.$$

Now it is the first task of positive non-welfare economics to make the best possible estimate of the values of $dx_a/dT$, etc.; we must first know what will in fact be the significant effects of the tariff reduction on outputs and consumptions.

There remain the welfare weights ($\partial W/\partial u_a$ . $\partial u_a/\partial x_a$, etc.) to give to these changes. If citizen A is maximising his own ordinal utility index, then

$$\frac{1}{\varrho_{x_a}} \cdot \frac{\partial u_a}{\partial x_a} = \frac{1}{\varrho_{y_a}} \cdot \frac{\partial u_a}{\partial y_a} \equiv \mu_a$$

where $\varrho_{x_a}$ represents the money marginal revenue obtained by A from $x_a$ if he is selling $X$ or the marginal money charge incurred by A from buying another unit of $X$ if he is buying $X$ (and similarly for $\varrho_{y_a}$), and where $\mu_a$ is the marginal utility of money to A measured in the arbitrary units of his ordinal utility index. In other words, A buys and sells what he does buy and sell until the marginal utility of $1s$. to him is the same in his net outlays on everything he buys and in his net revenues from everything he sells. The evaluation of the $\varrho$'s is the second great task of positive economics; we must know the market valuations which everyone puts on everything.

We can now write our marginal welfare criterion as

$$\varrho_{x_a}\frac{dx_a}{dT} + \varrho_{y_a}\frac{dy_a}{dT} + \frac{\omega_b}{\omega_a}\left(\varrho_{x_b}\frac{dx_b}{dT} + \varrho_{y_b}\frac{dy_b}{dT}\right) < 0.$$

where $\omega_b = \partial W/\partial u_a$ . $\mu_a$ and $\omega_b = \partial W/\partial u_b$ . $\mu_b$.

It is now the task of the welfare policy-makers to allot the social welfare weights $\omega_a$ and $\omega_b$. In other words, someone must decide whether in present circumstances we should give the same importance to an additional £1 of income to A as to B ($\omega_b/\omega_a = 1$) or should give twice as great an importance to an additional £1 of income to A as to B ($\omega_b/\omega_a = 1/2$).

A special case of the above type of analysis is the old-fashioned welfare function in which the total utility of society is the sum of the cardinal utilities of A and of B ($W = U_a + U_b$). In this case $\omega_a = \mu_a$ and $\omega_b = \mu_b$; or, in other words, the social-welfare weights are simply the marginal utilities of money to A and to B. It was more or less in terms of this kind that the present reviewer analysed the problem in his *Trade and Welfare* [*The Theory of International Economic Policy, Volume II*, London: Oxford University Press, 1955] referring to $\mu_a$ and $\mu_b$ as 'distributional weights'. But, as the above analysis shows, the method of analysis can be extended to cover the case of a general social welfare function, requiring from the policy-maker only the allotment of social-welfare weights to increments of money income for different classes in the community. Although such a method will deal only with marginal, and not with structural, problems, it would seem to the reviewer to be, in many cases, of greater promise for practical use than the more general structural analysis of Mr Little's book, which, if the above criticisms are accepted, boils down almost to the trivial conclusion that we must decide whether we prefer $Q_2$ or $Q_1$.

# 9

# The Theory of Indicative Planning

*Meade's famous lectures at the University of Manchester were, after some revision, published by Manchester University Press in 1970. The origins of the ideas in the lectures are explained in Meade's preface (dated March 1970) which is therefore included here.*

## Preface

I would like to thank the University of Manchester and Professor Prest in particular for their hospitality in inviting me to give the three lectures on *The Theory of Indicative Planning*, the substance of which is reproduced in the following pages. This has given me the opportunity to try out in a rather compressed form some of the ideas which I hope later to incorporate in a volume on *The Controlled Economy* on which I am at present working to form Volume 3 of a *Principles of Political Economy* [London: Allen & Unwin, 1971].

The ideas are not basically novel. What I have tried to do in these lectures is, first, to express by a very simple illustrative example the method of treatment of uncertainty which is used in the famous Arrow–Debreu analysis of this subject and then, second, to comment on a number of more specific practical problems which arise in the application of this treatment of uncertainty to the problems of planning in a basically free-enterprise economy.

The idea of 'residual uncertainty' used on pages 134–36 and 152 was suggested to me in conversation by Professor Lombardini. The criticism of one-path indicative planning on pages 128–29 was formulated as a result of reading Dr Vera Lutz' *Central Planning for the Market Economy: An Analysis of the French Theory and Experience* (London: Longman Green & Co., 1969). In general I have had great help in studying these problems from many of my colleagues in Cambridge over the last few years, particularly in an informal group in which we have been discussing the application of control theories to economic systems. I would like to acknowledge in particular the detailed help which I have received in the preparation of these lectures from A. B. Atkinson and G. M. Heal. Moreover, to my great good fortune, three of the most distinguished arts of the mathematical treatment of these problems, namely Professors Radner, Scarf, and Stiglitz, have been simultaneously visiting Cambridge; and I would like to thank them very sincerely for all their help and suggestions. I cannot refrain from adding that Professor Arrow himself will shortly be joining this formidable list of visitors; but, alas, by that time I fear that I shall already have committed myself to the printed words which follow in this book.

I

## 'Market' and 'Environmental' Uncertaintities

These lectures are concerned with problems which arise in planning to meet the future in an economy such as our own – developed, industrialised, essentially free enterprise, but with a considerable element of state activity and intervention of one kind or another. How best to plan for the future raises some quite basic theoretical issues which are at present debated in a highly sophisticated manner by modern mathematically minded economic theorists; it also raises a number of unanswered practical questions as is testified by recent attempts at national economic planning in this and other similar economies.

The subject is very important; but remains difficult, complicated, and confused. I do not pretend to know the answers and I do not claim to be able to throw new light on the subject. All I shall try to do is to present in a non-mathematical form a number of basic elements of the theory of the subject and of the unresolved issues. My method will be as follows. I shall start by constructing an absurdly abstract model of a competitive economy based on a number of extreme simplifying assumptions. Its purpose will be to isolate in the simplest and most intelligible form what I think is probably the crucial issue, namely how to deal with uncertainty in planning to meet future developments. This model will be extremely abstract; but for two reasons I beg you not to be put off too easily by its unreality. In the first place, the problems concerning the treatment of risk and uncertainty which it will, I hope, help to pinpoint, are highly relevant in the real world; and, in the second place, I shall proceed later in my lectures to the removal of my most extreme simplifying assumptions and to a discussion of the complications which thus arise.

The outrageous simplifying assumptions which I am going to make at the outset may be grouped under four heads.

First, there is perfect competition throughout the economy.

Second, there are no externalities or public goods; no indivisibilities, monopolies, or increasing returns to scale; and no inequities in the distribution of income and wealth between citizens of different classes or of different generations. In short, there is no call at all for state intervention in the economic sphere except in so far as it may be able to help private economic agents (i.e. individuals as consumers, merchants, entrepreneurs, investors, or producers) to plan to meet the future more efficiently.

Third, the world will last for a definitie period and will then come to an end with a loud bang at a known date in the future which I will call Kingdom Come. Thus every individual economic agent knows precisely what future time span there is to be covered by his plan.

Fourth, every private economic agent who will transact any business at all between Now and Kingdom Come is already alive and transacting business; and, on the other hand, every economic agent now alive will live until Kingdom Come. This means, I suppose, that there are to be no births or deaths between Now and Kingdom Come, and also that all citizens are already adult and do not age so as to become senile before Kingdom Come. But do not press me too keenly on the implications of this strange demographic assumption. I shall remove it before we are done. What I want for my present simplified model is to be able to assume that the whole of any plan covering the period from Now to Kingdom Come will be relevant for every economic agent now alive and for no one else.

Apart from these four groups of assumptions – and I realise that it is a very big 'apart' – the economy can be as complicated as you like, covering markets for lending and borrowing, and for insurance and betting; production and trade carried out by joint-stock companies, co-operatives, partnerships, private businesses; men and women at work with different skills in many occupations; and innumerable types of consumption good and service, of capital goods and intermediate products, and of natural resources. The essential feature which I wish to stress is that all concerned are faced with an uncertain future.

I wish to distinguish between two types of uncertainty, which I will call market uncertainty and environmental uncertainty respectively. A homely example may serve to explain the difference. A manufacturer of sunshades and umbrellas in forming his plans this year as to how many sunshades and how many umbrellas he will produce this year to put on the market next year does not know whether it will be Wet or Fine and this is an environmental uncertainty. The manufacturer also does not know what the market demand for umbrellas and for sunshades will be if it is Wet nor what the demands will be if it is Fine; but the consumers of sunshades and umbrellas may know very well how many of these objects they will buy next year at given market prices for these objects if it is Wet and how many they will buy at given prices if it is Fine. This lack of knowledge by the producer is a market uncertainty; and, to anticipate my argument, it is the sort of uncertainty which can be removed by a system of forward markets or of indicative planning. Forward markets and indicative planning are in fact information systems which reduce uncertainty by passing to producers the knowledge which consumers have about future demand conditions and passing to consumers the knowledge which producers have about future supply conditions. But no one has any certain knowledge to pass on about future environmental uncertainties.

Environmental uncertainties cover a very wide class of events. Some are obvious exogenous events: the future state of the weather may affect the harvest or the demand for bathing dresses; or, in the case of a single economy, the future state of economic activity and of price inflation or deflation in the outside world may affect the demand for a country's exports. In other cases, it is the parameters in production or consumption functions which are basically uncertain: future technical progress may affect the real input cost of nuclear power and the course of such progress may not be known with certainty even to the experts most closely concerned; or future changes in fashion may affect the demand for mini-skirts in ways which at present are still obscure to the consumers themselves.

This distinction between market uncertainties (about things which some people know for certain and others do not know at all) and environmental uncertainties (about things which nobody knows) should not in reality be drawn too sharply. There are some things which are relevant to the plans of many individual agents, which are not known for certain by anyone, but about which some agents can form a much better opinion than others. An obvious example is the difference in knowledge between the producers and consumers of a product about the probable effect of technical progress on the future cost of the product. A consumer's choice between an electric and a gas heating installation will depend upon his estimate of the probable future course of relative costs of electricity and of gas; but this may depend upon whether or not some expected technological breakthrough is successfully carried out in the production of electricity. No one may know for certain whether and, if so, when this will happen. But the producers of electricity may be able to estimate the probabilities much better than the consumers. A diffusion of knowledge from producers to consumers about their estimates of probabilities of environmental change is thus important. But for the time being I shall draw a rather sharp distinction between those things about which one group is pretty certain while another group is very uncertain, and those things about which everyone is inevitably very uncertain; and I shall call these 'market' and 'environmental' uncertainties respectively.

## II

### Forward Markets, Indicative Planning, and Econometric Forecasting in the Absence of Environmental Uncertainties

Let us first consider what the position would be in such an economy if there were no environmental uncertainties. It may at first sight appear that since the absence of environmental uncertainties implies the absence of uncertainties about changing fashions and changing technical knowledge, and since we are making the strange demographic assumption of no births or deaths, there would in fact be no change going on in the economy at all. But this is not so for two reasons. First, it is, I suppose, conceptually possible to imagine a state of affairs in which technical progress is taking place but in which it is precisely and exactly known in advance when each particular bit of increased technical knowledge will occur. In this case there would be technical progress without any uncertainty about its occurrence. But if it stretches your powers of abstraction a bit too far to imagine that the precise date and form of a future invention can be known without the invention having already been made, we can fall back on the second reason for change, namely savings, investment, and capital accumulation. We have not ruled these out; and as the amount of man-made capital equipment of various kinds changes per head of the population and per acre of natural resources, so market conditions will change. Rates of wages and rents will probably rise; the rate of interest will probably fall; some goods will become more costly to produce relatively to other goods; and some goods will be in greater demand relatively to others as the real incomes of consumers rise. Producers and consumers will be faced with all sorts of market uncertainties about the future course of the prices of their inputs and outputs, of their incomes, and of the prices of their final consumption goods and services.

In order that our competitive economy should move efficiently through time it is necessary that every decision-maker should be able to foresee correctly the future prices that will rule for the goods and services in which he is interested. Whether or not it is economic to set up a new steel mill will depend upon the future prices of the inputs of labour and of the outputs of steel which will be associated with that mill if it is installed. But the future demand for steel will depend upon the future plans of the users of steel to make machine tools, the worthwhileness of which will depend upon the still more distant prices of the inputs and outputs associated with the use of the machine tools; and so on. The economic system is a general system of interrelationships in which every price is directly or indirectly related to every other price, prices of steel to prices of labour and – the point which is most pertinent for our present enquiry – present prices to future prices.

Now if, as we are assuming, all future decision-makers are already alive and operating in the market and there are no unforeseen changes in technical knowledge or tastes, we can imagine a comprehensive set of forward markets which would remove all remaining market uncertainties. By one once-for-all gigantic market higgle-haggle everyone could buy and sell forward for all periods of time from Now to Kingdom Come everything in which he or she is interested, including the hire of his or her own labour and the purchase or sale, and the lending or borrowing, of different forms of property. When the market has settled down, everyone would know precisely the future course of his income, the prices of what he would buy and sell, the future level of his consumption of every good and service, the amounts of capital equipment of various kinds he would install at every future date, and so on and so on. Future prices and quantities would only settle down at levels at which competitive supply was equal to competitive demand at every point of time. No expectations would ever be disappointed; and as time passed there would be no need to supplement in spot markets the obligations already entered into in past forward contracts. Relative prices of different products and of the same product at different points of time would in the free competitive forward markets measure both the marginal rates of substitution in any one citizen's consumption plan and the marginal rates of transformation in any one citizen's production plan; and thus – for the reasons which are familiar in static analysis – we would have a Pareto optimum in the sense that we would achieve a development of the economy through time such that it would be impossible to make one citizen better off without making someone else worse off.

There are two different ways in which one can imagine the money payments being made in such a comprehensive set of forward markets. One must in any case imagine that the forward markets cover not only the prices of goods and services at each future date, but also the rate of interest at which money can be lent or borrowed at each future date. If people were uncertain about the market rate of interest which they could get on their savings at future dates, they would be uncertain about the market offers which they could afford to make for various goods at different dates. Market uncertainties would not be eliminated. Consider a two-period future of the following kind:

| Today<br>Day 0 | Tomorrow<br>Day 1 | The Next Day<br>Day 2 |
|:---:|:---:|:---:|
| $\longmapsto\!\!\!\longrightarrow$ | $\longmapsto\!\!\!\longrightarrow$ | |
| $i(0)$ | $i(1)$ | |

The forward markets for loans must have determined a rate of interest – $i(0)$ – which will clear the market for loans of money from day 0 to day 1 and another rate of interest – $i(1)$ – which will clear the market for loans from day 1 to day 2. Suppose that the great and glorious higgle-haggle takes place on day 0, and that as part of this higgle-haggle I purchase forward from you 1 unit of steel to be delivered on day 2 at a price of $P(2)$. Then our contract may take the form either that on day 2 I pay you $P(2)$ in money and you give me 1 unit of steel or else that I pay you today $\dfrac{1}{1 + i(0)}\dfrac{1}{1 + i(1)}P(2)$ units of money and you give me 1 unit of steel on day 2.

Let
$$\hat{P}(2) = \frac{1}{1 + i(0)}\frac{1}{1 + i(1)}P(2).$$

If the latter form of contract is used, you can (i) today lend the $\hat{P}(2) = \dfrac{1}{1 + i(0)}\dfrac{1}{1 + i(1)}P(2)$ today at an interest of $i(0)$ and receive $\dfrac{1}{1 + i(1)}P(2)$ tomorrow and (ii) at the same time today lend this sum of $\dfrac{1}{1 + i(1)}P(2)$ at interest $i(1)$ in the forward market for loans from tomorrow till the next day, thus receiving $P(2)$ the day after tomorrow. It is a matter of indifference which form of contract is used. Thus we can envisage *either* a once-for-all payment of money from buyers to sellers on day 0 of prices like $\hat{P}(2)$ in which case all that happens as time passes is that the sellers have to provide the goods and services at the appropriate dates *or else* a once-for-all fixing of contracts which require buyers to pay prices like $P(2)$ at the future appropriate dates for the goods and services then to be supplied. With our comprehensive set of forward markets, covering interest rates as well as commodity prices, the difference is a formal one. But it will prove a useful distinction later on when we come to consider environmental uncertainties.

Whichever form of contract was used, prices would provide a fully efficient signalling system horizontally over time as well as vertically between one product and another. The price of steel in the future markets would thus bring together the specialised knowledge of the producers of steel about the future supply and the specialised knowledge of the users of steel about the future demand in such a way that present investments in steel-making equipment and in steel-using equipment were consistent, on an economically efficient scale, and in an economically efficient form.

It should be observed that if all future prices both for goods and for loans could somehow be foreseen accurately and for certain, then exactly the same result could be achieved without any forward contracts of either of the two kinds which we have described. Thus suppose that the actual rate of interest ruling for a day's loan today is $i(0)$, that it is known for certain that the rate of interest tomorrow will be $i(1)$, and that it is known for certain that the price of a unit of steel the day after tomorrow will be $P(2)$. Then I can invest $\dfrac{1}{1+i(0)} \dfrac{1}{1+i(1)} P(2)$ today and get $\dfrac{1}{1+i(1)} P(2)$ tomorrow. I know that I shall be able to invest this $\dfrac{1}{1+i(1)} P(2)$ tomorrow so as to get $P(2)$ the day after tomorrow; and I know that $P(2)$ will then buy me a unit of steel.

It is precisely this forecasting of future market conditions which one can try to achieve by a mimicry of forward markets through a form of governmental indicative planning. Let me caricature the procedure by sketching it in a complete, ideal, but patently absurd form. The government summons to a meeting in the Albert Hall every citizen in the country; at this meeting every citizen is provided with a list of prices of every conceivable good and service, including, of course, wage-rates, rates of interest, security prices, etc. for every day in the future from Now till Kingdom Come, these prices being initially, if you like, simply the current market prices of everything. Every citizen is then required to write down for every day in the future how much he or she would buy or sell of every good or service at these prices, including, of course, the amounts which he or she would wish to borrow or lend on any future day at the stated rates of interest. There is then a coffee break during which the bureaucrats add up the total supplies and demands of every good and service for every future day. They then prepare a revised schedule of forward prices, having put up the prices for which demand exceeded supply and having put down the prices for which supply exceeded demand. The citizens are then recalled, confronted with the new price lists, and asked to revise their schedules of amounts supplied and demanded. This process is repeated until hopefully a series of price lists, one for every future day, is found at which the supply–demand position is balanced for every good and service at every future point of time.

You have, I hope, marked my use of the word 'hopefully'. Our sophisticated highbrow mathematical colleagues tell us that the particular process which I have described for groping towards the equilibrium set of prices which will bring all supplies and demands simultaneously into balance cannot be relied upon to converge on to that equilibrium solution except in the rather special circumstances in which every good is a substitute for every other good. This is because of the interaction of one market on another. The reason for this can, I think, be suggested intuitively in the following way.

Suppose that our process has succeeded in making aggregate demand equal to aggregate supply, but that it has not yet succeeded in bringing equilibrium to all particular markets, so that while some goods are in excess supply, others are in excess demand. Suppose these two classes of goods to be good substitutes for each other, such as white bread which is in excess supply and brown bread which is in excess demand. Then putting down the price of white bread which is in excess supply will help not only to increase the demand for white bread but also to reduce the demand for brown bread which is in excess demand. Conversely putting up the price of brown bread because it is in excess demand will not only reduce the demand for brown bread but will also stimulate the demand for white bread which is in excess supply. Each price adjustment will thus help to restore equilibrium in both markets.

But suppose that the two groups of commodities were complementary. Petrol is in excess supply and motor cars are in excess demand. Putting down the price of petrol decreases the cost of motoring, increases the demand for cars, and thus increases the excess demand for cars. Putting up the price of cars reduces the demand for cars, but by so doing reduces also the demand for petrol and thus increases the excess supply of petrol. Complementarity in production can lead to a similar perverse result. Suppose that wool is in excess supply and mutton in excess demand. A fall in the price of wool reduces the profitability of rearing sheep which reduces the supply of mutton and accentuates the excess demand for mutton. The appropriate price adjustment for the market directly concerned worsens the position in the other related market. In this case the process cannot be relied upon to lead to an equilibrium.

In such cases more subtle processes for finding the equilibrium set of prices would be necessary; but I fear that I have neither the time nor the ability to tell you what they are. I must confess that I am merely going to assume that some modified form of the simple process which I have described can be relied upon to find the equilibrium set of prices which balances supplies and demands for all goods at all points of time; but for the sake of simplification I shall talk of this as if it were the very simple process which I have described.

If this process is successfully carried out, the result will be the same as that achieved by a comprehensive set of actual forward markets. Both procedures indicate what set of spot prices at each given date in the future will in fact clear all markets; and if all the citizens really make their plans in the expectation of these prices, then these prices will in fact result in balanced supply and demand positions. Both procedures are mechanisms for forecasting balanced market conditions; and this is the essence of the matter. The difference of form is simply that with a set of forward markets actual contracts will have been entered into, these contracts being of a kind which no one will wish to alter when the time comes to fulfil them, whereas with the indicative plan citizens will have undertaken no contractual obligations in advance, but will in fact have planned freely to enter into these same contracts when the time comes.

The essence of the matter then so far is to find a procedure which will give citizens a foresight of future market prices so that they can make their present plans in the knowledge of what future costs of inputs, selling prices of outputs, and so on will in fact be. Now there is a third way, in addition to the methods of forward markets and of indicative planning, of trying to make such a forecast, namely the building of an econometric model of the economy and its use to forecast future market developments. If one knows all the technological and behavioural relationships in the economy – that is to say, what outputs can be produced with what inputs and how citizens as entrepreneurs, workers, savers, consumers, etc., react to changes in prices, costs, incomes, interest rates, etc. – if one knows the starting point of the economy – that is to say the existing capital equipment and so on – and finally if one knows how the future exogenous variables will behave – and we are in fact assuming that there are no environmental uncertainties – then theoretically, since one thing necessarily leads to another according to the known technological and behavioural relationships, one should be able to forecast the future course of all prices and quantities in all markets.

Consider the use of this method by envisaging the situation of an individual producer of steel in the absence of forward markets or of an indicative plan. He must now make his decisions on the basis of his own unaided best guess about the future. I have already alluded to the fact that the economic system is a general system in which the price of any one particular thing at any one particular time is related to the price of every other thing at every other point of time. The future price obtainable by our citizen for his output of steel will, for example, depend upon the price of alternative materials which will depend upon the price of the inputs used to produce those materials which will depend upon the future demand for those inputs in alternative uses to produce, say, equipment to produce in the more distant future some range of consumption goods. Thus in principle each individual business would need to have its own economic section to study the future development of the whole economy in order to consider its impact upon the particular business concerned.

It would obviously be very inefficient for every citizen to build his own econometric model in order to improve his own knowledge of future developments. Apart from the obvious duplication of effort, not every citizen would be as good as every other citizen in building comprehensive econometric models. If some central organisation – the government's Economic Section or Central Statistical Office or National Economic Development Council – constructed such an econometric model calling on the specialist knowledge of, for example, steel producers in constructing that part of the model which dealt with the supply of steel and of steel users in constructing the demand schedules of steel, a better model might hopefully be achieved at a lower cost which, if published, could be used as a forecasting tool by all private decision-makers.

But the construction of an econometric model for forecasting – quite apart from the very great statistical-econometric problems of estimation involved – raises one issue which differentiates it sharply from the methods of forward markets and of indicative planning. Economic behaviour depends in part on economic expectations. Thus the present demand for durable goods is likely to be higher if purchasers expect their cost to go up than if they expect it to go down. In constructing an econometric model it is not possible to measure expectations directly; we cannot measure the effect of past events on present expectations and then the effect of present expectations on present decisions. One can only take the short cut of observing the indirect effect of past events on present decisions, observing perhaps that if prices of durables have been going up in the past people buy more of them now and merely surmising that this is because a recent rise of price makes buyers expect a future rise of price. In the absence of forward markets, of an indicative plan, and of an econometric forecast, citizens will form their expectations somehow in the light of past experience; and it is virtually certain that they will not foretell the future correctly. Expectations will be disappointed and the economy will move in a disequilibrium way through time.

Introduce now an econometric forecast on the scene. Suppose it correctly estimates the effects of the existing method of formation of expectations. It will then predict the future disequilibrium path for the economy. If its forecasts are now believed by the citizens, they will see that their expectations are going to be disappointed. If they now believe the predictions of the econometric forecast, they will alter their expectations and so alter the behavioural relations on which the econometric forecast is built. The predictions of econometric forecasts will be falsified and perhaps they will not be believed in the future. In any case the econometric model builders must revise the behavioural relationships making the predictions of the model themselves explanatory variables in the explanation of the citizens' behaviour. There is, of course, nothing conceptually impossible in this; and if the predictions of the econometric forecast do come to be more and more trusted, and if the econometric model builders can introduce the forecasts which result from the econometric model as explanatory variables into the behavioural relationships of the model, and if they can thus succeed gradually in improving the fit of their behavioural relationships to the changed formation of expectations, one might perhaps in due course hope to converge on to the point at which all private decision-makers expected the predictions of the model to be true, and the econometric model builders simultaneously correctly estimated the effect of this on the behaviour of the private decision-makers. One could then hope to achieve the same final equilibrium result as through a comprehensive system of forward markets or of indicative planning.

But the process would at the very best be a very prolonged and unreliable one. Econometric forecasting involves both estimating indirectly the formation of expectations and their effect on behaviour and also altering the way in which expectations are formed. Forward markets and indicative planning kill both birds with one stone. They find out directly how private decision-makers will behave if they expect prices to move in the way in which they will in fact move.

III

## Environmental Uncertainties and Forward Markets

So much for the function of forward markets, indicative planning, and econometric forecasting in the absence of any environmental uncertainties. Let us now introduce such uncertainties, retaining for the time being the four sets of outrageous simplifying assumptions made at the beginning of this lecture. The situation becomes much more complicated. If I were a highly sophisticated mathematician and if you were an audience which enjoyed that sort of thing, it would probably be desirable for me at this stage to consider in a very generalised form the basic modifications which environmental uncertainties introduce into the analysis which I have just presented. But whether you would like it nor not, I am afraid that I am incapable of doing it. I shall, therefore, proceed by giving one very simple example of an economy with environmental uncertainties. I am not very ashamed of this piece of simplification because I think that this simple example does adequately illustrate the principles involved and that it is intuitively clear that the conclusions could be generalised to cover the more complicated forms of the problem.

Let us suppose then that the only environmental uncertainty is whether from day to day it will be Wet or Fine and that the world will last for only three days, today, tomorrow, and the next day, or – to be sophisticated – day 0, day 1, and day 2, coming to a certain end at midnight between day 2 and day 3. The BBC tells us at 7.45 each morning whether the day is Wet or Fine, but we do not know until 7.45 tomorrow whether tomorrow will be Wet or Fine. We stand then at 8 a.m. on day 0, knowing already for certain whether day 0 is Wet or Fine, but confronted with four possible future environmental paths. (See next page.)

The future two days may be WW, WF, FW, or FF and these weather paths are numbered 1, 2, 3, and 4 respectively. There are seven environmental points: today we are on all four paths and I will call this point 1234; tomorrow if it is Wet, we shall know that we are on either path 1 or 2 and I will call this point 12; and so on for the other points.

What I do today may depend very much upon my expectations about the environmental paths. Thus an umbrella may be reasonably durable, and if it is Wet today I may think of replacing my already shabby and worn umbrella. If I knew I was on path 1 and that it would also be Wet tomorrow and the next day, I would certainly do so. I would be somewhat

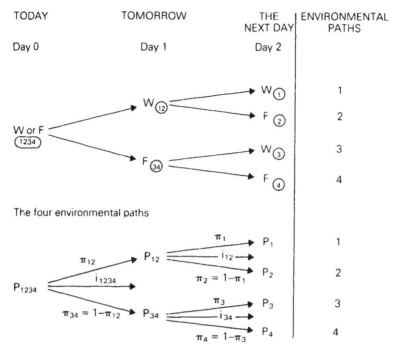

The four environmental paths

The market conditions on the four environmental paths

less inclined to do so if I knew that I was on path 2, i.e. that while it would be Wet tomorrow it would be Fine the next day. I would be still less inclined to do so if I knew that I was on path 3, i.e. that it would be Fine tomorrow and Wet the next day, so that my investment in an umbrella would lie idle for one Fine day though it would still be useful the day after that. I would be least inclined to do so if I knew that I was on path 4, so that a new umbrella would have no use after today. But I do not know and *ex hypothesi* cannot know for certain which path I am on. I can only make my own assessments of the probabilities of the four possible weather paths.

I hope that my frivolous example of the choice between sinking my money in an umbrella or a sunshade will not lead you to think that this problem is itself a frivolous one. In the real world it is of the greatest importance. Whether the community should sink durable resources on a vast scale in producing equipment to promote travel by air or by a renewed railway system, or to produce electrical power from coal-fired or nuclear stations, are questions which may depend in large measure upon the assessment of the probabilities of important future and uncertain technological advances. These issues are merely exemplified by the choice between umbrellas and sunshades in view of the uncertainty of the weather.

There are conceivable types of forward markets which could in theory cope with the tractable parts of the problems raised by environmental uncertainties. We can see the possibilities best by realising that not only is an umbrella tomorrow a different good from an umbrella today, but equally well an umbrella-tomorrow-if-it-is-Wet-tomorrow is a different good from an umbrella-tomorrow-if-it-is-Fine-tomorrow. We will call these goods 'contingency' goods. Thus there are seven different 'contingency' umbrellas, one at each of the seven points on the weather paths in my diagram. Suppose now that there was today a market in all contingency goods; that is, suppose, for example, that by paying a definite sum of money to you today I put you under an obligation to give me an umbrella-at-point-1, i.e. an umbrella on day 2 if, but only if, it is Wet on day 1 and Wet on day 2. This sum of money may be called today's 'contingency' price for an umbrella to be delivered at point 1, and I shall represent such a price by $\hat{P}_1$. This price is a price paid for certain now in return for a good which will be provided in the future and then only if some defined environmental event occurs. It is, therefore, in some way an amalgam of the value of an umbrella at point 1, of the rates of interest at which this future value must be discounted to obtain its present value, and of the allowance for the risk involved in the fact that I may never get my umbrella because we may never reach point 1. These relations between spot prices, interest rates, and allowances for risk are of central importance, and it is as well to get them clear at once.

The prices and money transactions of one day are now bound to the prices and money transactions of the next day by two links. In the first place, there is the tie of the rate of interest. We are at point 1234 on my diagram. At this point there will rule a rate of interest – call it $i_{1234}$ – at which I can lend money for one day at 8 a.m. today and receive principal and interest at 8 a.m. tomorrow. But at 8 a.m. tomorrow I may be at point 12 or at point 34; that is to say, it may be Wet or it may be Fine, and the rate of interest which will rule tomorrow if we are at point 12 – call it $i_{12}$ – is not necessarily the same as the rate which will rule tomorrow if we are at point 34 – which we will call $i_{34}$. That this is so is obvious if, for a moment, we suppose that the difference between points 12 and 34 is not whether it is Wet or Fine, but whether some very extensive technological invention making it profitable to borrow huge sums of capital for some vast new developments has taken place or not. Thus we imagine a rate of interest for a day's loan of money, ruling at 8 a.m. on every day, the level of the rate depending among other things upon the environmental conditions ruling at that point of time.

But the prices and money transactions of one day must now be regarded as being bound to the prices and money transactions of the next day not only by the rate of interest but also by an insurance or betting market on which one can cover the risk of movement from any given point on any one day on the environmental time paths to any feasible point on the following day. On day 0 we are at point 1234 and on day 1 we may move to point 12 or to point 34. We suppose for the time being that all risks are insurable so that for the payment of a premium (say $\$\pi_{12}$) you can insure for \$1 against the risk of moving from point 1234 to point 12 (i.e. you can insure today against the risk that tomorrow will be Wet). Such a contract is made at 8 a.m. on day 0 (i.e. at point 1234); but the actual premium is payable at 8 a.m. on day 1. Thus at 8 a.m. on day 1 if you are at point 12 you pay the premium of $\$\pi_{12}$ but receive the insured sum of $1, a net receipt of $\$(1 - \pi_{12})$; whereas if at 8 a.m. on day 1 you are at point 34, you pay the premium of $\$\pi_{12}$ and receive nothing. Thus we can also think of the contract as a bet entered into at 8 a.m. on day 0 such that you will receive $\$(1 - \pi_{12})$ if tomorrow is Wet but will pay $\$\pi_{12}$ if tomorrow is Fine. Thus we can talk of $\pi_{12}$ as the rate of insurance premium payable to insure against a movement from point 1234 to point 12 or we can talk of $(1 - \pi_{12}/\pi_{12})$ as the betting odds as between moving to point 12 or to point 34 from point 1234. We suppose that at 8 a.m. on every future day there will be a similar insurance or betting market which will enable anyone to insure against, or to bet as between, its being Wet or Fine on the subsequent day, though the rate of premium or betting odds which will have to be paid may well depend upon the environmental conditions as well as the date of the transactions. Thus we envisage in our diagram that at point 12 there will be rates of premium of $\pi_1$ and $\pi_2$ respectively for insurance against the next day being Wet and Fine respectively, and that at point 34 these rates will be $\pi_3$ and $\pi_4$.

Now if by some means or another I could foresee precisely and exactly what these spot interest rates, insurance premia, and commodity prices would be at each future point on the environmental paths in my diagram, then I would know exactly how much I must set aside today in order to be in a position to purchase any given commodity at any given future point on the environmental paths. Suppose $P_1$ is what the price of an umbrella will be at point 1. Then if I set aside $\dfrac{\pi_{12}}{1 + i_{1234}} \dfrac{\pi_1}{1 + i_{12}} P_1$ today and invest this sum at the current rate of interest $i_{1234}$, I shall have $\dfrac{\pi_{12}\pi_1}{1 + i_{12}} P_1$ tomorrow.

If today I have undertaken to pay an insurance premium of $\dfrac{\pi_{12}\pi_1}{1 + i_{12}} P_1$ tomorrow against its being Wet tomorrow (i.e. against our reaching point 12), I shall receive $\dfrac{\pi_1}{1 + i_{12}} P_1$ tomorrow if we do reach point 12. But this sum I shall be able to invest at point 12 at a rate of interest $i_{12}$ to get $\pi_1 P_1$ at 8 a.m. the day after tomorrow; and if I have undertaken at point 12 to pay a premium of $\pi_1 P_1$ on the following day as an insurance against Wet weather (i.e. against reaching point 1), I shall receive $P_1$ if we reach point 1, with which sum I can purchase my umbrella at point 1.

Thus we may write

$$\hat{P}_1 = \frac{\pi_{12}}{1 + i_{1234}} \frac{\pi_1}{1 + i_{12}} P_1$$

if $\hat{P}_1$ is today's price for the contingent commodity, namely an umbrella-at-point-1, and if individuals can correctly foresee the future loan, insurance, and commodity markets. For in these conditions it is a matter of indifference to me whether (i) I operate in today's contingent forward market and pay down $\hat{P}_1$ to someone today who in return promises to give me an umbrella if and when we reach point 1 or (ii) I put aside

$$\frac{\pi_{12}}{1 + i_{1234}} \frac{\pi_1}{1 + i_{12}} P_1 \text{ and undertake the necessary operations on the day-}$$

to-day loan and insurance markets, as described above, so as to obtain $P_1$, the price which I shall have to pay for an umbrella if and when we reach point 1. Arbitrage should imply that the two ways of acquiring today an umbrella-at-point-1 should cost the same.

The question then arises whether there are any means whereby I can accurately foresee what the relevant future rates of interest, rates of insurance premia, and commodity prices will be. One method might be through a form of indicative planning which took account of environmental uncertainties; and this is the possibility which I wish to examine at length in due course. But another possibility would be through a system of what I will call conditional forward markets.

At point 1234, i.e. at 8 a.m. on day 0 where we now stand, there will be an actual loan market which will determine the rate of interest ($i_{1234}$) for a loan for the duration of day 0. This we can call today's spot loan market. But let us envisage also the existence of what we may call a conditional forward loan market in which at 8 a.m. today I can enter into the following sort of contract with you: 'At 8 a.m. tomorrow I will lend you \$1 and in return you will pay me \$$(1 + i_{12})$ at 8 a.m. the day after tomorrow; but this bargain is on only if it is Wet tomorrow (i.e. only if we are then at point 12); otherwise no payment will be made in either direction.' Similar conditional loan markets must be available for every other day in the future, in each of which I can today undertake to lend or borrow money at a stated rate of interest at the stated date if, but only if, we are then at a stated point on the environmental time paths.

At point 1234, i.e. at 8 a.m. on day 0 where we now stand, there will also be an actual insurance market which will offer rates of insurance premia ($\pi_{12}$ and $\pi_{34}$) payable to insure against movements to points 12 and 34 respectively. This we can call today's spot insurance market. But let us envisage also the existence of what we may call a conditional forward insurance market in which it would be possible for me at 8 a.m. on day 0 to make the following sort of contract: 'At 8 a.m. on day 2 I will pay you \$$\pi_1$, if but only if we have been at point 12 on day 1. In return you will pay me \$1 at 8 a.m. on day 2 if but only if we are then at point 1.' This is simply a forward contract to insure against a movement from point 12 to point 1. If we never reach point 12 the whole contract is inoperative.

We can also envisage a conditional forward market for commodities in which I can enter into a deal of the following kind: 'I undertake now at 8 a.m. on day 0 that I will pay you $P_1$ at 8 a.m. on day 2 if, but only if, we are then at point 1 and in return you will provide me with an umbrella at 8 a.m. on day 2 if, but only if, we are then at point 1. If we are not then at point 1, the whole contract lapses.'

These conditional forward markets would simply be mechanisms whereby the future spot prices, including interest rates and insurance premia as well as commodity prices, were fixed in advance; and if all future transactions were on day 0 once and for all settled in such markets in conditions in which all possible environmental developments were taken into account, the result would correspond to a state of affairs in which all equilibrium spot prices were accurately foreseen along all possible environmental paths. In my formula

$$\hat{P}_1 = \frac{\pi_{12}}{1 + i_{1234}} \frac{\pi_1}{1 + i_{12}} P_1$$

$i_{1234}$ and $\pi_{12}$ would be the actual rates ruling in today's spot markets for loans and insurance, while $i_{12}$, $\pi_1$, and $P_1$ would be an interest rate, an insurance premium, and a commodity price at which I could make suitable firm contracts now in the relevant conditional forward markets. Thus I would know for certain how much money I must put aside now in order that, by fulfilling my contracts in the relevant conditional forward markets as and when the conditions arose, I might obtain my umbrella at point 1.

If any of you have not followed the details of the formula which I have just presented, please do not despair. For my present purpose the formula itself is immaterial. But it is important to accept intuitively that there is a relationship of the following kind. In order on day 0 to ensure that I shall obtain an umbrella at the end of weather path 1 (i.e. an umbrella on day 2 if it is Wet on day 1 and on day 2) I can calculate how much money I must put aside on day 0 if I know three things: (i) the rates of interest at which I shall be able to invest this capital sum from day to day at each stage along weather path 1, (ii) the insurance premia or betting odds at which I shall be able at each stage to allow for the risk of not reaching the next stage on path 1, and (iii) the price which I shall have to pay for an umbrella if and when I do reach the end of weather path 1.

If this is so, then, it follows – and this is the crucial point – that one can remove all market uncertainties even in the presence of environmental uncertainties by any one of the following three mechanisms. *First*, one can have a single gigantic once-for-all forward market higgle-haggle in which all contingent goods and services (i.e. all goods and services at each possible time-cum-environmental condition) are bought and sold once and for all now for money payments made now; *second*, one can have a single gigantic once-for-all forward market higgle-haggle in which what I have called conditional forward contracts for loans, bets, and goods are settled once for all; *third*, one can rely on a mechanism analogous to the indicative planning procedures already outlined for the case of no environmental uncertainties, which will reveal what future spot prices, interest rates, and insurance premia will in fact balance supplies and demands for goods and services and for loans and bets from one day to the next at every future date in every possible environmental condition. Theoretically all three methods should lead to the same results.

Let us first consider some of the implications of the first method. Suppose that I personally feel virtually certain that it will be Fine. I am free to sell my labour in the Wet weather markets and to buy my sunshades in the Fine weather markets, i.e. to sell labour at points 12, 1, and 3 and to purchase sunshades at points 34, 2, and 4. In these circumstances I receive now a given price for undertaking to work on days 1 and 2 if, but only if, it is Wet on those days; and I use this money to pay now to a sunshade manufacturer who undertakes to provide me with sunshades on days 1 and 2 if but only if it is Fine on those days. If my expectations are correct and it turns out Fine, then I can take a perpetual holiday in the sun parading up and down with a fine collection of sunshades; but if it turns out Wet, I must toil away without receiving any sunshades or umbrellas in return. If everybody felt like me, then the current price of future labour-if-Wet would be very depressed, and the current price of future sunshades-if-Fine would be much pushed up; and conversely the current price of future labour-if-Fine would be pushed up, and of future umbrellas-if-Wet would be depressed. At some point those who were not quite so sure that it would be fine would sell labour-if-Fine (thereby enabling entrepreneurs to plan to produce some sunshades-if-Fine), and would purchase umbrellas-if-Wet (thereby giving some employment opportunities for the many offers of labour-if-Wet). The contingency prices would settle at levels which cleared the contingency markets.

But would there be any virtue in this state of affairs? Is there any sense in which it is an economically efficient outcome? In the case in which there were no environmental uncertainties we argued that a comprehensive set of competitive forward markets would lead to an efficient solution in the sense that it would be impossible to change the use of the community's resources in such a way as to make one citizen better off over the period from Now to Kingdom Come without making any other citizen worse off. We cannot any longer apply this criterion without modification. For suppose that the community's resources are being used today partly to prepare for the production of sunshades in case it turns out to be Fine and partly to prepare for the production of umbrellas in case it turns out to be Wet. If it turns out Fine, then everyone could have been better off if today none of the community's resources had been devoted to the production of umbrellas. But to say that today's use of resources is inefficient because in fact no umbrellas turn out to be wanted would be comparable to saying that it is inefficient to have insured one's house except for the year in which it is actually burned down.

But suppose that every citizen today has a preference ordering between different collections of contingent goods. That is to say, suppose that he can say as between two different sets of goods, A and B, which he has the prospect of receiving if and when he passes through the points 12, 34, 1, 2, 3, and 4 on my diagram whether he prefers prospect A or prospect B. Then one can conclude that a comprehensive set of competitive contingent markets will lead to an efficient state of affairs today in the sense that no citizen could today look forward to a preferred set of possibilities without someone else having to look forward to a less preferred set of possibilities for himself. I hope that this conclusion is sufficiently clear intuitively, because I have no time to pause to demonstrate it at all vigorously. Perhaps it is sufficient to remember that in today's comprehensive contingency forward market there will today be uniform market prices quoted for every good and service at every future date-cum-environment point. Each consumer can today trade these contingent goods and services for each other freely at these uniform market prices in order to move as far as possible up his own preference ordering of future prospects for the various environmental outcomes, and entrepreneurs can plan to purchase inputs of various resources at each future time-cum-environment point to produce various outputs at each such future time-cum-environment point in such a way as to maximise today's net receipts or profits from the prices which they pay today for these contingent inputs and the prices which they receive today for these contingent outputs. The familiar types of analysis of a competitive system can now be applied to show that this will result in a Pareto optimum in the sense that no one can get a preferred bundle of contingent goods without someone else being left with a less preferred bundle.

There are two important features of this outcome which should be noted in passing.

First, entrepreneurs as such bear no risks. They purchase and sell for fixed and known prices today all their future contingent inputs and outputs. They can thus make their future production plans for each of the various environmental paths in such a way as to maximise today's riskless net value of these plans and they can then, as ordinary consumers, spend this net sum on the purchase of contingent goods and services for their own personal future use. In this respect they, like all other citizens, do face risks. Just as I, if I sell all my labour in the markets for Wet weather and spend all the resulting income on sunshades in the markets for Fine weather, stand to fare badly if it turns out in fact to be Wet, so the generality of citizens as earners of income and as consumers of goods and services (including leisure) must bear risks. It may be Wet or it may be Fine. This is a risk which must be faced, though any gains or losses from the risk may, of course, be spread or otherwise traded through insurance and betting markets. But entrepreneurs simply as the organisers of productive processes bear no risks in the conditions so far assumed. The risk-bearing function of entrepreneurial activity must wait on the modification of some of the far-reaching assumptions which I made at the beginning of these lectures.

Secondly, it is not assumed that all citizens must form the same assessment of the probabilities of the different environmental paths. On the contrary, I may expect Fine weather and sell labour-if-Wet and purchase sunshades-if-Fine, while you expect Wet weather and sell labour-if-Fine and purchase umbrellas-if-Wet. I stress this obvious point because it becomes important when we turn, as I shall now do, to a discussion of indicative planning as an alternative means for dealing with conditions of environmental uncertainty.

# IV

## Environmental Uncertainties and Indicative Planning

The planning procedure would now have to be modified in the following way. The government, as before, summons all the citizens to a meeting in the Albert Hall. In the absence of environmental uncertainty it issued to everyone merely a single questionnaire, showing a price for every good and service and an interest rate for loans for every day from Now until Kingdom Come, and asking each citizen to write down for each day how much of each good or service he would buy or sell and how much capital he would lend or borrow if these prices in fact ruled. Now it must issue not merely a single questionnaire, but as many questionnaires as there are environmental paths, each such questionnaire suggesting a course which the prices of every good and service, the rates of interest for the loan of a day's money, and each day's insurance premia or betting odds on moving from that day's point on that path to the next day's point on that path might take along that particular path.

Each citizen must now write down how much of each good he would buy or sell, how much capital he would borrow or lend, and how much he would bet on or against moving from one point to the next on each particular path, if the prices, interest rates, and betting odds in the market did move in the specified way. The government officials must then add up the total demands and supplies for goods and services, loans, and bets along each environmental path; they must then put up the price, interest rate, or insurance premium at any point on any environmental path where the demand for goods, the loan, or the insurance exceeded the supply; and *vice versa*. The procedure is then repeated; and this process goes on until hopefully – and once more I stress the significance of this word 'hopefully' – there is a balance between supply and demand in every market at every point on every environmental path.

The result is, as it were, as many indicative plans as there are environmental paths – one plan for each path. If the game has been played properly, that is to say, if each decision-maker has truthfully stated how he would behave on each path if prices moved as indicated along that path, then in fact supplies and demands will balance at those prices along each path and the prices will, therefore, in fact behave as indicated in the plan. The conditional future spot prices will have been accurately forecast and all market uncertainties will have been eliminated.

For the reasons which I gave at some length previously, the result will in theory be exactly the same as would be achieved from a comprehensive set of competitive contingency markets. Three features of the result may be mentioned. First, the outcome will be an efficient use of resources in the sense that no one citizen could look forward to a preferred set of possible outcomes without some other citizen being faced with a less preferred set of possible outcomes. Secondly, the entrepreneurs of production as such will face no risks; by planning to insure at each point against each environmental development they can plan in a way which will maximise their own certain profit. Thirdly, in the formation of the set of indicative plans, the individual decision-makers need not be persuaded to form any agreed or single view about the probability of each environmental path.

There is one implication of this last feature which should be stressed.

Indicative planning has been severely criticised on the following grounds. Does not the formation of an indicative plan necessarily involve the formulation of a common view about the probable course of future events in order that a single indicator of the probable future course of prices, incomes, employments and so on may be provided to guide and to make consistent the plans of all the individual participants? But is this not very undesirable? Surely, it is argued, it is better in a free competitive system that different individuals should be free to form different opinions about the probabilities of different outcomes rather than that all should be persuaded to act on a single view. Is it not a basic virtue of the competitive system that we do not put all our eggs in one basket, that different economic agents can bet on different outcomes, and that the risk-taking agents who best foresee the outcome can thrive and take over more and more decision-making at the expense of those who are not so successful in their speculations?

I will consider later how far this criticism is justifiable in the case of much actual indicative planning which has in fact been based upon a single most likely path for the environmental conditions, and has then produced only one single indicator for the future. But it would certainly not be relevant to the ideal type of indicative planning under uncertainty which I have just outlined and which would result, as it were, in as many indicative plans as there were environmental uncertainties. In this case it is not merely that there are many possible outcomes considered in the plan; it is not even necessary that all participants should take the same view about the probability of each outcome. On the contrary, each citizen would be free to form his own subjective assessment of the probability of each environmental path, though, for the reasons which I gave early on in these lectures, it might well be useful for the government in the formulation of the indicative plan to arrange for an exchange of views about the subjective assessments of the different environmental paths, so that the less expert could hear the opinions of the more expert on such topics as the probabilities of a particular technological advance or of a particular change in fashion. The basic point of the ideal type of indicative planning under uncertainty which I have outlined is that it would leave complete competitive freedom for economic agents to act on their own diverse assessments of future changes in the environment, but at the same time it would remove the unnecessary uncertainties about the combined market implications of the diverse plans of these free economic agents. One would know, given the diverse views and plans of the various economic agents, what these implied for the future development of market conditions along each environmental path.

I have spoken of the ideal type of indicative planning as if it consisted of the construction of a set of separate plans, one for each future possible environmental path. In a sense this is a fair description of the end result of the process; but in their construction this set of plans makes a single interdependent whole. Let me illustrate from my simple example of the three-day four-weather-path economy. Consider any one citizen who, during the Albert Hall meeting, is being asked to fill in four question-naires, the first stating how much of everything he will buy and sell at each point on path 1 – i.e. at points 1234, 12 and 1 – given the prices assumed on the questionnaire, the second asking for the same information for the points on path 2, i.e. for points 1234, 12 and 2, and so on. The point 1234 is common to all four questionnaires; the point 12 is common to the first two questionnaires; and the point 34 is common to the last two questionnaires. In filling up his information for point 1234 on questionnaire 1, our citizen must declare not what he would do today if he knew he was on path 1, but what he would do today in the absence of any knowledge about which path he is on. In filling up his information for point 12 on questionnaire 1, our citizen must declare not what he would do tomorrow if he knew that he was on path 1, but what today he thinks he would do tomorrow if he did not know today what path he was on, but tomorrow found that he was on either path 1 or path 2. And so on. The separate plans for the different environmental paths in fact form such an interrelated whole that we may refer to them as a single plan; and in what follows when I talk of a plan I mean a set of plans covering the various possible environmental paths, and when I wish to refer to the action planned along only one of the possible environmental paths I shall use the term 'a sub-plan'.

I have spoken so far as if it were the easiest thing in the world for the citizen to formulate his own total plan, that is to say, his own set of interrelated sub-plans. Far from it. It raises all the deep problems involved in how to formulate decisions in conditions of uncertainty, which I simply cannot tackle in these lectures. All that the ideal type of indicative planning can do is to reduce, perhaps greatly reduce, the amount of uncertainty with which each individual decision-maker has to cope by indicating what price paths will be connected with what environmental paths. It can, that is to say, eliminate market uncertainties, but not environmental uncertainties.

## V

### The Demographic Turnover

So much for the pure theory of ideal indicative planning in conditions of uncertainty. The time has now come for me to relax the four sets of extreme simplifying assumptions which I made at the outset of these lectures, to see what practical snags and difficulties are thereby introduced into the picture, and to consider what – if anything at all – of practical usefulness remains from the theoretical conclusions so far reached.

Let me start by relaxing my strange demographic assumption that there are no births or deaths or ageing between Now and Kingdom Come. If new citizens are still to be born or existing children are to grow up, then there will in the future be new economic agents buying and selling, lending and borrowing, taking and making bets in the future, who just do not enter the market now. This means that there cannot now be a comprehensive set of future markets covering all transactions from Now till Kingdom Come; the transactions of those who are at present infants or are as yet unborn cannot now be expressed in today's forward markets. The demographic turnover of economic decision-makers thus makes a quite fundamental difference to the situation. It is one, though as we shall see it is not the only, sufficient reason why a market price mechanism cannot be used in a system of forward markets to signal market information horizontally over time as it can be used to signal market information at any one time vertically as between one good and another.

This demographic situation thus provides an argument for supplementing the market mechanism with some procedures for indicative planning or forecasting. But it implies, of course, that in any such procedures the infants and the unborn, who cannot be present in the Albert Hall themselves, should be represented by someone else. Perhaps the Central Statistical Office might undertake this task. In order to do so it will have to insist on the introduction of some additional demographic environmental paths into the set of indicative plans, since nobody knows for certain now what will happen to future fertility, mortality, and nuptiality. And it is not only the size, and the sex and the age composition of future generations which constitute environmental uncertainties for the indicative planners. No one can say for certain what the inborn capabilities or psychological preferences of the future citizens will be, and these things could clearly have important market implications.

In shouldering this task of representing future generations in the formation of an indicative plan the Central Statistical Office would have to employ some econometric techniques. In trying to estimate how much individual citizens would work, save, spend on this good and on that good in future years given the ways in which incomes, prices, wealth, interest rates, family size and structure, etc. may develop along the various environmental paths, the statisticians would have to start by fitting parameters to the past changes in these variables and extrapolating the results. For how else could they make a start?

There are in fact further practical problems, which mean that, quite apart from the unborn citizens of the future, not all existing individual economic decision-makers could possibly take part directly in the formation of an indicative plan. Limitations on the size of the Albert Hall, quite apart from anything else, would prohibit a town meeting of all the UK citizens; and the mind boggles at the problems involved in trying to carry out the Albert Hall iterative planning procedure by post. Many citizens must in fact have their future market transactions expressed in an aggregative way by representatives who, in many cases, will have to rely on some form of econometric estimation to formulate their representations of their constituents' probable future transactions at future dates in the various market conditions and environmental backgrounds as stated in the plan.

Considerations of this kind tell strongly in favour of using actual forward markets wherever possible, since the market mechanism is a really rather remarkable signalling system in that every single individual, however unimportant, can take part in the expression of his decisions.

But, as we have just seen, a comprehensive set of forward markets is ruled out. To fall back on some procedures for indicative planning means to fall back on procedures in which many economic agents will be merely represented in the aggregate, their intentions being diagnosed in large measure by econometric techniques.

In the construction of an indicative plan some economic agents may take part individually. Thus all the individual firms producing steel or cars or aeroplanes might be present. In other cases they might be represented by, for example, a trade association which did not itself have to rely on econometric estimation but could consult each of its constituent members individually in order to form an aggregative picture of the future transactions of the whole industry. In other cases, for example in the case of the purchases of consumption goods by the individual housewives, the representation of total consumers' demands for various goods in different future situations would have to be undertaken on the basis of econometric studies of demand functions by some body like the Central Statistical Office.

One must then imagine the indicative plan being formed not in the Albert Hall but in the committee rooms of Whitehall where this limited number of individual decision-makers or their representatives are gathered together. But in principle the same procedure of indicative planning can be applied. The government planners start the dialogue by saying: 'Suppose market conditions to be such-and-such on each of the various environmental paths, how would each of you expect your constituents to behave on each of those paths?' The representatives reply: 'In this and that manner.' The government planners then adjust appropriately their market assumptions, and the dialogue is renewed until market consistency between the transactions suggested by the representatives of the different sectors of the economy is obtained. The total plan, containing one sub-plan for each environmental path, is then published in order to enable each individual decision-maker to formulate his own plans and decisions with a better guess as to what the future holds in store for him.

# VI

## The Multiplicity of Environmental Time Paths

A further complexity in indicative planning of the type which I have outlined arises in the enormous multiplicity of relevant environmental time paths. In my previous simple example with two future days on each of which it might be Wet or Fine, there were four such paths. Let us first be quite clear that there are four separate relevant paths. I indicated in my diagram that there were four possible price constellations on day 2 – namely, $P_1$, $P_2$, $P_3$, and $P_4$. At first sight it might appear that there are in fact only two price constellations to be considered. On day 2 it will be either Wet or Fine. Can we not be satisfied with a Wet-weather set of prices for umbrellas and sunshades and a Fine-weather set of prices for these objects? Can we not assume $P_1 = P_3$ and $P_2 = P_1$? Alas, no. $P_1$ occurs in Wet following Wet and $P_3$ in Wet following Fine. If day 1 has been Wet the umbrella producers may have made production arrangements on day 1 in order to make it easier to produce umbrellas on day 1 and these arrangements may carry over in part till the next day making it easier to produce umbrellas on day 2. Moreover, if umbrellas are at all durable, consumers may have a stock of umbrellas on day 2 which they have bought on day 1, because day 1 was Wet. Thus Wet following Wet may imply a day 2 in which umbrellas are cheap to produce and the demand is low as compared with Wet following Fine, which may imply for day 2 a productive apparatus not so well suited to produce umbrellas and a set of consumers with fewer umbrellas already in their possession. $P_1$ may be very different from $P_3$.

These interconnections between events in different years make our procedure very complicated in fact. Suppose there were only three uncertain exogenous variables, for example, rainfall, the fashion for skirt lengths, and the rate of technical progress in the engineering industry. Suppose each of these variables could have one of three values in each year, namely High, Medium, and Low. Suppose that there were only five periods in the plan, e.g. a five-year plan. Then instead of the four weather time paths of my simple example there would be $3^{3 \times 5} = 14,352,807$ different time paths for the environmental uncertainties; and it is, of course, a gross simplification of reality to assume that there are only three factors about which one is basically uncertain. The implications of this are far-reaching. A set of 14,352,807 interdependent indicative sub-plans would have to be worked out; and in making use of them each private decision-maker would have to consider the various paths and express in 14,352,807 fractions which added up to unity his subjective assessment of their probabilities. In fact the task might not be as difficult as it appears because no one would have any time to do anything but to consider the probabilities of future events and to calculate, so that all actual transactions at every point in every sub-plan might be written down as zero. But this would simply mean that the cost of constructing any such indicative plan would clearly be prohibitive.

It is obvious that if an indicative plan is in reality to be constructed to cope with conditions of environmental uncertainty there must be a process of gross simplification. This can take two forms.

In the first place, it is clear that only a very limited number of possible time paths for the environmental uncertainties can be taken into account. Two possible time paths for the external demand conditions for the country's exports plus two possible time paths for the course of general labour productivity plus two possible time paths for the growth of the population would alone necessitate a set of eight indicative sub-plans.

The implications of limiting in this way the number of environmental paths in an indicative plan are very far-reaching. Clearly the planners should try to choose for consideration one or two representative possible time paths which are typical of likely developments, but of developments which are unlike each other. But having chosen these environmental time paths for consideration, what should be the rules of the game? Suppose, by way of illustration, that the planners have chosen to consider only two such possible time paths. At the Albert Hall meeting, or in the committee rooms of Whitehall, they must explain to the assembled economic decision-makers exactly what are the assumptions about future environmental change on which the two paths are based. They must then, as before, start by enunciating two patterns of market prices which are to be assumed to rule along the two environmental paths which are being considered; and, as before, they must ask each economic agent to report how much of everything he would buy or sell along each path if the stated prices in fact ruled along each path. In the light of the replies they must revise appropriately the price paths along each environmental path.

But in making their replies what are the private citizens to assume about the probabilities of the two environmental paths? If the purpose of the indicative plan is really to discover how people would react along various environmental paths, then, as before, each citizen must be free to ascribe his own subjective probability to each of the two paths under consideration. Each private citizen will realise that the two paths are merely typical and do not by any means exhaust the possibilities. If there are really only two paths under consideration, then there can be only one environmental variable (say, the foreign demand for the country's exports) which is being allowed to take two different courses. For all the other environmental variables (such as the growth of population, the rate of technical progress, and so on) there must be only one single path assumed in the plan. But many citizens whose situation may be much affected by these other variables will want to plan their activities on the assumption that some of these other environmental variables (for example labour productivity) may develop in a more or less favourable way than that assumed by the planners.

The rules of the planning game could be so devised as not to allow the private citizens to take these other possibilities into account. They might be asked by the planners to say how they would react along each path if they were certain that either the one path or the other would in fact develop. Perhaps they could be persuaded to play this unreal hypothetical game and give accurate answers. But in that case the answers would not correspond to what they would in fact do along either of these paths if it did in fact materialise. To return to my frivolous example, the two paths might refer to two different developments of the rate of technical progress in the sunshade–umbrella industry, but in that case there could be only one assumption made about the future course of the weather. If the producers of sunshades and umbrellas had to say what they would do if they were certain that this would be the actual course of the weather, they might report quite properly the installation of some very expensive, specialised, technically efficient, long-lasting plant to produce sunshades and umbrellas in rigid proportions exactly suitable for that one weather path. But this is not what they will in fact do, since they realise that it may be much Wetter or much Finer than is assumed in the single weather path for the plan, and they will therefore install much less specialised, cheaper, short-lived but flexible plant which can be used to produce either sunshades or umbrellas.

An indicative plan based on a limited number of environmental paths must, therefore, leave a large amount of what may be called 'residual uncertainty'. The planners must ask the private citizens how in fact they would act along each of the representative environmental paths when they are free to make their own assessment of how probable these paths are and of the possibilities that the environment may in fact develop along other paths. Along these other paths the private citizens will, of course, be left with market uncertainties as well as with environmental uncertainties. On weather paths not covered by the plan the manufacturers of sunshades and umbrellas will not be told what prices for these objects will rule on these unconsidered paths. The manufacturers will have to make their own guesses about the possibilities of different price paths being connected with each unconsidered weather path.

But while an indicative plan which covers only a very few environmental paths cannot remove such market uncertainties, it may well reduce them very considerably. If the producers of sunshades and umbrellas learn from the indicative plan the market prices which will rule for these objects in the particular weather conditions covered by the plan, they have, as it were, a bench-mark from which they can make for themselves more accurate guesses as to what the prices would be if the weather were so much Wetter or so much Finer than the plan assumed. The indicative plan will no longer eliminate, but it can still hope greatly to reduce, market uncertainties.

In trying to cover these residual uncertainties each private economic agent will in turn be left with a vast number of possible future courses of the market and environmental factors which are relevant for his own operations. He in turn, in drawing up his own individual plans for the future, cannot hope to calculate meticulously what it will be best for him to do along each of the possible paths. He may himself take one or two additional representative paths for more detailed consideration. For example, the producer of sunshades and umbrellas might take one typical weather path which was Wetter by a given amount than the single path considered in the plan and one typical path which was Finer by a given amount than that considered in the plan. We may call these his representative sub-paths. For these sub-paths he might make his own carefully calculated guesses about the associated price paths. But there would always remain some large measure of residual uncertainty which he would find it too laborious or indeed quite impossible to cover by any form of detailed calculation. He would have to form his plans in the light of the market conditions which he thought would be associated with these typical sub-paths as well as with the path assumed in the indicative plan, but always making some allowance for the fact that things might work out differently in quite uncalculated ways.

The inevitability of much residual uncertainty is due not only to the mere multiplicity of possible environmental paths, but also to the fact that the very possibility of some future environmental developments may not even occur to anyone today. For example, someone in the future may think of some entirely new product the very idea of which is conceived by no one today; indeed, if anyone had conceived the idea today, the product would already have been invented. There is thus residual uncertainty because of possible developments which no one has even imagined, as well as because of possible developments about which one has not had the time to think and calculate precisely. Every economic decision-maker must make allowance for the unexpected.

How should he make such allowance? I fear that I have nothing precise or very helpful to say on this point. But it is at this point that the general desire to remain liquid and to be ready for anything which may turn up comes into the picture. In particular the private economic agent will want his capital resources to be in general more flexible and liquid than would be the case if he knew that every possibility was covered by the representative sub-paths which he had considered in detail and in view of which he could have made his betting, insurance, and other hedging arrangements to meet each calculated risk. He will want his real capital equipment to be more diversified, more flexible between uses, and less long-lived than would otherwise be the case, and he will wish to keep more of his total capital resources in forms (of which money is, of course, the extreme example) which can readily at short notice and at small transactions cost be used in the market to meet all sorts of eventualities. But quite in what forms and to what degrees he should devise this extra flexibility and how far he should sacrifice probable profit to liquidity are matters which, I am relieved to say, I have no time to try to discuss.

The planners will have to cultivate the art of selecting a number of environmental paths which are typical and yet sufficiently limited to be practicable. It is possible that the right number of environmental paths to consider will turn out to be one. A single 'most-likely' time path to cover all the environmental variables could be useful in giving a bench-mark for market developments from which private individuals could make measurements for their own market and environmental sub-paths and thus for the construction of their own plans. But it would be of use in this indicative way only if the planners did not require the private citizens to assume that the path used for the plan was the only environmental path which could actually materialise. If the private citizens are all left free to say how they would behave on this one environmental path if they made their plans and decisions on their own estimates of the probability of this one path and of any other representative sub-paths which they cared to construct and consider for themselves, then a one-path indicative plan could have a real, though limited, use in removing market uncertainties. On these conditions, but only on these conditions, it would not be open to the criticism of one-path indicative planning to which I have already referred (see pages 128–29 above).

Besides the limitation of an indicative plan to a small number of representative environmental time paths, there is a second consequence of the great multiplicity of environmental possibilities which we must now consider. It is clear that the time period of the plan must be limited. We can now drop our assumption that the world will come to an end with a loud bang at a definite moment in the future called Kingdom Come. If Kingdom Come is a far distant date, it will be certain that to cover the whole period from Now till Kingdom Come by a meaningful indicative plan would be impossible because of the multiplicity of environmental paths. To avoid impossible complexity the indicative plan must cover a shorter time period. In settling on such a time period two conflicting influences must be borne in mind.

On the one hand the longer the period of the plan the more do the environmental uncertainties multiply. This means that the cost of planning becomes rapidly inflated as the time period is extended, since it becomes more and more meaningless to plan in terms of only one or two limited time paths for the environmental uncertainties. After a limited period uncertainties become so great that numerical estimates become really meaningless; the cost of extending the period of the plan has become more or less infinite.

On the other hand, since, as we have already argued, the economic system is a general equilibrium system, ideally an indicative plan should cover the quantities and prices of every good and service for every future day until Kingdom Come. In any case, so long as the decisions which one would rationally take today are at all sensitive to what may reasonably happen after the end of the time period of the plan there is much to be gained by extending the planning period. We need, therefore, to consider whether the extension of the period of the plan to cover, say, the next six years instead of only the next five years will have much effect upon what one would decide to do this year. This is a question of fact which depends upon such matters as whether the plan, and equipment which one installs this year, is very long-lasting or very short-lasting, whether it is flexible or inflexible in the uses to which it can be put, and so on. It depends also in a crucial way upon the extent to which the extension-makers discount future utilities; if we don't really care much about the welfare of the next generation, we need not worry too much about the state in which we leave the economy in the distant future.

The optimum time horizon for a plan is that at which the improvement in today's decisions achieved by adding another unit of time to the period covered by the plan is just offset by the additional cost of that extension of the time covered by the plan. If conditions are such that today's decisions are sensitive to far-distant future events, but, at the same time, the cost of planning as a result of environmental uncertainties mounts very quickly as the time period of the plan is extended – that is just too bad. It simply means that planning will be difficult and that today's decisions will not be much improved by formal attempts at planning. But as far as I can see, there is nothing much that one can do about it.

The limitation of the period covered by the indicative plan means, of course, that the private economic agents will have no indication of what market conditions will be after the close of the plan period. In some cases this will be an important source of remaining market uncertainty even for the period and the representative environmental paths covered by the plan. An entrepreneur who is installing a steel mill now will want to know the demand for steel, say, three years hence. This future period may be covered by the plan; but the demand for steel three years hence may contain, as an important element, the demand for steel to produce machines to produce products for sale six years hence – a later date which is not covered by the plan period. The reports given to the planners for the demand for steel three years hence may thus depend upon private, unaided guesses by the purchasers of the steel about market and environmental developments after the end of the plan period. It is, of course, quite possible that these purchasers of steel when the time comes three years hence will have revised their guesses about the future market and environmental conditions which will determine their decisions about the purchase of the steel to build the machines to produce the products to sell in another three years' time. Thus in a plan with a limited time span even the market conditions which will be associated with the representative environmental path or paths considered in full detail in the plan cannot be estimated with certainty. Some market uncertainty remains attached even to these paths.

There is one extremely important implication of what I have just said, namely that any indicative plan should be subject to continual revision. We argued that when an ideal comprehensive set of indicative sub-plans could be formed covering all environmental paths over the whole period from Now to Kingdom Come, a once-for-all planning procedure was all that was needed. No revision need ever be made in the total plan because all eventualities had been covered for all time. But this is no longer so. Consider the scheme of my simple two-period four-weather-path model. Suppose we are restricting our plan to cover only two periods, not as was previously assumed, because Kingdom Come will occur for certain at the end of day 2, but because we cannot cope with more than four environmental paths. Today we are at point 1234 with four paths possible up to the end of day 2. But tomorrow we shall know for certain whether we are at point 12 or point 34 and we can then add another day to the planned period without increasing the number of weather paths above four. It should thus never be forgotten that, in conditions of environmental uncertainty, the sole purpose of today's indicative plan is to enable one to take wiser decisions today. Tomorrow the plan should be extended to cover another day and should be revised in view of all additional available information, but solely in order to enable tomorrow's decisions to be more wisely based. And so on until Kingdom Come.

## VII

### A Network of Plans

There is yet another source of complexity which we must now examine. I have so far spoken as if only one single national indicative plan was being prepared, this being comprehensive in the sense that, even if it could not cover every possible environmental path, yet it did cover in full and separate detail every industry, every region, every product, every quality of labour, and so on. And this is as it should be ideally since, as we have argued, for general equilibrium purposes the price and quantity of every good and service is directly or indirectly related to the price and quantity of every other good and service. But if every commodity, every industry, every occupation, every use of a product, every locality, every type of consumer, in short every possible relevant variable were to be expressed separately, the system of interrelationships in the econometric model would become impossibly complicated. It would be impossible to cope with it for at least two reasons. First, the number of independent variables in each relationship would become so great relatively to the number of observations or of other pieces of information about that relationship that it would be impossible to obtain reliable values for the parameters of the system. Second, even if reliable estimates of the relationships could be obtained, the number of relationships and their complexity would be so great that even with the most sophisticated techniques and equipment for simulation and calculation the system could not be handled. Thus no worthwhile forecasts could be obtained from such a system.

This means that the national indicative plan must be a plan for a much simplified model of the whole economy in which groups of relevant variables are consolidated into statistical aggregates and in which simplifying assumptions are made about the relationships between these various aggregates. Thus products may be broken down simply into agricultural products and manufactured products; income recipients into wage-earners and owners of property; uses of products into consumption, investment, and government use; workers into skilled, semi-skilled, and unskilled; the capital market into banks and other financial institutions; and so on. Even with very broad categories such as these the number of variables of prices and quantities in an economic model soon becomes surprisingly large.

But, it may be asked, if this is the best that can be expected of a national indicative plan, is it really any use? After all, the individual farmer is interested in forecasts of the markets for particular agricultural products – wheat, beef, butter, cheese, etc – and in the availability and price of labour of particular agricultural trainings and skills, not in general indices of the price of agricultural goods as a whole or of skilled or semi-skilled labour as a whole. The answer is that a general aggregative plan will reduce some of the market uncertainties, and against this background other less aggregated organisations or indeed particular individuals can make their own subsidiary forecasts and plans.

Let me continue the agricultural example. On the basis of a national framework plan a more detailed agricultural indicative plan could be formulated. Such an agricultural plan would take as exogenous variables (i.e. as already determined data) many of the variables which were endogenous (i.e. as needing to be determined) in the framework plan. Thus the total purchasing power of consumers and the price of manufactured consumption goods as a whole, the competing wage levels offered by industry for labour of various general grades, these and many other relevant factors which were outputs of the framework plan would be taken by the agricultural planners as given exogenous inputs into the agricultural plan. The agriculturalists could then break down their agricultural products into many more detailed categories and still have a manageable number of endogenous variables within their own plan. They would be making detailed forecasts for their particular agricultural products on the assumption that the general trends of the framework plan were correct.

There could then be a feedback from the agricultural plan to the framework plan. To take the clearest example, suppose that there was not only a subsidiary agricultural indicative plan but also subsidiary steel industry, textile industry, car industry plans and so on for all the main industries. Each industry takes as exogenous to it the main relevant indices produced by the framework plan. Each industry from this builds up its own particular demand for labour, for example. But the future demands for labour estimated by the sum of the separately planned industrial demands may not tally with the future demand for labour resulting from the framework plan. Clearly something is wrong with the aggregative behavioural or technical relationships assumed for the framework plan, and these must be altered at the next revision of the framework plan to take account of the discrepancy. But this in turn will affect the results of the framework plan so that the general indices which the individual industry plans take as exogenous data will be changed. This will affect the results of the industry plans which will feed back once more in due course into the framework plan.

Nor are industrial plans the only possible form of subsidiary plan. Another obvious example is regional planning. An indicative plan could be formed for one region taking as exogenous variables many of the general indices resulting from the framework plan and also perhaps some of the results of some of the subsidiary industrial plans. For example, the general national activity likely in a particular industry may be a very relevant datum for indicative planning for a region which was particularly dependent upon that industry. The combined results of a number of regional plans could then well lead to a modification of the relationships assumed in the framework plan.

Nor are there necessarily only two layers in the hierarchy of indicative plans. Not only can large Neddies have little Neddies on their backs to fight them, but little Neddies may have smaller Neddies and so on, not *ad infinitum*, but rather down to the individual decision-maker. Thus, to continue the agricultural example, in the light of the results suggested by the agricultural plan the individual farmer can construct his own plan for his own particular farm.

I have spoken of this system of indicative planning rather as if it were something novel and *sui generis*. But this is really not so. Even if the government does nothing about it, academic economists and financial journalists are likely on the basis of the more or less explicit assumptions of more or less sophisticated models to make general forecasts about the general future course of the economy in its broad aggregates, based partly upon forecasts made by particular trade associations or particular business concerns about the future of their particular markets. But these particular forecasts will often have been influenced by the results of the more general forecasts of the academics and journalists. An unorganised iterative feedback mechanism will be at work building up an interrelated network of indicative forecasts between a large number of planners ranging from the individual plans of the individual decision-makers to the sophisticated generalised econometric model of the high-powered academic research institution. All this can itself be regarded as a partial substitute for a system of forward markets; it does help to confront the anticipated future transactions of different sectors of the economy. The United States economy, for example, is not perhaps so unplanned as the absence of a formal national plan might suggest. In this sort of case we may say that national indicative planning is informal rather than formal; and I will be considering some of the relative merits of informal and formal national planning at a later stage in my lectures.

There is, however, one very important point to add. If a system of formal indicative planning is to be decentralised in this manner and if it is at the same time to cope at all adequately with environmental uncertainties, then, it would seem, each constitutent plan must be made up of a set of sub-plans based upon the same – or at least a very similar – set of environmental paths. If, for example, the national framework aggregative plan is based upon four possible environmental paths, it will show four separate sets of indices of the movement of its broad aggregates like total expenditure on consumption, the general level of wage-rates, the volume of employment, and so on. If these four sets of indices are to be useful for the detailed plan of, say, the steel industry, then that industry's plan also must consider these four separate environmental possibilities; and, what is equally important, if the results of the steel plan – such as the outputs of steel resulting from given levels of employment in the steel industry – are to be usefully fed back as aids to improve and correct the parameters used in the national framework plan, then they must refer to the same four environmental paths as are used in the national framework plan.

It is this feature of decentralised formal and informal indicative planning – namely, sets of alternative sub-plans all based upon more or less similar alternative environmental paths – which at the moment is conspicuous by its absence. Whether or not any useful advances can be made in this direction is one of the many questions arising from my lectures which I leave to you to answer for yourselves.

# VIII

## *Indicative Planning with Monopolists and Oligopolists*

There is another fundamental reason which we have not so far considered why in indicative planning great reliance must in fact be placed upon econometric model building. So far I have based the whole of my analysis upon the assumption of perfect competition. In fact, of course, much private enterprise is monopolistic or oligopolistic. This makes a quite fundamental difference to our analysis. In perfect competition the only market conditions which are relevant for any one economic decision-maker are prices. No individual producer, consumer, worker, saver, insurer, etc. can affect the prices of his inputs or outputs, or of his purchases for final consumption, or the wage-rate he can obtain from his work, or the rate of return he can get on his property, or the insurance premium for any particular risk. It is for this reason that the indicative planning procedure could take the form of a duet between the planning authority and the private citizens in which the planning authority simply states a set of prices, the private citizens reply with a set of quantities, the planning authority replies with a revised set of prices aimed at bringing the quantities into balance, the citizens reply with a revised set of quantities, and so on.

Where competition is not perfect, this procedure just will not work. Consider the simplest classical theory of monopoly pricing. It is not sufficient to tell a monopolistic producer what the market price for his product will be and then ask him how much he will produce. The market conditions relevant for the sale of his product are described not by a demand price but by a demand curve. Consider then the possibility that the planning authority should open the planning duet by saying, as before, to the *purchasers* of the product, 'How much of this product would you purchase at each point on each environmental path if its price moved in such and such a way?' but saying to the *producer*, 'How would you behave at each point on each environmental path if the demand schedule for your product were such-and-such at each point?' The producer if he was a price-taker could answer with the quantities he would put on the market, or if he was a price-maker with the prices which he would charge; given the assumed demand schedule the quantity put on the market implies the price and *vice versa*, so that in either case the planning authority could estimate the market disequilibrium involved in its first guesses. Moreover, the statements of the consumers as to how much they would purchase at each point at the price announced by the planning authority would inform the planning authority about one point on the demand curve at each point on the various environmental paths. At its next round in the planning dialogue the planning authority could revise the prices announced to the purchasers in a direction which would help to close any gaps between supplies and demands and it could revise the demand schedules announced to the monopolistic producer in a way which would make them consistent with the new information obtained from the purchasers in the first round of the dialogue.

This sort of procedure would obviously be much more complicated than that which was relevant in conditions of perfect competition when only market prices need be announced by the planning authority. But let us leave these practical complications on one side for the moment. The procedure is in any case much less reliable than the perfect-competition procedure. Suppose that every participant plays the game according to the rules, and suppose that the procedure does converge on to a set of sub-plans and that at every point on every environmental path the quantity which the monopolist will produce and the price which he will charge are equal to the quantity which the consumers will purchase at that price. 'Playing the game according to the rules' means that the producer must truthfully report what he would do if the demand schedule were as announced by the planning authority; but he may not in fact believe that the demand schedule is truly estimated by the planning authority. The only firm estimate which the planning authority will have is of certain points on the demand curve; and if the producer is not convinced that the demand curve is properly estimated, then he will not in future behave as he quite truthfully reported that he would have behaved if the demand schedule were as announced. The moral of this is that it would not be sufficient for the planning authority simply to announce its own revisions of the demand curve, though it is sufficient in conditions of perfect competition for it simply to announce its own revisions of the market price. It would now be necessary to discuss and agree its revisions of the demand curve with the monopolist.

These difficulties are multipled a thousandfold when one allows for the fact that one has not got to cope just with a classical monopolist but with a whole range of oligopolistic activities. I cannot possibly go into the general analysis of oligopolistic behaviour in these lectures. But the sort of problems which arise are familiar. In the first place the oligopolist will be able to affect his sales by advertisement and other selling expenditures; and the levels of advertisement expenditure must be added to the planning picture. This means, of course, that the consumers must now be asked in the planning procedure not merely how much they would buy at given prices but how much they would buy from each oligopolist at given combinations of prices charged by the different oligopolists and of levels of informative and of bamboozling advertisement by each oligopolist. The oligopolist in his turn has to consider not simply how his customers will react directly to a change in the prices he charges or in his advertisement and other selling expenses. He must also consider how his closest competitor or competitors will react in their prices and selling expenditures to any changes in his own marketing policies, which depends, of course, upon how they think that he will react to their reactions. We are in the realm of the theory of games, of bargaining, of conventional good behaviour among potential and powerful rivals, of letting sleeping dogs lie, of tacit or open collusion, and so on. In such conditions it is clearly not sufficient for the planning authority to announce an assumed demand schedule for the product of an oligopolist in order to find out what the oligopolist would do in various situations. The market conditions facing an oligopolist have to be described in a much more complicated fashion which includes such matters as the assumed reactions of his closest competitors to changes in his own marketing policies.

In these circumstances, there is, as far as I can see, only one possible promising line of procedure, a procedure which, I suspect, is in certain respects much more like what actually happens in the real world in the formation of an indicative plan. The planning authority must start by constructing its own econometric model whereby, on the best estimations it can make from past statistical information and other evidence, it states how it expects prices, quantities, loans, interest rates, bets, betting odds, advertisement expenditures, etc., etc. to develop along each specified environmental path. The planning dialogue now takes the form of showing the econometric forecasts to the various economic agents or their representatives and asking for their answers to the following question: 'If the different variables in the economy, in so far as they are outside your control or direct influence and are relevant to your own actions, behaved in the way suggested by our econometric forecast, would you behave as we have said you would behave and would you expect those whose actions are most closely affected by your own action to behave as we have said they would behave? If not, please tell us how you would behave, and how you would expect those most closely affected by you to behave, if the other general conditions behaved as we forecast?'

The answers to this question would all be of a form which suggested revisions in the structure of relationships or in the parameters in the existing relationships of the planning authority's econometric model. The model could be revised and resubmitted with the same question. Theoretically one might apparently hope to converge on to a solution such that everyone agreed that the forecast did show accurately how he would behave if everyone else behaved as forecast along each specified environmental path.

But this hides a basic difficulty. Consider two duopolists A and B, the only two producers of motor vehicles in the economy. Suppose the planning authority to produce at some stage a forecast on which A comments: 'Yes, that is how I would behave if I thought that B was going to behave like that, but I don't think he would,' and on which B similarly comments: 'Yes, that is how I would behave if I thought that A was going to behave like that, but I don't think he would.' A and B must have misjudged each other's market strategies since if each did think that the other would so behave, each would in fact so behave. But in fact neither A nor B will base their plans on these forecasts since neither believes that the other will so behave.

What should the planning authority do? There is in fact a remaining market uncertainty – namely, how B will in fact react to A is unknown to A and *vice versa*. Could not this market uncertainty be removed in the process of forming the indicative plan? Should not the planning authority get A and B together so that they could inform each other of their reactions to each other's strategies or, failing that, might not the planning authority reveal to B what it has learned during the planning process about A's reactions and *vice versa*?

This suggestion presents us with a dilemma. In an oligopolistic situation there are many trade secrets which a particular producer will not want to reveal to his rivals, such as his marketing strategy or the probability of his achieving a particular technological breakthrough in the near future. Surprise may be an important weapon in achieving commercial success. It is naïve, therefore, to expect that the planning authority will readily obtain unbiased information from big private concerns about their future prospects of cost reductions, introduction of new products, commercial strategies, and so on, where this information might serve to inform their competitors of their future plans and prospects. Or, alternatively, the provision of such information might depend upon the formation of collusive monopolistic arrangements between the competing concerns which made innocuous the sharing of trade secrets among the producers concerned. Indeed there may be a serious risk that the dialogue between the government, on the one hand, and trade associations or other representative bodies of industrial and commercial groups on the other might encourage the formation of open or tacit monopolistic arrangements. Sharing of information about their investment plans by all the producers of a particular product may help to make their plans more consistent, but it might also encourage them jointly to make quite sure that the market was not oversupplied with their product.

I do not pretend to know the answer to this dilemma. Individual decision-makers should certainly be able to make better decisions if through something corresponding to a comprehensive set of forward markets they are given information about the supply–demand situations likely to be caused by the decisions of their competitors as well as of their customers. But, for reasons which we have examined at length, such a forward market mechanism does not exist. Any official formalised planned exchange of information instituted to take the place of a forward market mechanism is difficult to separate from monopolistic restrictive collusion. It can be argued that for this reason we should rely not upon formal, but upon what I have called informal, indicative planning, where unofficial bodies are left to make forecasts which will naturally interact on each other. I leave it to you to make up your own minds on this issue.

## IX

### The Absence of an Insurance Market

When the relevant environmental uncertainties are so numerous that they cannot all be considered or, what comes perhaps to much the same thing, when any particular environmental risks are so hard to define and to distinguish from each other that it is impossible to base a firm betting or insurance contract upon the occurrence or non-occurrence of any one of them, then for this reason alone it is impossible to have a system of contingency or of conditional forward markets. In terms of my previous formula

$$\hat{P}_1 = \frac{\pi_{12}}{1 + i_{1234}} \frac{\pi_1}{1 + i_{12}} P_1$$

it is impossible to make a contract involving $\hat{P}_1$ or $P_1$ simply because one will not on day 2 be able to decide precisely enough for the purpose of a firm legal contract whether or not one is in fact at what each party to the contract considers to be point 1.

There is, however, another possible state of affairs in which it would be possible to make a contract in terms of the conditional forward price $P_1$ but not in terms of the betting odds or insurance premia (i.e. the $\pi_{12}$ and $\pi_1$), and thus not in terms of the contingency forward price $\hat{P}_1$. This is the case where what is known as the 'moral hazard' rules out insurance and betting, even though the risk can be precisely defined. Let me take an example. An entrepreneur is undertaking research into a new technological process. If his research is successful, the result will be of great value. It may be quite possible to lay down an exact criterion as to whether or not the new process has been found by next year to perform in a precisely defined manner. But the entrepreneur will not necessarily be able to lay a bet of $1 million that he will not discover the process by next year. He might be too much tempted to relax his inventive endeavours and take a year's rest.

In this sort of case it may be quite possible to develop a system of conditional forward markets. Our entrepreneur, for example, may quite well be able to make forward contracts in the form that he will sell to a particular customer $Q_1$ units of his product at a price $P_1$ if he is successful in his invention, but $Q_2$ units at a price $P_2$ if he is unsuccessful. This will remove some degree of market uncertainty for him as well as for his customers, and this may affect the nature of his research activities. But if the quantities $Q_1$ and $Q_2$ and the prices $P_1$ and $P_2$ correspond to what he thinks they would be in any case in the two possible eventualities of the outcome of his research, his incentive to research will not be bascially blunted.

What he cannot do without seriously blunting his incentives is to sell $Q_1$ for $\hat{P}_1$ and $Q_2$ for $\hat{P}_2$ in the contingency market, since this means that he will receive $Q_1\hat{P}_1 + Q_2\hat{P}_2$ for certain now, but will have to provide $Q_1$ if the research is successful and only $Q_2$ if the research is unsuccessful. If $Q_2 < Q_1$, this could introduce some element of disincentive for his inventive efforts. This simply corresponds to his inability to bet that he won't succeed in his research.

The moral for indicative planning is that, where environmental uncertainties can be reasonably well defined but where the moral hazard rules out insurance or betting, one can still have a set of indicative sub-plans, one for each well-defined environmental path. These sub-plans will help to predict what will actually happen in the future to spot prices including interest rates (i.e. the $P_{12}$, $P_{34}$, $P_1$, $P_2$, $P_3$, $P_4$, $i_{12}$, and $i_{34}$ of my simple example). But there will be no betting odds or insurance premia to predict (the $\pi_{12}$, $\pi_{34}$, $\pi_1$, $\pi_2$, $\pi_3$, and $\pi_4$, of my example). The planning procedure must aim at discovering what will be the course of prices and interest rates along each environmental path when the individual economic agents are unable to place bets on or to insure against these environmental uncertainties.

For the ordinary citizen as worker, saver, and consumer this means in theory that he will be able to foresee his future along each environmental path, but will be unable to transfer by betting or insurance his resources from one such path to another. Previously, to repeat my extreme but homely example, I could sell my labour in Wet weather markets and buy my sunshades in Fine weather markets thereby working if, and only if, it was Wet and consuming if, and only if, it was Fine. I had only one budget constraint covering all contingencies; what I earned in Wet weather markets limited my purchases in Fine weather markets. With a reliable indicative plan, but in the absence of betting markets, I would know what I could earn by my labour or gain in interest on my savings on each weather path and I would know at what prices I could purchase goods on each weather path; but what I earned on each weather path would limit my consumption on that weather path; I should be subject to a separate budget constraint for each weather path; I would have to earn in Fine weather in order to be able to spend in Fine weather. It would be impossible for someone who expected Fine weather to exchange income-if-Wet for income-if-Fine with someone who expected Wet weather.

But while there would now no longer be a straightforward market in which resources-if-Wet could be traded directly for resources-if-Fine, there would still exist limited possibilities on the production side of transforming resources-if-Wet into resources-if-Fine, just as a farmer who is precluded from trading corn for clothes can start to produce his own clothes as well as his own corn. In my homely example a person who expects Fine weather can concentrate on producing sunshades for which there will be a high price if it is Fine, while a person who expects Wet weather can concentrate on the production of umbrellas. By shifting from the production of umbrellas to the production of sunshades, an entrepreneur is shifting from profits-if-Wet to profits-if-Fine.

Thus the entrepreneur of production now starts to have to take risks. Previously, with a complete comprehensive set of contingency markets or – as we saw, what comes to the same thing – with a comprehensive indicative plan with comprehensive betting markets, the entrepreneur as such took no risks. He could plan his operations so as to get now a certain revenue for all his contingency outputs and to pay now a certain cost for all his contingency inputs; he could maximise the excess of certain revenue over certain cost; and as an individual he could then lay out his maximised certain net resources through the betting markets or contingency markets as he thought best in view of his own (and not his customers') expectations of Wet or Fine.

This is no longer possible to him. He cannot produce sunshades at a high and certain price because other citizens are foolish enough to expect Fine weather and use the proceeds to purchase for himself umbrellas at a certain low price because he and he alone knows that it will be Wet. To make a big income if it is Wet he must now produce umbrellas, however much other people may think that it will be Fine, simply because if it is in fact Wet he will get a low price for any sunshades he produces and a high price for any umbrellas. The entrepreneur must now bear the risk. It is in these conditions that the great entrepreneurial function of judging what the future market and technological developments will be comes into its own. The successful entrepreneur is now the one who is best at judging what the future market-cum-environmental paths will be and is, therefore, more likely than others to plan to produce what will in fact turn out to be wanted. The ordinary citizen as consumer will no longer determine in the contingency and betting markets through his own expectations the eventualities for which the entrepreneur should plan; the entrepreneur takes over from the run of citizens this function of assessing the probabilities of the various environmental paths.

But cannot the ordinary run of citizens share in this entrepreneurial function of assessing the probabilities of the various outcomes? With the existence of joint-stock companies with equity shares and with a well-organised stock exchange, an ordinary citizen can invest his savings in a company producing sunshades which will declare a high dividend if it is Fine or in a company producing umbrellas which will declare a high dividend if it is Wet. He is in fact participating in the entrepreneurial risk-bearing function by choosing, as it were, to use some of his productive resources to produce a Fine-weather product or a Wet-weather product. By a judicious mix of his portfolio he can vary the extent to which he is thereby betting on Wet weather or on Fine weather.

But, for two basic reasons, this provides only a very partial substitute for a straightforward betting or insurance market on which one might exchange direct income-if-Wet for income-if-Fine.

The first reason is that it can be operated only by the use of an individual's property and property income. It cannot be operated by the use of his labour and his wages. With a stock exchange I can without too much cost spread my capital over many uses and thus to some extent place bets of various sizes on many different environmental outcomes. But I cannot without intolerable cost work part of the day in a sunshade factory, part of the day in an umbrella factory, and so on. Nor is it easy for me to shift from day to day from one occupation to another. I cannot, therefore, readily as a worker distribute my productive effort in whatever parcels I choose over the various environmental outcomes, whereas with comprehensive betting or insurance markets I could so distribute my wage income. And if I own little or no property I shall not in fact be able to raise the funds or credit to speculate on the Stock Exchange. The entrepreneurial alternative to betting and insurance markets is broadly speaking open to property and not to work.

The second reason is that productive techniques may be such that it is impossible to use shifts of production instead of shifts of trade to exchange income-if-Wet for income-if-Fine. This would be so if umbrellas and sunshades were for technical reasons joint products. Let us again illustrate from a homely but simple example. Let us suppose that the only physical difference between a sunshade and an umbrella is that the former object is covered with a bright material whereas the latter is always covered in sombre black. Let us then suppose that the whole of the population is smitten with colour blindness. There is now no relevant physical difference between a sunshade and an umbrella, so that we may call the resulting single object a sunbrella. Suppose, however, that the consuming population is divided into those who expect Fine weather and have skins which are exceptionally liable to blister if exposed to the sun and those who expect Wet weather and are exceptionally liable to catch cold if exposed to the rain. There will be all the difference in the world to both groups between a sunbrella-if-Fine and a sunbrella-if-Wet. The two groups would dearly love to exchange sunbrellas-if-Wet for sunbrellas-if-Fine; that is to say, both would today face a preferred set of possible future outcomes if it could be so arranged that the sunbrellas all went to the first group if it were Fine and to the second group if it were Wet, but there are no contingency markets or betting or insurance markets in which this trade can directly take place. And, as far as the productive side is concerned, producers can produce today for sale tomorrow only sunbrellas; that is to say, for every sunbrella-if-Wet produced there will be one sunbrella-if-Fine produced. People cannot purchase ordinary shares in companies producing sunbrellas-if-Fine as opposed to companies producing sunbrellas-if-Wet. If any of you have ever studied the theory of international trade, it may not come as a complete surprise to learn that there are conditions of production in which the movement of productive factors is not a complete substitute for trade in the products of the factors.

A less extreme, though still very simple example, may be useful. Suppose mutton to sell well in Fine weather (because it is a good picnic food) and wool to sell well in Wet weather (because it makes good raincoats). Suppose that one can invest in three types of sheep — type A which produces 2 units of mutton + 1 unit of wool, type B which produces 1 unit of mutton + 2 units of wool, and an intermediate type C which produces 1¾ units of both products as illustrated in the graph below.

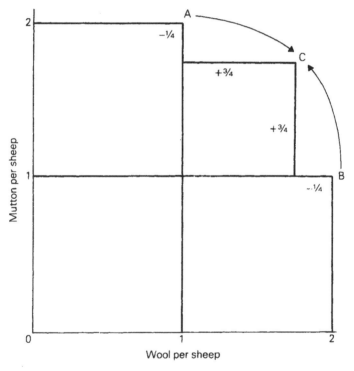

One can now have two independent farms, one producing with sheep of type A and the other with sheep of type B. Those who wish to bet on Fine weather can invest their money in Farm A and those who wish to bet on Wet weather in farm B. This enables some betting on the environmental outcome to take place but only at the expense of productive efficiency. For if farm A and farm B both exchanged one of their sheep for a type-C sheep, there would be a net gain of ½ a unit of both mutton and wool. The change in farm A would cause an increase in wool of ¾ and a loss of mutton of only ¼, but the change in farm B would cause a fall in wool of only ¼ but an increase in mutton of ¾. The flocks may properly be concentrated on types A and B on the different farms in order to be able to place different bets against weather risks. But this is a second-best arrangement. If people could use a betting or insurance market to make direct exchanges of income-if-Wet for income-if-Fine, while all farmers concentrated on producing that type of sheep which provided the highest certain income when consumers had made their bets, everyone could be better off.

## X

### *A Governmental Control Plan*

There remains one of the most outrageous simplifying assumptions made at the outset of these lectures which I must now do something to relax. You will have observed that in my discussion of a national indicative plan I have so far said nothing about governmental controls. The government has not as yet put any tax or subsidy or interest rate up or down as a means of influencing the economy; it has had no programmes for expenditures on defence, roads, schools, and so on. It has merely organised economic forecasts and a mimicry of forward markets in order to improve the efficiency of the market price mechanism in signalling over time. But there are, of course, other well-known reasons why in a basically competitive free-enterprise economy the public authorities should intervene by taxes, public expenditures, control of interest rates, direct controls, etc. Let me simply enumerate these reasons under four headings.

First, there are externalities and public goods. Public authorities must intervene to prevent smoke nuisance, to provide law and order, and defence.

Second, there are indivisibilities and monopolistic conditions. Here again there is a strong case for governmental intervention by state operation of public utilities, by price control, by appropriately designed taxes and subsidies, and so on.

Third, society may well decide that steps should be taken to affect the distribution of income and wealth between the rich and poor of the present generation or between present and future generations.

Fourth, there are all sorts of frictions in economic markets. In pure theory in a perfectly competitive economy there would, I suppose, never be any unemployment of labour except when the wage-rate was zero. All workers would come into the labour market at the beginning of the day or week and offer their services in competition with each other to a set of competing employers; and the wage would very quickly be reduced so long as it was positive and any worker remained without work. In fact, of course, workers set a price for their work (which may well, of course, as Professor Phillips suggests with his famous curve, be influenced more or less sluggishly by past and expected levels of unemployment) and there results from week to week a certain level of employment and a certain level of unemployment. Similarly many producers of manufactured products set prices for their goods (which also may be influenced over time by the level of demand for them) and there results from week to week a level of productive activity and a level of unused capacity in the business concerned. The fact that many producers of goods and suppliers of labour react to a change in demand, not by an immediate change in the price of the good or the wage of the labour, but by a change in the amount of goods sold and the amount of labour which finds employment, can lead to large cumulative swings – an initial change in demand leading to a change in output and employment, leading to a change in real income, leading to a change in demand, and so on in a cumulative vicious circle. But these swings could be offset by governmental measures, which affect the level of demand for goods and services and so for labour at any given level of money wage-rates and prices.

Even if we avert our gaze from the balance of payments, this implies a huge bag of problems which must be handled in a dynamic setting. The government's controls today (its expenditures, tax rates, interest rates, etc.) will affect the situation tomorrow. Thus the optimum level of today's controls will depend upon what is expected to happen tomorrow; but a large part of what happens tomorrow will depend upon tomorrow's governmental controls and these in turn should presumably also be set at their optimum levels. Thus the optimum level of today's controls will depend upon the optimum level of tomorrow's controls which will depend upon the optimum level of the controls of the day after tomorrow, and so on in a continuous series till Kingdom Come. This is the problem of optimum dynamic control. I will give three illustrative examples.

A government may have a policy of social services and benefits and of direct taxes and subsidies on income and wealth in order to affect the distribution of income and property. If so, one of the matters with which it will be concerned will be the distribution as between present and future generations. To what extent, for example, should it take steps to raise the current standard of living of the poorest members of the community if this necessarily implies some reduction in current savings and investment and thus in the rate of growth of the total resources which will be available to the next generation of citizens? The optimum present fiscal policy will be that which achieves the best available balance between this year's standards and next year's standards. But next year's standards will depend among other things upon next year's fiscal policy, which in turn will hopefully be set at its optimum level. Thus this year's optimum fiscal policy will depend, among other things, upon what is decided to be the optimum fiscal policy for next year, which in turn will depend upon what is decided to be the optimum fiscal policy for the year after next, and so on far into the future. Thus the choice of an optimum fiscal policy cannot be reduced simply to finding separately the optimum policy for each year as it comes along; it must take the form of finding an optimum plan for the development of fiscal policy over time.

Let us take a second example of a very different kind. Road transport provides an outstanding example of the need for governmental controls on grounds both of indivisibilities and of externalities. The road network itself is an indivisible whole and for that reason must be controlled by a public authority; and motor vehicles impose great external costs on the community of congestion, noise, poisonous fumes, and danger to life and limb, to say nothing of costs of doctors, hospitals, and undertakers. These are costs for which the individual user of the roads will pay nothing if the use of the road is free, unless there is an appropriate level of taxation on the use of motor vehicles.

What then should be the government's optimum policies of road-building and of motor-vehicle taxation? Clearly what it is best to do in the one sphere depends upon what is being done in the other. Thus there is no sense in reducing motor-vehicle taxation if its essential effect is merely to encourage more traffic on an unchanged network of already overcrowded and congested roads. Even more important for our present purpose is the fact that the optimum present road-building programme depends upon the future density of traffic which will depend upon current motor-vehicle taxation (since the present demand for new cars will affect the future stock of cars in existence) but also upon future road-building and upon future levels of motor-vehicle taxation. But if, as is to be hoped, these future programmes of road-building and motor-vehicle taxation will be at their optimum levels, we reach once more the conclusion that the present optimum levels of road-building and motor-vehicle taxation depend upon next year's optimum levels, which depend upon the following year's optimum levels, and so on. An optimum plan for road-building and motor-vehicle taxation stretching over the years would seem to be required.

A third example of optimal control planning can be taken from the widely recognised function of government today to control the total level of demand for goods and services in order to avoid inflations and deflations and to stabilise the economy. It may, for example, attempt to offset fluctuations in private demand by raising income tax and thus reducing tax-free spendable incomes when private demand threatened to be excessive and lowering income tax when private demand threatened to be deficient. But suppose that there are time-lags in the effect of changes in income tax on private expenditure; suppose, that is to say, that a rise in this year's rate of tax with a consequential reduction in this year's spendable income will cause only a moderate reduction in this year's spending but will cause a much larger reduction in next year's demand as consumers have time to adjust their expenditure habits. Suppose then that at the beginning of year 0 the government foresees a moderate deficiency in demand for year 0. If it attempts completely to offset this, then a large reduction in tax in year 0 may be required so that the moderate immediate effect of this large tax reduction in stimulating demand will restore the moderate deficiency of demand in year 0. But the delayed large effect in year 1 of the large tax reduction in year 0 might threaten to cause a large excess demand in year 1. To offset this a very large rise of tax in year 1 is required so that its moderate immediate effect will suffice to offset the threatened large inflation of year 1. But this very large rise in tax in year 1 may cause the threat of a very large deficiency of demand in year 2, which could be offset only by the moderate immediate effect of a very, very large reduction of tax in year 2.

Clearly ever-increasing swings in tax rates of this kind must be avoided. This means, of course, that this year's tax rates must be planned with an eye to the needs of next year, which will depend among other things upon the level of tax planned for next year, which level must be planned with an eye to the needs of the year after next, and so on into the future.

The need for governmental control plans of this kind raises many extremely important and difficult problems of theory and of application. I can do no more on this occasion than to mention one or two of them.

In the first place, all these governmental control plans must take account of uncertainties. Each of them should ideally consist of a set of sub-plans, one for each environmental path; each should be continually revised; and each should be used only to help to determine the best use of today's controls. Thus in the case of the distribution of income and wealth, the needs of future generations will depend upon future uncertain rates of growth of the population itself. Similarly, the future road requirements will depend upon future uncertain developments affecting the rates of growth in the real demands for transport and upon future uncertainties about the technical development of alternative forms of transport. Finally, the overall level of demand in the future will be subject to all sorts of environmental uncertainties which must be considered in drawing up its control plans. The treatment of uncertainty in governmental control planning raises problems very similar to those which I have discussed at length in connection with indicative planning.

In particular it is clear that governmental control plans cannot possibly be formulated so as to cover all possible environmental developments. This means that the government must cope with a lot of residual uncertainty. Like those who plan fixed capital investments in the private sector, it also in its own plans for fixed capital investments in the public sector must put an additional emphasis upon general flexibility of use. But there is, I think, one rather special implication for governmental control planning. All sorts of unexpected environmental events may directly or indirectly cause fluctuations in the total demand for goods and thus threaten to put into operation a cumulative positive-feedback cycle of inflation or of deflation and unemployment. Just as private citizens must carry cash to meet many uncalculated contingencies, so the Government must be ready with what may be called a stabilisation programme, namely with some set of fiscal and/or monetary control weapons with which it can rapidly react so as to stimulate total demand when an unexpected decline occurs and *vice versa*. A calculated governmental control plan is needed to shape the general structure of governmental policies over the coming years; in addition to this a stabilisation programme for quick reaction to uncalculated instabilities is needed. The two types of control plans or programmes are separate, but complementary, entities.

A second basic problem in governmental control planning is due to the fact that it is impossible to separate into unconnected water-tight apartments the use of controls by the government for different purposes such as (i) affecting the distribution of income and property, (ii) coping with indivisibilites and externalities, and (iii) stabilising total demand. The controls which are employed primarily for the one purpose will in almost all cases have some effect upon the other purposes. Thus, to take only one example, changes in tax designed primarily to help to stabilise total demand will almost certainly have some significant effects upon the distribution of income and perhaps also upon the balance between expenditure on road-building and expenditure upon vehicles to use the roads. And yet a modern government is such a big affair that there must be much decentralisation of planning among different departments and agencies of government. One of the most important topics for further economic investigation is the theory and practice of moulding these various governmental control plans into a single coherent whole.

This raises a third basic problem in governmental control planning. It is not just a question of considering how one governmental agency can best communicate with another and on what principles one governmental plan should react on another in its formation and application. There lies behind it all a basic problem in political philosophy. In the end a single government has to decide, for example, what the rate of income tax and the levels of governmental expenditures shall be. This may affect the distribution of income and wealth, the stabilisation of the economy – that is to say the level of total employment and the rate of price inflation – and many of the various departmental plans for roads, defence, schools, etc. The narrowly defined objectives of the various departmental plans may well conflict. How does the government judge how much extra employment is worth in extra price inflation, how much it is worth in a given change in distribution, how much education is worth giving up for how much extra in the battle against pollution, and so on? Can the government be thought of as having a single social welfare function (the value of which gives due and balanced weight to all the different objectives in the various departmental plans) and of setting its controls (always with a view to the many various possible future environmental paths) at levels which will maximise total future expected social welfare? Moreover, what is the legitimate use which, in a democratic society, one government may make of its own social welfare function? Should it rigidly commit resources to uses which will satisfy its own ideas about future social welfare without leaving any flexibility for them to be turned to the satisfaction of alternative objectives favoured by the opposition party which may well in turn become the government – presumably because of some change of social values among the electorate itself?

Probably we must anyhow be satisfied with something a good deal less tidy than a formal social welfare function. In any case it is not my intention to discuss in these lectures the problems involved in the formulation of optimal governmental control plans, nor to consider how far it is practicable to go in this ideal direction. I shall simply assume, as is in fact the case, that on whatever principles they may construct them, the governmental authorities do have programmes for future expenditures on various public goods and do have views about what is likely to have to be the future course of tax rates, subsidies, interest rates, etc., in order to keep the economy in balance and to attain the government's various social objectives; and in formulating these programmes the governmental authorities must, of course, have had in mind some ideas about the ways in which the private sector of the economy would develop along the various environmental paths, given the levels of the governmental controls themselves. I shall give this package of governmental programmes and policies, together with the forecasts of the private sector on which it is based, the resounding title of the national control plan.

The purpose of such a national control plan is different from that of a national indicative plan. It is not designed to enable private decision-makers to make better-informed or more consistent decisions. It is designed to enable the authorities to set their own controls at levels which will more effectively attain the social objectives of the politicians. But while the two sorts of plans are conceptually distinct, there are, of course, certain very close connections between them.

I have already stated that a government cannot formulate a sensible control plan without taking into account how the private sector of the economy is likely to develop on various assumptions about the levels of its own controls; and this means that a control plan cannot be formulated without there being some governmental forecast of the future development of the economy derived either from a national indicative plan or else from a governmental econometric model of the economy.

On the other hand – and this is the relationship with which I am particularly concerned in these lectures – it is impossible logically to formulate a national indicative plan without there being something in the nature of a governmental control plan and without this control plan being in large measure revealed to the public.

It is obvious that governmental expenditure programmes, as well as private demands, must be considered by the indicative planners in estimating future market excess demands and supplies. It is equally true that private decision-makers in announcing their future plans and intentions to the indicative planners must make assumptions about future levels of tax rates, subsidies, interest rates, etc.; and to get the most rational and consistent plans would involve the revelation to the private sector of the government's expectations about the future course of those controls.

An indicative plan is, as we have seen, a process whereby a number of decision-makers can inform each other about their expectations of market conditions and about their own plans, so that their plans and market expectations can be made consistent. In fact the government can be regarded simply as one decision-maker – albeit, of course, an immensely important one – whose expectations and plans must be put, like everyone else's, into the pool for the formation of a consistent indicative plan. The government must reveal its secret hopes and fears.

It is, of course, possible to reveal such secrets and in this way to marry the ideas of an indicative plan and of a control plan and I will call the offspring of this marriage a national indicative-control plan. Let us consider what the child would look like and whether it would be a healthy creature.

In order to bring out some of the basic problems involved let me caricature the formulation of a national indicative-control plan in the same way in which I previously caricatured the formulation of a national indicative plan. I leave it to you to make all the necessary modifications for a practical procedure. The government summons to a meeting in the Albert Hall all the citizens in the country. Each citizen is then presented with a list of every price for every good and service, and also a list of every tax rate and every rate of subsidy, and of every rate of interest for every day in the future. Each citizen then writes down how much of everything he or she would plan to buy or to sell at every future date if these prices and controls were operative. There is then a prolonged coffee break. It is necessary as before for the bureaucrats to add up the supplies and demands of each good or service for each future day including any future governmental demands in order to estimate the planned excesses of demand or supply. But now it is not sufficient for the planners simply to adjust upwards or downwards the future price of any good for which there is an excess demand or supply and to return to the meeting with a new price list for a second round of estimations. The planners can now attempt to remove an excess demand either by raising the price or by raising a tax or by reducing a public expenditure. In other words, at each round of indicative estimation the planners must present a future schedule of control levels as well as a future schedule of prices; and they must decide which type of adjustment they will suggest to the assembled citizens in the light of an answer to the question which type of adjustment will help most to attain the ultimate economic and social goals of the government. And this, of course, brings us back to all those problems involved in governmental optimal control planning to which I have already referred.

Is this process of national indicative-control planning healthy or not? The arguments in its favour are obvious, I think, and I will not dwell on them. Indeed the whole purpose of my discussion of planning has been to show how control planning may be useful for a good choice of today's controls and how indicative planning may help to remove market uncertainties due to the absence of forward markets. Since one cannot have a meaningful indicative plan without taking into account the future level of taxes and other controls, the case for an indicative-control plan is apparent.

But there are important snags which I will point out under three heads.

First, I have already pointed out in my earlier remarks about a purely indicative plan that the formal organisation of such a plan by a governmental authority will lead to the danger that private producers in order to avoid losses due to the revelation of trade secrets may either supply misleading and biased information to the planners or will be encouraged to form collusive monopolistic groups in which trade secrets can be shared, but which may have other obvious dangers to the public interest. When one allows for the fact that the indicative-control plan will involve and affect the government's control strategy these dangers are much increased. In an indicative-control plan the rate of tax or subsidy which will be imposed on a given activity may well depend upon the assessment by the governmental authorities, from information gathered in conversations with the private entrepreneurs concerned, of its effect on the relevant activity. Clearly there may be a strong incentive for the private entrepreneurs concerned to present a united front in persuading the authorities concerned that a low tax or a high subsidy is required to obtain a socially desirable result. The processes of an indicative-control plan may greatly encourage such collusive action.

The second set of problems arises from the possible political effects of the revelation of the probable future level of the controls by the authorities concerned. This might cause adverse inflexibilities of policy. The revelation of future budgetary plans could readily be interpreted as having implied certain moral commitments by the government to certain policies, whereas, as I have already argued, the purpose of the forecasts of future controls should be only a means for deciding upon the best level of today's controls. As the environment changes so control plans must be flexibly revised; and the publication of control plans might endanger this flexibility. This danger of political inflexibility will be the smaller, the greater the number of representative environmental time paths covered by the plan. For when there is more than one such time path, all commitments become conditional in form from the very outset; and a number of alternative paths for the controls will be stated in the plan itself.

Finally, there are serious speculative problems. These are particularly marked in the case of controls whose levels cannot be, or by convention are not, changed except at rather infrequent intervals and then by appreciable steps. This is the basic reason for budget secrecy. With a Budget coming in April the Chancellor of the Exchequer does not get up in the House of Commons in October and say that as at present advised he thinks that the purchase tax on cars will have to be raised by 50% in six months' time in April. Or rather he does not do so unless for economic control reasons he wishes to cause a six months' buying spree. But this would be just the sort of statement which would in effect be made if there were a completely open marriage between a control plan and an indicative plan. If this course were really adopted, it would be necessary to build in to the behavioural relationships of the econometric model some very important speculative parameters. Thus the demand for cars would have to be made dependent upon the future course of the purchase tax on cars as predicted in the control plan itself. It is not difficult to see how greatly this would complicate the problem of control. The speculative rather than the currently operative effect of controls might become of paramount importance.

If these difficulties in a complete marriage between indicative and control plans are considered decisive, then one is left with two possibilities. It may be wise to go to the other extreme, to keep the control plans as strict state secrets, and on the lines already mentioned to allow indicative planning to remain an iterative unorganised and informal conversation between academic research institutes, financial journalists, business concerns, etc., all guessing what the future rates of tax may be. On the other hand, it may be possible to compromise, and for purposes of indicative planning to reveal from the government's control plan some general indications of probable directions of the controls without specific information about those particular controls where speculative effects would be important. But I fear that I have no precise solution to recommend. I have come to that elderly stage of life in which I can only see the difficulties of every course of action. I leave the choice to my youngers and betters.

I would, however, like to add one concluding remark. I realise that these lectures have consisted in large measure in pointing out the many theoretical and practical snags and difficulties in any form of indicative planning. But I do not intend thereby to leave a negative impression. In the modern world the government properly undertakes many far reaching economic activities in dealing with the distribution of income and wealth, with external economies and diseconomies, with structural indivisibilities, and with the general stabilisation of the economy; and for all these purposes it should, indeed it must, plan ahead. Similarly private economic agents must properly plan their future activities with various degrees of sophistication ranging from the giant modern industrial corporation to the individual housewife; and with the modern specificity, rigidity, and durability of much large-scale equipment such planning is increasingly important. My only concern in these lectures is how such plans can best be organised and co-ordinated, particularly in view of the increasing uncertainties that surround human activities. Inevitable environmental uncertainties become more marked as the pace of technological development quickens; but this makes it all the more important to do what one can to lessen market uncertainties which are in principle avoidable. Future uncertainties can undoubtedly be reduced by some forms of swapping of information between economic agents about how they will react in the future to different situations. This swapping cannot in fact be done through a comprehensive set of forward markets; and there are great difficulties in finding a consciously planned and institutionalised alternative. My sole purpose in exploring these difficulties is to understand them so that we can devise the formal or informal planning arrangements which are most likely to overcome them.

# 10

# The Theory of Labour-Managed Firms and of Profit Sharing[1]

*From* The Economic Journal, *vol. 82 (March 1972 Supplement: Special Issue in honour of E. A. G. Robinson), pp. 402–428.*

I

One important problem in industrial economics which deserves more attention from economic theorists than it has received in the past is the effects of different forms of industrial organisation upon economic efficiency. To take one such question, what would happen if workers hired capital instead of capitalist entrepreneurs hiring workers? Professor J. Vanek has recently made an important contribution to this subject. Building on the work of two other economists,[2] he has produced a full-scale textbook on the theory of labour-managed economies.[3] In this book he investigates the properties of a system in which workers get together and form collectives or partnerships to run firms; they hire capital and purchase other inputs and they sell the products of the firm at the best prices they can obtain in the markets for inputs and outputs; they themselves bear the risk of any unexpected gain or loss and distribute the resulting surplus among themselves, all workers of any one given grade or skill receiving an equal share of the surplus; their basic objective is assumed to be to maximise the return per worker. For shorthand we will in what follows refer to this as the Co-operative system.

Professor Vanek contrasts the micro- and macro-results of such a system with those of the textbook capitalist model in which an entrepreneur hires all the inputs (including labour) and sells all the outputs of a firm at market prices, bears the risk and runs the firm in such a way as to maximise the total surplus of revenues from the sale of outputs over costs

[1] The author would like to thank Professors A. B. Atkinson, E. H. Phelps Brown and R. C. O. Matthews for many helpful comments in the preparation of this article.
[2] Benjamin Ward, 'The Firm in Illyria: Market Syndicalism', *American Economic Review*, vol. 48 (September 1958), pp. 566–89; Benjamin Ward, *The Socialist Economy* (New York: Random House, 1967); Evsey D. Domar, 'The Soviet Collective Farm as a Producer Cooperative', *American Economic Review*, vol. 56 (September 1966), pp. 734–57.
[3] Jaroslav Vanek, *The General Theory of Labor-Managed Market Economies* (Ithaca, NY: Cornell University Press, 1970).

of the purchase of inputs. For ease of reference I shall call this the Entrepreneurial system.

Many essential features of the contrast between the two systems are not basically affected by the question whether the capital resources of the community are privately owned or are socialised and owned by the state. In the case of a co-operative the workers may be hiring their capital resources either in a competitive capital market fed by private savings or else from a central governmental organisation which lends out the state's capital resources at rentals which will clear the market. The contrasting features of the Entrepreneurial system are equally well portrayed by a system in which the managers of socialised plants are told to hire inputs and sell outputs at given prices, the managers operating so as to maximise the total surplus of the plant and the state setting the prices so as to clear the markets.

II

Let us start then with an enumeration of what appear to us to be the five main differences which Professor Vanek notes between the two systems.

### Difference (1):   Incentives

A worker hired at a given hourly wage in an entrepreneurial firm will have to observe the minimum standard of work and effort in order to keep his job; but he will have no immediate personal financial motive and, particularly in the case of a large concern, may well have little or no social participatory motivation to behave in a way which will promote the profitability of the enterprise. He may, of course, take a pride in his work; and he may well wish to stand well with his employer in order to achieve security and promotion in his job. But any extra profit due to his extra effort will in the first place accrue to the entrepreneur. It is difficult and in many cases impossible to overcome this problem by a system of piece-rate wages; and in any case the problem is not one simply of incentives to work harder and to produce more.

Let us go to the other extreme and consider a one-man co-operative, i.e. a single self-employed worker who hires his equipment. He can balance money income against leisure and other amenities by pleasing himself over hours of work, holidays, the pace and concentration of work, tea-breaks or the choice of equipment and methods of work which will make his work more pleasant at the cost of profitability. Any innovative idea which he has, he can apply at once and reap the whole benefit himself. And so on over a whole range of qualities and conditions of his working life.

The trouble is, of course, that there are economies of scale which mean that a one-man firm must normally be ruled out. In an $n$-man co-operative the individual worker who shares the profit with his fellows will still get some direct benefit from any additional profit due to his own effort; but it will be only $1/n$ th of the result of his own efforts. If to reap the technical advantages of scale *n* must be large, then the direct advantage in financial incentives of the co-operative over the entrepreneurial firm may be small. But even in this case the sense of participation may be greater and thus provide a stronger social motivation to do the best for the firm as a whole, i.e. for the whole partnership of fellow workers.

This last consideration takes one out of the realms of strict economic analysis into those of the industrial and social psychologists and sociologists; and it must be left to them to consider what is perhaps in fact the decisive question, namely whether or not there would be difficulties of disciplined administration in a self-governing co-operative which would offset in part or whole the improved incentives which it would enjoy. One conclusion, however, may be reached. The most efficient scale for a co-operative is likely to be smaller than for an entrepreneurial firm; for in the case of the former but not of the latter a reduction in the number of workers increases the direct economic incentives for efficiency of the individual worker.

So much for *difference (1)*. If we abstract from this difference in incentives and also from any differences due to the effects of risks, it can be shown that both the Co-operative and the Entrepreneurial systems will lead to the same Pareto-optimal equilibrium situations in the long run, provided that there is perfect mobility of factors, including perfectly free and costless entry and exit of new firms in any industry and that there is perfect competition in the sense that no individual economic agent can by his own decisions affect appreciably any market price. Differences become apparent, however, as soon as we (i) consider the short run, (ii) modify the assumption of free and costless entry of firms, or (iii) allow for monopolistic conditions. We will consider each of these three cases below under *differences (2), (3) and (4)* respectively. But before we do so, we must consider the long-run Pareto-optimal outcome of the two systems.

Let us do this first by considering a firm in an industry in which there are only two inputs – a homogeneous worker $(L)$ who works a given number of hours at a given intensity, and a fixed capital good $(K)$, these two factors producing an output $(X)$ with a production function $X = X(L, K)$ in which there is some substitutability between $L$ and $K$.[4] Let $P_x$ be the price of a unit of $X$ and $W$ the market wage-rate of labour in an entrepreneurial firm. If the price of a machine (a unit of $K$) is $P_k$ and if $i$ is

---

[4] The firm's production function may be such as to result, with given prices of the two inputs, in either a $U$-shaped or an $L$-shaped long-run cost curve:

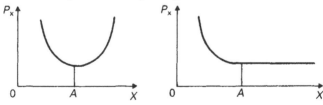

In order to rule out the one-man firm, the cost per unit must at first fall because of economies of large-scale production, but in order that perfect competition should be possible the total demand for the industry's output must be many times the amount $0A$ which, for an individual firm, is sufficient to lead to minimum cost per unit.

| | Entre-preneurial 2 | Co-operative 3 | Inegalitarian Co-operative 4 | Joint-Stock 5 | Inegalitarian Joint-Stock 6 | Inegalitarian Joint-Stock Co-operative 7 |
|---|---|---|---|---|---|---|
| Increase or Decrease $K$ according as $P_x \dfrac{\partial X}{\partial K} \gtrless$ | $iP_k$ | $iP_k$ | $iP_k$ | $\dfrac{P_x X - WL}{K}$ | $rP_k$ | $rP_k$ |
| Increase or Decrease $L$ according as $P_x \dfrac{\partial X}{\partial L} \gtrless$ | $W$ | $\dfrac{P_x X - iP_k K}{L}$ | $E_0$ | $W$ | $W$ | $E_0$ |

the market rate of interest, then $iP_k$ is the rental paid for the hire of a machine. In an entrepreneurial firm more (or less) labour will be hired if the value of the marginal product of labour $(P_x(\partial X/\partial L))$ is greater (less) than the wage-rate of labour $(W)$; and more (or less) machinery will be hired if the value of the marginal product of a machine $(P_x(\partial X/\partial K))$ is greater (less) than the rental payable for a machine $(iP_k)$. These relationships are shown in columns 1 and 2 of the Table on p. 161.

In a co-operative, machinery is hired in the same way as in an entrepreneurial firm and the same rule is, therefore, relevant. Machinery will be hired up to the point at which the value of its marginal product is equal to its rental. But the considerations governing the size of the labour force are different. If one more partner is accepted into a co-operative, he will add to the revenue of the co-operative an amount equal to the value of his marginal product $(P_x(\partial X/\partial L))$; in a co-operative he will receive the same share of the total surplus as do all the other partners $((P_x X - iP_k K)/L)$; if, therefore, $P_x(\partial X/\partial L) > (P_x X - iP_k K)/L$, he will add to the surplus of the co-operative something more than the existing surplus per head, so that the surplus per head can be raised for all the partners. Thus the existing partners will wish to build up the partnership until the value of the marginal product of labour is equal to the average earnings per worker. These relationships are shown for the co-operative in column 3 of the Table.

It is now easy to see why both systems lead to the same (i) long-run, (ii) free-entry-and-exit, and (iii) perfect-competition solution. As far as $K$ is concerned, in both cases it is attracted from points where the value of its marginal product is low to points where it is high by a competitive process in which either the entrepreneurial manager is attempting to maximise the surplus for the entrepreneur's or state's pocket or else the co-operative partners are attempting to maximise the surplus for distribution between them. As far as $L$ is concerned, in the entrepreneurial firm the same competitive process will attract it to the uses in which the value of its marginal product is highest. In the co-operative the process is different, but the final result the same. First, in each co-operative $L$ will be attracted until the value of its marginal product is equal to the average earnings of the existing workers in that firm. Second, if as a result of this the average earnings are higher in one industry than another workers will be attracted from co-operatives in the industry of low earnings to set up new co-operatives in the industry of high earnings; the output of the high-earning product will rise and its price will fall, until earnings, and so the value of marginal products of labour, are equalised in all industries.

### Difference (2):   Short-Run Adjustment

The short-run process of adjustment is, however, very different. Let us suppose that the capital is fixed in amount in each firm in the short run, but that the number of workers is variable. Suppose that we start in a full equilibrium and that then the demand price for the particular product $X$ rises, while all other demand prices remain unchanged. In the entrepreneurial system labour will be attracted into the $X$-industry, since the value of the marginal product of $L$ is now higher in the production of $X$; and this is a Pareto-optimal process of adjustment, since $L$ can be shifted from its low-valued to its high-valued uses, even though $K$ is *ex hypothesi* not shiftable immediately from its low-valued to its high-valued uses.

But the short-run effect in the Co-operative system will be to reduce, not to increase, the levels of employment and output which will maximise earnings per head in the $X$-industry firms. A rise in the selling price of $X$ will, of course, in itself raise both the value of the marginal product of labour and the average earnings per head in the $X$-industry firms; but it will raise the value of the marginal product of labour less than the average earnings[5] and it will thus mean that the average earnings could be still further raised if one worker was dismissed. The value of the reduction in the firm's output would be less than the amount paid by the co-operative to the dismissed worker; and the remaining partners would gain by his dismissal.

This relationship is shown in Figure 1.

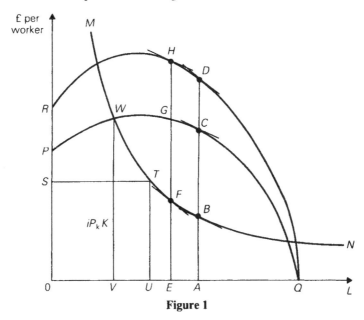

**Figure 1**

Measure the number of workers on the horizontal axis and money payments per worker on the vertical axis. Draw a rectangular hyperbola $MN$ such that the rectangle $STU0$ has a constant value of $iP_kK$, the total rental payable for the hire of $K$. Then $TU$ measures $iP_kK/L$ or the burden of debt payment per worker when the number of workers is $0U$. Draw a curve $PQ$ such that its height measures $P_xX/L$ or the total value of

---

[5] Suppose $P_x = £1$, $\partial X/\partial L = 1$, $X = 100$, $iP_kK = £50$, and $L = 50$.
Then $P_x(\partial X/\partial L) = £1$ and $(P_xX - iP_kK)/L = (£100 - £50)/50 = £1$.
If $P_x$ rises to £1·1, $P_x(\partial X/\partial L)$ rises to £1·1; but $(P_xX - iP_kK)/L$ rises to $(£110 - £50)/50 = £1·2$.

receipts per worker, i.e. output per head multiplied by the price of output. Net earnings per head are then the excess of the height of the curve $PQ$ over the height of the curve $MN$ (i.e. $(P_x X / L) - (iP_k K / L)$). These earnings are maximised at $CB$, where the slope of the curve $PQ$ is the same as that of the curve $MN$. The optimum number of worker-partners is thus $0A$.

Suppose now that $P_x$ rises by 10%, then the curve $PQ$ is replaced by the curve $RQ$ which is 10% higher than the curve $PQ$ at every value of $L$. Consider now a volume of labour $0E$ which is somewhat less than $0A$. Since $HG = 10\%$ of $GE$ and $DC = 10\%$ of $CA$ and since $GE > CA$, $HG$ must be $> DC$. In other words the slope of $RQ$ at $D$ is steeper than the slope of $PQ$ at $C$ which is equal to the slope of $MN$ at $B$. Since the slope of $RQ$ is greater than the slope of $MN$ with employment at $0A$, it will be possible by reducing the number of workers to $0E$ (where the slope of $RQ$ at $H$ is equal to the slope of $MN$ at $F$) to raise average earnings. The rise in $P_x$ will itself raise earnings ($DB > CB$); but these can be raised still more if the number of workers is reduced ($HF > DB$).

The common sense of this result can easily be seen in the following way. (1) With a fixed debt interest it is to the interest of the worker-partners to have a large partnership so that debt per head may be small. (2) With decreasing returns to labour applied to a given amount of capital it is desirable to have a small partnership so that the value of output per head may be high. A rise in the selling price of the product or a fall in the rental of capital will increase the importance of influence (2) relatively to influence (1) and will, therefore, work in the direction of a smaller partnership.[6]

[6] As a *curiosum* it may be noted that if the production function were of a Cobb–Douglas variety with $X = K^a L^{1-a}$, then the backward-sloping short-run supply curve of $X$ in terms of its price $P_x$ would take the form of a rectangular hyperbola. In a co-operative $L$ is always adjusted until the earnings of labour are equal to the value of their marginal product; with constant returns to scale this means that what is left over (namely $iP_k K$) will be just sufficient to pay to each unit of capital the value of its marginal product; and with a Cobb-Douglas function capital will in such an equilibrium always be paid a constant proportion $a$ of the value of the output; thus the equation $iP_k K = \alpha P_x X$ with $iP_k K$ as well as $\alpha$ constant in the short run provides the short-run supply curve for $X$, as depicted in Figure 2.

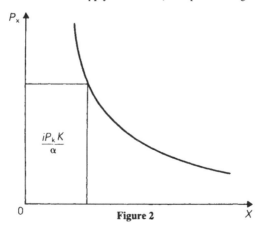

Figure 2

Professor Vanek seems to assume tacitly in most of his analysis that the rules of a co-operative would somehow permit the dismissal of a worker if it were to the advantage of the remaining workers, even if it were to the detriment of the dismissed worker.[7] In this case the short-run supply curve of $X$ would be backward-sloping; and this would be highly perverse and inefficient. Pareto-optimality requires that in the short run the variable factor $L$ should be attracted to, not pushed away from, its more highly valued uses.

At a later stage (Section V below) we will return to the question whether a rule which allowed the dismissal of a partner against his will is appropriate. But even if such dismissals are not allowed, there would be no mechanism inducing the existing partners to take the positive step of admitting more partners when the selling price of their product went up and when, in consequence, it would pay each existing partner to reduce rather than to increase the size of the partnership. The short-run supply curve of a co-operative would at least be highly inelastic – certainly less elastic than the Pareto-optimal entrepreneurial short-run supply curve.

The rather startling result that a rise in the selling price of a co-operative's product will in the short run lead to a reduction in the amount produced and a reduction in the volume of employment rests upon the assumption that the firm employs only one variable input, namely $L$, to produce only one product, namely $X$. But, as Professor Vanek points out, if we allow for the fact that the firm may well produce more than one product (e.g. products $X$ and $Y$) and may employ not only labour, $L$, but also a raw material, $M$, as a factor which is variable in the short run, these results may need to be modified.

The case of a multi-product firm is easy to understand. If the price of $X$ goes up, the co-operative may well shift from the production of the now relatively unprofitable $Y$ on to the now relatively profitable $X$. If $X$ and $Y$ are very easy substitutes in the firm's production programme, a rise in the price of $X$ may thus well lead to an increase in the output of $X$ even though, for the reasons already discussed at length, the co-operative were to reduce the absolute level of its employment and total production.

The case of a co-operative which uses inputs of materials as well as of labour needs a little more explanation. When the price of its output $X$ goes up, the co-operative which buys its material $M$ in the market will, just like an entrepreneurial firm, find that the cost-price of $M$ is now less than the value of the marginal product of $M$. For example, when the selling price of cars goes up, a firm assembling cars, whether it be a co-operative or an entrepreneurial firm, will wish to purchase more components to assemble because the profit margin on each assembled set

---

[7] Professor B. Ward makes the assumption explicitly when he writes (*The Socialist Economy*, p. 186, footnote 5), 'Conflicts might arise in case the criterion by the workers' council would lead to layoffs. But as long as these amounted to less than half the work force (and less than half of the members of the workers' council) a majority decision would still follow the criterion.'

Professor Joan Robinson very pertinently queries this assumption ('The Soviet Collective Farm as a Producer Cooperative: Comment', *American Economic Review*, vol. 57 (March 1967), pp. 222–3).

of components has risen. Suppose now (1) that the marginal product of $M$ does not fall at all rapidly as more $X$ is produced (that is to say, with the existing capital equipment $K$ a greater throughput on the assembly line is fairly readily possible); and suppose further (2) that labour $L$ and materials $M$ are rather highly complementary (that is to say, it is difficult to reduce the labour per car assembled). Then the possibility of extra profit because of the increased margin between the cost of $M$ and the selling price of $X$ may be more important in leading to an increased need for labour than the factors which we have previously examined can be in leading to a contraction in the labour force.

For these reasons with firms with many outputs and with many variable inputs the extreme paradoxical results of an increased selling price leading to reduced employment and output may disappear. But this in no way modifies what is the result of major importance which our previous analysis revealed. If the selling price of something produced by a co-operative does go up, clearly the workers in that firm can improve their average earnings whether this is accompanied by a rise or by a fall in output or in employment. Moreover, the new level of employment which will maximise earnings per head will always be that which equates the value of the marginal product of labour to its average earnings. This bit of our previous analysis is in no way modified; one can always raise earnings per head by taking on one more worker so long as what he adds net to total revenue is greater than the existing level of earnings per head. Thus in the new equilibrium situation the average earnings and so the value of the marginal product of labour in the firm in question will be higher than before and will thus be higher than it is in the other outside occupations whose situation has not been improved. The co-operative, unlike the entrepreneurial firm, will, therefore, fail in the short run to attract the variable factor $L$ from points in which the value of its marginal product is low to points where it is high. This is the essential point.

### *Difference (3): The Importance of Free Entry*

In the Co-operative system this situation is ultimately restored only by the free entry of new firms into any industry which has become exceptionally lucrative as a result of a rise in its selling prices. It is thus clear that the competitive pressures of free entry play a much more important role in a Co-operative than they do in an Entrepreneurial system. This can be illustrated in the following way. Consider a competitive industry with a large number of firms producing at constant returns to scale, i.e. firms with $L$-shaped cost curves of the kind shown in the footnote on page 160 above, each producing an output appreciably greater than $0A$. $P_x$ then rises. In an Entrepreneurial system firms take on more labour until the value of the marginal product of labour ($P_x(\partial X/\partial L)$) has fallen again to the ruling wage-rate ($W$) partly as a result of the reduction in the marginal physical product of labour ($\partial X/\partial L$) as more $L$ is applied to the fixed amount of $K$ and partly as a result of the reduction in $P_x$ as more $X$ is produced. The value of the marginal product of capital ($P_x(\partial X/\partial K)$) will now be greater than the ruling rental ($iP_k$) because $P_x$ will still be somewhat greater than before and the physical marginal product of capital $(\partial X/\partial K)$ will also have been raised because more $L$ is now applied to the given amount of $K$. The entrepreneurial firm will, therefore, invest in more $K$. The process will go on until $P_x$ has fallen to its initial level (since the long-run cost curve is horizontal) and an increased $X$ is produced by the use of more $K$ and more $L$, both $K$ and $L$ being increased in the same proportion as $X$. The process does not in this case require the entry of any new firms, though new firms may come in.

In the co-operative the first effect of the rise in $P_x$ is to reduce $L$ and $X$. This will go on until the marginal product of labour is so raised (as a result of the reduced application of $L$ to the given amount of $K$) that the value of the marginal product of labour $(P_x(\partial X/\partial L))$ has been raised once more as high as the amount of net average earnings per worker $((P_xX - iP_kK)/L)$.[8] If and when a new equilibrium is reached, the earnings of workers will be equal to the value of their marginal products. With constant returns to scale what is then 'left over' as a return to capital (namely, $iP_kK$) will be just sufficient to pay to each unit of capital the value of marginal product $(P_x(\partial X/\partial K)K)$. The reduction in the amount of $L$ will have reduced the marginal product of $K$ until $P_x(\partial X/\partial K)$, which had been raised above $iP_k$ by the rise in $P_x$, is once more reduced to equality with $iP_k$ as a result of the fall in $\partial X/\partial K$.[9] The situation will then be that the existing co-operatives are producing less $X$ with the same amount of $K$ and with less $L$ in circumstances in which (i) the value of the marginal product of labour is equal to the average earnings in the firms concerned but is greater than the value of the marginal product and the earnings of labour in other industries, and (ii) the value of the marginal product of capital is equal to the rental of capital, so that the existing firms have no incentive to invest in more capital. This is a Pareto non-optimal situation; restoration of the situation rests wholly upon the possibility of the free entry of new firms; and it should be emphasised that free entry involves workers who are unemployed as a result of the contraction of the firms in the $X$-industry getting together with workers in other industries who are earning less than the $X$-industry workers, and setting up new firms in the $X$-industry. The costs and institutional problems involved in such company promotion are not analysed in Professor Vanek's book.

## *Difference (4):   Monopolistic Behaviour*

A closely related difference is that in any given monopolistic conditions the co-operative will always be more restrictive than the corresponding entrepreneurial firm. The reason for this can be seen in the following way. Let us start with an entrepreneurial firm making a positive monopoly profit of $M = P_xX - iP_kK - WL$. If this firm has maximised its monopoly

---

[8] We must assume that the demand curve for $X$ is sufficiently price-elastic. If it were very inelastic, $P_x$ might rise so quickly as the output $X$ was reduced that, with a backward-sloping supply curve of $X$, the excess demand was not eliminated.

[9] $P_x(\partial X/\partial L) = (P_xX - iP_kK)/L$ as a result of the adjustment in $L$. Since with constant returns to scale $P_xX = P_xL(\partial X/\partial L) + P_xK(\partial X/\partial K)$, it follows that $P_x(\partial X/\partial K) = iP_kK$.

profit it will be in a position in which a small reduction in $L$ will cause no change in $M$. It follows that a small reduction in $L$ will cause a rise in $M/L$. But $M/L = (P_xX - iP_kK)/L - W$. With $W$ constant, it follows that a small reduction in $L$ will cause a rise in $(P_xX - iP_kK)/L$, *i.e.* in the average earnings of $L$ in a corresponding co-operative. In other words in any given monopolistic situation the co-operative will produce less than the corresponding entrepreneurial firm.

A particular example of this tendency may be of interest. Consider a case of a monopolistic entrepreneurial concern with an $L$-shaped cost curve facing a big demand, so that, as illustrated in Figure 3, it produces on the constant-cost part of its cost curve.

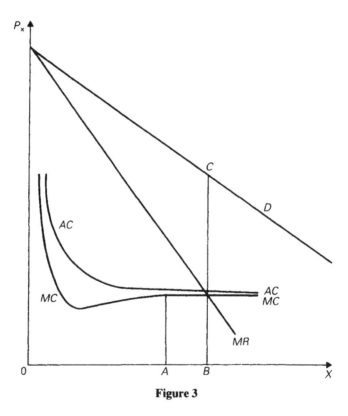

**Figure 3**

The entrepreneurial firm produces $0B$ where the marginal cost curve cuts the marginal revenue curve and sells the output at the price $BC$.

The co-operative will, however, always produce less than $0A$ (the output which is sufficient to make the average cost curve virtually horizontal), for the following reason. If there are constant returns to scale a 10% reduction in $L$ and $K$ would reduce $X$ by 10%. But if $P_x$ and $iP_k$ were both constant, this 10% reduction in $L$, $K$ and $X$ would leave $(P_xX - iP_kK)/L$ unchanged. But if as a result of the monopolistic situation $P_x$ goes up when $x$ is reduced by 10%, then $(P_xX - iP_kK)/L$ rises when $L$, $K$

and $X$ are all reduced by 10%. In other words, in order to maximise surplus per unit of $L$, there will always in monopolistic situations be an incentive for a co-operative to reduce output so long as there are constant returns to scale. Output will be reduced below $0A$, until the tendency for real costs per unit to rise as output is reduced offsets the tendency for a rise in the selling price of $X$ to raise income per unit of factor inputs.

Professor Vanek concludes from this analysis that in conditions of monopolistic competition each co-operative will tend to be smaller than the corresponding entrepreneurial firm; but, he argues, in the Co-operative economy there will be more competing firms than in the Entrepreneurial economy. This argument rests on the assumption that there will be full employment in the Co-operative economy or, more precisely, that there will not be more unemployment in the Co-operative economy than in the Entrepreneurial economy. If there were the same number of firms but each firm were smaller then there would be more unemployment in the Co-operative economy. If these unemployed got together and set up new firms, then there would be more, but smaller, firms in the Co-operative economy.[10] This in Professor Vanek's view justifies the view that in a very real, and desirable, sense the Co-operative economy will be more competitive than the Entrepreneurial economy. This is a somewhat paradoxical, but to the present reviewer a convincing conclusion.[11]

## *Difference (5): Macro-Economic Effects*

As a result of the great difference in the short-run behaviour of firms (see *difference (2)* above), the problems of macro-economic control of inflations and deflations of price and employment would be strikingly different. A fluctuation in the total money demand for goods as a whole would cause much greater fluctuations in price in the Co-operative than in the Entrepreneurial economy. In an Entrepreneurial economy an increase in total money expenditure engineered through monetary or fiscal policy may lead to some increase in prices, but if there is any considerable initial volume of unemployment it will lead also and importantly to increased employment and output. In a Co-operative economy it will not give any incentive to existing firms to increase output and may indeed, for the reasons discussed in connection with *difference*

[10] This conclusion is reinforced by the argument (see pp. 159–60 above) that because of the effect on incentives the most efficient size of the firm is likely to be smaller in the Co-operative than in the Entrepreneurial economy.

[11] Professor Vanek also claims that there will be less expenditure on advertisement in the Co-operative economy. The relevant question here is presumably not whether the individual small co-operative will spend less absolutely on advertisement than the individual large entrepreneurial firm, but whether advertisement expenditure per unit of total output will be smaller in the Co-operative than in the Entrepreneurial economy. After covering many sheets of paper with clumsy and inelegant differential calculus the present reviewer can find no plausible reason for giving an emphatic answer 'Yes' to the latter question. It seems to him that it might go either way.

*(2)* above, lead to a reduction in employment and output.[12] Prices are thus likely to fluctuate up and down much more in a Co-operative than in an Entrepreneurial economy, as total money expenditures fluctuate.

But Professor Vanek argues that at the same time it may be much easier in a Co-operative system to avoid a continuing upward inflation of money prices, since there can in a Co-operative economy *ex hypothesi* be no simple straightforward wage-cost inflation. Workers take what money earnings are left over after the firm has conducted its operations; they do not set money wage-rates on which employers construct their cost prices. But may not this argument be too *simpliste*? In an Entrepreneurial system wage-earners push up money wage-rates; employers then push up prices to maintain their profit margins; and the government permits or engineers a rise in total money expenditures sufficient to maintain full employment at the higher money price level. In a Co-operative system may not workers push up their selling prices directly and the government then permit or engineer a rise in total money expenditures sufficient to equate demand to supply at the higher price level?[13]

But however that may be, the implications for employment policy are very far-reaching. To rely in a Co-operative system on Keynesian policies to expand effective demand in times of unemployment would be at best ineffective, and at worst might lead to a reduction in output and employment. Indeed, as a short-run policy to induce existing firms to give more employment it would be necessary to *decrease* total demand or to *increase* the fixed overhead cost which firms had to face, for example by *raising* some fixed tax on each firm. But it is pretty clear that such policies would be ill-advised. If the short-run elasticities of supply of existing firms are low, then employment cannot be substantially increased except by setting up new firms, a process which may take considerable time both because of the organisational–promotional problems involved and also because of the gestation period for the production of the necessary new fixed capital equipment.

---

[12] Whether it causes an actual decline in output will depend *inter alia* upon the way in which the hire of $K$ by the co-operative workers is financed. *(a)* At the one extreme let us suppose that the existing $K$ is financed by a long-term debt whose service is fixed in terms of money. In this case the workers will have a fixed sum $(R)$ to pay in the service of debt. *(b)* At the other extreme let us suppose that the workers pay a rental of $iP_k$ per unit of $K$, the terms $i$ and $P_k$ being adjusted from day to day to correspond to market changes in the short-term rate of interest $(i)$ and the market price of a machine $(P_k)$. We start with a firm in equilibrium with

$$P_x \frac{\partial X}{\partial L} = \frac{P_x X - R}{L} \text{ in case } (a) \text{ and } \frac{P_x X - iP_k K}{L} \text{ in case } (b).$$

If $P_x$ and $P_k$ are both inflated by 10% while $R$ remains unchanged the equilibrium is not disturbed in case $(b)$, but in case $(a)$ $P_x(\partial X/\partial L)$ rises less than $(P_x X - R)/L$ and there will be an incentive to reduce the size of the firm of the kind examined in connection with *difference (2)* above. Thus in case $(b)$ a general inflation of commodity prices will leave output unchanged, while in case $(a)$ it may actually cause a reduction in output and employment.

[13] With some possible adverse effect on total employment if the finance of fixed capital is by long-term fixed interest loans as in case $(a)$ of the previous footnote.

In a Co-operative economy unemployment may well exist. If it does exist, its cure must be found in a longer-term structural policy aimed at promoting the institution of new firms by the unemployed in order to help them in their desire to enjoy the average earnings of an employed worker rather than the pittance of unemployment benefit. This relative short-run intractability of the unemployment problem may seem to be a serious disadvantage of the Co-operative system. But as Professor Vaneck rightly points out one must set on the other side of the balance sheet the fact that, if a long-run structure is achieved which gives full employment, then it will be much easier to maintain full employment than is the case in an Entrepreneurial system, since fluctuations in total demand will no longer lead to large fluctuations in output and employment. Prices, not output, will bear the brunt of the change.

So far only the macro-economic effects of effective demand on output and employment, but not those of output and employment on effective demand, have been considered. We may perhaps assume that the consumption function (the effect of real income and employment on consumption) would be the same in both systems. As for the incentive to invest in new capital goods by existing firms, perhaps we might also consider it to be the same, namely a function of the relationship between the cost of financing new capital goods and the value of the marginal product of new capital goods, investment by an existing firm being greater, the lower was $iP_k$ and the higher $P_x(\partial X/\partial K)$.[14] If this is so, it points to a very fundamental difference in the workings of the two systems. Suppose that there is an initial increase in effective demand. As we have seen (pages 169–70) in an entrepreneurial firm this will lead to an increase in output and employment and will also thereby lead to an increase in the value of the marginal product of capital in existing firms who will then (in the absence of any rise in the rate of interest) have an incentive to expand their capital equipment. In the co-operative, however, there will be no increase in employment and, therefore, no rise in the physical marginal product of capital. Indeed, in the case in which labour can be dismissed from an existing partnership and in which there were constant returns to scale, employment and output would be reduced until the value of the marginal product of capital were equal to its rental (see page 167 above). There would be no incentive to invest by existing firms as a result of an increase in effective demand.

But as we have seen, in a co-operative we must rely much more on investment to set up new firms as a means for coping with unemployment. Suppose then that there is some automatic or government-sponsored mechanism for promoting the setting up of new firms, such promotion being intensified as the volume of unemployment grows. Then if there were a reduction in employment and output, there would be a rise in the scale of investment to set up new firms to cope with the increased volume of unemployment.

---

[14] Professor Vanek (*op. cit.*, pages 168–172) discusses at length possible differences in the case of investment by co-operative and entrepreneurial firms. There is no space to discuss his views in this article.

But what a perverse universe this is! With the Entrepreneurial system a fall in effective demand reduces employment which reduces the marginal product of capital which reduces investment which reduces effective demand which reduces employment . . ., a vicious circle of positive feedback. With the Co-operative system a rise in effective demand reduces employment which increases unemployment which increases investment to set up new firms which increases effective demand which increases unemployment . . ., another vicious circle of positive feedback. The stability conditions of these two systems might be compared with some interest.[15] But on the face of it the devil seems to win whichever institutional arrangement we may adopt.

### III

So much for the main features of Professor Vanek's analysis. It is interesting to consider what are the basic institutional features which give rise to these differences in the workings of the two systems. We may ask whether the differences are due (i) to the fact that in a co-operative the objective is to maximise a residual surplus per unit of a factor input (i.e. earnings per worker) whereas in an entrepreneurial firm the objective is to maximise a residual total surplus (i.e. total company profit), or (ii) to the fact that in a co-operative the factor which is variable in the short run $(L)$ is the hiring factor whereas in an Entrepreneurial system it is a hired factor.

We can answer this question by considering an institutional set-up in which owners of machines $(K)$ get together, put their machines into a common enterprise, hire labour $(L)$ and sell the output $(X)$ on the best terms which they can obtain on the market, and run the concern so as to maximise the return per machine. This system which for ease of reference we will call a Joint-Stock system is exactly analogous to a Co-operative except that it is the factor which is fixed in the short run $(K)$ which hires the factor which is variable in the short run $(L)$ instead of the other way round. In conditions of perfect competition the management rules for maximising the return per unit of $K$ for the existing $K$-partners will be (i) to hire more labour until the value of the marginal product of labour is equal to the market wage-rate and (ii), if possible, to expand the size of the partnership by getting more adventurers to put machines into the enterprise so long as the value of the marginal product of machines $P_x(\partial X/\partial K)$ is greater than the average return per machine in the enterprise as it exists at present $((P_x X - WL)/K)$. These rules are shown in column 5 of the Table on page 161.

As far as labour incentives are concerned (*difference (1)* above), joint-stock and entrepreneurial firms are similar, since in both of these labour is hired at a given wage and told what to do. Moreover, in so far as the short period in which $K$ is fixed is concerned, the objective of an entrepreneurial firm to maximise a total surplus leads to exactly the same

---

[15] The reader is referred to Professor Vanek's consideration of the stability of his labour-managed economy (*op. cit.*, pp. 204–9).

result as the objective of a joint-stock firm to maximise surplus per unit of the fixed amount of $K$. For this reason, as far as the short-run competitive behaviour of the systems is concerned (*differences* (2), (3) *and* (5) above), once more Joint-Stock and Entrepreneurial economies are similar and are to be contrasted with a Co-operative economy in which the variable factor ($L$) does the hiring.[16]

But so far as monopolistic behaviour is concerned (*difference* (4)) a joint-stock firm is very similar in its effects to a co-operative. A joint-stock firm and a co-operative are more restrictive than an entrepreneurial firm because they aim at maximising a surplus per unit of a factor input instead of the total surplus of the firm. The similarity in this connection between a joint-stock firm and a co-operative can be appreciated by simply substituting $K$ for $L$ and $L$ for $K$ in the analysis given above on pages 167–69. For example, a monopolistic joint-stock firm like a monopolistic co-operative will always have an incentive to reduce output so long as it is producing with constant returns to scale. For if a 10% reduction in $K$ and $L$ would lead to a 10% reduction in $X$, then the return per machine $(P_x X - WL)/K$ would remain unchanged if the market prices $P_x$ and $W$ remained unchanged. But if $P_x$ rose as $X$ was reduced, $(P_x X - WL)/K$ would rise. Output would be reduced until the increase in real cost due to the low scale of operations offset the ability to raise earnings per machine by raising the price of the output.

In monopolistic conditions there is thus a real difference between an entrepreneurial firm and a joint-stock firm. In what does this consist? An entrepreneurial firm may be typified by a capitalist firm in which all the capital has been financed by the issue of fixed-interest debentures, the entrepreneur being someone who simply bears the risk that the difference between the revenue of the firm and the total bill for interest and wages may be a high or low positive or negative figure. At first sight it might be thought[17] that a joint-stock firm could be typified by a capitalist firm in which all the capital was financed by the issue of ordinary shares and in which, therefore, the existing shareholders would wish to maximise surplus per existing share rather than total surplus and would issue new shares to finance an increase in $K$ if and only if this would raise the return per existing share. For reasons which will become clear later, we will refer to such a firm as an Inegalitarian joint-stock firm.

[16] At first sight it seems very paradoxical that when $P_x$ rises because of an increased demand for $X$, there should in the short run be an increase in the production of $X$ if the fixed factor ($K$) hires the variable factor ($L$) but a reduction in the production of $X$ if the variable factor ($L$) hires the fixed factor ($K$). But when one factor hires another factor, a rise in the selling price of the product by reducing the real cost of the hired factor will induce each unit of the hiring factor to employ a greater amount of the hired factor. Thus when $K$ is the hiring factor a rise in $P_x$ will induce a rise in $L/K$ which, in the short run with $K$ constant, means a rise in $L$. But when $L$ is the hiring factor, a rise in $P_x$ will induce a rise in $K/L$ which, in the short run with $K$ constant, implies a reduction in $L$. In the long run, of course, in both systems if there are constant returns to scale $L$, $K$, and $X$ will all increase in the same proportion until the selling price of the product, $P_x$, has fallen once more to the old unchanged long-run cost of production.

[17] The author of this paper presented this thought to a seminar at the Delhi School of Economics, but realised his mistake as he lay in bed that evening. He was thus fortunately able to correct his mistake when the seminar met again on the following day.

In fact, however, this is not so: there is a world of difference between a joint-stock firm in which the objective is the maximisation of return per machine and an inegalitarian joint-stock firm in which the objective is the maximisation of return per share. Let us consider the rules which an inegalitarian joint-stock firm must follow. Since labour is hired at a wage-rate $W$, in perfect competition labour will be hired in the same way as in an entrepreneurial firm or a joint-stock firm up to the point at which the value of its marginal product is equal to the wage-rate $(P_x(\partial X/\partial L) = W)$.

As far as capital is concerned, we assume that there is a perfectly competitive capital market in which there rules a price $(P_s)$ at which the ordinary shares $(S)$ of the firm can be sold. We are assuming that all capital is financed by the issue of ordinary shares, i.e. that all profits are distributed in dividends and none used for the internal finance of development. The yield on the ordinary shares $S$ is thus $(P_xX - WL)/P_sS$, let us call this $r$. The total return per existing ordinary share $(P_xX - WL)/S$ can be raised by the issue of new shares to finance new capital equipment if the value of the marginal product of a machine $P_x(\partial X/\partial K)$ is greater than $rP_k$. For suppose that £100 worth of new shares are issued. This enables £100/$P_k$ new machines to be purchased and this will add $(£100/P_k)P_x(\partial X/\partial K)$ to total revenue at the current marginal productivity of machines. But the dividends which must be paid out to the new shareholders at the current rate of dividend per share will be $r$£100. If $(£100/P_k)P_x(\partial X/\partial K) > r$£100, i.e. if $P_x(\partial X/\partial K) > rP_k$, there will be some net gain which can be used to raise the dividend for all shareholders. These rules are shown in column 6 of the Table on page 161.

It is clear that the rule for investing more capital in an inegalitarian joint-stock firm is quite different from that for investment in a joint-stock firm but is very similar to that in an entrepreneurial firm with the exception that we are concerned with the earnings yield on ordinary shares $(r)$ instead of the rate of interest on debentures $(i)$.[18]

Why is this so? The answer becomes clear when we substitute the value $r = (P_xX - WL)/P_sS$ in the expression $P_x(\partial X/\partial K) \lessgtr rP_k$ and obtain

$$P_x\frac{\partial X}{\partial K} \lessgtr \frac{P_kK}{P_sS}\frac{P_xX - WL}{K}.$$

There are now two influences at work tending to lead to an increase in $K$:

(i) As in a joint-stock firm there is an incentive to increase $K$ if the value of the marginal product of a machine $(P_x(\partial X/\partial K))$ is high relatively to the existing return per machine $((P_xX - WL)/K)$.

---

[18] This similarity applies to monopolistic as well as to competitive conditions. Let $P_x[1 - (1/ed)]$ represent the marginal revenue obtained from the sale of an additional unit of $X$. The entrepreneurial firm will wish to invest in more $K$ so long as the marginal revenue from the marginal product of $K$ is greater than the rental for a unit of $K$, i.e. so long as $P_x[1 - (1/ed)] > iP_k$. The inegalitarian joint-stock firm will wish to invest in more capital so long as the marginal revenue from the marginal product of $K$ is greater than the additional dividends which must be paid on the value of the shares issued to finance the purchase of $K$, i.e. so long as $P_x[1 - (1/ed)] > rP_k$.

(ii) But now there is an additional incentive to expand $K$ if the valuation ratio $(P_sS/P_kK)$ is high, i.e. if the market value of the share capital is high relatively to the market price of the machinery which it finances.

Point (ii) means that, while shareholders are treated equally, not all shareholders 'own', as it were, the same number of machines per £100 subscribed in money capital. Suppose that an inegalitarian joint-stock firm is set up. The original shareholders purchase 100 shares at £1 a share and with the £100 so subscribed purchase 100 machines at £1 a machine. The company does well and the market value of a share rises from £1 to £2. Another 50 shares are issued raising £100 with which 100 additional machines are purchased again at £1 a machine. The company now owns 200 machines and has issued 150 shares. The first shareholders who own 2/3 of the shares 'own' as it were 2/3 of the 200 machines, i.e. 133½ machines as a result of subscribing £100 which financed the purchase of only 100 machines; the second lot of shareholders own 1/3 of the shares and thus 'own' as it were 1/3 of the 200 machines, i.e. 66⅔ machines as a result of subscribing £100 which financed the purchase of no less than 100 machines.

It should now be clear why we have nicknamed this an *inegalitarian* joint-stock firm. Partners do not participate in the partnership according to the amount of real resources which they have put in. Early partners (the original shareholders) can determine the conditions on which new partners (the later shareholders) can come in; and if the early partners, having taken the first risks, find that they are on to a good thing they may admit new partners on less favourable terms than those which they enjoy themselves. It is interesting to see the effects of applying this principle to a co-operative; and this we shall do in Section VI.

## V

Before we outline the structure of what we will call an Inegalitarian co-operative it will be useful to consider in more detail some of the rules which are appropriate for the running of all forms of labour co-operatives.

(i) It is clear that in order to give some security to those owners of capital who lend capital to a co-operative there must be some regulations governing the use of its real capital by a co-operative. In this respect a co-operative is in the same position as an entrepreneurial firm. It must not be possible for a group of workers any more than for an entrepreneur to borrow money, use the proceeds for riotous living, and then go bankrupt. While the commercial decisions as to what is the most profitable form for the use of the borrowed funds must be left to the worker-managers, there must clearly be some 'company-law' regulations which require the labour-managers to make proper use of proper depreciation allowances to maintain the capital of the concern intact in some accepted accounting sense; and if the concern should go bankrupt, then the capital assets would revert to the ownership of those who had lent funds to the concern. The loans to the concern would be secured on the real capital assets of the concern, which the labour-managers would be required by law to maintain intact in some accepted accounting sense.[19]

(ii) As for the rules governing the expansion of the number of worker-partners in a co-operative, it would seem obvious that a new partner should enter the concern only if two conditions are fulfilled, namely (a) that the new partner wished to come in and (b) that the old partners wish to accept him.

(iii) The rules under (ii) seem obviously fair and acceptable. We will now argue, what is not perhaps quite so obvious, that there must be two analogous conditions for the withdrawal of an existing partner from a co-operative, namely (a) that the partner concerned wishes to leave and (b) that he should obtain from the remaining partners permission to withdraw.

Rule (iii)(a) is incompatible with the rule of the dismissal of partners by majority decision mentioned in the footnote on page 165. There is presumably no absolute right or wrong about such a rule; but it would appear to the present reviewer that a fully participatory co-operative must have a rule like (iii)(a). In any case the following analysis is an analysis of what will occur if one does have such a rule.[20]

Rule (iii)(b) requires somewhat more discussion. Why should any individual worker-partner not be free to leave any co-operative at any time if he so wishes without any cost to himself? Consider the following case in terms of Figure 1 on page 163 above. Suppose the co-operative to be confronted with the curve $PQ$ for its average revenue per head $((P_x X)/L)$. Suppose that it starts with the optimum size of the co-operative (namely, $0A$) at which its average earnings $(CB = (P_x X - iP_k K)/L)$ are at a maximum. But suppose that the average earnings which

---

[19] This points to an important consideration concerning incentives. We have already argued (page 172 above) that as far as labour incentives are concerned, entrepreneurial and joint-stock firms are similar (in that labour is hired at a given wage and is told what to do), and are to be contrasted with a co-operative (where labour manages itself). But economic efficiency depends not only on labour incentives, but also upon incentives to maintain the value of the real capital stock. In this respect entrepreneurial and co-operative firms are similar (in that those who receive the residual profit on the firm's operations have no direct interest in the wealth of the ultimate owners of the capital) and are to be contrasted with joint-stock firms (in which those who enjoy the residual profit themselves own the capital and have, therefore, a much more direct incentive to pay regard to the maintenance or improvement of its value).

[20] Incidentally the existence of such a rule removes a serious problem which would otherwise arise from self-financing of co-operatives to which Professor Vanek draws attention (*op. cit.*, p. 307). Consider a co-operative which puts aside undistributed profits and thereby pays off the whole of its outside indebtedness. In terms of Figure 1, $iP_k K$ is reduced to zero and the curve $MN$ collapses to coincide with the two axes. The size of a competitive partnership which will maximise earnings per head is now that which will maximise output per head, which, in the absence of any increasing returns to scale, would with any given amount of real capital involve the reduction of the partnership to one man. With no debt there is no incentive to enlarge the partnership in order to share the debt burden; and the remaining partner will be left endowed with an enormous equipment of real capital financed out of the savings of his previous partners who have been dismissed without compensation.

partners might be able to get if they were free to join new co-operatives in other industries were greater than the earnings inside the existing partnership (i.e. $E_0 > CB = (P_x X - iP_k K)/L$ where $E_0$ measures the average earnings available outside the partnership). Some workers might be better able than others to take the opportunity of withdrawal to a more remunerative co-operative. Suppose the size of the co-operative is reduced to $0E$; then the remaining partners can earn only $GF$ so that $E_0$ is now even greater than before relatively to $GF = (P_x X - iP_k K)/L$. This may go on until what may be called the starvation–bankruptcy size of the co-operative is reached at a co-operative size $0V$ where the revenue is just sufficient to cover the debt interest and the remaining workers' earnings are zero.

The point is simply that as partners withdraw the remaining partners are left to hold the debt baby. If the debt obligation has been willingly incurred by all the partners, it is not a true participatory co-operative if any individual partner can without any obligation just walk out and leave his other partners with the full debt burden. All must sink or swim together.

What then should be the rules for the closure of a co-operative? What does bankruptcy mean?

One possibility would be that the partners could always in agreement decide to close down the concern leaving the debt holders with the ownership of the capital assets of the concern. Or, in the interests of the debt holders, it might be ruled that the existing partners could not take such action simply because they could do better elsewhere, but only if their earnings, after paying debt interest and maintaining capital intact, fell below some stated level. Indeed different rules, giving different degrees of security to the debt holders, might be freely negotiable between the partners and the debt holders when the partnership was first formed.[21]

# VI

Let us then consider a co-operative with rules (i), (ii)($a$), (ii)($b$), (iii)($a$), and (iii)($b$); and let us with these rules contrast the operation of a co-operative (as described on pages 158–9 above) with that of an inegalitarian co-operative whose mode of working is as follows. Each individual $L$-partner on joining the partnership is allotted a share $l$ in the total surplus $(P_x X - iP_k K)$ of the partnership. This share is such that ($a$) it pays the new partner to come in and ($b$) it pays the existing partners to let him in. A partner once in can (apart from death and retirement for reasons of age or ill-health) withdraw only if ($a$) it pays him to do so and ($b$) he can make it worthwhile for the remaining partners to release him. The shares allotted to the individual partners are not necessarily the same. They may

---

[21] Such rules would make schemes for capital reorganisation possible. If the debt holders were as a result of a 'bankruptcy' left holding the real assets of some defunct concern, they might by cutting the debt interest (reducing $iP_k K$ and so the curve $MN$ in Figure 1) bring the concern to life again with a different, or indeed the same, set of worker-partners.

differ because different partners with different skills and trainings may have different values to the partnerships, but they may also differ for partners with the same skills and trainings, because the partners have joined the partnership at different times.

The objective of the inegalitarian co-operative as it exists at any moment of time will be to maximise the return per share

$$a = \frac{P_x X - i P_k K}{l_1 + l_2 + \ldots + l_n}$$

where $l_1 \ldots l_n$ are the shares allotted to individuals $1 \ldots n$ who make up the existing partnership. Given the distribution of the shares, it is a fully participatory partnership in the sense that every partner has the same motive that the concern should be so managed as to maximise the return per share.

Let us consider the operation of rules (ii) and (iii) above for the expansion and contraction of such an inegalitarian co-operative.

The rules for expansion are straightforward. Suppose that $E_0 < P_x (\partial X / \partial L)$, i.e. that the average earnings outside are less than the value of the marginal product of labour in the partnership. Then all that is necessary is for the existing partners to agree on a share $l_{n+1}$ for a new partner such that

$$E_0 < a l_{n+1} < P_x \frac{\partial X}{\partial L}.$$

The new partner will wish to join because $E_0 < a l_{n+1}$. The existing partners will wish him to join because $a l_{n+1} < P_x (\partial X / \partial L)$; for since the addition to the revenue of the concern as a result of his joining will be greater than his share of the surplus, the return to all existing workers will be raised.

The rules for withdrawal are a little more complicated. Let us suppose that $E_0 > P_x (\partial X / \partial L)$. Now there are three cases to be considered.

(i)   Suppose that some existing partner $j$ has a share in the partnership $(l_j)$ such that

$$E_0 > a l_j > P_x \frac{\partial X}{\partial L}.$$

Then the partner will wish to withdraw because $E_0 > a l_j$; and the existing partners will willingly let him go because $a l_j > P_x (\partial X / \partial L)$, that is to say, they will lose less in revenue than they save on his share of the surplus.

(ii)   But suppose that for all the existing partners

$$a l > E_0 > P_x \frac{\partial X}{\partial L}.$$

The existing partners would like to see any individual partner withdraw because $a l > P_x (\partial X / \partial L)$; but no existing partner will wish to go because

$al > E_0$. However, there is a net gain to everyone concerned of $E_0 - P_x(\partial X/\partial L)$ if one partner does withdraw, since that partner will earn $E_0$ and the existing partnership will lose only $P_x(\partial X/\partial L)$. In this case the existing partners might bribe one of their number to withdraw, perhaps by allowing him to retain some of his shares in the partnership even if he goes and works elsewhere. In this case $L$ will be reduced so long as $E_0 > P_x(\partial X/\partial L)$.

(iii)   Suppose that for all existing partners

$$E_0 > P_x \frac{\partial X}{\partial L} > al.$$

Then an individual partner will want to withdraw because $E_0 > al$, but the other partners will not want to release him since $P_x(\partial X/\partial L) > al$. But once again there is a net gain of $E_0 - P_x(\partial X/\partial L)$ and an individual partner should be able to purchase his release from his colleagues.[22] Once again $L$ will be reduced so long as $E_0 > P_x(\partial X/\partial L)$.

An inegalitarian co-operative, in the same way as a co-operative, will have an incentive to borrow money to expand its capital equipment so long as the value of the marginal product of machinery is greater than its rental $(P_x(\partial X/\partial K) > iP_kK)$. The resulting rules for an inegalitarian co-operative are shown in column 4 of the Table on page 161.

For simplicity of exposition we have presented the argument without reference to the fact that not only the particular partnership which we have been examining, but also all the other concerns in the community, may be organised as inegalitarian co-operatives. Suppose this to be so and that the value of the marginal product of labour in one industry is greater than in another (e.g. $P_y(\partial Y/\partial L) > P_x(\partial X/\partial L)$). Then there is a net gain for everyone concerned of $P_y(\partial Y/\partial L) - P_x(\partial X/\partial L)$ if one unit of $L$ moves from the $X$- to the $Y$-industry. There must be some bargain which will involve the choice of the share which the migrant worker will receive in the $Y$-industry and which may involve him in purchasing his release from his $X$-colleagues which improves the lot of everyone – the existing $Y$-partners, the migrant worker and the remaining $X$-partners. Thus labour will move from $X$ to $Y$ if $P_y(\partial Y/\partial Y) > P_x(\partial X/\partial L)$. The short-run adjustment process of the inegalitarian co-operative, unlike that of the co-operative, becomes Pareto-optimal.

But this result is achieved only at the expense of a distributional principle which may involve two workers of equal age, sex, ability, skill, etc., working side by side at the same job at the same work-bench, but receiving different shares in the product. As with the shareholders in the inegalitarian joint-stock firm, the worker–partners in an inegalitarian co-operative who come in early bearing the initial risks in a concern which turns out to do well will earn more than those workers who come in later when the success of the enterprise is already established.

---

[22] For example, if the withdrawing partner pays to the partnership the present value of earnings of $E = \frac{1}{2}[E_0 + P_x(\partial X/\partial L)] - al$, the gain will be shared equally between the withdrawing partner who will gain $E_0 - al - E = \frac{1}{2}[E_0 - P_x(\partial X/\partial L)]$ and the remaining partners who will gain $al - P_x(\partial X/\partial L) + E = \frac{1}{2}[E_0 - P_x(\partial X/\partial L)]$.

## VII

There is no reason why one should not go the whole hog in participation and profit-sharing and apply the same principle both to those who supply the capital and to those who supply the labour. Such a set-up would be a combination of an inegalitarian joint-stock firm (as far as the supply of capital was concerned) and an inegalitarian co-operative (as far as the supply of labour was concerned). Let us call the resulting structure an Inegalitarian Joint-Stock-Co-operative firm. Let $S$ represent the number of shares issued to those who have subscribed capital. Let there be three skills or types of labour ($L$, $M$, and $N$) and let $l_1$, $l_2$ . . ., $m_1$, $m_2$ . . ., $n_1$, $n_2$ . . . represent the shares issued to individual workers $L_1$, $L_2$ . . ., $M_1$, $M_2$ . . ., $N_1$, $N_2$ . . . Then the objective of the existing partners at any one time will be to maximise the return per share or

$$a = \frac{P_x X}{S + l_1 + l_2 + \ldots + m_1 + m_2 + \ldots + n_1 + n_2 + \ldots}.$$

This will be achieved by following the rules (which are summarised in column 7 of the Table on page 161):

(i)   increase or decrease $S$ and so $K$ as $P_x \dfrac{\partial X}{\partial K} \gtrless r P_k$

(ii)  increase or decrease $L$ as    $P_x \dfrac{\partial X}{\partial L} \gtrless E_{0l}$

(iii) increase or decrease $M$ as    $P_x \dfrac{\partial X}{\partial M} \gtrless E_{0m}$

(iv)  increase or decrease $N$ as    $P_x \dfrac{\partial X}{\partial N} \gtrless E_{0n}$

Reductions in $L$, $M$, $N$ must be associated, as far as is necessary, with bargains by which existing partners buy their way out or are bribed by the remaining partners to withdraw.

The analysis which leads to these results is exactly the same as that which has been given above for an inegalitarian joint-stock firm and for an inegalitarian co-operative.

Nor is this the only possibility of combination of structures. There is nothing in the nature of things to prevent some capitalists and some workers getting together and forming a partnership (on inegalitarian joint-stock-co-operative principles), but nevertheless borrowing some additional capital at fixed interest and hiring some additional labour at a fixed wage (thus introducing entrepreneurial elements into the concern). Or, as with the usual profit-sharing arrangement, we may find labour being rewarded in an ordinary company partly with a fixed wage-rate and partly with shares in the concern, which introduces a co-operative element into an inegalitarian joint-stock firm. All sorts of participatory profit-sharing combinations are theoretically possible.

There is no place in the present article to discuss the historical and empirical questions as to which of these structures have flourished in which conditions. But it is interesting to ask why the co-operative structure is not more common than it is in fact in the free-enterprise world. Two factors spring to mind.

First, there is the basic, though not strictly economic question whether a workers' co-operative organisation is compatible with the maintenance of the discipline needed to ensure the efficient operation of a concern which employs a large body of workers.

Secondly, while property owners can spread their risks by putting small bits of their property into a large number of concerns, a worker cannot easily put small bits of his effort into a large number of different jobs. This presumably is a main reason why we find risk-bearing capital hiring labour rather than risk-bearing labour hiring capital. Moreover, since labour cannot spread its risks, we are likely to find co-operative structures only in lines of activity in which the risk is not too great, and this means in lines of activity in which two conditions are fulfilled: first, the risk of fluctuations in the demand for the product must not be too great; and, secondly, the activity must be a labour-intensive activity in which the surplus accruing to labour does not constitute a small difference between two large quantities, the revenue from the sale of the product and the hire of capital plus the purchase of raw materials.[23] This may help to explain why such labour partnerships as do exist are usually to be found in labour-intensive services, such as lawyers, accountants, doctors, etc.

## VIII

Many questions remain unconsidered. Neither Professor Vanek nor the author of the present article has attempted to answer a very important question concerning risk, namely whether, if a workers' co-operative did exist in any given situation, it would (in its decisions concerning output, price, investment, employment, etc.) react differently from an entrepreneurial firm in the face of a given set of risks. Nor has any systematic attempt been made to compare the behaviour of a Co-operative system with that of managerial capitalism,[24] though Professor Vanek does claim (*op. cit.*, page 119) that the Co-operative system would be less prone to the temptations of 'gigantism' than any other economic regime.

In this article the author has made no attempt to argue for or against the institution of labour partnerships. Professor Vanek in his book which inspired this article professes himself to be a keen advocate of such

---

[23] In terms of Figure 1 if the *MN* and the *PQ* curves were both raised substantially so as to leave the difference *CB* unchanged, a 1% fall in the *PQ* curve would have a much more marked effect in reducing *CB*.

[24] Of the kind described by such authors as Berle and Means, Burnham, Galbraith, and Marris.

participatory organisations; but in spite of this he maintains a most admirable scientific frankness in exposing the weaknesses as well as the strengths of such organisations. It has not been possible in this article to review all of Professor Vanek's arguments; his book should be read by all economists interested in the subject. The purpose of this article has been merely to analyse some of the implications of labour partnerships or profit-sharing structures. It may well be the case that the merits of participation should be so highly prized as to make the encouragement of such institutions a major objective of governmental policy. For governmental encouragement of one kind or another will almost certainly be necessary because of the natural tendency for risk-bearing capital to hire labour rather than the risk-bearing labour to hire capital.

If such governmental policies are to be devised, there are at least three main problems to be borne in mind.

First, as we have tried to show, the effective workings of labour partnerships will depend very much upon easy conditions for the formation of new partnerships to enter any profitable industry. But easy company promotion of this kind by unemployed or ill-paid workers will certainly be impossible without appropriate governmental interventions of a most extensive character – leading perhaps inevitably to a socialist ownership of the main capital resources of the community as in Yugoslavia.

Second, the labour partnership presents in its own special form a conflict between efficiency and equality. Some compromise rule on the distribution of the surplus among new and old workers must be found which does not introduce excessive inequalities on the one hand or excessive inefficiencies on the other.

Third, thought must be given to the extent to which labour partnerships involve workers risking all their eggs in one basket. Some compromise between the degree of participation and the degree of the spreading of risks would have to be sought.[25]

---

[25] In this connection it would be helpful to encourage a wide distribution of the ownership of property (what the present reviewer has called a Propdem in another connection [*The Growing Economy* (London: Allen & Unwin, 1968), Chapter III, 'Of Propdems, Plantcaps and other states of society']) so that the representative worker is also a representative property owner. A citizen could then at least spread his property in small parcels over a lot of other concerns, even though he had to concentrate his earnings from work on one particular concern.

# 11

# The Optimal Balance between Economies of Scale and Variety of Products: An Illustrative Model

*From* Economica, *vol. 41 (November 1974), pp. 359–67.*

In conditions of monopolistic competition there is a number of independent producers each producing its own particular brand or quality of a class of products which, while they are not exactly identical, are nevertheless partial substitutes for each other. A well-known problem in the economics of welfare then arises which can be expressed by asking the following two questions. First, is each producer producing the optimal output of his particular brand? Second, are the best number and assortment of brands being produced, or should there be more or less variety of products to meet the consumers' needs?

The answer to the first of these two questions is reasonably straightforward. Since each producer will be faced with a less than infinitely elastic demand curve for his particular brand, his selling price will be above his marginal revenue and, therefore, above his marginal cost. He must produce more if he is to equate marginal cost to selling price.

This proposition is, of course, subject to all the familiar limitations of the 'second best'. In particular, in a world of monopolistic competition the proposition that marginal costs should be equated to selling prices will hold good only if it is applied simultaneously in all lines of production; and if it is so applied and if we start from a position of full employment, it will clearly be impossible for all producers to expand their outputs simultaneously. What will happen as every producer simultaneously attempts to expand output will be a bidding up of the prices of the variable factors so that relationships between marginal costs and prices will be altered in the various lines of production. As a result some outputs will be increased and others decreased. Equilibrium will be reached only when outputs have been so adjusted that in each line of production marginal cost equals selling price.

But what about the second question? Will the number and variety of products being produced be optimal? The marginal conditions for optimality may be satisfied; but is the structure of production optimal? The answer to this question is not so straightforward or familiar. The number and variety of products produced may in fact turn out to be greater or to be less than optimal. Variety is desirable from the consumer's point of view if the products are not very good substitutes for each other; variety is costly if the economies of large-scale production are great. The degree of variety which it will pay uncontrolled competitors to produce and the degree of variety which it is in the social interest to produce are both influenced by these two factors; but as we shall see, the actual degree of variety provided by an uncontrolled market will not always coincide with the socially optimal degree of variety.

In a recent article Stern (1972) has provided a precise and formal solution to what is basically the same problem. He takes the geographical size of markets as the particular topic for his analysis. Products are differentiated by the location at which they are provided; variety is increased by increasing the number of points of production and reducing each producer's market area; and substitutability between products at different localities is greater, the smaller the cost of transport from one locality to another. Stern shows the conditions in which uncontrolled monopolistic competition will lead to market areas above the optimal size (too little variety) and to market areas below the optimal size (too much variety). Stern's article involves a sophisticated mathematical analysis. The present article attempts through a greatly simplified example to give the more humdrum economist an intuitive sense of the economic factors which lie behind the analysis.

I

Suppose then that in a particular township there are two possible supplies of energy for domestic purposes – gas and electricity. These two forms of energy are imperfect substitutes for each other from the housewife's point of view. Our structural question then takes the form of asking whether the township should be provided with a gasworks alone or an electricity works alone or with both a gasworks and an electricity works simultaneously.

In order to simplify the model as much as possible, we will assume:

(a)    that the township consists of a number of consumers with identical incomes and tastes, so that we can neglect effects on the distribution of welfare between the citizens;

(b)    that each consumer's utility function can be divided into two separate additive parts

$$U(E, G) + U(X, Y, Z, \ldots)$$

where $E$ and $G$ are the amounts of electricity and gas consumed by a representative consumer and $X$, $Y$, $Z$, etc. are the amounts of all other commodities consumed; and

(c)    that the amount spent by a consumer on $X$, $Y$, $Z$ is very large compared with the amount spent on $E$ and $G$.

These assumptions allow us to assume that the marginal utility of money income is the same for each citizen and is unaffected by any relevant changes in the total amounts of $E$ and $G$ which are produced and consumed; and they allow us to consider the total utility derived from the consumption of $E$ and $G$ independently of the amounts of $X$, $Y$, $Z$, etc. which are consumed.

But of course the total utility derived from the consumption of a given amount of $E$ is not independent of the amount of $G$ which is being consumed, and *vice versa*. If a given amount of $G$ is available, then the total utility of $E$ will be less than it would otherwise have been, and *vice versa*. There is, however, a single relationship of substitutability between $E$ and $G$. The effect of a given amount of $G$ on the total utility derived from a given amount of $E$ is not independent of the effect of a given amount of $E$ on the total utility derived from a given amount of $G$; these two effects are in fact only different facets of the same single substituta-bility relationship. This is illustrated in Figure 1.

Let $D_{e0}$ represent the demand curve for $G$ when no electricity is produced ($E = 0$). Suppose then that an amount of electricity equal to $E'$ is produced. The demand curve for $G$ will be reduced from $D_{e0}$ to $D_{e'}$, because the need for $G$ is less intense when some $E$ is available. The degree to which the demand curve for $G$ will be reduced will be the greater, (a) the greater is the quantity $E'$ of the competing fuel which is put on the market and (b) the greater the substitutability between $G$ and $E$. Similarly let $D_{g0}$ be the demand curve for $E$ when $G = 0$ and let $D_{g'}$ be the reduced demand curve for $E$ when $G$ is raised to $G'$. Because the relationship between $E$ and $G$ is a single relationship of substitutability, the relationship of $D_{e0}$ to $D_{e'}$ is not independent of the relationship of $D_{g0}$ to $D_{g'}$. In fact the relationship is such that the area $A$ in Figure 1(a) is necessarily equal to the area $B$ in Figure 1(b).

The proof is as follows. We assume that it makes no difference whether $G$ is introduced first and then supplemented by $E$ or whether $E$ is introduced first and then supplemented by $G$. Let us consider the total utility derived from $G'$ plus $E'$, when $G$ is introduced first. Since the

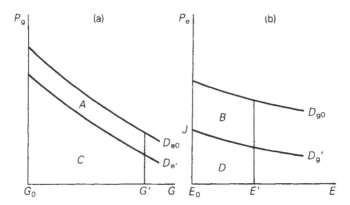

**Figure 1**

marginal utility of money income is given and constant, we can measure total utility by the areas under the relative demand curves. The problem is simply to decide which are the relevant demand curves.

Starting with no $G$ or $E$, consumers obtain a total utility equal to the area under the demand curve $D_{e0}$ (that is the area $A + C$) when an amount $G'$ is put on the market without any $E$. Suppose then that one unit of $E$ is put on the market. Consumers obtain an addition to their total utility equal to the price which they will pay for this unit of $E$, namely $E_0 J$ in Figure 1(b). As $E$ is increased to $E'$, they acquire less and less marginal increments of utility for each additional unit of $E$, until in the end the introduction of $E'$ units of $E$ has provided a total addition to their utility equal to the area under the curve $D_{g'}$ (that is, the area $D$). Their total utility is thus $A + C + D$.

Start now with $E'$ introduced first, giving a total utility under the $D_{g0}$ curve (i.e. equal to $B + D$); and then let this total utility be supplemented through the introduction of $G'$ by an addition to utility represented by the area under the $D_{e'}$ curve (i.e. the area $C$). Total utility is now measured by $B + D + C$. But if the order in which $E$ and $G$ are introduced makes no difference, these two sums should come to the same total, so that $A + C + D = B + D + C$ or $A = B$.

## II

There are four structural possibilities: (a) no gas and no electricity; (b) gas without electricity; (c) electricity without gas; (d) gas and electricity. Our first question is a question of marginal adjustment, that is, to determine how much gas and how much electricity should be produced under each of these structural arrangements. Our second question is the structural question, that is, to choose which of these structural arrangements gives the best results, given that the optimal marginal conditions are satisfied for each structural possibility.

The answer to the first marginal question in structural cases (a), (b) and (c) presents no problems:

(a)  *Ex hypothesi $G = E = 0$.*
(b)  *Ex hypothesi $E = 0$;* and $G$ should be produced up to the point at which the marginal cost of gas equals the demand price for gas, that is, up to the point $G^*$ in Figure 2(a) where $M_g$ is the marginal cost curve for gas.
(c)  Similarly $G = 0$ and $E = E^*$ as in Figure 2(b).

But the answer to the marginal question in structure (d), that is, when both gas and electricity are being produced, presents somewhat more difficulty. Given any initial outputs of $G$ and $E$, the excess of utility over cost will be increased by an increase in $G$ without any change in $E$, if the demand price for $G$ (at the initial given outputs of $G$ and $E$) is in excess of the marginal cost of $G$. Conversely, $E$ should be increased (given the initial outputs of $E$ and $G$) if at those outputs the demand price for $E$

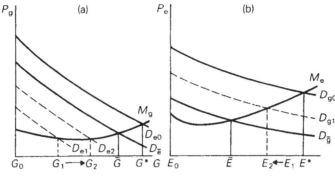

**Figure 2**

exceeds its marginal cost. A necessary condition, therefore, for the optimum combination of $E$ and $G$ is that the outputs of $E$ and $G$ should be such that the marginal cost of $G$ equals the price of $G$ and the marginal cost of $E$ equals the price of $E$.

The situation is illustrated in Figure 2(a) and (b). Suppose we start with the large output $E_1$, which is only a little less than $E^*$, the marginally correct output for $E$ when $G = 0$. This reduces the demand curve for $G$ to $D_{e1}$; but with this demand curve the optimal output for $G$ is $G_1$. But with $G = G_1$, the demand curve for $E$ falls to $D_{g1}$, and the optimal output for $E$ is then $E_2$. With $E$ reduced to $E_2$ the demand curve for $G$ rises to $D_{e2}$ and the optimal output for $G$ becomes $G_2$. And so on until we reach the values of $\bar{E}$ and $\bar{G}$. At these outputs the price of $E$ equals the marginal cost of $E$ and the price of $G$ equals the marginal cost of $G$.

### III

We turn next to the structural questions: 'Which combination of products (gas and electricity) should be produced?' and 'Which combination of the products will it be profitable to produce in an unregulated free market?' In this section we intend to consider the reasons why the combination which is actually put on the market may differ from the combination which should be put on the market by means of examples illustrating the three following possible cases:

*Case 1.* Neither product can be produced without loss, but at least one product ought to be produced;
*Case 2.* Both products should be produced, but loss can be avoided only if both are not simultaneously produced;
*Case 3.* Only one product should be produced, but both can be produced simultaneously without loss.

For purposes of simplification we assume that the marginal cost of each product is constant, but that there are economies of large-scale production because there is a fixed overhead cost which is not affected by the level of output, but which must be spread over whatever output is produced. Thus in Figure 3 we measure the output of $G$ along the horizontal axis and the cost of $G$ up the vertical axis. The constant marginal cost of $G$ is equal to $G_0 0$. There is a fixed overhead cost equal to the sum of the areas $A_g + J_g$. The average cost of any output $G$ is then obtained by adding to the marginal cost $G_0 0$ an amount equal to $(A_g + J_g) \div G$. This is obtained by drawing the curve $AC$ such that the area $(A_g + J_g)$ remains constant. The curve $AC$ is thus a rectangular hyperbola on the axes $0 - MC$ and $0 - P_g$.

*Case 1.* In Figure 3 when the marginally optimal output $G^*$ is produced without any $E$ being produced, the total utility (i.e. area under the demand curve $D_{e0}$) is equal to $J_g + H_g + K_g$. The total cost is equal to $K_g$, the total variable cost, plus $(A_g + J_g)$, the fixed overhead cost. Utility exceeds cost, therefore, if $H_g > A_g$. In Figure 3 this is clearly so. But at every point the average cost curve $AC$ lies above the demand curve $D_{e0}$. $G$ should be produced, but it will not pay to do so.

This is a familiar case. It is useful as an introduction to Cases 2 and 3 because we shall apply criteria similar to the criterion $H_g > A_g$ in these more complicated cases. From Figure 3 it is clear that the areas $J_g$ and $K_g$ are areas representing costs and also making up part of the area under the demand curve; they cancel out on both sides of the balance between total utility and total cost. But the area $H_g$ is an area of utility which does not coincide with the areas representing cost, and the area $A_g$ is an area representing cost which does not fall under the demand curve. The net excess of utility over cost is, therefore, $H_g - A_g$.

*Case 2.* In Case 2 the demand conditions for $G$ are the same as in Case 1; the marginal cost of $G$ is the same as in Case 1; but the overhead cost of

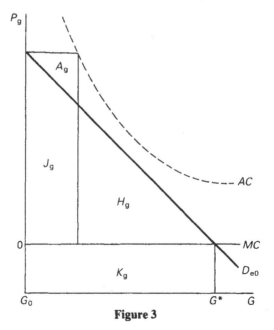

**Figure 3**

$G$ is lower than in Case 1, so that at an output $G = \hat{G}$ it is just possible to produce $G$ without loss, provided that no $E$ is produced. But while it is possible to produce $G$ without loss provided that $E$ is not produced, it will become unprofitable to produce $G$ if any $E$ is produced. For since $E$ is a partial substitute for $G$, the existence of $E$ will lower the demand curve for $G$ below $D_{e0}$ and $G$ will immediately become unprofitable.

Suppose for simplicity (as is shown in Figure 4 (b)) that the conditions of supply and demand for $E$ are exactly symmetrical with those for $G$. In this case, just as $G$ is profitable without $E$ but unprofitable with any $E$, so $E$ is profitable without $G$ but unprofitable with any $E$. The market cannot produce both simultaneously without loss; but in the conditions shown in Figure 4 both should nevertheless be produced. The calculus is as follows.

If both are produced, there is a pair of values $\hat{G}$ and $\bar{E}$ shown in Figure 4 at which the selling prices of both $G$ and $E$ are simultaneously equal to their marginal costs of production. Let $S_{g^*}$ be the net surplus of utility over cost if $G$ alone is produced at its marginally optimal level $G^*$ and let $S_{\bar{g}\bar{e}}$ be the net surplus of utility over cost if $G$ and $E$ are produced simultaneously at their marginally optimal levels $\hat{G}$ and $\bar{E}$. Then by the process of analysis used in consideration of Case 1 we have

$$S_{g^*} = C_g + F_g + H_g - A_g$$

since $C_g + F_g + H_g$ is the area under the demand curve not balanced by costs and $A_g$ is the cost area not balanced by area under the demand curve.

We now calculate $S_{\bar{g}\bar{e}}$. First introduce $G$ up to a level $\hat{G}$ instead of $G^*$ and the net excess utility is

$$C_g + F_g - A_g.$$

Then introduce $E$ up to a level $\bar{E}$ and the additional net excess utility is

$$F_e - (A_e + B_e)$$

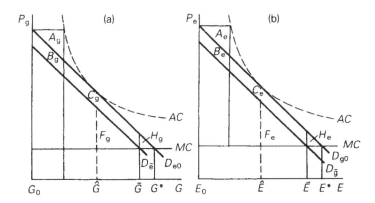

**Figure 4**

where $F_e$ is the area under the curve $D_{\bar{g}}$ not balanced by cost and $A_e + B_e$ is the cost area not balanced by area under $D_{\bar{g}}$. It follows that

$$S_{\bar{g}\bar{e}} = C_g + F_g + F_e - (A_g + A_e + B_e).^1$$

It follows that

$$S_{\bar{g}\bar{e}} - S_{g^*} = (F_e - A_e - B_e) - H_g.$$

In the case of Figure 4 this is clearly greater than zero. Both products should be produced, although it is possible to cover costs only if one alone is produced.

*Case 3.* In Case 3, depicted in Figures 5(a) and (b), the demand curves for $G$ in the absence of $E$ and for $E$ in the absence of $G$ (i.e. $D_{e0}$ and $D_{g0}$) are once again the same as in Cases 1 and 2. But in Case 3 $E$ and $G$ are much closer substitutes than in Case 2. This can be seen from the fact that although the marginally optimal value of $E$, namely $\bar{E}$, is lower in Case 3 than in Case 2, yet in spite of this $D_{\bar{e}}$ is much further below $D_{e0}$ in Case 3 than it is in Case 2. In other words, a smaller output of $E$ causes an even bigger fall in demand for $G$; and similarly for the greater impact of $G$ upon the demand for $E$ in Case 3.

On the cost side the marginal costs of $E$ and $G$ are once more the same as in Cases 1 and 2. But the fixed overhead costs are assumed to have been halved between Cases 2 and 3.

Indeed, in Figure 5 the fall in overhead cost is so substantial that it is just possible to produce both $G$ and $E$ simultaneously without loss, even though the demand curves for $G$ and $E$ are both much reduced because $E$ and $G$ are now close substitutes for each other. As is shown by the broken lines in Figure 5, at the pair of values $\hat{G}$ and $\hat{E}$ the average cost curve for

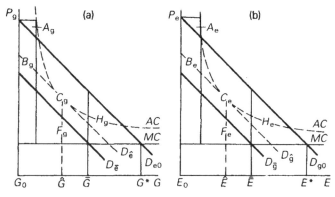

**Figure 5**

---

[1] If we calculate $S_{\bar{e}\bar{g}}$, namely the net surplus from $\bar{E}$ and $\bar{G}$ after introducing first $\bar{E}$ and then $\bar{G}$ we obtain $S_{\bar{e}\bar{g}} = C_e + F_e + F_g - (A_e + A_g + B_g)$ so that $S_{\bar{g}\bar{e}} - S_{\bar{e}\bar{g}} = (C_g + B_g) - (C_e + B_e)$. But in all cases, however different the supply–demand conditions for $\bar{E}$ and $\bar{G}$ may be, $C_g + B_g = C_e + B_e$ as is shown in the proof that in Figure 1 the area $A$ = area $B$.

each product is just tangential to the relevant demand curve for each product.

Nevertheless, although both products can be simultaneously produced without loss, only one should be produced. *E* and *G* are such good substitutes that the loss in variety for the consumers is more than compensated by the saving in overhead costs due to the concentration of output, even though overhead costs are less important than in Case 2. This can be seen by means of the same type of analysis as that which was applied to Case 2. By the same process of analysis as in Case 2 we have in Case 3 also

$$S_{\bar{g}\bar{e}} - S_{g \cdot} = (F_e - A_e - B_e) - H_g.$$

which, while it is positive in Case 2 (Figure 4) is clearly negative in Case 3 (Figure 5).

## IV

The example which we have developed in this paper illustrates the interaction between two major forces: on the one hand, the need for variety of products, a need which is greater the smaller the degree of substitutability between products; on the other hand, the cost advantage from concentrating productive effort on a limited number of products, an advantage which is greater the higher are the overhead costs in production. High substitutability and high overhead costs will both be factors inducing producers to concentrate production in an uncontrolled market economy. These same two factors – namely high substitutability and high overheads – will also both be reasons for concentrating production in the interests of maximising social welfare.

But these two factors do not pull with the same force in affecting private uncontrolled market decisions and public welfare decisions. To put the matter in an oversimplified manner it would appear that the market will overemphasise the factor 'overhead costs' relatively to the factor 'degree of substitutability'. Thus Case 2 illustrates a case in which, because overhead costs are high, the market will concentrate production in spite of low substitutability between products, whereas the socially optimal solution would introduce variety because substitutability was low, in spite of heavy overhead costs. Case 3 on the other hand shows a situation in which the market would introduce variety because overhead costs were low in spite of high substitutability between products, whereas the socially optimal solution would concentrate production because of high substitutability, in spite of low overhead costs.

## Reference

Nicholas Stern, 'The Optimal Size of Market Areas', *Journal of Economic Theory*, vol. 4 (1972), pp. 154–73.

# 12

# Labour-Managed Firms in Conditions of Imperfect Competition

*From* The Economic Journal, *vol. 84 (December 1974), pp. 817–824.*

In a previous article,[1] I outlined Professor Vanek's analysis of the reasons why in conditions of short-run competitive equilibrium a rise in the demand price offered for the product of a labour-managed or co-operative firm would lead to a reduction in the number of workers which would maximise average income per worker. The present note extends the analysis to the case where the firm is selling its product in an imperfect market.

Let

$$P = P(\alpha, X) \tag{1}$$

where $P$ is the selling price of the firm's output $X$ with $\partial P/\partial X < 0$ and where $\alpha$ is a shift parameter with $\partial P/\partial \alpha > 0$. An increase in $\alpha$ thus represents a rise in the market demand curve for the firm's output.

Let $V$ be the marginal revenue which the firm derives from additional sales of $X$, so that

$$V = \frac{\partial(PX)}{\partial X}. \tag{2}$$

Let $R$ represent the profit earned in an entrepreneurial firm. This is expressed by

$$R = PX - WL - F \tag{3}$$

where $$L = L(X) \tag{4}$$

represents the number of workers employed which depends solely upon

[1] 'The Theory of Labour-Managed Firms and of Profit Sharing', *The Economic Journal*, vol. 82 (March 1972 Supplement), pp. 402–28 [Chapter 10 above, pp. 159–82]. I am greatly indebted to Professor D. G. Champernowne for suggesting many improvements in the exposition of my argument.

the level of the output $X$, $W$ is the given market wage-rate, and $F$ is a given overhead cost due to interest on the firm's fixed debt.[2]

Thus $R$ is a function of $X$ and $\alpha$; and the entrepreneurial firm in the short run will adjust $X$, given $\alpha$, so as to maximise $R$. The first- and second-order conditions for this are

$$\frac{\partial R}{\partial X} = 0 \quad \text{and} \quad \frac{\partial^2 R}{\partial X^2} < 0.$$

This first-order condition is given by

$$\frac{\partial R}{\partial X} = V - W\lambda = 0 \tag{5}$$

where $\lambda = dL/dX$ or the short-run marginal labour cost of $X$. From (5) we derive

$$W = V\frac{1}{\lambda} \tag{6}$$

which states that in equilibrium the wage-rate $(W)$ will be equal to the marginal revenue $(V)$ value of the marginal product of labour $(1/\lambda)$.

From (5) we derive the second-order condition which is given by

$$\frac{\partial^2 R}{\partial X^2} = \frac{\partial V}{\partial X} - W\frac{d\lambda}{dX} < 0$$

so that, using (6),

$$\frac{\partial^2 R}{\partial X^2} = V\left\{\frac{1}{V}\frac{\partial V}{\partial X} - \frac{1}{\lambda}\frac{d\lambda}{dX}\right\} < 0. \tag{7}$$

Equation (7) expresses the fact that for entrepreneurial short-run equilibrium the marginal labour cost curve must cut the marginal revenue curve from below.[3]

From (5) we may also derive

$$\left.\begin{aligned}\frac{\partial^2 R}{\partial X\,\partial \alpha} &= \frac{\partial V}{\partial \alpha} \\[2mm] \frac{\partial^2 R}{\partial X\,\partial F} &= 0\end{aligned}\right\} \tag{8}$$

and

---

[2] $F$ was expressed by the term $iP_kK$ in my earlier article.

[3] It is normal to draw the marginal revenue curve as well as the demand curve as negatively inclined. But this is not necessarily so; $V = P[1 - (1/e)]$, where $e$ is the numerical value of the elasticity of demand. If $e$ rises sufficiently when $X$ increases $V$ may actually rise $(\partial V/\partial X > 0)$ even though $P$ falls $(\partial P/\partial X < 0)$. Equation (7) states that the marginal labour cost must be falling less quickly (or rising more quickly) than the marginal revenue curve.

We next consider a co-operative firm; and let $A$ represent the income per worker in such a firm. Ths is expressed by

$$A = \frac{PX - F}{L}. \tag{9}$$

In (9) $A$ is a function of $X$ and $\alpha$; and the co-operative firm, if it is free in the short run to choose the number of workers so as to maximise income per worker, will adjust $X$, given $\alpha$, so as to maximise $A$. The first- and second-order conditions for this are $\partial A/\partial X = 0$ and $\partial^2 A/\partial X^2 < 0$.

This first-order condition is given by

$$\frac{\partial A}{\partial X} = \frac{LV - \lambda(PX - F)}{L^2} = 0 \tag{10}$$

or using (9)

$$\frac{\partial A}{\partial X} = \frac{V - \lambda A}{L} = 0. \tag{11}$$

From (11) we derive

$$A = V\frac{1}{\lambda}. \tag{12}$$

If one more worker is admitted to the co-operative, he will add the marginal revenue value of his marginal product $(V(1/\lambda))$ to the total net income for distribution between himself and his fellow workers. If this additional revenue is greater than the existing net income per worker $(A)$, then his joining the firm will raise the average net income per worker. Equation (12) expresses the fact that new members will be admitted until these two terms are equal.

From (11) we derive the second-order condition

$$\frac{\partial^2 A}{\partial X^2} = \frac{1}{L}\left\{\frac{\partial V}{\partial X} - \lambda\frac{\partial A}{\partial X} - A\frac{d\lambda}{dX}\right\} - \frac{\lambda}{L^2}\{V - \lambda A\} < 0.$$

But from (11) $\partial A/\partial X = 0$ and $A = V(1/\lambda)$ so that

$$\frac{\partial^2 A}{\partial X^2} = \frac{V}{L}\left\{\frac{1}{V}\frac{\partial V}{\partial X} - \frac{1}{\lambda}\frac{d\lambda}{dX}\right\} < 0. \tag{13}$$

This condition is similar to the corresponding condition given for the entrepreneurial firm in (7).

From (10) we can also derive

$$\frac{\partial^2 A}{\partial X \partial \alpha} = \frac{1}{L} \left\{ \frac{\partial V}{\partial \alpha} - \frac{\lambda X}{L} \frac{\partial P}{\partial \alpha} \right\} \Bigg\}$$

and
$$\frac{\partial^2 A}{\partial X \partial F} = \frac{\lambda}{L^2}$$
(14)

Note (from (6) and (12)) that the short-run equilibrium of the entrepreneurial firm and of the co-operative firm would be the same if $A = W$. From (3) and (9) it can be seen that this would be the case if $R = 0$. It is thus convenient to continue the analysis by supposing that an entrepreneurial firm is transformed into a labour-managed co-operative, the co-operative incurring a debt of interest which accounts for the whole of the current profits of the entrepreneurial firm. In consequence there will be no immediate effect upon employment or output. We then compare the effect on output (and so on employment) of a rise in the demand schedule under the two different forms of management.

Consider first the entrepreneurial firm. If equilibrium is to be maintained in such a firm when $\alpha$ changes there must be an offsetting change in $X$ which allows the equilibrium equation (5) to continue to be satisfied. We need to find the relationship between $dX$ and $d\alpha$ when the equilibrium condition $\partial R / \partial X = 0$ remains satisfied. Differentiating $\partial R / \partial X$ in respect of $\alpha$ and $X$ we have

$$\frac{\partial^2 R}{\partial X^2} dX + \frac{\partial^2 R}{\partial X \partial \alpha} d\alpha = 0 .$$
(15)

Using (7) and (8) we thus obtain

$$\left( \frac{dX}{d\alpha} \right)_{\text{Ent}} = \frac{\dfrac{1}{V}\dfrac{\partial V}{\partial \alpha}}{\dfrac{1}{\lambda}\dfrac{d\lambda}{dX} - \dfrac{1}{V}\dfrac{\partial V}{\partial X}} .$$
(16)

Consider next the co-operative firm. In this case we need to find the relationship between $dX$ and $d\alpha$ when the equilibrium condition $\partial A / \partial X = 0$ continues to be satisfied. We thus have

$$\frac{\partial^2 A}{\partial X^2} dX + \frac{\partial^2 A}{\partial X \partial \alpha} d\alpha = 0 .$$
(17)

Using (13) and (14) we thus obtain

$$\left( \frac{dX}{d\alpha} \right)_{\text{Co-op}} = \frac{\dfrac{1}{V}\dfrac{\partial V}{\partial \alpha} - \dfrac{\lambda PX}{VL}\dfrac{1}{P}\dfrac{\partial P}{\partial \alpha}}{\dfrac{1}{\lambda}\dfrac{d\lambda}{dX} - \dfrac{1}{V}\dfrac{\partial V}{\partial X}} .$$

If we write $\theta = PX/(PX - F)$ for the ratio of gross revenue $(PX)$ to net revenue available to the workers after paying debt interest $(PX - F)$, we obtain from (10) $\lambda PX/VL = \theta$ so that

$$\left(\frac{dX}{d\alpha}\right)_{\text{Co-op}} = \frac{\dfrac{1}{V}\dfrac{\partial V}{\partial \alpha} - \theta\dfrac{1}{P}\dfrac{\partial P}{\partial \alpha}}{\dfrac{1}{\lambda}\dfrac{d\lambda}{dX} - \dfrac{1}{V}\dfrac{\partial V}{\partial X}} . \tag{18}$$

The expressions in (16) and (18) measure the response of output to an increase in demand in the entrepreneurial and the co-operative firms respectively.

From the familiar relationship $V = P[1 - (1/e)]$, where $e$ is the numerical value of the elasticity of demand, we note that the ratio between marginal revenue $(V)$ and selling price $(P)$ depends upon the elasticity of demand $(e)$. If the change in demand raises the price without changing the elasticity of demand, the ratio of $V$ to $P$ will remain unchanged. In other words, with unchanged elasticity of demand $V$ and $P$ will change in the same proportion, so that

$$\frac{1}{V}\frac{\partial V}{\partial \alpha} = \frac{1}{P}\frac{\partial P}{\partial \alpha} .$$

It follows from (16) that in this case (given the second-order condition of (7)) an increase in demand $((1/P)\, \partial P/\partial \alpha > 0)$ will cause an increase in the output of the entrepreneurial firm $((dX/d\alpha)_{\text{Ent}} > 0)$.

In the case of the co-operative firm it can be seen that with

$$\frac{1}{V}\frac{\partial V}{\partial \alpha} = \frac{1}{P}\frac{\partial P}{\partial \alpha} > 0 \quad \text{and} \quad \theta > 1$$

the numerator of (18) will be $< 0$, so that (given the second-order condition of (13)) an increase in demand $((1/P)\, \partial P/\partial \alpha > 0)$ will cause a decline in the output of the co-operative firm $((dX/d\alpha)_{\text{Co-op}} < 0)$.

But a rise in the demand curve may be associated with a change in the elasticity of demand. If the elasticity of demand were sufficiently reduced by the change in demand conditions, a firm's marginal revenue might fall absolutely even though its selling price rose. In this case the entrepreneurial firm as well as the co-operative firm would reduce its output when the demand rose. At the other extreme, if the elasticity of demand were sufficiently raised when the demand increased, the co-operative firm's marginal revenue might be so increased that it had an incentive to admit more partners in order to increase output. $V = P[1 - (1/e)]$ expresses the relationship between marginal revenue $(V)$, price $(P)$, and the numerical value of the price elasticity of demand $(e)$.

Differentiating this expression we obtain

$$\frac{1}{V}\frac{\partial V}{\partial \alpha} = \frac{1}{P}\frac{\partial P}{\partial \alpha} + \frac{1}{e-1}\frac{1}{e}\frac{\partial e}{\partial \alpha}.$$

Using this result we can see that the numerator in (16) is negative if

$$-\frac{1}{e}\frac{\partial e}{\partial \alpha} > (e-1)\frac{1}{P}\frac{\partial P}{\partial \alpha}$$

and the numerator in (18) is positive if

$$\frac{1}{e}\frac{\partial e}{\partial \alpha} > (\theta - 1)(e-1)\frac{1}{P}\frac{\partial P}{\partial \alpha}.$$

Thus the entrepreneurial firm will contract output if the proportional fall in the elasticity of demand is greater than $(e-1)$ times the proportional rise in price, and the co-operative firm will increase output if the proportional rise in the elasticity of demand is greater than $(\theta - 1)(e-1)$ times the proportional rise in price.

But from (16) and (18) we have

$$\left(\frac{dE}{d\alpha}\right)_{\text{Ent}} - \left(\frac{dX}{d\alpha}\right)_{\text{Co-op}} = \frac{\theta\dfrac{1}{P}\dfrac{\partial P}{\partial \alpha}}{\dfrac{1}{\lambda}\dfrac{d\lambda}{dX} - \dfrac{1}{V}\dfrac{\partial V}{\partial X}} > 0.$$

From this it follows that the entrepreneurial firm will always expand more or contract less than the co-operative firm when the demand rises.

So far we have compared the reactions to an increase in demand by an entrepreneurial firm and by a co-operative firm which start in the same equilibrium position. We turn now to a comparison of the reactions to a reduction in the fixed debt interest by an entrepreneurial firm and by a co-operative firm which start in the same equilibrium position. This amounts to starting once more with a level of fixed debt interest, $F$, which reduces the net profits of a profit-maximising entrepreneurial firm to zero ($R = 0$ in (3) as well as $\partial R/\partial X = 0$ in (5)) and then asking what would be the effect on each of the two firms of a small reduction in $F$.

Consider first the entrepreneurial firm. We wish to find the relationship between $dX$ and $dF$ when the equilibrium condition $\partial R/\partial X = 0$ (equation (5)) is maintained with a change in $F$ but with $\alpha$ constant. Differentiating $\partial R/\partial X$ we have

$$\frac{\partial^2 R}{\partial X^2}dX + \frac{\partial^2 R}{\partial X \partial F}dF = 0.$$

But from (8)

$$\frac{\partial^2 R}{\partial X \partial F} = 0 \quad \text{so that} \quad \left(\frac{dX}{dF}\right)_{\text{Ent}} = 0 .$$

This expresses the well-known fact that a change in a lump-sum charge on total gross profits will not affect the conditions which maximise total net profits.

Consider next the co-operative firm. We wish now to find the relationship between $dX$ and $dF$ when the equilibrium condition $\partial A / \partial X = 0$ (equation (10)) is maintained. Differentiating we have

$$\frac{\partial^2 A}{\partial X^2} dX + \frac{\partial^2 A}{\partial X \partial F} dF = 0$$

or from (13) and (14)

$$\left(\frac{dX}{dF}\right)_{\text{Co-op}} = \frac{\lambda}{LV\left\{\dfrac{1}{\lambda}\dfrac{d\lambda}{dX} - \dfrac{1}{V}\dfrac{\partial V}{\partial X}\right\}} > 0 .$$

Thus a reduction in debt interest will leave the short-run output of the entrepreneurial firm unchanged but will give the co-operative firm an incentive to reduce output and employment.[4]

The basic fact that the prosperous co-operative firm will be more restrictive than the prosperous entrepreneurial firm can be readily demonstrated diagrammatically.[5] Along the horizontal axis in Figures 1 and 2 we measure the amount of labour ($L$) employed and up the vertical axis we measure the total gross revenue of the firm ($PX$). Since output ($X$) depends in the short run only upon the labour employed ($L$) and since with any given demand curve the price ($P$) depends only upon the amount sold ($X$), we have $PX$ dependent only upon $L$. We assume that as $L$ increases, so $PX$ increases but at a diminishing rate.[6]

---

[4] The conclusions reached about the reactions of the two types of firm to changes in demand or in the fixed debt charge are subject to the condition that $d\lambda/dX < \infty$. If the firm were producing up to the absolute limit of short-run capacity, then $d\lambda/dX = \infty$ and output would not be affected by a small change in demand in either kind of firm.

[5] I am indebted to Avinash Dixit for suggesting to me the use of this very simple diagram. I have thought it worthwhile to retain the more clumsy algebraic expressions given earlier in this note because they express precisely the relevant relationships between the level of the demand curve, the elasticity of the demand curve, the elasticity of the short-run labour cost curve, and the proportion of the firm's revenue which is absorbed by the fixed debt charge.

[6] The assumption that the rate diminishes corresponds to our earlier stability assumption that

$$\frac{1}{\lambda}\frac{d\lambda}{dX} - \frac{1}{V}\frac{\partial V}{\partial X} > 0.$$

In the case of the entrepreneurial firm the wage-rate is represented by the slope of the line $AC$ in Figure 1($a$). The firm maximises its profit by choosing that point on the $PX$ curve at which $AC$ is tangential to it. It thus maximises $0A$ which measures its gross profit ($PX - WL$). The wage bill ($WL$) is measured by $AB$. In the case of the co-operative firm the distance $0'A'$ measures the fixed debt charge ($F$). The firm now wishes to maximise the slope of the line $A'C'$, which represents the net income per worker. This it does by choosing the point at which the line $A'C'$ is tangential to the $PX$ curve. $A'B'$ then measures ($PX - F$) or the total net revenue available to the workers. We start our comparison of the two firms with the assumption that $0A = 0'A'$, i.e. that the gross profit of the entrepreneurial firm is equal to the fixed debt charge of the co-operative firm.

Figure 2($a$) then compares the effect on the two firms of a rise in the demand curve of a sort which raises $P$ for every value of $X$, i.e. raises $PX$ for every value of $L$. The entrepreneurial firm, being faced with an unchanged wage-rate, will move from the original position at $C$ to the new position at point $D$ where the line $ED$ has the same slope as the line $AC$ and tangential to the higher $PX$-curve. The co-operative firm, being faced with an unaltered fixed debt charge ($F$), will move to the point $G$ where the line $AG$ is tangential to the higher $PX$-curve. The point $G$ is necessarily to the left of the point $D$. In Figure 2($a$) we have shown $D$

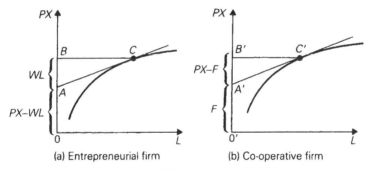

(a) Entrepreneurial firm    (b) Co-operative firm

**Figure 1**

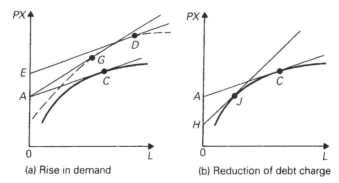

(a) Rise in demand    (b) Reduction of debt charge

**Figure 2**

to the right of *C* and *G* to the left of *C*, but both might lie to the right or both to the left of *C*.

In Figure 2(*b*) we illustrate the case in which *F* is reduced from 0*A* to 0*H*. The equilibrium point of the entrepreneurial firm remains unchanged at *C* since the wage-rate (slope of *AC*) and the *PX* curve are both unchanged. The co-operative firm reduces its employment and output from the point *C* to the point *J* because its fixed debt charge (*F*) has fallen from 0*A* to 0*H*.

The tendency for the prosperous co-operative firm to restrict output is likely to result in a misallocation of resources. This could be countered only by two types of institution: first, by making it easy for the entry of new co-operatives into the prosperous industry; or, second, by reserving decisions about the hiring and firing of workers to some outside authority which can require the co-operative to take on more labour so long as the value of the marginal product of labour in the co-operative is high relatively to its productivity in the rest of the economy. Both of these solutions would be extremely difficult in conditions in which the labour-managed concern was in an industry in which economies of large-scale production were so great that there was not room for more than a very limited number of efficient concerns. Competition from newly established competitive co-operatives would obviously be an inappropriate safeguard.

On the other hand, outside control by the state of the level of employment would inevitably lead to something approaching outright nationalisation. As long as increasing returns to scale persist, total output is less than sufficient to pay to all factors rewards equal to the value of their marginal products. If in such an increasing-returns co-operative the state always insisted on an expansion of employment so long as it estimated that the value of labour's marginal product in the co-operative firm were appreciably above labour's productivity in the rest of the economy, then some state remission of the co-operative's debt burden or some other form of subsidy might well be required to maintain earnings in the co-operative at a level equal to earnings in other outside employments. A co-operative for which the state decided the level of employment but was ready to subsidise any shortfall of the workers' earnings below some level which it considered appropriate (presumably on the condition that it was satisfied that the concern was efficiently managed) could hardly remain a truly independent labour-managed enterprise.

Fully independent labour-managed co-operatives are thus appropriate only in those industries in which there is room for many small-scale enterprises of an efficient scale and in which entry for new competing concerns is easy.

# 13

## The Adjustment Processes of Labour Co-operatives with Constant Returns to Scale and Perfect Competition

*From* The Economic Journal, *vol. 89 (December 1979), pp. 781–8. This was reprinted as an 'appended mathematical note' to Meade's paper, 'Labour Co-operatives, Participation, and Value-Added Sharing', in Alasdair Clayre (ed.),* The Political Economy of Cooperation and Participation: A Third Sector *(Oxford University Press, 1980), pp. 89–118.*

### I

Assume a large number of competing labour co-operatives in a perfect market. Each co-operative is producing an output ($X$) under constant returns to scale with only two factors, labour ($L$) and capital equipment ($K$).

For each co-operative we have the production function

$$X = X(L, K),$$ (1.1)

which by differentiation gives

$$dX = ldL + kdK,$$ (1.2)

where $l = \partial X/\partial L$ and $k = \partial X/\partial K$, the marginal products of $L$ and $K$ respectively.

Since there are constant returns to scale we have also

$$X = lL + kK.$$ (1.3)

### II

Consider any one of these competing co-operatives facing a market with a selling price $P$ for the product $X$ and a price $R$ for renting a unit of capital equipment $K$. (It can be assumed either that the co-operative rents each machine for a payment of $R$ per annum or that $R$ measures the interest payable on any sum borrowed for the purchase of a machine.) $P$ and $R$ may vary in the market from time to time but each co-operative acts on the assumption that it cannot affect the level of $P$ or $R$ through its own individual decisions.

Income per head in the co-operative (which we will call $W$) is given by

$$W = \frac{PX - RK}{L}. \qquad (2.1)$$

Given $P$ and $R$, the co-operative can affect $W$ by varying $K$ and $L$, and so $X$.

Differentiating (2.1) with $P$ and $R$ constant and using (1.2) and (1.3) we obtain

$$dW = \frac{(Pk - R)(LdK - KdL)}{L^2}. \qquad (2.2)$$

From (2.2) it can be seen that if $Pk > R$ (i.e. the value of the marginal product of capital equipment $>$ than its rental cost) $W$ can be raised either by increasing $K$ or by decreasing $L$. With constant returns to scale and with $P$ and $R$ given it is only the ratio of labour to capital which is relevant for the level of income per head.

Clearly the existing members of the co-operative can gain by taking on more capital so long as the marginal product of capital is greater than its rental ($Pk > R$). It is also true that income per head can be raised in the co-operative by taking on less labour so long as the value of the marginal product of labour (i.e. what will be lost to output by losing one member) is less than the existing income per head (i.e. what is saved to the remaining members of the co-operative by the departure of one member). But with constant returns to scale, if one factor is paid the value of its marginal product then what is left over is just sufficient to pay the other factor a reward equal to its marginal product. If in (2.1) we substitute $Pk$ for $R$ and use (1.3), we obtain $W = Pl$. In other words, there is only a single criterion for the maximisation of income per head in a constant-returns-to-scale competitive co-operative, namely: 'Adjust the capital–labour ratio until the value of the marginal product of capital is equal to its market cost.' The average income of each member of the co-operative will then be at a maximum equal to the value of each member's marginal product.

### III

We consider next the equilibrium conditions for an industry producing an output $NX$ by means of a large number $N$ of perfectly competing identical constant-returns-to-scale co-operatives of the kind described in Sections I and II above, each of which produces $X$. We assume that the number of co-operatives remains constant at $N$; there is no entry of new or exit of old co-operatives. We assume further that each co-operative adjusts itself to any change in the industry's market condition (i.e. to any change in $P$ or $R$) so as to maximise its income per head $W$ by keeping $Pk = R$. By differentiation we obtain

$$\frac{dR}{R} = \frac{dP}{P} + \frac{dk}{k} . \tag{3.1}$$

Assume a demand curve for the output of the industry of the form $P = m\check{P}(NX)$, where $m$ is a shift parameter, the underlying demand function $\check{P}$ remaining unchanged. By differentiation we have

$$\frac{dP}{P} = \frac{dm}{m} + \frac{NX}{\check{P}} \frac{d\check{P}}{d(NX)} \frac{NdX}{NX}$$

or

$$\frac{dP}{P} = \frac{dm}{m} - \frac{1}{\varepsilon} \frac{dX}{X} \tag{3.2}$$

where $\varepsilon$ is the arithmetical value of the elasticity of demand for the industry's product.

From (1.2) we obtain

$$\frac{dX}{X} = \lambda \frac{dL}{L} + (1 - \lambda) \frac{dK}{K} , \tag{3.3}$$

where $\lambda = (lL/X)$, i.e. the proportion of the product which will go to labour when, in equilibrium, labour is paid a reward equal to its marginal product; and similarly $(1 - \lambda) = (kK/X)$.

By differentiation of (1.3) and use of (1.2) we obtain

$$\frac{dl}{l} = -\frac{1 - \lambda}{\lambda} \frac{dk}{k} . \tag{3.4}$$

We define $\sigma$ (the arithmetic value of elasticity of substitution between $L$ and $K$) as the ratio of the proportionate increase in $L/K$ to the proportionate decrease in $l/k$ with which the change in $L/K$ is associated, so that

$$\sigma = -\frac{(dL/L) - (dK/K)}{(dl/l) - (dk/k)} . \tag{3.5}$$

It was shown in Section II that a single co-operative could adjust to a change in market conditions (i.e. a change in $P$ or $R$) by adjusting $K$ or adjusting $L$, since it is the ratio of $L/K$ which matters for the maximisation of income per head. Suppose that $Pk > R$. If it is easy to increase $K$ quickly and it is not desired to expel existing members from the co-operative, $L/K$ will be reduced by increasing $K$. But if it were less easy to increase $K$ rapidly and if at the same time $L$ were being reduced automatically by death and retirement, $L/K$ might rather be reduced by a decrease in $L$. We will consider the two extreme cases in which

either 
$$
\left.
\begin{aligned}
\frac{dL}{L} &= 0 \\[2ex]
\frac{dK}{K} &= 0.
\end{aligned}
\right\}
\tag{3.6}
$$
or

Finally from (2.1) by differentiation, with $\lambda = (PX - RK)/PX$ and $(1 - \lambda) = PkK/PX$, we obtain

$$
\frac{dW}{W} = \frac{1}{\lambda}\left(\frac{dX}{X} + \frac{dP}{P}\right) - \frac{1 - \lambda}{\lambda}\left(\frac{dK}{K} + \frac{dR}{R}\right) - \frac{dL}{L}.
\tag{3.7}
$$

We can then use equations (3.1)–(3.7) to solve for $dK/K$, $dL/L$, $dk/k$, $dl/l$, $dP/P$, $dX/X$, and $dW/W$ in terms of $dm/m$ and $dR/R$.

## IV

With adjustment wholly through changes in $K$ we obtain the following solutions:

$$
\frac{dK}{K} = \left(\frac{dm}{m} - \frac{dR}{R}\right)\frac{\varepsilon\sigma}{\varepsilon\lambda + \sigma(1 - \lambda)},
\tag{4.1}
$$

$$
\frac{dL}{L} = 0,
\tag{4.2}
$$

$$
\frac{dk}{k} = -\left(\frac{dm}{m} - \frac{dR}{R}\right)\frac{\varepsilon\lambda}{\varepsilon\lambda + \sigma(1 - \lambda)},
\tag{4.3}
$$

$$
\frac{dl}{l} = \left(\frac{dm}{m} - \frac{dR}{R}\right)\frac{\varepsilon(1 - \lambda)}{\varepsilon\lambda + \sigma(1 - \lambda)},
\tag{4.4}
$$

$$
\frac{dP}{P} = \frac{dm}{m}\frac{\varepsilon\lambda}{\varepsilon\lambda + \sigma(1 - \lambda)} + \frac{dR}{R}\frac{\sigma(1 - \lambda)}{\varepsilon\lambda + \sigma(1 - \lambda)},
\tag{4.5}
$$

$$
\frac{dX}{X} = \left(\frac{dm}{m} - \frac{dR}{R}\right)\frac{\varepsilon\sigma(1 - \lambda)}{\varepsilon\lambda + \sigma(1 - \lambda)},
\tag{4.6}
$$

$$
\frac{dW}{W} = \frac{dm}{m}\frac{\varepsilon}{\varepsilon\lambda + \sigma(1 - \lambda)} - \frac{dR}{R}\frac{(\varepsilon - \sigma)(1 - \lambda)}{\varepsilon\lambda + \sigma(1 - \lambda)}.
\tag{4.7}
$$

All the signs in these equations are what common sense would suggest with the possible exception of the sign of $dR/R$ in (4.7).

Thus a rise in the demand curve relatively to the cost of capital (i.e. an initial rise in $P$ and/or fall in $R$) will upset the existing equilibrium by making $Pk > R$. Each co-operative will have an inducement to increase $K$ which will cause an increase in output $X$, a fall in the marginal product of capital $k$, and a rise in the marginal product of labour $l$; and the increase in output will exert a downward influence on demand price $P$. $Pk$ will fall back until equality with $R$ is restored. There will finally be a net rise in $P$ in so far as it was an upward shift in the demand curve which caused $Pk$ initially to exceed $R$, but a net fall in $P$ in so far as it was a reduction in $R$ which caused the initial change.

In a perfectly competitive capitalist economy with constant returns to scale and given market prices for the factors, an upward shift in the demand curve would induce an equal proportionate increase in both $K$ and $L$ until output at a constant cost per unit was so increased that the demand price had fallen back to its initial level. With a labour-co-operative economy an upward shift of the demand curve may also give an inducement to expand output, but by taking on more $K$ without taking on more $L$. In this case the expansion of output will not be on a sufficient scale to bring the price down to its old level, since if the old price were so restored the whole of the inducement to employ more $K$ with the given amount of $L$ would have disappeared. The price would remain at a higher level than before the change, and income per head in each co-operative would be raised above its previous level. Only if new entrants were attracted by the prospect of this higher income per head to set up new additional co-operatives would the price be brought down once more to its previous level.

The importance of ease of entry for new co-operatives becomes even more marked when one considers the sign of $dR/R$ in equation (4.7). An upward shift in the demand curve will raise the average income in each co-operative. But the effect of a change in the cost of hiring capital equipment is uncertain. If $\varepsilon > \sigma$, then a rise in $R$ will reduce $W$. But if $\sigma > \varepsilon$, it will have the less obvious opposite effect of raising $W$.

Thus suppose $\sigma$ to be very large and $\varepsilon$ to be very small. An increase in $R$ causes $R$ to exceed $Pk$. As a result in each co-operative $K$ is reduced. But since $\sigma$ is very large, the reduction in $K$ causes a very small rise in $k$; on the other hand, since $\varepsilon$ is very small, the reduction in the industry's output causes a large rise in $P$. In the new equilibrium with $Pk = R$ once more, $W$ will again be equal to the value of the marginal product of labour $Pl$. But $l$ will have fallen little (because $\sigma$ is large) and $P$ will have risen much (because $\varepsilon$ is small). Thus $W = Pl$ will have risen.

In perfect competition in capitalist production with $\sigma > \varepsilon$ a rise in $R$ would cause a fall in output, a fall in $K$, but an *increase* in $L$. The main effect would be a substitution of $L$ for $K$ (with $\sigma$ large) rather than any reduction in output resulting from the net rise in cost ($\varepsilon$ small). This case emphasises the much greater importance of entry of new firms in the labour-co-operative economy than in the capitalist economy. In the latter each existing firm would have had an incentive to take on more labour if the change raised the value of the marginal product of labour above its reward in other occupations. This is not the case with the labour co-operative, where the industry must rely on the entry of new co-operatives if conditions raise income per head within the co-operative above the level ruling in other occupations.

## V

With all adjustment carried out by changes in $L$ we have:

$$\frac{dK}{K} = 0, \tag{5.1}$$

$$\frac{dL}{L} = -\left(\frac{dm}{m} - \frac{dR}{R}\right)\frac{\varepsilon\sigma}{\lambda(\varepsilon - \sigma)}, \tag{5.2}$$

$$\frac{dk}{k} = -\left(\frac{dm}{m} - \frac{dR}{R}\right)\frac{\varepsilon}{\varepsilon - \sigma}, \tag{5.3}$$

$$\frac{dl}{l} = \left(\frac{dm}{m} - \frac{dR}{R}\right)\frac{\varepsilon(1 - \lambda)}{\lambda(\varepsilon - \sigma)}, \tag{5.4}$$

$$\frac{dP}{P} = \frac{dm}{m}\frac{\varepsilon}{\varepsilon - \sigma} - \frac{dR}{R}\frac{\sigma}{\varepsilon - \sigma}, \tag{5.5}$$

$$\frac{dX}{X} = -\left(\frac{dm}{m} - \frac{dR}{R}\right)\frac{\varepsilon\sigma}{\varepsilon - \sigma}, \tag{5.6}$$

$$\frac{dW}{W} = \frac{dm}{m}\frac{\varepsilon}{\lambda(\varepsilon - \sigma)} - \frac{dR}{R}\frac{\varepsilon(1 - \lambda) + \sigma\lambda}{\lambda(\varepsilon - \sigma)}. \tag{5.7}$$

The outcome is in this case dependent in a much more fundamental way upon the sign of $\varepsilon - \sigma$. In fact the industry's output would, in the absence of the entry of new co-operatives or the exit of existing co-operatives, be unstable if $\sigma > \varepsilon$.

This can be seen by supposing the industry to be initially in equilibrium with $Pk = R$ but then to experience an upward shift in the demand curve ($dm/m > 0$). The immediate effect of this is to raise $Pk$ above $R$. $K$ is then being paid less than the value of its marginal product, so that $L$ will be receiving a $W$ which exceeds its marginal product. In this case it pays each co-operative to reduce its membership. As a result $X$ is reduced. But with $\sigma$ large and $\varepsilon$ small, this causes a large rise in $P$ but only a small fall in $k$, so that $Pk$, far from being reduced again towards $R$, rises still further above $R$. As a result $W$ exceeds still more the value of $L$'s marginal product. The position is an unstable one. Equality between $Pk$ and $R$ could in fact be restored only by an increase in $L$ which would cause a large fall in $P$ (with

$\varepsilon$ small) and only a small rise in $k$ (with $\sigma$ large). Equilibrium requires an increase in $L$; each co-operative has an incentive to reduce $L$.[1]

Once more in these conditions in a perfectly competitive capitalist industry there would be an incentive to employ more labour so long as the upward shift of the demand curve caused the return to labour to be above its reward in other occupations; but with a labour-co-operative structure the expansion of the industry would, with $\sigma > \varepsilon$, rely in a quite basic way upon the entry of new co-operatives. Indeed stability might well require that the entry and exit of co-operatives was easier and more prompt than the adjustment of the size of membership within each co-operative.

With $\varepsilon > \sigma$, the system of equations (5.1) to (5.7) would be a stable one. But an upward shift of the demand curve $(dm/m > 0)$ or a fall in the cost of capital $(dR/R < 0)$ would have the perverse effect of causing a reduction in $L$ and in $X$ – the well-known perverse backward-sloping supply curve of labour-managed economies. Only ease of new entry for new co-operatives would offset this effect.

There is one further important feature of the situation in which labour co-operatives rely upon adjustment of $L$ rather than upon adjustment of $K$ to maximise income per head, namely the greater sensitivity of the level of income per head to variations in demand or in the cost of capital. In the case of a capital-intensive industry this sensitivity can become very great indeed.

The situation is illustrated by the following numerical example. Assume a 1% upward shift in the demand curve $(dm/m = 1\%)$ in an industry in which $\varepsilon = 2$ and $\sigma = $ either 1 or 1·5. We ask what will be the resulting percentage rise in $W$ on the alternative assumptions that the industry is labour-intensive $(\lambda = 0\cdot9)$ or capital-intensive $(\lambda = 0\cdot1)$ and that the adjustment is made wholly by increasing $K$ or wholly by decreasing $L$. The following table derived from equations (4.7) and (5.7) gives the resulting percentage increases in $W$:

|  | $dL/L = 0$ | | $dK/K = 0$ | |
|---|---|---|---|---|
|  | $\sigma = 1$ | $\sigma = 1\cdot5$ | $\sigma = 1$ | $\sigma = 1\cdot5$ |
| $\lambda = 0\cdot9$ | 1·05 | 1·03 | 2·2 | 4·4 |
| $\lambda = 0\cdot1$ | 1·8 | 1·29 | 20·0 | 40·0 |

The variability of $W$ is in each case greater with $dK/K = 0$ than with $dL/L = 0$. This is to be expected. With, for example, a rise in the demand curve and $dL/L = 0$, $K$ will be increased, which will increase $X$ and tend to moderate the rise in $P$. On the other hand, with $dK/K = 0$, $L$ will be reduced, which will decrease $X$ and accentuate the rise in $P$. It is also clear that the variations in $W$ will be greater with $\lambda = 0\cdot1$ than with $\lambda = 0\cdot9$. The variation in $W$ depends *inter alia* upon the difference between $PX$ and $RK$; and with $PX$ or $RK$ varying by a given proportion the difference

---

[1] If $\varepsilon = \sigma$, there would be no equilibrium point in either direction. With a change in $L$ in either direction the change in the price of the product just offsets the change in the marginal product of capital so that the excess of $Pk$ over $R$, and thus of $W$ over $Pl$, remains unchanged.

between them will show a larger proportionate change the smaller is $PX - RK$ relatively to $PX$ or to $RK$.

What is most marked in the above numerical example is the extreme variability of $W$ when we combine $dK/K = 0$ and $\lambda = 0 \cdot 1$. It is quite probable that in the real world it would be difficult for new co-operatives to be set up in very capital-intensive industries in which a large amount of capital must be borrowed per member of the co-operative; and it may be more difficult also in such a case for members of an existing co-operative to make any substantial changes in their capital stock. If this is so, then we must expect the incomes of the members of capital-intensive co-operatives to be subject to extreme variability in the face of market changes.

From the above table it can be seen that a high $\sigma$ will moderate the variability of incomes in a co-operative which adjusts to an increase in demand by expanding $K$. The resulting fall in $k$ will be moderated so that the needed reduction in $Pk$ back to the ruling $R$ must be achieved by a greater increase in output and reduction in $P$. On the contrary a high $\sigma$ relatively to $\varepsilon$ will cause great variability if adjustment is through a reduction in $L$. If $\sigma$ is high, then $k$ will be little lowered by any given reduction in $L$ and the membership of the co-operative will have to be very greatly reduced to restore equilibrium. There will be a substantial fall in $X$ which will accentuate the rise in $P$ so that income per head is greatly raised. Indeed, we have already seen that if $\sigma > \varepsilon$ the position will be an unstable one. In the above numerical table with $dK/K = 0$, $\lambda = 0 \cdot 1$, $\varepsilon = 2$, and $\sigma = 1 \cdot 5$ a 1% upward shift in the demand curve would suffice to cause a 40% upward shift in the income per head for the co-operatives' remaining membership.

## VI

The above analysis is much restricted by the two assumptions of perfect competition and of constant returns to scale. Nevertheless it is suggested that it points to three very important basic differences between a free-enterprise market economy of the familiar capitalist type and one based upon competing labour co-operatives, particularly for those real world situations in which there is a fair measure of competition and in which economies and diseconomies of mere scale are not of great importance over a fairly wide range of a firm's size.

First, ease of entry and exit of firms plays a much more vital role in maintaining a balance between supply and demand in the case of labour co-operatives than it does in the case of capitalist enterprises.

Second, within any one labour co-operative appropriate adjustment to market changes can often be made either by changing the amount of capital employed in one direction or alternatively by changing the number of members in the co-operative in the opposite direction. Perverse effects can occur if the individual co-operatives choose to react by adjusting the number of workers in their membership rather than by changing the amount of capital employed. Since a co-operative may find it particularly difficult to attract new members just when market forces have reduced its earnings per head or to persuade members to leave just when market forces have raised its earnings per head, there may be some general tendency for each co-operative to react by adjusting the amount of capital employed by it. However, perverse reactions through adjustment of the size of membership are not to be ruled out if, in an activity in which fixed capital cannot be very readily and rapidly changed, old members happen to be retiring just at the time that market conditions improve or an exceptionally profitable co-operative still remains attractive even after some deterioration in its market conditions. In such cases perverse adjustments of the size of membership can be offset only by the entry of new or exit of old co-operatives.

Third, there are serious dangers of extreme fluctuations in income per head in labour co-operatives in industries which are capital-intensive, for which entry of new co-operatives is difficult, in which substitutability between labour and capital is high, and for the products of which the elasticity of demand is low.

## VII

A reading of the classical literature on the theory of labour co-operatives (for example, Ward, 1958, Vanek, 1970) may suggest that a competitive economy made up of such co-operatives would lead to a quite different equilibrium from that which would result in a competitive economy managed by independent entrepreneurs, one possible difference being the existence in the labour-managed economy of perverse backward-sloping supply curves with increases in demand leading to reductions in supply. This result has been challenged by Pearce (1977) on the grounds that an examination of the general equilibrium conditions shows that (given the same production functions in the two economies) the ultimate outcome is unaffected by the question whether it is the owners of labour, the owners of capital, or independent entrepreneurs who take decisions.

The present paper is intended to elucidate this apparent contradiction by emphasising two points:

(1) Ease of entry of new concerns into an industry plays a vital role in the labour-managed economy, a role which can be played by the expansion of existing competitive concerns with the alternative entrepreneurial arrangements. Such ease of entry is basic for Pearce's conclusions.
(2) It is the ratio of capital to labour which is of central importance in the individual competitive labour co-operative, a ratio which can be adjusted by altering the amount of labour or the amount of capital. The perverse backward-sloping supply curve occurs if (as may well be the case in certain conditions) the entry of new concerns is difficult and adjustment of the size of membership in existing co-operatives is easier than adjustment of the amount of capital equipment.

## References

I. F. Pearce, 'Participation and Income Distribution', in David F. Heathfield (ed.), *The Economics of Co-Determination* (London: Macmillan, 1977)

J. Vanek, *The General Theory of Labor-Managed Market Economies* (Ithaca, NY: Cornell University Press, 1970)

Benjamin Ward, 'The Firm in Illyria: Market Syndicalism', *American Economic Review*, vol. 48 (September 1958), pp. 566–89.

# 14

---

# Different Forms of Share Economy[1]

---

*This paper is an expanded version of the eighth Barnett Shine Foundation Lecture, delivered at Queen Mary College, London, on 25 February 1986, and was published as a pamphlet by the Public Policy Centre (London, 1986). The earlier version was also discussed at a meeting of the Bank of England's Panel of Academic Consultants on 28 February 1986.*

## 1 Three Basic Objectives

There is at present a widespread feeling of the need for some change in the way in which labour is remunerated. We are sailing between Scylla and Charybdis. On the one side is the whirlpool of *laissez-faire* competitive conflict between labour and capital. On the other side are the jagged rocks of centralised, bureaucratic socialist planning. A primary aim is to seek alternative ways of organising productive enterprises so as to maintain the advantages of market competition between independent business concerns but at the same time, within each such business concern, to put more stress on the common interests of labour and capital in the successful conduct of business and thus to improve industrial relations and to raise productive efficiency.

A second pressing problem arises from the phenomenon of stagflation. We need to ensure that an expansion of money expenditures brought about by expansionary fiscal and monetary policies stimulates an increase in output and employment rather than an inflation of money wage-rates, prices, and profit margins. Since real output and the available real income of the community would thus be increased, it ought to be possible for everyone to be better off. May there not be alternative ways of the individual enterprise which would at least help to achieve this result, without embarking on the horrors of a centralised, bureaucratic, statutory incomes policy?

A third *desideratum* which many have in mind in discussing alternative forms of workers' remuneration is concerned with the distribution of income, wealth, and power. This concern has two rather different origins.

[1] I am indebted to Henry Phelps Brown, Ronald Dore, Christopher Dow, John Flemming, Robin Matthews, Mario Nuti, Robert Oakeshott, Ugo Pagano, and Martin Weale for important comments on an earlier draft of this paper; but I am, of course, alone responsible for the views finally expressed in it.

In the first place, there is the strand of thought of the Owenite socialists who consider that some form of co-operative organisation of productive enterprises would result in a fairer and less unequal distribution of income, wealth, and power. In the second place, there are those who are convinced that a competitive capitalist organisation is desirable but would like to see workers owning capital as well as their ability to work and thus in a property-owning democracy entering fully into the ethos of the free capitalist enterprise society.

Inspired by one or other of these three main objectives there is now under discussion a bewildering variety of proposals about alternative forms of organisation (organisation of work councils, worker representatives on boards of directors, development of employee share ownership schemes, the formation of labour-managed co-operatives, profit-sharing or value-added-sharing schemes, other forms of partnership between labour and capital with a wide range of further variety within each of these main types). It is the purpose of this paper to pick out some of the most important distinguishing features of these different proposals and to assess their relative merits in the light of these three main objectives.

There are already in this country, as in many other countries, a number of developments of different kinds in this general field; and the sensible general policy would, no doubt, be to encourage a wide range of experimentation in various alternative forms and to let experience show which forms prove to be the most acceptable, the easiest to operate, and generally the most successful. But systematic analysis and discussion of the various possibilities could be of real help in the design of forms during the present experimental period.

## 2   Risk-Bearing in a Share Economy

There is one feature which all the schemes discussed in this pamphlet have in common. They all result in some form of sharing between labour and capital of the revenue produced by the concern in which they are employed; and, as an inevitable consequence of this, labour and capital must at the same time share the risks of fluctuations in that revenue.

A basic driving force behind all such sharing proposals is the desire to reduce the sense of alienation between 'us', the workers, and 'them', the capitalist bosses, and to raise productivity through an improvement in incentives. There are two closely related approaches to this problem.

The first is to stress the possibility of straightforward economic incentives which in one way or another relate workers' pay to workers' effort. Payment by piece-rate is the obvious and crudest example of this approach. But arrangements such as profit-sharing schemes, which make individual workers' incomes depend in part upon the general success of the whole enterprise, are often advocated for this purpose. It is true that in any large enterprise there will be a large number of workers among whom must be shared any extra profit due to a single worker's effort, so that the direct incentive for extra effort to the individual workers will be greatly diluted. But nevertheless the final result may not be negligible. Each individual worker may monitor the activities of his colleagues in the knowledge that his own income will be affected by their efforts as well as by his own, and thus the general atmosphere will discourage the slacker. Furthermore for much the same reasons workers will be more willing to co-operate with the management if their incomes all depend upon the success of the enterprise.

The second approach is to lay stress on the fact that human beings are not merely selfish individuals but have strong social loyalties which greatly affect their behaviour. To feel a loyalty to the whole enterprise rather than to an association of the workers whose purpose is to fight the management is perhaps of even more importance than any purely economic incentive relating to the level of the individual worker's pay. There is, however, no conflict between the two approaches of taking steps to promote the psychological feeling of membership of and loyalty to the concern as a whole and of arranging that economic rewards for the individual are related to the success of the whole enterprise. Indeed the two approaches would appear to be highly complementary.

In this connection there are many admirable proposals for consultation between workers and management and for the information of workers by management of the relevant facts about the fortunes of their business. There is no wish to depreciate the importance of such developments; but this paper is confined to a discussion of suggestions which are being made for more basic institutional changes of business structures including, in particular, formal arrangements for labour as well as capital to share in any financial gains due to the firm's success.

## Conflict and Co-operation

When labour and capital come together to make and sell some product there are two elements, one of co-operation and one of conflict, in their relationship. The larger the sales value of their joint co-operative output, the larger will be the cake to be divided between them; but, given the size of the cake, labour's share will be in conflict with capital's share. If the absolute size of labour's slice is fixed in advance, labour will have a minimal incentive to concern itself with the co-operative aspect of its relationship with capital, since it is promised the same sized slice regardless of the size of the cake which they manage together to bake. If, however, the contract between labour and capital involves in whole or in part, directly or indirectly, the payment to labour of an agreed fraction of the total revenue co-operatively produced, labour will be much more directly interested in the co-operative aspect of its relationship with capital in baking the largest possible cake.

For this very obvious and familiar reason all the proposals under discussion introduce some feature which causes labour's income to vary directly to some extent with the fortunes of the business in which it is employed, though, as we shall see, there is very great variety in the degrees to which, the forms in which, and the mechanisms by which labour's share in the firm's revenue is determined.

There is, however, an inescapable connection between the co-operative element in labour-capital relations and the bearing of risk. If the worker's income is to depend to some extent in one way or another on the fortunes of the firm in producing a large or small net revenue,[2] then obviously the worker must bear risk connected with the firm's operations. This raises the question of the extent to which the avoidance of risk for the workers should set a limit to the introduction of sharing arrangements; for there is a very good and familiar reason for believing that capital is better able to bear risks than is labour.

## Risk and Labour's Share of Revenue

An owner of capital can spread his risks; if one enterprise goes bust, it is not the end of the world for him. An owner of working ability, however, is unlikely to be able to apply that ability to more than one, or possibly two, forms of employment at the same time. Thus, in so far as imperfections in the labour market impede the immediate and costless movement to other jobs of equal value, all the worker's eggs, so far as his work is concerned, are in one basket. This does not mean that one must abandon all ideas of a share economy. But, as is so often the case in this wicked world, one must consider the balance of pros and cons; and it may not be wise to go too far in the sharing direction. A move in the sharing direction by stimulating the co-operative element in labour-capital relations may well raise productivity and the size of the cake and so of labour's slice on the average, but it will at the same time increase the risk of fluctuation in the size of that slice for the worker who cannot diversify his work risks or move easily to other jobs.

How far one should go must thus be influenced by the trade-off between average size of slice and fluctuations of size of slice; and this trade-off is likely to vary from firm to firm. Consider two extreme cases. In firm A output depends very much upon the individual care and effort put into the work by the individual craftsmen, and the market for the product is a very stable and certain one. In firm B the work is very automatic and routine and there is relatively little scope for increased

---

[2] Throughout this paper the following definitions will be used for a firm's revenue and its distribution:

Gross Revenue (i.e. Sale Proceeds) *less* Purchases of Intermediate Products used in Production and *less* depreciation of Fixed Capital = Value Added.
Value Added *less* the Firm's Tax Liability = Net Revenue.
Net Revenue *less* Payments of Fixed Wages, Fixed Interest and Fixed Rents = Distributable Surplus.
Net Revenue *less* the Amounts (Wages, Rent, Interest) which the Firm's Factors (Labour, Land, Capital) could earn on the average in other Activities = the Firm's Pure Profit or Loss.

An attempt is made to use as little technical jargon as possible in this paper. One term, however, which will be used refers to a factor's 'Marginal Revenue Product'. By the marginal revenue product of labour, for example, is meant the amount which could be added to the firm's net revenue by employing one more additional worker.

productivity from any change in the workers' motivation, but the market for the product is an uncertain and risky one. In case A a share economy may lead to a considerable rise in the average size of the worker's slice with little uncertainty about the size of that slice. In firm B there would be little increase in the average size of that slice combined with a great risk of its fluctuation. It is in firms of type A that the introduction of a share element in pay is most clearly advantageous.

Even in those cases (as in case A above) in which it is useful that the worker should bear some of the risk, it is important to avoid the imposition of excessive risk upon the worker. The amount of risk which the worker will be called upon to face in any particular case will depend upon both the structure of costs in the firm in which he works and the form of sharing arrangement which is applied to the firm. For this purpose it is useful to think in terms of two quantities: (1) the average share and (2) the marginal share of labour in the firm's net revenue.

Thus in one firm labour's pay in equilibrium may account for 90 per cent of the firm's net revenue. This could be true in a very labour-intensive service activity which did not involve using much capital equipment for its operation. At the other extreme, for a very capital-intensive activity labour's pay might account for only 10 per cent of the firm's net revenue. We may say that labour's *average* share is 90 per cent in the former case but only 10 per cent in the latter.

Labour's *marginal* share may be defined as the proportion of any fluctuation in the firm's net revenue which would be added to, or subtracted from, labour's pay if there were no change in the level of employment in the firm. This clearly depends upon the form of the sharing arrangement, if any, which has been adopted by the firm in question. If labour is paid a fixed money wage, then labour's marginal share is zero; the whole of any rise or fall in net revenue will be added to, or subtracted from, the owner's profit. At the other extreme consider a labour co-operative in which the whole of the needed capital equipment has been financed by borrowing at fixed interest and in which the worker co-operators simply divide among themselves any net revenue which remains after allowing for the depreciation of fixed capital and the service of their fixed-interest loans. In this case the workers' marginal share will be 100 per cent; they will add to or subtract from their residual earnings the whole of any fluctuation in the firm's net revenue. There are, of course, many intermediate types of payment which will be described in what follows; the feature which is relevant for our present purpose is the degree to which the scheme in operation will cause any fluctuation in the firm's net revenue to fall on the workers' rather than the capitalist's income.

The degree of risk to which the worker's income is subject depends upon the relation between the average and the marginal shares of labour in the firm's net revenue. Thus consider the effect of a 10 per cent fall in a firm's net revenue. If labour's average share were 10 per cent and its marginal share were 100 per cent, the decline in the firm's net revenue would reduce labour's income to zero. If, however, labour's average share had been 90 per cent and its marginal share 100 per cent, labour's income would have been reduced only in the proportion of 90 to 80 (i.e. by one ninth). If labour's average share were 50 per cent and its marginal share also 50 per cent, then labour's income would be reduced in the proportion of 50 to 45 (i.e. by one tenth). And so on. What is clearly to be avoided is a high ratio of labour's marginal to labour's average share in the firm's net revenue; and this means that some high marginal share arrangements which might be acceptable for labour-intensive activities should not be applied in capital-intensive activities.

## The Risk of Unemployment and the Share Economy

So far the analysis has ignored the fact that even in a capitalist firm which pays labour in the form of a riskless fixed wage labour does nevertheless bear risk in the real world of imperfect competition, the risk taking the form of the threat of unemployment. If there were perfect competition in the labour market a worker could always get an alternative job at the going outside market rate of pay, and the employer could always hire additional workers at that rate. The greater the degree of monopolistic element in any particular section of the labour market, the greater the degree of risk which may fall on workers in the form of becoming unemployed or accepting a cut in rates of pay if things go badly or in being able to press successfully for a higher rate of pay if things go well for the firm.

The introduction of a share element may not only increase the risks of fluctuation in the income of an employed worker. It may also shift the nature of risks from fluctuations of employment to fluctuations of income; for with a share element in workers' pay a given fall in the demand for labour may well cause an automatic reduction in the rate of pay per unit of work and thus lead to a small reduction in the number of units of work demanded. In assessing any share arrangements one must take account of any reduction in the risks of unemployment as well as of any increase in the risks of fluctuations of the pay of the employed.

In general one may feel that a situation in which a few persons risk a total loss of employment is worse than a situation in which a partial reduction in pay is spread over a large number of persons. But there are other considerations which may lead one to modify this conclusion.

In the first place, the relative burden of the two forms of risk will be affected by the elasticity of demand for labour in the particular firm in question. Consider a reduction in the demand for labour which would call for a 10 per cent reduction in the rate of pay to maintain employment. If the elasticity of demand for labour were unity, this would call for a 10 per cent reduction in employment if the rate of pay is to be maintained. But it might call only for a 1 per cent reduction in employment if the elasticity of demand were very small. The balance of advantage to the work force shifts from pay flexibility to employment flexibility if the elasticity of demand is small; and *vice versa*.

Among other factors the elasticity of demand for labour in any one business will depend upon the importance of the labour costs in relation to the gross revenue of the firm. Consider a firm which purchases an intermediate product and works it up for sale to the final consumer. The value added by the finishing firm represents, say, only 10 per cent of the price to the consumer of the finished product. Even if the whole of this value added represented labour cost, a 10 per cent cut in the cost of labour in the finishing firm would lead to only a 1 per cent cut in the price of the finished product to the consumer, and the elasticity of demand for labour in the finishing firm would be only one tenth of the elasticity of demand for the finished product. If there were a fall in demand for the finished product, a cut in the rate of pay confined alone to the firm which finished the product would have little effect in restoring demand for the finished product and thus in maintaining employment. From their own narrow point of view the workers in the finishing firm would gain little in security of employment from greater flexibility in their own rates of pay.

The situation would, however, be very different if at the same time the workers in the firm producing the intermediate product also accepted flexibility in their rates of pay. Any fall in demand for the finished product will lead to a fall in demand for the intermediate product, the cost of which in our example accounts for 90 per cent of the price of the finished product. If this fall in demand led to a reduction in the money pay of the workers concerned so that the cost of the intermediate product also fell as well as the cost of the labour directly employed in finishing the product, the effect of downward flexibility in rates of pay in the finishing firm would be ten times as great. Thus the effect of pay flexibility in reducing the risks of unemployment depends not simply for each firm on the flexibility of pay in that firm but on the adoption of the same principle of flexibility in other parts of the system.

Second, suppose that the elasticity of demand for labour were unity and that the risk of a 10 per cent cut in pay per worker or of a loss of employment by one out of every 10 workers were the same. In the ordinary risk-averse case an individual would be more willing to face a certain 10 per cent cut in his income than a 10 per cent chance of losing the whole of his income if he loses his job. There is the possibility of getting another job, and there is the certainty of unemployment support of one kind or another if he fails to do so. The greater the chance of getting another job and the higher the rate of unemployment support, the less certain is it that the flexibility of pay will be preferred by the individual worker.

Third, it is very probable that in most firms different workers face different chances of unemployment. It is the less reliable, most recently engaged, and less efficient workers who are likely to be made redundant. They may be clearly distinguishable among the work force. While this particular minority of workers whose employment is most at risk might prefer the flexibility of pay due to a share economy, the majority of workers who do not feel any risk of unemployment may prefer the certainty of a given fixed rate of pay.

For these three reasons, quite apart from any conservative unwillingness to venture on new and unknown possibilities it may well turn out that the majority of workers will prefer fixed wages to any very extensive move in the direction of a variable share in the firm's fortunes, even if the latter will reduce the risks of unemployment.

## 3   Entrepreneurial Risk-Bearing and the Principle of Non-Discrimination

For reasons discussed above, it is probable that the workers in a firm who have all their work eggs in one basket will be more risk-averse than the capitalist entrepreneurs who will have placed only some of their eggs in this particular basket. If this is so, a share arrangement which shifts some risk-bearing on to the workers' shoulders may well lead the workers to be concerned about the firm's policies in embarking on risky new adventures. If the workers have no risks at all, they would have no concern with the degree of riskiness of the firm's business; but the greater their marginal share in risk-bearing, the more direct will their interest be in the firm's choices between safe low-yielding business and risky high-yielding business. This is one, but only one, reason why the introduction of a share arrangement is likely to lead to a demand by workers that they should also participate in the making of decisions about the firm's policies.

This feature of any far-reaching extension of share arrangements is of the greatest importance. In a very wide range of business activities, particularly in modern conditions of rapid development of new products and new technologies, success depends upon venturesome and decisive action by managers with flair and the courage of their convictions. It may well be argued that in such conditions there must be a strong 'them' to tell 'us' what we must accept and carry out for the success of the business. There is a clear danger that in conditions of far-reaching share arrangements with the workers averse to risk but participating in the firm's policies the economy might fall further and further behind in innovation of products and techniques and generally in industrial efficiency. Does this mean that extensive sharing arrangements must be confined to what one may call sedate business activities? Or is it possible to set limits on the direct intervention of workers in managerial decisions, just as they are in fact set on the direct intervention of shareholders?

The possibility of workers becoming entrepreneurial risk-bearers raises another most important issue. If existing entrepreneurs in a successful business – whoever they may be – aim at maximising their own incomes, they should be prepared to admit newcomers into the business at rates of reward which are not necessarily as high as the rewards being earned by themselves. Otherwise, if the non-discrimination principle that newcomers from outside should invariably be treated as favourably as existing insiders is immutably applied, expansion of a successful business may be seriously impeded.

It is notable that the principle of non-discrimination is not applied as between the capitalist entrepreneurs in an ordinary company. Thus consider a successful firm run by the capitalists or their representatives in which capital equipment costing £100,000 is producing a profit for the capitalists of £20,000 a year, a return of 20 per cent. Suppose that an additional investment of £100,000 would add £10,000 per annum to the firm's net revenue, a yield of 10 per cent per annum. The capitalists would undertake this extra investment if they could persuade new outside investors to provide the necessary funds either by lending them the necessary £100,000 at a rate of interest less than 10 per cent or by purchasing newly issued shares from the firm at a price which would raise the necessary capital sum of £100,000 at the cost of dividend payments of less than £10,000 a year. This would mean that of the £30,000 total profit being made (£20,000 on the original investment of £100,000 and £10,000 on the additional investment of £100,000) the new investors would be receiving something less than £10,000 while the old investors would be receiving something more than £20,000 even though both groups of investors had provided the finance for the same amounts of real capital equipment.[3] We may call this the principle of discrimination, since the existing capitalists pay to the new capitalists a sum which, while it is sufficient to attract them into the concern, is nevertheless less than what the existing successful capitalists are themselves enjoying.

If we apply this same analysis to the employment of additional workers by the existing workers in a successful labour-managed concern, we see that it would involve a discrimination between the higher pay of the existing workers and the lower pay of the new workers. The principle of equal pay for equal work would have to be abandoned. Our story would now read as follows.

Consider a successful labour-managed firm in which 100 workers are producing a net income for themselves of £200,000 a year, i.e. an annual income of £2,000 for each worker. Suppose that an additional 100 workers would add £100,000 a year to the available surplus, i.e. an additional £1,000 a year produced by each additional worker. If the new outside workers in the less successful outside world were willing to be employed for something less than £1,000 a year, the existing workers would gain the difference; their income per head would rise something above £2,000 a year while that of the new workers would be at a rate of something less than £1,000 a year. This is the principle of discrimination between the pay of the existing successful insiders

---

[3] Any new shareholders would, of course, be receiving the same rate of dividend as old shareholders; but the old investors would own more shares than the new investors even though they had each financed the same amount of capital equipment. Thus suppose that the market rate of discount were 10 per cent. If the old investors had bought 100,000 shares at £1 a share to finance the £100,000 spent on the first batch of machines, they would have made a capital gain; the value of a share would have risen from £1 to £2, since the yield of £20,000 produced by the first batch of machines discounted at 10 per cent would give a value of £200,000. It would be necessary at £2 a share to issue only £50,000 new shares to finance the second batch of machines, which would produce a yield of £10,000 or 10 per cent of this cost, equivalent to the ruling market rate of of discount. The 150,000 shares would together earn dividends of £30,000 and would thus at the market rate of discount of 10 per cent maintain the value of £2 a share. But the old investors would own two thirds of the shares and receive two thirds of the profits, even though they have, in the first place, financed only half the capital equipment.

and that of outsiders admitted from the less successful parts of the world.

But suppose that the concern is run on the non-discriminating principle of 'equal pay for equal work'. The employment of the additional outsiders will have raised the total surplus available for labour from £200,000 (originally divided between the 100 existing workers) to £200,000 + £100,000 = £300,000 (to be divided between the new total labour force of 200). The average annual income per worker would be reduced from £2,000 to £1,500. If the existing workers (i) desired to maximise their own incomes per head and (ii) if the non-discriminatory principle of equal pay for equal work had to be maintained, the expansion of the labour force would not take place, even though outside workers would be willing to gain by joining the labour force at a lower rate of pay which would preserve the existing rate of pay for the lucky existing insiders.

The successful capitalist firm with a fixed money rate of pay would expand employment without breaking the non-discriminatory principle for labour because it would keep down the rate of pay for all workers to a level compatible with that earned in the less successful outside world. At the same time it would expand its capital investment on a discriminatory basis by offering new outside investors less attractive terms than those enjoyed by the existing lucky inside investors. The original successful capitalists would thus retain the profits of success for their own enjoyment. The labour-managed firm would keep the profits of success for the existing workers. It would employ new capital so long as the addition to the value of the firm's net product was greater than the cost of borrowing capital; but the existing workers would have an incentive to restrict employment to the level which maximised the average profit per worker so long as they observed the non-discriminatory principle of 'equal pay for equal work'.

These implications of the application of the non-discriminatory principle of 'equal pay for equal work' are relevant for all forms of concern in which labour takes, or participates in taking, decisions about the firm's expansion. But they have a special relevance for the problems of a share economy because participation by labour in control of the business is a natural feature of many forms of share-economy arrangements.

## 4 Different Types of Sharing Arrangement

There are so many different forms of sharing arrangement that it is impracticable to consider systematically all the features which may distinguish one form from another. It is impossible to do more than analyse a limited number of special cases, chosen to exhibit some of the most important features. This paper will accordingly confine itself to examples of the four main types described in the following box diagram:

|  |  | Is Labour Required to Own All or Part of the Capital Invested in Bsiness? | |
|  |  | Yes | No |
| Does Labour Control or Participate in Control of the Business? | No | ESOS | PS/RS |
| | Yes | LMC | LCP |

From the discussion in the preceding section it is clear that there is a very important distinction between those cases in which labour does not and those in which it does play an important role in the control of the business; this distinction is drawn between the cases in the top and the bottom rows of the diagram. An equally important distinction can be drawn between those schemes which do and those which do not involve labour in being the beneficial owners of part of the capital funds invested in the business; and this distinction is drawn as between the two columns of the diagram.

In what follows we will discuss in some detail four cases which are representative of the distinction:

1  Employee Share Ownership Schemes (ESOS) in which workers share in the fortunes of the firm by owning part of the ordinary shares in the business but do not in fact exercise any decisive control over the firm's operations.
2  A Labour-Managed Co-operative (LMC) in which the workers own all or the greater part of the equity of the concern and play the predominant part in the control of the concern's operations.
3  Profit-Sharing or Revenue-Sharing arrangements (PS/RS) in which labour is paid wholly or in part by a share in the firm's profit or net revenue but does not take part in the control of the firm's operations.
4  A Labour–Capital Partnership (LCP) in which the workers are not required to own any of the capital invested in the business but in which both workers and capitalists share the firm's revenue and play a part in the control of the firm's operations.

## 5  Forms Involving Workers in the Provision or Ownership of Capital Invested in the Business Where They Work

### Employee Share Ownership Schemes

We will start by considering what is widely known as an Employee Share

Ownership Scheme (ESOS). In this case a firm which is otherwise a familiar capitalist wage-paying firm introduces a scheme whereby part of the payment to labour takes the form of money used on the behalf of the workers to purchase the company's ordinary shares, these shares being either newly issued shares to finance new capital development or else existing shares purchased at market prices from the existing owners of the shares. The shares thus acquired on behalf of the workers are then either held in a special trust fund on behalf of the workers as a whole or are allocated in personal accounts to individual workers.

In the present section it is assumed that the funds needed for the purchase of the worker shares are raised by a given contribution charged in respect of wage payments just like a compulsory pension contribution. In fact in many schemes the necessary funds are raised by devoting a certain share of the firm's variable profit to this purpose. This introduces an element of profit-sharing which will be the subject of discussion in section 6 below.

SCHEMES WHERE SHARES ARE HELD IN TRUST

If the shares are held in a general trust, the dividends on the shares so held will be used to supplement the wages of the existing workers with a bonus distribution or else to plough back into the company for the company's further development and for the further enlargement of the workers' trust fund. During the process of build-up of the trust fund there is a clear conflict of interest between the present and future generations of workers. Existing workers will be receiving less in wages or bonus than would otherwise be the case in order to build up a permanent fund, the perpetual yield on which will benefit future workers. An existing worker – particularly an older worker who is about to retire – will be asked to make a sacrifice of present income in order to yield a benefit which will accrue largely to future workers. It is then a matter of great importance whether or not in such a scheme the workers have a say in the decisions made by the management about the running of the firm. The existing worker shareholders will be less enthusiastic than the other non-worker shareholders about the ploughing back instead of the distribution in dividends of the profits available to the shareholders.

This disincentive against the build-up of the trust fund does not, of course, exist in those admirable cases in which the owner of a successful capitalist enterprise has in effect given a large part of the assets of the firm to a trust fund to be held for the benefit of present and future workers. But however the fund is built up or acquired, there remains one further, though probably less important, distortion which it may introduce into the economy. Consider a case in which a worker in such a firm is receiving an income of £100, of which £80 is his fixed wage and £20 is the bonus paid to him from the yield of the shares in the workers' trust fund. Compare his position with that of an outsider who is employed in some other firm at a rate of pay of £90. The non-worker capitalist shareholders will want to attract this outsider to the firm provided that his product would cover the £80 cost of his wage to the firm, and the outsider will want to join the firm because he can raise his income thereby from £90 to £100. He will in fact be attracted from an occupation where he was paid £90, to one in which his product has the lower value of £80, because the move entitles him to the enjoyment of the income due to the yield on part of the firm's capital. The supplement to the new worker's wage which is paid from the income of the workers' general trust fund is equivalent to a subsidy paid on the employment of labour.

But, in contrast to this over-expansion of employment, if the non-worker shareholders are taking the decisions, there may well be a strong incentive to restrict employment on the part of the existing workers. The yield on the shares held in the workers' trust fund will be diluted by being shared among a larger number of workers. The subsidy to the employ-ment of a new worker will be financed by a reduction in the existing rate of subsidy paid on the employment of the existing workers. Thus in so far as the existing workers wish to maximise their income per head and in so far as the principle of non-discrimination between the pay of existing and of new workers must be observed, they will have an incentive, similar to that discussed in section 3, to restrict new entrants into employment. Employment decisions could thus constitute a bone of contention between workers and non-worker shareholders.

SCHEMES WHERE SHARES ARE INDIVIDUALLY ALLOCATED

We turn to the case in which the shares acquired on behalf of the workers are not held by a general trust fund but are allocated in personal accounts to the individual workers part of whose potential pay has been used for the purchase of the shares. The worker-shareholders, like any other shareholders, will receive any dividends payable on their shares so long as they continue to hold them. However, in order to ensure that this does truly lead to an ownership of shares in the company by the individual workers employed in the company, it will be ruled that the individual worker owners of these shares cannot immediately sell them. They must be held by the workers for at least a given number of years or, as will be assumed for illustrative purposes, until the worker concerned leaves the firm for retirement or for another occupation. The scheme can then be thought of as constituting an additional pension scheme financed by extra contributions deducted from each worker's pay, the proceeds being invested in the shares of the company which will be sold in the market when the worker retires, in order to pay to the worker the value of his 'extra-pension-fund' assets. In any stable situation, when the scheme is in full operation, the shares being so realised by, or on behalf of, the retiring workers will be being acquired for crediting to the individual accounts of the remaining workers including those newly recruited to replace those who are retiring.

Firms are not, however, always in a stable position. There may well be occasions on which an abnormally large number of retirements occur at more or less the same time, for example because of a bunched age-distribution of the work force. If this were to occur, the shares being realised by the retiring workers would exceed the shares being purchased out of the savings of the new and remaining work force, and thus the business would have to face a crisis of decapitalisation. Such a crisis would be mitigated in so far as workers' shares were held in a continuing trust fund. For this reason it may be desirable that part at least of the workers' shares should not be credited to individual accounts.

On the other hand, in so far as the workers' shares are allocated to individual accounts, many of the problems associated with the holding of shares in a general workers' trust fund will be avoided. It is no longer true that present workers will be building up a fund for the benefit of future workers. As with a pension fund they will be building up a fund for the benefit of their own future. They will, however, be participating in a scheme for *compulsory* savings to be invested *specifically* in the assets of the firm in which they are themselves working. Both these aspects of the scheme present certain disabilities. The amount that must be compulsorily saved may not be very acceptable to many workers particularly in certain cases which will be discussed later; and to hold one's capital wealth specifically invested in the firm in which one works is, as has been argued in section 2, undesirable from the point of view of the risks involved in having all one's eggs in one basket.

Arrangements of this kind for the holding of the worker shares in individual accounts also avoid the distortion which may arise in the trust fund case from the fact that a worker is attracted to employment not only by what his work will contribute to the firm's product, but also by his adventitious temporary enjoyment of part of the yield on the firm's capital. In the case of the individual-account arrangement this extra attraction will not exist, since the worker will have to pay through deduction from his pay for any future enjoyment from his ownership of shares in the company. Conflict of interest between non-worker shareholders and workers about the scale of employment due to a desire on the part of existing workers to maximise income per head on a non-discriminatory basis, as discussed in section 3, will of course persist. But it will not be intensified, as it would be intensified in the trust fund case, by the existence of a given parcel of shares, the yield on which is to be divided by the number of workers in employment.

### ESOS and Labour-Managed Co-operatives

Schemes for employee share ownership can be carried to the extreme case in which all the ordinary shares (the whole of the firm's equity) are owned by the workers in the firm, once again either in the form of a workers' trust fund or in the form of individual accounts. Radical reform has often been preached in this form of ownership by the workers concerned. Such concerns may be called Labour-Managed Co-operatives (LMC), though their legal form may be that of a company and not of a co-operative. The basic economic implications do not depend essentially upon their legal form. Such a form of organisation can raise some of the problems discussed above in a very acute form particularly in the case of a highly capital-intensive form of activity.

What then are the merits and demerits of schemes of this kind which rely upon the beneficial ownership by the workers of some or all of the firm's equity capital? It is impossible to cover all possible cases; the analysis will be confined to the two examples of, on the one hand, a partial Employee Share Ownership Scheme in which the non-worker capitalist shareholders continue to hold a predominant part of the share capital and retain all the powers of control over the firm's operations and, at the other extreme, a Labour-Managed Co-operative in which the workers own virtually all of the equity capital and alone control the business.

Both types of scheme are designed to mitigate the feeling of alienation between 'them', the bosses, and 'us', the workers and thus to improve both work incentives and industrial relations. On the other hand, both types of scheme constitute a form of sharing which involves the risk of putting all one's labour eggs and a substantial part of one's capital eggs in one and the same basket. As has been shown in section 2, the element of risk may become very great indeed in a concern in which a large part of labour's income takes the form of a share in the net revenue of a firm in which fixed-interest payments constitute a large part of the firm's costs.

CAPITAL INTENSITY AND CO-OPERATIVE STRUCTURE

A partial share ownership scheme can, of course, be applied in any enterprise, however capital-intensive the operations of that enterprise might be. In principle all workers in all enterprises could accumulate in employee share ownership schemes the same absolute amount of wealth; this would merely imply that in a capital-intensive enterprise the workers would own a much smaller fraction of the company's shares than would be owned by other workers who were employed in a less capital-intensive concern.

The full application of the labour co-operative structure may well be feasible in relatively labour-intensive lines of activity. But in capital-intensive activities they may well be impracticable simply because any amount which workers could possibly be asked to save out of their earnings in the firm would be insufficient to finance that proportion of the firm's capital which it would be impossible, or from the risk-bearing point of view unwise, to finance from outside funds through fixed-interest borrowing.

Consider, for example, the amount of compulsory savings needed under an individual-account form of labour-managed co-operative, in which the co-operators as they leave the firm are paid the value of their individual shares, the ownership of which must be replaced by the compulsory savings of new and existing co-operators. The proportion of pay which must be compulsorily saved will depend upon (1) what proportion of the capital assets of the firm cannot be financed by outside fixed-interest debt but must be financed by share ownership, (2) how capital intensive is the firm's activity, i.e. how much capital must be employed per head, and (3) how rapidly the labour force is likely to turn over, since the shorter the period any individual remains in the firm the smaller the amount of capital ownership which will have been accumulated per head of existing workers. In a concern which was very capital intensive with a relatively rapid turnover of employment and for which outside capitalists would be unwilling to cover a large part of the capital with fixed-interest debt, the needed compulsory savings by each worker might well be impossible to contemplate.[4]

In any case, as a general system it is clearly anomalous that the amount of compulsory capital accumulation required of any individual citizen should depend upon the nature of his employment. The steel worker would be obliged to accumulate the property of a millionaire; a worker in a service industry would be allowed to be a spendthrift. In the case of a trust-fund arrangement in which by one means or another the trust fund had in the past been built up to a sufficient size to cover the whole of the concern's equity, the worker who was lucky enough to get a job in a steel mill could live on a millionaire's income from somebody's previous savings while the worker in a service industry would enjoy little more than the value of his earnings.

These anomalies which arise from differences between labour-intensive and capital-intensive forms of business are to some extent overcome in the famous Mondragon co-operative community by the grouping of co-operative activities of different kinds (e.g. labour-intensive banking with more capital-intensive manufactures) for the investment of the co-operators' savings. But this principle cannot be carried too far without serious dilution of the incentive advantages of the co-operative principle, since the individual worker's return on his capital will not be mainly determined by the success of the particular enterprise in which he is employed. The dilution can be successfully carried only so far as the co-operative spirit itself extends. In this respect the pioneering spirit of Mondragon in building up a whole co-operative community may be of essential importance.

RAISING CAPITAL FUNDS

In raising capital funds from outside sources for capital development, there would seem to be little difference between the incentives of a capitalist-controlled fixed-wage firm, on the one hand, and those of a capitalist-controlled ESOS or a Labour-Managed Co-operative, on the other hand. In principle all three types of business would have an incentive to borrow outside funds to finance capital developments so long

---

[4] A numerical example may help. Consider an enterprise with a stable work force earning a constant annual rate of pay with a ten-year turnover of labour (i.e. with each individual worker leaving after ten years and being replaced by a new entrant). If each worker saved the whole of his pay in a fund which earned a return of 5 per cent per annum, he would, on leaving the enterprise after ten years have accumulated a sum equal to 13.2 times his annual wage. At any one time, with one tenth of the workers having accumulated for ten years, one tenth for nine years, . . . and so on, the total accumulation in the fund would be 6.72 times the annual wage bill of the enterprise.

Thus if the workers saved 50 per cent of their wages in such conditions, each would accumulate for his retirement a capital sum equal to 6.6 times his annual wage income and this would enable the fund to provide capital for the firm equal to 3.36 times the firm's wage bill. If, however, the fund could accumulate at 10 per cent instead of 5 per cent per annum and if the labour turnover period were 20 years instead of ten years, a 50 per cent saving from wages would provide a worker on retirement with a capital sum equal to 31.51 times his annual wage and would at any time finance a capital fund for the firm equal to 11.84 times its annual wage bill.

as the cost of servicing the outside funds was less than the marginal revenue product of the additional capital equipment, though a labour co-operative may, of course, have more difficulty than does an ordinary capitalist concern in raising funds on the capital market. But capital finance must probably also come from the ploughing back of some part of the firm's revenue; and in this case the incentives of the existing members of a labour co-operative may differ from those of the shareholders in a capitalist enterprise in that the working members may be less willing than the capitalist to sacrifice present spendable income for a given future return, and any such unwillingness would be further reinforced in so far as any funds which were ploughed back were to be held in a general trust fund for the benefit not only of existing workers who had provided the savings but also of future generations of co-operators.

IMPLICATIONS FOR EMPLOYMENT AND INCOME LEVELS

As far as the firm's incentive to employ labour is concerned the capitalist-controlled ESOS will not differ from the ordinary capitalist-controlled fixed-wage firm if the compulsory saving of the workers is financed from a part of what is in effect a fixed money wage-cost per worker. Workers will be employed up to the point at which their marginal revenue product is equal to this final wage-cost (inclusive of the fixed compulsory contribution for the purchase of the worker shares). If the demand for the firm's product falls, the marginal revenue product of labour will be reduced below the fixed wage-cost and the employers will have an incentive to reduce the labour force.[5]

The Labour-Managed Co-operative, on the other hand, will probably introduce an important element of stability in the sense that the immediate impact effect of a fall in the demand for the product of the co-operative is more likely to fall on the variable earnings of each co-operator than lead to the dismissal of a number of them.

However, for the reasons explained in section 3 a successful and profitable Labour-Managed Co-operative is likely to have a direct incentive to restrict the level of employment below the level which would be provided by a capitalist fixed-wage firm if (1) the existing workers aim at maximising their own income per head and (2) the concern is run on the non-discriminatory principle of equal pay for equal work for new and old workers.

Thus consider a co-operative in which, due to exceptional success, the existing co-operators are earning £200 a head, while the outside market rate of pay is only £100. By taking on an additional partner, the average earnings per co-operator will be reduced unless the additional worker adds at least £200 to the firm's net revenue. In an equally successful competitive capitalist firm, however, all workers will in any case be earning only the going wage of £100 and the exceptional surplus profit will accrue to the existing capitalists. As a result the capitalist managers would

---

[5] This conclusion needs to be modified in the case of a scheme which has already resulted in the building of a workers' general trust fund, the dividend income from which in fact constitutes a subsidisation of labour's income in the way described earlier in this section.

not stop at the point at which an additional worker would add £200 to the firm's net revenue, but would have an incentive to expand the firm's employment so long as an additional worker would add anything more than his wage cost of £100 to the firm's net revenue.

This does not, of course, mean that all labour co-operatives will in fact be restrictive. A co-operative may not be conducted with the overriding objectives of maximising the incomes of the existing members. Thus a concern such as the John Lewis Partnership may have inherited from a previous regime a more conventional form of management which is somewhat detached from workers' control and which puts a strong emphasis on growth and expansion. Or in some co-operatives which are subject to more direct workers' control the accepted philosophy may be expressly to restrain the pay of existing co-operators in order to encourage growth so as to expand the co-operative principle throughout the community, to promote the employment of new co-operators and to improve the prospect of the coming generation of children. This indeed appears to be the philosophy behind the success of the Mondragon co-operative movement.

Alternatively a labour co-operative could well be conducted on the principle that newly admitted co-operators would not necessarily enjoy the same share in the concern's revenue as the existing co-operators who have built the success of the concern; and indeed there appears to be some element of such discrimination in the Mondragon co-operative movement, where there are modest annual increments of pay for length of service and specially low rates of pay in start-up ventures and in ventures which are going through a crisis.

EMPLOYEE OWNERSHIP AND PROPERTY REDISTRIBUTION

One of the arguments often adduced for schemes of the kind discussed in this section is that they respond to the present great and growing interest in possibilities of redistribution of the ownership of property. Such a redistribution would tend to diminish the existing great difference of power and influence, as well as of income and standards of living, as between the wealthy and the less wealthy members of society. But the argument for change rests also on the idea that conflicts of interest and of political ideologies would be greatly diminished in a property-owning democracy in which every citizen was a capitalist as well as a worker.

Such a development in society can be brought about by changes in taxation of income, wealth and inheritance which encourage the growth of property ownership among the less wealthy relatively to the more wealthy. A distinction should be drawn between general measures of this kind which aim at a general redistribution of property and measures of a kind which are designed to stimulate the ownership by particular workers of a part or whole of the capital invested in the particular business in which they are themselves employed.

The argument for schemes of this latter kind is that such share ownership by workers may give psychologically a strong feeling of being an integral part of the enterprise.[6] It may greatly increase an appreciation of the problems and of the importance of managerial decisions. A movement towards a property-owning democracy of the more general kind may result in workers owning their houses, having the prospect of enjoyment in the future of the wealth held on their behalf by a pension fund, or possessing fixed money balances in a savings bank or a building society. None of these forms gives a direct appreciation of the marketing, technological and managerial problems involved in the employment of real capital in a productive concern; but it is just such an appreciation which is required to break down unnecessary conflicts between labour and capital and which can be provided by the ownership by workers of the capital at risk in their own business.

Employee ownership schemes should not be regarded as having important redistributive effects except in so far as they have their origin in the transfer of shares by what amounts to a free gift from successful owners to their work force. Otherwise they can lead to a redistribution in the ownership of capital only in so far as they cause the workers concerned to save more and thus to own more wealth than would otherwise be the case; and this effect is subject to severe limitatons. In the first place, many workers – for example, public servants – will inevitably be outside the reach of such schemes. Secondly, on the principle of spreading risks such schemes should not be carried too far since they involve workers in committing any capital which is accumulated in this way to the same basket as their labour eggs. Thirdly, in many cases the compulsory investment by the workers of their savings in the shares of the concern in which they are employed may represent merely a change in the form in which their savings are held rather than a net increase in their ownership of wealth. Such a shift may, as has been argued above, have a beneficial effect upon incentives and industrial relations, but it would have no significant net effect upon the general distribution of wealth.

## 6 Profit-Sharing and Revenue-Sharing

For the reasons given in the previous section forms of share economy which rely on the workers' ownership of the capital invested in the firm in which they work cannot be expected to cover more than a limited range of economic activities. We turn to forms of the share economy which do not rely on employee ownership. Of these also there are a very large number of possible varieties. We will illustrate the problems which may arise by concentrating on two possible extremes, which we will call cases of Pure Profit-Sharing and of Pure Revenue-Sharing.

---

[6] This raises an important question for the social psychologists to answer. Is the actual ownership of part of the capital of a firm needed to integrate the workers fully into an enterprise? Or would a complete partnership between labour and capital in the control of a firm's operations and in sharing its net revenue, as suggested below in section 7, be equally effective?

## Pure Profit-Sharing

By a case of Pure Profit-Sharing we mean a firm which pays its workers a fixed wage at the full market rate of pay which the workers might obtain elsewhere and which also deducts from the firm's net revenue a full market rate of return on the replacement value of its physical capital equipment. The resulting amount represents the firm's pure profit (i.e. the excess of its revenue over the full market cost of its factors of production) or, of course, its pure loss if the figure is negative. A pure profit-sharing arrangement is one in which this net pure profit or loss is divided on a predetermined share ratio between a bonus to or charge on wage payments and a bonus to or charge on the return on capital. But in many profit-sharing arrangements it is only a positive profit which is shared between workers and capitalists, any negative loss being borne by the capitalists alone.

From the point of view of risk-bearing, incentives and the relationship between workers and employers there is much to be gained from such arrangements. If the proportion in which any pure profit or loss is divided between pay of labour and return on capital is the same as the average overall ratio in the firm between pay and return on capital, the risks of fluctuation in the firm's fortunes will be distributed evenly over pay and return on capital. But it would be possible for workers and employers to agree on any alternative proportion for the division of the pure profit or loss if, in the particular circumstances of the case, some higher or lower marginal share for labour were thought appropriate.

There is in fact little more to be said for or against such pure profit-sharing schemes which are certainly to be welcomed on grounds of incentive and industrial relations with minimal adverse effects upon the distribution of risks. But they are not likely to have any very outstanding effect upon a firm's employment or investment plans or upon the distribution of the ownership of property. In a pure profit-sharing scheme the worker will be paid a fixed wage equal to the outside market rate. The employer will have every incentive to employ labour up to, but not beyond, the point at which any additional worker's marginal revenue product has fallen to equality with the fixed wage-rate, since the employer will enjoy the employer's share of any addition to the firm's pure profit which would arise if the worker's marginal revenue product exceeded the wage-rate. Moreover, since *ex hypothesi* the wage-rate is as high as the outside market rate of pay, the employer will be able to attract labour up to this point.

But no cushion will then remain in the form of an excess of the worker's marginal revenue product over the fixed money wage-rate. If as a result of a fall in demand for the firm's product the worker's marginal revenue product is reduced below the fixed money wage-rate, the employer will have an incentive to reduce employment just as would be the case in a firm without any profit-sharing arrangement.

As far as investment decisions are concerned, since the firm can deduct the full market cost of servicing any extra capital development before assessment of any pure profit which must be shared with labour, there will always be some incentive left for the employer to undertake any capital development whose marginal revenue product would exceed its cost. The incentive may be slightly blunted in that any net profit so earned must be shared with labour; but the employer will always get the advantage of his pure-profit share if the investment will more than cover its cost.

Finally there is no reason to believe that a pure profit-sharing scheme will have any decisive effect upon the distribution of the ownership of property. It may well have admirable effects on productivity and labour relations. But it is not to be regarded as a major instrument for promoting employment without inflation or for the redistribution of capital ownership.

## Pure Revenue-Sharing

A Pure Revenue-Sharing arrangement is a very different animal which may have some very different effects upon relations between labour and capital and upon decisions about employment and investment. By a Pure Revenue-Sharing Scheme we mean an arrangement whereby there is no fixed-wage payment and the whole of the pay of labour takes the form of a given share (e.g. 80 per cent) of the firm's net revenue. The remaining proportion (20 per cent) of the net revenue is then available to meet any fixed-interest obligations and for the rest to be allocated to the benefit of the owners of the firm's equity capital.

The immediate effects on risk-bearing and incentives for the existing work force would be very similar to those of a pure profit-sharing scheme in which negative losses as well as positive profits were allotted to labour in the same proportion as their average earnings, namely at 80 per cent in my numerical example. The existing net revenue of the firm and any fluctuations in that revenue would be divided at the same 80:20 ratio between labour and capital. But the implications for decisions about changes in the levels of employment and about capital development and for the effects of such decisions upon relations between workers and employers will be very different.

Indeed Professor Martin Weitzman has recently put forward a very strong and cogent argument that revenue-sharing arrangements would make a very important, indeed he argues a decisive, contribution to the cure of the problem of stagflation, that is to say, to the reform of society in a way which would make it possible to maintain a high and stable level of employment without the danger of a runaway inflation. The argument runs as follows.[7]

If a worker's pay consisted entirely of a share in the firm's revenue, the capitalist employer, it is argued, would have an incentive to expand employment so long as an additional worker would add anything, however small, to the firm's net revenue, since the employer would enjoy his share of that increment of revenue. The firm's employment would be restricted only by the employer's inability to attract more labour to his employment.

[7] Martin L. Weitzman, *The Share Economy: Conquering Stagflation* (Cambridge, Mass.: Harvard University Press, 1984).

In circumstances such as this, a reduction in the demand for the firm's product will not cause the employer to dismiss any workers until it has gone so far as to reduce the marginal revenue product of labour to zero. Or to take a less extreme form of sharing arrangement in which the worker was paid in part by a share in the firm's revenue and in part by a fixed wage payment, employment would be maintained so long as the marginal revenue product of labour remained at least high enough to cover the fixed-wage element in the worker's pay. Until this point was reached workers would not be dismissed but they would, of course, be free to move. If the fall in demand was not universal, workers might seek jobs elsewhere as their incomes in the depressed profit-sharing firm fell below the pay which they could earn elsewhere; there would be movement of labour but no involuntary unemployment. If the fall in money demand for the products of industry was general and if all firms paid their workers wholly in the form of a share in the firm's revenue, then there would be no incentive for movement from one firm to another and no unemployment. The general depression would take the form of a general cut in money prices and incomes rather than in employment and output.

This claim by the proponents of the share economy that it would help to stabilise employment against downward fluctuations of money expenditures is a true and important one. But it is not the end of the matter. It is not just stability of employment that we seek. What one has to ask is whether share-economy arrangements will lead to a high as well as to a stable level of employment.

In the pure share economy in which workers are paid solely by a share of the firm's revenue employers will, as has just been argued, wish to take on workers so long as they add anything, however small the amount may be, to the firm's revenue. This would indeed set a high, full-employment target level for the employers' demand for labour. But one must consider also the supply side. Would the workers who were already in employment, whom we may call the 'insiders', in fact willingly allow the employers to take into employment all the available involuntarily unemployed workers, whom we may call the 'outsiders', regardless of any effects upon the average rates of pay of the 'insiders' in the firm concerned?

Consider a firm which is paying its workers solely in the form of a share of the firm's revenue. Beyond a certain point the average revenue produced per head is likely to fall as more workers are employed, partly because as more and more labour is applied to a given amount of capital equipment output per head will fall after capacity output is reached but, probably more importantly in normal conditions of imperfect competition, also because selling prices will have to be cut or more intensive selling costs incurred in order to expand the market for the firm's product. But as revenue per head is reduced so, with any given share of revenue going to labour as a whole, pay per head will be reduced. The unemployed outsiders may be willing to come into employment at the reduced pay per head; but the insiders who are already in employment may wish to take action to offset the reduction in their own rate of pay. If, for example, they insist through trade union action that labour's share of the revenue should be increased sufficiently to maintain their rate of pay whenever it is threatened by the entry of more workers, the employers will lose the incentive to take on more workers. The high level of employment will not be achieved. Outsiders will remain involuntarily unemployed.

If, however, the workers' share of the firm's revenue could not readily be renegotiated, a serious conflict of interest between workers and owners could arise over employment plans. If the whole of the workers' pay took the form of an inflexible share of the firm's net revenue, the employers, as we have seen, would have an incentive to employ any workers who were willing and available to join the work force, provided only that they would add something positive, no matter how small, to the firm's net revenue. But the existing workers, each of whom received the same non-discriminating fixed share of the firm's revenue per worker, would, as explained in section 3, have an interest in seeing that employment was not expanded beyond the point at which the firm's net revenue per worker was maximised. In a successful firm in which a very high revenue per head could be earned if the sales of the product were not unduly expanded, there could be a very marked gap between the number of workers at which the net revenue per head would be maximised and the enlarged number of workers at which the revenue had been so reduced that the pay of the workers in the successful revenue-sharing firm had fallen to correspond with the pay needed to attract them from other less successful competing occupations.

A similar conflict of interest between workers and owners could arise over decisions to invest in new capital equipment. If the agreed share ratio of the firm's revenue – the 80:20 ratio of the example used above – were at all rigidly fixed, there would be a serious disincentive for the owners to embark on capital developments. Thus suppose that a firm is considering whether to embark on an investment costing £1,000,000 and expected to add £100,000 to the firm's net revenue. The owners would receive a return of only 2 per cent instead of 10 per cent on the investment if there was an inflexible agreement with labour that it should receive 80 per cent of the firm's net revenue.

The pay of the workers would thus be raised if the investment were carried out; and it would therefore be possible to reduce the share of revenue allocated to labour below the original 80 per cent without in fact reducing the pay which each worker would receive. Thus the disincentive to investment could be removed if in some way or another the employers could rely in advance on a reduction in the workers' share ratio which would offset the adventitious increase in their pay which would otherwise result from the investment of the new capital in the business. In a highly competitive economy in which each individual firm felt confident that it would always be able to set the share ratio which it offered to its own employees at whatever level was needed merely to maintain the workers' rate of pay at the rate ruling outside in the competitive labour market, the managers of a firm might have sufficient confidence in the possible downward flexibility of labour's share ratio not to be deterred from plans for capital development which would otherwise have been profitable. But if conditions were such as to preclude reliance upon such flexible competitive downward adjustment of share ratios, some method of introducing more automatic flexibility into pay contracts would need to be devised.

An alternative way of removing this disincentive to capital investment could be devised, at least in so far as it was financed by ploughing back industrial profits into the expansion of the firm's capital. Suppose that the firm's net revenue which was divided inflexibly 80:20 between labour and capital was defined as the firm's net revenue after deduction of any sums ploughed back for capital development. In this case the employers would in fact finance only £200,000 of the £1,000,000 cost of a capital investment and they would receive an annual return of £20,000 out of the £100,000 increase in the annual value of the firm's product. Labour would in fact have had its pay reduced by £800,000 by losing its 80 per cent of the funds which were ploughed back and in return it would in future gain £80,000 a year, i.e. its 80 per cent of the extra £100,000 a year of revenue. Each party would be receiving the full yield of 10 per cent on its share of the capital cost.

This sort of arrangement would in fact be the equivalent of a compulsory saving scheme for both the capitalists and the wage-earners. To this extent it would have the same effect as an Employee Share Ownership Scheme in enabling workers to enjoy a future return on that compulsory investment in the firm's capital resources; but it would have the same effect as employee shares which are held in a general trust fund for the benefit of future as well as present workers, since the continuing yield of £100,000 a year of which the workers would receive their £80,000 would be a yield which was not allocated to individual workers in individual personal accounts, but which was available for all workers present and future. Present workers might well have less incentive than the capitalists to have their income ploughed back into capital development, since the latter would receive their benefit in the form of a capital gain in their individually held shares which they could sell or leave to their heirs.

Thus there would inevitably be conflict of interest between workers and capitalists about investment plans if the share ratios of division of the firm's revenue were at all inflexible. As far as investment was financed out of the capitalists' resources, the capitalists would face a strong disincentive against capital development, the total cost of which they would have to meet while receiving only their allotted share of the yield. On the other hand, in these conditions workers would be in favour of capital development provided it added anything to the firm's revenue. If, however, a plough-back arrangement were made whereby the workers and capitalists shared the cost of investment in new capital in the same ratio as they shared the yield of the new capital, the capitalists' disincentive against capital expansion would be removed. But in this case the existing workers – and particularly those near retiring age – might well be much less attracted by an investment project partly because they had a smaller desire than the capitalists to save for the future but also because the yield on their savings would be enjoyed in large part not by them and their heirs but by other future employees of the firm.

Since the existing workers' interests would be so directly affected in a revenue-sharing economy by the management's decisions about capital investment and levels of employment it is most probable that in any such firm labour would insist more and more on participating in some way or another in the decision-making about such matters; and in this case the revenue-sharing arrangements could well intensify conflicts between capital and labour. The essential need would then be to find a form of partnership between labour and capital in which (1) the labour-capital share ratios in the division of a firm's revenue could be adjusted to take account of changes in the quantities of capital and of labour which were invested and employed in the firm, (2) arrangements could be made for the workers in employment to play a full part in decision-making about the firm's activities with a minimum of conflict between the workers' and capitalists' interests, and (3) any resulting conflicts of interest could be resolved as between prosperous 'insiders' in employment in a successful firm and less prosperous 'outsiders' who were unemployed or employed in less successful businesses. The following section of this pamphlet is devoted to the search for some such form of partnership.

## 7  Discriminating Labour–Capital Partnerships[8]

The easiest way to explain the basic idea of such a partnership between labour and capital is to imagine it to be suddenly applied to an existing firm in a completely undiluted form. Consider then a capitalist wage firm of the familiar kind. Suppose that of its revenue 80 per cent is being paid to the employees and the remaining 20 per cent is accruing to the capitalists. Simple conversion of this into a pure Labour-Capital Partnership would consist of the issue of two kinds of share certificates, namely:

1  Capital share certificates which would be distributed to all the persons who were in fact receiving directly or indirectly through profit, interest, rent, etc., the capitalists' 20 per cent share of the firm's revenue, this distribution to each beneficiary being *pro rata* to his or her existing income from the business; and
2  Labour share certificates which would be distributed to all employees *pro rata* to their individual earnings of the remaining 80 per cent of the firm's revenue.

All share certificates, whether capital or labour, would carry an entitlement to the same rate of dividend.

The immediate result of this conversion would be that everyone concerned would receive an unchanged income, but in every case in the form of a dividend on a shareholding, which would replace all interest, rent, wages, etc.; but everyone concerned in the operation of the business

[8] See Chapter 7 of J. E. Meade, *Alternative Systems of Business Organization and of Workers' Remuneration* (London: Allen & Unwin, 1986), of which the present section of this pamphlet is an abbreviated version.

would now have a share in the future success or failure of the enterprise.

There would, however, be one basic disctinction between capital share certificates and labour share certificates. Capital share certificates would correspond more or less exactly to a company's existing ordinary shares. They could be freely traded on the Stock Exchange or elsewhere in the market and could be transferred from one owner to the other.

Labour share certificates on the other hand would be tied to the individual employee and would be surrendered and cancelled when the employee retired or voluntarily left the business. They would not, however, be cancelled if the employee left the firm involuntarily (e.g. because of redundancy), unless the dismissal was due to grave misconduct or illness which incapacitated the worker for his job. The worker would thus normally be guaranteed his employment, or at least his appropriate share of income from employment until retirement. His claim on the firm would, however, be tied to his availability to perform the work for which the dividend on labour share certificates was the reward. There could, of course, as now be separate pension arrangements for those who had retired together with separate arrangements for the support of worker-partners in ill health.

With these arrangements major decisions about changes in the scale of employment or of capital investment could be taken in such a way that any action would be to the advantage of all shareholders, whether capitalists or workers, since, if a high dividend is to result, it will result for all owners and all employees.

The managers of the firm would be free to decide to employ an additional worker by offering to him or her a new issue of labour share certificates which was sufficient to attract the worker to the enterprise; if the expected dividend on these shares, while sufficient to attract the worker, was nevertheless lower than the expected marginal revenue of the new worker, all existing shareholders, whether capitalist or worker, would stand to gain by the decision, since the addition to the firm's revenue available to be paid out in increased dividends on all shares of both kinds would be greater than the additional dividend payable to the new worker on the newly issued share certificates. Since the new worker would presumably be attracted only if there was some advantage in accepting the offer, everyone would gain from such a decision.

Exactly the same considerations would be relevant for decisions to invest in more capital equipment. The purchase of a new machine could be financed by issuing and selling on the market an issue of additional capital share certificates sufficient to raise the necessary funds. All existing shareholders, whether capital or labour shareholders, would gain if the dividend payable on the new additional capital share certificates was less than the addition which the new capital equipment would add to the firm's net revenue. Thus the answer to a question whether to carry out an investment plan would depend upon a judgement whether it was to the advantage or disadvantage of all persons, whether capitalists or workers, who were concerned with the firm's activities.

Plans for a firm's expansion may often involve the simultaneous investment in new capital equipment and the employment of additional labour and this may be so not only to expand current activities but also for the improvement of the quality of the product, for diversification into new products, for greater flexibility, for improvement of managerial control systems and so on. Moreover, much of the expenditures involved may not be on physical equipment but on the work of design and development engineers, market researchers, and other specialists. The general principle, however, remains the same. If the dividends payable on the extra labour and capital share certificates needed to attract the resources required for the firm's new plans are expected to be less than the additional net revenue which will result from the firm's new plans, the development will be to the advantage of all existing shareholders, whether workers or capitalists.

There remain, however, two basic problems which will be discussed later in this section. First, special problems will arise in the case of any plans or programmes which in effect make any existing workers redundant, since in the way described earlier a Labour-Capital Partnership will involve some degree of security of tenure for existing worker-partners.

Second, it is not always easy to decide which elements of cost should be regarded as current expenditures needed to sustain the firm's current income and which should be treated as present outlays on capital account undertaken to obtain future returns. As will be shown later in this section, the distinction between capital and current expenditure acquires a special importance in any Labour-Capital Partnership.

## Modified forms of partnership

In many cases, of course, it is unlikely that the partnership principle would be applied in the undiluted form which has just been described. Thus a partnership may well need to be free to borrow some capital funds on fixed-interest contracts with the creditors (e.g. bank loans, debentures, etc.). On the labour side the partnership may well desire to be free to hire some forms of labour – temporary or part-time workers or consultants, for example – on fixed-wage contracts. One can also well imagine a Labour-Capital Partnership requiring all new workers to start on a fixed-wage basis and only later offering them the option of converting a part or the whole of their pay into dividends on labour share certificates.

Even more importantly some of the existing workers might prefer to remain on fixed-wage contracts and, indeed, all the workers might desire, as an insured fall-back in the case of the firm's poor performance, to remain for part of their reward on fixed-wage contracts and only for the remaining part of their reward on participation in a share of the firm's net revenue. It was suggested earlier that a worker who was voluntarily dismissed would nevertheless normally retain his labour share certificates until the age of retirement. In this case existing shareholders would have an incentive to dismiss a worker as redundant only if they judged that what he contributed to the firm's net revenue had fallen below the amount of the fixed-wage element in his pay, since any dividends payable to him would remain a charge on the partnership's income, whether he was made redundant or not. Thus a worker by choosing any given mix between a fixed-wage payment and a dividend on labour share certificates would thereby in effect have chosen to distribute his risks in a corresponding mix between unemployment and fluctuations in the inclusive rate of pay. The higher the fixed-wage element, the greater the risk of unemployment but the lower the risk of a drop – or indeed of a rise – in his inclusive rate of pay.

All of these various mixes between fixed payments and share dividends, in the case both of capitalists and workers, can be incorporated in the structure of a Labour-Capital Partnership. We have defined a firm's 'distributable surplus' as the value of its net revenue less expenditure on fixed interest, fixed rents, and fixed wages. Capital and labour share certificates can then be issued and distributed to those who have a claim on the firm's distributable surplus. The rules and activities of the partnership can then proceed on the principles already discussed for a pure undiluted Labour-Capital Partnership. All share certificates, whether capital or labour, would receive the same rate of dividend; in effect those who had a claim on the distributable surplus, whether capitalists or workers, would be the risk-bearing entrepreneurs.

The partnership mechanism would be unchanged, but whether or not it would carry with it to any substantial degree the advantages of the partnership principle would, of course, depend upon whether or not a substantial proportion of the incomes of workers as well as of capitalists had been transferred to the share principle.

If, however, there was a substantial shift from fixed-wage to partnership shares, the advantages of the new organisation could be very substantial. Many basic conflicts of interest between labour and capital in reaching decisions about employment and investment would be resolved. Decisions to expand employment so long as there were available unemployed workers would not be impeded by the need to negotiate a reduction in pay for existing workers. Any reduction in demand for the products of the industry would be met not, as in a capitalist wage economy, by a reduction in employment and growth of unemployment but by a reduction in prices and in the dividends payable to all workers and capitalists. The prospects of attaining and preserving a high and stable level of employment would be greatly improved, stability being promoted by the shift from fixed-wage payments to variable dividends on shares and economic expansion to a high level being attained by the automatic flexibility of share ratios and the abandonment by the worker entrepreneurs of the principle of non-discrimination.

## Problems with the partnership principle

### CONFLICT OVER REDUNDANCY

There are inevitably some costs to be set against the advantages of the partnership principle. The introduction of new and risky innovations might be discouraged if worker-partners, who had all their work eggs committed to the single basket of the concern in which they worked, were more averse to taking risks than the capitalists who could spread their risks.

Moreover, an effective application of the partnership principle implies – as has been proposed earlier – some security of tenure for the labour partners and this implies some cost to the owners of capital invested in the firm. Thus suppose a partnership to be exceptionally successful. Any profit over and above what is needed to recompense the labour and capital in employment at the current outside market rates will be distributable *pro rata* at the same rate on all share certificates, whether held by labour or by capitalist shareholders. But as the existing workers retire and surrender their profitable share certificates they will be replaced by new workers at ruling market rates of recompense. The distributable surplus thus released will be available to swell the incomes of all existing partners, both capitalists and workers. As a consequence all existing workers, including newcomers to the work force, will enjoy their share of the surplus so long as the incomes of the 'old hands' who are retiring exceed the starting pay of the 'new hands' who replace them. Thus 'new hands' as they gradually become 'old hands' will obtain their increasing share of the surplus.

But the existing capitalists will also receive their share of any surplus released by the retirement of old hands; thus not the whole of the surplus enjoyed by retiring workers will be transferred to other workers. As a result any pure profit enjoyed by a successful concern will bit by bit gradually seep away from the workers to the holders of capital share certificates. This process will be a very prolonged one; but in the very long run the whole of the profit will be enjoyed by the holders of the capital which, unlike the retiring workers, is not withdrawn from the business. But in comparison with a capitalist wage firm the capitalists in a successful partnership will be worse off in so far as they have to share the pure profit arising from successful business with the workers who have taken part in that success and, over a prolonged period, with the successors of such workers.

In the case of an unsuccessful venture the loss will be shared between the capitalists and the worker-owners of share certificates. Workers whose incomes are thereby reduced below the outside market level would enjoy the degree of security of tenure provided by their ownership of share certificates. But while to that extent they could not suffer from involuntary redundancy, they would nevertheless be perfectly free to leave the unsuccessful partnership in order to take better-paid employment elsewhere, leaving the capitalist shareholders immediately to carry the whole of the loss. To this extent the risks of the capitalists are increased; they must share with the existing workers any profit due to a success, but the existing workers are not tied to stay in the partnership to share with the capitalist any losses if the partnership is unsuccessful.

Security of tenure for worker-partners could also delay what would otherwise be a profitable introduction of certain new technologies. The replacement of existing workers by a machine or by workers of a different skill would be profitable in a capitalist fixed-wage firm if the wages payable to the existing workers were greater than the current costs of the new machine or of the new team of workers; such a replacement could be held up in a partnership in which the dismissal of an existing worker would, up to his retirement age, save only the fixed-wage element but not the share-dividend element in his pay. Any such delay would be mitigated in three ways: first it would operate only in so far as it would otherwise be desirable to introduce the new technology more rapidly than could be covered by the normal ageing and retirement of the work force; second, the extra cost of replacement of an existing worker would refer only to that part of his pay which took the form of a dividend on labour share certificates; and, third, it would be wholly avoided by any new firm which was set up to exploit the new technology.

The net loss arising from any such impediments to risky enterprise and the introduction of new technologies should not be exaggerated. There are already in a normal capitalist wage firm some serious impediments on account of trade union and similar pressure to preserve existing jobs and demarcations of work. It is indeed possible that in certain respects a change-over to partnership arrangements would result in a diminution of workers' resistance to risky change; in a partnership the worker-partners would have the promise of participation in the profits of any success together with greater security of tenure in the event of relative failure, whereas in the capitalist wage firm there is no guarantee of participation in the profits of success and no guarantee against involuntary redundancy in the case of relative failure.

In order to lighten the cost imposed upon a concern from its obligation to continue to pay dividends on labour share certificates to redundant workers, it might be proposed that such payments should cease if the worker in question was offered an alternative comparable job. In this case the redundant worker's labour share certificates would be cancelled if the concern which was making the worker redundant could find the worker an alternative comparable job or if the worker himself subsequently found and accepted an alternative job. Arrangements of this kind would represent an attempt to apply the principle stated earlier in this section that the worker's claim on the partnership 'would be tied to his availability to perform the work for which the dividend on labour share certificates was the reward'.

There would, however, be some serious problems in the application of such a rule. Clearly a comparable job implies one in which the worker is offered a rate of pay comparable not merely to the dividend payments which he was receiving on his labour share certificates, but to the whole of his previous pay inclusive of any fixed-wage element. But to what extent does a comparable job imply one with comparable prospects and security of tenure? Suppose a redundant worker to have found employment in an alternative job and as a result to have surrendered his labour share certificates but then to be made redundant in his new job. Does the original firm then have an obligation to restore his labour share certificates to him? Does the principle in fact mean that a redundant partner's future career must be continually kept in review up to his retirement age?

A simpler method of applying an 'availability' test might be merely to rule that a partnership which made a worker-partner redundant could at any time ask him to return to the partnership on the terms which he previously enjoyed with it. If the worker concerned declined the situation, then his labour share certificates would be cancelled. The existence of this rule would ensure that a redundant worker who did subsequently find an alternative post which held out more attractive prospects of future work could be effectively asked once and for all to surrender his existing labour share certificates.

The application of this simpler 'availability' test, however, raises one important and far-reaching problem. In the case of a worker who had been receiving the whole of his pay in the form of dividends on labour share certificates, there would be no problem in defining 'the terms which he had previously enjoyed' with the partnership. He would be offered a post with the reinstatement of the number of labour share certificates which he held when he was made redundant. But in the case of a worker who had received a fixed-wage element in his previous pay in the partnership, the problem would arise as to what level of fixed pay he should be offered on his reinstatement. The same money rate of pay might well be unfair if, for example, inflationary developments during the period of his absence from the partnership had substantially eroded the value of money. Since the partnership is founded on the principle that fixed money wages are not intended to represent the whole of, or indeed any specific proportion of, the real pay of any individual worker, there would be no obvious 'rate for the job' on which to base the new offer. It would be necessary to rely on some rather general definition such as 'the rate which the worker could reasonably be expected to be receiving if he had continued an unbroken membership of the partnership', backed by some form of arbitration or review by an independent tribunal in the case of disagreement.[9]

There is one further source of trouble which may arise in the treatment of redundancy. It is proposed that a worker who leaves the firm voluntarily to seek a better-paid job should surrender his labour share certificates, whereas a worker who is dismissed as redundant should at least for the time being retain them. It would thus be to the interest of a worker who wished to move elsewhere to be dismissed as redundant rather than himself to resign his membership of the partnership. For this purpose he might make himself as useless as possible to the management

[9] In a Partial Labour–Capital Partnership a large element of pay may take the form of fixed-wage payments which are not designed to cover the whole of the worker's pay for the job, and which may represent very different levels for different individual partners. Adjustments in such payments to existing partners would in principle be subject to criteria of the kind descibed earlier for the employment of new partners: 'Is the increase in pay needed to retain and to motivate the worker's contribution to the firm's product and is the value to the partnership (i.e. to all the other owners of share certificates, whether workers or capitalists) of that contribution at least as great as the adjusted pay of the worker partner?' But a criterion of this kind would not be suitable for the offer of reinstatement to a previous partner. The question in this case is not: 'What level of pay is needed to attract the worker?' but 'What level of pay could the worker be expected to be receiving from the partnership if he had continued to be a member of the partnership?'

without stepping over the borderline which would justify his dismissal for misconduct with consequential surrender of his labour share certificates. The conflict of interest in this case would be between the delinquent worker on the one hand and all other shareholders on the other hand; but there is clearly here the possibility of tiresome disputes requiring judgement by some form of industrial tribunal. This particular problem would, however, be greatly eased if the simple test of availability proposed above were adopted, since a worker who obtained a more attractive job and who retained the labour share certificates issued by the partnership in which he previously worked could always be induced to surrender them by being invited to rejoin the partnership on his original but now unattractive terms of service.

In considering the treatment of the problems which arise in cases of redundancy it is important to remember that any conflict of interest between the partnership and the potentially redundant partner is not, as it would be in a capitalist wage firm, a conflict between capital and labour. It involves a conflict of interest between the potentially redundant individual (a potential 'outsider') and all existing shareholders, whether capitalist or worker shareholders ('insiders'). Thus to cancel a redundant worker's dividend income will be to the disadvantage of that individual, and may or may not be 'unfair'; but the cancellation will be to the advantage of all remaining workers as well as to the beneficial owners of the firm's capital equipment, since the reduction of the redundant worker's claim on the firm's disposable surplus will leave a larger amount to be distributed on the share certificates held by all existing workers and capitalists.

Conflicts of interest over redundancy in a Labour-Capital Partnership will thus not represent direct conflict of interest between capitalists and workers. Indeed we have argued above that the great merit of a Labour-Capital Partnership would be the avoidance of the most direct conflicts of interest between existing capitalists and existing workers about decisions affecting levels of employment, investment and output. This does not, however, mean that there would never be any remaining areas of direct conflict of interest between worker-partners and capitalist partners.

OTHER CONFLICTS OF INTEREST

The basic reasons for avoidance of conflict of interest in decisions about employment and investment, as argued at the outset of this discussion of Labour-Capital Partnership, refer to the running of a partnership when it has been set up. But the initial conversion of a capitalist fixed-wage firm into a Labour-Capital Partnership would, of course, involve a once-for-all conflict of interest between labour and capital. Should the ratio of numbers of labour share certificates to capital share certificates be 75:25 or 80:20 or 85:15? A division precisely equivalent to last year's division of the net revenue between the two classes of beneficiaries might be very seriously disputed on many grounds: Did the accountant's definition of net revenue properly represent the underlying reality? Ought not labour to increase its share if it undertakes more of the risk? What are the underlying prospects for future growth in labour earnings and capital profits? Was last year a typical year? And so on. But once the initial big bang of conflict in the original distribution between existing workers and existing owners had been overcome, continuing operations would involve little further direct conflicts.

At the other extreme of a concern's life, namely on the voluntary liquidation of a partnership, conflict might well once more emerge. Should the owners of the capital in the concern have the power through voluntary liquidation of selling off the concern's assets and using the funds for a new purpose, leaving the worker-partners redundant and without any remaining claim on any labour share certificates? In the case of a large concern with many capitalist shareholders it might be practicable to rule that voluntary liquidation should be arranged only with the agreement of the majority of worker-partners as well as of the majority of capitalist partners. In this case there would have to be some reasonable agreed treatment of the interests of the worker-partners. But in the case of, for example, a one-man capitalist setting up a retail shop and taking on assistants as worker-partners endowed with labour share certificates, it would be unreasonable – indeed perhaps impracticable – for the worker-partners to be able to prevent the one-man owner from retiring and taking his capital out of the business. Could there be for such cases some rule which required the capitalist partner on liquidation of the business to devote some share of the value of the concern's assets to the compensation of the worker-partners?

There are, however, some possible remaining conflicts of interest between labour and capital in the continuing day-to-day running of an existing partnership.

One obvious case would be a decision to devote part of the firm's resources to the provision of social amenities or fringe benefits of a type (such as canteen facilities) which would be valued by the workers but which would not confer any direct benefits on the owners of the capital invested in the business.

A more serious and direct conflict of interest could arise from decisions to promote workers from one grade to a higher grade of work. Promotions are, of course, a proper and desirable phenomenon – indeed, a necessary one if able persons are to be retained in the firm's service. In such a case promotions involving the raising of a worker's pay by a rise in his fixed-wage payment or by the issue to him of additional labour share certificates, would, of course, be of ultimate benefit to all shareholders. But they could in theory be misused; if they were made on a wholesale scale which was unnecessary for the success of the firm's activities, they would result simply in a shift of part of the revenue of the firm from capital shareholders to labour shareholders.

One possible source of conflict could arise from the fact that labour share certificates give entitlement to a dividend only until retirement age, while capital share certificates give an entitlement to a dividend for the indefinite future. A worker, particularly a worker near retiring age, is naturally less concerned than is a holder of capital share certificates with the effect of management decisions on the future fortunes of the firm and is more concerned with their more immediate present effects.

Such a conflict of interest could be wholly avoided if it were possible always to adopt an accounting procedure which would give a clear and unequivocal definition of what was the firm's distributable surplus in any period, in the sense of the amount of dividends that could be distributed to the shareholders and yet leave enough funds to ensure that the real capital resources of the firm were so maintained as to allow this same level of real distributable surplus to be sustained indefinitely in the future. If less were distributed, then capital resources would be more than maintained so that some part of current distributable surplus should be treated as a net saving by the firm. If more were distributed in dividends, then the firm would be dissaving and living on its capital to that extent.

In these conditions an appropriate arrangement would be that there should be an issue of additional capital share certificates equal at current valuations to the amount of distributable surplus which was not distributed in dividend, and that these additional capital share certificates instead of being sold in the market should be distributed in lieu of dividend *pro rata* to all existing shareholders whether workers or capitalists. Thus workers as well as capitalists would acquire capital share certificates (which they would be perfectly free to hold or to sell as they chose), to represent that part of the firm's income which had been held back from distribution on their existing share certificates. Alternatively it would be possible to arrange for the dividend on capital share certificates to be cut without cutting the dividend on labour share certificates and to issue the additional capital share certificates solely to the existing holders of such certificates, so that it was only the capitalists who financed and who benefited from the ploughing back of revenue into an expansion of the capital resources of the business.

Unfortunately, however, it is notoriously difficult in a number of cases to obtain a clear-cut distinction for accounting purposes between revenues and expenditures on capital account and those on current account; but for the reasons just given this distinction is of crucial importance for a Labour–Capital Partnership.

In this connection there is one tiresome complication which might have to be introduced into the accounting procedures of a Labour–Capital Partnership. If workers relied for a main part of their pay on labour share certificates it would be necessary to pay such dividends at frequent intervals, possibly even weekly, and at rates which were reasonably stable and reliable. Any such distribution would involve some administrative costs and accounting problems, even though dividends on capital share certificates could continue to be paid yearly or half-yearly. But more importantly rates of dividend would have to be announced some time in advance of payment so that workers had some knowledge of the incomes on which they could rely at least for a number of months in advance. This would involve for accounting purposes some kind of dividend equalisation fund into which distributable surplus could be paid subject to inevitable variation between good and bad periods and from which more stable, reliable and frequent dividends could be paid.

Such an accounting arrangement would itself inevitably complicate somewhat the distinctions to be drawn between capital and current payments and receipts. But the problem in fact goes much deeper in trying to make a fair calculation of the probable level at which real distributable surplus could be sustained. Quite apart from problems which arise as a result of monetary inflation, the problems are especially great in cases where future risks and uncertainty are important. Suppose that the management of a partnership were confronted with the possibility of replacing part of the firm's capital equipment with equipment based on a new technology which would admittedly not produce a very high return in the near future period of inevitable teething troubles but which *might* if successful produce an exceedingly high return in future years. The holders of labour share certificates – and in particular those nearing retiring age – would have every justification in demanding that an accounting procedure should be adopted which treated the low returns expected during the immediate low years as due to savings which were being made in order to lead to the uncertain, but hoped-for, high returns of the successive years. But quite what allowances should be made for the uncertainty surrounding these venturesome new technologies and what rates of discount should be used to evaluate them in order to make the relevant calculations would be a matter for somewhat arbitrary choices.

In so far as the Labour–Capital Partnership principle removes direct conflicts of interest between labour shareholders and capital shareholders the way is open for a full participation of labour in the running of the firm. If all occasions of conflict were removed, the simple answer would be to arrange that all share certificates, whether held by the worker or by capitalist shareholders, carried an entitlement not only to the same rate of dividend but also to the same voting power at shareholders' meetings. But, as we have seen, some areas of conflict will inevitably remain, and to resolve these it might be wise for a partnership to rule that certain decisions – or indeed that all decisions – would require the agreement of representatives of both types of partner or in the case of dispute would be referred to some form of agreed arbitration. In any case it is clear that Labour–Capital Partnerships of the kind discussed in this pamphlet could work only in a general atmosphere of mutual trust in which the partners wished to make the partnership work and were prepared to accept some machinery for sensible compromise in any such cases of dispute.

The following arrangement would perhaps provide a reasonably independent management together with a workable process for the resolution of any conflicts of interest between workers and capitalists. The capitalist shareholders and the labour shareholders would each separately elect the same number of full-time members for a board of directors. These directors would appoint by agreement an additional chairman with a casting vote who would thus act as an 'arbitrator' in the case of a conflict between the two sets of directors. The board would appoint a general manager who would be responsible for the day-to-day conduct of the business, the agreement of the board of directors being required only for major policy decisions.

## 8   Some Concluding Remarks

Sharing arrangements in industrial concerns should not be relied upon to provide a decisive instrument for promoting a property-owning democracy. There are strong arguments in favour of moving towards a society in which the representative citizen is both capitalist and worker; but for the reasons given at the end of section 5, society must rely primarily on general fiscal, social benefit, inheritance, and social welfare reforms for this purpose.

Sharing arrangements may, however, have important merits for the improvement of incentives and of industrial relations and for the promotion of a high and stable level of employment.

There are, however, three possible basic snags which must be faced. First, any effective sharing arrangement implies that the workers become risk-bearers together with the entrepreneur capitalists. Do workers really want to share the risks? May the majority not greatly prefer work at a fixed wage? In some arrangements, such as the Labour–Capital Partnerships outlined in section 7, it may be possible to offer workers a reduction in the risk of unemployment in return for their accepting a greater risk of variation in their pay. But this may not be an attractive offer to the majority of workers because it may be a known minority of the least established workers in any team who are likely to be made redundant if trade is bad so that the majority face little risk of unemployment.

Could this be overcome by offering individual workers the choice between a fixed wage and a variable dividend? Those most liable to the risk of redundancy might then choose to accept a variable dividend together with the resulting security of tenure. The next layer of relatively less well-established workers would thus move into the category of those most liable to the risks of redundancy, and thus they in turn might favour a variable dividend with the greater security of tenure. Could the variable dividend thus be generally promoted through the domino effect of individual freedom of choice of regime? But in the case of a partnership which was going through a bad period of low profitability would such an arrangement be too liable to lead to the retention of the 'duds' on variable incomes and the redundancy of the 'winners' who had remained on a fixed-wage or salary basis?

Second, if workers come to bear serious risks in the outcome of the firm's operations they will inevitably wish to play their part in influencing the firm's policies. Is it possible to envisage such worker participation being compatible with decisive and strong action by managers with the necessary flair, ability, and expertise, particularly in the case of concerns whose success must rest on risky innovation? Is workers' risk-bearing compatible with a limitation of workers' intervention to an ultimate say in the appointment of managers, as in the case of the normal capitalist fixed-wage firm? Or are the worker-partners likely to be in such daily contact with the management that such a remote relationship would be impossible?

Third, if workers are participating in the firm's affairs, will they aim at the maximisation of the incomes of the existing workers in such a way as to impede the expansion of the business? It is precisely the successful business which should expand and thus help to achieve a high level of employment for the economy as a whole, but it is precisely in a successful business that a conflict may arise between using the profits of success to maintain at an exceptionally high level the incomes of the existing 'insiders' in the firm or using them to expand output and the employment of 'outsiders' at uninflated money prices, money profits, and money rates of pay. How far in a sharing arrangement can one rely on growth rather than maximisation of income per head as a motive force? Or would it be possible in certain forms of successful Labour–Capital Partnership to arrange for the employment of 'outsiders' on less favourable terms than the existing 'insiders'?

These questions raise an important issue which has not been discussed in this pamphlet. Are the advantages of sharing arrangements such that the state should take positive action to promote them (e.g. through some tax advantage on incomes which are paid in the form of a variable share of revenue or profit rather than in the form of a fixed wage or salary)? There are two quite distinct types of reason which might justify the answer 'yes' to this basic question.

In the first place, it may be necessary simply to overcome conservative inertia. Sharing arrangements may well in fact bring great benefits directly to the business which introduces them, but their introduction may be held up very reasonably because of their unfamiliarity and the surrounding uncertainty about their effects. Thus temporary subsidies to provide experimentation with new forms may well be socially desirable with the intention that only those forms which turned out to be directly advantageous to the firms which introduced them should ultimately survive.

But, secondly, there can be a case for permanent subsidisation of new forms if a substantial part of the benefits arising from the adoption of the new form by a particular business or individual in fact accrues indirectly to other businesses or individuals. Such social or 'external' benefits may result from the introduction of sharing arrangements in at least three ways:

1  The majority of workers who feel well established in their jobs may be unwilling to accept the risks involved in receiving a share in the firm's variable revenue in place of a fixed wage or salary payment. But the widespread acceptance of such substitution may be necessary to ensure stability of general employment, particularly for less well-established workers.

2  As has been shown in section 2 (pp. 216–17 above) the introduction of a share arrangement in a firm, a very large part of whose costs represent the purchase of semi-finished products or raw materials, may have little attraction unless the firms supplying the semi-finished products or raw materials are also introducing sharing arrangements which will make the prices which they charge for those semi-finished products and raw materials more flexible.

3   For reasons given in section 6 (p. 232 above) stabilisation of general employment in face of a general fall in expenditures on the products of the economy will be much simpler if a large number of concerns have introduced suitable sharing arrangements than will be the case if it is left to a limited number of 'sharing' concerns to mop up redundancies resulting from the contraction of activities in the 'fixed-wage non-sharing' firms.

If the snags mentioned above can be overcome and if firms can be induced from self-interest or otherwise to introduce them, there is much to be said for suitable sharing arrangements. Employee Share Ownership Schemes, Profit-Sharing Schemes, Labour Co-operatives, and Flexible Revenue-Sharing Schemes – such as those outlined in the description of Labour–Capital Partnerships – may all have a role to play with their different limitations which, as described in this paper, vary according to the nature of the activity to which each form of sharing arrangement is applied. Surely the right policy at present is to encourage experiment with the various types – paying, of course, due attention to the merits of Discriminating Labour–Capital Partnerships.

PART II

# Distribution

# 15

# The Post-War Treatment of
# the National Debt

*As a member of the official National Debt Enquiry established in early
1945 to consider post-war monetary and debt management policy,
including the possibility of a capital levy, Meade wrote the Economic
Section's memoranda for the committee on 'The Fiscal Problem set by
the Debt', 'The Capital Levy' and 'Debt Management and Employment
Policy'. Since Meade began drafting them as a single paper on 'the post-
war treatment of the national debt' they are printed together here.
Meade's memorandum on the capital levy, after some revision by other
members of the Enquiry, became the committee's report on the subject to
the Chancellor of the Exchequer in June 1945. (The National Debt
Enquiry included Keynes, Treasury and Inland Revenue officials,
Meade and Lionel Robbins whom Meade succeeded as Director of the
Economic Section at the end of 1945.) (Public Record Office T230/95,
NDE Papers 4, 5 and 6, and Meade Papers 3/10; Public Record Office
T230/94 and T233/159; Meade Diary, 28 January and 26 February
1945).*

## The Fiscal Problem set by the Debt

1   In considering the problem of the National Debt a distinction must be
drawn between internal and external debt. To finance interest payments
on the latter revenue must be raised by way of taxation and must be paid
over to the foreign debt holders. In order to transfer these payments to
the foreigner an excess of exports must be generated; and this clearly
involves a real burden on the community, since goods and services must
be handed over to the foreigner without any equivalent return. The
payment of interest on internal debt, on the other hand, represents
merely a transfer of resources from the taxpayer to the debt holder,
and there is no direct drain of resources from the community as a
whole. There will not even be any transfer of resources from one class to
another within the community in so far as the taxpayer is also the debt
holder.

2   It would, however, be going too far to conclude from this that the
existence of an internal debt makes no difference to the community. Even

if the taxpayer were precisely the same person as the debt holder, the raising of the taxation necessary to finance the national debt would impose a real hardship on the community. This point may be illustrated by means of a simple numerical example.

(i)   First, suppose that a community has a net national income of 4,500 and that there is no question of state expenditure other than on national debt interest. Then if it has no national debt, its taxable income is 4,500. But in this case no taxation is required for the finance of debt so that citizens are free to spend the whole of their 4,500 as they please.

(ii)  Secondly, suppose the same community with the same net national income of 4,500 to have a national debt interest of 500 to finance. Then the community's taxable income will be 5,000 (4,500 net national income plus 500 national debt interest). But an average rate of tax of 10 per cent on this 5,000 will be necessary to raise the funds to finance the national debt, leaving the citizens as before with 4,500 to spend as they choose.

3   These two cases are the same in that in each case there is a net national income of 4,500 which the citizens may spend as they please. But there is this vital difference. In the one case there is no taxation and in the other there is an average rate of tax of 10 per cent. But since people have in each case the same real income, they will be less inclined to exert themselves to add to their income in the case in which they can retain only 90 per cent of any additional income which they earn than in the case in which there is no taxation on their earnings. The precise effects will depend upon the form of taxation imposed; but, whatever the form, it is almost certain to reduce the real satisfaction which the taxpayer can obtain from any addition to his income, and thus to reduce the real reward obtained from additional work or from additional enterprise. This is particularly the case with progressive taxation, when the net amount left over to the taxpayer from any additional income may be very small. The internal debt presents a problem in so far as the rates of taxation which its payment necessitates have adverse effects upon the incentives of the taxpayer to work, to undertake risks, to invest and to choose between present and future consumption.

4   The actual hardships imposed on the community by the necessity of raising taxation to meet the payment of interest on the debt depends upon the structure of taxation. Certain taxes have a much more adverse effect upon economic incentives than others. The degree of reliance upon taxes assessed on income, taxes assessed on capital (such as death duties or an annual capital tax) or taxes on expenditure; the degree of progression of the various taxes; and the precise way in which the object of tax is defined; – all these considerations will affect the extent to which the raising of any given revenue has adverse effects upon economic incentives. This general problem requires separate study. The present note is confined to a discussion of the fiscal problem set by the debt (of which the ratio of debt

interest to total taxable income is taken as a rough measurement) and does not deal with the type of tax which is best suited to meet this problem.

5   The following figures[1] illustrate the extent of the fiscal problem of the debt in the past and give a rough estimate of its probable extent after the end of the war.

|  | *Interest on National Debt* | *Total expenditure by the Central Government* |
|---|---|---|
|  | *As a percentage of the taxable income* | |
| 1818 | 7.3 | 13.5 |
| 1913 | 0.7 | 8.7 |
| 1924 | 7.3 | 19.2 |
| 1938 | 4.1 | 20.1 |
| 1943 | 4.1 | 66.3 |
| 1948 | 6.7 | 25.0 |

It will be observed that the interest on the national debt had risen to some 7 per cent of the taxable income by the end of the Napoleonic Wars, was reduced to less than 1 per cent of taxable income by the outbreak of the first German War, rose again to rather more than 7 per cent of taxable income as a result of that war, had fallen again to rather more than 4 per cent of the taxable income before the outbreak of the present war and is likely to have risen again to nearly 7 per cent of taxable income by 1948.

6   At first sight it might appear that the fiscal problem set by the debt is likely to be a little less serious after this war (when the interest on it will amount to rather less than 7 per cent of the total taxable income) than after the Napoleonic Wars or the first German War (when national debt interest amounted to rather more than 7 per cent of taxable income). Quite apart from the fact that the estimates for the early years are very uncertain, this is not necessarily the case. After this war other forms of Government expenditure are likely to impose a considerably higher charge on the taxable national income than they did after the last war, as the following figures show:-

| | *Percentage of taxable income required to meet total expenditure by the Central Government* | | |
|---|---|---|---|
| | *(a)* *Actual* | *(b)* *Assuming no national debt* | *(c)* *Difference (a) − (b)* |
| 1924 | 19.2 | 12.8 | 6.4 |
| 1948 | 25.0 | 19.7 | 5.3 |

[1] See Appendix [pp. 261] for the figures on which these and the following estimates are based.

The existence of the national debt in 1924 raised the proportion of taxable income required for the finance of central government expenditure from 12.8 per cent to 19.2 per cent, and in 1948 it is likely to raise it from 19.7 per cent to 25.0 per cent. From the point of view of its ill effects upon incentives the latter movement may well be more disadvantageous than the former, since the evil effects of any given addition to taxation are likely to be greater, the higher the existing level of taxation on which they are imposed.

7    This point may be illustrated by means of an extreme example. An increase in the rate of taxation of 1*s* 0*d* in the pound would be very significant if it meant an increase from 18*s* 0*d* to 19*s* 0*d* in the pound; in this case it would represent a 50 per cent decrease (from 2*s* 0*d* to 1*s* 0*d*) in the tax-free income which a man could enjoy by earning another £1. But if it represented merely an increase in the rate of taxation from 1*s* 0*d* to 2*s* 0*d* in the pound, it would represent a decrease of only 5 per cent (from 19*s* 0*d* to 18*s* 0*d*) in the taxpayer's net reward for earning an additional £1. At the higher rates of taxation which are probable after the war any additional fiscal problem set by the debt (even if it were of quite moderate dimensions) is a matter of considerable importance. The increase in the average rate of tax (from 19.7 per cent to 25.0 per cent) which the existence of the post-war debt may involve represents a reduction in the *average* tax-free portion of taxable income of 6.5 per cent (i.e. from 80.3 per cent to 75 per cent). On the higher ranges of income where rates of taxation will be much above the average, it is likely to represent a much greater percentage reduction in the tax-free portion of the last units of income.

8    Obviously the most important single factor affecting the fiscal problem set by the debt is the size of the debt itself. The accumulation of debt is essentially a war phenomenon, as the following figures show:-

|  | *Total National Debt at 31st March £m.* |
|---|---|
| 1776 | 131 |
| 1818 | 840 |
| 1913 | 618 |
| 1924 | 7,535 |
| 1938 | 7,663 |
| 1943 | 15,594 |
| 1948 | approximately  23,250 |

9    During the wars with France the debt rose from £131 m. in 1776 to £840 m. in 1818. During the succeeding period of almost a century without a major war the debt was moderately reduced, but increased more than tenfold during the first German War. There was some slight increase in the inter-war years; but as a result of the present war the total debt may well become three times as great as it was when war broke out.

10    While war is clearly the outstanding factor affecting the size of the debt, peacetime policies also have their effect. Later sections of this note are devoted to a discussion of the question whether special *ad hoc* measures should be taken after the war to repay a large proportion of the debt; whether there should be a steady and continuing repayment of debt by means of an annual sinking fund; and whether the requirements of employment policy will lead inevitably to a further rise of debt during the years of peace.

11    Apart from the size of the debt, there are a number of factors which affect the fiscal problem set by a debt of any given size. If we adopt as a rough index of this fiscal problem the ratio between the interest on the debt and the total taxable income from which it must be financed, the fiscal problem will be reduced *first* by a reduction in the rate of interest payable on the debt and, *secondly*, by any developments (such as an increase of population, a higher level of employment, an increase in output per head, or a rise in the general level of money prices) which raise the total money income on which taxation may be levied.

## (i)    The Rate of Interest

12    The movement of rates of interest is illustrated in the following figures:-

|      | Yield on 2½% Consols % | Yield on 3 months fine Bank Bills % | National Debt interest as % of National Debt[2] |
|------|------|------|------|
| 1913 | 3.4  | 4.39 | 2.6  |
| 1924 | 4.4  | 3.47 | 4.1  |
| 1938 | 3.4  | 0.63 | 2.7  |
| 1943 | 3.1  | 1.03 | 2.3  |

13    During the last war, it will be observed, the long-term rate of interest was allowed to rise very considerably. This had a most marked effect upon the burden of the debt contracted during the last war. If, for example, in 1924 the average yield on the national debt had been at the 1913 level, the national debt interest would have represented only 4.8 per cent instead of 7.3 per cent of the national taxable income in 1924. Between 1924 and 1938 the average yield on the debt fell from 4.1 to 2.7 per cent; and if it had not done so, the debt interest in 1938 would have amounted to 6.1 instead of only 4.1 per cent of the total national taxable income.

14    An outstanding feature of the present position is that during this war the debt has been financed, not only without a rise, but even with an appreciable decline (from 2.7 in 1938 to 2.3 in 1943) in the average yield on the debt. If in 1948 the average yield were at the 1924 level of 4.1 per

---

[2] This column represents interest, management and expenses on the debt as a percentage of the nominal value of the outstanding debt.

cent instead of the 1943 levels of 2.3 per cent, the proportion of the national taxable income necessary to cover the national debt interest would be raised from 6.7 per cent to 11.3 per cent. This estimate, although very approximate, may serve to illustrate the important part played by low interest rates.

15   The fact that interest rates have been kept relatively low and, it is expected, will continue to be relatively low suggests that we cannot hope in the years following this war to obtain the same relief as we did in the inter-war years from the conversion of debt to lower rates of interest. But, while it is certainly true that we cannot expect to gain as much from this factor as before, it would be unwise to conclude that in no circumstances is any further appreciable relief from reduced interest rates to be anticipated.

16   In the years immediately after the war, it is generally recognised, there will be no reason to take measures in the interests of employment policy for a still further reduction in interest rates. The problem will rather be to find ways other than by a rise in interest rates to restrain excessive expenditure of all kinds. But at a later date, when the more pressing projects of capital replacement and development have been completed, the problem may be completely changed. The need may be to find means for stimulating expenditure without running into a continuing budget deficit and increase in debt. One of the most important measures for this purpose may be a reduction in interest rates which, by cheapening the terms on which funds can be borrowed, will help to stimulate expenditure on capital works.

17   Such a development would have the effect of further relieving the burden of the debt. The yield on 2½ per cent Consols is at present 3 per cent and on Treasury Bills about 1 per cent. Reductions of the rate of interest on long-term loans can affect the burden of national debt interest only when and in so far as the debt falls due for repayment or conversion. It is a matter worthy of further study how quickly the debt interest could in fact be reduced if, for example, the long-term rate of interest fell to a 2 per cent basis and the short-term rate to, say, ½ per cent. But as a preliminary measure of the order of magnitude of the change involved, the debt interest envisaged for 1948 would amount to only 5.3 per cent instead of 6.7 per cent of the total national taxable income if the average yield assumed on the debt were reduced by ½ per cent (i.e. from 2.3 to 1.8 per cent).

### (ii)   Population and Employment

18   The fiscal problem set by the debt is also diminished by any rise in the money income on which the necessary taxes must be levied; and the level of the taxable income in turn depends upon the size of the population, the degree of employment, the productivity of labour and the level of money prices.

19  As far as population and employment are concerned, we cannot hope to obtain the great relief from debt which, in the course of the last century, resulted from the enormous growth in the working population and, in consequence, in the national income. The following figures illustrate this development:

| | Total population | National Debt interest | National taxable income | National taxable income at 1818 population | National Debt interest as percentage of | |
|---|---|---|---|---|---|---|
| | | | | | c | d |
| | £m. | £m. | £m. | £m. | | |
| | a | b | c | d | e | f |
| 1818 | 17.0 | 31 | 431 | 431 | 7.3 | 7.3 |
| 1913 | 45.6 | 16 | 2,316 | 873 | 0.7 | 1.8 |

Between 1818 and 1913 the total population increased from 17.0 millions to 45.6 millions. On the assumption that no increase in population had taken place but that the net money income per head of population had increased between 1818 and 1913 in the way in which it did in fact increase, the national debt interest in 1913 would have represented as much as 1.8 per cent instead of 0.7 per cent of the total national taxable income. Such was the importance of the growth of population.

20  We cannot expect a similar development in the coming century. The demographic situation has entirely changed. There is not likely to be any appreciable increase in the population after the middle of this century, and in the last half of the century (unless there is a revolutionary change in existing demographic trends) there is likely to be an appreciable decline. The Registrar-General (Cmd 6358 [*Current Trend of Population in Great Britain*, May 1942]) has estimated that the total population of working age (15–65) may fall by 2.0 per cent between 1951 and 1961 and by some 7.3 per cent between 1951 and 1971. Assuming income per head to be unchanged, a reduction of 7.3 per cent in the working population would raise the 1948 proportion between national debt interest and total taxable income from 6.7 per cent to 7.2 per cent.

21  As far as the numbers of available workers are concerned, it is improbable that any relief to the burden of the national debt will be forthcoming. But it is the number of workers in employment who affect the national income; and for this reason, whatever may be future demographic movements, it is of the first importance to maintain a high and stable level of employment if the burden of the national debt is to be kept at a minimum. A general economic depression results in a reduction in employment and so in the national income produced, but it does not automatically result in any reduction in the national debt interest. The estimate of the national taxable income for 1948 which has been used above is based upon the assumption of an unemployment percentage of about 7½ per cent. If instead an unemployment percentage of 12½ per cent had been assumed, the national debt interest would have repre-

sented about 7.0 per cent instead of 6.7 per cent of the total national taxable income.

## (iii)   Productivity

22   While no very marked relief can be expected to result from an increase of national income due to a growth of population, it is to be hoped and expected that there will be further technical improvements and developments of capital equipment which will result in increased output per head. There is some evidence that in the period from 1911 to 1938 there was a cumulative increase in output per head of about 1 per cent per annum. If this were to continue after 1948 (with a constant debt interest, constant population and a constant level of commodity prices), the effect on the fiscal problem set by the debt would be as follows:-

| *National Debt interest as a percentage of total taxable income (assuming output per head to increase by 1½ per cent per annum)* | |
|---|---|
| 1948 | 6.7 |
| 1958 | 5.9 |
| 1968 | 5.1 |

This is clearly one of the most important factors which may operate to give relief.

## (iv)   The Price Level

23   The size of the national debt depends, of course, upon the level of money prices at the time at which it is contracted, while the real value of the interest payments on the debt depends upon the level of prices at the time when the interest payments are made. The fiscal problem set by the debt is, therefore, liable to be much increased in so far as (i) the debt is contracted during periods of high prices (such as is likely to be the case in war-time) and (ii) the general level of prices is permitted to fall during the subsequent years of peace.

24   The following figures suggest that in the case both of the Napoleonic Wars and the First World War debt was accumulated at high prices during war-time and that interest was paid on it at lower prices during the subsequent periods of peace:

| | Wholesale prices | Cost of living |
|---|---|---|
| | *1938 = 100* | |
| 1818 | 175 | — |
| 1913 | 93 | 65 |
| 1915–18 | 162 | 105 |
| 1924 | 152 | 112 |
| 1938 | 100 | 100 |
| 1940–43 | 168 | 125 |
| 1948 | — | 135[3] |

[3] The index assumed for the calculation of the 1948 taxable income.

25    Between 1818 and 1913 the general level of wholesale prices fell by 47 per cent. If the net national income of 1913 were revalued at the price level of 1818 the debt interest paid in 1913 would have represented only 0.4 per cent instead of 0.7 per cent of total taxable income, a difference which may be taken to represent the increase in the burden of debt which was allowed to occur as a result of the fall in prices over these years. Similarly, the cost of living fell by 11 per cent between 1924 and 1938; and if the net national income of 1938 is revalued at 1924 prices, the debt interest paid in 1938 would have represented only 3.7 per cent instead of 4.1 per cent of the total taxable income. Thus the deflation of prices after the last war added an appreciable burden to the country's finances.

26    In the previous paragraphs of this note calculations have been based on the assumption that the level of prices in 1948 will be 35 per cent above 1938. It is already doubtful whether this is realistic. The cost-of-living index now stands at 129 per cent of 1938, and some appreciable further rise must probably be expected during the readjustments of the transitional period. If the level of estimated net national income for 1948 were revalued at a level of prices 50 instead of 35 per cent above 1938, the debt interest payable in 1948 would represent only 6.1 instead of 6.7 per cent of total taxable income.

27    It is impossible to forecast the future trend of prices. But the trend is not as likely as after the last war to be in a downward direction. It is unlikely that any Government in this country will so tie the currency to an external standard (such as gold or the dollar) as to remove the ultimate power of the authorities in this country to determine our internal economic and financial policy without undue regard to movements in external prices. If this greater freedom in domestic policy is successfully used to maintain a high and stable level of employment, declining prices resulting from deficiency of general demand will be avoided. Indeed, if the employment policy is fully successful in maintaining demand, the problem may rather be to avoid an inflation of costs and prices. The decisive factor in this respect will be wages policy. How far will those responsible for fixing money wage-rates act moderately in circumstances in which there is a consistently high demand for labour? It will not be dangerous (indeed, in the interests of the problem of the national debt it will be positively advantageous) if wage-rates rise as fast as productivity increases, so that increased real standards are attained through a rise in money wages rather than through a fall in prices.

28    In the interest of the debt problem there is much to be said for allowing prices to settle at the end of the transitional period at a level somewhat higher than the 35 per cent above pre-war which has been assumed in previous calculations. It is another matter to decide whether it would also be useful thereafter to permit a steady upward movement of prices so as gradually to reduce the real value of the debt interest. A gradual rise of prices, if it were taken into account by the business community, would itself increase the incentive to spend money on capital

development; and (provided that the community was not threatened with a general problem of unemployment) it might accordingly be necessary to allow interest rates to rise to higher levels than would otherwise be the case in order to prevent an excessive inflationary development. The extent and the speed with which any such rise in interest rates would add to the budgetary burden of the debt interest would depend upon the proportion of the debt which was in short-dated stock on which higher yields would quickly have to be paid. If much of the debt was in this form, the increased burden of the debt due to the higher rates of interest payable on the debt might, in the early years at least, easily outweigh the reduction in the real burden of the debt due to higher money prices; for the rate of interest might have to be raised promptly to a substantially higher level in order to avoid undue inflation as soon as it was realised that prices were rising and were likely to continue to rise, whereas the relief to the real burden of the debt would materialise only after prices had risen to substantially higher levels. On the other hand, if there is a threat of general unemployment which it is technically impossible to cure by a reduction of rates of interest to still lower levels, a steady rise in money prices will bring an unequivocal advantage from the point of view of the fiscal problem set by the debt, since in this case it need not be accompanied by higher rates of interest. In this case the rising level of money prices takes the place of a lower rate of interest both as a measure for stimulating employment and also (incidentally) as a means of reducing the fiscal problem set by the debt.

## (v)   The Combined Effect of Interest Rates, Productivity and Prices

29   It would be foolish to attempt to forecast the development of the economy in the post-war years. Movements in many of the most important relevant factors will depend upon conscious acts of policy. Nevertheless, merely by way of hypothetical illustration, it may be useful to consider the effect of a possible combination of the various factors discussed above. If between 1948 and 1958 (i) the total outstanding debt were constant, (ii) the working population declined by 2.0 per cent, (iii) the average yield on the debt fell by ½ per cent from 2.3 to 1.8 per cent, (iv) productivity increased by 1½ per cent per annum, and (v) the level of prices rose from 135 to 150 per cent of the 1938 level, the effect would be that the percentage of total taxable income necessary to cover the debt interest would fall from 6.7 to 4.3 per cent. If thereafter in addition to these changes, between 1958 and 1968 productivity per head continued to increase by 1½ per cent per annum but the working population declined yet further to 92.7 per cent of the 1948 level, the percentage of total taxable income required to finance the interest on the 1948 national debt would fall to 3.9 per cent. This result rests, of course, on a combination of favourable circumstances: no increase in the size of the debt after 1948; a decline of ½ per cent in the already low average yield on the debt; the maintenance of prices at 150 per cent of the 1938 level; and, above all, a continued cumulative increase in productivity per head at 1½ per cent per

# Appendix   The National Debt 1818–1948

| | National Debt at 31st March[1] year beginning 1st April | Interest on National Debt year beginning 1st April | Total Government expenditure year beginning 1st April | Taxable income[2] | Interest on Debt | | Total Government expenditure | Population | Wholesale Prices | Cost of Living |
|---|---|---|---|---|---|---|---|---|---|---|
| | £m. | | | | As % of National Debt | As % of taxable income | As % of taxable income | Millions | 1938 = 100 | |
| 1818 | 810 | 31 | 58 | 431 | 3.7 | 7.3 | 13.5 | 17.0 | 175 | — |
| 1913 | 618 | 16 | 202 | 2,316 | 2.6 | 0.7 | 8.7 | 45.6 | 93 | 65 |
| 1924 | 7,535 | 306 | 806 | 4,206 | 4.1 | 7.3 | 19.2 | 44.9 | 152 | 112 |
| 1938 | 7,663 | 206 | 1,013 | 5,048 | 2.7 | 4.1 | 20.1 | 47.5 | 100 | 100 |
| 1943 | 15,594 | 356 | 5,782 | 8,721 | 2.3 | 4.1 | 66.3 | 48.2 | 182 | 127 |
| Estimate 1948[3] | (23,250) | 535 | 2,003 | 8,000 | (2.3) | 6.7 | 25.0 | 48.4 | — | 135 |

Notes

1  These figures are the nominal amount of the debt and 'interest management and expenses' as shown in the Reports of the Commissioners for the National Debt adjusted to exclude the debt held by certain Government departments. Interest paid to these departments is estimated at about £1 million in 1913, £6 million in 1924, £13 million in 1938 and £29 million in 1943.

2  The figures for 1938 and 1943 are based on the White Paper on the National Income 1944 [*An Analysis of the Sources of War Finance and Estimates of the National Income and Expenditure in the Years 1938 to 1943*, Cmd 6520, April 1944] with certain minor adjustments. Those for earlier years represent the net national income *plus* interest on the national debt, the net national income figures for 1818 and 1913 being those quoted in the *Report of the Committee on the National Debt and Taxation* [1927, Cmd 2800] (para. 679), and the 1924 figure being A. L. Bowley's estimate ('National Income in America and the United Kingdom', *Economica*, vol. 9 (1942), pp. 227–236).

3  The estimates for 1948 are based on those contained in WP (44)353 and PR(43)35 ['Post-war Financial Commitments', Memorandum by the Chancellor of the Exchequer', 28 June 1944, CAB66/52, and 'Influences affecting the Level of the National Income', 24 June 1943, CAB87/13] but certain small changes have been made in the calculations although the basic assumptions remain the same. It has been assumed that in 1948 national debt interest paid to Government departments, and therefore excluded from these figures, will be about £15 millions.

annum between 1948 and 1968. In spite of these developments the debt interest would still impose a charge on taxable income which (in view of the high rates of taxation required for other purposes) it might be very desirable to reduce.

## The Capital Levy

1   As a means of meeting the fiscal problem set by an internal debt, it has often been proposed that there would be a once-and-for-all levy on all capital, the proceeds of which would be used for the redemption of debt. The following paragraphs first state the general case for a capital levy and then proceed to discuss the various difficulties and disadvantages of a levy. Apart from its administrative practicability, the following questions arise: Would the levy be equitable? Would its impact on the capital and money markets cause intolerable disturbance? Would it produce a worthwhile yield to justify its inconveniences and disadvantages?

### (i)   The Case for a Levy

2   The annual transfer of income from the taxpayer to the recipients of debt interest involves real disadvantages because of the adverse effect upon economic incentives of the taxation required to finance these transfers. But to produce a true budget surplus from which repayment of debt may be financed involves raising rates of taxation to higher levels than those which are necessary merely to finance the interest on the debt. The period of debt repayment thus imposes higher rates of taxation on the community in order that rates of taxation may thereafter be lower than they would otherwise be.

3   Moreover, quite apart from the adverse effect of higher rates of taxation on incentives to work, to take risks and to undertake investment, the raising of additional revenue from the public for the purpose of debt repayment will almost inevitably lead to a reduction in private expenditure on goods and services; and, for this reason, attempts to repay debt are liable to make the problem of the maintenance of employment more difficult, if there is already any general tendency towards economic depression.

4   The strength of the general case for the once-for-all surgical operation of a capital levy is that it will bring with it the advantages of an immediate reduction of debt (and so of the taxation necessary to finance the interest payable on the debt) without involving a prolonged period of even higher taxation while the debt is being repaid. Repudiation of the debt would also, of course, have this effect. It would mean that rates of taxation could be reduced, since it would no longer be necessary to finance the interest on the debt. But repudiation is inequitable, because it falls on the holders of the debt but not on other property-owners; dishonourable because it breaks the state's contract with the debt holder; and liable in consequence

to lead to lack of confidence and financial disorder. A capital levy, the proceeds of which are used to repay the national debt, is a comparatively equitable, honourable and orderly cancellation of debt. If it is sufficiently equitable, and practicable; if it affords a worthwhile yield; and if it has not unduly disadvantageous effects of its own on economic incentives, its imposition will be justified by the advantageous effects on economic incentives caused by the reduction in annual taxation which its yield will make possible.

## (ii) The Question of Equity

5   If there is to be a swift reduction of debt on a substantial scale, the levy must fall on capital, since it is only from accumulated capital that it will be possible for the payers of the levy to finance their payments. This means that those who have substantial incomes from work but little or no property will go untouched (indeed, they are likely actually to gain as a result of the reductions in taxation which follow the levy); while those who have only a small income from property and little or no income from work may lose more from the levy than they gain from any subsequent reduction in taxation.

6   Generally speaking high earnings and the ownership of property go together, and for this reason (in the long run at any rate) a general levy on capital, even if it is not very progressive, is likely to improve the distribution of income. Alternative methods of obtaining a more nearly equal distribution of income are likely to involve highly progressive rates of income taxation and may, therefore, have seriously adverse and continuing effects upon economic incentives. It is arguable, therefore, that the more rough and ready method of a once-for-all levy on capital may provide a method of helping to equalise incomes with the minimum of continuing adverse effects upon economic incentives.

7   On the other hand, serious hardships and inequities are bound to result in a number of cases from a levy. Persons (for example the widows and orphans of middle-class professional men) who are solely dependent for their support upon relatively small incomes from property may be very badly hurt, while persons receiving very large incomes from work go scot-free or are positively advantaged by the subsequent reduction of taxation. And these hardships will be the more keenly felt in that they represent a sudden break in legitimate expectations and follow close upon the quite considerable rise in the cost of living which has resulted from the war. In later paragraphs it will be argued that at present rates of interest and rates of annual taxation the yield from a capital levy will certainly not be worth while if the levy is highly progressive and fails to reach down to quite moderate properties. This makes the problem of equity all the more important, since inequities and rough and ready means of assessment which might be bearable if the levy related only to the largest properties might become intolerable if they seriously affected the smaller properties.

8   The hardest cases might be partially met (a) by some degree of progression in the levy itself which results in the exemption (or taxation at only low rates) of the smaller properties or even perhaps of the properties of those with the smallest total incomes, and (b) by the use of an adequate part of the budgetary savings which result from the levy for the reduction of taxation on the lowest incomes. It might be possible partially to restore the balance between the charge on earned and unearned incomes, by imposing a special tax on high earned incomes for a short period of years after the levy as a means of making those with 'brain capital' contribute towards the levy. But there would in any case be limits to the amount of any such special contribution from earned incomes if seriously disadvantageous effects upon the incentive to work are to be avoided. Broadly speaking, it remains true that the levy is a tax on property-owners for the benefit of all recipients of income, whether earned or unearned; and while in the long run this is likely to have an equalising effect upon incomes, it is bound to involve (particularly in the short run) serious hardships and inequities in many cases.

9   There remains a rather different question of equity, namely equity between different classes of property-owner. In this respect the levy might be seriously inequitable if it took place in a period of rapidly changing property values. In order to assess the liability of each property-owner a fixed date must be taken at which each property is valued. Suppose this fixed date turned out to be at a point which marked the beginning of a serious economic depression, in the course of which reasonably safe fixed-interest securities rose in value while equity shares collapsed in price. The man who owned fixed-interest property would turn out, by the mere accident of choice of a particular date for the valuations, to be treated incomparably more lightly than the man whose property was invested in more risky forms of property.

10   Even within the class of owners of equity shares there might in these circumstances be considerable differences of treatment, if different methods of paying the levy are permissible. Suppose one man to own shares, part of which he can and does realise on the Stock Exchange to pay the levy. Suppose another man to own a participation (of equal value) in a private company which he cannot readily realise, but which he therefore mortgages in order to pay the levy. A general fall in equity values will then hit the first man much more lightly than it will hit the second, who has had to incur a fixed money charge in order to finance the levy payment.

11   Finally, the levy itself may affect the value of different types of property differently. It is liable to lead to a purchase of gilt-edged fixed-interest securities (as the Government repays debt) and to a sale of other forms of property (as individuals who cannot meet the levy by handing over government debt realise other assets for this purpose). If valuations of property are based on pre-levy values, those who own their property in the form mainly of fixed-interest property may benefit

substantially at the expense of holders of other forms of property. The effect of the levy on the prices of different types of assets is discussed in more detail below, where the conclusion is drawn that there is almost bound to be some lasting rise in the price of fixed-interest securities as compared with the values of more risky assets.

12    The Government is now committed to an internal financial policy for the avoidance of inflation and deflation; and the successful prosecution of such a policy will mean that the economy does not suffer from the extreme fluctuations in property values to which it has been subject in the past. A later section of this note is devoted to a discussion of the means by which the immediate disturbances to property values which would result from the levy may be mitigated. By these means it might be hoped to avoid the worst inequities as between various classes of property-owner; but the conclusion is inevitable that to some extent owners of fixed-interest securities would be bound to suffer less heavily than the owners of equities.

## (iii)    The Impact of the Levy on the Capital and Money Markets

13    Much of the discussion of the levy after the last war centred round the question whether its payment would cause a widespread deflationary movement. In so far as the individuals subject to the levy possessed holdings of Government securities which they could surrender in payment of the levy, there would be no very serious financial disturbance. Disturbance might be caused in those cases in which holdings of Government securities were inadequate and other assets had to be realised, or funds had to be borrowed, in order to meet the immediate call of the levy. It is true that even in those circumstances the Government would be redeeming debt and so providing funds for reinvestment on the capital market as other persons were selling assets in order to raise cash to pay the levy. But in two ways there might be difficulty. In the first place, there might be a serious time-lag between sales and purchases, if the Government waited to receive cash from the levy-payers before it in turn entered the market to buy up Government debt. In the second place, there might be a serious discrepancy between the type of assets (for example, industrial ordinary shares) which the levy-payers would be selling and the gilt-edged fixed-interest debt which the Government would be buying.

14    The levy would be payable by individuals in accordance with their individual holdings of property. Thus the levy would not be payable by business concerns as such. But in the case of private business difficulty would arise if the private business man did not own, outside of his trade, sufficient realisable assets to pay the levy. There would be a danger that in such cases the payment of the levy might lead to a serious interference with the finance of private business and to a consequent deflationary movement.

15   In many cases these difficulties will not arise. By the end of this war, a very high proportion of the capital in private hands will take the form of Government debt. In 1932–34 British and foreign Government securities have been estimated to represent 28.7 per cent of total private property;[1] during this war most of the greatly inflated personal savings have gone into Government securities and a number of requisitioned assets, such as foreign securities, have been replaced by Government debt, with the result that the ratio of Government debt to other forms of property will have been much increased.

16   It is also probable that most private business would be in a position to meet a considerable levy without impinging upon their trading assets. Evidence examined by the Colwyn Committee ([*Report of the Committee on National Debt and Taxation*, Cmd 2800, 1927] paras 779 ff) suggested that the majority of owners of private businesses in 1919 and 1923 had assets outside their business which would have been sufficient to meet their liabilities under the kind of levy then under discussion. As a result of the war certain private businesses in certain industries whose activity has been severely curtailed may find their outside assets insufficient. But the fact that saving has been much increased during the war but has found its way into Government securities rather than into business developments reinforces the view that as a general rule there will be no deficiency of outside assets.

17   Nevertheless, there will, of course, be a number of individual cases in which the levy will not be paid by the surrender of Government securities and in which it will impinge upon the trading assets of private businesses. Steps would, therefore, have to be taken: (i) to minimise the evil effects of any time-lag between the sale of assets by levy-payers and the purchase of assets as a result of the Government redemption of debt; (ii) to minimise the evil effects of any discrepancy between the type of assets which the levy-payers will be realising and the type of assets which will be in demand as the result of the repayment of debt; and (iii) to enable those with assets which it is difficult to realise (e.g. the trading assets of private businesses) to find means of financing their payments.

18   There are a number of mechanisms by means of which these financial disturbances may be mitigated. (i) An extensive list could be drawn up of securities and of other forms of assets acceptable to the state in payment of the levy, the state then having the duty of gradually realising these assets (other than Government debt) and using the proceeds to redeem debt. The more extensive this list, the less need would anyone have to sell inappropriate assets on a large scale at sacrifice prices in order to raise the funds required to pay the levy. (ii) Special arrangements might be made for the banking system to extend credit to the Government or to a special governmental agency, so that the state could begin buying up Govern-

[1] See H. Campion, *Public and Private Property in Great Britain* (London: Oxford University Press, 1939) p. 105.

ment debt in anticipation of its actual receipts of money from the levy, if this turned out to be necessary to avoid a time-lag between sales by levy-payers and purchases by debt holders who were being repaid. (iii) Arrangements might be made to extend credit on proper security to those who have to realise assets to pay the levy, so that the assets could be realised gradually over a considerable period. Such credit might take the form of bank credits or, in appropriate cases, of arrangements between the state and the levy-payer that the levy should be paid in instalments.

19 By devices of this kind it should be possible to reduce the time-lag between purchases and sales of assets, to ease the impact of the levy on private businesses which had not sufficient assets outside the business to meet the levy, and (in so far as the state was willing temporarily to hold a large variety of assets) to postpone the effects of any discrepancy between the type of assets which levy-payers would wish to realise and in which debt holders would wish to reinvest the proceeds from redeemed debt. But unless the state was willing permanently to hold a large variety of different assets, sooner or later a capital levy used to repay debt must have the effect of disturbing the proportions in which various assets are held by the public. There will be less fixed-interest debt of high security to be held, while the amount of other assets – land, buildings, equities and cash – will not be directly affected. Somehow or another persons who hitherto have held a high proportion of their property in the form of fixed-interest debt must be persuaded to hold a smaller proportion in this form and a larger proportion in other forms.

20 This shift will only be brought about by a change in the relative prices of different types of asset. For the present purpose it is probably sufficient to distinguish between three types of assets: cash; fixed-interest securities; and other more risky types of assets. For shorthand, let us call these assets Money, Bonds and Shares respectively. The direct result of the levy is to reduce the supply of Bonds without any direct change in the supply of Money or of Shares. This reduction in the relative supply of Bonds will lead to a rise in their price in terms of Money and of Shares, and the yield on Bonds will fall.

21 At first sight this might appear to be an inflationary influence, since the cheapening of the cost of borrowing by means of Bonds might in itself be expected to encourage expenditure on capital development. In some cases (e.g. public investment by municipalities) this will be the probable result. But in the case of industrial development, where there is an important element of risk in investment, it is the price of Shares (and so of the machinery and plant which lies behind the Shares) rather than the price of Bonds which determines the value of real capital investment. The price of Shares (the supply of which is not reduced) will not rise with the price of Bonds; and the increased differential between the yield on Bonds and the yield on Shares will represent the increased risk premium necessary to induce people to shift from fixed-interest Bonds to variable-

dividend Shares. To some extent the increased differential between the yield payable on Bonds and on Shares may induce businesses to undertake capital development through the issue of Bonds. But this automatically increases the risk borne by the existing shareholders and will, therefore, be a strictly limited development.

22   It seems probable that the Money price of Shares will actually decline. Whether the price of Shares falls or rises will depend upon whether property-owners, being starved of Bonds, shift rather to Money or to Shares as the alternative form of property to hold. When the supply of Money is plentiful and interest rates are low, Money is probably a better substitute for Bonds than are Shares. In the opposite circumstances Shares may be a better substitute than Money for Bonds. If, when Bonds become scarce, property-owners shift more readily from Bonds to Money, then the Money prices of Shares will fall, and there will be a deflationary influence. If they shift more readily from Bonds to Shares, the Money price of Shares will rise though not, of course, as much as the price of Bonds, and there will be an inflationary development. The former development would appear to be the more probable in present conditions of low interest rates and plentiful monetary supplies.

23   Any long-run deflation that might be brought about through this type of development might, in certain circumstances, be countered by a banking policy which increased the supply of Money. Such an expansion in the supply of Money could be brought about by the banks purchasing Bonds on the open market. The public would thus have to be persuaded to hold more money and less Bonds, which would cause the price of Bonds to rise still further and the yield on them to decline still lower. This would tend to raise the differential between the yield on Bonds and the yield on Shares, and there would accordingly be a sympathetic rise in the price of Shares. If such a development could be continued until the Money price of Shares was restored to its previous level, the deflationary effects upon capital development would be avoided.

24   Such offsetting monetary action may, however, be difficult if the rates of interest on Bonds are already very low. For in such circumstances the owners of Bonds will readily hold the new supplies of Money without any further substantial rise in Bond prices and, therefore, without any very appreciable sympathetic restoration of Share prices. It is in these conditions (of low interest rates) that (a) a capital levy by removing Bonds from the market is most likely to cause a depression of Share prices and that (b) it will be most difficult to offset such a depression of Share prices by an expansion in the supply of Money. The conclusion would seem to be that it is in conditions of low interest rates (when the yield on the capital levy will in any case be low) that there is the maximum danger of difficult deflationary consequences from the imposition of a levy.

25   On the other hand, the final effect of a levy, the deflationary effects of which were in fact successfully offset by monetary policy, would be that the price of the remaining Government debt would be raised and the yield on it would be lowered. This fact is of considerable significance. It means that in these circumstances a capital levy, in addition to the budgetary saving which would directly result from the saving of interest on that part of the debt which was redeemed, would enable the yield on all the remaining debt to be substantially reduced without any untoward effects. In this case the capital levy sets the stage for conversion of debt to lower yields.

26   The above paragraphs are written on the assumption that there are no violent shifts on the part of property-owners in attempts to evade the levy. If the levy were foreseen, or if a repetition of it were expected, by property-owners and if administrative difficulties made it difficult to detect and assess certain types of assets, there might be a considerable shift into these assets. The two most important possible movements would presumably be a flight of capital from the country or the large-scale hoarding of bank-notes. The former would depend upon the possibility of evading any exchange control and, perhaps, of the property-owner himself leaving the country with his capital. It is difficult to see how the latter, which would certainly represent a strong deflationary influence, could be administratively entirely avoided.

## (iv)   The Yield of the Levy

27   In assessing the net annual relief to the Budget which is likely to result from a capital levy, account must be taken of the rate of interest saved on the capital sum of the repaid debt. This determines the gross annual budgetary saving of debt interest; but account must be taken also of the reduction of tax revenue which will result (a) because there is less interest from debt to assess for income tax and sur-tax and (b) because there is less debt to be assessed for death duties. The gross and net annual budgetary savings from the redemption of any given volume of debt are likely to be much lower after this war than after the war of 1914–18. For, in the first place, the rate of interest on the debt is now much lower; and secondly, rates of income and capital taxation are now much higher. With the present structure of taxation the loss of revenue caused by the redemption of debt may be very great indeed. If, for example, the capital levy is very progressive so that practically all the saving of debt interest is in respect of interest received by owners of large properties; and if – at the same time – income tax, sur-tax and death duties are all very progressive, so that recipients of large incomes from large properties already pay 19s 6d in the pound on their last units of income and 65 per cent in death duties on their last units of capital; the loss of annual revenue from income tax, sur-tax and death duties will exceed the saving of interest on the debt which was redeemed.

28   There are a number of factors which together determine the net degree of relief obtained from any given capital levy.

(i)   The higher is the total of taxable property (i.e. of property in private hands which might be charged to the levy) in relation to the total of taxable income, the greater (it may be shown) will be the improvement to economic incentives (measured by the proportionate increase in the tax-free part of income) which will be brought about through the reduction of taxation resulting from any given proportionate levy on capital. The following figures (which are very rough approximations) show that total taxable property after this war, as a result of the very large increase in savings during the war, is likely to be greater in relation to the total of taxable income than it was immediately before the war. But it is not likely to be much greater than it was in 1924. While, therefore, on the ground mentioned above the case for a levy is stronger than it was immediately before the war, the position is not probably much different in this respect from that after the last war.

| | Taxable property (a) | Taxable incomes (b) | (a) as a multiple of (b) |
|---|---|---|---|
| | £m. | | |
| 1924 | 18,000 | 4,200 | 4.3 |
| 1938 | 20,000 | 5,000 | 4.0 |
| 1948 | $(35,000)^2$ | 8,000 | $(4.4)^2$ |

(ii)   It is probable, however, that as a result of the measures which have been taken during the war to prevent the growth of large incomes, small holdings of properties have grown more than large holdings. This means that any given scale of progressive levy would raise a smaller average amount from all property taken together and *pro tanto* would produce a smaller net yield for the relief of taxation.

(iii)   An outstanding change since the last post-war period and the present time is the reduction in the rate of interest. In 1924 the yield on 2½ per cent Consols was 4.4 per cent and now it is only 3 per cent. Nor is there any reason to expect that it will be appreciably higher after the war. This reduction of interest rates means that the annual yield from any capital sum raised by a levy is so much the less, and makes the levy so much the less effective in making possible a reduction of tax rates.

(iv)   The second outstanding change since the last post-war period is the greatly increased rates and degree of progression of existing taxes on income and capital. It would, of course, be unfair to

---

[2] Very uncertain.

compare existing tax schedules with those of 1924, since there is bound to be some reduction in war-time rates of taxation soon after this war. Moreover, the net annual budgetary saving to be obtained from a capital levy should be reckoned not at the rate of taxation operative at the moment of the levy but at the average of rates likely to be operative over the future period of years in which the benefits of the levy will be enjoyed. It is, of course, impossible to foretell what these rates will be; but in the paragraphs which follow the results have been calculated on the assumption (a) of 1936/37 rates of income tax, sur-tax and estate duty and (b) of present rates of sur-tax and estate duty combined with income tax at the level of the first Finance Act of 1940 (i.e. a standard rate of 7s 6d in the £). It is, perhaps, unlikely that we can very soon expect anything better than the reduction of income tax to this lower level or that we can expect even ultimately to go back as far as the pre-war rates of 1936/37. Perhaps some intermediate point would be the most likely for the average of post-war years. The following tables give some comparison of these rates with those of 1924/25.

| | *1924/25* | *1936/37* | *1944/45 rates of sur-tax and estate duty and first Finance Act 1940 rates of income tax* | *1944/45 rates of income tax* |
|---|---|---|---|---|
| Standard Rate of Income Tax (Shillings in the Pound) | 4s 6d | 4s 9d | 7s 6d | 10s 0d |
| Rates of Tax on Income within the Sur-tax Range (Shillings in the Pound) | From 6s 0d on incomes of £2,000 to £2,500 to 10s 6d on incomes above £30,000 | From 5s 10d on incomes of £2,000 to £2,500 to 13s 0d on incomes above £50,000 | From 9s 6d on incomes of £2,000 to £2,500 to 17s 0d on incomes above £20,000 | From 12s 0d on incomes of £2,000 to £2,500 to 19s 6d on incomes above £20,000 |
| Rates of Estate Duty (Percentages) | From 1 per cent on estates of £100 to £500 to 40 per cent on estates above £2,000,000 | From 1 per cent on estates of £100 to £500 to 50 per cent on estates above £2,000,000 | From 1 per cent on estates of £100 to £500 to 65 per cent on estates above £2,000,000 | |

It is clear that rates of taxation on income and rates of death duties are likely after the war to be very considerably higher and more progressive than in 1924/25. For this reason the loss of revenue (both from income taxation on the debt interest and from death duties on the debt itself) is likely to be much more significant this time, particularly if the levy is itself a very progressive one.

29   An attempt has been made to assess the gross and net annual saving from different types of levy on the basis of the value and distribution of private property in 1936 assuming revenue to be raised (a) at 1936/37 tax rates and (b) at the 1944/45 rates of sur-tax and estate duty with income tax at the rates of the first Finance Act 1940. Two different types of levy are examined: (a) the highly progressive scale of levy proposed by the Labour Party after the last war[3] and (b) a levy which exempts small properties of £1,000 (or alternatively of £5,000) but which levies a fixed proportion of 25 per cent (or alternatively of 33⅓ per cent) of all individual property holdings above this exemption limit.

30   In making these calculations it has been assumed that the debt which is redeemed yields 3 per cent. This is more or less the present yield on long-term debt. If the proceeds of the levy were used to redeem short-term and long-term debt in existing proportions, the gross and net yield from the debt would be correspondingly lower. If, however, higher rates of interest were anticipated for the future, the yield on the levy would be correspondingly higher.

31   The methods of the calculations are discussed in Appendix I [pp. 276–77]. The working is, of course, rough and approximate and has been done without consultation with the Board of Inland Revenue. It is hoped, however, that the order of magnitude of the results is not wildly wrong. The following table summarises the results:-

[3] This scale, which is the same as Scale I of the Colwyn Committee (see paragraph 723 of the Colwyn Report), is as follows:-

| Slice of estate | | | Rate per cent on slice | Average rate per cent on estate |
|---|---|---|---|---|
| First £5,000 | | | nil | nil |
| Next | £1,000 (up to | £6,000) | 5 | 0 – 0.8 |
| Next | £2,000 (up to | £8,000) | 10 | 0.8 – 3.1 |
| Next | £2,000 (up to | £10,000) | 15 | 3.1 – 5.5 |
| Next | £5,000 (up to | £15,000) | 20 | 5.5 – 10.3 |
| Next | £5,000 (up to | £20,000) | 25 | 10.3 – 14.0 |
| Next | £10,000 (up to | £30,000) | 30 | 14.0 – 19.3 |
| Next | £20,000 (up to | £50,000) | 35 | 19.3 – 25.6 |
| Next | £50,000 (up to | £100,000) | 40 | 25.6 – 32.8 |
| Next | £100,000 (up to | £200,000) | 45 | 32.8 – 38.9 |
| Next | £300,000 (up to | £500,000) | 50 | 38.9 – 45.6 |
| Next | £500,000 (up to £1,000,000) | | 55 | 45.6 – 50.3 |
| Remainder | | | 60 | 50.3 – 60 |

| Scale of levy | | | Annual yield of levy At 1936/7 tax rates | At rates of sur-tax and estate duty of 1944/45 and income tax of the first Finance Act 1940 |
|---|---|---|---|---|
| A. Colwyn Report Scale I | (a) (b) (c) | Gross Net (b) as % of (a) | £96m. £26m. 27% | £96m. −£11m. −11% |
| B. Levy of 25 per cent on all property above £1,000 | (a) (b) (c) | Gross Net (b) as % of (a) | £113m. £54m. 47% | £113m. £22m. 19% |
| C. Levy of 25 per cent on all property above £5,000 | (a) (b) (c) | Gross Net (b) as % of (a) | £80m. £30m. 38% | |
| D. Levy of 33⅓ per cent on all property above £1,000 | (a) (b) (c) | Gross Net (b) as % of (a) | | £151m. £29m. 19% |

32   It is clear from the above table that at rates of the height and of the degree of progressiveness of the kind probable after the war little or no net saving to the Budget could be anticipated from a capital levy as progressive as the Colwyn Report Scale I. If the goose which lays the golden eggs is killed by high and progressive income taxes and death duties, she cannot be persuaded to lay much (if anything) more through a highly progressive capital levy. On the other hand, a levy of 33⅓ per cent, with an exemption limit of the first £1,000 of each holding of property, would result in some net saving. The conclusion stands out sharply. If any appreciable net saving is to be gained from a capital levy with present progression in rates of income tax and death duties, the levy itself must fall in large measure on the relatively small and medium-sized properties as opposed to the very large properties.

33   The figures given in the above table refer to 1936 properties and incomes. As a result of the rise in capital values and of the great increase of savings during the war, the value of privately held properties may be some 75 per cent greater than in 1936. The yield from the levy after the war would be proportionately greater except in so far as it was affected by changes in the distribution of property. Allowing for such an increase, the yield of a levy on scale D of paragraph 31, might give a net yield of about £50 millions at present rates of sur-tax and estate duty and a standard rate

of income tax of 7s 6d in the pound. This would represent about 6d off the income tax. Its yield at 1937/38 rates has not been calculated, but on the evidence of scale B it might be twice as much, thus making possible a reduction in income tax of about 1s 0d in the pound. At all events it is clear that even with the stiff and unprogressive levy of scale D the net saving is likely to allow for a reduction of income tax only within the range of 6d to 1s 0d in the pound.

34    This would certainly be a disappointingly small result from so vast an operation. The picture is not, however, quite as bad as may at first sight appear. It must be remembered that net yields are low because existing rates of taxation are high; but it is also true that when rates of taxation are high, small reductions in rates of taxation are most significant. The highest rate of income tax and sur-tax in 1924/25 was 10s 0d in the pound and with present rates of sur-tax and a standard rate of income tax of 7s 6d would be 17s 0d in the pound. A reduction of 6d in the rate of tax in the former case would increase the tax-free reward for earning an additional unit of income from 9s 6d to 10s 0d or by 5 per cent, whereas in the latter case it would increase the tax-free reward from 3s 0d to 3s 6d or by 16⅔ per cent.

35    Moreover, even if there were no net annual saving from the capital levy it would produce some improvement in economic incentives. What is important from the point of view of economic incentives is not the average rate of tax which a taxpayer has to meet but the marginal rate of tax which he has to pay on the last units of his income. It is a question of the amount which he will be able to retain from the last pounds which he earns; and in highly progressive tax systems such as ours this marginal rate is considerably higher than the average rate of tax. A capital levy, by reducing the gross income of the taxpayer, will shift the taxpayer into a lower tax bracket; and with a highly progressive structure of income taxation this very fact will reduce the rates of tax which taxpayers have to meet on their last units of income, even though the scales of the rates of income tax and sur-tax are not themselves reduced. In this way a capital levy may appreciably reduce marginal rates of income taxation without any reduction in the schedule of tax rates. This factor can be of a very considerable importance if the levy itself is highly progressive. Where the levy is not very progressive the shift of recipients of higher incomes into lower tax brackets will be less marked.

36    The quantitative importance of this factor is illustrated for a levy of scale D of paragraph 31 in the tables and diagram of Appendix II [pp. 277–79]. The results may be summarised as follows.

The following table shows the effect of the automatic reductions of marginal rates of tax on incomes within the sur-tax range which would have taken place on 1936 incomes as a result of a levy of scale D of paragraph 31 at rates of income tax of the first Finance Act of 1940 and rates of sur-tax of 1944/45:-

| Range of total income before the levy | Automatic increase in tax-free proportion of marginal income | Percentage increase in tax-free proportion of marginal income | Personal incomes affected as percentage of: | |
|---|---|---|---|---|
| £ | | | total sur-tax incomes | total personal incomes |
| 10,000 – 11,650 | from  4s 3d to  5s 6d | 29.4 | 3.7 | 0.8 |
| 4,000 –  4,300 | from  8s 3d to 10s 6d | 27.2 | 3.7 | 0.8 |
| 8,000 –  9,250 | from  5s 6d to  6s 9d | 22.7 | 3.0 | 0.6 |
| 15,000 – 17,500 | from  3s 6d to  4s 3d | 21.4 | 3.0 | 0.6 |
| 2,000 –  2,250 | from 11s 9d to 13s 9d | 17.0 | 8.2 | 1.7 |
| 20,000 – 23,350 | from  3s 0d to  3s 6d | 16.7 | 1.5 | 0.3 |
| 3,800 –  4,000 | from  9s 3d to 10s 6d | 13.5 | 3.0 | 0.6 |
| 4,300 –  4,550 | from  8s 3d to  9s 3d | 12.1 | 2.2 | 0.5 |
| 6,000 –  6,850 | from  6s 9d to  7s 6d | 11.1 | 3.7 | 0.8 |
| 5,000 –  5,750 | from  7s 6d to  8s 3d | 10.0 | 5.9 | 1.2 |
| 3,000 –  3,400 | from 10s 6d to 11s 6d | 9.5 | 5.9 | 1.2 |
| 2,500 –  2,800 | from 11s 6d to 11s 9d | 2.2 | 4.5 | 0.9 |
| | | TOTAL | 48.3 | 10.0 |

On the average of all incomes this would have represented a tax reduction of between 1d and 2d in the pound; but from the point of view of economic incentives such an average is, of course, misleading since the reductions would have been concentrated on incomes subject to sur-tax where, existing rates of taxation being high, reductions are most needed from the point of view of economic incentives.[4]

37   Finally, as has been argued in paragraph 25 above, the levy may enable rates of interest on government bonds to be reduced in circumstances in which it would otherwise be inflationary to reduce them. It may, therefore, set the stage for a successful all-round conversion of debt to lower yields, thereby indirectly causing a considerable net budgetary saving.

38   These various indirect consequences must be considered before the levy is dismissed on the grounds of its disappointingly small direct net yield. Certainly no very progressive levy is worth while. It is doubtful whether even an unprogressive levy would be worth while unless circumstances were such as to ensure that it could be carried out with a minimum of financial disturbance, of personal hardship and of administrative difficulty.

[4] There would also be similar automatic reductions in the marginal rates of death duties as a result of the reduction in gross properties liable to such duties, but it is difficult to judge whether the effects on economic incentives of such reductions would be important or not.

## Appendix I    The Calculation of the Yield of a Capital Levy

1    The basis of the calculations of the gross and net yields of a capital levy at alternative scales of levy and rates of taxation is Mr Campion's estimate of £19,665 – 21,400 millions as the value of property in private hands in 1936.[5] As the levy at the scales considered in this paper has no effect on very small properties, all property in estates of £100 or less has been excluded. Mr Campion estimated this at £580–1,150 millions in 1936 so that the total value of property in private hands in estates exceeding £100 in value has been assumed to be £19,668 millions.

2    Mr Campion has also estimated the distribution of the number and total value of estates held by persons aged 25 and over in England and Wales in 1936.[6] The total number of properties in Great Britain exceeding £100 in value has been estimated from Mr Campion's figures on the assumption that the increase is proportionate to the assumed increase in value. This gives a figure of 7,650,000 for the total number of estates in private hands exceeding £100 in value.

3    The distribution of private property given by Mr Campion was not sufficiently detailed to cover all the different ranges of value affected by the capital levy scale proposed after the last war by the Labour Party (scale A). It has therefore been assumed that within each of the grades shown in Mr Campion's table the distribution of the number and total value of estates was the same as that of estates passing at death as shown in the Report of the Commissioners for Inland Revenue for 1936/37.

4    From the figures obtained in this way it was possible to calculate the yield of various capital levies and the total and average unearned incomes in each grade before and after the levies. The estimated capital proceeds of the levies were as follows:

|   | Scale of levy | £ millions |
|---|---|---|
| A | Labour Party Scale | 3,210 |
| B | Levy of 25 per cent on all property above £1,000 | 3,780 |
| C | Levy of 25 per cent on all property above £5,000 | 2,660 |
| D | Levy of 33⅓ per cent on all property above £1,000 | 5,040 |

It was assumed that the yield on these capital values was 3 per cent and that the average pre-levy income from property was 5 per cent. The loss of income resulting from the levies was assumed to be equal to their yield.

[5] H. Campion, *Public and Private Property in Great Britain* (London: Oxford University Press, 1939), p. 24.
[6] *Ibid.*, p. 109

5   The annual loss of estate duty resulting from a capital levy was calculated on the assumption that the value of estates liable to estate duty in each grade in 1936/37 was reduced as a result of the levy in proportion to the calculated reduction in the value of all estates in the same grade. The loss of duty was then estimated by calculating the total duty payable before and after the levy at 1936/37 rates and at 1944/45 rates.

6   In order to estimate the annual loss of income tax and sur-tax resulting from each capital levy it was necessary to estimate the average total income corresponding to the average unearned income in each grade. This was done by interpolating for each value of unearned income, already obtained from the estimated distribution of the number and total values of estates, in the table given by Findlay Shirras and L. Rostas[7] of the investment income corresponding in 1937/38 to various levels of total income ranging from £100 to £50,000. In the highest ranges of income, the estimates supplied to the Colwyn Committee[8] were also used as a guide.

7   The total income tax and sur-tax payable on unearned incomes before and after each capital levy was then calculated (a) at 1936/37 rates of income tax and sur-tax and (b) at 1944/45 rates of sur-tax with income-tax rates of the first Finance Act 1940. It was then possible to estimate the net gain from each of the scales of capital levy proposed at both levels of income taxation and estate duty.

## Appendix II   Marginal Rates of Taxation and the Effects of a Capital Levy

1   From the estimates of earned and unearned incomes before and after the imposition of a capital levy, which have been obtained in the course of calculating the gross and net yield of the levy, it is possible to estimate approximately the changes in marginal rates of income tax and sur-tax which would occur as a result of the levy, and the proportion of total personal incomes which would be affected. This has been done for the capital levy scale D, and for 1944/45 rates of sur-tax with income tax rates of the first Finance Act 1940.

2   Within the range of incomes affected by the capital levy all changes in the marginal rate of tax, other than the change which occurs when the earned income allowance reaches a maximum, are due to changes in the marginal rate of sur-tax. The earned-income allowance reaches a maximum when earned income is £1,500 and this was estimated to correspond with an income from property of about £2,300 and a total income of £3,800.

---

[7] G. Findlay Shirras and L. Rostas, *The Burden of British Taxation* (Cambridge: Cambridge University Press, 1942), Table 13.

[8] *Report of the Committee on National Debt and Taxation* (Cmd 2800, 1927), Appendix XV, Table 1.

3   By charting the available estimates of corresponding pre-levy and post-levy total incomes and comparing them with the marginal rates of tax payable on those incomes, it is possible to observe to what extent the reduction from pre-levy to post-levy incomes would involve a shift to lower marginal rates of tax. The results, which are necessarily subject to a considerable margin of error, are as follows:-

| Marginal rate of tax | | Income range | Pre-levy income required to yield income within range after levy |
|---|---|---|---|
| s | d | £ | £ |
| 6 | 3 | 300 but under 2,000 | 300 but under 2,250 |
| 8 | 3 | 2,000 but under 2,500 | 2,250 but under 2,800 |
| 8 | 6 | 2,500 but under 3,000 | 2,800 but under 3,400 |
| 9 | 6 | 3,000 but under 3,800 | 3,400 but under 4,300 |
| 10 | 9 | 3,800 but under 4,000 | 4,300 but under 4,550 |
| 11 | 9 | 4,000 but under 5,000 | 4,550 but under 5,750 |
| 12 | 6 | 5,000 but under 6,000 | 5,750 but under 6,850 |
| 13 | 3 | 6,000 but under 8,000 | 6,850 but under 9,250 |
| 14 | 6 | 8,000 but under 10,000 | 9,250 but under 11,650 |
| 15 | 9 | 10,000 but under 15,000 | 11,650 but under 17,500 |
| 16 | 6 | 15,000 but under 20,000 | 17,500 but under 23,350 |
| 17 | 0 | 20,000 and over | 23,350 and over |

4   From this table it is possible to construct the attached chart which shows more clearly the extent of the changes in the marginal rates of tax and the ranges of income within which these changes occur.

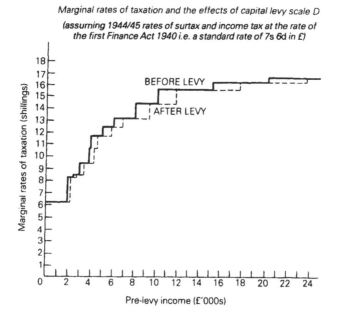

Marginal rates of taxation and the effects of capital levy scale D

(assuming 1944/45 rates of surtax and income tax at the rate of the first Finance Act 1940 i.e. a standard rate of 7s 6d in £)

5   The following table gives an estimate of the total personal incomes affected by these changes:-

| Range of total income before levy £ | Reduction in marginal rate of tax from | to | Increase in tax-free portion of marginal income from | to | Percentage increase | Estimated total personal incomes within range £m. | % of incomes within sur-tax range | % of all personal incomes |
|---|---|---|---|---|---|---|---|---|
| 2,000 – 2,250 | 8s 3d | 6s 3d | 11s 9d | 13s 9d | 17.0 | 55 | 8.2 | 1.7 |
| 2,500 – 2,800 | 8s 6d | 8s 3d | 11s 6d | 11s 9d | 2.2 | 30 | 4.5 | 0.9 |
| 3,000 – 3,400 | 9s 6d | 8s 6d | 10s 6d | 11s 6d | 9.5 | 40 | 5.9 | 1.2 |
| 3,800 – 4,000 | 10s 9d | 9s 6d | 9s 3d | 10s 6d | 13.5 | 20 | 3.0 | 0.6 |
| 4,000 – 4,300 | 11s 9d | 9s 3d | 8s 3d | 10s 6d | 27.2 | 25 | 3.7 | 0.8 |
| 4,300 – 4,550 | 11s 9d | 10s 9d | 8s 3d | 9s 3d | 12.1 | 15 | 2.2 | 0.5 |
| 5,000 – 5,750 | 12s 6d | 11s 9d | 7s 6d | 8s 3d | 10.0 | 40 | 5.9 | 1.2 |
| 6,000 – 6,850 | 13s 3d | 12s 6d | 6s 9d | 7s 6d | 11.1 | 25 | 3.7 | 0.8 |
| 8,000 – 9,250 | 14s 6d | 13s 3d | 5s 6d | 6s 9d | 22.7 | 20 | 3.0 | 0.6 |
| 10,000 – 11,650 | 15s 9d | 14s 6d | 4s 3d | 5s 6d | 29.4 | 25 | 3.7 | 0.8 |
| 15,000 – 17,500 | 16s 6d | 15s 9d | 3s 6d | 4s 3d | 21.4 | 20 | 3.0 | 0.6 |
| 20,000 – 23,350 | 17s 0d | 16s 3d | 3s 0d | 3s 6d | 16.7 | 10 | 1.5 | 0.3 |
| Total personal incomes affected | | | | | | 325 | 48.3 | 10.0 |
| Total personal incomes within sur-tax range | | | | | | 673 | 100.0 | |
| Total personal incomes* | | | | | | 3,233 | | 100.0 |

* This is, in fact, an estimate of total personal incomes of not less than £100.

## Debt Repayment and Employment Policy

1   In the past the most normal instrument for repaying the debt has been the annual Sinking Fund. Revenue is raised each year in excess of budgetary expenditure, and the surplus is allocated to the repayment of outstanding debt. The Sinking Fund is, of course, effective only in so far as there is a true excess of revenue over expenditure. Where this is not the case, funds must be borrowed to meet the Sinking Fund and in effect no reduction of debt is achieved.

2   The principle of an annual excess of revenue over expenditure which remains unchanged year after year is incompatible with the general policy outlined in the recent White Paper on *Employment Policy* [Cmd 6527, 1944]. In that document the Government accepts responsibility for ensuring that, as far as possible, the general level of total national demand shall be maintained at a high and stable level so as to prevent mass unemployment on the one hand and inflation on the other hand. It is recognised that the carrying out of this policy will almost certainly involve the stimulation of public investment at times when activity in the private sector of the economy threatens to fall off, and the retardation of such public expenditure when there is a threat of general inflation.

3   Such a policy involves incurring a budget deficit and borrowing in those years in which it is necessary to stimulate expenditure on public investment. This effect may be partially disguised if the Central Government stimulates public investment, not by making a capital grant to the authority concerned, but by the promise of a future annual subsidy on the municipal authority's investment. In this case there is no immediate growth of the nominal Central Government debt; but the obligation of the Central Government to raise revenue in the future to meet the annual subsidy payable by the Central Government to help service the debt incurred by the local authority will present the same fiscal problems as the raising of the revenue to service increased Central Government debt.

4   It may be that the planning and timing of public investment will be sufficient to preserve a high and stable level of aggregate demand. But this may not always be so. There are many technical and administrative obstacles setting limits to the speed with which the flow of investment expenditure may be turned on or off. It may, therefore, at times be necessary deliberately to reduce rates of taxation in order to stimulate private buying (or to raise rates of taxation to restrict private buying) in the interests of stabilising total aggregate demand and without undue regard to the effect upon the balance of the Budget in any one year.

5   Whether or not tax policy on these lines will be necessary to supplement the effects of public investment policy, it is clear that the idea of a steady annual surplus of revenue over expenditure is out of place. This much is now a matter of general agreement.

6   There remains, however, a more controversial issue. It is agreed that budget deficits in certain years are admissible. But what of the balance of the Budget over a series of years? If, as has been suggested in the note on 'The Fiscal Problem set by the Debt', it is desirable to reduce the total outstanding national debt, it would follow that the budget surpluses in years of good trade should be greater or more frequent than the budget deficits which are permitted in years of bad trade, so that over the average of good and bad years together there is a net repayment of debt. But is this compatible with a financial policy for the maintenance of a high and stable level of employment? If in each year expenditure on public investment is maintained at such a level (and rates of taxation are fixed at such a level) that aggregate national expenditure is sufficient to maintain employment without the threat of inflation, what guarantee is there that the budget deficits of bad years will not be greater than the budget surpluses of good years? What reason is there to believe that there will be no conflict between the apparently quite separate objectives (i) of a net budget surplus over the average of years and (ii) of the maintenance of employment in each particular year?

7   This is likely to be a crucial issue of post-war debt policy. In the short run (that is to say, in the formulation of budgetary policy from year to

year) the problems of employment policy and of the avoidance of inflation are likely to take pride of place. In other words, the general level of expenditure on public investment and the general level of taxation are likely to be determined each year primarily with a view to maintaining total national expenditure at the high and stable level necessary to preserve employment without running into inflation. If, however, short-run budgetary policy is planned solely on these lines, long-term corrective measures may have to be taken if there appears to be any serious danger that, on the average of years, such a budgetary policy will lead to budget deficits or to an inadequate rate of debt repayment. Appropriate long-term correctives may be discussed under the headings of Interest Policy, Price Policy, Foreign Investment and Tax Structure. The purpose of this paper is merely to indicate the relevant fields of appropriate policy; and no attempt is made to discuss them at all fully.

## (a) Interest Rates

8   The essential feature of a situation in which on the average of years, in the interests of employment policy, new public debt is being contracted or old public debt is being repaid less rapidly than would otherwise be desirable is that private expenditure on capital development is not sufficient to make use of all the savings which are forthcoming from the national income which is associated with a high level of employment. The fundamental cure is to stimulate additional expenditure on new capital development by reducing the rate of interest. An appreciable reduction in interest rates will help to stimulate capital expenditure by private business, by local authorities and by other public authorities, particularly on housing, the capital development of public utilities and various forms of municipal works in which the interest charge is an important element of the total cost. Moreover, a reduction in the rate of interest may have a noticeable effect on private expenditure on durable consumption goods (such as motor-cars, furniture, household equipment, etc.) in so far, for example, as it reduces the cost of hire-purchase finance.

9   Thus a reduction of interest rates, by stimulating private expenditure, will bring it about that the state need not go to the same lengths in expanding public expenditure or in reducing rates of taxation in the interests of employment policy. It will, therefore, help to set the stage for a budgetary policy which reconciles repayment of debt with the preservation of employment.

10   In the note on 'The Fiscal Problem set by the Debt' it is shown that a reduction in interest rates will diminish the burden of the existing debt. Here, therefore, is an instrument which will both lighten the burden of interest on existing debt and also, by making budget deficits less necessary on grounds of employment policy, will help to keep down the size of the debt in the future.

11   No attempt will be made in this note to discuss the monetary and

banking problems involved in a reduction of long-term rates of interest. It is, however, generally agreed that when interest rates have been reduced to very low levels it may become very difficult to effect still further reductions by orthodox monetary measures. At this point it may become necessary to find other means of making capital expenditure more profitable.

## (b)  Price Policy

12  A second fundamental factor affecting the profitability of capital expenditure is internal price policy. A general downward movement of prices causes businesses to refrain from expenditure on replacements or extensions of plant, machinery and other capital equipment, in the expectation (a) that such equipment may be purchased more cheaply if its purchase is postponed and (b) that further falls in the prices which the businesses can obtain for their products may cause the return on any such investment to turn out to be unprofitable. Private consumers may also be influenced, in their expectation of future price falls, to postpone their purchases of many durable goods (houses, cars, furniture, household equipment, etc.) in the hope of obtaining them cheaper at a future date.

13  If at any point it is, on financial grounds, technically impossible to bring about a further reduction in interest rates, it may be possible to produce a rather similar stimulation to the economic activity of business men by adopting a policy for a gradually rising level of the money prices received for their products. Low interest rates on borrowed money on the one hand, and rising prices for the products produced on the other hand, are alternative methods of increasing the rate of money profit on capital developments. A rapid inflation of prices is certainly to be avoided. Even gradually rising prices are probably less desirable than lower interest rates as a means of economic stimulation, particularly if such a development might lead to a movement of United Kingdom prices out of harmony with world prices in circumstances in which it is desired to avoid an adjustment of the foreign exchange rate. But if interest rates have reached their technical minimum, a gradually rising trend of prices may become desirable in the interests of domestic employment policy.

14  Reference is made in the note on 'The Fiscal Problem Set by the Debt' to the desirability of preventing a decline in the general level of prices (or even of allowing some gradual rise) in order to keep down the burden of the interest payable on existing debt. For the reasons given above a price policy on these lines, in addition to its advantageous effects on the existing debt, will also serve to stimulate private expenditure and will thus help to set the stage for a long-run budgetary policy in which the repayment of debt is compatible with the maintenance of employment. Interest Policy and Price Policy are both means of simultaneously reducing the burden of existing debt and diminishing the need to accumulate further debt.

## (c) Foreign Investment

15 Steps may also be taken to increase the balance between the foreigners' expenditure on our goods and services and our expenditure on foreign goods and services. Any increase in this balance represents a net increase in demand for our goods and services. The higher, therefore, is this balance, the less necessary will it be to run a budget deficit in order to maintain the total demand for our goods and services at an adequate level.

16 To attempt to cure domestic unemployment by increasing foreign investment may in certain circumstances be tantamount merely to the 'export of unemployment' to other countries, since it involves buying less from or selling more to other countries. In other circumstances an increase of one country's foreign investment may not only help the domestic employment situation in the country concerned but may also be in the interest of the rest of the world. It is clear that foreign investment is a matter of international and of domestic concern; and it is of importance that some set of guiding principles should if possible be internationally agreed on the use of this instrument of employment policy.

## (d) The Tax Structure

17 Different types of taxation have different effects upon private expenditure. Some taxes may take a form which is peculiarly discouraging to business enterprise (and thus to the willingness of private business concerns to spend money on new capital development) or which is peculiarly adverse to expenditure by consumers on private consumption. Other forms of tax, although they raise no less in revenue, may be much less deterrent to private expenditure on investment or consumption. If a situation develops in which it becomes difficult simultaneously to maintain a high level of employment and to repay debt, a fundamental cure may be so to revise the structure of taxation as to raise revenue with a less restrictive effect upon private expenditure on investment and consumption.[1]

18 There are a number of ways in which this objective may be achieved. In the first place, it is often argued, a system of more progressive taxation which takes more income from the rich and less from the poor will stimulate total private expenditure on consumption because the rich will pay a considerable proportion of their additional taxation by cutting down, not their consumption, but their savings, whereas the poor will spend a larger proportion of their additional net incomes on consumption. This argument is probably correct as far as it goes. But an increased

[1] The tax structure needs to be considered from other points of view as well. Thus the effect of different types of taxation on the balance between work and leisure or between present and future enjoyment of income is a matter of considerable importance. For the purpose of the present note, however, attention is limited to the effects of different types of taxation in stimulating or restricting total expenditure on goods and services and so the total demand for labour.

progressiveness in the structure of taxation has counteracting disadvantages. At the extreme limit (at which people with incomes above a certain level had to pay 20s 0d in the £ on the whole of their incomes above that level) progressiveness in taxation would completely dry up the sources of revenue. No one would bother by work, enterprise or investment to earn an income beyond the point at which the whole increment must be paid over to the state. As a result, therefore, such a tax would raise no revenue and in consequence would not enable the rate of tax on the lower incomes to be reduced. And even before this extreme limit is reached, there are likely to be seriously adverse effects on enterprise and private investment. It is no use encouraging consumption by a means which would simultaneously discourage investment.

19    Apart, however, from changes in the structure of taxation which are designed to encourage consumption expenditure by distributing income more equally, there are other modifications which, may, nevertheless, help to encourage private consumption. Suppose, for example, that a specially heavy rate of tax were levied on the profits of business concerns which were not distributed to shareholders. In such circumstances, business concerns would have a clear incentive to distribute their profits to shareholders and this would stimulate private expenditure on consumption.[2]

20    Changes in the tax structure may also be considered from the point of view of stimulating expenditure on private investment. One method of doing this might be to raise a given tax revenue by means of a tax assessed on capital values instead of on income. Taxation assessed on income falls on the yield of capital, while taxation assessed on capital falls on assets which yield no income as well as on those which do. The latter, therefore, is likely to encourage a shift from holding cash to holding other types of asset. Accordingly it may help to reduce interest rates and to encourage investment. This tendency is likely to be accentuated if a flat-rate capital tax takes the place of a progressive income tax. A progressive income tax is likely to discourage the holding of risky assets (and all forms of real investment must involve some degree of risk), since it taxes exceptionally high profits at exceptionally high rates. If it is replaced by a flat-rate tax on capital (or, for that matter, by a flat-rate tax on income) the incentive to put money into real capital development rather than to hold fixed-interest bonds would be increased.[3]

---

[2] Any restrictive effect which such a tax might have on private investment could be offset by confining it to undistributed profits which were not used for the finance of real capital development by the business in question.

[3] The above paragraph is not, of course, intended to pass final judgement on the merits of capital taxation. The equity of such taxation, its administrative practicability – would it, for example, be easy to evade the tax by holding bank notes? – and its economic effects other than on investment expenditure all require consideration.

# 16

# Next Steps in Domestic Economic Policy

*This article, written originally as a memorandum for the Labour Party's Research Department in November 1948 (Labour Party Archives), appeared in the* Political Quarterly, *vol. 20 (January–March 1949), pp. 12–24.*

## I Introductory

My object in this article is to discuss the broad principles which should underlie the domestic economic policy of the Government over the next five years or so. But it is not possible reasonably to discuss even in broad outline the *means* of economic policy which should be adopted without relation to the *ends* which it is desired to achieve; and accordingly I will start by enumerating what I am assuming to be the most important basic aims of policy.

These I assume to be fourfold:-

(i) *Social Equity*  The first assumed objective is to prevent the return of those great inequalities of income, of property and of opportunities which marred the community before the war.

(ii) *Personal Freedom*  The second assumed objective is that we intend to achieve our economic ends by means which allow the maximum freedom to consumers to decide what shall be produced for their satisfaction and to workers to decide what jobs they want to undertake.

(iii) *Full Employment*  The third assumption is that we will no longer tolerate the stupid and stultifying wastes of large-scale involuntary idleness when there are still many goods and services which people would like to consume in greater abundance.

(iv) *Economic Efficiency*  Lastly, I assume that we seek for arrangements which will enable us out of our limited resources to produce in the greatest quantities those things which consumers most desire to have.

There may, of course, be conflict between these ends; some measure of economic efficiency may have to be sacrificed in order to obtain some further measure of social equity or *vice versa*; and in such cases a political decision is required as to which is the most important end. But wherever it is possible technically to devise economic measures which will enable us to achieve more of one of these ends without sacrificing any of the others, I take it that we should be prepared to accept them uninhibited by any presuppositions about methods.

This does not, however, mean that we must be completely agnostic about methods. It is not possible in the confined space of a single article to discuss this issue in detail;[1] but in my opinion we shall get nearest to the achievement of our aims if we base our choice of methods on the following broad principles.

First, a wide use must be made of general financial policy. For example, full employment in a free society can be achieved only if financial policy is such as to maintain a total monetary demand for goods and services high enough to prevent mass unemployment but not so high as to cause a general inflation. Or, to take another example, social equity can be promoted by a system of progressive taxation and social security benefits, without so large an adverse effect upon personal freedom or economic incentives as might be involved in alternative means.

Secondly, a clear distinction should be drawn between public and private enterprise. Those plants are most suitable for socialisation which, like the railways or the generation of electricity, are bound in any case on technical grounds to be monopolies. But those plants which are left in private hands should be freed from stultifying interferences which prevent the more efficient from driving out the less efficient. This does not, of course, mean that socialised and unsocialised enterprise should never be found together in the same industry. Far from it. Such competition between different forms of enterprises might, for example, in the steel industry be most fruitful and revealing. What it does mean is that in those productive *firms* which are not socialised the creative forces of private enterprise and competition should be allowed real free play.

Thirdly – a matter which has in my opinion been much neglected – in a mixed economy including much private enterprise there is bound to be much private property. But there is no reason at all why the division of such property should be so markedly unequal as it has been in the past.[2] If private property were much more equally divided we should achieve the 'mixed' citizen – both worker and property-owner – to live in the 'mixed' economy of public and private enterprise. The ownership of private property could then fulfil its useful functions of providing a basis for private enterprise and for individual security and independence without carrying with it the curse of social inequality. The class conflict between labour and capital would in large measure disappear. And it would thus gradually become easier to deal with a situation, for example, where an industry to be economically efficient needs reorganisation by having more capital equipment and less labour; the rise in profits and the fall in

[1] I have tried to do so, however, in my recent book, *Planning and the Price Mechanism* (London: Allen & Unwin, 1948).

[2] In 1936 the wealthiest 5 per cent of all adults in England and Wales owned more than 75 per cent of all property in private hands. At the other end the poorest 75 per cent of the population owned little more than 5 per cent of such property. See H. Campion, *Public and Private Property in Great Britain* (London, Oxford University Press, 1939).

wage-rates which, in the absence of compulsion, may be necessary to attract additional capital into the industry and to persuade labour to seek other occupations, would not raise such acute social problems where every citizen had interests both as a worker and as an owner of property.

Finally, in considering the economic policy of the next five years we must bear in mind the essential economic conditions which will form its background. We have no unemployed resources which we can call into production. We cannot expect to swell the output of civilian industry any further from men and material demobilised from the armed forces and their supply; indeed in present conditions rearmament is more likely to be necessary. Between 1947 and 1948 we experienced great increases in productivity due to the removal of reconversion troubles which were holding up production over wide areas, and in particular the removal of the bottleneck of coal supplies. We cannot expect similar factors to cause any startling increase in our productivity over the coming years. And yet we are living at the moment on American charity.

This being so, it is not difficult to see what must be the general shape of any realistic programme for domestic economic policy in the next five years. It must be concentrated upon measures for increasing economic efficiency in the broadest sense by means which do not prejudice the increased social and economic equity which the last years have brought with them. The extension of social services, including health and education, and the improvement in the general distribution of income must be consolidated; but except in one respect to which I will now turn, no very great further improvements in social equity can be expected. Our immediate need is to devise measures for increasing our power and our incentives to produce so as to stand on our own feet at our existing standards of living.

## II  Measures for Achieving a More Equal Distribution of Property

In later paragraphs of this article some suggestions are made for measures designed to improve economic incentives. Some of these might inevitably mean the relaxation of controls or of interferences at present designed to improve social equity; but any adverse effects of such proposals could be more than counterbalanced by some redistribution of ownership of property, which in my view is in present conditions the best way of ensuring social equity with the minimum of other adverse effects.

One factor is already at work. During and since the war, as a result of fiscal measures such as income tax and sur-tax rising to 19s 6d in the £ on the highest incomes together with extensions of social security and improved wage-rates at the other end, net income (after payment of tax) has been much more equally divided than before the war. The wage-earner has had a greater power to save relatively to the property-owner than he did before the war. The accumulation of small savings during and since the war, together with the lesser ability of the very rich to accumulate, has already led to some improvement in the distribution of property. But could not further steps be taken to make it attractive to the small man to save? We need all the savings we can obtain in order to reduce the present inflationary pressure on our economic resources; and if the small man can be persuaded to save now it will also improve the future distribution of property. Why, for example, should not financial arrangements be made to enable the occupiers of municipal houses to purchase their homes by saving and paying a weekly sum in addition to the rent?

A second means of redistributing property would be by means of a radical reform of the laws of inheritance. An upper limit might be set to the total amount of property which any individual could receive by way of gift or inheritance. Under such a system a man would be free to accumulate any property he could by his own efforts; moreover he would be free to bequeath all his property at his death to whomsoever he pleased provided that he gave his property in small enough parcels to persons who had not already received large gifts or inheritances. To avoid the total loss of death duties which this scheme in its simplest form would involve, it might take the alternative form of a death duty levied on gifts and bequests at a progressive rate according to the amount of property which each beneficiary had received up to date from this and other sources by way of gifts or inheritance. Such a reform would not necessarily involve any higher taxation of property at death than is at present imposed, but it would increase the incentive to split up large properties. It might, however, necessitate a considerable reform in the laws relating to property, and it would involve administrative difficulties including the tracing of gifts *inter vivos* – a problem which, however, will almost certainly arise in any case if death duties are continued at their present rate. But if these difficulties can be faced, this reform in a generation could transform society in so far as the ownership of property is concerned.

A more rapid redistribution of property would require an immediate large-scale capital levy. A large and progressive capital levy would promote social equality more effectively than any other single measure. It would remove a part of the power of the rich to make excessive claims on our strained resources by spending their capital funds. It would remove a large part of the national debt and thereby, as is noted below, remove one of the main factors preventing the use of higher interest rates as a means of restraining inflationary pressures. On the other hand, one must not, of course, overlook the immense administrative difficulties of such an operation, and the adverse effects which it would have on the incentives to accumulate if it was thought that the levy would be repeated. Nor in present conditions when the reduction in the property owned by the rich would be largely matched by a reduced payment by the rich of income tax, sur-tax and death duties must one expect a highly progressive capital levy to lead to any very substantial net budgetary saving, since the saving of interest on the national debt would to a very surprising extent be offset by a fall in tax revenue.

## *III    The Rationalisation of Income Redistribution*

Let us next consider those reforms whose main purpose is to increase economic efficiency.

First, I would put forward for consideration the complete overhaul of our present machinery for the redistribution of income.[3] At the moment we have the most cumbersome and complicated machinery for this purpose. There is the income tax and sur-tax with its various allowances for dependents, for earned income, etc., and with the complicated machinery of pay-as-you-earn with its codings, tax tables and the rest. Quite separate from this is the whole machinery of national insurance with its separate machine for collecting national insurance contributions and for the payment of benefits of various kinds, including the payment of family allowances. Then there are the mechanisms of food subsidisation and housing subsidies designed to redistribute real income by keeping down the price of the necessities of life to needy families at the expense of the taxpayer.

A host of departments are concerned with this Heath Robinsonian machine for income distribution: the Treasury and the Inland Revenue with income tax; the Ministries of Food and of Health and the Treasury with housing and food subsidies; the Ministries of National Insurance, of Labour and of Health and the Post Office with the administration of various 'social security' benefits. Businesses must provide manpower to help to assess and to administer pay-as-you-earn and national insurance contributions; and the ordinary citizen must be prepared to cope with the complexities of these strange arrangements.

Moreover, many of these devices are very uneconomic. The subsidisation of food helps the millionaire without dependents as well as the wage-earner with a large family; by keeping food artificially cheap, it removes the incentive to avoid every kind of food waste; and by necessitating the continuation of high rates of income tax to raise the necessary funds, it may impair general economic incentives for work and enterprise. No household need be worse off if the food subsidies were removed and the price of food allowed to find a more natural level, provided that the £450,000,000 so saved were distributed directly in support of the households which needed the help.

Why not scrap pay-as-you-earn, national insurance, family allowances and the food and housing subsidies, and substitute the following scheme to be carried out by a single department such as a reformed Board of Inland Revenue? Pay every man, woman and child in all circumstances an unconditional 'social dividend' which would support them in unemployment or ill-health and would take the place of family allowances, national insurance benefits and allowances under the income tax. Charge a single standard rate of tax on all earnings, thereby avoiding all the complications of pay-as-you-earn. Charge a higher standard rate of tax on all unearned income. Charge, if necessary, a fixed weekly basic contribution

---

[3] See pp. 42–46 and 105–107 of my *Planning and the Price Mechanism*.

on every earner,[4] and levy sur-tax from all incomes of £500 or more (in place of £2,000 or more).

Such a reform would release a large amount of manpower not only from Government departments but also from businesses which have at present to cope with the complexities of pay-as-you-earn. There would be less interference with the ordinary citizen. It would also introduce a great improvement into the incentives of the ordinary earner who would be faced with a charge of 3s or 4s in the £ on all earnings as compared with the present pay-as-you-earn position in which the tax may fall exclusively and at a higher rate on additional earnings, thus reducing the incentive to add to earnings by regular attendance, higher piece-rate output, etc. Moreover, when the new scheme was devised, rates for the social dividend, for the standard rates of tax on earned and unearned incomes, for the basic weekly charge on earnings and for the levies under the new sur-tax schedules, might well be chosen so as to bring some improvements in the distribution of income from the point of view of 'social equity', particularly in the form of relief in the higher as well as the lower income grades to the married persons with children or other dependents. The introduction of the new scheme would present the opportunity for a rational reconsideration of the whole problem of redistribution.

## IV   Public Enterprise

It would not appear to me wise to socialise more industries over the next five years. The present choice of industries for socialisation is probably imperfect. I can think of some, for example the trade in raw cotton and certain forms of road transport, which I, for one, would like to see returned to private enterprise. On the other hand, there are probably other industries which in the end should be socialised in the ideal mixed economy. But there are strong reasons against further socialisation in the immediate future. It is doubtful whether it could make any substantial contribution to the immediate objective of greater economic efficiency; it would disturb industry in the change-over; and with the nationalisations of the last five years enough has been bitten off to require careful chewing and digesting by the state over the next five years.

This process involves many problems of administering the industries which have been nationalised. How far should the different regions or the different plants be independent? What is to be the relation between labour and management in the nationalised industries? Where is the administrative personnel to come from for all the higher positions on the boards, etc.? How can it be best assured that the greatest technical efficiency is forthcoming in the production?

On these vital questions I have no knowledge and no suggestions to make. But there is another, more particularly economic, aspect of the

---

[4]   Such a basic fixed charge on earnings would be necessary to replace in part the present national insurance contribution and to offset in part the unconditional 'social dividend' which under the above proposal the wage-earner would continue to obtain when he was in work. Without such a basic charge the standard rate of tax on earnings might have to be set so high as to have serious disincentive effects.

consolidation of the already nationalised industries. The next years might profitably be used to make a conscious effort to see that the prices offered and charged by the boards of the nationalised industries should be such as to provide the maximum incentives to economic efficiency in the broadest sense of that term.

For example, in the prices charged for electricity, how can the charge best be related to the cost of producing the current? There are at present vast schemes on foot for the development and extension of electrical generating plant so that all over the country the peak load for electricity can be met. But it would be very wasteful of our most precious resources (steel, labour, engineering products, etc.) to carry out any parts of such a programme, if it were in fact cheaper to persuade the industrial or domestic consumer to shift his demand from the peak to the off-peak load so that the new plant is not necessary. And the consumer of electricity can be given the full incentive to do so only if he is charged for electricity at the peak an amount which allows for the whole of the costs of the new construction necessary to meet the peak and if he is charged for off-peak consumption a price which does not include any of these capital costs. There are devices for distinguishing between peak and off-peak consumption; and the socialised electricity industry could make a major contribution to economic efficiency by their introduction.

Or, to take another example, consider the problem of road and rail competition. The community will be able to transport a given amount of ton-miles at a lower real cost in fuel, steel, labour, etc., if goods are sent by rail rather than by road, whenever the additional cost to the railway system involved by taking on that traffic is less than the additional cost incurred on the roads by doing so. In order, therefore, to get the proper incentives for the maximum economy of effort, road and rail charges must be set so that each measures, not the average total cost of providing transport on that system, but the additional social costs involved by adding the additional traffic to the existing activities of each system. The setting of proper transport charges combined with the free choice of the users of the various means of transport might appreciably increase the real productivity of the country.

The above examples are only two out of many. The principle pervades all the nationalised industries. The charges set for different grades and qualities of coal in different regions will help to determine the amount of effort which will be expended in mining and transporting fuel to obtain a given result. Charges for gas as compared with those for electricity will have similar results. The iron and steel industry produces a myriad products in many various regions, and with many different types of plant. Its economic effectiveness would be greatly raised by offering its alternative products in the different regions to the final users at prices which reflect the additional costs involved in producing more of each product by each alternative means at each alternative point of production. One of the main purposes of socialisation, which it must be a chief objective of policy now to ensure, is that it will make possible a greater degree of economic efficiency by a proper use of the price mechanism. Too little attention has been paid to this fact.

## V   Private Enterprise

Increased economic efficiency must also be sought, though by other means, from that sector of industry which is left to private enterprise. Fundamentally the method must be to restore and perpetuate conditions for fruitful competition in this sector of the economy. Business men are all too apt to get together to protect their interests. Each producer, sheltered by some agreement with his competitors, need no longer fear that he will be driven out by his competitors if they become more efficient than him; nor can he expect to be able so easily to capture his competitors' markets if he reduces his own costs of production. An extension of competition in the private sector of industry is the surest guarantee of increased economic efficiency in that sector, since each producer will be striving to produce at the lowest cost those products which the consumer most wants.

The first means to this end lies ready to hand. Parliament has just enacted a new Monopoly Act which will enable the Government to enquire into, and to discourage, the various restrictive practices of private industry. The fullest use should be made of this Act.

The other main remedy lies equally ready to hand. It is a main disadvantage of direct quantitative controls over industry (including such devices as the administrative allocation of raw materials between different firms) that they stereotype the existing situation. Not only is each particular producer unable to expand rapidly (since his material allocation will not permit it) so as to drive out his more costly competitors, but the allocation of materials itself is likely to be based upon some base period – often the pre-war situation – which becomes progressively less and less appropriate but which it is administratively difficult, if not logically impossible, to replace with anything better. The policy of removal of the direct controls over competitive industry, already initiated by the Board of Trade, should be progressively developed. It will add to the community's economic efficiency in two ways. It will improve incentives in private industry by restoring the possibility of fruitful competition; and it will economise in administrative manpower both in the Government departments which run, and in the businesses which suffer,[5] the various controls.

In present circumstances of inflationary strain on our resources and of acute balance-of-payments difficulties some controls are inevitable. We must control the end uses of goods, whether for consumption or for investment in capital development at home, in order to prevent an inflationary excess of demand for goods and services and in order to economise on goods and services which might be used for export or to replace imports. And we must continue for some time to control the

---

[5] The suffering is, however, often very bravely borne by the business man who enjoys the security from the worries of competition and the safeguards from excessive enterprise or progressiveness by newcomers, which control from Whitehall confers upon him. The business man is too apt to like the allocated quota which is, after all, the device of monopoly cartels. Businesses should be either socialised or made to compete, though the business man may dislike either prescription.

volume of imports. But there is no reason why the control of the end uses of goods should not be progressively achieved by financial means – by the direct and indirect taxation required to limit consumption and by a rise in the rate of interest at which new funds can be borrowed, which would discourage investment in capital equipment at home and whose evil budgetary consequences would be avoided if the national debt were much reduced by a capital levy. Nor is there any reason why the raw materials which are allowed to be imported should not then be sold in a free market to the highest bidder in private business. The controls over intermediate products could be progressively scrapped; licensing of building and other capital goods would become less exacting as higher interest rates had their effect;[6] and, in addition to the rationing to consumers of certain essentials such as basic foods and clothing so long as they remained really scarce, tax restraints could be used to limit consumption. In the greater freedom for private initiative and in the smaller demands on manpower for administration which such a policy of rational decontrol would bring with it, there lies an important potential stimulus to economic efficiency.

## VI   Wages Policy and Labour Incentives

In order to obtain the greatest possible increase in economic efficiency incentives must be as effectively applied to the payment for work as to other parts of the economic system.[7]

It is essential that all forms of restrictive practice among wage-earners should disappear. It is to be hoped that the proposals which have already been made would help to create a favourable atmosphere in this respect. In continuing conditions of full employment it should not be difficult for a worker to find alternative work; and it is, therefore, less important from his point of view to spread the work. Moreover, in a world in which property was more equally divided and workers received income from property as well as from work and in a world in which basic industries have been socialised so that the profits from them accrue not to private owners but to the state, there is less occasion for workers to adopt practices which are aimed at ensuring that benefits from increased effort do not accrue to the owners of property.

There remain two important connections between wage-rates and economic efficiency. It is economic inefficiency that labour should be unemployed; and it is economic inefficiency that labour should be employed in a less essential use when more labour is required in more essential uses. Yet both these inefficiencies may result from an inappropriate wages policy. If money wage-rates were pushed up whenever, and as rapidly as, bargaining power made it possible, this might lead

---

[6] Any encouragement which, on social grounds, it was desired to give to one form of activity as against another (e.g. for building hospitals rather than breweries) could be achieved through the general fiscal policy of taxing the production or consumption of beer and subsidising medical services.

[7] The reform of taxation proposed in section III above would, as has already been pointed out, assist in the attainment of this end.

to a vicious inflationary spiral of upward-moving wage-costs and money prices. Quite apart from the added difficulties to our balance of payments which would be caused by the increased prices of our exports, this might bring with it the threat of large-scale internal inflation with all its evil consequences. The Government would in such cases be faced with the tragic dilemma of adopting *either* an inflationary financial policy which would enable money demand to rise rapidly enough to cover the ever-increasing money costs *or* an anti-inflationary policy of stabilising total money demand, in which case as wage-costs rose there would undoubtedly develop a serious threat of unemployment.

Moreover, in a free society reliance cannot and should not be placed upon the direction of labour to obtain the most effective allocation of labour. The only effective alternative is that wage-rates should rise relatively in those industries which are short of labour as compared with those industries from which labour should move, so that workers have an incentive to move occupationally and, if necessary, geographically to the more attractive employments. Such movement is essential if we are to achieve a significant increase in economic efficiency.

Both these wage problems call for the same remedy. The Government through its general financial policy must ensure that the total money demand for goods and services is neither so great as to cause general inflation nor so low as to cause general unemployment. Wage-rates must then rise relatively in any occupation or region in which there is a local shortage of labour, and must fall relatively in any occupation or region in which there is a local surplus of labour. Such a combination of financial policy and wages policy will help to avoid general inflation or deflation on the one hand and the misallocation of labour on the other hand.

But to achieve this it is necessary that each particular wage-rate should not be fixed solely by the bargaining power of the particular bodies connected directly with that particular wage-rate, but should be raised or not according as there is an appreciable and lasting excess of demand over the supply of labour in that occupation. This will not be the automatic result of wage bargains between associations of workers and of employers possessing as they do very varying degrees of control over the supplies of, or the demands for, the labour involved and its closest substitutes. Very great restraint has, of course, in fact been observed by those responsible for wage-fixing in the existing inflationary situation. But it is nevertheless questionable whether more might not be achieved in obtaining the relativity between wage-rates which is desirable from the community's point of view; and, after all, trade union officials are appointed to promote the interests of their particular members rather than to plan the wage arrangements of their industry in the interests of the whole community.

It is difficult to avoid the conclusion that the submission of wage claims to arbitration should as far as possible become the general rule and that the arbitral bodies should be expressly entrusted with watching the community's interest. It would then be their duty to ensure that – subject to some basic minimum – rates of wages should in each particular case be so adjusted as to attract labour to those industries in which the demand for labour exceeded the supply and from those industries in which the labour supply exceeded the demand. Here again a redistribution of property which in general gave workers an interest in income from property as well as in income from work should ease the process of reform.

# 17

## Is the National Debt a Burden?

*This article, from* Oxford Economic Papers, *vol. 10 (June 1958), pp. 163–183, is reprinted here with Meade's 'Correction' published in* Oxford Economic Papers, *vol. 11 (February 1959), pp. 109–110.*

I

The view is sometimes expressed that a domestic national debt means merely that citizens as potential taxpayers are indebted to themselves as holders of government debt, and that it can, therefore, have little effect upon the economy, except in so far as it may lead to a redistribution of income and wealth between taxpayers and owners of property. It is my purpose to refute this argument; to show that, quite apart from any distributional effects, a domestic debt may have far-reaching effects upon incentives to work, to save, and to take risks; and to examine the nature of these effects.

I shall say very little about the distribution of income and property. My thesis is that if the national debt could be removed in such a way as to leave the distribution of real income totally unchanged, then in certain specified ways it would improve economic incentives. In economic policy there is very frequently a conflict between the objectives of efficiency and of equality. Measures which improve incentives often increase inequalities; and measures which increase equality often blunt economic incentives. If it can be shown that the removal of the national debt in a way which did not affect the distribution of income would improve economic incentives, then it would not be difficult to show that the removal of the national debt in a way which did not affect incentives could be used to improve distribution.

This paper is concerned only with domestic debt. It is well known that an external debt is a burden on a community, since there must be a transfer of real goods and services from the debtor to the creditor country in payment of interest and sinking fund on the debt. A domestic debt, on the other hand, means merely a transfer from citizens as taxpayers to citizens as property-owners, so that there is no direct loss of real goods and services to the citizens as a whole.

But one must not conclude from this that a domestic debt has no adverse economic effects.[1] In order to examine these effects, a comparison will be made between two societies which are in every respect similar except that the one has a large domestic national debt and the other has no debt. This idea is a useful analytical device to isolate certain factors at work in society; but the concept is an artificial one and needs careful definition, in particular in respect to the effect of the presence or absence of a national debt upon the distribution of income and property.

We can apply this concept by supposing that we move by means of a capital levy from a society with a national debt to a society without a national debt. But this capital levy is a purely analytical device.[2] We are really imagining two different societies, otherwise the same, except that history has left one with and the other without a national debt; and this is put in terms of assimilating the position of the former to that of the latter by means of a capital levy merely as a way of explaining in what sense they are otherwise the same.

Let us then consider a society with a large national debt. We will make one and only one simplifying assumption about distribution, namely that all citizens in any one given income bracket have the same ratio of income from work to income from property. The rich man may have a higher ratio than the poor man of unearned to earned income, but each rich man has the same ratio as every other rich man and each poor man has the same ratio as every other poor man. Suppose then that there is a capital levy of any degree of progression, the total levy being on a scale sufficient to redeem the whole debt. After the levy any citizen in any one income bracket will have a lower gross income according to the amount of income from property in that bracket and according to the progressiveness of the levy on property. Let us suppose that the scale of taxation on income is then so adjusted that each citizen in each income bracket gains in reduced taxation on income exactly what he loses in income from property.[3] Each citizen's net tax-free income remains exactly the same as before, so

---

[1] Some excellent articles have been written to remove fears about the evils to be expected from an ever-growing debt. For example, Professor A. P. Lerner ('The Burden of the Debt' in *Income, Employment, and Public Policy [Essays in Honor of Alvin A. Hansen*, New York: Norton, 1948, pp. 255–75]) shows that there is no reason to believe that the debt will grow without limit, even if a debt is always created to finance a budget deficit so long as total demand is deficient; for when the debt has grown to a certain size its 'Pigou-effect' (see p. 299 below) will serve to raise demand without further growth of debt. Professor Domar ('The Burden of the Debt and the National Income', *American Economic Review*, vol. 34, December 1944, pp. 798–827) has shown that even if debt grows without limit, the rate of tax necessary to service it may not grow beyond a certain limit, if the national income is also growing. But these articles show only that the debt is unlikely to grow without limit relatively to the national income. They do not show that a given debt has no adverse effects.

[2] For the reasons given below (p. 312) I would not personally advocate an actual capital levy.

[3] This involves the assumption that each citizen is paying sufficient in income taxation for it to be possible to offset by a remission of such tax his loss of income from property resulting from the levy on his capital. But this assumption can be safely made in conditions in which (i) income taxation accounts for a large proportion of government revenue and debt interest for a small proportion of government expenditure, so that much revenue from income tax is needed even after the capital levy; and (ii) income taxation and the capital levy are both progressive and people with large incomes hold large amounts of property, so that the people who lose income from property are also the main payers of income taxation.

that the capital levy has left the distribution of personal incomes unchanged. If the capital levy was a proportionate one, it would also have left the distribution of property unchanged, in the sense that it would have reduced all personal properties in the same proportion. If the capital levy was a progressive one, it would *pro tanto* have diminished the inequality of ownership of property.

There is, of course, a relationship between the degree of progression of the levy and the modification of the progressiveness of the existing taxation on income which is necessary to leave each citizen's net income unchanged.[4] But for our present purpose we can be content to conclude that on our assumptions in the society without the national debt (i) every citizen will own a smaller amount of property, (ii) every citizen's gross income will be lower, (iii) every citizen's average rate of taxation on income will be lower, but (iv) every citizen's net income will be unchanged.

## II

What would be the effects of these changes on the citizen's behaviour? The first and foremost effect, but a strangely neglected effect, is the increased incentive to save which would be caused by the fact that each citizen's net income was unchanged while the value of his property had been reduced. Imagine the same individual in two situations: in both situations he has a tax-free income of £1,000 to spend or save; but in situation 1 he has £10,000 worth of property and in situation 2 he has only £5,000 worth of property against a rainy day, or for his old age, or to leave

---

[4] Let $e + pr$ be an individual's gross income, where $e$ is income from work, $p$ the value of property, and $r$ the rate of interest on property. Let $i$ be the rate of tax on his income before the capital levy, $c$ the rate of levy on his capital, and $i'$ the rate of tax on his income after the levy. For his net income to remain unchanged we have

$$(e + pr)(1 - i) = \{e + (1 - c)pr\}(1 - i'),$$

or $(1 - i')/(1 - i') = 1/(1 - ck)$ where $k = pr/(e + pr)$ or the proportion of his income which is unearned. Consider now an individual with a large total income denoted by subscript ¹ and an individual with a small total income denoted by subscript ². Then $(1 - i_1')/(1 - i_1)$ is $> (1 - i_2')/(1 - i_2)$ if $c_1 k_1 > c_2 k_2$. The modification in the degree of progression of the income tax is thus seen to depend on the progressiveness of the capital levy ($c_1$ and $c_2$), and on the factors determining $k_1$ and $k_2$ which are the distribution of income from work ($e_1$ and $e_2$), the distribution of property ($p_1$ and $p_2$), and the yield of income from property ($r$). Now if the rich man has a higher ratio of unearned to earned income ($k_1 > k_2$) and the capital levy is progressive ($c_1 > c_2$), then $c_1 k_1 > c_2 k_2$. In this case taxation of income must be so adjusted that the tax-free proportion of gross income goes up in a greater proportion for the rich than for the poor (i.e. $(1 - i_1')/(1 - i_1) > (1 - i_2')/(1 - i_2)$). In this sense the taxation of income must become less progressive; and its degree of progression will be reduced the more, the more progressive *ceteris paribus* is the capital levy, i.e. the greater is $c_1 c_2$. But the mere fact that the rich man has a greater *absolute* amount of property than the poor man (even if the capital levy remains progressive) is not sufficient to cause the post-levy taxation of income to become less progressive in the sense defined above. A man with a large income may have a larger absolute income from property and yet a smaller proportion of his income coming from property than in the case of a poor man, i.e. $k_2$ can be greater than $k_1$. If the capital levy is only slightly progressive ($c_1$ only slightly $> c_2$), it is possible that $c_1 k_1 < c_2 k_2$.

to his family, or to supplement his present consumption by living on his capital. The amount which he would spend on goods and services would almost certainly be considerably greater in situation 1 than in situation 2; or, to put the same thing another way, a man's net savings will be higher or his net dissavings lower, the lower is the ratio of his capital to his tax-free income. We may call this the Pigou-effect.[5]

Professor Hicks[6] has estimated that in 1947–9 the domestic indebtedness of the government which was uncovered by any real assets (which I will call the 'deadweight debt') represented no less than 43 per cent of all privately owned property. The removal of the deadweight debt could thus be considered as capable in those circumstances of reducing the representative citizen's property by 43 per cent without reducing his tax-free income. This is what might be called a gigantic Pigou-effect and would clearly raise the incentive to save very greatly.[7]

This increase in the incentive to save is almost certain to represent an improvement from the point of view of society. If a reduction in the demand for consumption goods is desired either to reduce an inflationary pressure or to release resources so that investment can be raised in the interests of economic growth, the advantage is obvious. But even if no change in expenditure on consumption goods is desired, the increased incentive to save can be made to have advantageous indirect effects. For, in this case rates of taxation can be reduced so as to raise the citizens' tax-free incomes to the extent necessary to restore their demand for consumption goods; and these reductions in rates of tax will improve incentives for work and enterprise.[8]

Moreover, the fact that the removal of the deadweight debt would cause all personal properties to be smaller than before is likely to improve incentives for work and enterprise as well as for saving. Greater effort of every kind is likely to be made to be in a position to build up private fortunes when these are not already inflated by a deadweight debt.[9]

### III

The second major effect of the disappearance of the deadweight debt is the familiar one most usually discussed in this connection, namely the

[5] See Pigou, 'Economic Progress in a Stable Environment', *Economica*, vol. 14 (1947), pp. 180–8.

[6] See Hicks, *The Social Framework*, 2nd edn (Oxford, 1952), p. 109.

[7] We are not, of course, considering the effects of an actual capital levy, which might have other psychological repercussions upon the incentive to save, particularly if it were thought that the levy might be repeated. We are considering only how incentives in this country might differ from what they are if the past history of the country had been such as to leave it now with its present real income and real resources but without the deadweight debt.

[8] It should be noted that these reductions of tax rates made possible by the Pigou-effect are quite separate from, and additional to, any reductions in tax rates made possible through a saving of interest payments from the state budget, which are the subject-matter of the next section.

[9] Mr N. Kaldor has suggested this point to me. I shall refer to it as the Kaldor-extension of the Pigou-effect.

improvement to incentives to save, to work, and to bear risk brought about by the reduction in rates of taxation which it would make possible directly as a result of the saving of interest payments on the budget. The argument is in principle a very simple one. The redemption of the deadweight debt would mean a saving in budgetary expenditure on interest on the debt. This would make it possible to reduce rates of tax; and this would improve incentives to earn larger incomes by more effort and enterprise.

That there would be some incentive to more work and enterprise and that this would mark an improvement in economic arrangements is almost certain. We are assuming that when the deadweight debt disappears each citizen experiences a reduction in the rate of tax on his remaining income which exactly offsets his loss of income from property. So far he is in exactly the same real position with the same real income – neither better nor worse off. The only change is that if he earns an additional unit of income he will keep more of it. He will then take steps to earn more because he starts with the same real income and can get another unit of income more easily than before. And this change must be an improvement from his point of view because he could, had he so wished, have made no change in his income or leisure; and, so long as any positive rate of tax remains on income, he is likely by further effort to add more to the wealth of society than he takes from society after payment of tax on his additional earnings.

But how important are these effects of reduced rates of taxation on income likely to be? It has often been argued that they will be quantitatively very small if (i) the market rate of interest is low, (ii) the progressiveness of existing rates of taxation on income is high, (iii) there is a high correlation between large incomes and large properties, and (iv) the progressiveness of the capital levy is also high.[10] In these conditions a large redemption of debt is likely to lead only to a very small net saving of expenditure on the budget and so to make room for only a very small reduction of rates of taxation. If the rate of interest is low, a given redemption of debt will cause only a small gross saving of interest payments in the budget; if the levy on capital is progressive, if large properties are held mainly by people with large incomes, and if the marginal rates of tax on these incomes are very high, then most of this small gross saving of interest will itself be absorbed by a loss of revenue from the taxation of income. The net saving to the budget and so the consequential reduction in tax rates and so the consequential improvement in incentives to be expected from a redemption of debt will be very small.

---

[10] We are using the capital levy merely as an analytical device for comparing two otherwise similar societies, whose histories have differed in one way or another so that in one a large national debt has been contracted and in the other no debt has been contracted. Since a national debt involves the inflation of the total amount of privately owned property, the histories of our two societies must have differed in such a way that over the past years in one of them private citizens have been able to accumulate more savings than in the other. The assumption that the capital levy is progressive corresponds, therefore, to a difference in the past histories of our two societies such that it is those who were able to accumulate the largest sums in the one society who were most denied the opportunity to accumulate in the other.

The conditions which I have just enumerated existed in this country in the years immediately after the war; and for these reasons the existence of a very large national debt was not considered to have any seriously adverse effects on incentives. But, quite apart from the very important Pigou-effect, there are at least three reasons why the deadweight debt has been a more serious impediment to economic incentives than was generally recognised.

In the first place, the rate of interest was kept at a low level in large measure because of the existence of the national debt. These were years of heavy inflationary pressure. Reluctance to use monetary policy as one of the instruments to restrain inflation was greatly increased by the fact that an all-round rise in interest rates would immediately increase the budgetary burden of expenditure of interest on Treasury Bills and other short-term debt and would gradually lead to a rise in expenditure on longer-dated debt as it fell due for repayment.[11] With low interest rates a removal of the debt might cause only a small gross saving on debt interest; but it would mean that a rise of interest rates as an anti-inflationary device would no longer be open to the objection that it would seriously increase the budgetary problem. The removal of the national debt would thus have made it much easier to use the instrument of monetary policy flexibly for the control of inflation and deflation. Now that, for better or worse, interest rates have been raised to really high levels the argument can, of course, be put once more in its direct form. Rates of interest being high the redemption of national debt would mean a large saving of interest on national debt.

Our attitude to a deadweight debt must be much influenced by the surrounding economic climate. In times of economic stagnation like the 1930s, low interest rates and cheap money were most desirable in themselves to stimulate investment; this had the incidental result that a given national debt did not involve very high rates of tax for its service and, at the same time, the Pigou-effect of a high capital sum of the debt in discouraging savings was positively beneficial. But in the present (and so much more desirable) world climate of economic development and buoyancy, high interest rates may be desired as a means of discouraging the least productive investment projects, and the Pigou-effect of the debt in discouraging savings is most undesirable. A deadweight debt may have been a blessing in the 1930s, but it is a curse in the 1950s.

Secondly, the fact that a progressive capital levy combined with a progressive system of taxation of income means that there is little scope for subsequent reduction in the existing schedules of taxation on income does not mean that it gives no increased incentive at the margin for greater work and enterprise. A capital levy reduces the property-owner's

[11] It is not certain that a rise in interest rates increases the net burden of a given national debt. This depends greatly on the structure of the debt. If the debt consisted solely of short-term bills it would not affect the capital value of the debt but would add to the interest payments and so raise the rates of tax needed to service the debt. If the debt consisted solely of irredeemable bonds it would reduce the capital value of the debt without raising interest payments. In the former case there would be an unfavourable effect on tax rates with no favourable Pigou-effect; in the latter case there would be a favourable Pigou-effect with no adverse effects on tax rates.

gross income; with a progressive system of taxation of income the reduction in the amount of his gross income by putting him into a lower income bracket causes the rate of tax on his income to be reduced. For this reason, even if there were no reduction whatsoever in the schedules of taxation of income after the capital levy, there would nevertheless be an improvement in marginal incentive. Because he was now in a lower gross-income bracket the representative taxpayer could keep a larger proportion of each additional £1 which he earned.

Thirdly, there is some reason to believe that a given reduction in the marginal rate of tax will be more important from the point of view of economic incentives when tax rates are high than when they are low. Consider two situations which are otherwise the same. In situation 1 the rate of income tax is 19s 6d in the pound because the cold war is on and there is a great deal of government expenditure on armaments to finance in addition to interest on the national debt. In situation 2 real peace has broken out and the rate of income tax is only 2s in the pound because there is little government expenditure on armaments, though expenditure on interest on the debt remains unchanged. Now in situation 1 remove just sufficient national debt to make possible a reduction of 6d in the pound in the income tax while leaving every citizen with the same real income as before because his loss of interest on debt is just compensated by the fall in the rate of income tax. Then in situation 2 make a similar change; that is to say, remove that amount of debt which in situation 2 will permit a reduction of 6d in the pound while leaving every citizen with the same real income. In situation 1 out of every additional £100 which he now earns a citizen can keep £5 instead of only £2 10s. In situation 2 out of every additional £100 which he now earns he can keep £92 10s instead of only £90. The same reduction of tax of 6d in the pound has in both situations left the taxpayer's spendable income unchanged; but it has raised his *marginal* reward by 100 per cent in situation 1 and by under 3 per cent in situation 2. Since in the 'cold-war' situation our taxpayer is so much worse off than in the 'real-peace' situation we cannot say for certain that a 100 per cent increase in his marginal reward without any change in his total reward will have a greater effect on the amount of work which he does in situation 1 than a 3 per cent increase in his marginal reward without any change in his total reward in situation 2. But there is a strong presumption that he will increase his effort more in situation 1 than in situation 2.[12]

But even if he increased the amount of work which he did by the same

[12] If his elasticity of demand for income in terms of effort is equal to unity, then he is supplying the same amount of work in situation 1 as in situation 2. The outbreak of the cold war and the consequent increase in the rate of tax from 2s to 19s 6d in the pound will have raised the marginal utility of money income to him (by reducing his tax-free income) in exactly the same proportion as it has lowered his tax-free wage in terms of money. Since he is doing the same amount of work, the marginal disutility of work is in this case the same for him in situation 1 as in situation 2. In both cases when debt is removed and the tax rate is lowered by 6d the marginal utility of income is unchanged (because he loses interest as much as he gains by paying his tax); but in situation 1 his net reward for doing more work is doubled and in situation 2 it is raised by less than 3 per cent. He will be certain in this case to increase his supply of work more in situation 1 than in situation 2.

amount in situation 1 when his marginal reward was doubled as in situation 2 when his marginal reward was increased by only 3 per cent, the reduction in tax would be much more important in situation 1 than in situation 2. In both cases his wage before tax measures the value of his marginal product, while his wage after tax measures the marginal disutility of effort to him. In situation 1 our citizen is working to a margin at which the value of his marginal product is no less than 40 times as great as the cost of his marginal effort (£100 ÷ £2 10$s$ = 40). In situation 2 the value of his marginal product is only 1⅑ times as great as the cost of his marginal effort (100 ÷ £90 = 1⅑). In the former case society as a whole stands to gain much more from additional work than it does in the latter case.

Thus it is certainly true that if the initial taxation of income is high and progressive, then a progressive capital levy will lead to only a small budgetary saving of interest on debt and will therefore permit only a small reduction in tax rates. But it is precisely when marginal rates of tax on income are high that a small reduction in tax rates may do much good.

## IV

Up to this point the existence of death duties has been neglected. A removal of the deadweight debt would reduce the size of the average private holding of property; it would thus reduce the size of the average estate passing at death; and so with any given schedule of death duties it would reduce the annual revenue from such duties. This additional automatic loss of revenue, so it may be argued, still further weakens the case for a removal of the deadweight debt as a means of making possible a reduction of tax rates and so an improvement in incentives.

That one must be careful about this argument is forcibly demonstrated by the following consideration. If the rate of interest is sufficiently low, if the taxation of income is sufficiently high and progressive, if the capital levy itself is sufficiently progressive, if estates pass frequently enough by death from one owner to another, and if the rates of death duty are sufficiently high and progressive, then the removal of the deadweight debt may at existing tax rates cause budgetary revenue to fall by more than budgetary expenditure. The loss of death duties because of the reduction in the capital sum of personal properties may be greater than the small saving of interest after payment of income tax. To preserve the budgetary balance tax rates must be raised after the removal of the debt. The greater the national debt, the better the budgetary situation.

It is quite probable that in the years immediately after the war conditions were of this kind, so that the disappearance of the debt would have reduced budgetary expenditure less than budgetary revenue. Yet common sense rightly rebels against the conclusion that the great growth of debt during the war could have improved the budgetary situation in any basic sense. Where has the argument gone astray?

The answer is, of course, that there is no reason to believe that the balance between revenue and expenditure ought to remain unchanged when the deadweight debt is removed. In the modern economy the basic purpose of taxation is to restrain the demands of private citizens in order to release real resources from the production of goods and services for private consumption to the extent that they are needed to meet the demands of current government services and of the programme of capital development that, with given policies and institutions, the state and private enterprise plan to carry out. As a first approximation we should judge the extent to which tax rates can be reduced after the removal of the deadweight debt not by the criterion that the balance between budgetary revenue and expenditure should be unaffected, but by the criterion that the demand of private citizens for goods and services for private consumption should be unchanged. If this criterion is applied, there can be no doubt that the removal of the deadweight debt will permit some reduction of tax rates even in the extreme conditions which we have been envisaging, in which, because of the incidence of death duties, it will at unchanged rates of tax worsen the balance between budgetary revenue and expenditure.

This can be demonstrated by the following example. In both the pre-levy and the post-levy situations a representative citizen has a net tax-free income of £1,000, but in the former situation he possesses a property of £10,000 and in the latter he possesses only £5,000 of property. His consumption will be greater in the first than in the second case simply because he has so much more property; and if death duties are high and progressive, his consumption in the first situation may be higher still because he is allowed to consume all his property during his lifetime but cannot hand much of it on to his heirs. But in the first situation the state will be enjoying a large revenue from death duties (since some citizens will be dying each year and handing on their considerable properties), whereas in the second situation the state will receive much less revenue from death duties because there is only half as much private property to hand on at death. Now, since *ex hypothesi* our citizen has the same tax-free income in both situations, the state has already reduced rates of taxation of income between the first and second situation sufficiently to leave him with the same net tax-free income, even though he has lost half his income from property. This in itself will have left the balance of revenue and expenditure in the budget unchanged, since the state has lost in tax payments by him exactly as much as it has reduced its interest payment to him. But the state will also have lost a large part of its revenue from death duties since there is now only half as much private property to pass at death. Nevertheless, because of the Pigou-effect the reduction in our citizen's property will have reduced his expenditure on consumption and tax rates must be reduced still further if private consumption expenditure is to be maintained. In other words, when the deadweight debt is removed not merely should the loss of revenue from death duties be totally disregarded, but in addition rates of taxation on income can properly be reduced by more than would be sufficient to maintain the previous balance between revenue and expenditure even if there had been no fall in revenue from death duties.

## V

The disappearance of the deadweight debt would also have a revolution-ary effect in the capital and money markets through changes in the amount and the structure of capital assets available to be held by the banks and the rest of the private sector of the economy, and this would have some marked effects upon economic incentives which we must now examine.[13]

Let us divide the assets available to be held by the private sector of our community into four categories, namely: Money, Bills, Bonds, and Equities. Money includes coin, notes, and bank deposits, on all of which no interest is paid but all of which are fixed in money value and can be transferred at a moment's notice with negligible cost. Bills, of which the three-months Treasury Bill is the pure example, are reliable promises to pay a fixed sum of money in a short time; their capital value when that time comes will be certain, but there is some possibility of moderate variations in their value with variations in the rate of interest before they reach maturity. Bonds, of which 2½ per cent Consols are the pure example, are reliable promises to pay a fixed annual money income with no obligation to repay the capital sum; income from them is certain but their future capital value may vary widely with variations in the rate of interest. Equities include ordinary shares and real assets like machines; the income from them is uncertain and the rate of interest at which that income should be capitalised is also uncertain; their future capital value is subject to a double risk.

We will for the moment make two simplifying assumptions, both of which we shall in due course modify. First, let us assume that the disappearance of the deadweight debt does not disturb the banking system and that the total amount of coins, notes, and deposits made available by the banking system to the rest of the private sector of the economy remains unchanged. Second, let us assume that there is no attempt to keep the balance of revenue and expenditure in the budget unchanged, but rather that tax rates are reduced sufficiently to keep the total demand for private consumption goods at its previous level. In this case, since the market for finished goods is undisturbed, we can assume that there is no change in the absolute level of earnings expected on Equities.

There are two main ways in which the disappearance of the national debt might in these circumstances affect the incentive to invest, the first operating directly through the change in the amount of Bills-and-Bonds existing in the market and the second operating through the consequen-tial changes in the prices of Bills, Bonds, and Equities.

The Kaldor-extension of the Pigou-effect (p. 299 above) suggests that people might make all sorts of efforts to rebuild their private fortunes if they had been diminished by the disappearance of the deadweight debt. Such efforts might include greater activity on the part of business men,

---

[13] See E. Nevin, *The Problem of the National Debt* (Cardiff: University of Wales Press, 1954) for a stimulating description and discussion of the effect of the debt upon the assets held by the various sectors of the United Kingdom economy.

involving an increased incentive to invest in capital equipment. But there is an important influence operating in the opposite direction. The disappearance of the deadweight debt means that the entrepreneur (whether he be a private business man or be taken to represent the managing body of a joint-stock company) will have at his command a much smaller amount of assets – and precisely of assets like government Bills-and-Bonds on the security of which, or through the sale of which, it is especially easy to raise funds for the finance of capital development. Both because the ratio of his total assets to liabilities will be lower and because the ratio of his readily realisable assets to other assets will be lower, the typical entrepreneur will be less able to finance projects of capital development, and the risks involved in doing so will be greater. Thus the incentive to invest may be increased, but the ability to finance investment is likely to be reduced, simply by the changes in the quantity of assets.[14]

# VI

But the disappearance of the deadweight debt will affect the prices as well as the amounts of various assets; and these changes in price may also affect the level of investment. The disappearance of the deadweight debt represents, on the one side, a reduction by that amount in the total capital wealth of the private sector of the community and, on the other hand, an equal reduction in the Bills-and-Bonds available to be held by the private sector, the amounts of Money and of Equities available in the market, and the level of earnings expected on Equities being unchanged. But when a private citizen has £5,000 less capital to hold with asset prices and expectations unchanged, he is unlikely to choose to hold £5,000 less Bills-and-Bonds; although his reduction in holdings of Money, Bills, Bonds, and Equities will not necessarily all be in the same proportion, he is likely to want at current asset prices to hold somewhat less of each type of asset.[15] In other words the disappearance of the deadweight debt will cause a scarcity of Bills-and-Bonds relatively to Money and relatively to Equities; in an otherwise unchanged market situation, the price of Bills-and-Bonds will probably rise in terms of Money and in terms of Equities.

The rise of the price of Bills-and-Bonds in terms of Money represents a fall in the rate of interest. The rise in the price of Bills-and-Bonds relatively to that of Equities represents a rise in the risk premium. The margin between the rate of yield on Equities, on the one hand, and on Bills-and-Bonds, on the other hand, will be increased. It will be easier to borrow for capital development by the issue of fixed-interest debentures than by the issue of ordinary shares. There will be a premium on capital development of a safe kind.

---

[14] The argument in this paragraph was suggested to me in discussion by Mr N. Kaldor.

[15] He will presumably wish to reduce his holding of foreign assets as well as of domestic assets. In this way a reduction of domestic deadweight debt might cause some easement on the capital account of a country's balance of payments.

It would, of course, always be possible for the government to offset this change in asset prices by itself supplying risk-bearing. This it could do by issuing Bills-and-Bonds and investing the proceeds in Equities, so that, while the deadweight debt was eliminated, there remained a considerable governmental liability in the form of government Bills-and-Bonds balanced by an equal asset in the form of governmental investments in private industry.[16]

But suppose that the government took no such action. Then, as we have seen, there will be some rise in the price of Bills-and-Bonds in terms of Money; this will represent a fall in the pure rate of interest; and a lower pure rate of interest is a price change which may help to stimulate some extra investment in safe, long-term projects such as house-building.

But a change in the price of Equities (which represents the market valuation placed on machines and other real assets in industry) is more likely to affect investment than is a change in the price of Bills-and-Bonds. Bills-and-Bonds go up in terms of Money and in terms of Equities. But will Equities go up or down in terms of Money?

The outcome will depend upon whether Bills-and-Bonds are better substitutes for Money than for Equities or whether, on the contrary, they are better substitutes for Equities than for Money. When the government Bills-and-Bonds disappear, the amounts of Money and of Equities remaining unchanged, the representative private citizen has got to increase by a given amount the proportion of his assets which he holds in Money and by another given amount the proportion of his assets which he holds in Equities. If Bills-and-Bonds are a good substitute for Money, then only a small rise will be needed in the money price of Bills-and-Bonds to persuade the representative citizen to make the needful shift into Money; and if Bills-and-Bonds are a bad substitute for Equities, a large rise in the price of Bills-and-Bonds will be necessary in terms of Equities to bring about the needed shift into Equities. In these conditions there will be only a small rise in the money price of Bills-and-Bonds, i.e. only a small fall in the pure rate of interest; and the increase in the risk premium will be large and will be brought about by a fall in the price of Equities. Similarly, in the opposite conditions where Bills-and-Bonds are a bad substitute for Money but a good substitute for Equities, the price of Bills-and-Bonds will rise a lot and the rate of interest will fall a lot in order to cause the necessary shift to Money; but the risk premium will have to rise only a little to cause the necessary shift to Equities, so that the money price of Equities will rise almost as much as the money price of Bills-and-Bonds.

Which of these two things is likely to happen in fact? We must distinguish between Bills and Bonds. Bills are more like Money than are Bonds, and Bonds are more like Equities than are Bills. When the private

---

[16] In terms of our analytical capital levy this result would be brought about and all asset prices would remain unchanged if those liable to the capital levy were allowed at their choice to pay in Money, Bills, Bonds, or Equities, and if the government after cancelling any government Bills-and-Bonds which the payers of the levy surrendered, itself held on to the other private assets handed over to it, leaving outstanding in private ownership any government Bills-and-Bonds which had not been surrendered to it in payment of the levy.

citizen loses his Bills he is likely to go for Money. But in fact most government short-term debt is held by the banks. As long as we are assuming that the banks are not disturbed by the change but supply an unchanged amount of money, the effect of the disappearance of the national debt on the private sector's structure of assets will be mainly a loss of Bonds. When property-owners are starved of Bonds will they shift to Money or to Equities?

There is, I think, no simple answer to this question. One can imagine circumstances in a mature economy with a tendency to secular stagnation in which exceedingly low rates of interest are necessary to prevent deflation, so that a further fall in interest rates is almost out of the question. In this case an increased risk margin will show itself in a fall in the money price of Equities rather than in a rise in the money price of Bonds. The disappearance of the deadweight debt will have made an already deflationary situation still more deflationary. On the other hand, one can imagine a buoyant situation in which interest rates are very high and in which it is the scarcity of capital rather than of risk-bearing and of profitable opportunities for investment which holds back further development. In these circumstances a scarcity of Bonds might well cause a substantial fall in the rate of interest which might carry upwards the money price of Equities; and in this case, in so far as price effects in the capital market are concerned, the disappearance of the national debt would have made an inflationary situation still more inflationary.

But the analysis in the last paragraph has not allowed for the fact that substantial deflations or inflations of the general level of prices may be in progress and may be expected to continue. The capital value of Bills and the interest payable on Bonds are fixed in terms of Money; in the case of Equities, neither capital value nor yield is fixed. For this reason in times of rapidly changing money prices Bills and Bonds are likely to be better substitutes for Money than for Equities. This is an added reason why the disappearance of the national debt is likely to exert a deflationary influence on the price of Equities.

## VII

We have still to modify our two assumptions that the disappearance of the deadweight debt does nothing in itself to affect either the absolute level of earnings expected on Equities or the total supply of Money. In fact in both these respects also it might exert a strong deflationary force.

For the reasons developed in section II above, the disappearance of the deadweight debt would be likely to increase the propensity to save. The effects of this we have so far assumed to be offset by a reduction of tax rates by the government sufficient to restore private expenditure to its previous level. But, of course, tax rates might not be reduced in this way. The increase in savings and decrease in expenditure on consumption goods caused by the disappearance of the deadweight debt might be acceptable to the government if there was initially a strong inflationary pressure which it was desired to counteract. Or the reduction in the demand for consumption goods might be acceptable even in the absence of any inflationary pressure, if it was thought that too much of the community's resources was being devoted to consumption and too little to investment. In this case the reduced expenditure on consumption, by causing a fall in the absolute level of earnings expected on Equities would cause an undesirable deflationary pressure. In order that this should not cause an actual deflation of total demand, it would then be necessary for there to be an increase in total investment expenditure equal to the reduction in expenditure on consumption goods. To engineer an increased expenditure on capital development, when the market for finished consumption goods was actually being contracted, might require a very large increase in monetary liquidity and fall in interest rates or risk premium. In such circumstances the disappearance of the deadweight debt might well be deflationary unless the total supply of Money were considerably increased.

But how would the supply of Money react to the disappearance of the deadweight debt? At present the supply of Money depends upon the liquidity of the banking system which depends upon the issue of a sufficient amount of liquid Treasury Bills to be shuffled about between the Bank of England, the discount houses, and the clearing banks. If these higher banking mysteries remain unchanged, then the disappearance of the deadweight debt including the disappearance of all government Bills would make the banking system highly illiquid and would cause a reduction in the supply of Money.[17] This deflationary effect could be offset if the Government, while its net debt was zero, issued Bills to the banks and invested the money so borrowed in private Bonds or Equities. The government would buy private Bonds-and-Equities with government Bills in order that the banks might buy Bills with Money, unless there were a change in banking arrangements so that the banks themselves in these conditions bought Bonds and Equities with Money.

# VIII

Whether the net effect of the disappearance of the deadweight debt would be inflationary or deflationary rests upon a complex balance of forces. The outstanding deflationary possibility would be its effect upon the banking system. If all Treasury Bills disappeared there would in present conditions be a catastrophic monetary deflation. Let us leave this on one side and assume that some alternative method is found for controlling the supply of Money. This is a *sine qua non* for the removal of the deadweight debt.

There would remain a number of conflicting forces at work.

[17] If the national debt consisted entirely of Bills held partly by the banks and partly by private owners and if, as is probable, Bills are a good substitute for Money, then the disappearance of the national debt would cause a large reduction of Money-and-Bills with an unchanged stock of privately issued Bonds-and-Equities. In this case the money prices of Bonds and of Equities would fall. In other words, the pure rate of interest would rise because the change would be essentially one of reduced liquidity.

(i)	Because of the Pigou-effect people are likely to spend less on consumption and to save more, which in itself will be a deflationary force.

(ii)	Because of the Kaldor-extension of the Pigou-effect and because of reductions in marginal rates of tax people are likely to produce more goods and services. Since producers are likely to increase their expenditures by less than their incomes (particularly when rates of taxation on incomes are high and progressive), this is likely to increase supplies relatively to demand and to exert a deflationary influence.

(iii)	Entrepreneurs will have a smaller amount of easily realisable assets in their ownership and this will make the finance of investment more difficult.

(iv)	If Bonds are a good substitute for Money and a poor substitute for Equities, then the disappearance of government Bonds is likely to cause only a small rise in the price of Bonds but a large fall in the price of Equities. This would probably exercise a deflationary effect upon investment. If, on the other hand, Bonds were a bad substitute for Money and a good substitute for Equities, the prices of Bonds and Equities would both rise with a consequential inflationary effect upon investment. But, as we have seen, in periods of rapid fluctuations in commodity prices, Bonds are unlikely to be a good substitute for Equities, and the inflationary effect upon Equity prices is not very probable in such circumstances.

(v)	The desire to rebuild private fortunes which have been reduced by the disappearance of government debt might stimulate business men to greater risk-bearing and enterprise and thus to a higher level of expenditure on investment programmes.

On balance it would appear probable that, even apart from any effects on the supply of Money through the banking system, the disappearance of the deadweight debt would exert a significant deflationary influence. But, provided always that the government has a firm grip upon monetary institutions and policies and is prepared so to control its monetary and fiscal policies as to stabilise the total demand for goods and services, this in present-day conditions must be counted a great advantage of the removal of the debt. In present-day conditions of economic expansion and buoyancy interest rates and rates of taxation have to be kept at otherwise undesirably high levels in order to avoid the threat of inflation. The disappearance of the deadweight debt could provide just the occasion for an otherwise desirable relaxation of monetary and fiscal conditions.

The danger might, however, remain that through the increased difficulty of finding finance for risky investment projects and through an increase in the risk premium on Equities, there would be a special deterrent to innovation and to the application of new and risky techniques. To counteract such a tendency it might be necessary for the government to relax its monetary and fiscal policies in ways which specially favoured innovation and enterprise (e.g. by tax allowances for new investment), and to introduce new arrangements for the provision of risk capital through public or semi-public institutions. But, given this, the disappearance of the deadweight debt could be made the occasion for a great improvement in economic incentives.

## IX

This paper has been devoted to the question whether an internal national debt is an economic burden or not. The method of analysis of this problem has been to remove the debt by means of an imaginary capital levy to see what difference this would make to economic incentives, if everything also remained unchanged. Our analysis has suggested that in certain important respects the existence of a large deadweight debt seriously blunts economic incentives. But before we rush to rebuild society with a zero deadweight debt there are two further questions which would require extensive investigation. In this paper they can only be briefly mentioned.

The first remaining problem is this. Granted that a positive deadweight debt is a burden, it does not follow that the optimum size for the deadweight debt is zero. Perhaps a negative debt would be still better. Or in terms of our national capital levy, why should the total levy be just equal to the deadweight debt? Might there not be advantages if it were still bigger and left the state a net creditor instead of a net debtor to the private sector of the economy? The argument for such a development runs as follows. The government has expenditures to finance on defence, justice, police, education, health, and social security. For this it has to impose taxes. Rates of tax cause divergences between efforts and rewards and thus interfere with economic incentives. If the state was a net owner of property which it itself used productively or hired out to the private sector of the economy, it would itself obtain a net income from rents, interest, and profits which it could use to finance part of its expenditures so that rates of tax could be further reduced. Provided that the state's property was devoted to uses where the marginal social return on it was at least as high as it would have been if it had been left in private ownership, the reduction in tax rates would represent a further net improvement in economic incentives; and there would, of course, be a still greater Pigou-effect stimulating private savings.

There would remain the question of the kind of assets which the state should hold. Some assets, like roads, schools, and the equipment of nationalised industries, are obvious candidates. But for the rest should the state invest in private bonds or in private equities? If it invested its funds in fixed charges like ground rents, mortgages, and debentures, it would still further usurp the function of the private rentier. The private-property-owner would willy-nilly be forced to become more and more of a private risk-bearer, if not an actual entrepreneur. If, on the other hand, this would reduce the supply of risk-bearing too seriously, the state would have to hold private equities rather than private bonds; and an arrangement which was devised in the first place to give the state an income from property would have the indirect effect of forcing the state into participation in the management of private industry.

But with the present gigantic deadweight debt these problems are all ones for a still far-distant Utopia. We should be happy enough to see a substantial reduction in the debt without demanding even its total elimination, much less its replacement by a net ownership of property by the state. Even so, there remains the great practical question: how is the reduction to be effected? The fact that the deadweight debt is a serious and real economic burden does not itself prove that it should be removed or even reduced. It might be a good thing if it had never existed; but it does exist and the best cure might be worse than the disease.

The first possibility is to use the capital levy not merely as a tool of economic analysis, but also as a practical means of debt redemption. I have been persuaded that we should not.[18] We have to face the following dilemma. A levy can be successful only if it is not expected that it will be repeated, since the expectation of a further levy would destroy all incentives to save. A successful levy will lead to the expectation that it will be repeated unless it is on such a scale that there remains no case for a repeat. But a levy on this scale would present such problems of administration and valuation, would so disturb the structure of the capital market, and would involve such vast changes in personal wealth that it really lies outside the range of what is practicable or suitable in our evolutionary methods of social and economic reform.

But alternative and less revolutionary methods are available to reduce the burden of the national debt. We may perhaps take the ratio of deadweight debt to total privately owned property as an index of the relative size of the debt. There remain three ways of reducing this proportion, namely: inflation, private savings, and public savings through budget surpluses.

First, it can be very effectively reduced by inflation. This has in fact been happening since the war. In the nine years since 1947-9 the general level of money prices of fixed assets in this country has risen by some 45 per cent. In 1947-9 43 per cent of private property was deadweight debt.[19] If this 43 per cent remains fixed in money values and the other 57 per cent rises by 45 per cent in money values, then the deadweight debt represents only 34 per cent instead of 43 per cent of total private property.[20]

Second, the relative importance of the deadweight debt can be reduced by the accumulation of private savings.[21] Such savings, matched by an

[18] The argument is exceedingly well put by Mr C. A. R. Crosland in pp. 311-18 of his *The Future of Socialism* (1st edn, London: Jonathan Cape, 1956).

[19] J. R. Hicks, *loc. cit.*

[20] I would like to thank Mr J. Longden of the Faculty of Economics and Politics, University of Cambridge, for help in the preparation of the estimates in this and the following paragraphs.

[21] For this and the following paragraph the total savings of the community have been divided between private and public savings. Private savings include the surpluses of public corporations as well as the undistributed profits of ordinary companies. The realisation of assets for the payment of death duties has been treated as a reduction of private savings and accordingly the receipt of death duties has been allowed to swell the budget surplus. The current revenue of the public authorities and so their savings also includes the receipts of foreign aid. Public savings include the surpluses of local authorities as well as of the central government.

expansion of the community's real capital assets, represent a growth of total privately owned property, so that any given amount of deadweight debt will represent a smaller proportion of total privately owned property. In the nine years 1948–57 total private savings reckoned at 1948 prices amounted to about £6,100 million, which represents an addition of some 15 per cent to the £40,500 million of total privately owned property which was estimated to exist in 1947–9.[22] Such an increase would reduce the proportion of deadweight debt to total privately owned property from 43 per cent to 38 per cent.

Third, there is the old-fashioned method of debt reduction through an annual surplus of revenue over expenditure in the state budget. Such public savings have a double effect in reducing the proportion of total privately owned property which takes the form of deadweight debt. Suppose that the government has an excess of revenue over current expenditure of £1 million. If the government invests this sum in new public works like schools, then £1 million of existing government debt ceases to be uncovered by real assets. Privately owned property remains unchanged in total, but it consists of £1 million less of deadweight debt and £1 million more of claims backed by real assets. If the government uses its surplus of £1 million to redeem outstanding national debt, then private owners must hold £1 million less of government debt and they must invest this sum in £1 million worth of additional private real assets. The ratio of the former to the latter has fallen both because the former has decreased and also because the latter has increased. During the nine years 1948–57 public savings amounted at 1948 prices to some £3,100 million. If we subtract this figure from the £17,500 million of deadweight debt outstanding in 1947–9 and add it to the £23,000 million of other privately owned property, outstanding at that time,[23] the ratio of deadweight debt to total privately owned property is reduced from 43 per cent to 36 per cent.

Nowadays, the desirability of a budget surplus is often argued on one or both of two grounds: first, that high levels of taxation and low levels of governmental expenditure are desirable in order to exert a disinflationary pressure in an inflationary situation and, second, that public savings through a budget surplus are a desirable supplement to private savings in order that, in the interests of economic growth, more resources may be devoted to capital development at the expense of immediate consumption. I would like to restore a third old-fashioned argument for a budget surplus, namely, that it will help to reduce the national debt and thereby improve economic incentives in the future.

Additional taxation even if it were paid wholly out of savings (i.e. even if it caused no reduction at all in private consumption and therefore served no useful purpose in fighting inflation or promoting economic growth) would nevertheless serve a useful purpose in debt redemption. It would reduce the amount of national debt held by individuals even though it caused no net increase in their holding of other assets. Of

[22] J. R. Hicks, *loc. cit.*
[23] J. R. Hicks, *loc. cit.*

course, taxes imposed for this purpose as for all others should have as little adverse effect as possible upon current incentives for work and enterprise; the point is only that, if taxes are imposed for debt redemption, they are not to be ruled out because they are paid out of private savings. Death duties and annual taxes assessed not on income but on the value of privately owned property may fall into this category. Such taxes may have the smallest adverse effects upon work and enterprise (though it would be rash to claim that they have no such effects), but they are likely to be paid wholly or in large part out of private savings. It might be wise to build up a considerable budget surplus financed out of these taxes and to use it for the redemption of the national debt.[24]

A budget surplus can also be achieved by a reduction in budgetary expenditure in so far as this is not offset by a reduction in rates of taxation. If expenditure is reduced for the purpose of debt redemption, the future advantages of a lower national debt are gained at the expense of the present restriction of government expenditure below the level which would otherwise be considered desirable.

Indeed we are faced, as so often in economic policy, with a dilemma. There would be great future advantages in improved economic incentives if the debt were reduced. But the methods of doing this are likely to worsen economic conditions in the immediate present. Inflation is the great debt-reducer, but has many other bad marks to be set against it. Private savings may be stimulated, but after a point only by means of systems of taxation which involve a reduction in public savings or are undesirable on distributional or similar grounds.[25] A budget surplus can be achieved only by further increases in tax rates or by a reduction in other budgetary expenditures – when it is a main purpose of debt reduction to enable a given level of other budgetary expenditures to be maintained without the disincentive effects of high taxation. The purpose of this paper is the limited one of showing in what ways the existence of a large national debt blunts economic incentives; it has not attempted to assess the balance between the immediate costs and the ultimate gains of different methods of debt reduction.

---

[24] Taxes of this sort (and in particular death duties) are not of the kind whose rates can appropriately be frequently varied. In so far as variations in tax rates are needed to control total expenditure in order to avoid inflations and deflations of demand, alterations in rates of taxation on income or on purchases are more appropriate. But if, over and above such taxes, there is a considerable and fairly stable revenue from death duties and other taxes which are paid out of savings, it should be possible normally to run a considerable budget surplus. Any reductions in other taxes which may then at any time be needed to offset the threat of a general deflation will involve the reduction of a budget surplus rather than the incurring of an actual deficit. Revenue from taxes paid out of savings thus allows fiscal measures to be used for reflationary purposes without a budget deficit and thus without building up once more a deadweight debt.

[25] I would exempt from this criticism any shift from a progressive tax on income to an equally progressive tax on expenditure which, if administratively practicable, should greatly stimulate savings without other seriously adverse effects.

## Is the National Debt a Burden? A Correction

In my article in the *Oxford Economic Papers* for June 1958 I made a serious mistake.[26] The point which I overlooked is one which would tend to raise the money price of privately held assets after their quantity had been reduced by the capital levy. The total value of the remaining capital assets would thus be greater than I allowed in my article; but, as I argue in this note, the rise in their price would not normally be great enough to restore the total value of privately held assets to their pre-levy value. Some element of the Pigou-effect (discussed in section II of my article) would remain.

My blunder was as follows. In section VI of my article I argued as if the functional relationship expressing the demands for Money, Bills, Bonds, and Equities in terms of the total money value of assets to be held and of the money prices of Bills, Bonds, and Equities would be the same before and after the levy. But this is not so because of the lower rate of tax on interest and dividends after the levy. The gross (or *cum* tax) and net (or *ex* tax) yield on Money is always zero; with a gross yield on bonds of 4 per cent, the net yield is 2 per cent with a rate of tax of 10s in the £ and 3 per cent with a rate of tax of 5s in the £. This means that, after the levy, income-yielding assets become so much the more attractive at any given price in terms of Money. This will cause their price to be driven up (i.e. their gross yield or the rate of interest to be driven down) not only because they are now scarce relatively to Money (the point which I made) but also because their net yield is now higher while that on Money remains zero (the point which I overlooked in my article).

Nevertheless, I think that there remains a presumption that the price of income-yielding assets (Bills, Bonds, and Equities) will not rise to the extent necessary to restore the total value of such assets to the pre-levy total. The argument may be put in the form of a *reductio ad absurdum*. Suppose that the rate of interest did fall to the extent necessary to restore the pre-levy total value of all assets. Then there are two reasons why it would rise again.

First, the net rate of yield on such assets would now be *lower* than in the pre-levy situation and this would cause people to desert income-yielding assets for Money, i.e. would cause some rise in the rate of interest. The reason for this is that, while the loss of interest on the national debt is exactly counterbalanced by a reduction of income tax (assuming income tax to be the only form of tax and a balanced budget to be maintained), the loss of interest on debt is wholly a loss of income from property but the gain through lower tax is spread over earned and unearned income. Thus the tax-free income from property is lower post-levy than pre-levy, so that if the total market value of property is to be the same post-levy as pre-levy the net rate of return on income-yielding property must be lower post-levy than pre-levy. If the tax remission were confined to the remission of tax on income from property, it might be argued that the first presumption in the capital market is that the total value of income-

---

[26] This mistake has come to light as a result of a correspondence with Mr John Spraos, to whom I would like to acknowledge my indebtedness.

yielding assets will be exactly restored by a fall in the rate of interest; for in this case the amount of Money, the value of other assets, and the net yield on other assets would all remain unchanged; but in so far as some of the tax remission is on earned income the net yield on income-yielding assets is reduced and their value will tend to fall.

Second, suppose that the tax remission were confined to taxation of income from property so that the above considerations would not prevent the value of assets being restored to their pre-levy level. There would now be no Pigou-effect to cause a rise in savings and so a deflation in the demand for consumption goods, and for exactly the same reason there would be no deflationary influence damping down investment of the kind which I mentioned on pages 305, 306 in my article. But in so far as the rate of interest affects investment, there would now be an inflationary demand for investment goods because it is the *gross* and not the *net* rate of yield which affects investment incentives. So far nothing would have happened to make people expect a lower gross rate of profit on any given new investment, but the gross rate of interest would have fallen so as to keep the net tax-free rate of yield unchanged. The fall in the rate of interest would cause an inflation; and if monetary policy and not budgetary policy were used to prevent this the amount of Money would have to be reduced and the rate of interest raised again somewhat, so that the total value of assets would fall. Indeed, if on these grounds monetary policy was so devised as to keep the gross rate of interest at its pre-levy level, there would be a completely unmitigated Pigou-effect; the total value of privately held assets would fall by the amount of the levy.

The net effect of this correction is, therefore, to suggest that, while there would still be a Pigou-effect, it might be less marked than I supposed it to be in my article.

# 18

# Poverty in the Welfare State

*From* Oxford Economic Papers, *vol. 24 (November 1972), pp. 289–326. As Meade explained,*

'This paper is an expanded version of the Sidney Ball Lecture delivered in Oxford on 3 May 1972. No attempt has been made to refer to any developments since that date. In writing this paper I have made free use of Professor A. B. Atkinson's book *Poverty in Britain and the Reform of Social Security* [Cambridge: Cambridge University Press, 1969] both for describing the present position and for the discussion of proposals for reform. Professor Atkinson and Mr Alan Harrison have also undertaken for me the calculations presented in the Appendix to this paper. I have been much helped by comments from that remarkable triad of Professors – Titmuss, Townsend and Abel-Smith – who were responsible for putting this subject back into the political arena and to the work of that remarkable pressure group, the Child Poverty Action Group which, working from a tiny, dingy, meanly equipped office, has had a profound effect on policy – would that all such organizations had such a high ratio of effectiveness to overhead costs. *Family Poverty*, a collection of essays by members of the Child Poverty Action Group [ed. David Bull, London: Duckworth, 1971] has helped me to bring the story up to date. I am indebted to many others, including Dr G. M. Heal, Miss T. Cooper, Professor T. H. Marshall, Mr D. F. J. Piachaud, Professor A. R. Prest, Mr A. Seldon, Sir Brandon Rhys-Williams, and a number of officials in various Departments for helpful comments and information.'

One should, I suppose, start by saying a word or two about what one means by 'poverty'. Rowntree in his classic investigation into the degree of poverty in York in 1899 used an absolute measure. Those in primary poverty were defined as those whose income fell below what was required to purchase the absolute essentials of food, clothing, shelter, warmth, etc.; and those in secondary poverty were defined as those who through inappropriate or inefficient use of their income – betting or drinking by the husband, ignorant housekeeping by the wife, and so on – failed to acquire these essentials, even though their income would have sufficed to do so.

The Rowntree inquiry of 1899 was repeated in 1936 and again in 1950. The percentages in poverty were found to be[1]

| 1899 | 1936 | 1950 |
|------|------|------|
| 28   | 18   | 2    |

This great change had occurred even though the 1899 original austere standard of absolute poverty was somewhat relaxed for the later inquiries. General economic progress and the institutions of the welfare state had together resulted in a dramatic reduction in the degree of poverty; and, indeed, there is no doubt that in absolute terms the real grinding destitution of the poorest sections of the community is much less now than in the England of Dickens's novels. There has been great real progress.

But is the Rowntree-type of definition of poverty in absolute terms all that we have in mind when we talk about certain people living in poverty in the community? There are in fact some very real difficulties with the absolute measure.

In the first place, even if we limit essentials to what is needed to keep body and soul together, we are in difficulties. A diet may be sufficient to keep a person alive for the time being; but improvements in the diet may decrease the liability to disease and increase the expectation of life. What is the cut-off point in reduced diets and worsened expectation of life at which poverty begins? There is no absolute answer.

Secondly, suppose that being without warmth did not affect one's health (though in fact lack of warmth is almost certainly a contributory factor to some deaths of impoverished old age pensioners); but suppose that being cold merely made one shiver miserably, incapable of enjoyable activity. Would we be prepared to say that someone without any warmth was not in poverty because his life was not thereby endangered? I think not. But suppose the greater the warmth, the more the enjoyment. At what point in the scale of enjoyment (if one could measure enjoyment, which one can't) does a man become poor?

The answers which would be given to questions of this kind in fact depend upon the general standards of the community in question. In a society in which everyone took it for granted that he had to shiver throughout the winter and in which everyone had learnt to make the best of life in these conditions, a shiverer might not be considered poor. But in a society in which everyone except Tom Jones lived with enjoyable central heating, while Tom Jones had to shiver, Tom Jones might well be considered to be living in poverty.

Poverty as we generally think of it has, I am sure, an element of the relative about it. People are poor if they are much worse off than the other members of the community in which they live; and the fact that as the Rowntree investigation of 1899 was repeated in 1936 and 1950 the list of minimum necessities in the family budget itself lengthened is not

[1] Figures quoted from Peter Townsend, *Poverty, Socialism and Labour in Power*, Fabian Tract 37 (Fabian Society, 1967).

without significance. The absolute standard could not resist altogether the temptation of the relative.

But to give any precision to a definition of relative poverty we must ask at least two questions: first, how seriously short of the average must a man fall to be considered poor? and, second, what is the society against whose average this shortfall is to be reckoned? There can in the nature of things be no scientific, objective answers, independent of the states of mind and of the value judgements of the individuals concerned. Is a family to be regarded as poor because it cannot afford a motor-car? Not yet, I think, in this country, but perhaps the answer would be 'Yes' in some communities in the United States. Is a family on a given housing estate poor because it cannot afford a TV set so that its children cannot discuss last night's programme with their playmates? Or must its children have to go to school in rags and tatters before it is regarded by its neighbours or by itself as being in poverty? A family which is regarded in this country as being in poverty may well have a real standard of living above the world average; it is regarded as poor because our frame of reference is British society, not the world society. Certainly many of the poor in this country would be regarded as affluent on the streets of Calcutta.

On the other hand, impoverishment is not merely a question of relative lack of money. A neighbourhood may be poor because its schools and hospitals are below standard, its general medical practitioners over-worked, its atmosphere polluted by industry, and so on. Impoverishment is also not merely a question of material conditions. Loneliness is an important factor in the real poverty of many old people.

There are so many rather intangible social, psychological, and moral issues involved that I cannot offer you a fundamental definition of poverty. I must proceed by limiting my subject matter very strictly. The political process in this country produces for the use of the Supplementary Benefits Commission a scale of the minimum levels below which incomes should not be permitted to fall. With some very important exceptions to which I will refer in due course, every family in this country has the right to obtain from the Supplementary Benefits Commission whatever supplement is needed to bring its income up to this minimum level. Parliament has thus defined a level, which we may call the 'minimum standard', below which it considers it undesirable that any family's income should fall.

This 'minimum standard' is itself somewhat elastic in terms of money income. There is a basic scale of money payments[2] which is intended to cover needs other than housing, which are met by additional payments

---

[2] These are at present:

|  | £ per week |
|---|---|
| For a single adult | 5·80 |
| For a married couple | 9·45 |
| For a married couple with three children (aged between 5 and 10) | 15·45 |

plus an additional £0·50 a week for all pensioners on Supplementary Benefits and for all those who have been in receipt of benefit for two years or more.

(with certain necessary safeguards) to meet the rent and rates actually paid by the family concerned. Certain further additional payments may be made to meet exceptional needs; and certain small elements of income or other resources may be disregarded in assessing the amounts of benefit needed to bring the recipients up to the 'minimum standard'.

I shall define being in poverty as falling below this minimum standard of income. In doing so I am conscious of having very severely limited my subject matter. To bring all incomes up to this minimum standard is a necessary, but by no means a sufficient, condition for the elimination of poverty. Social conditions, personal difficulties, financial arrangements between husband and wife, and similar factors, may make it difficult for families at this level so to use this income as to avoid real poverty. The need would remain for all sorts of social services. All that I am claiming is that to ensure to everyone a money income at least equal to this minimum standard is a necessary aid to the relief and elimination of poverty.

If we accept this working definition of poverty we shall, of course, find ourselves in the apparently paradoxical position that any rise in the Supplementary Benefit Scales itself automatically increases the amount of poverty requiring Supplementary Benefit for its relief. But this is really a quite reasonable implication of our definition. If a rise in the general average standard of living in the community does in fact cause an increase in relative poverty, then a rise in the Supplementary Benefit Scale is required to recognise and (with our usage) to define the increase in poverty.

If we accept the definition of those in poverty as those whose income falls below the Supplementary Benefit Scale, it is clear that we are not dealing with any definition of absolute poverty. The basic scale for the assistance of poverty was first introduced in 1948 as a result of the Beveridge Report. But the scale has been greatly raised since 1948. Thus between October 1948 and 1970 the weekly rate for a three-child family (excluding any allowance for rent) has been raised from £3.35 to £13.90, a rise of 315 per cent. Between these dates the cost-of-living index (excluding housing) rose only by 134.7 per cent, so that in real terms the rate of benefit has risen by 77 per cent.

Indeed, the Supplementary Benefit rates have risen even more rapidly than the disposable income of the average wage-earner. In October 1970 the disposable income of the wage-earner with average gross earnings and with three children (i.e. earnings plus family allowances less tax, national insurance contributions, average housing costs, and employment expenses) was £20.50. Thus the corresponding Supplementary Benefit rate of £13.90 was 68 per cent of this average disposable income. This percentage was only some 57 per cent in 1948.[3]

But if poverty is defined as being below the minimum standard set by the Supplementary Benefit Scale and if the Supplementary Benefit system were simply a system for guaranteeing everyone an income at least as high as this minimum standard, would it not follow that there could by

---

[3] See p. 2 of 'Two Parent Families', Department of Health and Social Security Statistical Report Series No. 14 (HMSO, 1971). The estimate for 1948 has been kindly provided by the Department.

definition be no poverty in Britain? We might still ask whether the scale was adequate and we might still ask how many people need the assistance of the Supplementary Benefit system to keep them out of poverty. But there would be no point in discussing the amount of poverty in Britain.

In fact a substantial number of people do fall below the Supplementary Benefit level. The relief of poverty is in a terrible muddle in this country; and the object of my paper is to explain the nature of that muddle and to suggest a way out.

To understand the nature of the problem let us start by considering the nature of the system as it developed from the end of World War II up to the beginning of the 1960s. Beveridge's famous plan of 1942 was based on three ideas: first, social insurance for Sickness, Unemployment, Industrial Injuries, Widowhood, and Old Age whereby in return for compulsory insurance contributions payable by insured persons and their employers together with contributions from the state out of general tax revenue, everyone was to receive weekly benefits in times of these defined categories of need; second, family allowances were to be paid to parents to help with the support of all dependent children after the first dependent child; and, third, national assistance – what was later to be called Supplementary Benefit and what I will therefore inaccurately call Supplementary Benefit throughout this paper – was to be available on a scale calculated to avoid absolute poverty to anyone not in work who for one reason or another fell into poverty through the social-insurance–family-allowance net.

If social insurance benefits and family allowances were paid on scales at least as generous as those of Supplementary Benefit and if everyone in employment earned an income which after payment of tax, insurance contributions, and working expenses was at least equal to the Supplementary Benefit of a married couple plus one child (subsequent children being eligible for adequate family allowances), very few would have been in poverty and in need of Supplementary Benefit, which would have been confined to a few special groups not covered by national insurance, such as deserted families and the congenitally disabled.

But there were two reasons why this was not so. In the first place the scales of social insurance benefits and of family allowances in particular were initially set, and have ever since continued to be set, on a scale appreciably below the entitlements to Supplementary Benefit (including rent allowances), so that many who were sick, unemployed, retired, disabled, widowed, or in work with large families may need supplementation to bring them up to the minimum standard.

Secondly, there is an acute problem of rents. At present there is an enormous range of variation in the rents charged for very similar dwellings and rent is a very important part of the cost of living of a poor family. As a result social insurance benefits and family allowances, if they were paid at the same money rate to all beneficiaries, would have to be at an extravagant rate in order to meet the needs of those who had to face the highest rent charges. These fixed money benefits must be geared to some average money rent. But even if they were sufficient to keep the payer of average rent out of poverty (which they are not), they would have to be supplemented in the case of people who have to meet a much higher rent. The Supplementary Benefit Scales are in fact for this very reason expressed in terms of a fixed money scale to meet other needs plus an additional variable sum to meet whatever rent the particular family (with adequate safeguards) has to pay.

The result of all this is that the Supplementary Benefit system, instead of being as Beveridge intended a safety net which was scarcely ever used, has become an institution of central importance. Yet in spite of the fact that many do receive Supplementary Benefit there are still many familes whose incomes remain below the Supplementary Benefit level. These families fall into three main classes.

First, some people who are eligible for Supplementary Benefits do not in fact claim them. This is partly due to ignorance of their rights and the procedures for making a claim, and party due to a very laudable, but unfortunate pride which makes people unwilling to admit poverty and to seek means-tested aid. There still surrounds the Supplementary Benefit system an atmosphere of the old poor law, under which every kind of social stigma was deliberately attached to the workhouse in order to minimise reliance on that system of relief. The post-World War II reforms completed the break-up of the old poor law and introduced a national assistance board in the place of the local poor law. In 1966 the Labour Government, in an attempt to remove the atmosphere of social stigma, changed the name of the institution from national assistance to Supplementary Benefits, transferred responsibility for the institution to the same department as that which handled the acceptable social benefits under the social insurance schemes, and relaxed some of the rules attaching to the supplementation of benefits. But there are still those who fail to claim the benefits which are due to them.

There is a second category of people whose incomes remain below the poverty level. Supplementary Benefit cannot be paid to anyone who is in full-time employment. There are persons in such employment with net incomes below the Supplementary Benefit scale for a married couple with one child; and since the family allowances payable for additional children are below the Supplementary Benefit allowances for children, a man earning a low wage but with a large family will fall well below the minimum standard.[4] Moreover, it is a general principle of the Supplementary Benefit system, the 'wage-stop' rule, that if a man is out of work he must not be paid in Supplementary Benefit an amount which would bring his income above that which he would receive in work, so that an unemployed man with a large family whose normal work was in a low-paid occupation must continue below the minimum standard.

There is a third category to be considered. Supplementary Benefit is not payable to those who refuse suitable available work. It is not payable to men on strike, though it is payable in respect of the dependents of those on strike. Moreover, in the case of unmarried unskilled men under 45 in districts in which there is deemed to be no surplus of such labour Supplementary Benefit may be payable in the first instance only for the

---

[4] This deficiency is reduced but not necessarily removed by the scheme for Family Income Supplement, introduced in 1970 and described below (p. 325).

first four weeks of unemployment, it being assumed that any person in this category in this district can find a job in that time. Renewal of payment at the end of the four weeks is subject to special control.

One may well ask why social insurance benefits and family allowances have been consistently kept below the Supplementary Benefit entitlements since the end of World War II. A main reason has been the cost of their finance at the Supplementary Benefit levels; and one reason for the considerable cost involved is that they are payable to everybody who is in the defined category. A rich man, a moderately well-off man, and a poor man will all receive additional income from the raising of national insurance benefits and family allowances. If these benefits were payable only to those who needed them to bring their other incomes up to the poverty level, the cost would, of course, be reduced. But this would be equivalent to scrapping the whole of the national insurance and family allowance parts of the Beveridge scheme (which were intended to deal with the whole problem) and to rely solely on Supplementary Benefits (which were expected to be an almost negligible part of the system). We have an apparent dilemma between the universal principle which is more expensive and the means-tested assistance principle, which is less expensive but also less effective because some people are too proud to use it and which many others dislike because it divides the nation into two groups – paupers and non-paupers.

There is one important feature in the definition of needs and resources for the purposes of Supplementary Benefits which may cause us to exaggerate the amount of poverty in Britain. Since World War II needs and resources have been assessed on a 'family', as contrasted with a 'household', basis. Let me illustrate the point. Husband and wife and dependent children make up the family. Granny, who lives with them, is a member of the 'household', but not of the 'family'. Suppose husband and wife to be earning a large income, while granny has no income. On a household basis granny is not in need, since the household's income is fully sufficient to support granny comfortably. On the present family basis granny is in desperate poverty since she constitutes a separate family and has no income. But she may in fact be living in decent comfort.

But when all is said and done there is now considerable evidence that a substantial number of families are living below the minimum standard. We used to think that the post-World War II reforms, summed up in the phrase 'the Welfare State', had eliminated poverty. Work since the early 1960s by Titmuss, Townsend, Abel-Smith, Dorothy Wedderburn, Atkinson, and others has now disabused us of this comfortable myth. The Child Poverty Action Group has put the subject on the political map. A number of special official inquiries into retirement pensioners in 1965, into families receiving family allowances in 1966, and into two-parent families in 1971 have revealed substantial groups in poverty. In the event, during the last decade, there have been a large number of piecemeal reforms, which I can do little more than catalogue.

1   In 1961 a scheme of graduated pensions was introduced, whereby in return for additional contributions during working life, geared to the insured person's earnings, a pension on retirement which is related to the

pensioner's previous income is added on top of the existing flat-rate pension. This scheme, however, adds only a small amount to the pre-existing state flat-rate pension. Moreover, the amount so added will be greater for those who had higher earnings during their working life and are, one would expect, the least likely to be in want on retirement. The scheme is not designed to be, and will not in fact turn out to be, an important element in the elimination of poverty. Moreover, in my opinion governments would be well advised to concentrate on measures which will ensure incomes to everyone at the basic minimum standard and to leave supplementation above this to private savings without any special governmental assistance or tax privileges. But the organisation of individual savings and pensions is another long story that I cannot tackle on this occasion.

2   In 1965 the Government introduced a scheme of redundancy payments whereby persons dismissed from their jobs because work was no longer available for them received certain payments which were the larger (i) the higher their pay in work and (ii) the longer they had served in their present employment. Such payments may well take the edge off poverty that might otherwise have been experienced while another job was being found. There is, thus, some effect in the relief of poverty; but this again is not a scheme which will have a very large effect on the number in poverty nor indeed is it designed expressly for that purpose.

3   In 1966 a scheme was introuduced for income-related benefits for unemployment, sickness, and widowhood under which (as in the case of graduated pensions) in return for additional contributions benefits related to earnings are paid for a limited period in addition to the flat-rate benefits. Once again this scheme will make a small, but only a small, dent into poverty.

4   Over the post-war years there has grown up a whole host of different, particular schemes for the relief of low income earnings, each subject to its own particular test of means and definition of what constitutes needs. Thus there are means tests for maintenance allowances for children who stay at school beyond school leaving age, for school dinners, for school uniforms and essential clothing, for day nurseries, for grants to students in places of higher education, for fees for boarding schools, for direct grant school fees, for home helps, for dental services, spectacles, and medical prescriptions, for legal aid, for rebates of rents and of rates, as well as for the payment of income tax and the receipt of Family Income Supplements which I will discuss in due course. Many of these schemes lie in the province of local governments. Such schemes may exist in one locality and not in another, and where they do exist the definition of needs and the scales of benefit may well differ as between one authority and another. Indeed it has been estimated that if one takes all the different schemes in all the different authorities into account there may well be about 3,000 different forms on which claims can be made in this country for means-tested help of one kind or another.[5]

5   In the course of 1967/68 family allowances were raised by £0.50 a

[5] Mike Reddin, 'Local Authority Means-tested Services', in *Social Services for All?*, Fabian Tract 382 (Fabian Society, 1968), pp. 7–15.

week from £0.40 to £0.90 for the second child and from £0.50 to £1.00 for all subsequent children. A large part of the cost of this operation was covered by what came to be known as the 'clawback', which involved a simultaneous reduction in the allowances for children under the income tax of such a kind that a person who paid income tax at the standard rate lost in tax relief almost exactly as much as he gained in higher family allowances. As a result the relief to large families, although it was paid out in the form of universal family allowances to all families rich or poor, was felt only by those whose incomes were below the levels at which they became liable to pay income tax at the standard rate. In effect this was using the income tax machinery as a means-test for family help. The new and higher family allowances still remained appreciably below the Supplementary Benefit scales for children which now range from £1.70 a week for a child between 0 and 5 to £3.00 for a child between 13 and 15 years of age, whereas family allowances are zero for the first child, £0.90 for the second child, and £1.00 a week for all subsequent children. The increase in family allowances did not, therefore, eliminate poverty in large families with low earnings but it was an important move in this direction.

6   In 1970 the present Government introduced the Family Income Supplement scheme which was expressly designed to relieve poverty in families with low earnings relatively to the size of their families. For the purpose of this scheme a schedule of notional family incomes is laid down, this notional income being the higher the larger the number of children in the family. Those whose actual income from earnings, family allowances, or other sources falls below the notional income relevant for their family size can apply for a supplementation of their actual income by an amount equal to one-half of the deficiency of their actual income below the scheduled notional income. This scheme also makes an important contribution to the relief of poverty. But it is by no means a complete cure. In the first place the scales in the scheme are such that these family income supplements may make up only a part of the deficiencies of family incomes below the supplementary benefit levels especially in the case of a family with an above-average rent to pay. Secondly, the scheme involves the introduction of yet one more major means test[6] and by no means all of those families who are eligible for Family Income Supplements have applied for them. Thus the Minister concerned stated that by December 1971 only 68,000 families out of an estimated total of 140,000 eligible families had taken up their rights.

7   The present Government has before Parliament a most important Housing Finance Bill a main part of which is designed to have, and will in fact have, far-reaching effects upon poverty. This bill is such a major measure, the market for housing is in such a complicated muddle, and rent is so important an element in the family budget of those at or near the poverty level that I must make a considerable digression at this point into a discussion of the present housing situation.

---

[6] At the same time it simplifies some other means tests since any family which qualifies for Family Income Supplement is automatically entitled, without further test, to free school meals, welfare milk and welfare foods, and exemption from prescription, dental, and ophthalmic charges.

There are three main sources of supply of housing.

(1)    Owner-occupied houses.
(2)    Lettings of furnished and unfurnished dwellings by private landlords.
(3)    Lettings of unfurnished dwellings by local councils.

In the case of owner-occupied houses a very substantial and in my view most unfortunate tax relief is given to anyone who owns his own house by exempting the annual value of the house from liability to income tax and sur-tax.[7] Consider sur-tax payer A using Stock Exchange dividends to rent a house from sur-tax payer B. A will pay income and sur-tax on his investment income and will pay rent to B out of the remainder of his tax-free income. B will then pay income and sur-tax on the rent received from A. This is as it should be; there are two rich men and two incomes from two important real capital assets, one from the profits of the companies whose shares are held by A, and one from the annual value of the house owned by B. If now A hands over his securities to B and B hands over the house to A so that A is now an owner-occupier, no income or sur-tax will be paid on the annual value of the house, though income and sur-tax will, of course, still be payable on the investment income.

The undesirable results of this are fourfold: first, it is a way of giving tax exemption on a most important part of the real income of owner-occupiers provided they are rich enough to pay tax, an exemption which is the more important the richer the man concerned and the higher the rate of sur-tax to which he is liable; second, it encourages the demand for housing by the rich, since this form of investment has so important a tax privilege, and thus diverts building resources and available land to the rich end of the market and drives up the price of houses and building land against the poorer end of the market; third, it greatly discourages the building of houses for letting as contrasted with building for owner-occupiers; and, fourth, by reducing in an important way the tax base, it means that the rates of income tax and sur-tax on the remaining sources of income must be so much the higher in order to raise the total tax revenue which may be necessary on budgetary grounds.[8]

Privately owned houses for letting to tenants, on the other hand, have been granted no such tax privileges. On the contrary, they are subject to a tax disadvantage in that for tax purposes dwelling-houses are assumed to last for ever and no depreciation allowance may be deducted from the rent before tax liability is assessed. But, much more important than this, rent control legislation which has persisted in one form or another since World War I to prevent private landlords from exploiting situations of

[7] The owner-occupier is, of course, liable to pay local rates which are assessed on a notional annual value of his house. But other owners of real property are also liable to pay such rates in addition to income tax and sur-tax on the annual income earned on their property.

[8] If the annual value of owner-occupied houses were liable to tax, mortgage interest would, of course, be allowed as a deduction from the annual value before liability to income tax was assessed. The *raison d'être* of the present mortgage option scheme would disappear; and it should be allowed to lapse.

housing scarcity has in fact in many cases been so severe as to make private lettings totally unprofitable. With the Conservative Government's legislation of 1957 followed by the Labour Government's Fair Rent Act of 1965 there is in process a relaxation of rent control which will help to rectify this situation. But the rent of private lettings will still be regulated at a 'fair' level, while owner-occupied houses are totally unregulated and for the well-to-do carry the great tax advantages which I have outlined. It is not surprising that the proportion of all dwellings provided by private landlords fell from 90 per cent to 20 per cent between 1914 and the present day, whereas owner-occupation now makes up some 50 per cent of all dwellings.

The third great source is, of course, council housing. Here there is a notorious unfair muddle. Since World War I the building of council houses has been encouraged by a large number of different subsidy schemes. These subsidies have varied from time to time in a great number of ways.[9] The housing costs which each local authority must meet consist of the maintenance costs of their houses and, most important, the interest and debt service incurred on the loans in the past to finance the building of the houses. Against these costs the local authorities can set the various subsidies paid to them by the Central Government and any subsidies which they choose to contribute out of their own local rates. The balance must be met by charging rents to the tenants of the council houses. Each authority has great freedom in determining how to select the tenants for its houses and how to set the rents charged.

The general level of council house rents is at present kept substantially below the level of the regulated fair rents now being applied to private tenancies; this is possible partly because of the subsidies paid on council houses and partly because many of the money debt charges fixed in the past have been eroded in real terms by the process of general inflation. But the level of the rents charged varies in an arbitrary way from one local authority to another, the position of each authority depending upon historical accident – whether, when the particular houses were built, the money cost of building was high or low, whether at that time the rate of interest at which loans could be raised was high or low, and whether at that time rates of subsidy offered by the Central Government were stingy or generous.

But arbitrary variations in council house rents occur not only because the average level is higher in one locality than in another, but also because the principles on which rents are set may vary from one authority to another. Thus one council may charge the same rent for similar houses to all tenants, another may vary the charge from house to house according to the actual historical cost of building the particular houses concerned, and yet another authority in order to relieve poverty may vary the rents, under a rent rebate scheme, in accordance with the needs and the income of the particular tenants concerned; but at present only one-tenth of existing housing subsidies are used for this purpose of making rent rebates for the poorer tenants.

[9] See A. A. Nevitt, *Housing Taxation and Subsidies* (London: Nelson, 1966), Chapters 6 and 7.

The present bill before Parliament would have three main effects.

1   Council house rents will be moved gradually on to the same fair-rent basis as is now being applied to private lettings. This will be a step forward in removing anomalies as between different sections of the market for houses. A house of a given quality will tend to be charged much more nearly the same rent whether it be a private house or a council house or a house in one locality or in another. But it will involve an average rise of about 50 per cent in the rents of council houses. The present better-off tenants of low-rental council houses will be the losers.

2   There will be a national scheme of rent rebates for council housing and of similar rent allowances for private unfurnished lettings, similar in many ways to the Family Income Supplement scheme of which I have already spoken. That is to say, there will be a national scale under which, according to their income and the size of their family, tenants of both council houses and of private unfurnished dwellings will be able to apply for money allowances to meet part of these 'fair' rents of their dwellings.

3   All existing housing subsidies will be gradually removed. Part of the funds so saved will be used to help with the finance of the rent allowances paid according to the needs of the tenants and part will be used to pay subsidies on slum clearance and to pay subsidies for local authority housing accounts according to their needs for such subsidies to meet their finances after the introduction of the uniform fair rents which all authorities will have to charge. There will be a net saving to the Central Government in the sense that the cost of housing subsidies will be stabilised at its present level of some £200m instead of rising by another £300m over the next ten years as it would otherwise have done.

There are three aspects of this reform which are to be highly commended.[10]

First, the upward movements of the rents of council houses and of private dwellings in a direction which makes them approach more nearly to uniform market levels should do something to relieve the housing shortage which falls with such tragic incidence on those who have not merely missed the luck of becoming the secure tenants of a private dwelling at a low controlled rent or of a subsidised council house but can indeed find no dwelling at all. Some relief of an existing housing shortage can be obtained by making a more efficient use of the existing stock, by giving people an incentive to take lodgers into rooms which are not needed for the family or to move into smaller dwellings when their children have grown up and left the home and when, therefore, less dwelling-space is needed. An upward movement of rents in the direction of a freer market for houses will discourage people from the continued occupation of dwelling-space simply because they have secure possession of a particular dwelling at an exceptionally low rent.

Second, this development should not only help to relieve the housing shortage; it will also increase mobility. People will no longer be inhibited to the same degree from making a move, which they would otherwise have made in order to obtain better employment prospects, simply

[10] Cf. Norman Macrae, 'To Let?' in *Radical Reaction* (ed. R. Harris, London: Hutchinson for Institute of Economic Affairs, 1961), pp. 115–53.

because in their present dwelling they have secure accommodation at an exceptionally low rent.

Third, the equalisation of rents combined with a national scheme of rent rebates and allowances to give aid to poor families in meeting their rents, whether they be the tenants of private landlords or local councils, will enable housing aid to be concentrated on those who need it – provided that they do in fact take it up.

But there are aspects of the present proposals which give cause for concern.

First, I greatly regret that the exemption from tax of the annual value of owner-occupied houses is to continue. The removal of such exemption could help to divert land and building resources into the construction of more modest houses of all kinds for private letting away from the construction of more elaborate houses for purchase by the richer members of society who now receive so great a tax stimulus to spend their wealth on the purchase of more expensive dwelling-space than they would otherwise have wished to purchase. But it would be desirable if poorer owner-occupiers and poorer tenants of furnished accommodation could receive some assistance comparable to the rent rebates and allowances now proposed for the tenants of unfurnished houses.

Second, the scheme for rent rebates and allowances introduces yet one more major and complicated set of means tests with all the problems which we have come to associate with the multiplication of such tests.

Third, the costs of these important housing reforms will inevitably fall predominantly on the moderately well-off council house tenant who does not qualify for a rent rebate but whose rent will be substantially increased. Such tenants will be meeting not only the main part of the costs of the rent rebates and allowances, but also the future saving of £300m a year of housing subsidies. It is not, I think, unfair that the peculiar privilege of an exceptionally heavily subsidised council house should be gradually removed from the reasonably well-off council tenant. But what should be, and what will be, done with the £300m saved at their expense in future subsidies? This, of course, depends upon unknown future budgetary decisions. But if these sums were to be devoted to the relief of poverty, then we should have witnessed that rate event – an extension of the use of the price mechanism to promote the more efficient use of resources associated with a socially desirable redistribution of income.

The combination of all the various schemes which I have outlined for the relief of poverty has resulted in what can only be described as a great muddle.[11]

The basic fact is that, for the reasons which I have outlined, poverty is not abolished, in spite of great effort and much expenditure.

There is now a very large number of unrelated means-tested schemes of relief of poverty, which in spite of their number and complication do not cover all possible cases of poverty.

[11] For a description of many of the anomalies in the present position see A. B. Atkinson, 'Income Maintenance and Income Taxation', *Journal of Social Policy*, vol. 1 (1972), pp. 135–48.

Social stigma, ignorance, and procedural difficulties prevent the take-up of many of these schemes. But where the unrelated schemes are taken up, they can involve extremely high marginal rates of 'tax' on low incomes[12] in the sense that of an extra earning of £1 a large amount will be lost either in extra tax payments or loss of benefits. Indeed, marginal 'tax' rates can often be over 100 per cent, i.e. an extra £1 of earnings will lead to a reduction in net spendable income. Consider a married couple with one child earning £19.00 a week. If he earns an extra £1, he loses his entitlement to the Family Income Supplement, he pays a trifle more than 30 per cent in income tax, and he will have to pay more in graduated insurance contributions. These items alone account for nearly 85 per cent of his increased earnings. Other miscellaneous means-tested benefits, including rent and rate rebates, might well account for the remaining 15 per cent.

Cannot something be done to simplify the whole system of benefits, assistance, and taxation and, above all, in the process to ensure to *everyone* a level of income at least equal to the Supplementary Benefit Scales?

The Chancellor of the Exchequer announced in his recent Budget speech that a scheme of this kind was in preparation. Unfortunately I had committed myself to the Sidney Ball lecture in innocent ignorance of any such official undertaking; and now the time has come for me to deliver my lecture in the knowledge that such a scheme exists, but before any details have been made public. The Chancellor could not have treated me with less consideration! I intend to make the best of a bad job by confining myself to some of the more general problems involved in any such scheme in the hope that this may be of some help to some of you when the Government's proposals are published and you are able to consider them in detail.

I will raise these basic issues by considering in turn each of four basic types of scheme which I will call: (1) Unmodified Social Dividend, (2) Negative Income Tax, (3) Minimum Income Guarantee, (4) Modified Social Dividend.[13]

In order to bring out some basic features of these schemes I shall start with a very much simplified model which I will modify by degrees until I reach the actual situation in the UK in 1970.

Start then with the two assumptions:

(i)   that there is no governmental taxation or expenditure other than that which is needed to deal with the relief of poverty, and

(ii)  the population is made up of a number of families all of which in size and in age and sex composition are exactly the same.

---

[12] See A. R. Prest, *Social benefits and tax rates* published by the Institute of Economic Affairs, Research Monograph 22, 1970; A. Nevitt, 'A "Fair" Deal for Housing', *The Political Quarterly*, vol. 42 (October–December 1971), pp. 428–433.

[13] For a general discussion of such schemes see Christopher Green, *Negative Taxes and the Poverty Problem* (Washington, DC: Brookings Institution, 1967).

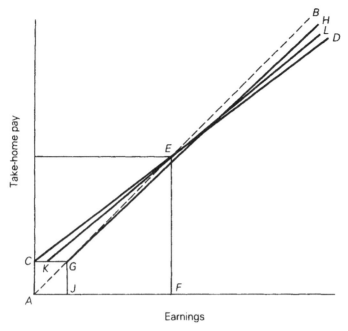

**Figure 1**

Minimum standard $(AJ)$ = ¼ of average earnings $(AF)$.

¹⁄₁₀ of families have no earnings.
²⁄₁₀ of families have earnings of ½ of minimum standard.
⁷⁄₁₀ of families have earnings above minimum standard.

*Line CD*   *Unmodified Social Dividend*. Social Dividend = $AC$.
Tax of 25 per cent on all earnings.
*Negative Income Tax*. Tax-free allowance of $AF$.
Tax of 25 per cent on excess of earnings above $AF$.
Subsidy of 25 per cent on deficiency of earnings below $AF$.

*Line CGH*  *Minimum Income Guarantee*. 100 per cent subsidy on deficiency of earnings below $AJ$.
6¼ per cent tax on excess of earnings above $AJ$.

*Line CKL*  *Modified Social Dividend*. Social Dividend of $AC$.
Flat-rate levy of 40 per cent of Minimum Standard $(CK)$.
Tax of 17½ per cent on excess of earnings above $CK$.

Figure 1 illustrates the four different systems under these very limiting assumptions. Along the horizontal axis we measure income per family before the fiscal measures for redistribution (which, for short, I will call Earnings although in fact it includes income from property as well) and along the vertical axis we measure income per family after the redistributive fiscal measures (which I will call Take-Home Pay for short). The broken line $AB$ at 45° shows the position if no redistributive system is applied; Take-Home Pay equals Earnings.

## (1)   Unmodified Social Dividend

With a pure social dividend scheme[14] every family receives weekly a tax-free social dividend equal to its 'minimum standard' which in Figure 1 I have have assumed to be set at $AJ = AC$, which is ¼ of average Earnings, $AF$. There is a proportional income tax on all Earnings set at a rate which will raise the funds necessary to pay the Social Dividends.

The arithmetic of such a scheme is very simple. If the Social Dividend is set at ¼ of average Earnings, then the rate of income tax must be set to raise a sum equal to ¼ of total Earnings, i.e. at a rate of 25 per cent. This means that every family starts with a Social Dividend equal to $AC$ and then keeps ¾ of its Earnings in addition. If from $C$ we draw $CD$ with a slope of 3 in 4, the height of $CD$ then shows the family's Take-Home Pay. Those who start with Earnings above the average will lose more in tax than they gain in Social Dividend and those with Earnings below the average will gain more in Social Dividend than they lose in tax. The system not only ensures that no family falls below the minimum standard; it also operates as a powerful instrument for the redistribution of income from everyone above the average to everyone below the average. But it involves a high rate of tax equal to the ratio of the minimum standard to average earnings.

## (2)   Negative Income Tax

The line $CD$ also illustrates the effect of a Negative Income Tax.[15] Suppose one operates solely through an income-tax machinery. One sets a tax-free allowance for every family equal to the average income $AF$. On all Earnings above $AF$ one levies a tax of 25 per cent of the excess of Earnings above $AF$, so that Take-Home Pay moves along the line $ED$. On all Earnings below $AF$ one pays a subsidy equal to 25 per cent of the deficiency of Earnings below $AF$, so that Take-Home Pay moves on the line $CE$. The redistributive effect is the same as with an Unmodified Social Dividend scheme provided that the tax-free allowances and the tax rate are set at levels which both balance the budget and also ensure the minimum standard to the family which has zero Earnings; but the administrative machinery differs in a very important respect which I will discuss later.

[14] This type of scheme was first proposed by Lady Juliet Rhys-Williams in *Something to Look Forward To* (London: MacDonald, 1943). A modern version of the proposal is to be found in C. V. Brown and D. A. Dawson, *Personal Taxation Incentives and Tax Reform*, Political and Economic Planning Broadsheet 506, Jan. 1969. See also Sir Brandon Rhys-Williams, *The New Social Contract*, Conservative Political Centre, 1967.

[15] Cf. Milton Friedman, *Capitalism and Freedom* (Chicago: University of Chicago Press, 1962); Dennis Lees, 'Poor Families and Fiscal Reform', *Lloyds Bank Review*, no. 86 (October 1967), pp. 1–15.

## (3) Minimum Income Guarantee

Both the Unmodified Social Dividend and the Negative Income Tax need a high rate of tax equal to the ratio of the minimum standard to the average Earnings and both have marked redistributive effects besides ensuring everyone a minimum standard. One can, however, devise a Minimum Income Guarantee system which confines itself to ensuring the minimum standard to everyone.[16] On Figure 1 we are now on the kinked line *CGH*. This represents a system where the tax-free allowance is set, not at the average Earnings, *AF*, but at the minimum standard, *AJ*. Those whose Earnings are below *AJ* receive an income subsidy equal to 100 per cent of the deficiency of their Earnings below the minimum standard, so that they move on the line *CG*. Those whose Earnings are above the minimum standard are taxed on the excess of their Earnings above the minimum standard at a proportional rate which is sufficient to raise the funds for the subsidisation of those whose Earnings are below the minimum standard.

With the Unmodified Social Dividend and the Negative Income Tax the actual distribution of Earnings made no difference to the proportional rate of tax. If a Social Dividend was to be paid universally at a rate equal to ¼ of average Earnings, then a proportional tax rate of 25 per cent on all Earnings is implied regardless of the original distribution of Earnings around the average. Let me take an extreme example. Suppose Earnings were in fact equally divided. Then no family would gain or lose. Every family would receive a Social Dividend equal to ¼ of its Earnings which it would finance by paying a tax of 25 per cent on its Earnings. The only result would be a marginal disincentive since any family which earned £1 more (or less) would gain (or lose) only 75p instead of 100p in Take-Home Pay. This system is clearly wasteful unless there are important inequalities to be corrected.

A Minimum Income Guarantee does not suffer from this disability. If there were no family Earnings below the minimum standard, a zero rate of income tax on Earnings above the minimum standard would be required. The necessary rate of tax depends upon the number and size of the various family Earnings which are below the minimum standard. I have in Figure 1 made up the story that 10 per cent of the families have no Earnings because of unemployment, sickness, old age, etc., and that 20 per cent have low Earnings which are equal only to ½ of the minimum standard, everyone else's Earnings being above the minimum standard. I need not bother you with the arithmetic[17] but if my arithmetic is correct this means that a rate of tax of only 6¼ per cent (instead of 25 per cent) would have to be imposed on these other Earnings. The slope of *GH* is drawn accordingly, 93¾ points up for every 100 points along.

The Minimum Income Guarantee scheme thus implies a much lower rate of tax on Earnings above the minimum standard. But, so far as

---

[16] It is the type of system suggested in *Policy for Poverty*, Research Monograph No. 20, published by the Institute of Economic Affairs, 1970.

[17] The relevant formulae are given in Appendix II [pp. 350–51].

disincentive effects are concerned, it does so with a much greater disincentive effect on Earnings below the minimum standard, since any family which adds £1 to its Earnings below the minimum standard will lose £1 in income subsidy – a marginal tax rate of 100 per cent instead of the 25 per cent of the Unmodified Social Dividend or the Negative Income Tax.

## (4)  A Modified Social Dividend

With a fairly simple modification of the Social Dividend Scheme of a kind which I proposed in 1948[18] it is possible to reach a solution between these two extremes. The proposal is to combine the Social Dividend payments with a lump-sum tax on those who have independent Earnings – or more accurately a tax of 100 per cent on the first slice of Earnings, this first slice being less than the Social Dividend itself. This I will call a 'flat-rate levy'. It all sounds complicated; but the basic idea is very simple. Every family receives a weekly tax-free sacrosanct lump-sum Social Dividend sufficient to cover its minimum standard; but those with adequate income pay back, as it were, a part of this in the form of a fixed 'flat-rate' levy. This raises part of the revenue required to finance the Social Dividend, and the remainder is raised by a somewhat lower proportional rate of income tax on all Earnings left after the payment of the flat-rate levy.

In Figure 1 this is shown by the kinked line *CKL*. I have assumed that the 100 per cent flat-rate levy is on a first slice of Earning equal to 40 per cent of the minimum standard. The proportional rate of income tax needed in this case will be 17½ per cent – something in between the 25 per cent of the Unmodified Social Dividend and the 6¼ per cent of the Minimum Income Guarantee. The family now receives its minimum standard in any case, pays 100 per cent tax on a first slice of its Earnings equal to 40 per cent of the minimum standard, and a rate of tax of 17½ per cent on the remainder of its Earnings.

The flat-rate levy under a Modified Social Dividend scheme might be operated as part of the income-tax machinery, in the form of a tax at 100 per cent on the first slice of all income other than the Social Dividend. An alternative possibility is that the flat-rate levy should be raised by continuing to charge the existing flat-rate national insurance contributions at an appropriately increased rate, the proportional rate of income tax then being levied on all income (other than the Social Dividend) remaining after payment of these flat-rate contributions.

There are many other possible ways in which a pure Social Dividend scheme might be modified. One which has much to recommend it is that in addition to a proportional rate of tax levied on all income other than the Social Dividend, there should be an additional levy which was proportional to Earnings but which would have an upper limit set to it – an arrangement comparable to the present wage-related insurance contributions. The line *CKL* of Fig. 1 would still be kinked at *K*, but the portion *CK* would slope upwards though less steeply than the remainder *KL*.

---

[18] See J. E. Meade, *Planning and the Price Mechanism* (London: Allen & Unwin, 1948), chapter III and Appendix I.

In Figure 1 I have assumed that no taxes were needed except those for the relief of poverty. I did this in order to emphasise some of the very simple underlying relationships which are implied in the use of fiscal measures solely for the purpose of redistributing income. But let us now allow for the fact that revenue must be raised for other expenditure as well. In Figure 2 I assume that a revenue equal to 25 per cent of the national income must be raised to finance other forms of government expenditure in addition to that needed for the relief of poverty and the redistribution of personal disposable incomes. The total income available for redistribution among families will thus be only 75 per cent of the total national income; and I assume that the minimum standard is now set at 25 per cent of this reduced average family disposable income. The result will be that the proportional rate of tax must be raised from 25 per cent to 44 per cent in the case of the Unmodified Social Dividend and the Negative Income Tax schemes, from 6¼ per cent to 34 per cent in the case of the Minimum Income Guarantee, and from 17½ per cent to 39½ per cent in the case of the Modified Social Dividend scheme. The results are shown in Figure 2.

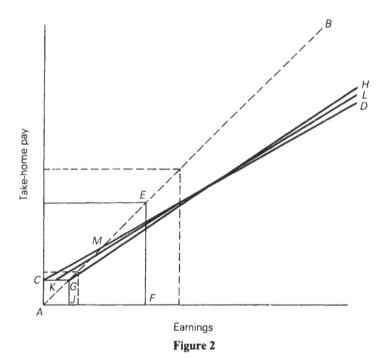

**Figure 2**

Same as Figure 1 except that additional revenue equal to 25 per cent of national earnings is raised for other government expenditures. Minimum standard and flat-rate levies are also reduced by 25 per cent in line with average family disposable income. Proportional tax rates raised to balance the budget.

*Line CD*    Tax rate raised from 25 to 44 per cent.
*Line CGH*  Tax rate raised from 6¼ to 34 per cent.
*Line CKL*  Tax rate raised from 17½ to 39½ per cent.

Let us next relax the assumption that all families are identical in size, age, and sex composition. We can in fact best do this by moving on to a consideration of the actual position in this country.

In the table on p. 337 I show certain results for an Unmodified and for a Modified Social Dividend scheme applied to the actual conditions of the United Kingdom in 1970. It is assumed for the Unmodified Social Dividend scheme

(i) that Social Dividends were paid to the various family groups which actually existed in 1970 at the rates of Supplementary Benefit (including average rents) which ruled in 1970 for the families of different sizes and compositions;

(ii) that national insurance and health contributions payable by insured persons, national insurance benefits, Supplementary Benefits, and family allowances were all abolished; and

(iii) that income tax and sur-tax were replaced by a proportional income tax on all incomes other than the Social Dividends, the rate of tax being that which was needed to maintain the 1970 balance between total governmental revenue and expenditure. This rate would have been about 53 per cent – or 10s 7d in the £.

In the case of a Modified Social Dividend scheme I have assumed that the flat-rate levies took the form of the retention of the flat-rate national insurance contributions by insured persons, these contributions being raised six-fold. This would have involved a fixed-rate levy of £275 a year for an adult male worker, in part repayment of his tax-free Social Dividend which would have ranged from £340 a year if he were unmarried to £845 a year if he had a wife and three children to support. In this case the proportional rate of tax required on all other income would be some 43 per cent (or 8s 7d in the £) as compared with the 53 per cent (or 10s 7d in the £) of the Unmodified Social Dividend scheme. These rates compare with the 1970 standard rate of income tax on earned incomes of 32 per cent (or 6s 5d in the £) and on unearned incomes of 41¼ per cent (or 8s 3d in the £).

Both Social Dividend schemes would thus require a considerable increase in the standard rate of tax. The effect on the Take-Home Pay of various families of different sizes and compositions and with different levels of Earnings is shown in the table. The main effects are not surprising. Both schemes would cause a marked rise in the standard rate of tax on earned incomes; and both schemes would redistribute income markedly from rich to poor and from small to large families. All these effects would be less marked in the case of the Modified than in the case of the Unmodified Social Dividend scheme.

There are in fact many other possible variants of schemes for the unification and simplification of our present jumble of arrangements for the relief of poverty; but we cannot discuss every possible variant. I shall confine myself to a discussion of my four basic types. This will, I hope, serve to bring out some of the main points; and I must leave you to build to your own particular design on these foundations.

**Take-Home Pay (£ per annum)**

| Earnings (£ per annum) | Single A | B | C | Married couple A | B | C | Married couple with one child A | B | C | Married couple with two children A | B | C | Married couple with three children A | B | C | Married couple with four children A | B | C |
|---|---|---|---|---|---|---|---|---|---|---|---|---|---|---|---|---|---|---|
| 500 | 426 | 575 | 468 | 452 | 753 | 646 | 452 | 862 | 755 | 499 | 971 | 864 | 551 | 1080 | 972 | 603 | 1189 | 1082 |
| 600 | 489 | 622 | 525 | 547 | 800 | 703 | 547 | 909 | 812 | 594 | 1018 | 921 | 646 | 1127 | 1030 | 698 | 1236 | 1139 |
| 700 | 552 | 669 | 582 | 610 | 847 | 760 | 642 | 956 | 869 | 689 | 1065 | 978 | 741 | 1174 | 1087 | 793 | 1283 | 1196 |
| 800 | 615 | 716 | 639 | 673 | 894 | 817 | 725 | 1003 | 926 | 784 | 1112 | 1035 | 836 | 1221 | 1144 | 888 | 1330 | 1253 |
| 900 | 678 | 763 | 696 | 735 | 941 | 874 | 788 | 1050 | 983 | 855 | 1161 | 1092 | 926 | 1268 | 1201 | 983 | 1377 | 1310 |
| 1000 | 742 | 810 | 753 | 800 | 988 | 931 | 852 | 1097 | 1040 | 919 | 1206 | 1149 | 990 | 1315 | 1258 | 1060 | 1424 | 1367 |
| 1200 | 872 | 904 | 867 | 929 | 1082 | 1045 | 982 | 1191 | 1154 | 1049 | 1300 | 1262 | 1120 | 1409 | 1372 | 1190 | 1518 | 1481 |
| 1400 | 1002 | 998 | 981 | 1059 | 1176 | 1159 | 1112 | 1285 | 1268 | 1179 | 1394 | 1377 | 1250 | 1503 | 1486 | 1320 | 1612 | 1595 |
| 1600 | 1132 | 1092 | 1095 | 1190 | 1270 | 1273 | 1242 | 1379 | 1382 | 1309 | 1488 | 1491 | 1380 | 1597 | 1600 | 1451 | 1706 | 1709 |
| 1800 | 1268 | 1186 | 1209 | 1326 | 1364 | 1387 | 1378 | 1473 | 1496 | 1445 | 1582 | 1605 | 1516 | 1691 | 1714 | 1586 | 1800 | 1823 |
| 2000 | 1404 | 1280 | 1323 | 1461 | 1458 | 1501 | 1514 | 1567 | 1610 | 1581 | 1676 | 1719 | 1652 | 1785 | 1828 | 1722 | 1894 | 1937 |
| 2500 | 1743 | 1515 | 1608 | 1801 | 1693 | 1786 | 1854 | 1802 | 1895 | 1921 | 1911 | 2004 | 1991 | 2020 | 2113 | 2062 | 2129 | 2222 |
| 3000 | 2083 | 1750 | 1893 | 2141 | 1928 | 2071 | 2193 | 2030 | 2180 | 2260 | 2146 | 2289 | 2331 | 2255 | 2398 | 2401 | 2364 | 2507 |
| 4000 | 2762 | 2120 | 2463 | 2820 | 2398 | 2641 | 2872 | 2507 | 2750 | 2939 | 2616 | 2859 | 3010 | 2725 | 2968 | 3081 | 2834 | 3077 |

Figures in italics show those who lose by introduction of Social Dividend Schemes.

A = 1970 situation. National insurance contributions, family allowances, and income tax at 1970 rates.

B = Unmodified Social Dividend scheme. Social Dividends equal to 1970 Supplementary Benefit rates (including average rent allowance) with tax at 53 per cent on all earnings.

C = Modified Social Dividend scheme. Social Dividends as in B with £275 a year national insurance contribution and tax at 43 per cent on all earnings.

All of these four schemes are attempts to mould the many existing independent schemes of social benefits, means-tested aid to the poor, and taxation of incomes into a single consistent unit. But in present conditions they would all of them need to be combined with special arrangements for housing costs in order to meet the widely discrepant needs of families, otherwise similarly situated, arising out of the great divergences in rents or other costs of housing. It would be possible to include in the Social Dividend or in the Minimum Income Guarantee or in the tax-free allowances under the Negative Income Tax an amount to cover the average rent payable by the size of family concerned. But in all cases one would have to continue with some special administrative arrangement to make payments in individual cases to help meet above-average rents in the case of poor families. This element of the present miscellany of schemes could not be fully integrated into any single unified scheme until the process of integration of conditions in the different sectors of the housing market had gone very much further than at present.

The problem of rents for housing is common to all these schemes. But it is interesting to go on to consider some of the ways in which they differ.

In the first place, there is a most important administrative difference between the Social Dividend schemes on the one hand and the Negative Income Tax and Minimum Income Guarantee schemes on the other hand. With the Social Dividend schemes a minimum-standard allowance is paid out weekly to everybody rich or poor through the Post Office or other similar administrative arrangements; and it is then the job of the tax authorities to extract revenue according to the level of the other income of the citizens concerned. With the Negative Income Tax and Minimum Income Guarantee schemes a single tax authority has to pay out in income subsidy, or to levy in income tax, a given net amount according as the citizen's income falls below or above a pre-determined level. The Social Dividend type of administrative arrangement involves a much larger gross turnover of funds than do the Negative Income Tax or Minimum Income Guarantee types of system. In spite of this, however, the Social Dividend type of administrative arrangement is, in my opinion, to be preferred. Citizens' needs and cash receipts may vary from week to week; and with self-employed or part-time workers or casual workers or persons with small incomes from property it may be very difficult to make a prompt weekly adjustment of any net income subsidy or tax under an income-tax administrative machine. With the Social Dividend type of arrangement everyone is guaranteed the minimum-standard income every week; there is no problem of people not taking up their rights; and the means-tested adjustment is then carried out solely by the taxation of their other income through the accepted machinery of the income-tax authorities on a basis which does not require the same degree of precise, prompt response to meet a sudden or irregular change of income flow.

The administration of a Social Dividend scheme should be feasible.

The payment of a weekly Social Dividend to every family in the country would be a massive affair and would involve keeping up to date the recording of all changes in family circumstances which involved changes in Social Dividend payments. The levying of a proportional tax on all other incomes would mean that the income-tax authorities would have to extend the scope of their operations over all families whereas at present many whose incomes are below the tax exemption limit file no tax return. On the other hand, the income-tax authorities would no longer have to cope with so complicated a pattern of tax allowances, and the apparatus of administration of national insurance and of Supplementary Benefits could for the most part be disbanded, though – as long as the present lack of uniformity in rents persists – some special machinery for rent allowances would have to be continued.

The administration of a Modified Social Dividend scheme would be somewhat more complicated, since there would be the additional task of assessing and raising the flat-rate levies, either through the income-tax machinery or else by maintaining the machinery for the collection of national insurance contributions. In the latter case, the very marked rise in the size of such contributions would intensify the problem of devising special rules for reduced contributions by part-time workers or other special categories of persons whose incomes (other than their Social Dividend) might be very low relatively to these high national insurance contributions. It is most undesirable to introduce arrangements which make it difficult for employer or worker to arrange for part-time or intermittent work in appropriate cases. For this reason there is much to be said in favour of basing a Modified Social Dividend scheme (as suggested on p. 334 above), not on increases in the flat-rate national insurance contributions, but on the total replacement of flat-rate contributions by graduated contributions. The graduated contributions would, as at present, be subject to an upper limit, but would be levied at a much higher rate than at present. In this case the contributions of part-time or casual workers would be automatically adjusted to their earnings.

As far as the distribution of income is concerned, the effects of the Unmodified Social Dividend and of the Negative Income Tax can be identical. Both are represented by the line *CD* on Fig. 2. But this identity holds only if both schemes are so devised as to ensure the same minimum standard, namely *AC*, to those whose Earnings are zero. This means that the tax-free allowances under the Negative Income Tax must be at the level represented by the point *M* in Fig. 2 where Take-Home Pay is equal to Earnings. If, however, the tax-free allowances under the Negative Income Tax were in fact set much lower than this, the Negative Income Tax would operate with a somewhat lower proportional rate of tax but would ensure a lower standard than the 'minimum standard' *AC* to those whose Earnings were zero. In fact the income-tax arrangements in this country in 1970 were such that the tax-free allowances for families of various compositions were not vastly different from the Supplementary

Benefit entitlements (including average rents) of similar families.[19] If the tax-free allowances exactly coincided with the minimum standard incomes, then in terms of Fig. 2 the line $CD$ would have been lowered until the point $M$ moved down the $AB$ line and coincided with the point $G$. Clearly those with Earnings less than the minimum standard would have had only a fraction of this deficiency made up in income subsidies. Thus while there is no structural difference between the Unmodified Social Dividend and a Negative Income Tax in so far as their distributional effects are concerned, they will in fact have the same effect only if the tax-free allowances under the Negative Income Tax are raised sufficiently far above the minimum standard which it is intended to ensure even to those with zero Earnings. As between the Unmodified Social Dividend and the Negative Income Tax the administrative structure is very different but the distributional structure is the same.

Similarly, the difference between a Minimum Income Guarantee scheme and a Modified Social Dividend scheme is essentially an administrative one, and not one which has any necessary implication for its distributional effect. Thus the kinked line $CKL$ (the Modified Social Dividend scheme of Figure 2) can be made to correspond with the kinked line $CGH$ (the Minimum Income Guarantee scheme of Figure 2) by raising the flat-rate levy under the Minimum Income Guarantee scheme from $CK$ to $CG$.

There is, however, a structural distributional difference between Negative Income Tax and Unmodified Social Dividend schemes on the one hand and Minimum Income Guarantee and Modified Social Dividend schemes on the other. The Negative Income Tax and Unmodified Social Dividend schemes both imply a single proportional rate of tax on all earnings, while the Minimum Income Guarantee and Modified Social Dividend schemes both imply a 100 per cent rate of tax on the lowest earnings and in consequence a lower rate of tax on higher earnings.

The Modified Social Dividend scheme is the most flexible of all the four schemes in its effect on distribution. An Unmodified Social Dividend scheme allows only a single choice of the balance between two sets of policy instruments, namely (*a*) the scale for Social Dividend payments and (*b*) the level of the proportional rate of tax. The modified scheme allows in addition for a third set of policy instruments, namely (*c*) the scale for the flat-rate levies. Social Dividend payments could be

---

[19] In fact in 1970 the two scales were as follows:

|  | Supplementary Benefit (including allowance for average rent) | Personal, children's, and earned income allowances for tax-free income under the income tax |
|---|---|---|
|  | £ per annum | |
| Single person | 340 | 418 |
| Married couple | 518 | 598 |
| Married couple and one child | 627 | 746 |
| Married couple and two children | 736 | 840 |
| Married couple and three children | 845 | 934 |
| Married couple and four children | 954 | 1028 |

differentiated not only by age and marital status of the recipients, but also by other categories as well, such as blindness, disability, and so on. With a modified scheme the flat-rate levies or national insurance contributions would also, as at present, be differentiated into various categories, by age, sex, part-time workers, self-employed, etc. But these categories could themselves be varied and new distinctions introduced. A modified Social Dividend scheme with possible variations in the balance between (*a*) Social Dividend scales and categories, (*b*) social insurance contribution scales and categories, and (*c*) the rate of tax on other income can become a very flexible instrument.

The table on p. 337 shows the effects which an Unmodified Social Dividend scheme and a Modified Social Dividend scheme, of the kinds described in detail in Appendix I [pp. 347–50], would have had in 1970 on the distribution of income both as between rich and poor families and also as between childless and fertile families.

These differences in their distributional effects are associated with differences in tax rates, which in turn will give rise to differences in incentives to work and to earn income. Indeed, the one great question mark which hangs over an Unmodified Social Dividend scheme is whether the high rate of tax of rather more than 50 per cent which it might involve on additional earnings might not have intolerable disincentive effects. There are two reasons why I personally believe that these dangers are frequently exaggerated.

In the first place, under existing arrangements with sur-tax rates for the rich and, as we have seen, with the cumulative effect of a whole host of means-tested schemes for the poor, marginal rates of tax are already much above 50 per cent both for the rich and the poor; it is only the middle-income classes which get away with lower marginal rates of tax; and neither the low-paid nor the high-paid workers would appear to be excessively idle relatively to the middle-rank earners.

In the second place, if in these middle-class incomes the higher rates of income tax did give some additional preference for leisure as contrasted with an incentive to earn more income in order to purchase more gadgets, I for one would not be dismayed. Indeed with our increasing awareness of the polluting, congesting, and resource-using features of much economic activity more leisure and less ironmongery may become a positive social target.

There are ways of reducing the high rate of tax of the Unmodified Social Dividend scheme. Indeed the flat-rate levies of the Modified Social Dividend scheme are devised for this express purpose and have the effect in the scheme examined in Appendix I of reducing the proportional tax rate from rather more than 50 per cent to rather more than 40 per cent. But this reduction is achieved at the cost of imposing what is in effect a 100 per cent rate of tax on the first slice of earnings. The result is that for a man whose earnings will in any case be moderate there will be a reduced incentive to take a job rather than to remain idle, since the excess of earnings (after meeting the extra travel and other expenses involved in working) over the flat-rate levy may be small; but if a job is taken, the marginal disincentive on adding to one's income by working longer hours or by seeking out a better-paid job will be reduced. Provided that the flat-rate levies are not raised to levels which remove all advantage in taking a job rather than remaining idle, the disincentive effects of the flat-rate levies are, I think, likely to be small; practically everyone, I imagine, would prefer a job to no job even if the financial gain were small; and in this case there would be a net advantage from the point of view of incentives from the lower rates of marginal tax on additions to income.

But there are also other ways of reducing the marginal rates of tax on earnings. The sums for the finance of the Social Dividend schemes have so far been conducted on the assumptions that no sur-tax rates were levied on higher incomes, that no supplementary tax was imposed on unearned as contrasted with earned income, and that there was no extension of the tax base, the imputed value of owner-occupied houses, for example, continuing to be free of tax. As is shown in Appendix I, by tax developments of this kind the rate of tax on the middle-class incomes might in the case of the Modified Social Dividend scheme be kept down to 40 per cent.

There is one further and in one sense much more basic possible development. It would be inappropriate on this occasion to enter into the dispute as to whether Spaceship Earth is threatened with Doom or not; but we are all quite properly becoming increasingly aware of the serious external diseconomies of congestion, pollution, and resource use which are associated with various economic activities. Now these activities positively ask to be discouraged, through, for example, the imposition of taxes and other forms of levy or charge which cause them to bear their full social costs. We should on pure efficiency grounds make a tour of our economy, imposing taxes on many particular activities in order to give the correct social incentives. The fact that a tax on earned income will, as I have already argued, give some increased preference for leisure over ironmongery is a crude, but much too crude an example of this sort of possibility. We should be much more discriminating by taxing the particular polluting, congesting, resource-using activities; and the more taxation that is raised in these ways whose incentive effects are wholly desirable, the easier it will be to finance Social Dividend schemes without the possible adverse incentive effects of high undifferentiated rates of tax on all earnings from every kind of activity.[20]

It is not only incentives to work and to save which might be affected by a Social Dividend scheme. Two other important sets of incentives might be much affected: namely the incentive to have children and the incentive of trade unionists to take industrial action to press claims for money wages.

A Social Dividend scheme, or indeed practically any scheme for the relief of poverty by means of the redistribution of income, will have the effect not merely of taxing the rich to subsidise the poor, but also of taxing

---

[20] The need for tax revenue for the relief of poverty makes it very important to tax the activities which pollute or congest rather than to subsidise activities which do not pollute or congest or which do so to a lesser degree. Thus we should greatly increase the taxation of private cars which congest our cities rather than subsidise public transport because it causes less congestion.

the childless in order to subsidise fertile families. Poverty depends so much upon the numbers in the family that need to be provided with a decent living that some element of this type of redistribution is inevitable; and this effect of Social Dividend schemes is well illustrated by the results shown in the table on p. 337. We are here faced with a choice of evils in this wicked world. On the one hand, if – as I and the Duke of Edinburgh and many Doomsters believe – we wish to reduce the growth rate of the population, we may consider a tax on children as a useful means of discouraging parents from breeding. On the other hand, the children, if they are produced, are after all human beings, and to give them a decent start in life we need to subsidise the larger families.

Can one square this particular circle? In the case of the Modified Social Dividend scheme (column C of the table) the extreme degree of redistribution from childless to large families could be moderated, without any reduction of the Social Dividend payable in respect of children, by means of an adjustment of the flat-rate levies. In the table the adult male worker is assumed to pay the same flat-rate levy of £275 a year regardless of the size of his family. But by charging a higher flat-rate levy from the heads of those families which contained many dependent children and which were, therefore, in receipt of a higher total Social Dividend, the effect of the scheme in taxing the childless in order to subsidise the fertile could be reduced. But the further one goes in this direction, the larger the first slice of wage earnings of a large family on which a 100 per cent rate of tax will be levied. At the extreme, if one removes in flat-rate levy from the workers in a family the whole of the Social Dividend payable to that family one is back at the dis-incentive effects of the Minimum Income Guarantee scheme (line *FDE* in Figure 1).

If poverty is to be reduced one cannot avoid subsidising large families to a smaller or greater degree. This means that population growth must be controlled by means other than the taxation of fertility. Some alternative policies can be designed to discourage fertility; and if such policies did result in a reduction in fertility in poor families without taxing fertility in poor families, the result will be the very beneficial one both of a reduction in the rate of population growth and also, at the same time, a relief of poverty, since a large number of children in a low-wage family is itself a cause of poverty. Sterilisation and abortion on demand, the development of family planning advice and services in all maternity hospitals, the complete incorporation of universal and free family planning into the National Health Service, the provision of extensive domiciliary family planning services, school education to the effect that sexual intercourse should never occur without contraception unless a child is positively planned – these are the sort of developments which could do something to offset the undesirable effects of the financial support of large families in encouraging procreation.

Such measures would, of course, themselves entail cost and some additional taxation. But the additional cost would probably be moderate in relation to the results which might be achieved; and there is evidence that in the not too distant future these costs would be exceeded by the savings in various social services due to the reduction in the number of unwanted and problem children.[21]

Whether such measures would prove to be an adequate offset to the subsidisation of procreation is another question. Perhaps in the end we shall need to adopt more authoritarian methods. But this possibility need not be contemplated until we have introduced, and seen the results of, effective measures designed to ensure that every birth is a planned birth.

One of the great advantages of a Social Dividend scheme – indeed, in my mind the outstanding feature of the scheme – is that, as ought to be the case in a society as prosperous as our own, everyone in the community would automatically receive the basic minimum standard income. I would like to be able to add the words 'without any exception whatsoever'. I would certainly myself allow anyone to be idle on this low income if they chose that way of life in preference to industrial activity on a higher income. I have little doubt that the community could well afford to carry any such passengers, and the increase in individual liberty and freedom from bureaucratic surveillance would in my opinion be worth the cost. It may be that citizens who are in prison, hospital, or other institutions should be required to contribute an appropriate part of their family's Social Dividend to their upkeep in the institution concerned. But apart from this there is one group to whom in present conditions it would be difficult to apply the principle of unconditional payment, namely to those monopolistic groups of citizens who organise a simultaneous cessation of work throughout a whole economic sector in order to press a particular wage claim. To subsidise all strikes on this scale would be an irresponsible encouragement of cost inflation. One must, I think, regretfully add a condition that, until some more equitable and socially efficient method of determining wage earnings is devised, the Social Dividend must be withheld or turned into a repayable debt in whole or in part in the case of those who take industrial action in support of wage claims which are ruled to be excessive. But this raises yet one more set of basic problems which I cannot discuss on this occasion.

I am myself much attracted by the merits of a Modified Social Dividend scheme; but it is clear that one would have to move by degrees through a series of transitional stages before arriving at the complete and final form of such a scheme. The first stages could take the form of a policy of what has been called 'Back to Beveridge',[22] whereby all national insurance benefits and family allowances, payable without means test, were raised up to the Supplementary Benefit levels.[23] In these conditions, as we have already argued, if all those in work (and therefore not in receipt of sickness, unemployment, retirement, or similar benefits) received a wage at least as high as the Supplementary Benefit entitlement for a married

---

[21] See W. A. Laing, *The Costs and Benefits of Family Planning*, Political and Economic Planning Broadsheet 534, February 1972.

[22] See A. B. Atkinson, 'Policies for Poverty', *Lloyds Bank Review*, No. 100 (April 1971), pp. 17–28.

[23] Including an amount designed to cover an average rent. The problem of special supplementation for above-average rents payable by poor families would remain.

couple with one child, virtually no one would be left below the Supplementary Benefit level, even without taking into account the effect of the present Family Income Supplement scheme.

The increased cost of the improved family allowances could in large measure be financed by the 'clawback' method of reducing *pari passu* the children's allowances under the income tax; and if the allowances were also made free of tax, they would correspond to a Social Dividend for the children concerned, financed largely by the standard rate of tax on Earnings which had previously been tax-free. If the increased cost of the higher national insurance benefits were financed by a combination of increased flat-rate insurance contributions and a higher standard rate of income tax, if the tax-free allowances under the income tax were adjusted to be equal to the Supplementary Benefit entitlements for all members of the family other than the children covered by family allowances, and if all national insurance and similar benefits (other than family allowances) were included in income for income-tax purposes, the system would in many ways be very close to a Modified Social Dividend scheme.

But there would still be one basic difference.

Consider the case of a married man with three children and no independent income from property passing from unemployment into a paid job. After the implementation of the Back to Beveridge policy he will in unemployment be receiving an income equal to the minimum standard through family allowances for the second and third child and through unemployment insurance benefit for himself, his wife, and the first child. If he moves into employment, he will retain the adequate family allowances for the second and third child; but he will exchange his wage earnings for the adequate unemployment benefit for himself, his wife, and the first child. If his wage (after deduction of any national insurance contributions and of extra travel and other expenses due to being in work) is less than this he will, in the absence of some other supplementation of his family income, fall below the Supplementary Benefit level of income.

The frequency of such situations in which the wage earned (after deduction of working expenses) was less than the minimum-standard income of the members of the family who were not covered by family allowances would, of course, be reduced if the Back to Beveridge moves were extended by making family allowances payable not merely in respect of children after the first child (as proposed in the Beveridge report) but in respect of all children in the family including the first. Being in employment could then cause the family income to fall below the Supplementary Benefit level only in those cases in which the wage (after deduction of working expenses) was less than the Supplementary Benefit level for a married couple.

It is sometimes proposed that the way to fill this final gap is by means of minimum wage legislation which ensures to all workers a wage at least as high as the Supplementary Benefit entitlement of a married couple or, if family allowances were not extended to cover all children including the first, of a married couple with one child.

But there are serious disadvantages in such minimum wage legislation.

First, minimum wage legislation can do nothing to help those self-employed persons whose earnings are low.

Second, to meet its purpose of ensuring a minimum standard of life for those who are employed by others the minimum wage would have to be set in terms of a minimum weekly earning. But if this were done, it would be unprofitable to employ part-time or casual workers, since to pay a full week's wage for a few hours' work would be out of the question. If, however, the minimum is set in terms of a minimum hourly wage rate, part-time work is no longer ruled out; but the person who can obtain only part-time work will not necessarily obtain an income sufficient to ensure the basic Supplementary Benefit standard.

Third, an effective minimum wage, whether it be on the basis of the hourly wage or of the weekly earnings, may deprive some persons of the possibility of obtaining employment. There are sectors of the labour market for relatively unskilled work – particularly for older workers, for workers in depressed occupations, industries, or localities, and for disabled workers – where the value of the output of the worker is low and where, therefore, employment opportunities will depend upon the wage payment being low. This does not imply that nothing should be done to push up low wages where low wages are due to the monopsonistic exploitation of the workers. Nor, of course, does it mean that nothing should be done to bring industry to depressed areas, to subsidise employment in such areas, to retrain labour, to enable workers to move to regions and occupations where prospects are better. But it does imply that it is better, if possible, to rely on other fiscal measures for the relief of poverty rather than upon any universal minimum wage legislation.

Fourth, there are serious difficulties in evaluating the true value of the wage where, as in the case of domestic service, a large part of the wage takes the form of a payment in kind.

Fifth, the interpretation and enforcement of the minimum wage raise serious administrative problems with yet one more apparatus of bureaucratic control.[24]

If one got as far as Back to Beveridge, one could take the final steps to a Modified Social Dividend scheme by paying minimum-standard Social Dividends to all citizens (and not merely to second and subsequent children in the form of family allowances) and by financing the additional cost by a corresponding reduction in all national insurance benefits and pensions, by a clawback of the personal allowances under the income tax, and for the rest partly by increased flat-rate levies similar to the national insurance contributions and partly by the increased taxation of other incomes. Is it not good to contemplate a society in which literally everybody – if for one moment I may close my eyes to the problems of strikes and wage inflation – was automatically ensured in all circumstances a weekly income at a predetermined minimum-standard level?

Finally, I would point out that in this paper I have been concerned only with the nuts and bolts of fiscal schemes for the redistribution of money income in such a way as to ensure that no income after the redistributive

[24] Cf. Department of Employment and Productivity, *A National Minimum Wage: An Inquiry* (London: HMSO, 1969).

mechanism has played its part should fall below the minimum standard. But there are, of course, much more fundamental questions concerning the forces in society which cause income and wealth to be so unequally distributed in the first place. These I have not considered at all; but let me close with a brief enumeration of some of the most important categories of policy which are important in this respect.

First, policies for the maintenance of full employment are clearly important to prevent the concentrated poverty due to inability to find work.

Second, the relaxation of restrictive practices in trade unions and professional bodies would make it easier for low-paid workers to move into high-paid jobs.

Third, the provision of greater educational opportunities will increase the supply of trained and skilled persons relatively to the unskilled and will thus help to equalise rates of pay. But in this connection we must be mindful of the possibility that an educational system which carefully selects all the ablest persons from all income and social classes, and which encourages these highly selected citizens to meet and to marry each other and thus to form themselves into a separate meritocratic élite may in the long run introduce an even more marked separation between the rich and successful and the poor and unsuccessful – what Tawney called an increase in equality of the opportunity to become unequal.

Fourth, a family planning policy which makes it possible for poor and unsuccessful families to limit the number of their dependent children will relieve poverty due to the combination of large families and low earnings.

Finally, the revision of laws relating to the acquisition by gift as well as by benefaction at death of large capital wealth might be designed so as to encourage a much more equal distribution of property.

But these basic policies are necessarily slow in their operation and in any case are never likely to do more than mitigate, perhaps to an important degree, the very strong forces in all societies which lead to inequalities and, at the bottom end, to what we have called relative poverty. For as long as we can look ahead we shall need some fiscal system for the day-to-day redistribution of income to bring those at the bottom end of the scale at least up to some currently agreed minimum standard.

The purpose of my paper has been to persuade you that in this country this system is in a terrible muddle and needs a rather radical overhaul. In my opinion this overhaul should take the form of a policy of Back to Beveridge leading ultimately to a Modified Social Dividend scheme.

## *Appendix I   The Finance of Social Dividends in 1970*

In order to illustrate in more detail the modified and unmodified forms of the Social Dividend schemes described in the main text, this appendix contains an analysis of what the financial implications of such schemes would have been if they had been in operation in 1970.

The following table gives the Supplementary Benefit scales for 1970:

| | Weekly payments £ per week | | Total Annual equivalent £ per year |
|---|---|---|---|
| | Without rent* | Average rent | |
| Single non-householder | 3·25 | .. | 169 |
| Single householder | 4·85 | 1·70 | 340 |
| Married couple | 7·95 | 2·00 | 518 |
| Children 5–10 | 1·70 | 0·20 | Av. 109 |
| Children 11–15 | 2·10 | 0·20 | |

* ⅚ of rate to 2. xi. 70 + ⅙ of rate after 2. xi. 70, excluding the £0·50 per week or £26 per annum addition payable if the family has been in benefit for a long period.

We will use the figures in the last column of this table as the annual values of the Social Dividends payable to all citizens but will allow an additional £26 per annum for all persons over 65 to correspond to long-period Supplementary Benefit.

The population at June 1970 may be estimated as:

| | Number of persons |
|---|---|
| Children aged 0–15 | 14·1 millions |
| Single non-householders aged 16–20 | 3·9 millions |
| Single under 65 | 6·1 millions |
| Single over 65 | 4·1 millions |
| Married under 65 (No. of couples 12·4m.) | 24·8 millions |
| Married over 65 (No. of couples 1·4m.) | 2·8 millions |
| Total | 55·8 millions |

If we apply the rates of Social Dividend payable in respect of these groups of persons, we obtain a total cost of £12,955m.

In 1970 income tax and sur-tax raised £6,083m. and the national insurance and health contributions payable by insured persons amounted to £1,300m. To replace these revenues and to finance the cost of the Social Dividends would have needed a revenue of £12,955m. + £7,383m. = £20,338m.

But the payment of the Social Dividends would have made possible a saving of £2,704m. on national insurance benefits, of £517m. on Supplementary Benefits, and of £351m. on family allowances, a total saving of £3,572.

The net amount to be raised for the finance of a Social Dividend scheme would have been £20,338m. − £3,572m. = £16,766m.

On the basis used by Brown and Dawson[25] the personal income base on which this sum could have been raised would have been in 1970:

[25] C. V. Brown and D. A. Dawson, *Personal Taxation Incentives and Tax Reform.*

|  | £ million |
|---|---|
| Wages and salaries | 26,816 |
| Pay in cash of HM Forces | 632 |
| Income from self-employment | 3,345 |
| Rent and net interest | 2,158 |
| Pensions and other benefits from life assurance | 2,161 |
| Total: | £35,112 |

The similar total for 1967 was £27,579m.; but this figure may well have been an overestimate, and on the basis of the Inland Revenue figures then available Professor Atkinson[26] used for 1967 an estimate of £25,000m. If we write down the estimate of £35,112m. for 1970 in the same ratio, we obtain a tax base of £31,800m.

To raise £16,766m. on a base of £31,800m. needs a tax rate of 0·53. We will accordingly illustrate an unmodified Social Dividend scheme for 1970 with a proportional income tax rate of 0·53 (the equivalent of some 10s 7d in the £).

For a modified Social Dividend scheme suppose that one raised the flat-rate social insurance contributions of insured persons to six times the levels ruling in 1970. In 1970 £1,300m. was raised in contributions by insured persons, but of this £404m. was revenue from graduated contributions, leaving £896m. as the revenue from the flat-rate contributions of insured persons. Increasing these rates sixfold would, therefore, have raised 6 × £896m. = £5,376m. If we subtract this figure both from the amount to be raised by the proportional income tax and also from the tax base (since the proportional income tax could be applied only to income remaining after payment of these contributions) we reach a rate of tax of

$$(16,766 - 5,376) \div (31,800 - 5,376) = 11,390 \div 26,424 = 0·43.$$

These rates may be compared with the 1970 standard rate of tax:

|  | Standard rates of income tax | |
|---|---|---|
|  | Unearned income | Earned income, i.e. after allowance of 2/9 of earned income |
| 1970 income tax | 0·4125 | 0·32083 |
|  | (8s 3d in the £) | (6s 5d in the £) |
| Unmodified Social Dividend | 0·53 (10s 7d in the £) | |
| Modified Social Dividend | 0·43 (8s 7d in the £) | |

The Social Dividend rates are estimated on the assumption that sur-tax is abolished, that there is no differentiation between earned and unearned income, and that no measures are taken to extend the tax base.

[26] See *Poverty in Britain*, p. 173.

If any of these assumptions were modified, the standard rate of tax on earned incomes could be *pro tanto* reduced. Suppose, for example, that a sur-tax on higher incomes was maintained and gave the same yield as in 1970, then the rate of tax needed for a Modified Social Dividend would fall to $(11,390 - 266) \div 26,424 = 0.42$. If in addition some £200m. were raised by taxing wealth or by taxing unearned income more heavily than earned income, the rate of tax would be $(11,390 - 266 - 200) \div 26,424 = 0.41$. Finally, if one maintained the sur-tax yield, raised £200m. by the taxation of wealth or of unearned income, and taxed the annual value of owner-occupied houses, the tax rate would be $(11,390 - 266 - 200) \div (26,424 + 1,154) = 0.39$ (the equivalent of 7s 10d in the £).

The columns marked $A$, $B$, and $C$ in the table on p. 337 illustrate the effect of $(A)$ the 1970 combination of national insurance contributions, family allowances, and income tax, $(B)$ an Unmodified Social Dividend scheme, and $(C)$ a Modified Social Dividend scheme on the net Take-Home Pay of adult male wage-earners with different earned incomes and different family responsibilities. Both Social Dividend schemes allow for social dividends paid on the Supplementary Benefit scales for 1970 (including average rent), as shown above. The unmodified scheme combines this with a tax rate of $0.53$ on all earned income. The modified scheme combines these social dividends with (i) the payment of £275 a year in national insurance contributions (i.e. the annual equivalent of six times the 1970 contribution of an adult male employee which was then £0.88 a week) and (ii) a tax rate of $0.43$ on all earned income in excess of £275 a year. The table illustrates how the burden of the Social Dividend schemes is concentrated on those families with (i) a high income and (ii) a small family to the advantage of those with (i) a low income and (ii) a large family. With a Modified Social Dividend scheme influence (i) can be moderated, without any reduction in the scale of Social Dividend payments, by a rise in the flat-rate levies combined with a reduction in the proportional tax rate. Influence (ii) can be moderated, also without any reduction in the Social Dividends payable to children, by raising the flat-rate levies for those with large families combined with corresponding reductions in the flat-rate levies for those with small families. But in both cases the adjustment if carried too far would increase the chances that, for those whose flat-rate levies had been raised and whose earnings were low, all incentive to earn would be eliminated.

## Appendix II

There are $N$ families of identical size and age and sex composition. Let $y$ be the average income of a family before tax or subsidy. Let $d$ be the proportion of total national income which must be raised in tax to cover governmental expenditure on purposes other than the relief of poverty and the redistribution of private disposable income, so that $(1 - d)yN$ is the total national income available for redistribution among private families for their free disposal. Let $s$ be the ratio of the 'minimum standard' to average disposable private income, so that the 'minimum standard' is set at $s(1 - d)y$.

Let there be $p_0 N$ families with no original incomes and $p_a N$ families with original incomes equal to a fraction $a$ of the minimum standard, i.e. with original incomes of $as(1 - d)y$. The remaining families, $(1 - p_0 - p_a)N$, all have original incomes greater than the 'minimum standard' $s(1 - d)y$.

For an Unmodified Social Dividend scheme the payment of Social Dividends will involve an expenditure of $s(1 - d)yN$; and expenditure on other purposes will be $dyN$. The base for the proportional income tax is $yN$. If this is taxed at a rate $t_1$ which equates revenue to expenditure we have

$$t_1 yN = s(1 - d)yN + dyN,$$

so that

$$t_1 = s(1 - d) + d.$$

For a Minimum Income Guarantee the subsidisation of low incomes will require an expenditure of $p_0 s(1 - d)yN + p_a(1 - a) s(1 - d)yN$ and other expenditure will be $dyN$. The base for the proportional income tax will be

$$yN - p_a as(1 - d)yN - (1 - p_0 - p_a)s(1 - d)yN.$$

If this is taxed at a rate $t_2$ to equate revenue to expenditure we have

$$t_2 = \frac{s(1 - d)(p_0 + p_a[1 - a]) + d}{1 - s(1 - d)(1 - p_0 - p_a[1 - a])}.$$

For a Modified Social Dividend scheme let us suppose that there are 'flat-rate levies' which are at a rate of 100 per cent on all original incomes up to a ceiling $bs(1 - d)y$, where $0 < b < a$. In other words, a zero flat-rate levy will be charged to the $p_0 N$ families with zero original incomes, but a flat-rate charge of $bs(1 - d)y$ will be levied on all the remaining $(1 - p_0)N$ families, since in all these cases the flat-rate levy is less than their original income. Expenditure on Social Dividends will be $s(1 - d)yN$ and on other purposes will be $dyN$. The flat-rate levies will raise $(1 - p_0)bs(1 - d)yN$. A tax at the rate $t_3$ on the remaining original incomes will raise

$$t_3(yN - [1 - p_0]bs[1 - d]yN);$$

if this tax is set to equate revenue to expenditure, we have

$$t_3 = \frac{s(1 - d)(1 - [1 - p_0]b) + d}{1 - s(1 - d)(1 - p_0)b}.$$

# 19

## The Inheritance of Inequalities: Some Biological, Demographic, Social, and Economic Factors[1]

*The British Academy's Third Keynes Lecture in Economics, delivered on 5 December 1973; from* The Proceedings of the British Academy, *vol. 59 (1973), pp. 355–81.*

In a society in which there were no governmental interferences with the operation of the competitive markets and no other artificial impediments to competition or mobility, persons who were similarly endowed would tend to receive the same incomes.

But if individual citizens are not equally endowed, then personal incomes may continue to be unequal even in a fully competitive, *laissez-faire* society with unrestricted mobility. The man with little skill and ability will not necessarily be able to undercut the man with great skill and ability, even though the earnings of the latter greatly exceed those of the former. The man with much property will have a higher income from property than the man with little property even though the rate of return on all properties were the same.

In this lecture I wish to isolate for examination some of the factors which would cause citizens to be unequally endowed and thus to receive unequal incomes even in a competitive, *laissez-faire* society with unrestricted mobility. For this purpose I shall proceed for the most part as if there were free competition, unimpeded mobility, and no governmental interference in the economy; and, on these assumptions, I shall inquire what influences one would expect still to remain to cause inequalities in personal endowments of income-earning factors of production. I am not thereby intending to assert that the actually existing structure of inequalities can be explained without allowing for the influence of such factors as customary ideas about fairness which may cause rigidities in pay differentials, or impediments to movement from a low-paid to a high-paid occupation, due, for example, to trade union or similar restrictions on the entry of outsiders into a protected occupation, or governmental tax

---

[1] The arguments in this lecture have been much stimulated by the ideas of others and in particular by the ideas of my professional colleagues: Professor Tony Atkinson, Professor Henry Phelps Brown, Professor David Champernowne, and Professor Richard Stone.

policies and similar measures many of which are expressly designed to affect the distribution of incomes and properties. I am merely engaged in one preliminary exercise of abstraction which may help to bring to one's attention certain important influences which must be brought into any final calculation.

A citizen in a *laissez-faire* competitive society would receive certain endowments from his parents which would help to determine the amount of income which he could earn and property which he could accumulate during his own lifetime. This in turn would affect the endowments which he could hand on to his children.

The endowments with which we will be concerned may be enumerated under four heads.

First, a citizen will be endowed with a certain genetic make-up. There is some genetic component in intelligence which may affect earning capacity. But it would be a mistake to forget other characteristics which probably have some genetic component and which may well exert a greater influence on earning capacity. Quite apart from straightforward bodily strength and health, there may be other relevant physical differences which have some genetic component; there may, for example, be some genetic influences affecting the vocal cords of Mr Fischer-Dieskau and Miss Janet Baker which help to explain their ability to earn income. There may also be genetic components in the determination of certain qualities of character which have an income-earning potential, though it by no means follows that all of these are desirable in themselves. Thus a certain streak of ruthlessness and aggression may be helpful to the accumulation of wealth without being in any basic ethical or aesthetic sense good or desirable qualities in and for themselves.

Second, a citizen may inherit a certain amount of income-earning property of one kind or another from his parents.

Third, a citizen will have received as a child a certain education and training. In a strictly *laissez-faire* competitive society this education and training will have been provided and financed privately by his parents, though this is, of course, one of the fields in which my neglect of governmental interventions and policies is especially significant.

Fourth, there are the rather less tangible advantages or disadvantages which accrue to a citizen through the social contacts which he makes with other persons, these social contacts being much affected by the social background into which he was born.

These two last elements of endowment – namely, education and social contacts – must in my scheme of things cover a very wide range of social phenomena. Education obviously covers an individual's formal education and training at school, university, or similar institution. Social contacts obviously cover a citizens' range of acquaintances who through their particular brand of the old-boy network can or cannot get him a good job or provide him with a favourable investment opportunity. But there are many other factors to be taken into account which in my limited scheme must be put into either the one or the other of the very general categories of 'education' and 'social contacts'.

I personally think of the category of education as covering practically all of the environmental influences which affect the development of an individual's knowledge, character, and motivation. He will thus receive much of his so-defined education directly from his parents as they bring him up in a certain way and from the acquaintances he makes – to say nothing of the education which a husband receives from his wife and, if Women's Lib will allow me to say so, which a wife may receive from her husband.

If education is defined in this very broad way, then social contacts must be narrowly defined and are reduced to little more than a catalogue of the sort of friends, acquaintances, neighbours, and colleagues with whom an individual spends his days.

A citizen is thus fortunate or unfortunate according as he starts out in life with a helpful or unhelpful endowment of genes, inherited property, education, and social contacts. But in addition to these initial structural elements of good or bad fortune which are determined by his family background, a citizen will also encounter many elements of good or bad luck in the course of his career. To take but one example, two men with the same inborn ability and the same initial advantages of education, property, and social contacts may end up with very different incomes and properties, simply because they embarked on careers in different lines of economic activity, one of which prospered and the other of which declined. And yet at the time of choice the prospects of the two activities may have seemed very similar to both of them and it may have been a matter of almost random chance which determined the choice of career. In what follows I shall use the term 'fortune' to describe the basic structural endowments of genes, property, education, and social contacts, and the word 'luck' to describe the many chances in life which determine the actual outcome within these structures of basic endowments. One cannot, of course, draw any hard and fast line between elements of fortune and elements of luck as I have tried to describe them; they are both mixtures of recognisable laws of cause and effect and of strokes of pure chance; but the nature of society – or should I say of the social studies? – is such that it seems to me useful to think in terms of some such broad distinction.

Social scientists examine the general genetic, demographic, social, and economic structure of society. They consider the characteristics of, and the factors affecting, various groups: income groups, property groups, IQ groups, social classes, age and sex groupings of the population, occupational classes, classes of educational attainment, and the like. $A$ may be born into one set of groupings and $B$ into another. When the souls of little $A$ and little $B$ were lining up in heaven to be sent forth on their sojourn in this wicked world, did they toss up as to which soul should occupy which niche in the social structure which they were joining? I do not know. But I shall refer to the structured endowments which $A$ and $B$ receive in society by joining whatever group they do join as their good or bad fortune.

However, different people within the same niche in the structure of society may fare very differently in the course of their lives. It is the causes of these divergences in the fates of two persons within the same fortunate or unfortunate structural niche which I shall call factors of luck. This is not to assert that these factors are in any fundamental sense less subject to laws of cause and effect than are the factors of fortune. My category of luck certainly contains all those causes of inequality which are not explained by the structured influences of what I have called fortune; and there may well be disciplines other than present-day economics and sociology which would help to explain why two persons with the same structured fortune fare differently in the outcome.

The basic structural endowments of good or bad fortune are handed down from parent to child; but the child as he grows up moulds and modifies the basic endowments which he received as a child from his mother and father, before he amalgamates them with those of his wife and passes this package of *modified* and *mixed* endowments of fortune on to his own children. I will start first with a consideration of the way in which an individual's initial endowments may be *modified* as he grows up; and I will turn later to the implications of the fact that he *mixes* these *modified* endowments with the already *modified* endowments which his wife received from her parents before the two of them hand on this modified mixture to the next generation.[2]

Let us then consider how a citizen's passage through life may affect the elements of basic structural fortune with which he was initially endowed. This is illustrated in my diagram in which I consider the way in which a particular citizen – let us call him Tom Jones – starting out as little Tommy receives his basic endowments from his home background, proceeds through life, and at length as poor old Tom or Thomas Jones Esquire or maybe even Sir Thomas Jones, CGB, himself contributes to a home background transmitting endowments to his children.

Tom Jones then starts in a home background ($H_1$) which is built up by his father and mother. We are concerned with his parents solely as instruments affecting his basic endowments of good or bad fortune; and in this sense his father and mother are themselves simply bundles of factors which will affect their ability to provide Tom Jones with his initial endowments of fortune. The parents' relevant factors I assume to be the mother's and the father's genes ($G_m$, and $G_f$) (line 1), education ($E_m$, $E_f$) (line 2), and social contacts ($C_m$, and $C_f$) (line 4), and their joint income ($Y_j$) and property ($K_j$) (lines 3 and 5). These together constitute the home background which provides Tom Jones with an endowment of genes ($G$), education ($E$), social contacts ($C$), and property ($K$). Thus in the diagram we look upon the home background as a *GEYCK* which produces a *GECK* for each child.

One must not, however, regard this endowment of Tom Jones by his parents as a once-for-all affair which occurs instantaneously at his birth. It is a continuing process; and this introduces two interacting dynamic factors. In the first place, Tom Jones will be susceptible to different endowments at different stages of his life: to his parents' genes once-for-all on his conception, to the qualities of his mother's care as an infant, to his parents' friends at a later stage, to his inheritance of

---

[2] I have put this example in terms of a boy only because the English language does not possess a pronoun which covers both male and female. Solely for this reason in what follows I shall analyse in terms of the male sex much that applies equally to the female sex.

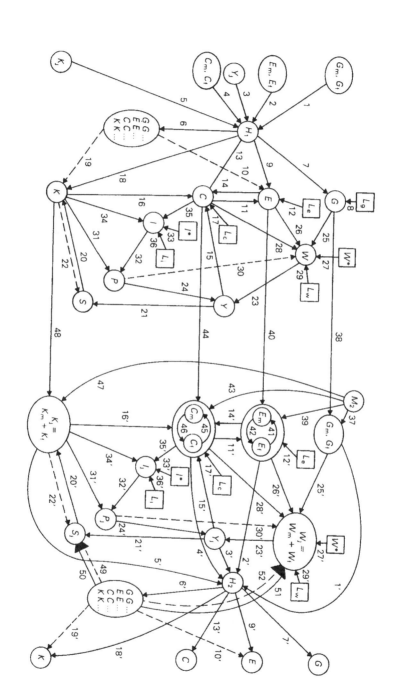

property on his parents' deaths, and so on. Second, his parents' own education, income, social contacts and property will be developing during their years as home-builders and parents, so that what they have to give as well as what Tom Jones is ready to receive will be changing over time.

I shall at first neglect the influences affecting what Tom Jones's parents have to contribute and shall take the nature and development of his parents' genes, education, income, social contacts, and property as given. I shall return to this set of problems when I close the cycle and come to regard Tom Jones himself as a parent. I will then consider his develop-ment as a provider of endowments for his children. For the time being I wish to consider him solely as a recipient of a given developing flow of basic endowments from his parents, which he himself then develops further.

To return to the diagram, Tom Jones's parents may produce brothers and sisters for him, and these are represented by the little *GECK*s which proceed from Tom Jones's home background $H^1$ (line 6). But the main purpose of my diagram is to put the individual Tom Jones under the microscope.

From his two parents Tom Jones receives his genetic endowment ($G$) (line 7). But while his genetic make-up is basically conditioned by that of his parents there is also an element of luck ($L_g$) (line 8). Two children of the same parents will not receive identical genetic endowments unless they are identical twins. Tom Jones can draw his genes only from those offered by his parents; but he may have good or bad luck in his draw from the parental stock.

Tom Jones will receive an education ($E$). In the absence of governmen-tal intervention not only much of his early upbringing but also his formal education and training will be provided for him by his parents (line 9). However, the greater the number of Tom Jones's brothers and sisters, the less his parents may be able to afford out of their given time, income, and property to invest in Tom Jones's individual education (line 10). In addition to his home background and formal education, much of what I have broadly defined as his education will be continued during his own career by his social contacts, that is to say, by the sort of friends and colleagues with whom he associates (line 11). But in all this there is a considerable admixture of luck ($L_e$) (line 12). To take only one example, his parents may make most carefully calculated decisions about the amount of money which they will invest in his education and about the educational institutions to which they will entrust him. But the outcome may be greatly affected in ways which it may be impossible to foresee by luck – as, for example, whether a particular teacher happened to fire young Tommy's imagination and interest in a particular subject or activity.

Tom Jones will inherit certain social contacts ($C$) from his parents (line 13), since the social environment of his home background will greatly affect his choice of friends and acquaintances. But as he grows up his social contacts will develop and will depend upon the way in which his own career develops. An important factor will be the social contacts which he makes at school or other educational institutions (line 14). Thereafter, the further development of his social contacts is likely to be affected by his material success in life. If he manages to earn a high income ($Y$) or to acquire much property ($K$), the fact that he is a man of riches will enable him to make contacts with people who will be useful to him in his career (lines 15 and 16). Finally, of course, there is an important element of luck ($L_c$) in the people he meets and the friends he makes (line 17).

From his parents Tom Jones may also receive property ($K$) (line 18). But once again the greater the number of Tom Jones's competing brothers and sisters, the smaller will be his own share of the family property (line 19). As time passes he may supplement this property from his own savings ($S$) (line 20). The level of these savings will be affected by many considerations; and in the diagram I have introduced only two of the most important.

In the first place, the higher is his income the greater will be Tom Jones's ability to save (line 21).

But, in the second place, the greater the property which he has already acquired (perhaps by inheritance) the smaller will be his need to save, since there will be less need to abstain from present consumption to acquire a property to support him in his old age or to give him security against adversity. This fact that the higher his property ($K$) the lower will be his savings ($S$) is represented by the broken line 22.

It remains to consider the factors determining the level of Tom Jones's income as he passes through life. His income ($Y$) is simply the sum of his earnings or income from work ($W$) and of his income from property ($P$) (lines 23 and 24).

His earnings will be affected by many factors. First of all there is his capacity to earn which will be affected both by his genetic endowment and by his educational endowment (lines 25 and 26). But, given his ability his actual earnings will depend upon the structure of wage-rates that exist in the market for different kinds of ability ($W^*$) (line 27). Earnings, however, are not determined exclusively by a given market wage-rate for a given ability. There is an element of fortune in that good social contacts may enable a man to make a more rewarding choice of job (line 28); and there is also an element of luck ($L_w$) in determining whether Tom Jones will be successful in his choice of occupation or in the development of his particular job (line 29).

There are other important influences in the real world which I am neglecting as a result of my assumption of free competition – influences such as trade union or similar restrictions on entry into protected occupations or customary differentials in pay which interfere with market forces. But there is one further consideration which I cannot neglect in my competitive economy.

Tom Jones's earnings will depend in part upon the amount of effort which he chooses to put into the business of earning a high income. This is influenced by many factors; but among these we may suppose that the higher is Tom Jones's income from property ($P$), the lower – other things equal – will be the effort which he puts into earning an income from work (line 3). Indeed if he has a sufficiently high income from property he may not bother to earn any additional income at all.

At this point I must digress to ask myself whether my diagram covers the undoubted fact that Tom Jones's own moral character and motivation will affect how hard he will work and what steps he will take to get on. Do not some people get on – and deserve to get on – because they try hard and others fail to make good – and deserve to fail – because they make little or no effort to help themselves? We are immediately faced by the riddle of free will. Do not a man's genetic and environmental endowments, together with some elements of pure luck, for which he can in no way be held responsible, determine his moral character and motivation as well as his ability? If so, it can all be comprehended in lines 25, 26, 28, and 29 of my diagram. But it would then seem meaningless to assert that Tom Jones was in any way a free agent in deciding whether to deserve success or failure. But if one does believe in some measure of free choice and personal responsibility for success or failure – and I cannot help doing so – there is something vital – but I do not quite know what – missing from my diagram. This is one of those many difficulties which I learned from Professor Sir Dennis Robertson to look squarely in the face and pass on.

Let us turn now from Tom Jones's earned income to his income from property $(P)$. This is simply his property $(K)$ multiplied by the average yield or rate of interest on it $(I)$ (lines 31 and 32). The yield on property will be basically determined by the structure of the ruling market yields on various types of property $(I^*)$ (line 33). But the actual yield obtained may well be affected by Tom Jones's investment opportunities. Thus the yield on property is likely to be higher for a man with much property to invest (line 34) and for a man with the right social contacts (line 35). A man with a large property can afford to take more risks in his investments, and the cost of advice from stockbrokers and of other investment services can be spread over a larger capital fund. For these reasons a large property normally obtains a higher yield than a small property. Moreover, a wealthy man is more likely to have those social contracts which will enable him to be better informed about the chances of profitable investment. Finally, let me point out, in case any of you have not operated on the Stock Exchange, there will be an element of luck in Tom Jones's choice of investments for his property $(L_j)$ (line 36).

Tom Jones grows up into mature manhood with a certain make-up of genes, education, income, property, and social contacts, these elements of his make-up being, as we have seen, partly inherited from his original home background and partly made up by his own social and economic development. He is now ready to marry a wife and to become a father; and together these two bundles of genes, education, income, social contacts, and property having joined together in holy matrimony, are ready to make up a second-generation home background for the next generation of children.

I will turn to their married life in a moment. Let me pause for a little to comment on my account of Tom Jones's bachelor life.

A very marked feature of the simple model which I have presented to the diagram so far is the amount of positive feedback which it contains, that is to say of self-reinforcing influences which help to sustain the good fortune of the fortunate and the bad fortune of the unfortunate.

Let me give two examples.

The first concerns job opportunities. A man who for any reason starts with a high income may be able to make appropriate social contacts which enable him to find exceptionally repaying jobs which will in turn help to raise his income still further (lines 15, 28, 23).

My second example concerns the accumulation of property. A man who for any reason of good fortune has a high income can save much and accumulate a large property (lines 21 and 20). But with a large property he has a high income from property (line 31) and thus a still higher income (line 24). Nor is that the end of the matter; with a high property he can probably get a high yield on his property, partly because a large property can be more cheaply and effectively managed than a small property (line 34) and partly because a man of wealth will be better able to make the sort of social contacts which will enable him to invest his property profitably (lines 16 and 35). Thus the yield on his property, as well as his property itself, will be raised simply because his initial fortune was good.

This particular set of positive-feedback relationships probably helps to explain one of the very pronounced phenomena in our type of society – namely, the very much greater degree of inequality in the distribution of the ownership of property and of income from property than in the distribution of earned income. An individual with a high income is able to save a higher proportion of his income than can an individual with a low income. A man with high earnings will thus accumulate a property which is high relative to his already high earnings. If, having a high property, he then gets an especially high yield on property, his income from property will become large relative to his property which will become large relative to his already high earnings. Conversely, for the citizen with low earnings, his income from property will be low relative to his property which will be low relative to his already low earnings. The discrepancy between high and low property incomes will be much greater than the discrepancy between high and low earnings; and to anticipate my analysis, these discrepancies are likely to be perpetuated from one generation to another through the inheritance of properties and earning capacities.

My diagram has many positive-feedback loops. It contains through the broken lines 22 and 30 only two examples of negative feedbacks, of influences, that is to say, which damp down rather than multiply the results of initial good or bad fortune. Thus it is probable that the higher is a man's property the smaller is his incentive to cut back his present consumption in order to save and accumulate; and this factor damps down the way in which large properties tend to lead to still larger properties (line 22). In a rather similar manner the existence of a high income from property reduces the need for income from work and may thus damp down the incentive to earn more (line 30); and this factor may reduce the positive, reinforcing effects which we have just examined, whereby high incomes lead to still higher incomes.

However, my assumption of *laissez-faire* has forbidden me to display on my diagram some fundamental elements of negative feedback which may be at work in the real world through governmental interventions. Progressive taxation, the provision of free education and medicine, and the payment of social security benefits or other supplements to the incomes of those who are less well off, in so far as they are effective in redistributing income from the rich to the poor, are outstanding examples of such negative feedbacks. In such circumstances a rise in a man's gross income and wealth (before governmental adjustment) causes a less than proportionate increase in his net income and wealth (after governmental adjustment); and this diminishes the multiplier whereby initial good fortune feeds upon itself and magnifies the final outcome.

But there remain in society very strong elements of positive feedback which I have illustrated in my diagram. Two results follow from this.

First, there is the obvious point that there are some apparently powerful built-in tendencies for the rich to sustain their riches and the poor their poverty, which one would expect to help in explaining the persistent continuation of the large inequalities in income and wealth which we actually observe in society.

A second major result may be expected from the intertwining of the many positive feedback loops in my diagram, namely that the various endowments passed from parent to child are likely to become highly correlated with each other. Thus if Tom Jones is born with a set of useful genes which help him to earn a high income this will enable him to make useful social contacts and to accumulate a sizeable property. Thus as a father he is likely to be a bundle not only of useful genes, but also of a useful income, a useful property, and useful social contacts. There will be a strong tendency in society for good or bad fortune to be handed on to the next generation in associated parcels of genes, incomes, property, and social contacts.

This tendency for the useful endowments of various kinds to become associated with each other will be further strengthened when we allow for the mixture of Tom Jones's endowments with those of his wife. Tom Jones marries Mary Smith. Tom Jones may be fortunately endowed with an educational and genetic make-up which turns him into an able, enterprising, perhaps ruthless, but anyhow successful businessman. Mary Smith may be fortunate in being the heiress to much property and endowed with the best social contacts. If in society there is a tendency for the fortunate to marry the fortunate and for the unfortunate to marry the unfortunate, whatever may be the primary cause of their good or bad fortune, then there will be a tendency for Tom Jones's useful genes and education to be joined with Mary Smith's useful property and social contacts. The various elements of basic endowments will become more highly correlated with each other.

But I am anticipating the next stage of my analysis. If the new biologists had already succeeded in getting rid of sex as a method of human reproduction, I would have little to add to the analysis presented in the first half of my diagram. If Tom Jones by some process of cloning could by himself produce a little son with an exact replication of his own genes, we could explain most of the factors affecting the development of inequalities of income and wealth as between various families by concentrating solely on the influences which I have discussed so far. Tom Jones would receive his endowments of genes, education, social contacts, and property from his father. He would hand these same genes on to his son; subject to all sorts of luck, he would develop his property and social contacts in the way which we have examined and, in the light of this development of his fortune, he would pass on the education, social contacts, and property to his sons. The situation could be much affected by the number of sons which he decided to clone – I will return to that subject in due course – but apart from that there would be little to add to the analysis.

But the fact that he has to marry Mary Smith and mix his genes, income, social contacts, and property up with hers before they jointly endow their sons and daughters introduces many basic modifications into the analysis. We will start the analysis of these problems by assuming that Tom Jones has chosen, or been chosen by, a particular Mary Smith with her own particular bundle of genes, education, social contacts, and property as they exist at the time of her marriage. I will discuss later the very important question what it was that brought Tom and Mary together. For the moment I am interested in the implications of their joint family life.

A family is more than a number of individuals. In the first half of my diagram we watched the development of Tom Jones as an individual bachelor. In the second half of the diagram we watch Tom and Mary Jones's family developing as a joint concern.

I represent Mary Smith as $M_2$, namely as a second-generation mother. For our purpose she is simply a bundle of factors relevant for the joint building of a second-generation home background $(H_2)$ for the endowment of the second generation of children. She brings into the marriage her genes, education, social contacts, and property, the nature of which depend upon what endowments she has received from her parents and the way in which she has developed them during her spinsterhood.

Thus Tom and Mary together provide a pool of mothers' genes $(G_m)$ and fathers' genes $(G_f)$ for use by the family (lines 37 and 38). They provide mother's education $(E_m)$ and father's education $(E_f)$ to form part of the family background (lines 39 and 40). Their educations in my broad sense of the term continue during their married life; and this is partly due to the fact that they educate each other (lines 41 and 42). They provide the mother's and the father's social contacts for use by the family $(C_m$ and $C_f)$ (lines 43 and 44); and Tom's contacts enlarge Mary's contacts and *vice versa* (lines 45 and 46). They both bring some property into the family $(K_m$ and $K_f)$ (lines 47 and 48); and I am assuming that they form a close-knit family in which the two properties are for practical purposes merged into a single joint family property $(K_m+K_f=K_j)$ with a corresponding joint family income from property $(P_j)$ derived from the yield on the joint family property $(I_j)$. Similarly I assume also that Tom and Mary merge their individual earnings into a joint family income from work $(W_m+W_f=W_j)$. Thus there is a joint family income $(Y_j)$ from which joint family savings $(S_j)$ are made.

The main relationships within this family are now exactly similar to those in the first half of my diagram. I will not bore you with a tedious repetition of the strokes of luck which Tom and Mary may find in their further education, their social contacts, their investments, or their jobs, nor with the way in which the various elements in their family structure feed back upon each other. The relevant lines in the second half of my diagram correspond exactly to the same relevant lines in the first half of my diagram.[3]

All that part of the second half of the diagram is a mere application to the joint family of the relationships considered at some length in the case of Tom Jones's bachelor life. But there is now an important additional consideration to be introduced.

At the far right of the diagram we have a new home background ($H_2$) made up of Tom's and Mary's genes, education, income, social contacts, and property as these develop during their married life (lines 1', 2', 3', 4', 5'); and these provide endowments of genes, education, social contacts, and property as Tom's and Mary's little *GECK*s are born and grow up. If we want now to consider the life-cycle of one of these in particular (for example, the life-cycle of Tom's and Mary's son Richard), we start from the large *GECK* at the far right of the diagram, which shows Richard Jones endowed with genes, education, social contacts, and property from his home background ($H_2$) (lines 7', 9', 13', and 18'), but competing for education and property (lines 10' and 19') with his brothers and sisters represented by the other little *GECK*s proceeding from the same home background (line 6'). We have in fact cycled back to the extreme left-hand end of the diagram, but for generation 2 instead of generation 1.

But the size of Tom's and Mary's family will feed back into their own development as parents. The larger their family, the greater their financial responsibilities for feeding, clothing, housing, entertaining, and educating their children. The greater these responsibilities, the more difficult will it be for them to save and accumulate property. The broken line 49 represents the fact that the larger is the number of their children the more difficult will it be for Tom and Mary to accumulate property during their married life. It is probable that they will in fact accumulate a smaller property. But this is not absolutely certain, since while their ability to save will be less, their motivation to save may be greater, since the larger the family the more they must accumulate in order to be able to give each child an inheritance of any given absolute size. This increased motivation for saving is shown by the continuous line 50.

The size of their family will also affect their earnings. A large family may make it more difficult for Mary to go out to work and earn an income. On the other hand it will increase the need for income and may increase the parents' motivation to seek as high an income from work as they can manage to earn. The net result is uncertain and I have represented this by a solid line 51 which represents the number of children as increasing the

[3] In the diagram I have made this clear by numbering the relevant lines on the right-hand half of the diagram with the same numbers as the corresponding lines on the left-hand half of the diagram. Thus line 1 on the left-hand is numbered 1' on the right-hand half; and similarly for the other numbers.

motivation to earn income and a broken line 52 as reducing the mother's opportunities to earn income.

My diagram is complicated enough; but even so it is a great simplification of reality. There are causal relationships which I have omitted from my diagram. Thus I have not allowed for the fact that a man's genetic and educational background may affect his ability and his effort in investing his property so as to obtain the highest possible rate of return on it; nor have I allowed for the fact that a man may during his career invest resources in his own further education and training, his ability to do so depending upon the level of his income and property. It would be easy to add the arrowed lines to my diagrams which would represent these further positive feedbacks; I have refrained from doing so simply in order to keep the picture clear.

Moreover there are certain other very important relationships which are perhaps implied in my diagrams but which are not very clearly represented in them and which I have not discussed. Thus my diagram fails to bring out the fact that the endowments which parents can give to their children may compete with each other. The more money a parent invests in a child's formal education $(E)$ the less he may be able to leave to him in the form of other income-earning property $(K)$. Moreover, parents who apply their minds to the direct care, education, and amusement of their children at home may have less time and energy left for making money to leave to them.

Above all I have not discussed what determines the number of children which a set of parents will produce. It may well be that the structured genetic, educational, social, and economic characteristics of the parents do influence the size of their families, some types of family having on the average a larger number of children than others. But there would almost certainly be important dispersions around these characteristic averages, the representation of which would need the introduction of yet another 'luck' factor. I shall have something to say later about the important effects of differential fertility between different types of family; but I have nothing to say about the *causes* of differential fertility. This is probably the most important omission from the general scheme of relationships which I am trying to put before you.

Finally, there is another very closely related demographic consideration. My diagram is based on the assumption of the permanent monogamous family in which Tom has children only by Mary and Mary has children only by Tom. This is still the basic pattern in our society, though the bonds of marriage are looser than they used to be. In a society in which human breeding pairs were frequently reshuffled the picture would be very different. In particular I would need to modify substantially what I am about to say on the mating patterns of husband and wife.

But let me return to my model with all its admitted deficiencies. I have now discussed how Tom as a bachelor and how Tom and Mary as a married couple develop the endowments which they received from their parents, mingle them into joint family endowments, and hand them on in turn to their children. Let me next turn to the important question of the factors which caused Tom and Mary to choose each other as mates in the first place.

I have already argued that there are strong forces at work in society causing the basic components of good or bad fortune – genes, property, and social contacts – to become highly correlated with each other; and I shall start my analysis of this question by talking of the fortune of a man or woman as if there were some single index of the amount of genetic–property–social–contact 'fortune' which a man or a woman possessed at the time of his or her marriage.

The fact that Tom Jones mingles his fortune with that of Mary Smith before he transmits endowments to the next generation will tend to limit the degree of inequalities in family backgrounds and endowments which would otherwise develop.

Let us imagine all the eligible bachelors drawn up in a strictly descending order of their fortunes and all the eligible spinsters similarly drawn up in a strictly descending order of their fortunes. We may say that there is perfect assortative mating if the most fortunate bachelor married the most fortunate spinster, the second most fortunate bachelor the second most fortunate spinster, and so on down the two lists.

In this case there would be no averaging of fortunes as the generations succeeded each other. But consider, simply as an intellectual exercise, what might be called perfect anti-assortative mating. Suppose that the most fortunate bachelor married the most unfortunate spinster, the second most fortunate bachelor the second most unfortunate spinster, and so on down the bachelors' list and up the spinsters' list. The net result would be a tendency for the complete averaging of family fortunes in one generation, each family ending up with the same joint fortune.[4]

Completely random mating may be defined as the case in which each pair of bachelor and spinster were drawn at random from the two lists.

In fact mating is somewhere between the completely random and the perfectly assortative. A bachelor at a given position in the bachelor's pecking order will not inevitably marry the spinster at the corresponding position in the spinster's pecking order; but the choice is not purely random; the nearer any given bachelor and any given spinster are to the same position in their two pecking orders the more likely they are to choose each other as mates.

But so long as mating is not perfectly assortative there is some averaging and equalising tendency at work. If Tom's and Mary's fortunes do not correspond, then the joint family's fortune will be an average of whichever is the greater fortune and whichever is the lesser fortune. This is an equalising tendency; and if this were the whole of the story, inequalities would progressively disappear as the generations succeeded each other. For as long as differences of fortune persisted there would be a force at work taking two different fortunes, joining them together, and averaging them. This force is known as the regression towards the mean. Exceptionally large fortunes would tend to be averaged with lower

---

[4] On the assumption that the fortunes of the bachelors and of the spinsters were symmetrically distributed.

fortunes, and exceptionally low fortunes with higher fortunes. Fortunes would regress towards the average of fortunes.

If this regression towards the mean were the whole of the story we would expect to find society continually moving towards a more and more equal distribution of endowments. But there is another set of forces at work tending all the time to reintroduce inequalities, forces which we may call the forces of dispersion around the average. These forces are expressed in all the elements of luck to which I have drawn attention in my diagram – genetic luck $(L_g)$, luck in education $(L_e)$, luck in social contacts $(L_w)$. If the genetic factors in ability were purely additive, then children would be likely on the average to inherit purely genetic factors for ability which were the average of their parents' genetic factors. But this is only an average. Unless they are identical twins, they will differ. Some will be lucky and some unlucky in the draw from their parents' pool of genes; and thus inequalities between the most and the least able in the family will be re-established. Moreover, in their careers some will strike lucky in education, social contacts, investments, and jobs and will go uphill, while others will go downhill.

The ultimate self-perpetuating degree of inequality in the distribution of fortunes can thus be seen as depending upon the interaction of three forces. The less assortative is mating, the greater will be the regression towards the mean, and thus the smaller the ultimate degree of inequality. But elements of random luck in genetic make-up and in social and economic fortune cause a dispersion about the average; and the more marked are these elements, the greater will be the ultimate degree of inequality in society. Finally, the more marked are the positive feedbacks and the less marked the negative feedbacks in my diagram of structured developments of endowments, the greater the ultimate degree of inequalities.

So far I have spoken in terms of a composite single index of fortune. But for many purposes it is necessary to break it down into its components. Consider the effects of changes in social habits which modify previously rigid social barriers. Suppose that members of different social classes begin to meet more frequently in clubs, sports, and other institutions.

Such changes would almost certainly make mating less assortative in terms of property and social contacts. The child of propertied parents with useful social contacts would be more likely than before to meet the child of propertyless parents with less useful social contacts.

But as far as ability to earn is concerned, whether this be due to genetic or environmental luck, the change might lead to greater assortative mating. In particular the introduction of a system of higher education which was less structured according to social class would tend to bring boys and girls together according to their intellectual ability. This would be particularly true of a university system which ceased to be a finishing school for the sons of gentlefolk and started to provide an education for the able sons and daughters of all classes. Only the able children of gentlefolk would get to the university where, for the first time, they would meet the selected able children of the working class – and this just at that impressionable age when it has been known for young men and young women to become fond of each other.

It would be tempting to conclude from this that such social changes might lead to a more equal distribution of property (as mating was less assortative according to property ownership) but a less equal distribution of earnings (as mating was more assortative according to those endowments which led to intellectual ability). But this overlooks the interconnections between the various endowments. High earnings lead to high incomes which enable large properties to be accumulated. It is possible, though not certain, that in the end the more unequal distribution of earning power leading to a more unequal chance of accumulating property would have so potent an effect in increasing inequalities in the ownership of properties that it would outweigh the equalising effects on property of less assortative mating according to property ownership. The easier rise of the meritocratic élite and descent of the aristocratic dud might in the end increase the concentration of property as well as of income at the upper end, unless, of course, offset by governmental measures for the redistribution of income and wealth.

I turn to a second reason why we must distinguish between the different elements of good fortune. Until the new biologists have made further advances in their art, it will remain impossible for Tom and Mary Jones to control the genes which they pass on to their children. They cannot decide that little Richard shall inherit all the good genes and little Jane all the bad genes; little Richard and little Jane must both take part in the same lucky dip. But Tom and Mary Jones can decide that little Richard shall inherit all the family property while little Jane shall have none of it; and the laws and customs which regulate the inheritance of property can have a very important effect upon the ultimate degree of inequality in society.

One can illustrate this by means of the following artificial, but nevertheless, suggestive, exercise.[5] Imagine a society in which there is no capital accumulation but a constant stock of property which passes by inheritance from generation to generation. Suppose this property to be shared initially in equal parcels among a privileged 5 per cent of the families. Suppose each set of parents in the community to produce the same number of children, equally divided in each family between boys and girls. Suppose every boy and girl to survive and to get married and to have in turn the same number of boys and girls as did their parents. If each family produces one son and one daughter, then the population will be constant. If each family produces 2 sons and 2 daughters, the population will grow, doubling in each generation.

We wish to watch the distribution of property as the generations succeed each other. The table illustrates the way in which the combination of the degree of assortative mating according to property ownership, the growth rate of the population, and the laws and customs affecting the inheritance of property will combine to affect the outcome.

---

[5] Based on the analysis on page 63 of Professor A. B. Atkinson's *Unequal Shares* (London: Allen Lane, 1972).

| | | Percentage of population owning property | | | |
| --- | --- | --- | --- | --- | --- |
| | | Perfect assortative mating | | Completely random mating | |
| | Properties left to: | Stationary population | Growing population | Stationary population | Growing population |
| 1. | First son (*or* first daughter) | Percentage constant | Percentage falls (absolute number constant) | Percentage constant | Percentage falls (absolute number constant) |
| 2. | First child whether son or daughter | Percentage falls rapidly towards zero (concentration on one family) | | Percentage falls slowly towards zero (concentration on one family) | |
| 3. | All sons (*or* all daughters) | Percentage constant | | Percentage constant | |
| 4. | All children whether sons or daughters | Percentage constant | | Percentage rises towards 100 per cent (equality of ownership) | |

In the first row of the table we consider the case in which parents always leave their property to the eldest son. In this case the absolute number of property owners each owning an unchanged amount of property will remain unchanged, since each property owner leaves it all to one son, who leaves it all to one son, and so on *ad infinitum*. In a constant population the percentage of families owning property will, therefore, also remain constant. But in a growing population the constant number of property owners will come to represent a smaller and smaller proportion of the population, as all sons after the first son in each family join the growing ranks of those without property. The analysis would be exactly the same if all families always left all their property to the eldest daughter instead of the eldest son.

In the second row we consider as an instructive intellectual exercise what is probably an unusual set of laws and customs, namely that the whole property is left exclusively to the eldest child whether a boy or a girl. In this case whether the population be stationary or growing the ultimate outcome will be for the whole property of the community to be owned by one single individual. Two properties can in this case be joined together in holy matrimony, but once joined they can never be separated, since death does not part them. If an eldest daughter with a property marries an eldest son with a property, this becomes a single property which will be left to the eldest child of the marriage. If that child marries a propertyless spouse, the enlarged property remains unchanged; but if he or she in turn marries a propertied spouse, then the already enlarged property is enlarged still further into a still bigger single property.

This process of concentration will continue indefinitely; but the speed with which it occurs will depend upon the degree of assortative mating. If there were perfect assortative mating among property holders, there would be a tendency for the number of property holders to be halved in each generation, since at every generation a male property and a female property would be merged into a single property. If mating were perfectly random, the process of property meeting property would be much slower. But the inexorable final result would be the complete concentration of all properties into a single ownership.

In row 3 of the table I consider the case where only men own property but where, unlike row 1, the property is divided equally among all sons instead of being left only to the eldest son. In the case of the stationary population where each father has only one son, the effect in row 3 is identical with the effect in row 1. But where the population is growing there is a difference between rows 1 and 3. Where only eldest sons inherit, the absolute number of families owning property will remain the same. Where all sons inherit, and where propertied and propertyless families are growing at the same rate, the percentage of families owning property will remain unchanged as its original 5 per cent. Once again the analysis would be unchanged if it was the daughters and not the sons who inherit the whole of the family property.

Neither in row 1 nor in row 3 does the degree of assortative mating have any effect upon the result. Indeed, the degree of assortative mating is in these cases meaningless; since either all women or all men are propertyless, there is no meaning to be attached to the degree to which men and women select spouses with properties similar to their own.

In row 4, however, the absence of perfect assortative mating is crucial. We consider now the case where properties are split up equally among all children, whether they be sons or daughters. If there were perfect assortative mating, properties would remain in the ownership of a privileged 5 per cent of the population as in row 3. It makes no difference whether a property is left only to the sons in a family, or whether it is left half to the sons and half to the daughters, provided that these sons and daughters take as spouses the similarly endowed daughters and sons of similarly propertied families. Whether a whole property passes from a father to his sons who then marry propertyless wives or whether a half property passes to his sons who then marry wives who have received a similar share of a similar half property makes no difference to the property which they can then hand on to their children.

But if mating is not perfectly assortative, the difference between rows 3 and 4 is decisive. When properties are divided equally between sons and daughters and when the propertied sons may marry the daughters of propertyless parents and the propertied daughters may marry the sons of propertyless families, properties will be spread over a larger and larger number of the population. In the end there will result a complete equalisation of property ownership. If any properties of unequal size remained, sooner or later they would meet, marry, and be averaged before being left to the next generation. Inequalities could thus be reduced; they could never be reintroduced. The smaller the degree of assortative mating, the quicker the process of equalisation.

I need hardly add that laws and customs relating to inheritance do not consist exclusively of one or other of these pure forms. Moreover, of course, in the real world inequalities would be reintroduced and maintained by the accumulation of new properties and by all those factors of what I have called luck which lead to a dispersion about the average as new properties are accumulated; and the higher the degree of assortative mating according to properties, the greater the ultimate degree of inequality that will be sustained. In my artificial, mechanistic model of inheritance, I concentrated on a limited number of pure rules of inheritance, assumed that no new properties were accumulated, and omitted all the factors of dispersion which tend to restore inequalities solely to give an intuitive idea of the important underlying forces which over time the laws and customs of inheritance may be exerting in the background in society.

I introduced this discussion of the importance of laws and systems relating to the inheritance of property by pointing out that, while parents could control the distribution of their property among their children, they could not control the distribution of their genes. There remains another very important reason for distinguishing between genetic inheritance and the inheritance of property. If Tom and Mary Jones decide to leave all their property to little Richard, they cannot leave any to little Jane as well. But if little Richard is lucky in the genes which he receives from his mother and father, this in no way reduces the chances of little Jane being equally lucky in the genetic draw. Or to put this in a somewhat different way, if a set of parents have four instead of two children, they can leave each child only one-quarter instead of one-half of their combined property; but they can endow each child with the same average genetic make-up however few or however many children they may have.

This distinction is of fundamental importance when we consider the effects of differential fertility upon inequalities of income and wealth.

Suppose that the fertility of the fortunate were to rise and that of the unfortunate were to fall. As I have already pointed out, the fortunate parents would probably be able to accumulate somewhat smaller properties since they would have to support more children (line 49 in my diagram) and, on the assumption that the custom was to leave property equally divided among all children in the family, these somewhat smaller properties would be split into a larger number of fragments (line 19' in my diagram). Thus if parents have more children, each child can inherit a smaller share of what is probably a smaller total property. Conversely the less fortunate families having a smaller number of children to support might be able to accumulate somewhat larger properties, and in any case whatever properties they did accumulate would be less liable to be split into small fragments on the death of the parents. The effect of the differential fertility would undoubtedly be to mitigate inequalities in the ownership of property.

But there would be no such tendency to equalise genetic endowment. Having a large number of children in no way diminishes a parent's total genetic stock nor does it mean that this stock must be split into smaller fragments. An increase in the fertility of the fortunate relative to that of the unfortunate may raise the average quality of genetic endowments. But to equalise genetic endowment one would need to reduce the fertility both of the exceptionally fortunate and of the exceptionally unfortunate relative to the fertility of those with average fortune.

Endowments in social contacts probably fall in this respect somewhere in between genetic and property endowments. There are certain elements of social contact and atmosphere in the home which, like genetic endowments, can be enjoyed by all the children in the family, however few or many they may be. There are others, like expenditure on educational and similar social contacts, which, like property, if spent on Richard cannot be spent on Jane. There are still other elements which are intermediate; to have four instead of two children probably means that each child gets somewhat less attention, but more than half as much, attention from his parents.

To conclude, my remarks on the various relationships which determine the transmission of personal endowments have, I fear, been rather disjointed; but I hope that I have said enough to make it clear that they are all interrelated in a rather complicated single biological–demographic–social–economic system.

In any case the analysis remains woefully incomplete unless one can estimate quantitatively the relative importance of the various factors. The difficulties of quantifying the relationships are immense. First, it is extremely difficult to get measurements of many of the relevant variables. For example, genetic endowment may affect many hitherto unmeasured characteristics which are economically much more important than the IQ scores which we can measure and which for that very reason have been so much examined. Second, the very marked correlation between the various components of good and bad fortune which I have emphasised in this lecture itself makes quantitative measurement of the separate importance of each component statistically very difficult. Third, the very complexity of the intertwining of so many genetic, demographic, sociological, and economic factors raises very formidable problems for empirical research in this field.

In their recent book entitled *Inequality* [London: Allen Lane, 1973] Professor [Christopher] Jencks and his colleagues at Harvard claim to have shown that the factors which I have called luck are immensely more important in the explanation of inequalities between individuals than the structured biological, demographic, social, and economic factors which I have called fortune and on which I have concentrated in this lecture.

This may well be so; and if it is so, it has very far-reaching implications for the design of policies if we want to reduce inequalities. Many people and not only Marxists have maintained that we must rely more on structural changes in society's institutions which will basically readjust what I have called the structural endowments of good or bad fortune. But if Professor Jencks is correct, we should on the contrary rely less on factors of educational, social, and economic reform which will equalise people's structured fortunes in life and should rely more on a continuing direct day-to-day redistribution of the unequal incomes and properties which the chances of luck will continually be re-establishing in society. Such measures – for example, progressive taxation of incomes and property, negative income taxes, social dividends and other social benefits, minimum wage-rates, free education and medicine – would be needed simply because of their immediate direct effect on the standards of the lucky and the unlucky within any one generation.

Perhaps in the present state of our knowledge we should put more emphasis on such direct measures. If Professor Jencks is correct, that is the only way. If he is incorrect, such measures, in addition to their immediate impact effect on the equalisation of incomes and property within any one generation, will also help to set in motion in the right direction many of the self-reinforcing influences in society which I have catalogued in this lecture, since more equal incomes and properties may lead to somewhat more equal educational, social, and economic opportunities and thus, for what it is worth, to a more equal intergenerational transmission of endowments.

But I confess that I am disinclined to rush to this conclusion. I understand that the results of the many valuable empirical studies on these matters which have been and are being conducted are still to a considerable degree uncertain, controversial, and sometimes inconsistent with each other. There remains the possibility that fortune is not quite so secondary to luck as Professor Jencks considers it to be.

Thus something may still be gained from considering carefully those factors whose importance Professor Jencks is denying; for they really do at first sight appear to be very influential factors. Indeed, I must confess that I do find Professor Jencks's conclusions very surprising, although I have not the competence to criticise his sophisticated, careful, and scholarly statistical work.

I have already chosen an epitaph for inscription on my tombstone, namely: 'He tried in his time to be an economist; but common sense would keep breaking in.' It certainly is a useful irruption when common sense breaks into a sophisticated economic model to point out that the assumptions of the model simply rule out all the factors which casual empiricism suggests are important in the real world. But I cannot apply my common sense in that manner to Professor Jencks's work which covers comprehensively, but finds unimportant, all the main factors which my casual empiricism suggests to be important. Alas, common sense may imply no more than the conservative conventional wisdom which refuses to face new hard facts because they are disturbing. I know that in the end I must face the facts; but meanwhile I am surrendering to my common sense to the extent of preserving an open mind for just a little longer.

# PART III

# Growth and Development

# 20

# Mauritius: A Case Study in Malthusian Economics

*From* The Economic Journal, *vol. 71 (September 1961), pp. 521–534.*
*In November 1959 Meade was appointed Chairman of a Commission*

'To survey the present economic and social structure of Mauritius and to make recommendations concerning the action to be taken in order to render the country capable of maintaining and improving the standard of living of its people, having regard to current and foreseeable demographic trends.'

*(J. E. Meade and others,* The Economic and Social Structure of Mauritius *(London: Methuen, 1961), p. xv).*

Mauritius is a small isolated island lying far out in the Indian Ocean off the east coast of Africa. It is the outstanding example of a monocrop economy. No less than 99% of her exports are sugar or direct by-products of sugar; and she relies upon imports for the vast majority of her foostuffs, clothing, other consumption goods, raw materials and capital equipment.

As a result of her history the population of Mauritius is very diverse in its racial, religious and linguistic composition. Some 5% of the population is made up of the Franco–Mauritian families, French in origin, using the French language, nursed in French culture, Catholic in religion, and owners and managers of the great sugar estates. About 25% of the population is Creole, an admixture of white and coloured races but based essentially upon the slaves who were brought in from Madagascar and Africa before the abolition of slavery to work in the cane-fields. Some 66% of the population is Indian, the descendants of the indentured labour which was brought in after the abolition of slavery to produce sugar. There is a small but vigorous and enterprising Chinese population which accounts for 3–4% of the population and which dominates the retail trade. The British population is almost too small to show in the statistics, but includes the Governor, the Colonial Secretary, the Financial Secretary and a few other senior public servants.

In this island there has, since the end of the Second World War, been a great population explosion; and the purpose of this article is to take the case of Mauritius as an example in order to discuss in general terms one problem of economic analysis and policy which arises in the case of underdeveloped countries which are threatened with rapid population growth.[1]

Immediately after the Second World War there were great improvements in public health; and, in particular, malaria was eliminated. These medical changes have resulted in a fall in the death rate from 28 per 1,000 in 1936–40 to 12 per 1,000 in 1958, and, since better health increases fertility, a rise in the birth rate from 33 to 41 per 1,000 over the same period. As a result, the population which before the war was rising by about ½% per annum, is now rising by about 3% per annum. Compound interest is a powerful force. It is reckoned that, if fertility rates remain at their present level and if mortality rates are brought down (and there is no medical obstacle to this) to the levels ruling in the Western developed countries, the total population of Mauritius, which is now somewhat over 600,000, will be 3 million by the end of the century.[2]

This demographic change has been very recent and very sudden. There is now an exceptionally large number of young children rising towards working age. If one looks ahead fifteen years to 1975 one can say that the number of persons of working age in Mauritius will, barring some unexpected major calamity, almost certainly be about 50% greater than it is now. All the persons who will be of working age in fifteen years' time have already been born; and Mauritius would be faced with this enormous increase in her working population for whom productive employment must be found even if no baby were born in the island from tomorrow onward. The demographers tell us that this particular figure is not likely to be affected much by what happens over the next fifteen years to mortality. If mortality is brought down farther towards the levels in Western developed countries, the number of workers fifteen years hence will, of course, be somewhat greater than it would otherwise be. But this is a minor consideration. The major consideration is that past demographic changes have already decreed that Mauritius must now prepare for a 50% increase in her working population over the next fifteen years.[3]

It is the purpose of this article to discuss certain problems involved in

[1] The author of this article was chairman of an Economic Survey Mission which visited Mauritius early in 1960 and has since then reported to the Government of Mauritius. Those who are interested in a more detailed examination of the economic problems of Mauritius can consult that report which is published by Methuen & Co. under the title *The Economic and Social Structure of Mauritius*. The academic generalisations in the present article are, of course, wholly the responsibility of the author of this article and do not necessarily represent the views of the other members of the Economic Survey Mission.

[2] These and the following demographic figures are taken from the report of Professor Titmuss on *Social Policies and Population Growth in Mauritius* (London: Methuen, 1961).

[3] This estimate of a 50% increase in the working population to be absorbed into productive employment allows nothing for the economic development which is necessary in order to take up any existing slack in the economy. There is almost certainly some considerable unemployment and underemployment in the economy. A recent survey suggested that there was heavy unemployment in the economy. This has been disputed, and the statistical evidence is not perhaps conclusive. But there are undoubted symptoms of at least some underemployment, such as the great pressure on the Government to pad the public service and the public works department with unnecessary posts.

absorbing so sudden and great an increase of the working population into the economy. The analysis will proceed on the assumption that emigration from Mauritius will be able to provide at best only a minor mitigation of the problem. The arguments for making this assumption cannot be developed here, but are discussed in the report of the Economic Survey Mission.

The analysis will also proceed without any consideration of the future course of fertility and births in Mauritius. This is not to suggest that this is in fact unimportant. On the contrary, it is likely to be decisive for the future welfare of Mauritius. For example, if fertility rates remain at their present level the number of children under fifteen years of age is likely to increase by some 66⅔% over the next fifteen years, thereby greatly increasing the burden of their support upon the present generation of working age and presenting the educational authorities with an almost insoluble problem. Moreover, fifteen years constitute a quite arbitrary and short period in the life of a community; although it is true that all the persons who will be of working age fifteen years hence have already been born, it is not a matter of indifference whether the rapid increase in the size of the working population will continue in the following fifteen-year period. By heroic measures it may be possible to cope with one 50% increase in the working population, although it may well take more than fifteen years to absorb all of it into productive employment; it is quite another matter to absorb indefinitely a 3%-per-annum increase of population.

Indeed, in the author's opinion, Mauritius faces ultimate catastrophe unless effective birth control can be introduced fairly promptly into the island. The problems of introducing family planning are discussed at length in the Titmuss Report (see page 387) and the ultimate economic necessity for family planning is a main topic of the report of the Economic Survey Mission. These problems will not be discussed in this article which is concerned with the limited question how to absorb a once-for-all 50% increase of workers into an economy which is already experiencing population pressure. Mauritius has got to face this limited problem whatever happens to the future of the birth-rate.

Even if she is not already, Mauritius will soon be a country with an excess working population seeking employment. What is the right way to cope with a situation of this kind? Let us consider what classical economic analysis would have to say on this issue. Mauritius will be an economy in which unskilled labour is extremely plentiful and land and capital equipment are scarce. Such a situation would be one in which, in the classical competitive economy, the rent of land and the rates of profit and interest would rise and the real wage-rate would fall. This would give every incentive to private producers as well as to public authorities to go in for the production of things which required much labour and relatively little land and capital for their production and, in the production of any product or service, to choose those processes and techniques which used much labour and little land and capital.

The ultimate purpose is, of course, not to give employment, but to obtain the largest possible output from the community's (scarce) resources of land and capital and (plentiful) resources of labour. And this is what the classical price mechanism might be expected to bring about. A rise in rent and interest and a fall in wage-rates will induce producers to employ more labour with a given amount of land and capital if, but only if, a larger output can thereby be produced. No entrepreneur will take on more labour with a given amount of land and capital in order to produce a smaller or less-valuable total output. Indeed, it is one of the main merits of this use of the price mechanism that it will not choose inefficient techniques in order to make work for work's sake.

There can be little doubt that this principle is of the utmost relevance in an economy such as that of Mauritius. A few examples must suffice. In cane-fields weeding can be carried out either by hand or else, in part at least, by the use of imported chemical herbicides. Which method it is profitable for the sugar estates to use depends essentially upon the wage and availability of labour. Another example is the handling of sugar when it has been produced. At present, sugar is put into bags at the factory on the sugar estate, transported by rail to Port Louis, carried by hand from the rail head on to the ship, where the bag is opened and emptied into the ship's hold. The alternative method of bulk handling, which is at present under discussion, would be to load the sugar automatically into special containers on road vehicles at the factory, to discharge the sugar from these vehicles automatically into silos at the quayside and to discharge the sugar automatically direct from the silos into the ship's hold at the quayside. This method would economise much labour in stevedoring at Port Louis, in handling the sugar in the factory and in the growing of the hemp and the manufacture of the hemp into bags, which is done at present at a government factory in Mauritius. On the other hand, it would involve very heavy capital expenditure on the new road vehicles, on deepening the harbour to bring the ships to the quayside, on the new equipment at the port and so on. Whether or not it is the cheaper method depends essentially upon the wage-rate of labour compared with the cost of acquiring the necessary capital.

A further example is given by the problems involved in the establishment of a tea industry in Mauritius. Tea is a rather labour-intensive crop and needs a higher level of employment per acre than sugar. There are prospects that Mauritius might be able to produce good-quality tea. Just because tea is a rather labour-intensive crop it is very appropriate as a way of saving land and using labour. But just because it is a labour-intensive crop the wage element in its cost is of great importance. At present the wage-rate in Mauritius is significantly higher than in Ceylon and East Africa, with whose teas Mauritian tea would have to compete. The success of this new venture for employment will be greatly affected by the cost of labour in Mauritius.

Mauritius will be able to find productive employment for a greatly increased working force only if she can establish and expand some manufacturing industries. She cannot rely on finding employment for a greatly increased population in her present staple industry, namely sugar. The sugar industry is a highly progressive one in which output per worker employed is constantly rising. At the same time the total amount of sugar which Mauritius may export is strictly limited under the Commonwealth and International Sugar Agreements. Though it is to be expected that the expansion of world demand will enable the Mauritian quotas under these Sugar Agreements to be raised, it would be foolhardy to assume that they will be raised much more rapidly than the output of the existing number of workers in the sugar industry. In any case, apart from these marketing problems there is a strict limit to the amount of land on which sugar can be grown, and this must set a strict upper limit to employment in the sugar industry in Mauritius. Other lines of agricultural production are capable of some significant expansion; but in the end limitations of land will make it impossible to find sufficient employment in these lines of agricultural production.

Mauritius must develop some industries. But in manufacturing industry the island starts with many disadvantages. She has little technical know-how in manufactures or experience, outside the sugar factories, in the conduct of industry; she has little technical training; she has few raw materials; she is not rich in capital; and her domestic market alone will not provide a sufficient market for large-scale production. She must emulate in a minor way economies such as Hong Kong, Jamaica, Japan and the United Kingdom, where raw materials are imported to be made into manufactures for export. But can Mauritius establish such manufactures except on the basis of cheap labour? Initially, at least, plentiful labour will be her one comparative advantage.

While the simple classical answer would be to reduce the wage-rate in Mauritius, in fact in recent years exactly the opposite has happened. After a considerable period of stability, both of the cost of living and of the money wage-rate, between 1956 and 1959 the wage-rate in the sugar industry (which sets the pattern for the rest of the island) went up by some 45%, while the cost of living remained constant. Here in a most marked form is the basic economic dilemma or paradox of such communities. The sugar industry was certainly very prosperous in the sense that the big sugar estates were making very good incomes from rent and profits, and the political awakening of the underdog in Mauritius has not unnaturally been associated with aggressive trade-union action, which has pushed up the wage-rate in the sugar industry as a method of redistributing part of the wealth of the island. But from the point of view of getting the best use of resources in Mauritius there is little doubt that the wage-rate ought to be very low.

Moreover, the effect of the wage-rate on the level of rents and profits in an economy like that of Mauritius will affect the rate of economic development in another way. In Mauritius the big sugar estates do in fact plough back a large part of their profits for the expansion of the sugar industry; the rate of profits tax is high, the rates of personal income tax on the higher incomes are high and progressive, and these direct taxes are collected by an efficient tax administration. The result is that a substantial part of the high gross profits and rents either goes direct into the capital development of the sugar industry or goes to swell the Government's budgetary revenue, from which capital development outside the sugar industry is largely financed by the state. A high wage-rate is also, therefore, liable to reduce the rate of economic development by reducing the sources of private and public capital accumulation.

This is perhaps the basic economic conundrum of such overpopulated underdeveloped countries. Let us take an extreme example and consider a country which is so overpopulated that if all available labour were employed the marginal product of labour would be zero. Then to get the most out of the country's resources and to maximise its national income labour should be free to all who want to use it. But, of course, if the wage-rate is set at zero, while the national income may be maximised it will all go in rents, interest, dividends and profits to the owners of property, and none of it will go to labour. If the wage-rate is set at a level which gives labour a reasonable share of the product, then there will be underemployment and unemployment; foreign capital will not be attracted as it might be by the high rate of profit which would result if the labour which it employed were freely available to it;[4] traditional labour-intensive processes and products will be discouraged; engineers and technicians, who in any case will normally have been trained in developed countries where the need is to save labour rather than capital, will not be encouraged to apply new scientific knowledge in devising new ways to enable much labour to work effectively with little capital equipment; the economy will not be able to compete as it should with foreign producers of labour-intensive products; and the sources of capital accumulation, and so of economic growth, may be dried up.

What are the theoretical possibilities of squaring this circle and of introducing an economic system which enables labour to be treated as a really cheap element in the cost of production but results nevertheless in a reasonable distribution of the national product? One can discuss such systems under six main heads.

1   Suppose that by some wave of a magic wand the ownership of a considerable amount of property could be transferred from the private citizen to the state without the state incurring any debt to the private citizen in respect of that property. The Government would have a considerable income from that property. If, then, there were a fall in the money wage-rate in order, in the ways discussed above, to promote economic efficiency and growth in the economy, the Government's income from profits and rents would be increased and it could use its income from property to distribute some form of social benefit to maintain the incomes of the workers whose wage income had fallen. Moreover, by deciding how much of its income from property should be so distributed in social dividend and how much should be saved and added to its budget surplus to finance capital development, the Govern-

---

[4] The fact that in many underdeveloped countries the wage-rate is higher than it would be in full-employment competitive equilibrium may be one of the main reasons which explains the paradox that capital appears to be attracted for investment into developed countries such as the United States, the United Kingdom and Germany, where the ratio of capital to labour is already high, rather than into underdeveloped countries where the supply of capital is low relatively to that of labour. The return on capital in such underdeveloped countries would be much higher if the wage-rate were reduced to correspond to the marginal product of labour in conditions of full employment.

ment would be in a good position to control the total amount of capital accumulation, and so the rate of economic growth.

But, in the absence of a revolutionary situation which on other grounds would, in Mauritius at least, do much more economic harm than good, this solution can be adopted only very gradually. For the Government can build up public ownership of income-bearing property unencumbered by an offsetting public debt only gradually as it uses an annual budget surplus to improve its capital position. In the long run this is an important way in which countries such as Mauritius can aim, at least in part, to make low wage-costs compatible with a reasonable distribution of income. But it can hardly be relied upon to make any very great immediate impact on the problem.

2    Suppose that by some wave of a similar magic wand the ownership of property could be made much more equal without in any way diminishing the efficiency with which land and capital were used for productive purposes. The direct conflict between the desire for a high wage-rate to give a reasonable distribution of income and for a low wage-rate to promote employment in an overpopulated economy would be solved. Suppose that the representative citizen were a representative property-owner as well as a representative wage-earner. If, on grounds of economic efficiency, the wage-rate must go down and the rate of profit up, the representative citizen would gain on the roundabout of his property what he lost on the swing of his labour. This sort of solution might have some social and political advantages over that of a wide extension of the state ownership of property; but, together with all the other solutions discussed below, it would have one economic disadvantage in that the state might have to raise substantial sums in tax revenue to provide a budget surplus for the public finance of much of the capital accumulation needed for economic growth. For all methods of redistributing income more equally will probably reduce private savings, and the state ownership of unencumbered income-bearing property is the only source of finance for an offsetting increase in public savings without having to impose additional taxes for this purpose.

It is impossible in this article to consider at length by what measures in a free society the ownership of property might be more equally spread among the citizens of that society. This is a badly neglected subject which merits very full treatment, and there is much to be said on the question. But once more, short of a sudden revolution, which on other economic grounds is greatly to be deplored, this is a solution which in developed and underdeveloped countries alike can be introduced only very gradually. It certainly cannot deal quickly with the pressing problems of Mauritius.

3    A third type of solution which is very closely connected with the one just discussed is the solution of self-employment. For example, in Mauritius, as already explained, the production of tea, which is labour-intensive, is probably very justified in terms of real comparative costs, but it may well be threatened by the height of the money wage-rate. One way round this problem would be the organisation of tea production on the basis of small-holdings in which the owner and his family produced tea

not for a given money wage but for what it would fetch on the world market. There are, of course, many problems of efficiency of production on small-holdings. In the case of Mauritian tea, for example, it is essential to ensure that only tea of a uniformly high quality is produced. Production of tea on small-holdings would have to be organised so that there were some centralised processing of leaves and some centralised supervision of the type of tea planted and of its mode of cultivation. But if these problems can be solved, the self-employment of the small-holder as compared with the employment of labour for a wage on the large estate certainly helps to get round the basic dilemma discussed in this article.

It is, however, important to realise what it does and what it does not do. Let us take a very simple numerical example. Suppose that in our economy labour is so plentiful that its marginal product would be zero if it were fully employed. Suppose that the owner of an acre of land would, if labour were available free, use 100 units of labour on his land to produce 100 units of product. His income as a landlord would be this 100 units of

|  | *I* | *II* | *III* | *IV* |
|---|---|---|---|---|
| Amount of land | 1 | 1 | 1 | 1 |
| Amount of labour | 100 | 50 | 100 | 100 |
| Output | 100 | 75 | 100 | 100 |
| Wage-rate at which a unit of labour is hired by the landlord | 0 | 1 | — | — |
| Total wage income | 0 | 50 | 75 | 0 |
| Rate of rent at which a unit of land is hired by the workers | — | — | 25 | 100 |
| Total income of landowner | 100 | 25 | 25 | 100 |

output, since his wage cost was zero (see column I of the table). Suppose now that the wage-rate is fixed not at zero but at 1 unit of output, and that in these conditions it would pay our landowner to employ only 50 units of labour to produce only 75 units of output. His total output is now 75, his wage bill is 50 and his income from land is therefore only 25. Suppose that this wage system of employment is in operation all over the economy. Then the income from a unit of land is 25, the wage of labour is 1 but at least half the labour force is unemployed or underemployed (see column II of the table). Suppose now that a worker were able to hire a unit of land at the current rent of 25 and applied to it 100 units of his own and his family's labour to produce 100 units of output. He is able to obtain an income of 75 instead of only 50 for himself and his family because – since he and his family are underemployed – he does not mind working on his land until there is no more productive work which he can find to do on it (see column III of the table). In other words, in a general milieu of wage employment, self-employment as an exceptional device is a way of expanding employment to the benefit of the workers without any detriment to the landlord and without any change in the ownership of the land.

But suppose that the system of self-employment became general throughout the economy. The position would be very different. We imagine now all landlords hiring out their land at a rent of 25 to self-employed workers who apply 100 units of labour to each unit of land and produce 100 units of output, of which they keep 75 for their own income (see column III of the table). But why should the landlords show such moderation? If there is a scarcity of land and plenty of working farmers there is nothing to prevent landlords from raising the rent from 25 much more nearly to the full 100 which represents its value to the working family. In this case the full shift from wage employment to self-employment will have increased output from 75 to 100: but it will have reduced the income of the workers from 50 towards zero (see column IV of the table).

This, of course, will not be the case if the change is combined with a total or partial shift in the ownership of the land to the self-employed worker. In our example, if the previous owner could by law get only a fixed ground rent of 25, while the new self-employed worker can otherwise do what he likes with the land, the shift from wage employment to small-holding self-employment would raise output from 75 to 100 and the worker's income from 50 to 75 (see column III of the table). In brief, the introduction of small-holding self-employed labour in an overpopulated country can help to solve the clash between the efficiency of a low wage and the equity of a high worker's income either if it is introduced merely as a marginal device in certain occupations or else if it is combined with some legal changes which in fact give the small-holder at least a partial interest in the ownership of the land. In the latter case it is, of course, to this extent a special form of the general principle of a wider spread ownership of property discussed under (2) above.

4    A fourth line of approach to the solution of our dilemma is the subsidisation of employment by the state. This can take many forms. It might mean that a state subsidy of so much a week was paid to every employer for every worker which he employed. Or the subsidy might be paid only in respect of workers employed in certain special lines of activity – for example, in all manufacturing establishments employing more than a certain number of persons. In all these cases it would, however, have the effect of making the wage received by the worker greater than the cost to the employer of employing an additional worker, and this is, of course, exactly what is needed to resolve the basic paradox.

But here again it is important to realise what the device does, and what it does not, achieve. The snag is, of course, the problem of raising the additional tax revenue needed to pay the subsidy on employment. Let us suppose that taxation is raised by an income tax on non-wage incomes, i.e. on profits and rents. Then the entrepreneur is favoured by the subsidy on the labour which he employs, but is hit by the additional tax which he must pay on the profits and rents which he makes, the subsidy in total amount just offsetting the extra taxation. Something is gained. The entrepreneur who goes in for a specially labour-intensive product or process of production will be favoured; he will have a specially high ratio of wage-cost (on which he receives subsidy) to income on land and capital (on which tax is paid). The system will give a definite incentive to employ more labour relatively to land and capital, which is what is wanted.

But what this system will not do is shown by comparing its effect with the effect of a straightforward reduction in the wage-rate and rise in the rate of profit on the attraction of outside capital into the economy in question. Suppose that the ownership of property in Mauritius were so widespread that the Mauritians could deal with their problems simply by reducing the wage-rate in Mauritius and permitting the consequential rise in profits and rents. This would give an added incentive for Mauritian and foreign owners of capital to invest their capital inside rather than outside Mauritius. But if the problem is met by a tax on profits and rents used to pay a subsidy on the employment of labour, the average owner of property will gain on the wage subsidy just about as much as he loses on the tax on income from property and, generally speaking, will have no more or less incentive to invest in Mauritius rather than elsewhere, though what capital is invested in Mauritius will be used to employ a larger amount of labour.

In conditions such as those of Mauritius there is a further reason why not too much reliance should be placed on this method of employment subsidies. This is the problem of administration. In a community where administrative experience is limited, and where loyalties towards the members of the same race and of one's own extended family are very strong, the problem of ensuring that an entrepreneur's wage list was not padded with otherwise underemployed cousins and second cousins whose main function in the firm was to be the occasion for a subsidy would be very difficult. It may be necessary for this reason to make use of this weapon of subsidies on employment only in much more limited and rough-and-ready forms. In an economy such as Mauritius, in which it is essential to introduce manufacturing industries in order to give employment, it will almost certainly be necessary to give infant-industry assistance of one kind or another to selected new enterprises which are considered promising, whether this help be given by tariff protection, by the subsidisation of output, by the provision of cheap loans, by remission of taxation or by other means. In the selection of the enterprises to be aided the authorities can give high weight to the probable labour-intensity of the enterprise. Other things being equal, the authorities in an economy such as Mauritius should choose for assistance those enterprises which are likely to use a high ratio of labour to capital and land in their production; and in appropriate cases, where administrative difficulties would not be too formidable, they may be able to go farther and to give their support in the form of a subsidy on the number of persons employed.

There is, in any case, one form of support which should be avoided in the Mauritian type of situation. At present in Mauritius, as in many other British overseas territories, following the United Kingdom pattern, assistance is given to the building up of new enterprises and the expansion of old enterprises through a system of investment and initial allowances. These are in fact tax remissions which depend upon investment in new capital equipment. They are, therefore, specially favourable to the industry and processes which use a high ratio of capital to labour. They may be appropriate enough in the United Kingdom or in the United States of America, where in conditions of full employment labour may be very scarce but capital relatively plentiful, so that it is difficult to absorb all new savings in new investments. But this is the precise reverse of the principle which it is desirable to apply in an economy such as Mauritius, where whatever form of assistance is given should favour the industries and processes which employ a high ratio of labour to capital. A general remission of taxation on all or selected new enterprises is to be preferred to a remission of tax which is geared to heavy expenditure on capital equipment.

5 A fifth device which might be used is the raising of revenue in order to subsidise the worker's cost of living. This policy has to a limited extent already been applied in Mauritius, where it has taken the form of government monopoly of the import of rice, the staple diet of the Mauritian, the authorities selling the imported rice at a low stable price, which for a number of years involved a loss on the import of the rice. Subsidies on the cost of living are administratively practicable; they can affect all workers in all occupations; and they effectively raise the real wage to the worker by reducing his cost of living without raising the money cost of employing labour by the entrepreneur. If a general subsidy on all employed labour is administratively impracticable it would seem that much the same result ought to be capable of achievement through a system of cost-of-living subsidies.

Such a system would, of course, not avoid the problem of raising tax revenue, though in his case the tax revenue would be needed to pay a subsidy to cover the loss in, say, the trade in rice rather than to pay a subsidy direct to the employer of labour. In this respect this system would have the same limitations as a system of subsidies on employment. But the policy of subsidising the cost of living would have two special disadvantages which could be avoided by a direct subsidy to employment if it were administratively possible.

The first of these two problems is probably of minor importance in the conditions of the Mauritian economy, but it may be worth mentioning for the sake of completeness of the analysis. For administrative reasons it is possible to subsidise the cost of living only by subsidising one or two particular but important items in the cost of living. In the case of Mauritius it would mean, above all, subsidising the cost of rice. This leads to some distortion of demand. The subsidised articles are made especially cheap to consumers relatively to the cost to society of acquiring them. Any consequential heavy shift of demand away from unsubsidised on to subsidised articles may involve a social loss because it involves a shift of consumers away from products which, relatively to their selling prices, cost little to society to acquire to products which cost much to acquire. This consideration is relatively unimportant, however, if the substitution in consumption between the subsidised and the unsubsidised products is low, so that there is in fact very little wasteful distortion of demand; and this is probably the case with rice in Mauritius, where the amount of rice needed by each consumer is a relatively fixed quantity.

But the second limitation to the use of the weapon of cost-of-living subsidies is a much more serious practical matter. In the case of direct subsidies on employment the cost of labour to the employer can be reduced by the amount of the subsidy without any reduction in the money wage-rate; the real wage to the worker is maintained because his money wage and the cost of living are unchanged. In the case of subsidy to the cost of living the cost of labour to the employer can be reduced only if the money wage-rate is reduced; the real wage to the worker is maintained because the cost of living is reduced *pari passu* with the reduction in the money wage-rate. In other words, in order to get a net reduction in the cost of labour to the employer the cost-of-living subsidy – unlike the direct subsidy to employment – involves getting the agreement of the trade unions to an actual reduction in money wage-rates.

This is likely to prove a very difficult operation in many countries, and Mauritius is no exception. If such agreement cannot be reached, the cost-of-living subsidy cannot be used to bring about any substantial reduction in money wage-costs, but must be relegated to the secondary role of helping to prevent increases in money wage-costs which might otherwise occur. This secondary role can be of extreme effectiveness in a general world inflationary situation. If all money prices and costs including wage-rates are going up by, say, 3% per annum, then to hold money wage-rates and the cost of living constant by means of a cost-of-living subsidy is in its effect more or less equivalent to reducing money wage-rates and the cost of living by 3% per annum in an environment in which all other money prices and costs are constant. But unfortunately from this point of view the post-war inflationary tendency of world prices has at least temporarily ceased; and if a country such as Mauritius intended now to obtain any marked effect from a cost-of-living subsidisation policy this would involve a conscious agreement between the government authorities who paid the cost-of-living subsidy and the trade unions and employers' federations who fixed the money wage-rate.

It would, of course, be possible to achieve the desired result by a once-for-all depreciation of the Mauritian rupee in terms of sterling and other foreign currencies, provided that the consequential increase in the prices of importable and exportable products in terms of Mauritian rupees were offset by increased cost-of-living subsidies and were not accompanied by a rise in the Mauritian money wage-rate. It would in Mauritian conditions be extremely dangerous to start a vicious circle of inflation – depreciation of the rupee leading to rising prices, leading to rising money wage-rates, leading to further depreciation and so on. An increase in cost-of-living subsidies to reduce wage-costs without a change in real wage incomes would have to be accompanied by the agreement of the workers to allow *either* a once-for-all reduction in the money wage-rate *or else* a once-for-all depreciation of the exchange rate without any rise in the money wage-rate.

6   A sixth device is the introduction of some element of social security benefits whereby the state raises revenue to pay out to the citizens unemployment benefit, sickness benefit, family allowances, old-age pensions and the like. With such a system the standard of living of the

workers could be maintained even though the money wage-rate, and so the cost of labour to the employer, were reduced. Like the methods of direct subsidies to employment and cost-of-living subsidies, it involves all the problems of raising the necessary tax revenue to finance the scheme; and like the method of cost-of-living subsidies, its introduction as a means of lowering wage costs would involve obtaining the agreement of the workers *either* that the money wage-rate should actually be reduced, *or else* that a depreciation of the rupee should be allowed to raise the cost of living without any accompanying rise in the wage-rate, when these social security benefits outside the wage-rate were introduced. In the absence of any such agreement one can only hope to achieve a much more moderate result from it – namely, that in future it will be easier to prevent further rises in the money wage-rate because of the existence of social security benefits outside the wage system. The method of social security benefits has, however, two possible advantages over that of cost-of-living subsidies. First, it does not lead to a distortion of demand on to any specially subsidised commodities; and secondly, it enables the benefits to be concentrated in a more direct manner on to those who most need help – the sick, the unemployed, the children, and so on.

This method of coping with the problem is particularly relevant in Mauritius at the present. At the same time that the Economic Survey Mission was making its enquiries in Mauritius, Professor Titmuss was in Mauritius with a Mission preparing a report for the Government of Mauritius on how they might introduce a social security system into the island. The first quarter of 1960 was indeed a heavy time for the island of Mauritius, which in that short period was visited not only by the two cyclones Alix and Carol but also by the two Professors Titmuss and Meade. The destruction that was started by Alix was completed by Carol. What about the relationships between the two professors? For the demographic reasons already explained at length, it is going to be a great achievement if Mauritius can find productive employment for her greatly increased working population without a serious reduction in the existing average standard of living. If money wage-rates are set at high levels and, in addition, heavy taxation must be imposed to finance new social security arrangements, the prospects in Mauritius will be bleak. But if a moderate element of social security can be used as a means of establishing a really effective policy of wage restraint, this is a system which makes very good sense in Mauritian conditions.

This is not, of course, the whole of the Titmuss story. The administration of public assistance in Mauritius was rapidly breaking down, and its costs rapidly mounting under the pressure of the growing population. Some extensive recasting of social security arrangements was, therefore, in any case essential. Moreover, there is now a chance to recast these arrangements in a way which helps to establish the pattern of a three-child family instead of making the very large family a financially paying proposition, as it was tending to become under existing arrangements. Family planning and family welfare can be co-ordinated. These matters are studied in detail in Professor Titmuss' report. For the purpose of this article it is necessary only to make the point that in an overpopulated underdeveloped country such as Mauritius low wage rates combined with a social security system constitute a very sensible economic framework.

As a practical policy in Mauritius in the immediate future probably the best that can be done is to aim at a mixture of various devices. Self-employment on small-holdings, together with a wide ownership of land, may in some cases be helpful, but it should be encouraged only if it can be organised in schemes which sufficiently ensure the efficient conduct of the small-holder's operations. Financial assistance to infant enterprises by way of tax remission, subsidisation or tariff adjustment can be given with special liberality to labour-intensive products and processes; and wherever possible forms of help which encourage capital-intensive production (such as investment allowances) can be avoided and forms of help which encourage the employment of labour (such as employment subsidies) can be used. Government trade in rice can continue to be used to stabilise the cost of living; and this, together with the introduction of social security benefits, might be used to get the effective agreement of the trade unions to a conscious policy of wage restraint. Meanwhile an annual budget surplus can be used by the Government to finance productive capital investment, which will gradually give the Government an income from property which can be used to support the standard of living of low-wage workers.

# 21

---

# The Effect of Savings on Consumption
# in a State of Steady Growth

---

*Meade contributed this article to the* Review of Economic Studies *Symposium on Production Functions and Economic Growth (vol. 29, June 1962, pp. 227–234). The other contributors were K. J. Arrow, N. Kaldor and J. Mirrlees, P. Samuelson, R. Solow, Joan Robinson, D. G. Champernowne, J. Black, Richard Stone and J. A. C. Brown.*

Assume an economy with one product $(Y)$ and three factors of production (capital $K$, labour $L$, and land $N$), capital being an accumulated stock of $Y$. Assume neutral technical progress at a constant rate $r$. Assume constant proportional marginal products of the factors in the sense indicated below. We have then a production function of the form:—

$$Y = R\, K^U\, L^Q\, N^Z\, e^{rt} \tag{1}$$

where $R$, $U$, $Q$, $Z$, and $r$ are all constant. $U = (\partial Y/\partial K)/(Y/K)$ and represents the (constant) proportional marginal product of $K$ or the (constant) proportion of income which will go to profits if capital is paid a reward equal to its marginal product; and similarly for $Q$ and $Z$. There are constant returns to scale if $U + Q + Z = 1$ and increasing returns to scale if $U + Q + Z > 1$.

Keep $N$ constant; differentiate (1); and write

$$y = \frac{1}{Y}\frac{dY}{dt},\ \ k = \frac{1}{k}\frac{dK}{dt},\ \text{and}\ l = \frac{1}{L}\frac{dL}{dt}.$$

We have:—

$$y = Uk + Ql + r. \tag{2}$$

Make now two alternative assumptions about $l$.

I.   $l$ is constant. In this case we assume that the growth of the population is at a constant rate, $l$, and that full employment is maintained.

II.   $l = y$. In this case we assume that the wage-rate paid is a fixed proportion, $j$, of the marginal product of labour. In perfect competition $j = 1$, but with given degrees of monopoly in the sale of the product and/or of monopsony in the hiring of labour $j < 1$. We assume further that there is a given real subsistence wage-rate $(W_s)$ and that the growth of population is such that there is always a reserve of labour available for employment at this fixed wage. Since total wages are $jQY$, total employment is $jQY/W_s$. If we now write $L$ for the demand for labour instead of for the supply of labour, $L = jQY/W_s$. Since $j$, $Q$, and $W_s$ are constants, we have $l = y$.

In case II with $l = y$ we can express equation (2) as $y(1 - Q) = Uk + r$, or

$$y = \frac{U}{1 - Q} k + \frac{r}{1 - Q}. \tag{3}$$

We assume that $U + Q < 1$ or in other words that, while there may be increasing returns to land, labour, and capital increased together, these are not so potent as to lead to increasing returns to labour and capital applied in increased amount to a constant amount of the fixed factor, land.

In both cases I and II we now have an equation of the form

$$y = \alpha k + \beta \tag{4}$$

where $\alpha$ is a positive constant fraction ($U$ in case I and $U/(1 - Q)$ in case II),[1] and $\beta$ is a constant growth rate ($Ql + r$ in case I and $r/(1 - Q)$ in case II).

Assume a constant proportion of income $(S)$ to be saved. Then $k = SY/K$. Since $S$ is constant, $k$ is constant only if $Y/K$ is constant, i.e. only if $y = k$. But if $k$ is constant, then from (4) $y$ is constant. We have, therefore, a constant rate of growth of output if $y = k$. From (4) we see that this constant rate of growth is given by

$$y = k = \frac{SY}{K} = \frac{\beta}{1 - \alpha}. \tag{5}$$

By integration of (4) one has $Y = R' K^\alpha e^{\beta t}$  (6)

where $R'$ is a constant. Confining our attention to values of $Y$ and $K$ in situations of a steady rate of growth, we have from (5) $K = [S(1 - \alpha)/\beta] Y$. Substituting this value of $K$ into (6) we obtain

$$Y = R'' S^{\frac{\alpha}{1 - \alpha}} e^{\frac{\beta}{1 - \alpha} t} \tag{7}$$

where $R''$ is a constant.

[1] Since $0 < U < 1 - Q < 1$, $U$ and $U/(1 - Q)$ are both positive fractions; but $U/(1 - Q) > U$.

From (7), keeping $t$ constant, we have

$$\frac{\partial Y}{\partial S} \bigg/ \frac{Y}{S} = \frac{\alpha}{1 - \alpha}. \tag{8}$$

But if we write $C$ for the level of consumption, $C = Y(1 - S)$ so that

$$\frac{\partial C}{\partial S} = \frac{\partial Y}{\partial S}(1 - S) - Y. \tag{9}$$

Substituting for $\partial Y/\partial S$ from (8) into (9) we have

$$\frac{\partial C}{\partial S} \bigg/ \frac{C}{S} = \frac{\alpha - S}{(1 - \alpha)(1 - S)}. \tag{10}$$

In other words at any one time in a state of steady growth a higher propensity to save would have resulted in a higher level of consumption if $\alpha > S$. In case I this would be so if $U > S$, i.e. if the proportion of income saved were less than the proportion of income going to profits, when capital is paid a reward equal to its marginal product.[2] But in case II the level of $S$ which maximises $C$ is higher than $U$, namely $U/(1 - Q)$.

\* \* \*

Since I wrote the above I have had the opportunity of reading Mrs Robinson's note on a 'Neo-Neoclassical Theorem' ['A Neo-Classical Theorem', *Review of Economic Studies*, vol. 29 (June 1962), pp. 219–26]. This has suggested to me the following way of expressing the above conclusions. From (5) above, we know that in a state of steady growth $SY/K = \beta/(1 - \alpha)$, i.e. $SY/K$ is a constant. If, therefore, $S$ were 1% greater, $Y/K$ would have to be 1% lower. $K$, owing to greater accumulated savings, would be greater; $Y$ would also be greater because $K$ was greater; but because of diminishing returns $Y$ would have grown in a smaller proportion than $K$ and $Y/K$ would be lower. Indeed, from (4) we know that the proportionate rise in $Y$ will be a fraction $\alpha$ of the proportionate rise in $K$. In other words, at any one point of time in a state of steady growth, the rate of growth of the capital stock $(k)$ is independent of the level of $S$, but the size of the capital stock $(K)$ which will have been accumulated will be greater, the greater is $S$. We can, therefore, transform the question whether a higher $S$ will lead to a higher $C$ into the question whether a higher $K$ will lead to a higher $C$.

Write $I \, (\equiv dK/dt)$ for investment. $C = Y - I$, so that $\partial C/\partial K = \partial Y/\partial K - \partial I/\partial K$. In other words, an increase in $K$ will lead to an increase in $C$ if $\partial Y/\partial K > \partial I/\partial K$, i.e. if the additional income produced by the greater amount of capital is greater than the additional investment out of income which is needed to maintain a constant proportionate rate of growth for

[2] I have already shown this case on page 112 of the second edition of my *A Neo-Classical Theory of Economic Growth* (London: Allen & Unwin, 1962).

the higher capital stock. Since the rate of growth is constant, $I/K$ (which is the same as $k$) must be constant. It follows that $\partial I/\partial K = I/K$, since it is only if $I$ and $K$ increase in the same proportion (i.e. if $\partial I/I = \partial K/K$) that $I/K$ will remain unchanged. The condition that $\partial C/\partial K$ will be $> 0$ can, therefore, be written as $\partial Y/\partial K > I/K$.[3]

Now $\partial Y/\partial K$ is the additional output due to a unit increase in the capital stock. In case I this is the marginal product of capital or – in competitive equilibrium – the rate of profit. In this case the condition for $\partial C/\partial K > 0$ becomes that the rate of profit should be greater than the rate of growth of the capital stock, i.e. that profits should be greater than investment.

There are four reasons for not interpreting 'savings = profits' as the universal rule for the optimum level of savings.

First, there are the possible conditions of case II.[4] If a unit increase in the capital stock is automatically accompanied by an increase in the employment of labour, then $\partial Y/\partial K$ must be interpreted not as the marginal product of capital but as the additional product due to the increase of capital and labour. Our formula tells us that in this case savings should be greater than profits.

This case would arise in a situation in which there was a reserve of unemployed labour available at a constant conventional wage-rate; in which the unemployed were maintained by gifts or taxes paid by capitalists, landlords, and/or employed workers; and in which there was an exogenously given rate of population growth continuously feeding the reserve of unemployed labour. The rational policy would no doubt be (i) to reduce the wage-rate sufficiently to induce employers to employ all labour which had any physical marginal product, and (ii) to control by fiscal measures the distribution of this maximised national product among savings, workers' consumption, and non-workers' consumption.[5] Such action would turn case II into case I.

But if for institutional reasons the cost to the employer of employing a worker cannot be reduced below the conventionally fixed wage-rate, then savings should be raised above profits in order to expand the demand for labour at the fixed wage-rate. If the exogenously given rate of population growth is sufficient to maintain an unexhausted reserve of unemployed labour, an $S$ equal to $U/(1 - Q)$ will maximise consumption in the state of steady growth. If $U/(1 - Q) < 1 - Q$, then these savings can be financed out of non-wage incomes, i.e. out of profits and rents. If $U/(1 - Q) > 1 - Q$, the desired level of $S$ can be achieved only if workers also save out of their conventionally fixed wage-rate.

Second, there may be a subsistence limit which prevents the raising of $S$

---

[3] $\partial Y/\partial K > I/K$ can be written as $K/Y . \partial K/\partial Y > I/Y$, i.e. as $\alpha > S$, which is the form used earlier in this note.

[4] I am indebted to Mr L. Pasinetti for far-reaching criticisms of my first attempt to apply my analysis to case II. The following paragraphs have been completely recast in an attempt to meet his criticisms, though I do not know whether he will agree that I have succeeded in doing so.

[5] For the sort of measures which would be involved, see J. E. Meade, 'Mauritius: A Case Study in Malthusian Economics', *Economic Journal*, vol. 71 (September 1961), pp. 521–34 [Chapter 20 above, pp. 375–88].

as high as would otherwise be desirable – $U$ in case I and $U/(1 - Q)$ in case II. With heavy population pressure, in case I the full-employment wage-rate might be below the subsistence level, or in case II there might be a subsistence wage-rate with a very large number of unemployed workers. In both cases profits and rents would have to be taxed to finance subsistence incomes for workers. In either case there might be a steady growth situation with $S$ below $U$ (case I) or $U/(1 - Q)$ (case II), but it might be impossible to raise $S$ up to the otherwise desired level because further savings out of profits and rents would reduce current consumption below the subsistence level. Indeed if the growth rate of population were sufficiently great, output per head of total population will be falling in the state of steady growth.[6] If this is so, it may be impossible to maintain $S$ even at an existing 'inadequate' level (i.e. below $U$ in case I or below $U/(1 - Q)$ in case II). There may have to be a cumulative decline in savings in order to keep the growing population from immediate starvation.

Third, the analysis has been based on the assumption that $S$ is kept constant. No doubt in the ultimate optimum steady-growth state $S$ should be kept constant at $U$ (in case I) or $U/(1 - Q)$ (in case II). But in the process of moving from an actual present situation to this ultimate 'blissful' state of affairs, there is no reason to believe that the best time pattern of savings implies a constant level of $S$. Suppose, for example, that in a case I economy there is a steady rate of growth but with $S < U$. If there were no population pressure setting a subsistence limit for $S$, $S$ should be raised. But it does not follow that $S$ should be instantaneously raised to $U$. How quickly one should raise $S$ to $U$ depends upon a balancing of present consumption against an earlier attainment of the ultimate 'blissful' state. The nature of the old optimum-savings problem remains to this extent unchanged.

Fourth, the argument has so far proceeded on the tacit assumption that the rate of profit actually earned is equal to the marginal social product of capital. But consider, for example, a socialist state in which, for purposes of achieving the most efficient allocation of resources among different uses, both labour and land are charged to the plant managers at prices equal to the values of their marginal products. If there were increasing returns to scale,[7] profits as the residual element of income would be less than corresponded to the marginal product of capital. If $U$ stands for the proportion of income actually left over for profits, $S$ would in this situation have to be raised above $U$ (in case I) or $U/(1 - Q)$ (in case II).

---

[6] From (5) it can be seen that this is so if the growth rate of population exceeds $r/(1 - U - Q)$. In case I $y - l$ is $< 0$, if $l > r/(1 - U - Q)$. In case II the steady-state rate of growth of demand for labour is $r/(1 - U - Q)$, so that the unemployment percentage grows and income per head therefore falls if population grows more rapidly than this.

[7] See the following note on 'Economic Growth and Increasing Returns to Scale' for the limitations which must be set to the degree of economies of scale to enable a state of steady growth to be attained. It is only in those cases in which a state of steady growth can in fact be attained that our present analysis is relevant.

## Economic Growth and Increasing Returns to Scale

It will be observed that in the above note on 'The Effect of Savings on Consumption in a State of Steady Growth' I have not assumed constant returns to scale. The purpose of this note is to consider the effect of increasing returns to scale upon the possibility of reaching a state of steady economic growth.

In accordance with that note we start with a production function of the form

$$Y = RK^U L^Q N^Z e^{rt} \tag{1}$$

where $R, U, Q, Z$, and $r$ are all positive constants, but there is no other limitation on the size of $U$ and $Q$.

From (1) we obtain

$$y = Uk + Ql + r. \tag{2}$$

In case I we assume $l$ as a given constant; but in case II we assume $l = y$ and obtain

$$y = \frac{U}{1-Q} k + \frac{r}{1-Q}. \tag{3}$$

Both (2) and (3) can be expressed in the form

$$y = \alpha k + \beta \tag{4}$$

where $\alpha$ and $\beta$ are both constants.

We can integrate (4) into

$$Y = \frac{Y_0}{K_0^\alpha} K^\alpha e^{\beta t} \tag{5}$$

Since investment = savings, we have $dK/dt = SY$ or from (5)

$$\frac{1}{K_0} \frac{dK}{dt} = k_0 \left( \frac{K}{K_0} \right)^\alpha e^{\beta t} \tag{6}$$

where $k_0 = SY_0/K_0$ and measures the initial rate of capital accumulation.

Integrating (6) we obtain

$$\frac{K}{K_0} = \left\{ 1 + \frac{1-\alpha}{\beta} k_0 (e^{\beta t} - 1) \right\}^{\frac{1}{1-\alpha}}. \tag{7}$$

Dividing both sides of (6) by $K/K_0$ and then substituting the value of $K/K_0$ from (7) into (6) we obtain

$$k\left(\equiv \frac{1}{K}\frac{dK}{dt}\right) = \frac{k_0\,e^{\beta t}}{1 + \dfrac{1-\alpha}{\beta}\,k_0\,(e^{\beta t}-1)}. \tag{8}$$

This expresses the equilibrium time-path of the rate of capital accumulation ($k$) given its initial value ($k_0$) in terms of the two parameters $\alpha$ and $\beta$. Our present purpose is to see whether $k$ will necessarily approach the steady-state rate of growth, namely $\beta/(1-\alpha)^1$ as $t\to\infty$, given the possible effects of various degrees of increasing returns to scale on the parameters $\alpha$ and $\beta$.

We will use the following terminology. There are constant or increasing returns to all factors together according as $U+Q+Z=$ or $>1$. There are constant or increasing returns to capital and labour together according as $U+Q=$ or $>1$. There are constant or increasing returns to capital (or labour) alone according as $U$ (or $Q$) $=$ or $>1$. All these cases, except only $U+Q+Z=1$, are cases of increasing returns to scale of different kinds or degrees.

Let us first confine our attention to cases in which there are decreasing returns to labour alone, i.e. $Q<1$. With $Q<1$, in both cases I and II $\beta$ will be a positive finite quantity. We will return later to the possibility that $Q\geqslant 1$.

Let us turn to the value of $\alpha$ in equation (8).

(i) Assume $\alpha=1$, i.e. assume in case I that there are constant returns to capital alone ($U=1$) and in case II that there are constant returns to capital and labour together ($U+Q=1$). Then (8) becomes

$$k = k_0\,e^{\beta t}.$$

The rate of capital accumulation and thus the rate of economic growth does not tend towards any finite steady-state level but itself grows without limit. If we started with case II, after a time the expansion would have absorbed any finite initial volume of labour and the rate of expansion would exceed any finite rate of population growth. We would in fact shift over to case I with $\alpha<1$. (With $\alpha=1$ in case II we have $U+Q=1$ so that $U<1$. In other words in case I $\alpha<1$.) The possibility that $\alpha=1$ is, therefore, relevant only if we are in case I with $U=1$.

(ii) Assume $\alpha<1$, i.e. assume that, while there may be increasing returns to all factors ($U+Q+Z>1$), yet there are decreasing returns to capital alone in case I ($U<1$) and to capital and labour together in case II ($U+Q<1$). Equation (8) can be expressed in the form:—

$$k = \frac{\dfrac{\beta}{1-\alpha}}{1 - \dfrac{1 - \dfrac{1}{k_0}\dfrac{\beta}{1-\alpha}}{e^{\beta t}}}.$$

[1] See equation (5) of the previous note.

The denominator of the expression in the RHS starts at $(1/k_0)$ $[\beta/(1 - \alpha)]$ when $t = 0$ and moves steadily towards the value 1 as $t \to \infty$, remaining positive throughout. $k$, therefore, starting at $k_0$ approaches steadily the steady growth rate $\beta/(1 - \alpha)$.

(iii) Assume $\alpha > 1$, i.e. in case I increasing returns to capital alone $(U > 1)$ and in case II increasing returns to capital and labour together $(U + Q > 1)$. Equation (8) can be expressed as

$$k = \cfrac{\cfrac{\beta}{\alpha - 1}}{-1 + \cfrac{1 + \cfrac{1}{k_0}\cfrac{\beta}{\alpha - 1}}{e^{\beta t}}}$$

where $\beta/(\alpha - 1)$ is a positive constant. The denominator of the RHS of this expression starts at $(1/k_0)[\beta/(\alpha - 1]$, when $t = 0$ and approaches $-1$

as $t \to \infty$. At some point of time $\left( \text{namely, } t = \cfrac{\log^e\left[ 1 + \cfrac{1}{k_0}\cfrac{\beta}{\alpha - 1} \right]}{\beta} \right)$

the denominator $=$ zero and $k$ therefore approaches infinity as this point of time is reached. If we started with case II, in fact we should have shifted over to case I before this critical point of time were reached. For at some previous point the expansion would have absorbed any unemployed labour and the rate of expansion would have risen above any finite rate of population growth. It is only in the extreme case of increasing returns to capital alone $(U > 1)$ that the ultimate Big Bang would take place.

So far we have assumed $Q < 1$. If $Q \geq 1$, this makes no essential difference to the analysis of case I. It merely causes $\beta$ to be a larger quantity than it would otherwise be, and this does not alter the main features of the time paths of $k$ according as $\alpha \lessgtr 1$. But in case II if $Q \geq 1$, there is an essential difference, since $\beta \to \infty$ as $Q \to 1$ and $\beta$ becomes $< 0$ as $Q$ becomes $> 1$. What is the meaning of this?

It implies that $Q \geq 1$ in case II we could not even start initially with a finite equilibrium rate of growth of output $(y_0)$. There would at the word 'Go' be an instantaneous Big Bang. We can see this by means of a *reductio ad absurdum*. Suppose we had an initial rate of growth of income of any finite magnitude, say 2% p.a. ($y_0 = 2\%$ p.a.). Since $l = y$ (because otherwise the real wage-rate will be rising), the volume of employment will be rising by 2% p.a. If there are constant returns to labour alone, output must therefore be rising by more than 2% p.a., because the rise in employment alone would cause output to rise by 2% p.a. and capital accumulation and technical progress $(Uk + r)$ will be adding to this rate of growth. *A fortiori* if there were increasing returns to labour alone, $y_0$ would exceed 2% p.a. In other words, choose any finite positive value for $y_0$ and it will in fact be found that $y_0$ must be greater than this. This means in fact that if $Q > 1$ we must *start* with case I and not with case II.

Otherwise an instantaneous expansion of $Y$ takes place to absorb any finite volume of unemployed labour, and then from the starting point onwards the rate of growth of demand for labour is greater than any finite rate of population growth. But even if $Q > 1$, we then reach the case I steady rate of growth $(Ql + r)/(1 - U)$, provided that $U < 1$.

# 22

# The Adjustment of Savings to Investment in a Growing Economy[1]

*From the* Review of Economic Studies, *vol. 30 (October 1963), pp. 151–166. This article was included in F. H. Hahn (ed.),* Readings in the Theory of Growth, A Selection of Papers from the Review of Economic Studies *(London: Macmillan, 1971), pp. 202–17.*

I

A major issue underlying the differences between what have come to be known as the Neo-Keynesian and the Neo-Classical theories of economic growth is the extent to which, and the mechanisms by which, savings and investment are brought into balance in a growing economy with full employment. To what extent for equilibrium growth must the level of investment be, somehow or another, adjusted to the level of the savings which the community is prepared to make in 'equilibrium' conditions? Or may the level of investment be determined independently (by government policy or the animal spirits of the entrepreneurs) with the level of savings adjusting itself to that level of investment? And, given these mechanisms, what will be the effect upon employment, output, growth, and price inflation of a policy which stimulates investment without affecting the citizens' propensities to save?

It is not the purpose of this paper to examine this central question in all its possible aspects. Our present objective is a very limited one. We shall assume that the level of money expenditure on investment is kept strictly equal to a given fixed proportion $(S_i)$ of the money national income. There is no time-lag and there are no mistakes. We shall not enquire how this occurs.[2] We are frankly not building a complete model of the economic system which would certainly require the inclusion of a more plausible investment function than this. Our purpose is merely to

---

[1] Mr F. H. Hahn has discussed with me many of the problems involved in the preparation of this paper and I would like to acknowledge the great help which he has given me.

[2] Those who like to have some institutional model in mind are advised to imagine a supremely efficient and well-informed government which is able by various devices (fiscal and monetary measures and planned socialised investment) to keep the level of investment expenditure in a planned ratio $(S_i)$ to the actual national income with negligibly short time-lags and errors of judgement.

examine the way in which the proportion of the national income which is saved may be adjusted to this given investment proportion.

Even here our objective is a very limited one. We shall concern ourselves with only two out of the almost infinite number of possible forms of behaviour which would help to adjust the savings proportion to the investment proportion. We assume that a fixed proportion $(S_w)$ of wages and a fixed proportion $(S_v)$ of other incomes are saved.[3] Let us suppose that if the labour market were in equilibrium (we will explain below more precisely what is meant by this) the proportion of the national product which would go to wages would be $EQ$ (we will explain below the reason for this apparently clumsy notation) so that the proportion going to non-wage incomes would be $1 - EQ$. It follows that the proportion of the national income which recipients of income would plan to save if there were an equilibrium distribution of income between wage incomes and non-wage incomes would be $EQ\ S_w + (1 - EQ)\ S_v$, which we will call $S_s$.

We assume that $S_i$ is set above $S_s$. Actual investment is greater than planned equilibrium savings. There is an inflation of total demand. This inflation of total demand has a two-fold effect in reconciling the proportion of income actually saved to the proportion actually invested. (1) In so far as recipients of income plan their consumption expenditures in terms of money, the inflation of their money incomes will tend to cause the actual proportion of income saved to rise above the planned proportion. (2) In so far as an inflation of total demand will in the first instance cause profits to rise, there will be an inflationary shift from wage incomes to non-wage incomes. If recipients of income plan to save a smaller proportion of wages than of other incomes $(S_w < S_v)$, this shift to profit will cause the proportion of income saved to rise above the equilibrium planned proportion.

Section II of this paper examines the possible interrelationships between these two mechanisms of adjustment.

---

[3] Mr Pasinetti ('Rate of Profit and Income Distribution in Relation to the Rate of Economic Growth', *Review of Economic Studies*, vol. 29, October 1962, pp. 267–79) has shown the great importance of distinguishing this assumption from the assumption that wage-earners save a proportion $S_w$ of their total incomes while non-wage-earners save a proportion $S_v$ of their incomes. For, if wage-earners save, they will receive profits on their accumulated savings, so that the proportion $S_w$ would have to refer to wages plus profits accruing to wage-earners. I have maintained the pre-Pasinetti Kaldorian assumption because it is a main purpose of this article to reconcile the clash between the 'neo-Keynesian' and the 'neo-classical' theories of distribution. I make no apology, therefore, for illustrating this clash by maintaining the 'neo-Keynesian' savings propensities in their most familiar Kaldorian form and by using later in this article the familiar Cobb–Douglas production function to represent the 'neo-classical' forces of marginal productivity. An institutional set-up which would lead to the Kaldorian savings propensities would exist if all individuals saved the same proportion $(S_w)$ of their incomes, while all non-wage incomes were in the first place earned by companies which placed to reserve a proportion $((S_v - S_w)/(1 - S_w))$ of their earnings before distributing the remainder in dividends to individual shareholders.

## II

The following four equations[4] show the basic relationships in our models:—

$$I = S_i\, Y \tag{1}$$

$Y$ measures the national income in money terms and $S_i$ is the proportion of this national income which is invested.

$$C = \frac{\mu}{D + \mu}\left\{ (1 - S_w)\, W + (1 - S_v)\, (Y - W) \right\}. \tag{2}$$

$W$ measures total money wage income, so that $(1 - S_w)\, W$ is desired consumption expenditure out of wages and $(1 - S_v)\, (Y - W)$ is desired consumption expenditure out of other incomes. But actual consumption expenditures $(C)$ may differ from these desired levels. Equation (2) is based on the very simple behavioural assumption that recipients of income never foresee a rise in their money incomes but simply adjust their expenditure on consumption with a time-lag to their actual incomes. In fact they are assumed to raise their expenditure on consumption at a proportionate rate which is equal to $\mu$ times the proportionate excess of desired consumption over actual consumption at any one time.

$$W = \frac{\theta}{D + \theta}\, EQ\, Y. \tag{3}$$

Let $Q$ = the proportional marginal product of labour (i.e. $(L/X)$ $(\partial X/\partial L)$ where $L$ is the amount of labour in employment and $X$ is physical output) so that $Q$ would be equal to the proportion of the national income which would go to wages if labour were paid a wage-rate equal to the value of its marginal product. We assume $Q$ to be constant.[5] But because of elements of monopoly and monopsony in the markets for the sale of the product of labour and for the hire of labour itself (i.e. because of the absence of perfect competition), the micro-economic conditions in our economy may be such that the markets are in equilibrium when labour is paid less than its marginal product. Let $E$ be a fraction expressing the proportion of its marginal product which labour

---

[4] In these and the following equations $D$ stands for the differential operator $d(-)/dt$. For the use of this operator see Appendix A of R. G. D. Allen's *Mathematical Economics* (London: Macmillan, 1956).

[5] This implies (i) a production function with unitary elasticities of substitution between the factors and (ii) neutral technical progress. See J. E. Meade, *A Neo-Classical Theory of Economic Growth*, 2nd edition (London: Allen & Unwin, 1962), Chapter 4 and Appendix I.

will be paid when micro-markets are in equilibrium.[6] We will at first assume $E$ to be a constant given by unchanging conditions of monopoly and monopsony in the individual markets, though later we will allow $E$ itself to be affected by the degree of inflationary pressure. Equation (3) assumes on the part of the employers the same sort of simple-minded behaviour as equation (2) assumed for consumers. Employers do not foresee future increases in their sales proceeds and profits; but with a time-lag they adjust their expenditure on labour to what it would be profitable for them to spend on labour in present conditions. They will be raising their expenditure on labour at a proportionate rate equal to $\theta$ times the proportionate excess of the equilibrium wage bill $(EQ\,Y)$ over the actual wage bill $(W)$ at any one time.

$$Y = I + C. \tag{4}$$

Equation (4) states the identity that at any one time the actual level of money income must be equal to the actual level of money expenditures on investment and consumption.

From equations (1), (2), (3) and (4) we can eliminate $I$, $C$ and $W$ and obtain

$$Y(1 - S_i) = \frac{\mu}{D + \mu} \left\{ (1 - S_v)\, Y + (S_v - S_w) \frac{\theta}{D + \theta} EQ\,Y \right\}.$$

Multiplying both sides by $(D + \mu)\,(D + \theta)$ and writing $S_s$ for $EQS_w + (1 - EQ)\,S_v$ we obtain:—

$$D^2 Y + \left( \theta + \mu \frac{S_v - S_i}{1 - S_i} \right) DY - \mu\,\theta \frac{S_i - S_s}{1 - S_i}\, Y = 0. \tag{5}$$

The roots of this equation are:—

$$\frac{1}{2}\left\{ -\theta - \mu \frac{S_v - S_i}{1 - S_i} \pm \sqrt{\left( \theta + \mu \frac{S_v - S_i}{1 - S_i} \right)^2 + 4\mu\theta \frac{S_i - S_s}{1 - S_i}} \right\}.$$

---

[6] If $-\varepsilon$ is the elasticity of demand facing the individual seller of the product and $\eta$ is the elasticity of supply facing the individual hirer of labour, then the marginal labour cost is $(1 + (1/\eta))$ times the wage-rate and the marginal revenue is $(1 - (1/\varepsilon))$ times the price of the product. Profit will be maximised when $\dot{W}(1 + (1/\eta)) = (1 - (1/\varepsilon))\, P\,(\partial X/\partial L)$ where $\dot{W}$ is the money wage-rate, and $P$ is the money price of the product, i.e. when

$$\dot{W}L = \frac{1 - \frac{1}{\varepsilon}}{1 + \frac{1}{\eta}} PX \frac{L}{X} \frac{\partial X}{\partial L} = \frac{1 - \frac{1}{\varepsilon}}{1 + \frac{1}{\eta}} QY. \quad \text{In other words } E = \frac{1 - \frac{1}{\varepsilon}}{1 + \frac{1}{\eta}}.$$

These roots are both real,[7] one positive and – provided that $S_i < S_v + [\mu/(\mu + \theta)](1 - S_v)$ – one negative. The larger of these two roots will measure the growth rate of the national income which will become the dominant rate of growth, which we will call $\pi$. If, as a numerical example, we assume $S_i = \frac{1}{3}$, $S_v = \frac{1}{2}$, $S_w = 0$, $EQ = \frac{1}{2}$ (so that $S_s = \frac{1}{4}$), $\mu = 1$, and $\theta = 1$, then this dominant rate of growth ($\pi$) will be $9\frac{3}{8}$ per cent per annum.

From equation (3) we can see that the proportion of income going to wages will approach $[\theta/(\pi + \theta)] EQ$ which, with our numerical example, will be equal to $1/1 \cdot 09375 \times \frac{1}{2} = 0 \cdot 457$, so that as a result of the inflation only $45 \cdot 7$ per cent of the national income in the state of steady inflation will be going to wages instead of 50 per cent. Thus we can say that, with our numerical example,

(i) the planned equilibrium proportion of savings is $S_w \ EQ + S_v (1 - EQ) = 0 \cdot 25$

(ii) the planned proportion of savings is

$$S_w \frac{\theta}{\pi + \theta} EQ + S_v \left( 1 - \frac{\theta}{\pi + \theta} EQ \right) = 0 \cdot 2715$$

and (iii) the actual proportion of savings is $S_i = 0 \cdot 3$.

The difference between (i) and (ii) marks the influence of the $\theta$-mechanism or of the shift to profit in raising savings and the difference between (ii) and (iii) marks the influence of the $\mu$-mechanism or of the lag of consumption on incomes in raising actual savings.

This general case when both the $\theta$-mechanism and the $\mu$-mechanism are operating simultaneously we will call Case I. Let us now consider two special cases, Case II where only the $\mu$-mechanism is at work and Case III where only the $\theta$-mechanism is operative.

Case II rests on the assumption that there is an instantaneous adjustment of actual wage payments to the equilibrium level, i.e. that $\theta \rightarrow \infty$. In this case equation (5) becomes

$$DY = \mu \frac{S_i - S_s}{1 - S_i} Y \tag{6}$$

[7] If one writes $S_s = S_v - EQ (S_v - S_w)$ in the expression given for these roots we obtain

$$\frac{1}{2} \left\{ -\theta - \mu \frac{S_v - S_i}{1 - S_i} \pm \sqrt{\left( \theta - \mu \frac{S_v - S_i}{1 - S_i} \right)^2 + 4\mu\theta EQ \frac{S_v - S_w}{1 - S_i}} \right\} .$$

From this it is clear that the roots are real except in the very peculiar case in which $S_w$ exceeds $S_v$ by more than $(1 - S_i)/4\mu\theta EQ$. $[\theta - \mu (S_v - S_i)/(1 - S_i)]^2$. If we rule out all cases in which $S_w > S_v$, the roots of equation (5) are real whether (as in the text) we confine our attention to situations in which the national income in money terms will be rising ($S_i > S_s$ and the dominant root is > 0) or whether we also consider cases in which the money income will be falling ($S_i < S_s$ and the dominant root < 0).

so that there is a single real positive rate of growth of $\pi = \mu (S_i - S_s)/ (1 - S_i)$. With our same numerical example (except that $\theta = \infty$ instead of $= 1$) $\pi$ is raised from $9\frac{3}{8}$ to $12\frac{1}{2}$ per cent per annum. The inflationary pressure is this much raised by the absence of any shift to profits. The proportion of income going to wages is, of course, equal to its equilibrium value of $EQ$ or $\frac{1}{2}$. Planned equilibrium savings are equal to $\frac{1}{4}$. The whole difference between this and the actual proportion of income saved ($S_i = \frac{1}{3}$) is closed by the higher rate of inflation ($12\frac{1}{2}$ per cent per annum) operating on the lag between income and expenditure on consumption.

It is of interest to note that if in Case I (equation 5) one writes $S_v = S_w$ so that $S_v = S_s$, the roots of the equation become $-\theta$ and $\mu (S_i - S_s)/ (1 - S_i)$. The dominant root in Case I is then the same as the single root in Case II. That is what one would expect. If the proportion of non-wage income saved were the same as the proportion of wage income saved (Case I with $S_v = S_w$), this would have essentially the same effect as the absence of the $\theta$-mechanism (Case II), since the distribution of income between wages and non-wage income would have no effect on planned consumption.[8]

Case III rests on the assumption that there is an instantaneous adjustment of actual consumption to planned consumption. Only the shift to profits caused by inflation maintains the balance between savings and investment by raising the proportion of income planned to be saved. In this case (with $\mu \to \infty$) equation (5) becomes

$$D Y = \theta \frac{S_i - S_s}{S_v - S_i} Y \qquad (7)$$

so that there is a single real root of $\pi = \theta (S_i - S_s)/(S_v - S_i)$. With our same numerical example $\pi$ is now raised to a growth rate of no less than 50 per cent per annum. From equation (3) we can see once more that the proportion of income going to wages will be equal to $[\theta/(\pi + \theta)] EQ^9$ which with our present numerical example is $1/1 \cdot 5 \times \frac{1}{2} = \frac{1}{3}$. The rate of inflation (of 50 per cent per annum) is sufficient to reduce the proportion of income going to wages from $\frac{1}{2}$ to $\frac{1}{3}$, and this is sufficient to raise the planned proportion of savings to income from $\frac{1}{4}$ to $\frac{1}{3}$.

If we compare equations (7) and (6), it can be seen that the difference in effectiveness between the consumption adjustment lag ($\mu$) and the wage adjustment lag ($\theta$) depends upon two things: first, the relative sizes of $\mu$ and $\theta$ and, secondly, the difference of $S_v$ from unity. In so far as $\theta$ were less than $\mu$, i.e. in so far as wage adjustments were less quick than consumption adjustments, the $\theta$-mechanism would be more effective in

---

[8] The only difference is the presence of a damped element in $Y$ associated with the root $-\theta$ in case I with $S_v = S_w$. In case II the initial growth rate of $Y$ cannot diverge from the root $\mu (S_i - S_s)/(1 - S_i)$. In case I with $S_v = S_w$, the initial growth rate of $Y$ can diverge from $\mu (S_i - S_s)/(1 - S_i)$. But any such initial divergence will be removed by the damping factor $-\theta$.

[9] If one substitutes the value of $\pi = \theta (S_i - S_s)/(S_v - S_i)$ into this expression for the ratio of actual wages to income one obtains the result $W/Y = (S_v - S_i)/(S_v - S_w)$ which is precisely Mr Kaldor's expression for the distribution of income.

checking inflation than the $\mu$-mechanism. But if these rates of adjustment were the same, the $\theta$-mechanism would be as effective as the $\mu$-mechanism only if the whole of profits were saved ($S_v = 1$). The $\mu$-mechanism works by the whole of an increase in income being temporarily added to savings, until actual consumption is adjusted to the higher incomes. The $\theta$-mechanism works by the whole of an increase in incomes being added to profits, until actual wages are adjusted to the higher national expenditure, but it is only if the whole of profits are saved that this causes an equivalent temporary increase in savings.

The following points about the $\theta$-mechanism of Case III are worth noting:—

1.  The mechanism will work only if $S_i < S_v$. From equation 7 it can be seen that as $S_i$ rises towards $S_v$, so the rate of inflation approaches infinity. It is only if the proportion of profits saved is higher than the planned proportion of income to be invested that a shift to profit of a sufficient magnitude can bring actual savings up to this planned investment proportion. This condition that $S_v > S_i$ is not necessary for the working of the $\mu$-mechanism.
2.  We are assuming that $S_i > S_s$. If $S_i < S_v$ then $S_v > S_s$. In other words, the mechanism will work only if a higher proportion of profits than wages is saved; for $S_s$ can be $< S_v$ only if $S_w < S_v$. Thus we must have $S_v > S_i > S_w$. The condition $S_v > S_w$ is not necessary for the working of the $\mu$-mechanism.
3.  With the numerical example which we have taken (i.e. with $\mu = \theta$ and $S_v = \frac{1}{2}$) the $\theta$-mechanism is much less effective than the $\mu$-mechanism in restraining inflation.

### III

The model which we have built has so far been entirely in terms of flows of money income and expenditure on consumption ($C$), on investment ($I$), on all goods and services ($Y$), and on labour ($W$). We shall proceed in this and the next section to split these money flows up into real quantities multiplied by their prices. In this section we shall deal with the labour market and split the total wage bill ($W$) into the volume of employment ($L$) and the wage per worker ($\bar{W}$), where

$$W = L\bar{W}$$

so that        $l = w - \bar{w}$                                      (8)

where          $l = \dfrac{1}{L}\dfrac{dL}{dt}, w = \dfrac{1}{W}\dfrac{dW}{dt}$, and $\bar{w} = \dfrac{1}{\bar{W}}\dfrac{d\bar{W}}{dt}$.

In all the three cases which we are considering there will, as we have seen, emerge a dominant rate of growth of the national income which we call $\pi$. Moreover, as this dominant rate of growth asserts itself the total wage bill will also grow at the same dominant rate, $\pi$, so that eventually $w$ will also equal $\pi$. The basic simplifying assumption about the labour market which we are making is that the employers raise their wage bills at a proportionate rate equal to $\theta$ times the proportionate excess of the equilibrium wage they would be willing to pay in current market conditions over the actual wage which they are paying. We are assuming that this rate of increase in their total money outlay on labour is the same whether in fact it results in an equivalent rate of rise in the volume of labour which they can employ at current wage-rates or an equivalent rate of rise in the wage-rate which they have to pay for an unchanged volume of labour or partly in the one and partly in the other. This assumption permits very great simplification of the analysis without necessarily being very unrealistic. We can write equation (8) as

$$l = \pi - \bar{w}. \tag{9}$$

We shall assume that the rate of rise of the money wage-rate, $\bar{w}$, depends upon the proportion of the labour force which is unemployed, $J$. We assume (i) that the lower is the unemployment percentage the higher will be the rate at which the money wage-rate is being raised through the competition of employers and employed, (ii) that there is a finite limit to the rate at which the money wage-rate can be lowered as the unemployment proportion rises towards unity, but (iii) that there is no limit to the rate at which the money wage-rate can be raised as the unemployment proportion falls towards zero.

One function which would satisfy these conditions is

$$\bar{w} = -\bar{w}_x \left\{ \left( \frac{J_x}{J} \right)^{\gamma} - 1 \right\} \tag{10}$$

where $-\bar{w}_x \, (>0)$ is the maximum rate of fall of the wage-rate as $J \to \infty$, $J_x$ is the unemployment percentage at which the money wage-rate is constant, and $\gamma$ is a positive parameter which measures the extent to which a fall in the unemployment proportion causes an increase in the rate of inflation of money wage-rates.[10]

If we write $L$ for the total demand for labour and $\bar{L}$ for the total supply of labour and if we assume that the available working population is growing at a constant proportionate rate, $\lambda$, so that $\bar{L} = \bar{L}_0 e^{\lambda t}$, we have $J = 1 - (L/\bar{L}_0 e^{\lambda t})$. We have then from (9) and (10)

$$l = \pi + (-\bar{w}_x) \left\{ 1 - \left( \frac{J_x}{1 - \dfrac{L}{\bar{L}_0 e^{\lambda t}}} \right)^{\gamma} \right\}. \tag{11}$$

Since $l = (1/L)\,(dL/dt)$, this gives us a differential equation in $L$ and $t$, the

[10] For a discussion of this function see Appendix at the end of this paper [pp. 414–15].

general solution of which would determine the behaviour of employment over time, starting from any given initial position.

The general solution of (11) is, however, not necessary for our purpose. We are concerned only with (i) what will be the rates of growth in a state of steady growth and (ii) whether the system, starting from any initial conditions, will always move towards this state of steady growth. In the case of equation (11) we wish, therefore, to know (i) whether there is a particular solution of (11) which gives a steady rate of growth of $L$ and (ii) whether the system is stable in the sense that it will always converge onto this rate of growth for $L$.

The first question is easily answered. The LHS of (11) is the rate of growth of $L$ and this will be constant only if the RHS of (11) is constant. But the RHS of (11) will be constant only if $L/\bar{L}_0e^{\lambda t}$ is constant, i.e. only if $l = \lambda$. If we write $l = \lambda$ in (11) we obtain

$$\bar{J} = \left( \frac{-\bar{w}_x J_x{}^\gamma}{\pi + [-\bar{w}_x] - \lambda} \right)^{\frac{1}{\gamma}} \tag{12}$$

where $\bar{J}$ is the equilibrium level of the unemployment proportion, $1 - (L/\bar{L}_0e^{\lambda t})$. This equilibrium unemployment proportion is the value of $J$ at which the rate of change of the money wage-rate ($\bar{w}$) would be such that, taken together with the rate of rise in the total wage bill ($\pi$), the volume of employment would rise at a rate equal to the rise in the supply of labour ($l = \lambda$), so that the unemployment proportion ($J$) would in fact stay unchanged.

Now we shall assume that $\pi > \lambda - (-\bar{w}_x)(1 - J_x^\gamma)$. It will be seen from (10) that $\bar{w}_x(1 - J_x^\gamma)$ is the value of $\bar{w}$ when $J = 1$. Our assumption therefore, implies only that the investment proportion is sufficient to raise $\pi$ (the dominant rate of growth of the money national income and so of the total money wage bill) to a sufficient degree to absorb the growing working population ($\lambda$) at least when the unemployment proportion is very high and the money wage-rate is itself already falling at nearly its maximum rate $(-\bar{w}_x)(1 - J_x^\gamma)$. If this were not so the unemployment percentage would rise continuously since the volume of employment would be growing less rapidly than the supply of labour.

Since $0 < J_x < 1$ and $\gamma > 0$, it follows that $0 < 1 - J_x^\gamma < 1$. Hence with $\pi > \lambda - (-\bar{w}_x)(1 - J_x^\gamma)$ we have $\pi > \lambda - (-\bar{w}_x)$. From this it follows that the equilibrium value of $J$ given in (12) lies between 0 and 1. In other words, there is an economically possible equilibrium value of $J$ which leads to a steady rate of growth of $L$ equal to $\lambda$.

From (12) it can be seen that this equilibrium unemployment proportion ($\bar{J}$) will be greater (or less) than the unemployment proportion required to keep the money wage-rate constant ($J_x$) according as the rate of growth of the money national income is less (or greater) than the rate of growth of the working population which has to be absorbed at the current wage-rate (i.e. as $\pi \lessgtr \lambda$).

From (12) it can also be seen that $\partial \bar{J}/\partial \pi < 0$. In other words, the more inflationary is the investment policy the lower will be the equilibrium unemployment proportion because a higher rate of inflation of the money wage-rate is compatible with the absorption into employment of the given growth in the working population.

We have shown that there is an equilibrium unemployment proportion ($\bar{J}$) and have considered some of its features. But will our system always approach this equilibrium level of $J$ if it started initially at some other level? It would appear intuitively probable that it would do so. Suppose by accident that one started with a value of $J$ far above the equilibrium level $\bar{J}$. Money wage-rates would be falling; the money wage bill would be rising at its given rate $\pi$ and this, combined with the fall in the money wage-rate, would cause the amount of employment to be rising at a higher proportionate rate than the supply of labour; $J$ would be falling towards its equilibrium level. Conversely, if $J$ were below $\bar{J}$, there would be forces at work tending to raise $J$.

This argument can be expressed rigorously in the following way. We know that $0 < J < 1$ or, what is the same thing, $0 < 1 - J < 1$.[11] We can, therefore, treat both $J$ and $1 - J$ as positive quantities.

Now $1 - J = L/\bar{L}_0 e^{\lambda t}$, so that

$$\frac{dJ}{dt} = -(1 - J)(l - \lambda)$$

or from equation (11)

$$\frac{dJ}{dt} = -(1 - J)(\pi + [-\bar{w}_x] - \lambda - [-\bar{w}_x] J_x^\gamma J^{-\gamma}).$$

Given $1 - J > 0$, it follows that $dJ/dt \lessgtr 0$, as

$$\pi + (-\bar{w}_x) - \lambda \gtrless (-\bar{w}_x) J_x^\lambda J^{-\lambda}.$$

Since, as we have explained above, we may assume $\pi + (-\bar{w}_x) - \lambda > 0$, $(-\bar{w}_x) J_x^\gamma > 0$, and $J > 0$, it follows that $dJ/dt \lessgtr 0$ according as $J \gtrless \bar{J}$, where $\bar{J}$ has the value given in equation (12). Moreover, $dJ/dt = 0$ only when $J = \bar{J}$. It follows that if $J$ starts above $\bar{J}$, $J$ will fall continuously so long as $J > \bar{J}$ but will never fall below $\bar{J}$. Similarly, if $J$ starts below $\bar{J}$, $J$ will rise continuously towards but never above $\bar{J}$. $J$ moves to its steady-growth level, $\bar{J}$.

---

[11] $1 - J = (L/\bar{L}_0 e^{\lambda t})$. Since $\bar{L}_0 > 0$ and $e^{\lambda t} > 0$, $1 - J > 0$ if $L > 0$. We assume $L_0 > 0$. Moreover we assume $\pi > 0$. It follows *a fortiori* that $\pi + (-\bar{w}_x) > 0$ and, therefore, that before $L$ falls to zero it will start to grow, since $l = \pi - \bar{w}$. Therefore, $L$ cannot fall below zero. Therefore, $1 - J > 0$. We can also show that $J > 0$. We assume that $J_0 > 0$. Given any finite value of $\pi$, there will always be a low enough positive value of $J$ to cause $\bar{w} > \pi - \lambda$ since $\bar{w} \to \infty$ as $J \to 0$. But if $\pi - \bar{w} < \lambda$, we have $l > \lambda$, since $\pi - \bar{w} = l$; and therefore $J$ will be rising. It follows that $J$, being initially $> 0$, must remain $> 0$.

## IV

Let us turn next to the market for goods and to the general level of money prices. Let us assume that the technical conditions of production are such as to enable a state of steady growth of real output to be reached when the proportion of income actually saved and invested is constant. A production function of the kind

$$X = R \, N^Z \, K^U \, L^Q \, e^{rt} \tag{13}$$

will have this effect, where $X$ is real output, $N$, $K$, and $L$ are the amounts of land, capital, and labour in employment, $r$ is the rate of technical progress, $Z$, $U$, and $Q$ are the proportional marginal products of land, capital, and labour respectively, and $R$ is the amount of output that could be produced by one unit each of land, capital, and labour in the state of technical knowledge at time $o$. $R$, $N$, $Z$, $U$, $Q$, and $r$ are assumed constant. Then if a constant proportion $S_i$ of real income $X$ is invested and added to the capital stock and if there is a constant rate of growth of the volume of employment, the economy, whatever its starting point, will in time reach a steady rate of growth equal to $(Ql + r)/(1 - U)$ where $l$ is the constant growth rate of employment.[12]

Now we know from the previous section of this paper that in our present model in time there will be a constant rate of growth of employment equal to the growth rate of the population, $\lambda$. It follows that the growth rate in real output will eventually be equal to $(Q\lambda + r)/(1 - U)$.

Now $Y = X P$ where $P$ is the money price of real output, so that $p = y - x$, where $y = (1/Y) (dY/dt)$, $x = (1/X) (dX/dt)$ and $p = (1/P) (dP/dt)$. We also know from section II of this paper that the growth rate of total money expenditure $(y)$ will eventually be at a constant rate $\pi$. It follows that

$$p = \pi - \frac{Q\lambda + r}{1 - U} \tag{14}$$

where $p$ is the rate of inflation of the general level of prices. Since $Q$, $\lambda$, $r$, and $U$ are all constant, it is clear that $\partial p / \partial \pi > 0$. In other words a more inflationary investment policy will eventually raise the rate of inflation of money prices.[13]

---

[12] See J. E. Meade, *A Neo-Classical Theory of Economic Growth*, 2nd edition, pp. 108 and 109.

[13] The immediate effect of an increase in the investment proportion would necessarily be to raise the absolute level of prices but it might also *temporarily* reduce the subsequent rate of rise of prices. The *temporary* effect of an increase in the investment proportion is to raise the rate of growth; but *ultimately* its effect is to raise the ratio of capital to output $(K/X)$ with the restoration of the original rate of growth. (See J. E. Meade, *A Neo-Classical Theory of Economic Growth*, Chapter 4.) During the temporary phase while the rate of growth of output is higher than normal, it is possible that the increase in the investment proportion raises $x$ (the rate of growth of output) more than it raises $\pi$ (the rate of growth of total money expenditure.) Consider Case II by way of example. We have then $\pi = \mu (S_i - S_s)/(1 - S_i)$

We have now shown the connection between investment policy and price inflation. To illustrate the connection let us suppose that the object of policy is to stabilise the price level and that we have to rely exclusively either on the $\mu$-mechanism (Case II) or on the $\theta$-mechanism (Case III) to keep actual savings in balance with actual investment. Setting $p = 0$ we have from equation (14)

(case II)
$$\frac{Q\lambda + r}{1 - U} = \mu \frac{S_i - S_s}{1 - S_i}$$

and (case III)
$$\frac{Q\lambda + r}{1 - U} = \theta \frac{S_i - S_s}{S_v - S_i} .$$

From these equations we can derive

(case II)
$$S_i - S_s = \frac{1 - S_s}{1 + \mu \dfrac{(1 - U)}{Q\lambda + r}}$$

and (case III)
$$S_i - S_s = \frac{E Q (S_v - S_w)}{1 + \theta \dfrac{(1 - U)}{Q\lambda + r}} .$$

These show the extents to which in the two cases the planned level of investment can be raised above the equilibrium planned level of savings while preserving a stable money price level.

We showed in the last section that a more inflationary investment policy (a rise in $S_i$), while it would raise the rate of rise in money wage-rates, would also have the effect of raising the employment percentage. Similarly, we can now show that a rise in $S_i$, while – as we have already seen – it will raise the rate of inflation of the money prices of goods, will also cause the real capital stock in equilibrium steady growth

and (see J. E. Meade, *op. cit.*) $x = U (S_i X / K) + Ql + r$ so that $p = \mu (S_i - S_s)/(1 - S_i) - U (S_i X / K) - Q\lambda - l$. In this case a rise in $S_i$ causes an immediate adjustment of the rate of growth of total money demand to the new value of $\pi = \mu (S_i - S_s)/(1 - S_i)$. Suppose that the adjustment in the labour market, examined in the last section, is also rapid so that $l$ is quickly restored to $\lambda$. The output–capital ratio $(X / K)$ will, however, change only gradually as the higher proportion of income saved causes capital to be accumulated more abundantly. Before $X / K$ has time to change significantly

$$\frac{\partial p}{\partial S_i} = \mu \frac{1 - S_s}{(1 - S_i)^2} - \frac{UX}{K} .$$

This might be $< 0$. But as time passes the rate of growth of $X$ would fall again to $(Q\lambda + r)/(1 - U)$ and ultimately, comparing one steady-growth state with another, $\partial p / \partial S_i = \mu (1 - S_s)/(1 - S_i)^2$ which is necessarily $> 0$.

to be higher than it would otherwise be. In the state of steady real growth we know that[14]

$$\frac{S_i X}{K} = \frac{Q\lambda + r}{1 - U} \quad \text{or} \quad K = \frac{1 - U}{Q\lambda + r} S_i X.$$ (15)

Since $L = (1 - \bar{J}) \bar{L}_0 e^{\lambda t}$ it follows from (13) and (15) that

$$K = \left\{ \frac{1 - U}{Q\lambda + r} S_i R N^Z (1 - \bar{J}) {}^Q L_0^Q \right\}^{\frac{1}{1-U}} e^{\frac{Q\lambda + r}{1 - U} t}.$$ (16)

It follows that a once-for-all permanent increase in $S_i$ will cause $K$ to be larger than it would otherwise have been at any point of time in the subsequent ultimate state of steady growth because on the RHS of (16) both $S_i$ and $1 - \bar{J}$ will be higher. In other words, at any one time the capital stock will be higher because in the past a greater proportion ($S_i$ higher) of a larger output ($\bar{J}$ lower) will have been invested. At the same time current output (though not necessarily consumption[15]) will be greater both because the capital stock will be greater for the two reasons just given and also because the fall in $\bar{J}$ will mean that a larger amount of employment is associated with this larger stock of capital.

## V

So far we have assumed that the degrees of monopoly and monopsony in the micro-markets for labour and for output are constant. But it is possible that the higher is the level of pressure of demand upon resources, the greater the degrees of monopsony in labour markets and/or of monopoly in product markets.[16] The smaller the general volume of unemployed labour, the more fearful will the individual employer become that attempts on his part to build up his labour force will involve driving up the wage-rate against himself. The greater the shortage of products relatively to final demand, the less will the individual producer fear that he will lose his market if he raises the price of his product. In our system $E$, which we have so far regarded as a given constant, is better regarded as itself a variable depending upon $J$, the unemployment percentage.

In this section we will briefly indicate the lines on which the preceding analysis might be modified in order to take account of this possibility. We will carry out this analysis only for our two special cases – Case II which

---

[14] See J. E. Meade, *A Neo-Classical Theory of Economic Growth*, Chapter 4.

[15] See J. E. Meade, *A Neo-Classical Theory of Economic Growth*, 2nd edn, pp. 110–113.

[16] Mr Kaldor has stressed the former possibility and Sir Roy Harrod the latter in his book, *The Trade Cycle* (Oxford: Clarendon Press, 1936).

relies solely on the $\mu$-mechanism to achieve equality between actual savings and investment and Case III which relies solely on the $\theta$-mechanism. Moreover, we will carry out the analysis solely for the purpose of examining the effect of an increase in $S_i$ on $y$, the rate of growth of total money national income, confining this analysis to steady-state equilibrium rates of growth.

In other words, we assume a steady-state rate of growth of national income. The actual investment proportion $(S_i)$ is then raised. As we have already seen in the previous sections, this raises the rate of inflation of the national income until a new and higher steady-state rate of growth of money national income is achieved. In the labour market there is a higher level of demand and a lower unemployment percentage. This causes a higher rate of rise of the money wage-rate, until the higher rate of rise of the money wage-rate combined with the unchanged rate of growth of the total working population enables the lower unemployment percentage to be maintained with a rate of rise of the total wage bill equal to the new and higher rate of inflation of the total money national income.

The modification which we are now making in this analysis is to add the fact that the lower unemployment percentage will cause a reduction in $EQ$, the equilibrium proportion of the national income which goes to wages. If $S_v > S_w$, this will cause a rise in $S_s$, the planned equilibrium proportion of the national income which is saved. The rise in $S_i$ will thus indirectly cause a rise in $S_s$; the rise in $S_i$ will, therefore, cause a smaller inflationary pressure in this case in which we allow $E$ to fall as $J$ falls; the effect of the increase in $S_i$ will therefore be to cause (i) a smaller increase in the rate of inflation of the national income and (ii) a smaller decrease in $J$ than would have been the case if $E$ were constant.

Let us apply this analysis more rigorously to the situation of Case II. An examination of equations (1) to (4) will show that, if we allow $\theta$ to approach $\infty$, we have

$$y = \mu \frac{S_i - S_s}{1 - S_i} \tag{17}$$

even though we no longer assume that $E$, and thus $S_s$, are constant. Since $S_s = S_v - (S_v - S_w) EQ$, it is no longer certain that $S_s$ is constant even though $S_v$, $S_w$ and $Q$ are all constant. $E$ may be changing. Consequently it is no longer certain that $y$ is constant even though $\mu$ and $S_i$ are constant, since $S_s$ may be changing as a result of changes in $E$.

But perhaps $y$ will in fact always reach a constant level given the values of $S_i$, $S_v$, $S_w$, $Q$, and $\mu$, because $E$ will always reach a constant level appropriate to those given values of $S_i$, $S_v$, $S_w$, $Q$ and $\mu$. Without giving a formal mathematical proof[17] we shall assume that this is in fact the case.

---

[17] A formal proof would require the re-writing of section III on the following lines. From equation 3 with $\theta = \infty$ we have $w = y + 1/E(J).dE(J)/dt$ where $J = 1 - (L/\bar{L}_0 e^{\lambda t})$. Using the value of $y$ from (18), taking a suitable function $E(J)$, and substituting the above value of $w$ and the value of $\bar{w}$ from (10) into (8), we should obtain a differential equation, the solution of which would give the path of $L$ over time. Our proof would require that as $t \to \infty$, $L/\bar{L}_0 e^{\lambda t} \to$ some constant value between 0 and 1.

The plausibility of this assumption can be seen in the following way. $E$ decreases as $J$, the unemployment percentage, decreases. If $J$ finds a constant level, $E$ finds a constant level and in consequence $S_s$ and $y$ find constant levels. Assume then certain values for $S_i$, $S_v$, $S_w$, $Q$ and $\mu$. Suppose $J$ to be very high. Then $E$ is very high. $S_s$ is very low. $S_i - S_s$ is very high and $y$ is very high. Now if $J$ were constant at this exceptionally high level, $E$ would also be constant. $EQ$ would, therefore, be constant. Since in our present case $\theta = \infty$, $EQ$ measures the proportion of income actually going to wages. This would be constant, if $J$ were constant, so that the total wage would be rising at the same exceptionally high rate as $y$. But with a very high $J$, the rate of rise of the wage-rate will be exceptionally low. The high rate of rise in the total demand for labour will, therefore, result in an exceptionally high rate of rise in the volume of employment. If this is higher than the rate of rise of the total supply of labour, $J$ will in fact be falling. Thus we may assume that if $J$ is 'too' high, it will fall, and – by a similar process of reasoning – that if it is too low it will rise. We assume that $J$ will remain at the steady-state level at which $E$, $S_s$, and $y$ will be constant. In this position $y$ will be equal to the sum of the growth rate in the total supply of labour plus the growth rate in the money wage-rate which is itself associated with this equilibrium level of $J$.

Let us write both $E$ and $\bar{w}$ (the growth rate of the money wage-rate) as functions of $J$, namely $E(J)$ and $\bar{w}(J)$, $\partial E/\partial J$ being $> 0$ and $\partial \bar{w}/\partial J < 0$. We have in case II by writing $S_s = S_v - (S_v - S_w) EQ$ in equation (17):—

$$y = \mu \frac{S_i - S_v}{1 - S_i} + \mu Q \frac{S_v - S_w}{1 - S_i} E(J). \tag{18}$$

In a steady-growth state we know that the growth rate of total national income must equal the growth rate of the wage bill, this latter growth rate being itself the sum of the growth rate of the supply of labour ($\lambda$) and the growth rate of the money wage-rate ($\bar{w}[J]$). We have, therefore,

$$\mu \frac{S_i - S_v}{1 - S_i} + \mu Q \frac{S_v - S_w}{1 - S_i} E(J) = \lambda + \bar{w}(J). \tag{19}$$

If we knew the form of the functions $E(J)$ and $\bar{w}(J)$, equation (19) would determine the unemployment percentage, $J$, ruling in the steady-growth state.

Let us now consider the effect of a small increase in $S_i$ on $J$ and on $y$, on the assumption that $\mu$, $S_v$, $S_w$, $Q$, and $\lambda$ remain constant. By partial differentiation of equation (19) we obtain:—

$$\frac{\partial J}{\partial S_i} = -\frac{\mu \dfrac{1 - S_s}{1 - S_i}}{\mu Q (S_v - S_w) \dfrac{\partial E}{\partial J} + (1 - S_i) \left( -\dfrac{\partial \bar{w}}{\partial J} \right)}. \tag{20}$$

We can see from (20) that if either $\partial E/\partial J = 0$ or else $S_v = S_w$ (in which case a shift to profit has no effect in stimulating savings and mitigating inflationary pressures), then

$$\frac{\partial J}{\partial S_i} = -\mu \frac{1 - S_s}{(1 - S_i)^2 \left( -\dfrac{\partial \bar{w}}{\partial J} \right)}. \tag{21}$$

In both cases a rise in $S_i$ causes a fall in the employment percentage; but this fall is less in equation (20) than in equation (21).[18]

By partial differentiation of (18), keeping $\mu$, $S_v$, $S_w$, and $Q$ constant, we obtain

$$\frac{\partial y}{\partial S_i} = \mu \frac{1 - S_s}{(1 - S_i)^2} + \mu Q \frac{S_v - S_w}{1 - S_i} \frac{\partial E}{\partial J} \frac{\partial J}{\partial S_i}.$$

Making use of the value of $\partial J/\partial S_i$ from (20) we obtain

$$\frac{\partial y}{\partial S_i} = \mu \frac{1 - S_s}{(1 - S_i)^2} \frac{1}{1 + \dfrac{\mu Q (S_v - S_w)\left( \dfrac{\partial E}{\partial J} \right)}{(1 - S_i)\left( -\dfrac{\partial \bar{w}}{\partial J} \right)}}. \tag{22}$$

If either $\partial E/\partial J = 0$ or $S_v = S_w$, then

$$\frac{\partial y}{\partial S_i} = \frac{1 - S_s}{(1 - S_i)^2}.^{19}$$

The value of $\partial y/\partial S_i$ in (22) is less than this. The fact that an increased inflationary pressure due to a rise in $S_i$ causes a shift to profit through the reduction in $E$ is itself a factor mitigating the inflationary pressure.

A similar process of analysis can be applied to the situation of Case III when we assume that $\mu = \infty$ and rely solely on the $\theta$-mechanism. Once again an examination of equations (1) to (4) shows that $y = \theta (S_i - S_s)/(S_v - S_i)$, even though we no longer assume $E$ and so $S_s$ to be constant, so that instead of equation (18) we have:—

$$y = -\theta + \theta Q \frac{S_v - S_w}{S_v - S_i} E(J). \tag{23}$$

---

[18] That is to say, on the assumption that $-(\partial \bar{w}/\partial J)$ is the same in the two cases. But the two cases may refer to very different market situations; and it is very questionable whether the relationship between pressure in the labour market and the rate of rise of wage-rates would be the same.

[19] This corresponds with the result already obtained at the end of footnote 13 on page 409.

If we consider only steady-growth states we have instead of equation (19):—

$$-\theta + \theta Q \frac{S_v - S_w}{S_v - S_i} E(J) = \lambda + \bar{w}(J). \tag{24}$$

From (24) by partial differentiation we can obtain instead of equation (21):—

$$\frac{\partial J}{\partial S_i} = -\frac{\theta \dfrac{S_v - S_s}{S_v - S_i}}{\theta Q (S_v - S_w)\left(\dfrac{\partial E}{\partial J}\right) + (S_v - S_i)\left(-\dfrac{\partial \bar{w}}{\partial J}\right)}. \tag{25}$$

Finally, by partial differentiation of (23) and use of (25) we have instead of equation (22):—

$$\frac{\partial y}{\partial S_i} = \theta \frac{S_v - S_s}{(S_v - S_i)^2} \frac{1}{1 + \dfrac{\theta Q (S_v - S_w)\dfrac{\partial E}{\partial J}}{(S_v - S_i)\left(-\dfrac{\partial \bar{w}}{\partial J}\right)}}. \tag{26}$$

In this case we must assume $S_v > S_i > S_w$. The $\theta$-mechanism depends upon this assumption. But the assumption that $\partial E/\partial J > 0$ instead of $= 0$ is seen once again to reduce the (numerical) values of $\partial J/\partial S_i$ and $\partial y/\partial S_i$.

## Appendix

The function given in equation (10) of the main text is the same function as that used by Professor A. W. Phillips in his 'The Relation between Unemployment and the Rate of Change of Money Wage Rates', *Economica*, vol. 25 (November 1958), p. 290. His equation is $y = -a + bx^c$ where $y$ is the percentage rate of rise of the money wage-rate and $x$ is the unemployment percentage and where $a$ and $b > 0$ and $c < 0$. His equation can therefore be written

$$\bar{w} = -\frac{a}{100} + \frac{b}{100^{1-c}}\left(\frac{1}{J}\right)^{-c}$$

As $J \to \infty$, $\bar{w} \to -(a/100)$, and we write $\bar{w}_x = -(a/100)$. We also have $0 = -a/100 + (b/100^{1-c})(1/J_x)^{-c}$ where $J_x$ is the value of $J$ which makes $\bar{w} = 0$, so that $b/100^{1-c} = -\bar{w}_x J_x^{-c}$. If in addition we write $\gamma = -c$ we have our equation (10)

$$\dot{w} = -\,\bar{w}_x \left\{ \left( \frac{J_x}{J} \right)^{\gamma} - 1 \right\}.$$

The interpretation of the parameter $\gamma$ can best be understood from the following diagram:—

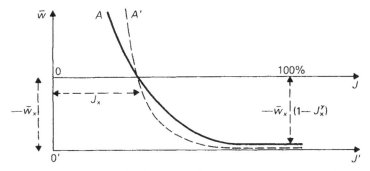

Measure along the $0J$ axis the unemployment percentage and up the $0\bar{w}$ axis the rate of rise of the money wage-rate. The curve $A$ showing this relationship falls as $J$ increases. It crosses the axis $0J$ at $J = J_x$. At $J = 100$ per cent it is $(-\bar{w}_x)(1 - J_x^{\gamma})$ below the $0J$ axis. But as $J \to \infty$ it approaches asymptotically a level $-\bar{w}_x$ below the $0J$ axis. Now

$$\gamma = -\,\frac{J}{\dot{w} + (-\bar{w}_x)} \quad \frac{d\,[\dot{w} + (-\bar{w}_x)]}{dJ}.$$

In other words, it is the arithmetical value of the negative elasticity of the curve $A$ if we measure its base not from the axis $0J$ but from the axis $0'J'$. The curve $A'$ has the same values for $\bar{w}_x$ and $J_x$ but a higher value of $\gamma$ than curve $A$. Professor Phillips' calculations make $\bar{w}_x = -\,{\cdot}009$ per annum, $J_x = {\cdot}054$, and $\gamma = 1{\cdot}394$.

# 23

# The Rate of Profit in a
# Growing Economy

*From* The Economic Journal, *vol. 73 (December 1963), pp. 665–74*

I

In recent years a group of economists, of whom my colleagues Joan Robinson, Richard Kahn, and Nicholas Kaldor are acknowledged leaders, have made notable contributions to new methods of analysing economic growth. Their work has revealed a number of fundamental relationships. The purpose of my book *A Neo-Classical Theory of Economic Growth* (London: Allen & Unwin, 1961; 2nd edn, 1962) was to inquire how far these new relationships are compatible with the orthodox classical assumptions of a simple production function. This article is intended to push that inquiry into one more set of relationships. My purpose is to shed light rather than to generate heat; and if I call my colleagues 'neo-Keynesians' and myself a 'neo-classicist' it is merely to use convenient labels rather than to suggest that there is any unbridgeable gulf separating the assumptions, methods or results of the analysis.

My present purpose is to discuss the two following propositions concerning the rate of profit in a state of steady growth which often appear in the 'neo-Keynesian' system of thought, namely: (1) that the rate of growth of the national output itself depends upon the rate of growth of population and the rate of technical progress, and is otherwise independent of the form of the production function; and (2) that the rate of profit depends upon the rate of growth of the national output and upon the thriftiness conditions in the economy and is otherwise independent of the form of the production function.[1]

In order to consider these propositions in the 'neo-classical' system of thought let us assume the most simple Cobb-Douglas production function in which there are: (i) constant returns to scale; (ii) three factors of production – land, labour and capital; (iii) constant and neutral technical

---

[1] These propositions are laid out in a form directly relevant for the 'neo-classicist' in the footnote on p. 276 of L. Pasinetti's 'Rate of Profit and Income Distribution in Relation to the Rate of Economic Growth', *Review of Economic Studies,* vol. 29 (December 1962), pp. 267–79. The ideas expressed in Section I of the present article spring from comments about that footnote made to me by Professor Trevor Swan.

progress; and (iv) unitary elasticities of substitution between factors, so that

$$Y = RK^U L^Q N^Z e^{rt} \tag{1}$$

where $Y$ = output; $K$ = amount of capital; $L$ = amount of labour; $N$ = amount of land; $R$ = an arbitrary constant; $U$, $Q$ and $Z$ = the proportional marginal products of $K$, $L$ and $N$ respectively which, in competitive conditions, are also equal to the proportions of income paid out in profits, wages and rents respectively; and $r$ = rate of technical progress. $N$, $R$, $U$, $Q$, $Z$ and $r$ are constant, and $U + Q + Z = 1$.

By differentiation of (1) we obtain

$$y = Uk + Ql + r \tag{2}$$

where $y = (1/Y)(dY/dt)$, $k = (1/K)(dK/dt)$, and $l = (1/L)(dL/dt)$.

There is a state of steady growth when $y = k$. Call the rate of economic growth in this steady state $y_s$ and we have from (2)

$$y_s = \frac{Ql + r}{1 - U}. \tag{3}$$

Now $U = (K/Y)(\partial Y/\partial K)$, so that the rate of profit can be expressed as

$$\frac{\partial Y}{\partial K} = \frac{UY}{K}. \tag{4}$$

In equilibrium growth to maintain full employment total investment must be kept at the right level and total savings will be equal to this investment. Define $S$ as the ratio of total savings to the national income. (We will discuss later what determines $S$.) We have then $SY = dK/dt$, so that $K = SY/K$. Now in the state of steady growth $k = y_s$, so that from (4) we have

$$\frac{\partial Y}{\partial K} = \frac{UY}{K} = \frac{U}{S} y_s. \tag{5}$$

Now our two 'neo-Keynesian' propositions are to the effect that in equation (3) the value of $y_s$ is independent of $Q$ and $1 - U$ and that in equation (5) $U/S$ is independent of $U$, since $Q$ and $U$ are parameters of the actual production function. How can this be so?

Equation (3) can be written as $y_s = [Q/(1 - U)]l + \bar{r}$, where $\bar{r} = r/(1 - U)$. If there are constant returns to scale and only two factors, labour and capital, then $Q = 1 - U$ and $y_s = l + \bar{r}$. The 'neo-Keynesian' proposition (1) thus depends: (i) upon there being no appreciable scarcity of land (which in some but not all cases may be a reasonable assumption), and (ii) upon the assumption that it is the degree of 'Harrodian' technical progress $\bar{r}$ and not of 'Hicksian' technical progress which is independent of the form of the production function. Those who prefer the Hicksian measure would argue that a given increase in technical knowledge is best measured as the increase in output one can get from the same amount of $L$, $K$ and $N$. When $K$ also increases in step with $Y$ there will be a larger rise in output if $U$ (the proportional marginal product of $K$) is large than if $U$ is small. With $r$ constant, $\bar{r}$ will be greater if $U$ is greater.

Equation (5) brings one to the second 'neo-Keynesian' proposition mentioned in the second paragraph of this paper. The 'neo-classicist' notes the term $U/S$ in equation (5). It implies that, given the rate of economic growth, the rate of profit $\partial Y/\partial K$ will depend upon the balance between the productivity of capital and thrift. For $U$ is the proportional marginal product of capital and $S$ is the proportion of income saved.

The 'neo-Keynesian' will point out that a higher share of profits in the national income (a higher $U$) is associated with a higher proportion of the national income being invested and saved (a higher $S$). $S$ and $U$ are thus interdependent in a way which may make $U/S$ a function only of the thriftiness conditions and not of the productivity conditions.

## II

We must look closer at the thriftiness conditions. Let us consider a number of representative possibilities.

1 If everyone (whether wage-earner, capitalist or landlord) saved the same fixed proportion, $S$, of income, then $S$ would be given independently of $U$ and the 'neo-classical' view would be correct in its simplest form.

2 If, on the other hand, neither wage-earners nor landlords saved anything, but capitalists (owning no land and doing no work) saved a fixed proportion $S_v$ of their incomes, then $S = S_v U$ and $U/S = 1/S_v$. In this case the 'neo-Keynesian' view would be true in its simplest form. A higher $U$ would represent a higher productivity of capital, but the accompanying shift to profit would represent a higher $S$ to an exactly offsetting degree.

3 Suppose fixed proportions $S_v$, $S_g$ are saved out of profits, wages and rents. Then

$$\frac{U}{S} = \frac{U}{S_v U + S_w Q + S_g (1 - U - Q)} = \frac{1}{S_v + S_w \dfrac{Q}{U} + S_g \dfrac{1 - U - Q}{U}}.$$

If $S_v$ were larger than $S_w$ and $S_g$ then a rise in $U$ would raise $S$. We would have a situation in between the 'neo-classical' and the 'neo-Keynesian' result. How near it was to the one or the other would depend upon the relative sizes of $S_v$, $S_w$ and $S_g$ and of U, Q and Z. One institutional arrangement which would give a result of this kind would be if all individuals saved the same proportion of their personal incomes, but if all profits (unlike wages and rents) passed through companies which placed a certain proportion of them to reserve before distributing the remainder as dividends to persons. Suppose $S_u$ of company profits are put to reserve, while $S_i$ of individual incomes are saved. Then we have $S_v = S_u + S_i (1 - S_u)$ and $S_w = S_g = S_i$, so that

$$\frac{U}{S} = \frac{U}{US_u (1 - S_i) + S_i}.$$

From this we obtain

$$\frac{U}{U/S} \frac{d(U/S)}{dU} = \frac{S_i}{US_u (1 - S_i) + S_i}.$$

Or, to take a numerical example, if $S_i = 1/9$ and $S_u = U = \frac{1}{2}$, the above expression for $[U/(U/S)] [d(U/S)/dU] = \frac{1}{3}$. In other words, a 3% increase in $U$ (from 50 to 51½%) would cause a 1% rise in $U/S$ (from 150 to 151½%).

4 Mr Pasinetti, in the article to which reference has been made above, stresses the very important fact that to assume (as we have done in the last paragraph) that certain fixed proportions of wages, profits and rents are saved is not the same thing as to assume that wage-earners, capitalists and landlords save certain fixed proportions of their incomes. For if wage-earners save, then wage-earners will accumulate property and will receive profits and/or rents. In consequence, the wage-earners' savings ratio ($S_w$) will apply to some of the income from property.

Following Mr Pasinetti, let us assume that there are only two factors, labour and capital, and that there are only two classes of persons – wage-earners, who save a fixed proportion $S_w$ of their incomes, and capitalists, who do no work and save a fixed proportion $S_v$ of their incomes. Wage-earners will accumulate capital; and wage-earners' property will be accumulating at a higher (or lower) proportional rate than capitalists' property according as to the ratio of wage-earners' savings to wage-earners' property is higher (or lower) than the ratio of capitalists' savings to capitalists' property. Since the yield on capital will be the same for both classes, the condition for the wage-earners' share of property incomes to be rising or falling will be

$$\frac{S_w (W + \pi P)}{\pi P} \gtreqless \frac{S_v (1 - \pi) P}{(1 - \pi) P} \tag{6}$$

where $W$ is the total wage bill, $P$ is the total of profits and $\pi$ is the proportion of property owned by, and so of profits received by, wage-earners. Since $W = QY$ and $(1 - Q) Y$, the condition for $\pi$ to be rising or falling is

$$S_w \left\{ 1 + \frac{Q}{(1 - Q)\pi} \right\} \gtreqless S_v. \tag{7}$$

There are now two possibilities.

First, if $S_v \leqslant S_w/(1 - Q)$, $\pi$ will go on rising so long as $\pi < 1$. In other words, capitalists' property will ultimately become a negligible proportion of total property. The community's savings will approximate to $S_w(W + P) = S_w Y$. The fraction $U/S$ will become $U/S_w$. If, for example, $Q = 2/3$, $S_v$ would have to be more than three times as great as $S_w$ for this result to be avoided.

Second, if $S_v > S_w/(1 - Q)$, $\pi$ will reach a value between 0 and 1 of $QS_w/[(1 - Q)(S_v - S_w)]$. The ratio of savings to property incomes will be $S_v$ for capitalists and $S_v$ for wage-earners also. So that for the community as a whole the ratio $U/S$ will equal $1/S_v$.

Thus, with unitary elasticities of substitution between the factors of production added to Mr Pasinetti's assumptions the 'neo-classical' result will be true in its simplest form if $S_v \leqslant S_w/(1 - Q)$, while the 'neo-Keynesian' result will be true in its simplest form if $S_v > S_w/(1 - Q)$.

Mr Pasinetti does not allow for income from rents on land, nor does he allow for the fact that capitalists may work. We can generalise his system by assuming $n$ different classes of persons who save fixed proportions $S_1$, $S_2, \ldots S_n$ of their incomes and who provide fixed proportions $\lambda_1, \lambda_2, \ldots \lambda_n$ of the wage-earning power of the community. Now the proportion of the total property owned by (and so the total of property incomes received by) any one class will be rising if the ratio of savings to property (and so to property incomes) is higher for that class than for the national average.[2] Let $\pi_1, \pi_2, \ldots \pi_n$ be the proportions of total property held by classes 1, 2, $\ldots n$. Then $\pi_j$ will be rising or falling as

$$S_j \left\{ \frac{\lambda_j Q}{\pi_j (1 - Q)} + 1 \right\} \gtrless \frac{S}{1 - Q} \tag{8}$$

where

$$S = \sum_{i=1}^{i=n} S_i \{ Q\lambda_i + (1 - Q) \pi_i \}.$$

It follows that $\pi_j$ will be rising or falling as

$$S_j \gtrless \frac{\sum\limits_{i \neq j} S_i \{ Q\lambda_i + (1 - Q) \pi_i \}}{Q\lambda_i + (1 - Q) \pi_i} \frac{\pi_j}{1 - \pi_j}. \tag{9}$$

From this a number of general conclusions can be reached.

First, if $\lambda_j > 0$, then the equilibrium value of $\pi_j$ must be greater than 0. If $\pi_j = 0$, then the condition for $\pi_j$ to be rising is only that $S_j > 0$. Every working class will own some property.

---

[2] This assumes that each class holds the same ratio of land to capital, so that a change in the relative prices of land and capital equipment does not alter the distribution of property.

Second, if $1 > \lambda_j > 0$, then the equilibrium value of $\pi_j$ must be less than 1. For if $\lambda_j < 1$, some other $\lambda$ must be $> 0$. If then $\pi_j = 1$, so that $\sum_{i \neq j} S_i \pi_i = 0$, the condition for $\pi_j$ to be falling would be simply that $S_j < \infty$. The only working class that could own all the property would be one which did all the work.

Third, suppose $\lambda_j = 0$. Then the condition for $\pi_j$ to be rising or falling is

$$S_j (1 - \pi_j) \gtrless \sum_{i \neq j} S_i \left( \frac{Q}{1 - Q} \lambda_i + \pi_i \right).$$

If $\pi_j = 1$, then $\pi_j$ would be falling. But however closely $\pi_j$ approached 0, $\pi_j$ would still be falling if

$$S_j (1 - Q) < \sum_{i \neq j} S_i \{ Q \lambda_i + (1 - Q) \pi_i \}$$

i.e. if $S_j$ were less than $1/(1 - Q)$ times the weighted average of the savings proportions of the other classes in the community.

Fourth, if $\lambda_j = 0$ and $S_j > 1/(1 - Q) \sum_{i \neq j} S_i \{ Q \lambda_i + 1 - Q \pi_i \}$, then $\pi_j$ will find an equilibrium level between 0 and 1. In this case we should have for the class $j$ the ratio of property incomes to savings equal to $1/S_j$ and since $\pi_j$ is constant, this would be the average for the economy, so that $(1 - Q)/S = 1/S_j$. If there were no land, so that $1 - Q = U$, we would have then $U/S = 1/S_j$.[3]

Fifth, if there were no class $j$ for which both $\lambda_j = 0$ and also $S_j > 1/(1 - Q) \sum_{i \neq j} S_i \{ Q \lambda_i + (1 - Q) \pi_i \}$, then the community would in equilibrium for all practical purposes contain only classes of persons who both worked and owned property.

As a special case of this last result, assume two classes 1 and 2, where $\lambda_1 + \lambda_2 = \pi_1 + \pi_2 = 1$. In equilibrium we would have from (8)

$$\frac{S_1 \{ \lambda_1 Q + \pi_1 (1 - Q) \}}{\pi_1 (1 - Q)} = \frac{S_2 \{ (1 - \lambda_1) Q + (1 - \pi_1) (1 - Q) \}}{(1 - \pi_1) (1 - Q)} = \frac{S}{1 - Q} \quad (10)$$

---

[3] Suppose we had another class $k$ for which $\lambda_k = 0$ but that this non-working class had a smaller savings ratio $(S_k < S_j)$. If $\pi_j$ is constant, then $S_j (1 - \pi_j) = S_k \pi_k + \sum_{\substack{i \neq j \\ i \neq k}} S_i \left( \frac{Q}{1 - Q} \lambda_i + \pi_i \right)$.

Therefore $S_k (1 - \pi_k) = S_k - S_j (1 - \pi_j) + \sum_{\substack{i \neq j \\ i \neq k}} S_i \left( \frac{Q}{1 - Q} \lambda_i + \pi_i \right)$.

Since $S_k < S_j$, $S_k (1 - \pi_k) < \sum_{i \neq k} S_i \left( \frac{Q}{1 - Q} \lambda_i + \pi_i \right)$

so that $\pi_k$ will be falling continuously. In other words, for long-run equilibrium we need consider only the non-working class with the highest savings ratio. The others will become negligible.

since the ratio of savings to property income must be the same for each class and the same for the national average if the distribution of property is to remain unchanged. From the two equations in (10) we can derive

$$\pi_1 = \frac{S_I \lambda_1 Q}{S - S_1 (1 - Q)} \tag{11}$$

and

$$S = S_1 \{ \lambda_1 Q + \pi_1 (1 - Q) \} + S_2 \{ (1 - \lambda_1) Q + (1 - \pi_1) (1 - Q) \} \tag{12}$$

so that, substituting for $\pi_1$ from (11) into (12) we have

$$S = S_2 + \lambda_1 Q (S_1 - S_2) + \frac{(1 - Q) (S_1 - S_2) S_1 \lambda_1 Q}{S - S_1 (1 - Q)}. \tag{13}$$

The solution of this quadratic for $S$ gives

$$S = \tfrac{1}{2} \{ S_1 (1 - Q + \lambda_1 Q) + S_2 (1 - \lambda_1 Q)$$
$$\pm \sqrt{[S_1 (1 - Q + \lambda_1 Q) + S_2 (1 - \lambda_1 Q)]^2 - 4 S_1 S_2 (1 - Q)} \}. \tag{14}$$

There would seem in general to be two possible values for $S$ and for $\pi$.[4] One of these solutions can, however, be neglected because it would involve one class in society having to own a negative amount of property. We can rewrite the solution for $S$ given in (14) as

$$S = S_1 (1 - Q + \lambda_1 Q) + \tfrac{1}{2} \{ S_2 (1 - \lambda_1 Q) - S_1 (1 - Q + \lambda_1 Q) \pm$$
$$\sqrt{[S_2 (1 - \lambda_1 Q) - S_1 (1 - Q + \lambda_1 Q)]^2 + 4 S_1 S_2 \lambda_1 Q^2 (1 - \lambda_1)} \}. \tag{15}$$

From this it can be seen that both the solutions for $S$ are real. The larger value of $S$ is $> S_1 (1 - Q + \lambda_1 Q)$, and the smaller value of $S$ is $< S_1 (1 - Q + \lambda_1 Q)$. But from (11) above it can be seen that this smaller value would imply $\pi > 1$ or $< 0$. We can therefore confine our attention to the higher value of $S$. From this we can derive $U/S$, which will clearly be dependent upon $U$ and $Q$.

Mr Pasinetti has done great service by bringing to the forefront of the discussion the long-run implications for the distribution of property of differences in the savings proportions and the working habits of different classes of the community. These matters are of the greatest interest, quite apart from their implications about the savings proportion $S$ for the community as a whole. The strict logic of his analysis would imply that if there were one single property-owner who did no work and saved a proportion of his income greater than $1/(1 - Q)$ times the average savings proportion of the rest of the community he would in the end accumulate so much capital that his savings proportion (say $S_j$) would impose itself so that for the community as a whole $(1 - Q)/S = 1/S_j$. Our

---

[4] If we write $\lambda_1 = 1$ and $1 - Q = U$ the two values of $S$ become $S_1$ and $S_1 U$, which are the strict neo-classical and neo-Keynesian results noted above (p. 420).

miser might have to live a long long time to achieve this result. In fact he would die, and death duties combined with the probably less austere and possibly less lazy life of his heirs would prevent the achievement of this result. For Mr Pasinetti's results to have practical use we must assume a self-perpetuating class of property-owners who do no work and who, even after allowing for death duties, save a proportion of their income greater than $1/(1 - Q)$ times the savings proportion of the rest of the community.

Moreover, it is, of course, only a first approximation to assume that some persons save a proportion $S_1$ and others a proportion $S_2$ of their incomes, no matter what happens to their incomes (either in real terms or relatively to their neighbours) as a result of the accumulation of property or the rise in the real wage-rate. The important path which Mr Pasinetti has pioneered needs now to be developed by means of an analysis which makes the proportion of income which any group will save depend upon their real income per head (either absolutely or relatively to the rest of the community) and which makes their real income per head depend upon their ability and willingness to work and upon the property which they have inherited and accumulated after allowance for recurrent taxation of income and the spasmodic taxation of wealth at death.

To what extent meanwhile each of us chooses to assume $S$ to be independent of $U$ and $Q$ must, I fear, remain largely a matter of taste.

## III

We may sum up so far by saying that the two 'neo-Keynesian' propositions with which we started are dependent upon two special assumptions about the production function (that there are only two factors of production and that it is the 'Harrodian' and not the 'Hicksian' rate of technical progress which is independent of the other features of the production function) and upon the assumption that the thriftiness conditions are such that $S$ can be expressed as a constant proportion of $U$.

These 'neo-Keynesian' propositions refer only to the state of steady growth. It can be shown that, if we are not in the state of steady growth with our simple Cobb-Douglas production function, the values of $Q$ and $U$ do affect $\partial Y/\partial K$ even when the conditions are fulfilled in which $Q$ and $U$ would not affect $\partial Y/\partial K$ in the state of steady growth.

From equation (37) on p. 110 of the second edition of my *A Neo-Classical Theory of Economic Growth* we have

$$k = \frac{y_s}{1 - \dfrac{k_o - y_s}{k_o e^{(r + Ql)t}}} \tag{16}$$

where $y_s = (r + Ql)/(1 - U)$ as given in equation (5) of this paper. As $t \to \infty$, so $k \to y_s$ in equation (16).

Since $SY/K = k$ and $\partial Y/\partial K = UY/K$, we have from (16)

$$\frac{\partial Y}{\partial K} = \frac{UY}{K} = \frac{U}{S} \cdot \frac{y_s}{1 - \dfrac{k_o - y_s}{k_o e^{(r + Ql)t}}}. \tag{17}$$

Let us assume $Q = 1 - U$, that $r/(1 - U)$ is given at the constant value $\bar{r}$, and that $U/S = 1/S_v$.[5] These are the conditions necessary for the two propositions under examination to be true in the state of steady growth. We then have from (17)

$$\frac{\partial Y}{\partial K} = \frac{1}{S_o} \cdot \frac{\bar{r} + 1}{1 - \dfrac{k_o - \bar{r} - l}{k_o e^{(1 - U)(\bar{r} + l)t}}}. \tag{18}$$

There is a $U$ in this expression which only time will remove.

Examination of (18) will show that the effect of a larger $U$ is to decrease the speed with which an initial rate of capital accumulation ($k_o$) is brought into line with its steady-state level ($\bar{r} + l$). As far as the rate of profit is concerned, this means that the effect of a larger $U$ is to decrease the speed with which the initial rate of profit $k_o/S_v$ is brought into line with its steady-state level $\bar{r} + l/S_v$. The reason for this is as follows. $k = SY/K = S_vUY/K$. Given $S_v$ and $U$, $k$ will be falling so long as $Y/K$ is falling, i.e. so long as $y < k$. Suppose we start with $k$ in excess of its steady-state level by a certain amount. If $y$ were at its steady-state level $Y/K$ would be falling with the most speed. But since $y = Uk + Ql + r$, $y$ will be above its steady-state level by $U$ times the amount by which $k$ is above the steady-state level. If $U$ is large $y$ will be only a little lower than $k$, so that $Y/K$, and thus $k$, will be falling only slowly. If $U$ is small $y$ will be only a little higher than its steady-state level, and will thus be much below $k$, so that $Y/K$, and thus $k$, will be falling rapidly. The form of the production function will thus in any case affect the speed of movement of the system towards its steady state, including the speed with which the rate of profit moves towards its steady-state level.

---

[5] We assume simply that a constant proportion of profits ($S_v$) and a zero proportion of wages ($S_w = 0$) are saved. In other words, this is an instance of case (2) (p. 418 above) and not the end result of the Pasinetti process of case (4) (p. 419 above). For the Pasinetti process does not imply that $U/S$ is constant at $1/S_v$ during the process of approach to the state of steady growth but only that $U/S$ becomes equal to $1/S_v$ at the end of the process. For example, the economy may have been pushed off its path of steady growth in the first instance by a change in thriftiness conditions. In case (4) above the restoration of the state of steady growth would involve not only the familiar process of adjustment of the capital-output ratio to the level appropriate to the new equilibrium ratio of savings to income but also a Pasinetti process which would adjust the distribution of property between workers and capitalists so as to make the ratio of workers' savings to workers' income from property equal once more to the proportion of income saved by capitalists. The Pasinetti process could be very prolonged. An investigation of the factors determining its speed of operation is badly needed.

# 24

# The Rate of Profit in a Growing Economy

*By J. E. Meade and F. H. Hahn, from* The Economic Journal, *vol. 75 (June 1965), pp. 445–48.*

In his article[1] Meade was concerned to show that the very long-run rate of profit in a golden age will depend upon technology, if, in that age, all people both work and own property. He also gave a simple account of how such a state might come about even if at some initial date there were people who only owned wealth and did not work. Dr Pasinetti, in his note:[2] (i) claims that these results depend upon the assumption of what he calls 'infinite substitutability' between labour and capital, and (ii) emphasises that he had in any case assumed that the people who both work and save can never save enough to allow full-employment growth. It is our object in this note to argue that the claim under (i) above is false and that, in an important respect, the assumption under (ii) above begs the real question at issue.

I

In order to get as far away as possible from any implication of 'infinite substitutability' between labour and capital let us consider a world of many goods where a finite number of discrete production processes are available (book of blueprints). In equilibrium, in all the activities used, selling prices must just, but only just, cover costs; and there must be no unused activities for which selling prices would more than cover costs. These 'supply' conditions are not alone sufficient to determine the whole structure of prices (i.e. of the wage-rate, of the rate of interest and of the commodity prices). This can be seen in the following ways. Let us take labour as our *numéraire*. Start with any given rate of interest, and given set of prices (in terms of labour) at which the commodities can be sold. If the rate of interest is sufficiently low, and the commodity prices sufficiently high, then there will be some activities in which the rate of

---

[1] J. E. Meade, 'The Rate of Profit in a Growing Economy', *Economic Journal*, vol. 73 (December 1963), pp. 665–74 [Chapter 23 above, pp. 416–24].

[2] L. L. Pasinetti, 'A Comment on Professor Meade's "Rate of Profit in a Growing Economy"', *Economic Journal*, vol. 74 (June 1964), pp. 488–89.

profit exceeds the rate of interest. Keep the prices of the commodities constant, but raise the rate of interest until there is no activity left in which profits exceed interest, but at least one activity in which profits equal interest. We can thus say that (within possible limits) to each structure of commodity prices there corresponds an equilibrium rate of interest. The converse will in fact also be true, namely, that to each rate of interest there will correspond an equilibrium set of prices. What we need to close our system is, of course, the 'demand' conditions. Assume that for consumption purposes our commodities are purchased in proportions which depend only on their relative prices. We need then to add only one more demand condition. How much of total income is saved and spent on commodities for investment in additions to capital stocks? If we know this, all the demand conditions and thus all the prices will be determined in our system. For the relative demand for different products for investment purposes will itself be determined by the structure of final demand for consumption purposes and by the technology of the profitable activities.

As is well known, if savings are proportional to profits the above system (like other systems) in a golden age will decompose in such a way that the equilibrium rate of profit is determined independently of the technology of the system. The golden age rate of growth will be the natural rate of growth $(g_n)$, which depends upon the growth of the labour supply and the rate of technical progress. The rate of growth of the capital stock $(I/K$ where $I$ is investment and $K$ the capital stock[3]) must be equal to this. But where savings $(=$ investment$)$ is a fixed proportion $(S_p)$ of profits $(P)$ we have $S_p P/K = I/K = g_n$ or $P/K$ (the rate of profit) $= g_n/S_p$. But, on the other hand, where $I$ is a fixed proportion $(S_y)$ of income $(Y)$ we have $S_y Y/K = I/K$ or $K/Y = g_n/S_y$. The income-capital ratio, but not the profit-capital ratio, is now independent of the technology. In this case to know the equilibrium rate of profit we must solve for the whole system, which will involve the technological aspects of the economy.

Let us now apply these familiar aspects of the theory of golden-age growth to the problem raised in Dr Pasinetti's original article. Suppose that there are two groups of people: pure capitalists and those who both work and own wealth. If they are accumulating property at different proportionate rates the asset distribution will vary. Three possibilities exist for a very long-run equilibrium where further changes in asset distribution cease to play a role: $(a)$ the proportion of assets owned by workers may become negligibly small; $(b)$ the asset distribution may remain constant through time; and $(c)$ the proportion of assets owned by pure capitalists may become negligibly small. In cases $(a)$ and $(b)$ the eventual rate of profit multiplied by the capitalists' saving propensity will equal the rate of growth. This is Dr Pasinetti's case. But in case $(c)$ savings will eventually become proportional to income. This is the case investigated by Meade. In this case the system does not decompose in the required manner. What we have now to do is to show that case $(c)$ does not depend upon the assumption of 'infinite substitutability' between

---

[3] $K$ is the capital stock of products measured at their equilibrium prices, and similarly for $I$, $Y$ and $P$.

labour and capital, but is compatible with the book-of-blueprints technology outlined earlier in this note.

It is not easy to trace the process of asset adjustment to an eventual very long-run equilibrium. But for our purposes we need only try the following experiment, in order to show that Dr Pasinetti's outcome is not the only possible one. Suppose for the sake of the argument: (i) that the economy is in a state of long-run golden-age growth, and (ii) that, in this state, the rate of growth is equal to the rate of profit multiplied by the capitalists' propensity to save $(S_p P/K = g_n)$, so that the rate of profit $(P/K)$ is set at a value given by two exogenous parameters $(g_n/S_p)$. Then, as we have argued above, all the price relationships in our system will be given. In particular, the distribution of the national income between wages and profits will be given. Let $Q$ be the ratio of wages to total income so determined. It is now quite possible that even though the proportion of income saved by pure capitalists $(S_p)$ were greater than that saved by those who work and own property $(S_w)$, yet $S_p(1 - Q)$ might be less than $S_w$. This is the inequality at the top of p. 420 of Meade's article. If this were so, and if the system approaches a very long run golden age, then it will approach one given by $(c)$ above, where the system cannot be decomposed in the required manner. Meade's conclusion does not depend upon the assumption of 'infinite substitutability' between labour and capital.

## II

Dr Pasinetti in fact rules out case $(c)$ by his assumption that the saving propensity $(S_w)$ of those who both work and own capital is less than the ratio of full-employment investment to income $(I/Y)$. We venture to suggest that this assumption begs the question. In golden-age growth $I/K = g_n$, so that $I/Y = g_n K/Y$. The condition assumed by Dr Pasinetti (namely $S_w < I/Y$) can be expressed as the assumption that in the golden age $S_w < g_n(K/Y)$ or $K/Y > S_w/g_n$. This assumption can legitimately be made *a priori* without investigating the general conditions of the golden-age equilibrium (which will depend upon demand conditions and relative prices as well as upon technological possibilities) only if the book of blueprints contains no set of activities which is sufficiently labour-intensive (capital-disintensive) to reduce the capital-output ratio below the given level $g_n/S_w$. This may, of course, be so if $S_w$ is negligibly small or if the available technology does not include any very labour-intensive methods. If this were the case Dr Pasinetti's results would, of course, follow. If we happened to start from a position in which a very small proportion of property were owned by the pure capitalists, then in these conditions the rate of investment would not be sufficient to keep the growth of the capital stock in line with the growth of labour, even when the most labour-intensive techniques were chosen. Unemployment would result. For full employment the real wage-rate would have to be reduced until the distribution of income were shifted to profits until the savings propensity of the community were sufficient to correspond to a rate of investment which generated a sufficient supply of real capital to employ all the available labour. The equilibrium value of $Q$ in our experiment would not be great enough to make $S_p (1 - Q) < S_w$.

But what if we look at the real world and find that the minimum technologically possible value of $K/Y$ is less than $S_w/g_n$? Dr Pasinetti can, of course, legitimately build a model in which this is just assumed not to be the case. But it may be the case; and Meade claims the right to examine the possibility.[4]

---

[4] It may be of interest to note that in the United Kingdom at present income from employment (including self-employment) is of the order of 85% of net national income. If this were the equilibrium value of $Q$, $S_p$ would have to be at least seven times as high as $S_w$ for Dr Pasinetti's result to follow.

# 25

# Life-Cycle Savings, Inheritance and Economic Growth[1]

*From the* Review of Economic Studies, *vol. 33 (1966), pp. 61–78. A revised version subsequently appeared as a note to Chapter XIII of Meade's* The Growing Economy (Principles of Political Economy, Vol. 2) *(London: Allen & Unwin, 1968), pp. 243–261. The correspondence with D. G. Champernowne in August 1944, referred to in footnote 9 on p. 442 below, concerned a paper by Meade on 'Increasing returns, monopoly and population' (Meade Papers 3/3).*

## I  The Assumptions

Our object is to present a model of the interrelationships between (i) certain macro-economic variables in a state of steady growth (in particular, $S$, the proportion of total national income saved) and (ii) the main forces determining personal motives for savings (in particular, saving for old age and saving to leave property to one's children). We shall be concerned only with the situation in conditions of steady growth. Moreover, while we shall be concerned with inequalities in the standard of living between citizens of one generation and those of another, we shall assume that all citizens of the same age at any one time are exactly equal in earning power and in the ownership of property. The model, therefore, cries out for elaboration in two ways: first to examine its behaviour when it is not on the steady-state path; and second, to build into it inequalities in earning power and in the ownership of property as between individuals of the same generation.[2]

The model is built on the following very strict assumptions:—

[1] I would like to thank my colleagues C. J. Bliss, M. J. Farrell, F. H. Hahn, and J. A. Mirrlees for much help and stimulation in discussion of the matters covered by this paper. I have been privileged to see in draft a paper by M. J. Farrell discussing the determinants of life-cycle savings, from which I have learned much for the writing of this paper. I am particularly indebted to J. A. Mirrlees. I had obtained the result embodied in equations (17) below in a clumsy manner. He showed me the much simpler approach adopted in equations (1) to (9) and – in consultation, I understand, with C. von Weizsäcker – prevented me from making a major blunder in their interpretation. He also gave me great help in considering the possible particular solutions which are examined in section IV of this paper.

[2] For example, on the lines discussed in J. E. Meade, *Efficiency, Equality and the Ownership of Property* (London: Allen & Unwin, 1964), Chapter V.

(1)    We assume a constant-returns-to-scale production function with Harrod-neutral (i.e. labour-expanding) technical progress with only two factors, labour and capital, and only one output which can be used for consumption or for addition to the capital stock. There are diminishing returns to each factor taken separately and there is perfect competition, so that each factor receives its marginal product. We shall make frequent use of the well-known propositions that with such a productive system in a state of steady growth (i) the rate of growth of total output, of total consumption, of total savings, etc., will be equal to the sum of the rate of growth of the working population and of the rate of technical progress and (ii) the rate of growth of output per head, of consumption per head, of the wage-rate, etc., will be equal to the rate of technical progress. We assume that the working population is growing at a constant proportional rate, $l$, and that the rate of Harrod-neutral technical progress (i.e. of labour-expanding progress) is a constant, $l'$, so that the rate of growth of total output is $l + l'$.

(2)    We make the following demographic and biological assumptions. (i) Citizens are born as fully trained adults ready to start earning. (ii) Each citizen then works for $F$ years and then retires. (iii) Each citizen dies at the age $G$ (i.e. he enjoys $G - F$ years of retirement). (iv) At the age of $H$ years each citizen produces $e^{lH}$ children ($e^{lH}$ not necessarily being a whole number), so that the number of births can rise at the constant rate of $l$. (v) There is no distinction between men and women. These assumptions enable one to consider both savings for old age and savings for one's heirs with the minimum of complication. It is not difficult to see how the following analysis could in principle (but at the expense of clumsy elaboration) be extended to cover more realistic biological and demographic assumptions.[3]

(3)    Each individual has certain and correct expectations. He knows that the rate of interest ($i$) will remain constant at its existing steady-state level, that he will have $e^{lH}$ children at the age $H$, that he will retire at the age $F$, that he will die at the age $G$, and that his wage-rate will rise at the rate $l'$. There is a perfect capital market on which he can lend his savings, or can borrow to finance his consumption, at the rate of interest, $i$. He can mortgage the future, but he cannot plan to leave an outstanding debt at his death. He may, however, plan to make a gift to his children; or his children may intend to make a gift to him, in which case he can foretell it exactly. Such transfers between generations are all made when the parent is aged $H$, i.e. children inherit at birth a gift from their parents or at birth children borrow and mortgage their own future earnings to help out their ageing parents. It is, in fact, quite immaterial at what stage any intergenerational transfer is made; this particular stage is assumed solely for convenience of exposition.

---

[3] It would, of course, be particularly easy to modify assumptions (iv) and (v) and to replace them with the assumptions that an equal number of boy and girl babies are born, that every man and woman marries a spouse of the same age as him- or herself, and that each set of parents have $2e^{lH}$ children when the parents are aged $H$ years. But it is so much simpler to speak of each parent having $e^{lH}$ children, of each child having one parent, and of each separate parent (or child) deciding whether he should support his children (or parent) that I have maintained the peculiar biological assumption (v).

(4)   With this background each citizen plans the pattern of his life's consumption. We shall assume that he always chooses to increase his consumption at a rate $\sigma i$, where $\sigma$ is a constant and $i$ is the rate of interest. His problem will always be to choose between (i) a high starting level of consumption which does not grow rapidly or (ii) a low starting level of consumption which grows rapidly over the years. If the rate of interest is high, he is more likely to choose (ii), since the higher the rate of interest the more future consumption he can gain at the expense of a unit of consumption today. We assume that he plans to raise his consumption at the steady rate $\sigma i$, i.e. at a constant multiple of the rate of interest.[4]

We now have three influences on a citizen's savings. (i) He may save to raise the rate at which his consumption rises over his life span. (ii) He may save in order to make a given time pattern of steadily rising consumption compatible with a time pattern of earned income which will rise with the wage-rate so long as he works but will fall to zero on his retirement. (iii) He may save to give property to his children.

## II   The Structure of the Model

Our first task will be to determine the total value of capital $(K)$ which will be owned by individual citizens at any one time, namely at $t = 0$. Consider first the amount of capital $(K_\theta)$ which is owned by any one individual born at $t = -\theta$ and therefore aged $\theta$ at $t = 0$. If he has planned his consumption correctly, the amount of his capital at any one time must be sufficient to finance the excess of his future consumption and of what he will hand over in the future to his children over his future earnings. Or, in other words, $K_\theta$ must be equal to the discounted value at time $t = 0$ of the future consumption plus the future bequests to his children minus the future earnings of a man aged $\theta$ at $t = 0$.

Let us start with the present value of the future bequests which he will make to his children. Let $I$ represent the amount of property which a citizen born at time $t = 0$ will receive at $t = 0$ from his parent.[5] In a state of steady growth the amount of property received by a citizen at his birth must grow (like the wage-rate, output per head, and similar *per caput* values) at the rate $l'$. The citizen aged $\theta$ at $t = 0$ will, therefore, have received $Ie^{-l'\theta}$ at his birth, and at $t = H - \theta$ will have to give to each of his children $Ie^{l'(H - \theta)}$. He will have $e^{lH}$ children at time $t = H - \theta$ and will, therefore, at that time have to give a total of $Ie^{lH + l'(H - \theta)}$. The present value at $t = 0$ of this sum at $t = H - \theta$, discounted at the steady-state rate of interest $i$, we can express by

$$I_\theta = Ie^{lH + (l' - i)(H - \theta)}. \tag{1}$$

---

[4] This is in fact equivalent to the assumption that he maximises his total utility over his life span in conditions in which the curve expressing the marginal utility of consumption as a function of the level of consumption has a constant elasticity with the (numerical) value of $1/\sigma$. For an alternative way of considering the meaning of the constant $\sigma$ see the Appendix to this paper [pp. 446–50].

[5] $I$ will have a negative value if it turns out that, instead of parents endowing their children, children help to support their parents.

This formula rules only for citizens who have not yet reached the age $H$; after that age they have no future bequests to make. Thus (1) is operative for $0 < \theta < H$; and the corresponding quantity is zero for $H < \theta < G$.

Next let us consider the value at time $t = 0$ of the future consumption of our citizen aged $\theta$ at time $t = 0$. Let $C$ represent the starting level of consumption of a citizen born and starting to consume at $t = 0$. This starting level of consumption must in a steady state, like all similar *per caput* terms, be rising at the rate $l'$. Thus our citizen born at $t = -\theta$ will have had a starting level of consumption equal to $Ce^{-l'\theta}$. This level he will have raised at the rate $\sigma i$ throughout his life and at time $T$ in the future, when he is aged $T + \theta$, his consumption level will be $Ce^{-l'\theta + \sigma i(T + \theta)}$. The present value at $t = 0$ of his consumption at $t = T$ is, therefore, $Ce^{(\sigma i - l')\theta + (\sigma - 1)iT}$, so that the value at $t = 0$ of all his coming consumption we can express

$$C_\theta = Ce^{(\sigma i - l')\theta} \int_0^{G - \theta} e^{(\sigma - 1)iT} dT. \qquad (2)$$

Finally let us consider the value at $t = 0$ of the future earnings of our citizen aged $\theta$. Let $W$ represent the wage-rate ruling at $t = 0$. The wage-rate at any future date $T$ will be $We^{l'T}$. The value at $t = 0$ of the wage to be earned at $t = T$ will, therefore, be $We^{(l' - i)T}$, so that the value to our citizen aged $\theta$ at $t = 0$ of all his earnings still to come will be

$$W_\theta = W \int_0^{F - \theta} e^{(l' - i)T} dT. \qquad (3)$$

There is a prospect of future earnings only for persons under the age of $F$ so that (3) is operative only for $0 < \theta < F$. For $F < \theta < G$ the corresponding figure becomes zero.

We have then

$$K_\theta = I_\theta + C_\theta - W_\theta,$$

where $I_\theta$, $C_\theta$, and $W_\theta$ have the values given in (1), (2), and (3).

Let $N$ be the number of births in the year $t = 0$. Then the number of births $\theta$ years before and so the number of persons aged $\theta$ at $t = 0$ will be $Ne^{-l\theta}$. The total property owned at $t = 0$ by all persons aged $\theta$ will be $Ne^{-l\theta}K_\theta$, so that the total property owned by persons of all ages at $t = 0$ will be

$$K = \int_0^H Ne^{-l\theta} I_\theta d\theta + \int_0^G Ne^{-l\theta} C_\theta d\theta - \int_0^F Ne^{-l\theta} W_\theta d\theta$$

$$= NIe^{(l + l' - i)H} \int_0^H e^{(i - l - l')\theta} d\theta$$

$$+ NC \int_0^G e^{(\sigma i - l - l')\theta} \int_0^{G-\theta} e^{(\sigma i - i)T} dT d\theta$$

$$- NW \int_0^F e^{-l\theta} \int_0^{F-\theta} e^{(l' - i)T} dT d\theta.$$

If one performs these integrations[6] and writes $\varphi_T(u)$ for $(e^{uT} - 1)/u$, then (a) when $i \neq l + l'$,

$$K = NI\varphi_H(l + l' - i)$$

$$+ \frac{NC}{i - l - l'} \left\{ \varphi_G(\sigma i - l - l') - \varphi_G(\sigma i - i) \right\}$$

$$+ \frac{NW}{i - l - l'} \left\{ \varphi_F(l' - i) - \varphi_F(-l) \right\} \tag{4a}$$

or (b) when $i = l + l'$,

$$K = NIH + \frac{NC}{\sigma i - i} \left\{ Ge^{(\sigma i - i)G} - \varphi_G(\sigma i - i) \right\}$$

$$+ \frac{NW}{l} \left\{ Fe^{-lF} - \varphi_F(-l) \right\}. \tag{4b}$$

$$\int_0^F e^{a\theta} \int_0^{F-\theta} e^{bT} dT d\theta$$

$$= \int_0^F e^{a\theta} \frac{e^{b(F-\theta)} - 1}{b} d\theta$$

$$= \frac{1}{b} \left\{ e^{bF} \frac{e^{(a-b)F} - 1}{a - b} - \frac{e^{aF} - 1}{a} \right\}$$

so that, if $a = b$, the above expression becomes

$$\frac{1}{b} \left\{ Fe^{bF} - \varphi_F(b) \right\}$$

but, if $a \neq b$, then the expression becomes

$$\frac{b(e^{aF} - 1) - a(e^{bF} - 1)}{ab(a - b)} = \frac{1}{a - b} \left\{ \varphi_F(a) - \varphi_F(b) \right\}.$$

We next proceed to determine the values of total wages, total profits, and total consumption at $t = 0$.

We have already seen that the number born at time $t = \theta$ and, therefore, aged $\theta$ years at time $t = 0$ is $Ne^{-l\theta}$. Therefore, the number of workers alive at time $t = 0$ is $\int_0^F Ne^{-l\theta}d\theta = N\varphi_F(-l)$. The total wage bill at time $t = 0$ is, therefore $WN\varphi_F(-l)$.

The total profits at $t = 0$ must equal $iK$. If we write $U$ for the proportion of the national income going to profits and, therefore, $1 - U$ for the proportion paid in wages, we have

$$\frac{iK}{WN\varphi_F(-l)} = \frac{U}{1 - U}. \tag{5}$$

We have also seen that the starting level at time $t = -\theta$ of consumption of a person born at time $t = -\theta$ (and therefore aged $\theta$ years at time $t = 0$) will have been $Ce^{-l'\theta}$. But such a citizen will have planned his consumption to rise at the rate $\sigma i$ so that the consumption level at time $t = 0$ of a citizen aged $\theta$ years at time $t = 0$ is $Ce^{(\sigma i - l')\theta}$. As we have just seen, there are at time $t = 0$ $Ne^{-l\theta}$ citizens born $\theta$ years ago. Therefore, the total consumption at time $t = 0$ of all citizens aged $\theta$ years at time $t = \sigma$ is $NCe^{(\sigma i - l - l')\theta}$. It follows that total consumption by all citizens at time $t = 0$ is $\int_0^G NCe^{(\sigma i - l - l')\theta}d\theta = NC\varphi_G(\sigma i - l - l')$.

Let $S$ be the proportion of total national income saved, so that $1 - S$ is the proportion of total national income spent on consumption. Then, since $1 - U$ is the proportion of the national income which goes to wages, $(1 - S)/(1 - U)$ is the ratio of consumption to wages, so that

$$\frac{C\varphi_G(\sigma i - l - l')}{W\varphi_F(-l)} = \frac{1 - S}{1 - U}. \tag{6}$$

With a constant-returns-to-scale production function with only two factors of production, labour and capital, the capital–labour ratio chosen for production at time $t = 0$ can be expressed as a function of the rate of interest. The higher the rate of interest, the more labour-intensive the technique of production. But the marginal product of labour and so the real wage-rate can be expressed at any one time as a function of the capital–labour ratio. Thus the wage-rate at time $t = 0$ can be expressed as a function of the rate of interest. Moreover, if to each level of the rate of interest at time $t = 0$ there corresponds a given ratio of capital to labour and a given wage-rate, then we can also express the ratio of profits (i.e. capital times the rate of interest) to wages as a function of the rate of interest. It follows that we can write

$$W = W(i) \tag{7}$$

and

$$U = U(i) \tag{8}$$

the nature of the functions $U(\ )$ and $W(\ )$ depending upon the nature of the production function.

If $Y$ is the total national income and $K$ the total national stock of capital, we can write $U = iK/Y$. Moreover we can write $SY/K$ for the proportional rate of growth of the capital stock; but in a state of steady growth the proportional rate of growth of the capital stock must equal the proportional rate of growth of total output, namely $l + l'$, so that $SY/K = l + l'$. It follows that in a state of steady growth

$$S = \frac{l + l'}{i} U .$$
(9)

We have now a system involving the determination of seven variables $(I, C, W, S, U, K, \text{and } i)$ in terms of seven parameters $(N, l, l', \sigma, F, G, \text{and } H)$ and of the form of the production function. We already have six independent equations between these variables, namely equations (4) to (9). A final equation can be devised to express how much property a parent will plan to accumulate to bequeath to his children (or alternatively how much a child will mortgage his future in order to make a gift to his parent). We will devote a separate section to this relationship, since it is the central purpose of this paper to build inheritance into the theory of personal savings.

## III   The Factors Determining Inheritance

The first possible assumption which can be made about inheritance is simply that of 'perfect selfishness', i.e. that a parent thinks only of himself and a child only of himself and there is no positive or negative inheritance, so that

$$I = 0.$$
(10)

Equations (4) to (10) will then determine the variables in our system, including the variable $i$.

Consider in these circumstances a citizen born at time $t = 0$, now aged $H$ years and producing $e^{lH}$ children at time $t = H$. This citizen's consumption will be $Ce^{\sigma iH}$, since he will have planned his initial consumption $C$ to rise at the rate $\sigma i$ over the first $H$ years of his life. But in a state of steady growth the initial starting level for consumption must rise at the rate $l'$, so that our citizen's children in the year $H$ will each of them start his consumption at a level equal to $Ce^{l'H}$. From then on the parent and each child will raise their consumption levels at the same rate $\sigma i$, so that from age $H$ to age $G$ (when he dies) the ratio of the son's to the parent's standard of living can be expressed by the equation

$$\beta = \frac{e^{l'H}}{e^{\sigma iH}} .$$
(11)

If $i$ as determined by equations (4) to (10) is $> l'/\sigma$, then $\beta < 1$ and the parent enjoys a higher standard than the son; and *vice versa*. The standard of living will progress in a zig-zag manner as depicted in Figure 1. The starting levels of consumption for each generation will lie on a curve (the broken line in Figure 1) which grows exponentially at the rate $l'$. But each individual's consumption through his life rises exponentially at the rate $\sigma i$, along lines such as $AB'$, $BC'$, $CD'$, $DE'$ if $i > l'/\sigma$ or lines such as $AB''$, $BC''$, $CD''$, $DE''$ if $i < l'/\sigma$. The ratio $\beta$ is shown by the ratio of the height of $B'$ (or $B''$) to the height of $B$ above the horizontal axis.

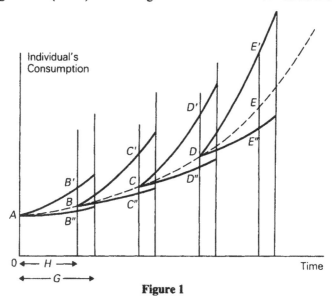

**Figure 1**

We are now in a position to introduce an alternative assumption about the factors influencing inheritance. Suppose that there is a given degree of altruism of parents towards their children and of children towards their parents. If a child's standard of living is at any given time much below the parent's, then the parent will aid the child by reducing his own consumption to provide for his child an inheritance sufficient to bring the child's standard up to what he regards as a tolerable fraction of his own. Let this fraction be $\beta'$. Then if $\beta$ as determined by equations (4) to (11) is $<\beta'$, the parent will give to his child a sufficient inheritance to make $\beta = \beta'$. Thus as far as the parent's plans are concerned we have the condition $\beta \geq \beta'$.

The parent will thus plan the starting level of his own consumption on the basis that he must transfer sufficient to each of his children to prevent the child's starting level of consumption falling below the fraction $\beta'$ of the parent's level of consumption at the time of the birth of his children. The parent has this degree of concern with his children's welfare, though he cares nothing for the welfare of his grandchildren. Nevertheless through his children's action the parent is indirectly affected by considerations for the welfare of the grandchildren. For the child will plan his own initial consumption level at a sufficiently low level to leave a suitable inheritance for the grandchildren. Thus when the parent passes to his child sufficient to raise that child's starting level to an adequate level, he is indirectly through the child helping to raise the standards of the grandchildren; and so on through the generations.

One can deal in an exactly similar manner with the case in which equations (4) to (11) would lead to a value of $\beta > 1$. Suppose that children are not prepared to see their own standard of living rise above $\beta''$ times that of their parents, where $\beta''$ is a parameter greater than unity. Then if $\beta$ as determined by equations (4) to (11) were $> \beta''$, children would cut down their consumption as a result of mortgaging their future to help their parents.

If parents are accumulating to bequeath property to their children, savings will be *pro tanto* increased, the capital–labour ratio in the state of steady growth will be higher, and the rate of interest will be lower. Thus $\beta$ as given in equation (11) will be higher. We will be in a steady state when inheritance ($I$) is positive and at such a level that the rate of interest has reached a level at which

$$\left.\begin{array}{l} \beta' = \dfrac{e^{l'H}}{e^{\sigma i H}} \\[3em] i = \dfrac{l'H + \log\left(\dfrac{1}{\beta'}\right)}{\sigma H} . \end{array}\right\} \qquad (12)$$

or

If children are mortgaging their future to finance the current consumption of the parents, national savings will be so much the lower, the capital–labour ratio will be lower, and the rate of interest higher. $\beta$ will be lower. We will be in a steady state with $I < 0$ and

$$\left.\begin{array}{l} \beta'' = \dfrac{e^{l'H}}{e^{\sigma i H}} \\[2.5em] i = \dfrac{l'H - \log \beta''}{\sigma H} . \end{array}\right\} \qquad (13)$$

or

With our assumption of partial altruism we reach the following conclusions. If equations (4) to (10) result in a value of $i$ such that $\beta' < e^{l'H}/e^{\sigma i H} < \beta''$, then there can be a steady state with no inheritance. 'Transport costs' between generations (as represented by the degrees of selfishness which still remain) are so great that no 'trade' (as represented by intergenerational transfers) takes place. But if the value of $i$ resulting from equations (4) to (10) causes $e^{l'H}/e^{\sigma i H}$ to be either $< \beta'$ or $> \beta''$, then we can have a steady state with *either*

$$I > 0 \text{ and } i = \frac{l'H + \log\left(\dfrac{1}{\beta'}\right)}{\sigma H}$$

*or*
$$I < 0 \text{ and } i = \frac{l'H - \log \beta''}{\sigma H}.$$

If we assume that there is perfect altruism then $\beta' = \beta'' = 1$ and from equations (12) or (13) we obtain

$$i = \frac{l'}{\sigma}. \tag{14}$$

Parents and children transfer property in the one direction or the other to the extent necessary to ensure that at any one time everyone enjoys the same standard of living. The value of $i$ obtained from (14) can then be used in equations (4) to (9) to determine $I, C, W, S, U$, and $K$. If as a result $I > 0$, then perfect altruism requires that parents help their children; and *vice versa*.

In this case of perfect altruism $i$ is determined solely by the two parameters $l'$ and $\sigma$. The values of the parameters $N, l, H, F$, and $G$ do not affect the value of $i$. Now given the value of $i$ and given the production function we will know the real wage-rate (equation 7) and the distribution of income between the factors (equation 8). If we also know the value of $l$, we shall know the proportion of total income saved (equation 9). Knowing the movements in the labour force, the rate of technical progress, the proportion of total national income saved, and the ratio of capital to labour $(K/N\varphi_p(-l)$ in equation 5), we shall then know all the macro-economic variables, and so the time paths in the state of steady growth of total capital, total income, total consumption, total investment, and the wage-rate. All this we know independently of the values of $H, F$, and $G$. The individual life-cycle problems do not affect the macro-economic outcome. They do of course affect the individual's life story – the starting level of consumption for each individual (equation 6) and the amount which each individual must leave to his children (or will receive from his children) (equation 4). If the parents refuse to die ($G$ is great) that will no doubt burden the population of working age, keep their consumption low, and make them support their parents (or receive less inheritance from them). But it will not affect the total level of consumption or the total stock of capital in the community at any one time.

Of special interest in the case of perfect altruism is the proportion of the national income which will be saved. From equations (9) and (14) this is seen to be

$$S = U\sigma\left(1 + \frac{l}{l'}\right). \tag{15}$$

Now the 'golden rule' tells us that the highest possible level of consumption at each point of time in a state of steady growth is obtained if $S = U$. If $S > U$, then total national consumption is held permanently below the level which it could at any one time have attained with a lower value of $S$. This will be so if $\sigma > l'/(l + l')$. Thus altruism by leading to parents saving to leave property to their children could possibly raise $S$ above the 'golden rule' level, $U$. If $S = U$, then from equation (9) we have

$$i = l + l'. \tag{16}$$

We will call the value of $i$ given in equation (16) the 'golden-rule' value of $i$; and we will call the value of $i$ given in equation (14) the 'perfect-altruism' value of $i$. This value of $i$ optimises the time path of each individual's consumption over his life-span and equalises the standards of living of all individuals at any one moment of time. But if $\sigma > l'/(l + l')$, this value of $i$ will not give an optimum solution; consumption will be kept permanently lower than it need be.[7] We shall call the 'perfect-altruism' value of $i$ the 'optimum' value of $i$, only if $\sigma \leq l'/(l + l')$.

## IV  The Solution of the System

We will now confine ourselves to the two extreme assumptions of perfect selfishness ($I = 0$) or perfect altruism ($i = l'/\sigma$). We are concerned then with a system expressed in equations (4) to (9) together with either equation (6) or equation (14). In particular we want to know in the case of perfect selfishness what will be the value of $i$ and in the case of perfect altruism what will be the value – or at least the sign – of $I$. From equations (4) to (9) we can obtain the following relationship between $I$ and $i$:—

(a)  When $i \neq l + l'$ we use equation (4a) with equations (5) to (9) and obtain

$$I = W(i)\varphi_F(-l)\frac{\varphi_G(\sigma i - i)}{\varphi_G(\sigma i - l - l')}\frac{a - b}{c} \tag{17a}$$

where

$$a = \frac{1 - \dfrac{l + l'}{i}U(i)}{1 - U(i)}$$

$$b = \frac{\varphi_F(l' - i)}{\varphi_F(-l)}\frac{\varphi_G(\sigma i - l - l')}{\varphi_G(\sigma i - i)}$$

and

$$c = 1 - e^{(l + l' - i)H}.$$

---

[7] J. A. Mirrlees in an unpublished paper has shown that savings according to a 'Ramsey' principle by immortal citizens in conditions otherwise similar to those assumed in this paper will always lead (whatever the starting point) to a state of steady growth in which $S$ has the value given in equation (15) above, provided that $\sigma \leq l'/(l + l')$. If this condition is not fulfilled, no 'Ramsey' optimum path exists.

(b) When $i = l + l'$ and, therefore, $S = U$, we use equation (4b) with equations (5) to (9) and obtain:—

$$I = \frac{W(i)\varphi_F(-l)}{H}\left\{\frac{1}{i}\frac{U}{1-U} + \frac{1}{l} - \frac{F}{e^{lF}-1} - \frac{1}{(1-\sigma)i} + \frac{G}{e^{(1-\sigma)iG}-1}\right\}.$$

But by differentiation of $a$ and $b$ in equation (17a) we have, when $i = l + l'$,

$$\frac{da}{di} = \frac{1}{i}\frac{U}{1-U}$$

and

$$\frac{db}{di} = -\frac{1}{l} + \frac{F}{e^{lF}-1} + \frac{1}{(1-\sigma)i} - \frac{G}{e^{(1-\sigma)iG}-1}$$

so that in this case

$$I = \frac{W(i)\varphi_F(-l)}{H}\left\{\frac{da}{di} - \frac{db}{di}\right\}. \qquad \text{17(b)}$$

We can observe the following characteristics of the expression for $I$ in (17a) and (17b):—

(1) Since $W(i)$, $\varphi_F(-l)$, $\varphi_G(\sigma i - i)$, $\varphi_G(\sigma i - l - l')$, and $H$ are all $> 0$, the sign of $I$ will be the same as the sign of $(a - b)/c$ if $i \neq l + l'$ or the same as the sign of $d(a - b)/di$ if $i = l + l'$.

(2) The term $c$ in (17a) is $\gtrless 0$ as $i \gtrless l + l'$. It follows that if $i > l + l'$, then $I \gtrless 0$ as $a \gtrless b$. But if $i < l + l'$, then $I \gtrless 0$ as $a \lessgtr b$.

(3) If, however, $i = l + l'$, then $I \gtrless 0$ as $d(a - b)/di \gtrless 0$.

(4) If we have perfect selfishness and $I = 0$, then we can have steady states either with $(a - b)/c = 0$ and $i \neq l + l'$ or with $da/di - db/di = 0$ and $i = l + l'$.

(5) Suppose that we have perfect altruism so that in the steady state $i = l'/\sigma$. Then if $F = G$ so that there is no period of retirement in old age, we have from (17a)

$$I = W\varphi_F\left(l' - \frac{l'}{\sigma}\right)\frac{U}{1-U}\frac{1 - \sigma\dfrac{l+l'}{l'}}{1 - e^{\left(l + l' - \frac{l'}{\sigma}\right)H}}.$$

From this it can be seen that if $l + l' \neq i = l'/\sigma$, $I$ must be $> 0$, whether $l'/\sigma$ is $\gtrless l + l'$, i.e. whether (see p. 439 above) the perfect-altruism value of $i$ is or is not also the 'optimum' value. Moreover, if $l'/\sigma = l + l' = i$ and $F = G$, then from (17b) we see that

$$I = \frac{W\varphi_F(-l)}{H}\frac{l}{l+l'}\frac{U}{1-U}$$

so that $I$ is also $> 0$ in this case. In other words, if parents have no period of retirement during which they need to live on their capital, perfect unselfishness implies that they will always accumulate something to bequeath to their children.

Let us next consider the form which $a$ and $b$ in equations (17) may take as functions of $i$.

One can say of $b$, (i) that $b$ is always $> 0$ whatever the value of $i$, (ii) that for each value of $i$ there is only one value of $b$, (iii) that when $i = 0$, $b$ has a finite positive value, (iv) that when $i = l + l'$, $b = 1$, and (v) that as $i \to \infty$ so $b$ also $\to \infty$. This does not, however, imply that $b$ rises monotonically, as $i$ increases. From the expression for $db/di$ when $i = l + l'$, given in equation (17b), one can see that it may be $>$ or $< 0$. For example with $F = 40$, $G = 50$, $l = .01$ and $l' = .04$, $db/di = +4.4$ if $\sigma = 0.8$ and $db/di = -2.24$ if $\sigma = 0.1$.[8] Thus the function $b$ has the general shape shown in Figure 2. At the point $i = l + l'$, $b = 1$, but at this point $db/di$ may be $< 0$ as in the case of the continuous line in Figure 2; or we may have $db/di > 0$ as in the case of the broken line in the figure.

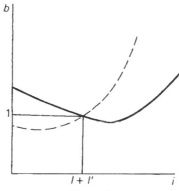

**Figure 2**

Two general statements can be made about the expression $a = (1 - S)/(1 - U) = (1 - [(l + l')/i]U)/(1 - U)$ in equation (17a). First, $a = 1$ when $i = l + l'$. Second, as long as we confine our attention to those cases (which are the only ones in which a steady-state equilibrium is economically possible) in which $1 > U > 0$ and $1 > S > 0$, then $a < 1$ when $i < l + l'$ and $a > 1$ when $i > l + l'$. This implies that in these cases (as can be verified from the expression for $da/di$ in equation (17b)), $da/di > 0$ at $i = l + l'$.

For the rest we will confine our attention to the particular case of a production function with a constant elasticity of substitution between the two factors, labour and capital. Such a function is given by $Y = R\{\bar{U}K^{(\mu-1)/\mu} + (1 - \bar{U})L^{(\mu-1)/\mu}\}^{\mu/(\mu-1)}$ where $Y$ is total output, $K$ capital, $L$ labour (in efficiency units which may be increased either by population growth or by Harrod-neutral labour-expanding technical

---

[8] As an interesting limiting case, if $F = G$ (i.e. there were no period of retirement) and if $i = l + l' = l'/\sigma$ (i.e. the 'golden-rule' level happened to coincide with the 'perfect-altruism' level of $i$), then $db/di = 0$.

progress), $\mu$ is the numerical value of the constant elasticity of substitution between $K$ and $L$, and $R$ and $\bar{U}$ are constants.[9] By differentiation of this function we obtain

$$U = \frac{K}{Y}\frac{\partial Y}{\partial K} = Bi^{1-\mu}$$

where $B$ is a constant with the value $\bar{U}^{\mu}R^{\mu-1}$. In this case the value of $a$ in equation (17a) can be expressed as

$$a = \frac{1-S}{1-U} = \frac{1 - \frac{l+l'}{i}U}{1-U} = \frac{1 - (l+l')Bi^{-\mu}}{1 - Bi^{1-\mu}}.$$

Differentiation of this expression gives

$$\frac{da}{di} = \frac{Bi^{-\mu}}{(1-U)^2}\left\{ (1-S)(1-\mu) + \frac{l+l'}{i}\mu(1-U) \right\}$$

$$= \frac{Bi^{-\mu}}{(1-U)^2}\left\{ 1 - S + \mu\frac{l+l'-i}{i} \right\}$$

from which it can be seen that $da/di$ is $> 0$ if either $\mu < 1$ or $i < l + l'$.

We must now distinguish two cases: (i) where $\mu < 1$ and (ii) where $\mu > 1$.

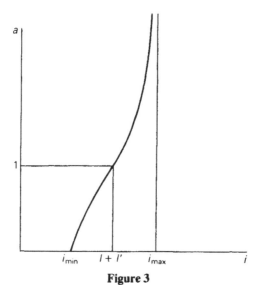

**Figure 3**

[9] Mr D. G. Champernowne devised this production function in a comment which he wrote on an unpublished paper of mine in 1944; but his note remained unpublished.

(i)   With $\mu < 1$, the steady-state equilibrium value of $S = (l + l')Bi^{-\mu}$ increases as $i$ decreases. In order that the steady-state value of $S$ should not exceed unity, $i$ has a minimum value of $\{(l + l')B\}^{1/\mu}$. But the value of $U = Bi^{1-\mu}$ increases as $i$ increases and in order that $U$ should not exceed unity we have a maximum value of $i$ of $B^{-1/(1-\mu)}$. A steady state is, therefore, possible only if this $i_{max}$ is greater than this $i_{min}$, i.e. if $l + l' < B^{-1/(1-\mu)}$, i.e. if $l + l'$ is less than the $i_{max}$. In this case we have a curve of the kind shown in Figure 3. When $i = i_{min}$, $S = 1$ and $a = 0$. Since $\mu < 1$, $da/di$ is throughout $> 0$. At $i = l + l'$, $a = 1$; and as $i \rightarrow i_{max}$, $U \rightarrow 1$, and $a \rightarrow \infty$.

(ii)   With $\mu > 1$, both the steady-state value of $S$ and the value of $U$ decrease and tend towards zero as $i \rightarrow \infty$. It follows that $a \rightarrow 1$ as $i \rightarrow \infty$. Moreover both $S$ and $U$ rise without limit as $i \rightarrow 0$. From this we have two minimum values of $i$, one set by the requirement that $S = [(l + l')/i] U < 1$ and one by the requirement that $U < 1$. We must now subdivide into two sub-cases: (iia) where $i_{min}$ is set by the requirement $S < 1$ and (iib) where $i_{min}$ is set by the requirement $U < 1$.

(iia)   In this case as $i$ decreases we reach $S = [(l + l')/i] U = 1$ with $U < 1$. Therefore, $i_{min} < l + l'$. At $i_{min}$ $a = 0$. $da/di > 0$ so long as $i < l + l'$. At $i = l + l'$, $a = 1$. With $i > l + l'$, $a > 1$. But as $i \rightarrow \infty$ $a \rightarrow 1$. The curve is of the kind shown in Figure 4.

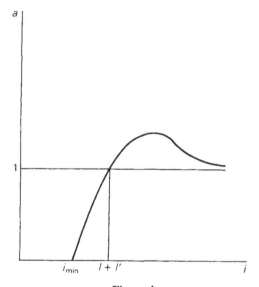

**Figure 4**

(iib)   In this case as $i$ decreases we reach $U = 1$ with $S = [(l + l')/i] U < 1$. Therefore $i_{min} > l + l'$. As $i$ falls towards $i_{min}$, $U \rightarrow 1$ so that $a \rightarrow \infty$. With $i > l + l'$, $a > 0$. But as $i \rightarrow \infty$, $a \rightarrow 1$, so that we have a curve of the kind shown in Figure 5.

If we put the curves $a$ and $b$ together, it is clear that the four types of case shown as Cases I, II, III, and IV on Figure 6 are all possible, though it

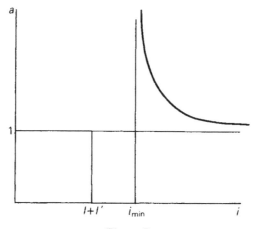

**Figure 5**

is not claimed that these are the only possible cases. In each case we have used propositions (2) and (3) on page 440 above to indicate the sign of $I$ for the different ranges of possible values of $i$.

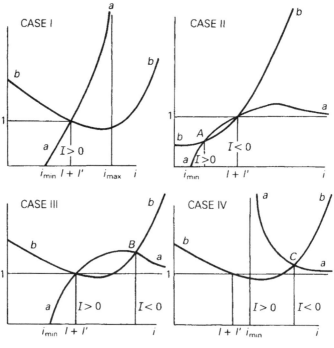

**Figure 6**

In Case I with perfect selfishness and $I = 0$, no steady-state position is possible. We could, however, have a steady-state position with perfect altruism and $i = l'/\sigma$, provided that $i_{min} < l'/\sigma < i_{max}$. But in this case we must have $I > 0$, so that in these conditions with perfect altruism parents would necessarily be accumulating to endow their children, whether $l'/\sigma$ were greater or less than $l + l'$.[10]

In Case II there is a perfect-selfishness steady-state position at the intersection $A$. This is at a value of $i < l + l'$ so that $S > U$ and perfect selfishness leads to more than golden-rule savings. Case III is similar to Case II except that the perfect-selfishness steady-state position at the intersection $B$ is at a value of $i > l + l'$, so that the level of perfect selfishness savings is now less than the golden-rule level. Inspection of Cases II and III shows that there could be an intermediate case at which the curves $a$ and $b$ happened to be tangential at the point $i = l + l'$ and $a = b = 1$. This is the fluke case where golden-rule savings and perfect-selfishness savings happen to coincide.

In Cases II and III and in this intermediate fluke case, a perfect-altruism steady-state is possible provided that $i_{min} < l'/\sigma$. According as $l'/\sigma$ corresponded to a value of $i$ above (or below) the perfect-selfishness value of $i$ (at the intersection $A$ or $B$), so perfect altruism would involve $I < 0$ and children helping their parents (or $I > 0$ and parents helping their children).

Case IV illustrates the possibility that no golden-rule steady state is possible since $i_{min} > l + l'$. In this case there is a possible perfect-selfishness steady state at the intersection $C$. Moreover, a perfect-altruism steady state with $i = l'/\sigma$ is also possible, provided that $l'/\sigma > i_{min}$. In this case parents will help their children if $i = l'/\sigma$ lies to the left of $C$ and children will help their parents if $i = l'/\sigma$ lies to the right of $C$.

The above perfect-selfishness steady-state points at the intersections $A$, $B$, and $C$ conform with common sense. Suppose that one starts in a perfect-selfishness steady state at one of the points, and that mankind is then converted to perfect altruism. Then on the lines of the argument in section III above, according as $l'/\sigma$ is greater (or less) than the initial perfect-selfishness value of $i$, this conversion will make children wish to help their parents (or parents wish to help their children). In the former case there is less net saving as children mortgage their future to help their parents; but in the latter there will be more saving as parents accumulate to bequeath to their children. In the former case $i$ rises towards $l'/\sigma$ and in the latter it falls towards $l'/\sigma$. Thus the movement is in the correct direction to attain the new perfect-altruism steady-state position. But this actual process of adjustment calls for more precise analysis.

---

[10] In all four cases I to IV it should be borne in mind that the perfect-altruism value of $i$ (namely, $l'/\sigma$) is the optimum value only if it is not less than the golden-rule value of $i$ (namely, $l + l'$). If $l'/\sigma < l + l'$, then $S > U$ and too much is saved. Also as noted in proposition (5) on page 440 above, if $F = G$ then the value $i = l'/\sigma$ can occur only within ranges with $I > 0$. The reader is left to apply these points himself to the discussion of Cases I to IV.

## Appendix on the Time Pattern of the Individual's Consumption

We assume that each individual citizen has a consistent set of preferences between various combinations of consumption levels at various points of time. Thus he knows whether or not he prefers the combination (a) of 100 units this year, 90 units next year, 110 units the year after and so on or the combination (b) of 98 units this year, 90 units next year, 113 units the year after, and so on. His preferences are consistent in the sense that if he prefers combination (a) to combination (b) and combination (b) to combination (c), then he also prefers (a) to (c). But we make two further special assumptions about his preferences. (i) We assume that he has no pure time preference. It makes no difference to him whether he has 100 this year and 105 next year or 105 this year and 100 next year. (ii) We also assume that his preferences between consumption in any one year and any other year are independent of the level of his consumption in other years. For example, if he prefers 100 this year plus 105 next year to 101 this year plus 102 next year, he will do so whatever has been the pattern of his consumption before this year and whatever may be the expected pattern of his consumption after next year.

These assumptions have the following implications. The citizen's total welfare over time will depend upon the levels of his standard of living in various years: one year at 100, one year at 105, two years at 106, one year at 110, and so on. But the order will make no difference: 100, 105, 106, 106, 110 is neither better nor worse than 105, 106, 100, 110, 106. But, of course, 50 followed by 150 is not the same as 100 followed by 100, although both combinations give a total of 200 for the two years. To fall from 100 to 50 this year may mean cutting into the most indispensable necessities, while rising from 100 to 150 next year may mean enjoying only a few unnecessary additional luxuries. 100 followed by 100 will probably be preferred to 50 followed by 150. But we assume that 50 followed by 150 has the same value as 150 followed by 50. The citizen does not mind in which year the stringency and in which year the surfeit comes.

Let us start by considering a citizen's preference between consumption in any one year and in any other year – for example between consumption this year (year one) and consumption next year (year two). This preference map is shown in Figure 7. We measure along the vertical axis the amount consumed by an individual in the year one ($\bar{C}_1$) and along the horizontal axis the amount consumed in year two ($\bar{C}_2$). Any point in Figure 7 represents a combination of consumption in year one and consumption in year two; for example, at $R$ our citizen is depicted as consuming $SR$ in year one and $0S$ in year two. Through $R$ we can draw our citizen's indifference curve $II'$ which shows the locus of all the points which describe combinations of $\bar{C}_1$ and $\bar{C}_2$ which have the same value to our citizen as the combination at the point $R$. Any combination of $\bar{C}_1$ and $\bar{C}_2$ to the North East of $II'$ would make our citizen better off than at $R$; any combination to the South West of $II'$ would make him worse off.

We draw $II'$ as having all the usual characteristics of a consumer's indifference curve. In particular we assume that $II'$ slopes downwards

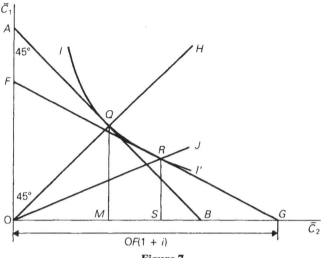

**Figure 7**

from left to right, since to be equally well off our citizen must have more next year if he has less this year. We also assume that the slope of *II'* becomes gentler and gentler as we move down from left to right. This means that for one reason or another our citizen prefers stability to variability in his level of consumption. The more we move South East from $Q$ (where $\tilde{C}_1 = \tilde{C}_2$) in the direction of $I'$, the greater is $\tilde{C}_2$ and the less is $\tilde{C}_1$; the greater, therefore, is the variability from year to year in consumption. Our citizen may simply just prefer sameness to variation. But there is perhaps another and more basic factor at work. The less our citizen has this year and the more he has next year, the less willing he is to give up still more of this year's consumption (which will now mean cutting into basic necessities) in order to raise next year's consumption (which will now mean adding only a few frivolous luxuries to his standard of living).

But in addition to these general characteristics the indifference map in Figure 7 has some special features due to two special assumptions which we have stated above. We are assuming that the map of preferences between $\tilde{C}_1$ and $\tilde{C}_2$ is independent of what is consumed in other years. In other words we can draw the indifference curve *II'* and it will remain unchanged whatever may have been the level of consumption in the years before year one and whatever may be expected to be the levels of consumption after year two. Moreover we are assuming that there is no time preference which implies that our citizen would be equally well off with 90 for $\tilde{C}_1$ and 110 for $\tilde{C}_2$ or with 110 for $\tilde{C}_1$ and 90 for $\tilde{C}_2$.

Geometrically this second assumption means that the curve *II'* would remain unchanged if we drew $\tilde{C}_1$ instead of $\tilde{C}_2$ along the horizontal axis and $\tilde{C}_2$ instead of $\tilde{C}_1$ up the vertical axis. If we draw the line $0H$ at 45° through the origin 0, cutting *II'* at $Q$, then the curve $QI'$ is a mirror image of the curve $QI$; that is to say, if we folded the page along the line $0H$, $QI$

would coincide with $QI'$. It follows from this that at the point $Q$ the curve $II'$ cuts the line $0H$ at right angles; [11] that is to say, the tangent $AB$ to the curve $II'$ at $Q$ itself makes angles of 45° with the vertical and the horizontal axes. The common sense of this is easily understood. At the point $Q$ our citizen will consume next year the same amount as this year; and at this point he will, therefore, place the same value on an additional unit of next year's consumption as he does on an additional unit of this year's consumption. The marginal rate of substitution between $\tilde{C}_1$ and $\tilde{C}_2$ is unity. In contrast to this at $R$ he would be expecting a higher level of consumption next year than he is enjoying this year, and he would therefore value an additional unit of consumption this year more highly than an additional unit of consumption next year; the tangent $FG$ at $R$ has a gentler slope than the tangent $AB$ at $Q$.

We can next introduce the idea of the elasticity of substitution between $\tilde{C}_1$ and $\tilde{C}_2$. How quickly does the marginal value of an addition to next year's consumption relatively to the marginal value of an addition to this year's consumption fall off as next year's consumption grows relatively to this year's consumption? This elasticity of substitution can be measured in the usual way. The slope of the lines such as $AB$ and $FG$ can be taken to represent the price of $\tilde{C}_2$ in terms of $\tilde{C}_1$. Thus the slope of $AB$ means to our citizen that he can obtain $0B$ more units of consumption next year for every $0A$ of consumption given up this year. In this case $0B/0A = 1$, which must mean that the rate of interest is zero; if he saves $100 this year he can as a result consume only $100 more next year. The slope of $FG$ is, however, less than this. This must mean that the rate of interest ($i$) is positive; for every $0F$ given up this year, he obtains $0G$ next year; and $0G/0F$ is greater than unity. For example, if he saves $100 this year, he can as a result consume $105 more next year without altering his consumption in any other year, if the rate of interest is 5 per cent annum. $0G/0F$ thus equals $1 + i$ or in our numerical example 105 per cent.

Now the numerical value of the elasticity of substitution between $\tilde{C}_2$ and $\tilde{C}_1$ is the proportional increase in the ratio of $\tilde{C}_2$ to $\tilde{C}_1$ divided by the proportional decrease in the price of $\tilde{C}_2$ in terms of $\tilde{C}_1$. Between the points $Q$ and $R$ the price of $\tilde{C}_2$ in terms of $\tilde{C}_1$ has fallen by a proportion equal to the rate of interest. [12] Between the points $Q$ and $R$ the ratio of $\tilde{C}_2$ to $\tilde{C}_1$ has changed from $0M/QM$ to $0S/RS$, so that the proportional change in this ratio is

$$\frac{\dfrac{0S}{RS} - \dfrac{0M}{QM}}{\dfrac{0M}{QM}}.$$

[11] If $II'$ cut $0H$ at any other angle, then in folding the page along the line $0H$ $QI$ would clearly not coincide with $QI'$.

[12] At $Q$ one can get one unit of $\tilde{C}_2$ for the price of one unit of $\tilde{C}_1$. At $R$ one can get $1 + i$ units of $\tilde{C}_2$ for the price of one unit of $\tilde{C}_1$; for example, with a rate of interest equal to 5 per cent per annum, one can get 1.05 units of $\tilde{C}_2$ for the price of 1 unit of $\tilde{C}_1$, and the price of $\tilde{C}_2$ relatively to the price of $\tilde{C}_1$ has fallen by 5 per cent.

But $0M/QM = 1$, so that the above expression becomes

$$\frac{0S - RS}{RS}.$$

But $0S - RS$ is the consumption between year one and year two and $RS$ is the consumption of year one. Thus the above expression is equal to the proportional rate of increase in consumption between year one and year two which will take place at the rate of interest $i$. Let us call this rate of growth of consumption $\tilde{c}$.

Let us use the symbol $\sigma$ for the (numerical) value of the elasticity of substitution between $\tilde{C}_2$ and $\tilde{C}_1$. This symbol $\sigma$ is simply defined as meaning the proportional increase in the ratio of $\tilde{C}_2$ to $\tilde{C}_1$ divided by the proportional decrease in the ratio of the price of $\tilde{C}_2$ relatively to the price of $\tilde{C}_1$. But between the points $Q$ and $R$ the proportional increase in the ratio of $\tilde{C}_2$ to $\tilde{C}_1$ is, as we have seen, simply the proportional rate of growth of consumption, namely $\tilde{c}$, while the proportional fall in the price of $\tilde{C}_2$ relatively to the price of $\tilde{C}_1$ is simply the rate of interest $i$. Thus we have

$$\sigma = \frac{\tilde{c}}{i} \text{ or } \tilde{c} = \sigma i$$

which is the formula used in the body of this paper.

What in the name of common sense does this mean? The problem with which our citizen is trying to cope is to plan the pattern of his consumption over the years. Shall he save little or much for the purpose of raising his future consumption little or much relatively to his present consumption? The rate of interest ($i$) tells him how much more he can consume if he consumes next year rather than this. The elasticity of substitution ($\sigma$) is numerically large (or small) according as the marginal value of next year's consumption falls off slowly (or rapidly) relatively to the marginal value of this year's consumption as he raises next year's consumption relatively to this year's consumption. There are thus two factors which should make him plan to raise his consumption rapidly from one year to the next: (1) a high rate of interest which will enable him to get much more consumption next year for a given sacrifice of consumption this year and (2) a high (numerical) value of the elasticity of substitution, which means that as he raises next year's consumption relatively to this year's consumption the valuation of yet more consumption next year does not fall much relatively to the valuation of a given further sacrifice of consumption this year. The formula $\tilde{c} = \sigma i$ tells us that the optimum rate of growth of his consumption at any point of time should be equal to $i$ multiplied by $\sigma$. If at any given point of time $i$ is 5 per cent per annum and $\sigma$ is ½, then he should plan his consumption pattern so that his consumption is at that point of time rising at a rate of 2½ per cent per annum.

In the main text of this article we assume that $\sigma$ is constant and does not depend upon the absolute level or rate of growth of the citizen's consumption. This is the final basic simplifying assumption required for the use made of the formula $\bar{c} = \sigma i$ in the main text.

# 26

# Population Explosion, the Standard of Living and Social Conflict

*Meade's Presidential address to the Royal Economic Society on 30 June 1966, published in* The Economic Journal, *vol. 77 (June 1967), pp. 233–255*

This year, 1966, is the two hundredth anniversary of the birth of Malthus; and possibly the most important political–social–economic development in the world today is the quite unprecedented explosion of population, particularly in many of the poor underdeveloped countries. It is, perhaps, therefore fitting that something should be said on population on this occasion. To set the general background the graph on p. 452 displays the total population of the world from 5500 BC to AD 2000. In 1963 we were at the point marked $D$ on the graph. In the year 2000, on the assumption that mortality continues to decline at rates which we now regard as normal, we should be at the point $A$ if fertility rates remained at their present high levels, at the point $B$ if fertility rates in the areas of high fertility started to decline after 1975 at rates previously experienced in the areas of low fertility, and at the point $C$ if such declines in fertility had started in 1950 and had continued without break until AD 2000. Even on this last most optimistic hypothesis, which events since the making of these projections have already proved to be false, the world's population would have doubled between 1950 and 2000. On the first and least optimistic hypothesis, which so far seems to be proving to be the most realistic the world's population would be almost three times as great in the year 2000 as it was in 1950.

Rates of growth of population of these orders of magnitude cannot, of course, in fact continue very much longer in terms of human generations. It was to me a rather surprising fact to learn that the 3,000,000,000 $(3 \times 10^9)$ of the world's present population could all find standing room – but admittedly not sitting or lying room – on the 147 square miles of the Isle of Wight, though they would – if my calculations are to be trusted – be uncomfortably packed, each person having only a territory of 14 inches by 14 inches on which to live and have his being. At the present rate of increase of the world's population of 1.7 per cent per annum, in 850 years the whole 196,836,000 square miles of the world's land surface would be needed to provide standing room on this same somewhat cramped scale for the then population of the world of about 4,000,000,000,000,000 $(4 \times 10^{15})$.

However much the skyscraper building and the synthetic production of foodstuffs and raw materials may be developed, we may safely conclude that long before any such degree of confinement were reached Malthus's preventive or positive checks, whether of vice or of misery, would have limited fertility or have raised mortality. I do not want to dwell on the fearsome possibilities of pestilence, famine and war, which one must hope will be avoided by the modern equivalent of Malthus's moral restraint – namely the widespread use of modern contraceptive methods. But contraceptive restraint cannot come quickly enough to prevent a very great increase in population densities in many parts of the world above their present levels; and in some parts of the world already these densities are such as to cause serious economic problems. I want today to talk about some of these more immediate problems – some of the economic and social problems involved in the movement from point $D$ to point $A$, $B$ or $C$ on the graph.

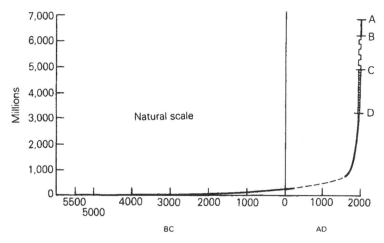

BC 5500–AD 400: Sir Julian Huxley, 'Sind zuviel Menschen auf der Welt?', *Der Monat*, 1950 [vol. 27, pp. 245–53, and vol. 28, pp. 386–93].

1650–1900: Sir Alexander Carr-Saunders, *World Population* [Oxford: Clarendon Press, 1936].

1900–2000: United Nations.

I shall do this by cataloguing briefly in very general terms the main economic problems which such a demographic situation may raise and then illustrating these problems by the particular example of the island of Mauritius.

What, then, in fact are the disadvantages of an excessively large population in an economy?

The first, simple and familiar – but not the less important – answer is the reduction in output per head, and so in the standard of living, due to the law of diminishing returns as more and more labour is applied to a given amount of natural resources. There are, of course, some important ways in which this tendency to lower output per head may be offset.

A first offset is the phenomenon of increasing returns to scale. Because of indivisibilities in human beings and, above all, in instruments of production a large absolute scale of production is often necessary in order to achieve a high output per head. I have no intention on this occasion of discussing in detail how large an economy must be in order to achieve the full advantages of large-scale production. The excellent report of the International Economic Association under the editorship of our Secretary, Professor E. A. G. Robinson, on *The Economic Consequences of the Size of Nations* [London: Macmillan, 1960] shows how difficult it is to reach a precise conclusion on this problem; but it leaves me with the following impressions, which I will state bluntly without argument.

In the first place, the extent to which it is desirable that the absolute size of any one national economy should be raised in order to enjoy the economies of scale depends upon the opportunities for international trade. Switzerland is a small country, but enjoys fully the economies of scale in a watch industry that supplies markets all round the world. It seems very improbable that if we allow for reasonable freedom of international trade, there is any serious argument for a growth in population in order to reduce costs by extending the market except in the case of those particular territories in which at present population is very sparse relatively to land area and natural resources. In those cases the large-scale economies of certain lines of production of goods and services which cannot readily be transported and traded – in particular, of many public services such as roads, railways, electricity – may still be so important that a higher density of population might in itself help to raise income per head.

But in this connection we should be careful not to forget one simple fact. It is not sufficient merely that there should still be scope for increasing returns to scale for a rise in the population in itself to lead to a rise in output per head. There are increasing returns to scale if a 1 per cent increase in every factor input – in land and natural resources and in capital equipment as well as in labour – would cause more than a 1 per cent increase in total output; but this does not ensure that a 1 per cent increase in labour alone will cause a more than 1 per cent increase in total output; the scope for increasing returns to scale will have to be very marked for this to be so. Accordingly I shall proceed on the assumption that the economies-of-scale argument is an argument for freer trade rather than an argument for a larger population, except in the case of territories in which there is a really sparse population covering an area of good inhabitable land.

Two other sets of forces which may prevent the pressure of a larger population on a given limited amount of natural resources from causing a fall in output per head are technical progress and capital accumulation. Scientific discovery and its technical application to industry and management; improved measures of business organisation, management and incentive; greater supplies of man-made capital resources for the equipment of workers; larger investment in the education and training of workers; all these will tend to raise output per head and to offset a fall due to increased pressure of numbers on land and other natural resources. Indeed, at present these ameliorative forces do seem to have the upper hand. In nearly all countries some net improvements in output and consumption per head are taking place. It would be rash to assume that these ameliorative forces will continue to prevail. But whether they do or not, the immediately alarming feature is that as a general rule the poorest countries now have the worst population explosion and – as I shall argue later – largely as a result of this have the slowest improvement in real income per head, with the result that the gap in standards of living between rich and and poor countries is not only enormously wide but is becoming wider rather than narrower not only in absolute but also in relative terms.

I have spoken so far as if the ultimate criterion were output per head of the population. But it is not in fact at all self-evident that the most desirable or optimum size for population is that which maximises output per head or consumption per head regardless of the absolute number of heads to enjoy that standard of living. Would the Council of the Royal Economic Society or the United Nations or God or whoever is to be the ultimate judge in these matters prefer a small population with a high standard per head or a larger population with a lower standard of living? And if the latter, how much increase in population compensates for how much fall in the standard of living? Are we selfish to take measures to avoid a fall in our own standard of living by preventing the birth of a human being who would prefer that lower standard of living to no living at all? Let us look these awkward questions squarely in the face and pass rapidly on, as Dennis Robertson used to say. I believe that in many parts of the world pressure of population on resources is already so great or threatens to become so great that, however we might define an optimum population, there would be a general consensus that the optimum was exceeded.

In such countries heavy population pressure is already an important cause of a low standard of living. This is the basic economic evil. But in many of these countries heavy population pressure leads to one or other or both of two further evils – to heavy unemployment and/or to great inequalities in the distribution of income. When land and real capital equipment are scarce but labour is very plentiful competition is likely to raise rents per acre and the return on capital and to lower the wage-rate. Producers will pay much to get hold of the scarce resources of land and capital equipment and will offer very little for the abundant supplies of workers seeking work. If it is left to a purely competitive labour market the wage-rate will fall sufficiently to cause labour costs to be low, even though in such economies labour productivity is low.

The resultant low wage-cost will help to expand employment and output. It will make attractive lines of production and methods of production which require relatively little land and capital equipment for their production, as witness the growth of labour-intensive textile industries in many underdeveloped countries with cheap and abundant labour supplies. Low wage costs and high profitability will attract the investment of capital into the country by capitalists from other countries where the pressure of population on resources is less and where, for that reason, labour costs are high and the profits on capital lower. High profits and low wages are likely to encourage savings and so to increase supplies of capital within the country itself, since a larger proportion of the profits of wealthy property-owners than of the wages of poor workers is likely to be saved and devoted to capital accumulation. Moreover, cheap labour and expensive capital and land will encourage technicians to find new methods of production which use labour and save other resources.

But these incentives to expand the demand for labour depend upon wages being low while rents, interest and profit are high; and this may involve a very unequal distribution of income between property-owners and wage-earners. If, however, the wage-rate is maintained at a high level in order to maintain a decent income for the wage-earner these incentives to expand employment and output will not operate. Thus *either* there is unemployment or underemployment of labour, since there is not enough land and capital to equip all available workers in current lines of production, *or else* the wage-rate must fall very low indeed to encourage the introduction of new lines of production, which employ much labour with little equipment of capital or land and which become profitable only when labour is very cheap relatively to capital and land. Such new lines of production are, of course, economically efficient in the sense that it will pay to introduce them only if a greater output can be produced by employing more labour with the given amount of other resources; but as a result of the lower wage-rate there is a very unequal distribution of income as rents and profits of property-owners rise and the wages of workers fall.

In a community in which there was an equal distribution of the ownership of property these concomitant evils of overpopulation – namely, unemployment or unequal distribution of income – might not be serious. A real wage-rate low enough to induce the necessary high ratio of labour to other resources in productive operations would as before lead to a low ratio of total wages to total property incomes, but if each citizen were a representative property-owner as well as a representative worker, what he lost in wages he would gain in property incomes. A community of peasant proprietors will be of this kind. A high density of peasant families on the land might reduce output per head to a low level; but the peasant family which was owner of the land as well as supplier of the working force would not be deterred from applying the maximum amount of effort to the land. The marginal product of labour might be low; but the peasant being worker and property-owner would be interested in the average and not the marginal product of labour.

These evils might also be avoided – at the cost perhaps of introducing some others – in a community in which all property was socially owned. The managers of the socialised concerns could be instructed to conduct their operations so as to maximise profit on the basis of a very low accounting or 'shadow' wage-cost for the abundant labour and a very high accounting or 'shadow' rent and interest cost for the scarce resources of land and capital. On the basis of these costs the socialised concerns would pay out little in wages and make high profits; but these profits earned by the state enterprises could be used to supplement, in one form or another, by social benefits or by direct supplements to wages, the low incomes that workers would otherwise receive from the plants in which they were employed.

But in a community in which one class owned the land and capital resources and another class provided the labour conflict of interest might be very acute. If by trade-union action, by governmental wage regulation or by custom the real wage-rate is kept up to provide a decent income to the worker, unemployment may result, in which case there may be acute tension between the workers as to who should get the work and who the unemployment. If the real wage is reduced, employment and output may be increased but the disparity between the poor worker and the rich owner may be much magnified. For these reasons social conflict may be especially acute in an overpopulated country.

So much for a simple catalogue of the evils which may result from having too dense a population. There are also certain evils which may result from having a rapid rate of increase of population, whether the existing density is already great or small.

In the first place, to prevent a fall in the standard of living a growing population must be equipped with its complement of real capital goods – with the tools, machinery and plant required to employ it in industry and agriculture, with the housing needed for the additional families, and with the hospital beds, school places and other public services required for the care of the additional young, old and sick persons. Such capital equipment in the absence of foreign aid or borrowing can come only out of a community's savings; the citizens must devote part of their incomes and resources to building new factories, etc., to serve the new population instead of to the production of goods and services for their own immediate consumption or for the raising of their own future standards of capital equipment. In any community the value of the stock of real capital equipment may be three or four times the value of the annual production of the community. It follows that if the population is growing at 3% per annum some 9–12% of the national income must be saved, not in order to raise the standard of capital equipment for each existing citizen, but in order to equip each additional citizen on the existing standard.[1] The higher the rate of population growth, the greater must be the cut into present standards of living in order to prevent a fall in future standards of living.

A second disadvantage of a rapid rate of rise of population is that it is likely to be associated with a high ratio of dependents to workers in the economy. Consider two countries which we will call Fertilia and Sterilia. In both of them specific mortality rates have been reduced to the same low norms which are quickly being spread by medical knowledge around

---

[1] Suppose the capital stock of a country to be worth £4,000 million and the annual income to be £1,000 million. Suppose the population to be growing by 3 per cent per annum. To achieve a concomitant 3 per cent increase of a capital stock of 4,000 one needs an addition of 120 units to the capital stock. But to save 120 units out of an income of 1,000 one must save 12 per cent of one's income.

the world. In Sterilia fertility rates have fallen in like manner, and the population is stationary or rising only slowly. In Fertilia fertility rates have remained much higher and the population is growing rapidly. In time, if its specific fertility and mortality rates remain constant, each country will settle down to a constant rate of growth (let us say ½% per annum in Sterilia and 3% per annum in Fertilia). Each after a time will also have a stable age distribution; but Fertilia will have a much younger age distribution than Sterilia. In both countries the number of citizens aged, say, 31 will be less than the number aged 30 for two reasons: first, because the 31-year-olds will have been subject to one more year's mortality than the 30-year-olds and second because the 31-year-olds will be the survivors of babies born 31 years ago, while the 30-year-olds are the survivors of babies born only 30 years ago, and in a growing population the number of babies born 31 years ago will be less than those born 30 years ago. Since in Fertilia the number of babies born is rising by 3% per annum and in Sterilia it is rising only by ½% per annum, the 31-year-olds will bear a smaller ratio to the 30-year-olds in Fertilia than in Sterilia. In this sense Fertilia will have a younger population than Sterilia; at any one point of time all up the age scale the ratio of older to younger persons will be smaller in Fertilia than in Sterilia. This means that the ratio of children to persons of working age will be higher in Fertilia than in Sterilia, while the ratio of old-age retired persons to persons of working age will be lower in Fertilia than in Sterilia. Now it so happens that in human populations mortality rates and the ages at which people start and end their working lives are such that the child population is normally a good deal larger than the population of retired persons. A higher ratio of dependent children to workers is more important than a lower ratio of dependent old-age persons to workers, so that Fertilia will have a higher ratio of dependents of all ages to persons of working age than will Sterilia. Moreover, a large number of children in the family makes it more difficult for women to go out to work so that the ratio of persons of working age available for work outside the home in industry, agriculture, or other occupations will also be less in Fertilia than in Sterilia. Thus there is a double reason why the ratio of mouths-to-be-fed to hands-to-do-the-work will be higher in Fertilia than in Sterilia.

This higher ratio of dependents to available workers in Fertilia will tend to reduce standards of living in Fertilia, and this in itself will tend to make it more difficult to save in Fertilia; but as we have just seen a larger volume of savings will be needed in Fertilia merely to maintain the existing standard of equipment per head. It is difficult enough in a poor country, where each worker has many mouths to feed and bodies to clothe, to save 5% of the national income; but, as we have seen, a savings ratio of some 10% may be needed simply to maintain existing standards of equipment for the growing population.

One must, however, be careful in considering this burden of dependency in Fertilia; and one should perhaps distinguish between two countries: on the one hand, Fertilia Densa, where not only is the population growing rapidly and the ratio of dependents to workers is high, but also the existing pressure of numbers on resources of land and capital equipment is already very heavy, and on the other hand, Fertilia Sparsa, where growth is also rapid and the dependency ratio is also high, but the existing population is still low relatively to the existing resources of capital and land. In Fertilia Densa, as we have already seen, there may well be unemployment of labour because there are not enough resources of land and capital to give employment to the available labour at an acceptable wage-rate. In this case to have one less child and one more worker in Fertilia Densa would not help; there might well be only one more unemployed, and therefore dependent adult, instead of one dependent child. In Fertilia Sparsa, however, where labour is scarce relatively to other resources, there can be full employment of labour at an acceptable wage, and to have one less child and one more worker would mean that more could be produced without any greater number of mouths to be fed; and thus a lower *ratio* of dependents to workers would enable the standard of living to be raised. In Fertilia Densa it is too great a total population and too rapid a rate of growth of population rather than too high a ratio of dependents to workers which holds down the standard of living at a very low level. In Fertilia Sparsa it is too high a dependency ratio and too rapid a rate of growth of population rather than too great a population which prevents the standard of living from being as high as it might otherwise be; indeed, it is possible in Fertilia Sparsa that because of increasing returns to scale a large population might *ultimately* help to raise the standard of living.

Finally, there is a third possible disadvantage of a rapid rate of growth of population, namely, the need for a rapid change in the structure of industry. Consider a community in which the population is growing at 3% per annum. If it manages to save 10–12% of its income it can equip each additional citizen with the same equipment as the existing citizens. This is admittedly a burden. But if this burden can be faced, is it not possible to envisage a 3% growth of every element of the existing economy – a 3% growth of schools and school teachers, a 3% growth of hospitals and doctors, a 3% growth of each industry and each occupation? Why should the industrial or occupational structure be changed? Cannot all sectors of the economy grow in their existing ratios at 3% per annum? Alas, this is impossible for two closely interrelated reasons: one connected with the existence of land and other natural resources which are fixed in amount and refuse to join in the harmonious 3% growth, and the other connected with the existence of foreign trade.

Since land and other natural resources are fixed in amount, a 3% per annum growth of population means that, if full employment and standards of living are to be maintained, there must be a shift in the economy away from lines of production and away from methods of production which use a high ratio of land and other natural resources to men and man-made capital resources on to lines of production and on to methods of production which use lower ratios of land and other natural resources to men and man-made capital resources. This necessarily involves learning new techniques, finding entrepreneurs who will run the risks of trying out new lines of production, and in general encouraging a society which will face a rapid change of industrial structure. And the more rapid the rate of population growth, the more rapid are the structural changes in industry and society which must be faced, and indeed somehow promoted, if unemployment and falling standards of living are to be avoided.

A similar need for rapid change in the structure of industrial activities may arise from international trade. Consider the trade between Fertilia and Sterilia. Suppose them to have the same rate of technical progress due to the inventiveness of their scientists, and the same willingness and ability to accumulate capital. Suppose, moreover, that in both countries land and natural resources are abundant. If the rates of population growth were also the same in both countries, then one might expect both economies to expand at the same rate. But in Fertilia the rate of population growth is higher than in Sterilia; and if by one means or another Fertilia manages to avoid growing unemployment the total national output and national income will be expanding more rapidly in Fertilia than in Sterilia, let us say at 4% per annum in Fertilia and at 2% per annum in Sterilia. But in general the demand for imports depends upon total income, and not merely on income per head; it is raised not only by a rise in the standard of living per head but also by a rise in the number of heads. We may expect Fertilia's demand for imports from Sterilia to be growing at 4% per annum, but Sterilia's demand for Fertilia's products to be growing only at 2% per annum. Fertilia is in for a balance-of-payments crisis which can be solved only by a structural change in her economy. She must shift resources into industries which produce for herself some goods of the kind which she would otherwise have imported from Sterilia, or she must develop new export industries so that she can expand her export sales to Sterilia at 4% per annum, even though Sterilia's total purchasing power is growing only at 2% per annum. And the more rapid is the excess of Fertilia's growth rate over that of Sterilia, the more quickly must Fertilia shift the structure of her industries if she is to avoid a balance-of-payments crisis and to maintain full employment of her labour force.

Such, then, is our general catalogue of problems. A heavy pressure of population on resources will depress output per head, and so the standard of living, and, particularly in a community in which property-owners and workers are sharply divided classes, it may lead also to unemployment and/or to great inequalities of income. Moreover, a rapid rate of growth of population will require a high level of savings (and so *pro tanto* a low level of consumption) to equip with capital the additional citizens; it will mean that there is a large ratio of dependents to workers; and it will necessitate rapid structural changes in industry, agriculture and other economic walks of life.

I now intend to illustrate these very big and general issues by the very small and particular example of the island of Mauritius.[2]

---

[2] The economic, demographic and sociological problems of Mauritius are fully discussed in three reports: J. E. Meade and others, *The Economic and Social Structure of Mauritius* (London: Methuen, 1961); R. M. Titmuss and B. Abel-Smith, *Social Policies and Population Growth in Mauritius* (London: Methuen, 1961); B. Benedict, *Indians in a Plural Society* (London: HMSO, 1962).

Let me start with a description of the Mauritian background. Mauritius is a small tropical island about the size of the county of Surrey in the Indian Ocean lying East of the island of Madagascar. It is more highly concentrated on one crop – namely sugar – than any other territory in the world. Some 98% of its exports are sugar, and sugar production accounts for 35% of its total domestic production of all goods and services. Since the Second World War it has been the scene of a classic population explosion. The island was discovered in the sixteenth century by the Portuguese; but it was first settled by the Dutch in the seventeenth century, who named it after their Prince Maurice. After the extinction of the Dodo the Dutch settlement was abandoned; and the island was first permanently settled and developed by the French in the eighteenth century, who started the cultivation of sugar and imported African and Malagassy slaves to work the estates. The island was acquired by the British during the Napoleonic Wars. The French language, French law and the Catholic religion remained; and they remain still as marks of what I will call the 'top-dog' culture in the island. On the abolition of slavery in the nineteenth century the African and Malagassy slaves deserted the sugar plantations and were replaced by indentured labour brought in from India. The result is a remarkable admixture of races, religions, languages and cultures.

At present about 5% of the population is true Franco-Mauritian. This includes the majority of the extremely rich owners of the large sugar estates; it includes also many professional men – lawyers, doctors, architects and so on. They speak French, are Catholic in religion, and conservative in much of their social, political and economic outlook. About 25% of the population is Creole. This group includes the descendants of the African and Malagassy slaves and the offspring of unions between them and the French. They are mainly Catholic in religion, and they provide many of the artisans and of the minor government servants. They speak Creole, which is a debased French patois – a sort of 'pidgin French'. About 66% of the population are Indian, mainly but by no means wholly Hindu, the offspring of the indentured labour. They still provide the main labour force on the sugar estates. This Indian population includes a substantial Moslem community (comprising 16% of the total population) which contains a few really wealthy merchants engaged in the import trade. Some 4% of the population are Chinese, who are enterprising, frugal and prolific and who have more or less monopolised the retail trade in the island. Nought per cent (to the nearest percentage number) of the population are British, including, however, the Governor, the Financial Secretary and one English family of sugar estate owners.

At this point it may be useful to give a rather miscellaneous catalogue of certain features of the society which result from this history and this mixture of peoples, features which are relevant for a proper understanding of the effects of the present population explosion in Mauritius.

First, inequalities in the distribution of income and wealth are extreme in Mauritius. The contrast between the extremely wealthy Franco-Mauritian owners of the sugar estates and the poverty-stricken

Indian cane cutter is something quite unlike the present position in this country.

Second, there is the language problem. English is the language of Government, French is the 'top-dog' cultural language, Hindi and other oriental languages are spoken by many members of the population, while Creole – which is hopelessly inadequate for literary, commercial, governmental or learned purposes – is the only language which everyone in the island can in fact speak. Apart from anything else, this diversity of language enormously complicates the educational problem.

Third, the history of the island has led to an association in the mind of the underdog between manual work and slavery. Everyone seeks education, but education of a cultural rather than a technical kind. There is a high Mauritian entry with an appalling failure rate for the Cambridge School Certificate examination. To obtain a pass in order to qualify for a job as a government clerk is the ambition of every Indian cane cutter's son. One result of this attitude is that there has been a frightening neglect of technical education, which is only now being gradually made good.

Fourth, the Catholic religion, though the religion of a minority, is of great importance in Mauritius. It is the religion of the top-dogs and has had all the power and influence which that carries with it. It has in the past been a serious obstacle to an effective family planning policy.[3]

Fifth, political parties are now more or less concentrated round two groups. On the one side is an alliance between three parties, one of which is exclusively a Muslim party, one of which is for practical purposes entirely Indian and the third of which – the Mauritian Labour Party – is predominantly but not exclusively Indian. On the other side is the Parti Mauricien, which is Creole and Catholic and financed by the wealthy Franco-Mauritians. It is fearful of the domination of the island by the majority of Indians, who it is feared will job their nephews and cousins into the posts now held by Creoles. It now possesses for the first time an effective radical orator who can bring the crowds out on to the streets. Recently in the discussions about political independence for the island (which the Creoles and the Franco-Mauritians fear as meaning their surrender to the Indian majority) there were disturbances which led to the sending of a small body of British troops to the island to maintain order.

Sixth, in Mauritius 'Sugar is King'. Sugar is planted by everyone from the owners of the large sugar estates down to the individual Indian who

---

[3] The Catholics in Mauritius are, however, now very conscious of the need for family planning; and there has recently been set up a very efficient organisation (Action Familiale) for promoting the rhythm method of family planning. This organisation is predominantly Franco-Mauritian and Creole in its leadership. Side by side with it is an active and much older Family Planning Association advocating all methods of family planning and run predominantly by the Indian community. Co-operation between these two organisations is difficult. Many Indians are suspicious that Action Familiale is a means whereby the minority French community is attempting to extend its influence into the Indian home; and there are, alas, some members in all the communities who feel that they should avoid too radical a control of their own numbers lest they should lose the contest for numbers and so for voting power to other races who control their numbers less effectively.

tends a few canes in, as it were, his backyard. This is partly because the market for sugar is so highly organised. There are a small number of large sugar estates which not only grow sugar but also possess factories which extract sugar from the cane. Everyone else who chooses to plant sugar is free to do so, but must take his canes to the factory-estate in his district; and that factory-estate is under an obligation to accept any canes so delivered to it. The resulting sugar is sold through a central agency, a large part at a stable price guaranteed to the Mauritians by the United Kingdom under the Commonwealth Sugar Agreement. There are elaborate rules to determine the proportion of the proceeds of the sugar sales which must be passed back by the factory-estate to each planter who has delivered canes to that factory. On the determination of this payment there is continual bickering, which is basically one between rich Franco-Mauritian owners of sugar factory-estates and smaller Indian planters. The result is nevertheless that the return on sugar is much more stable and secure for the individual planter than it is on any other agricultural or industrial product. This contrast is increased by the existence of an effective scheme for insurance against loss from drought and cyclone, which covers sugar but not other products. But the devotion to sugar is not only based on such rational economic calculus; it is partly irrational. The Franco-Mauritians have until recently tended to fight shy of other agricultural or industrial activities, and the rest of Mauritius has followed this lead. This attitude has seriously impeded the development of other lines of production.

Seventh, racial differences in Mauritius themselves present an important obstacle to economic development. It is difficult to conceive, for example, of a rich Franco-Mauritian putting money into a business conceived by an enterprising Chinese who relies on an English engineer for technical operation and upon an Indian for the daily management of the concern. A Mauritian business in its ownership and top management is almost invariably exclusively either Franco-Mauritian or Indian or Chinese. This introduces an element of inflexibility which is peculiarly disadvantageous to development in a small economy. To confine each business jig-saw to the pieces that can be fitted together within a single racial group of limited size artificially increases the difficulty of building new concerns.

This, then, is the sort of society into which the British have since the end of the Second World War introduced two new major features.

First, there has been a marked movement towards democratic self-government and independence – one-man, one-vote, more power to the elected members of the Legislative Council, discussion of and now decisions on a new constitution for an independent, democratic, self-governing Mauritius – with all the strains which this must in any case bring in such a multi-racial community.

But, secondly, the British at the close of the Second World War eliminated malaria and introduced other measures of preventive medicine with dramatic effects upon the growth of the population. It is the combination of these two simultaneous events which has caused such a potentially tense situation in the island.

Table I    *Population (thousands), birth-rates and death-rates (per thousand) in Mauritius*

|  | Total population | Birth-rate | Death-rate | Rate of natural increase |
|---|---|---|---|---|
| 1931–35 * | 401 | 31·1 | 29·6 | 1·5 |
| 1944–48 * | 429 | 41·5 | 27·2 | 14·3 |
| 1949–53 * | 484 | 47·4 | 15·2 | 32·2 |
| 1954–58 * | 575 | 41·6 | 12·9 | 28·7 |
| 1960 | 645 | 39·3 | 11·2 | 28·1 |
| 1961 | 662 | 39·4 | 9·8 | 29·6 |
| 1962 | 682 | 38·5 | 9·3 | 29·2 |
| 1963 | 701 | 39·9 | 9·6 | 30·3 |
| 1964 | 722 | 38·1 | 8·6 | 29·5 |
| 1965 | 741 | 35·5 | 8·6 | 26·9 |
| 1966 | 759 | 36·0 † | 8·9 † | 27·1 † |

* Average.
† Estimated on basis of first eight months of 1966.

The main demographic effects of these measures of preventive medicine are shown in Table I. As compared with the pre-war situation the crude birth-rate has risen somewhat to nearly 40 per thousand, the crude death-rate has been reduced from 30 per thousand to under 10 per thousand, with the result that the population which was practically stationary pre-war is now rising by nearly 3% per annum. Table II shows the effect of this population explosion upon the age distribution in Mauritius. The fall in infant mortality combined with no fall (indeed, with some slight increase) in fertility has had the familiar effect of greatly raising the proportion of young children to adults in the population. As a result, the proportion of the population which is of working age has fallen from 62% in 1944 to 51% in 1962, as compared with a proportion of about 66 per cent in the typical European country. Each worker in Mauritius has markedly more dependents to support than has the British worker.

The outlook for the future growth of numbers in Mauritius is illustrated

Table II    *Population of Mauritius – percentage distribution by age groups*

|  | Mauritius | | | European countries c. 1950 |
|---|---|---|---|---|
|  | *1944* | *1952* | *1962* |  |
| Under 15 | 35 | 40 | 46 | 25 |
| 15–64 | 62 | 57 | 51 | 66 |
| 65 and over | 3 | 3 | 3 | 9 |
| Total | 100 | 100 | 100 | 100 |

Table III    *Population of Mauritius – projections of numbers in age groups (thousands)*

|  | Actual 1962 | Projection A 1977 | Projection A 1987 | Projection B 1977 | Projection B 1987 |
|---|---|---|---|---|---|
| Under 15 | 313 | 514 | 776 | 356 | 385 |
| 15–64 | 351 | 579 | 813 | 579 | 757 |
| 65 and over | 22 | 37 | 51 | 37 | 51 |
| Total | 686 | 1,130 | 1,640 | 972 | 1,193 |

*Source:* Edith Adams, *Evaluation of Demographic Data and Future Population Growth in Mauritius 1962–1987* (New York: United Nations, 1966).

by the projections shown in Table III. Both projections are based on the assumption of a decline of mortality at a 'normal' rate which implies an annual gain of about one-half year in life expectancy. But while Projection A assumes a continuation of the 1961–63 levels of fertility, Projection B is based on the assumption that fertility is rapidly reduced between 1966 and 1972 until a level is reached at which no child is born beyond the third child in each family. Three outstanding differences between the results of Projections A and B are to be observed:

1   Fifteen years after the base date (i.e. in 1977) the only difference between the two projections is, of course, in the number of children (356,000 in Projection B against 514,000 in Projection A). All the adults in 1977 were already born in 1962.

2   Twenty-five years after the base date (i.e. in 1987) there would be a very large difference indeed in the number of children (385,000 against 776,000), but still only a relatively small difference in the number of adults of working age (757,000 against 813,000).

3   But thereafter the Projection-B population falls rapidly behind the Projection-A population, since the lower fertility rates begin to be combined with a smaller number of women of child-bearing age. Indeed, by the end of the century the total population might be less than 1,300,000 on the favourable assumption about the future course of fertility as contrasted with over 3 million on the unfavourable assumption.[4]

As I shall point out later, Mauritius is a community in which there is already a high level of unemployment. For this reason we cannot simply say that this high dependency ratio is itself a cause of poverty in Mauritius. For if there were one less child and one more man of working age in Mauritius the national product would probably not be increased,

[4] The projections for 1977 and 1987 are taken from Edith Adams, *Evaluation of Demographic Data and Future Population Growth in Mauritius 1962–1987* (New York: United Nations, 1966). The projections for the end of the century are from Titmuss and Abel-Smith, *loc. cit.* The two sets of projections are broadly comparable, though the bases for them are not precisely the same.

merely the number of unemployed workers might rise. The advantage (see Table III) which Mauritius would gain in 1977 from being on a Projection-B rather than a Projection-A path would not be so much from having a higher *ratio* of adult workers to dependents as from having a smaller *absolute* number of consumers (namely 356,000 instead of 514,000 children). The gain would be very great indeed. The total population (972,000 instead of 1,130,000) would be 16% smaller, and if total national production were unchanged this would make Projection-B income per head so much the greater than Projection-A income per head.

The simple fact is that there would be fewer dependent children to absorb resources in food, clothing, education, etc. Particularly striking would be the saving of resources on education. Mauritius has in any case a peculiarly difficult and intractable educational problem due to racial, cultural, religious and – above all – linguistic problems. On top of this, in the four years 1955–59 the numbers in the primary schools rose by 50% owing to the combination of growth of numbers in the population and an attempt to provide primary education for all children. A rise in the number of children over a fifteen-year period (1962–77) by 14% (Projection-B) instead of by 64% (Projection-A) would make an enormous difference to the tractability of the educational problem.

In Mauritius there is already a heavy pressure of numbers upon existing resources of capital equipment, land and other natural resources. The density is 1,000 per square mile, which is very high for an agricultural, unindustrialised community. Other factors (such as the level of technical training, the ability, enterprise and character of the people, the climatic conditions and so on) are, of course, of great importance in determining a community's productivity, and so its real income per head. But in addition to these factors a high ratio of population to other economic resources is undoubtedly an important cause of a low output per head,

Table IV  *International comparisons of income and growth*

| | Value of output per head ($ US) 1962/63 | Annual percentage rate of growth 1954–62 in | | Wages, salaries and income from unincorporated enterprises as percentage of total output 1961/62 |
| --- | --- | --- | --- | --- |
| | | Total output | Output per head | |
| Mauritius | 281 | — | — | 72 |
| Tanganyika | 66 | — | — | — |
| India | 76 | 3·5 * | 1·4 * | — |
| Kenya | 82 | — | — | — |
| Turkey | 230 | 5·0 | 2·1 | — |
| Japan | 589 | 10·1 | 9·1 | 78 |
| UK | 1,361 | 2·7 | 2·1 | 83 |
| France | 1,406 | 4·9 | 3·7 | 89 |
| USA | 2,790 | 2·9 | 1·2 | 83 |

\* 1953–60.

and so of a low standard of living; and there is no doubt that this factor is already operative in Mauritius. The first column of Table IV shows how low real income per head is in Mauritius as compared with highly developed countries such as the United Kingdom, France and the United States, although Mauritian standards are still high as compared with the poorest countries, such as India and East Africa.

I have already argued that in a community such as Mauritius, where there is a sharp distinction between property-owners and workers, population pressure may be accompanied by either or both of two concomitant evils – unemployment and great inequalities of income. In Mauritius both these evils are in evidence, and the pressure of population undoubtedly impedes their removal. The last column of Table IV gives some indirect statistical evidence of what every visitor to Mauritius can observe – namely, the great inequality of distribution of income. In Mauritius some 72% of the national income accrues in wages or small business incomes (e.g. one-man retail shops), whereas in the developed countries the corresponding figure is over 80%.

As for unemployment, a recent official estimate[5] suggested that in 1965 there were already some 20,000 unemployed, that between 1965 and 1970 38,000 additional workers would enter the labour market and that on present policies over the same period 21,500 additional jobs might be found, so that in 1970 there would be 36,500 unemployed. Only two comments are needed on these figures. First, relatively to the size of the adult population, an unemployment figure in Mauritius of 20,000 would correspond to a figure of some 1,750,000 in the United Kingdom, as compared with the 400,000 or so to which we are now accustomed. The Mauritian figure is already one of 'mass unemployment'. Secondly, a rise from 20,000 to 36,500 in five years represents a compound rate of growth of 12.8% per annum – that is to say, more than four times the rate of population growth. There is no doubt that pressure of numbers on resources in Mauritius is already a cause of a very unequal distribution of income and of a serious unemployment problem and that these problems threaten to become even more acute.

Mauritius is indeed an outstandingly good illustration of the clash between the use of the wage-rate to encourage the use of the abundant factor labour and the use of the wage-rate to achieve social justice. There are many cases in Mauritius in which a low wage might have an effect in encouraging a more economic use of resources. Thus low wage-rates encourage: (1) the weeding of sugar plantations by hand rather than by imported herbicides; (2) the loading of the sugar on to ships by hand rather than by the use of expensive capital equipment at the docks at Port Louis; (3) the growing of labour-intensive tea on suitable land in place of land-intensive sugar; and (4) the development of labour-intensive manufactures such as textiles to compete with the similar products of similar population-pressure territories, such as Hong Kong. But a wage-rate which is low enough to make these activities worthwhile may lead to a quite unacceptable inequality in the distribution of income.

[5] W. A. Hopkin, *Policy for Economic Development in Mauritius*, Mauritius Legislative Assembly, Sessional Paper No. 6 of 1966.

In fact, between 1956 and 1964 the wage-rate in Mauritius has been doubled, although prices have risen very little. This is a marked case of the employment of the wage-rate to obtain social justice in spite of its discouraging effects upon economic efficiency. The development was a very natural one. The political process of extension of the franchise and of movements towards self-government, majority rule and independence in Mauritius, combined with the 'wind of change' which is blowing throughout such communities, has made the underdog more aggressive in his claims. Trade unions and official wage boards have developed an upward thrust on wage-rates. But there can be little doubt that, taken alone, this development frustrates the growth of employment and output in Mauritius.

Heavy population pressure must inevitably reduce real income per head below what it might otherwise be. That surely is bad enough in a community which is full of potential political conflict. But if in addition, in the absence of other remedies, it must lead either to unemployment (exacerbating the scramble for jobs between Indians and Creoles) or to even greater inequalities (stocking up still more the envy felt by the Indian and Creole underdog for the Franco-Mauritian top-dog), the outlook for peaceful development is poor.

It is essential, therefore, that Mauritius, like many other communities of this kind, should find social institutions and economic policies which will square this circle – that is to say, which will cause labour costs to be very low from the employers' point of view and yet cause the labourer's income to be reasonably high. There do exist devices which will have this effect, ranging from a radical socialisation of private property to less-radical 'welfare-state' measures, such as the taxation of high personal incomes to finance either subsidies on employment or the cost of living or social security benefits for workers. But I have written elsewhere[6] at length on this aspect of the Mauritian problem, and will not repeat myself here.

We turn now to the problems connected with the high rate of growth of population in Mauritius. Suppose (what will very probably be near the truth) that all elements in the population will be 50% larger in fifteen years' time than they are now, i.e. that there will be 50% more children, 50% more adults of working age, 50% more old persons and so on. The standard of living would be unchanged if everything went up by 50% with the population, i.e. 50% more output, 50% more exports, 50% more consumption, 50% more employment and – of course – 50% more unemployment. What problems would be involved in attaining the 50% increase in production to match the 50% increase in population?

First, the economy would need a 50% increase in its capital equipment in order to keep the increased population equally well equipped. Apart from borrowing from abroad or foreign aid, this means devoting some 10% or more of the Mauritian national income to savings for the purpose merely of maintaining existing standards of equipment.

Second, it would be desirable to expand the resources of land and other

---

[6] Chapter 20 above, pp. 375–88.

natural resources also by 50% to match the 50% increase in the population: but this is, of course, impossible. In order to increase output by 50% without a 50% increase in the amount of land, reliance must be placed on technical progress. In Mauritius sugar comprises so much the most important use of natural resources that the answer must be sought in the sugar industry. The main figures are shown in Table V. The salient

Table V   *Sugar industry in Mauritius*

|  | *Production, thousand metric tons* | *Area thousand arpents* | *Employment, thousand persons* | $\frac{P}{A}$ | $\frac{P}{E}$ | $\frac{E}{A}$ |
|---|---|---|---|---|---|---|
| 1928–46 * | 267 | 137 | — | 1·95 | — | — |
| 1947–51 * | 419 | 156 | 56·7 | 2·69 | 7·4 | 0·363 |
| 1952–56 * | 517 | 178 | 54·2 | 2·90 | 9·5 | 0·304 |
| 1957–59 * | 556 | 189 | 56·3 | 2·95 | 9·9 | 0·297 |
| 1960 | 236 † | 202 | 56·7 | — | — | 0·281 |
| 1961 | 553 | 201 | 60·7 | — | — | 0·303 |
| 1962 | 533 † | 205 | 60·8 | — | — | 0·297 |
| 1963 | 686 | 204 | (60·1) | 3·36 | (11·3) | (0·296) |
| 1964 | 519 † | 207 | (63·7) | — | — | (0·306) |

* Average.
  † Production seriously reduced by cyclone damage.

features are that the output of sugar has risen rapidly in the past (column 1); that there has been some increase in the amount of land available for sugar production (column 2) due partly to the absorption of underused land into use and partly to the very expensive clearance of volcanic rocks from land which previously was unusable – processes which sooner or later must come to an end; that there has been little increase in the amount of employment in the sugar industry (column 3); but that the main increase in output has been due (column 4) to increased output per acre (P/A) and increased output per head (P/E), employment per acre (E/A) having remained stationary or actually fallen. In brief, we may be able to expect an increase even of 50% in the output of sugar over the next fifteen years; but if so, this will be achieved by increased productivity; and employment in the sugar industry is unlikely to rise appreciably.

Third, Mauritius produces sugar for export and exchanges it for imported supplies of food, clothing, raw materials, machinery, etc. It is not the quantity of Mauritian sugar exports that matters, but its value in terms of these other imported products. Even if Mauritius could increase the volume of her sugar exports by 50% *pari passu* with 50% increase in her population, could she sell this sugar on the same terms as at present so as to finance with the proceeds of her sugar exports a 50% increase in the volume of her imports? The answer is probably No. At present Mauritius sells some 60% of her sugar exports to the United Kingdom under the Commonwealth Sugar Agreement at a price (the 'negotiated price') fixed in advance, which is normally much more favourable than the 'world price' for sugar at which the rest of the Mauritian output must be sold. There is no prospect that the United Kingdom (unless there is a radical change in her policy of protection for domestic sugar beet) will radically increase the amount of sugar which she will import at the favourable price. Her total sugar imports are very stagnant, having averaged 2.18 million tons a year in 1960–64 as compared with 2.2 million tons a year in 1935–38. The United Kingdom market for Mauritian sugar is most unlikely to expand by 50% in fifteen years. In this case if Mauritius is to attain a 50% increase in her real supplies of the sort of products which she now imports she would have to produce other products for export or produce domestically for herself goods of the kind which she now imports.[7]

But export expansion and/or import substitution mean making things at home in face of foreign competition. Either domestic wage-rates must be kept low, or domestic labour productivity must be raised, or imports must be restricted by tariffs and import licensing, or exports must be subsidised, or the foreign-exchange value of the Mauritian rupee must be depreciated. The solution of this balance-of-payments problem would in any case involve a development of new industries, and in particular of new labour-intensive industries. Very little industry other than sugar exists in Mauritius at the moment; and the initiation of the necessary structural change is thus particularly difficult, since there is so little existing experience on which to build. The necessary structural change involves learning the necessary new skills and finding enterprising risk-bearers and able managers who will try out the new lines of production. But Mauritian technical education is backward and tends to be despised. Outside sugar, to which there is a traditional devotion, enterprise and good management is sadly lacking in Mauritius; and the inflexibilities due to racial traditions and divisions impede the necessary combinations of finance, enterprise and management. The necessary

---

[7] If the Mauritian output of sugar should in the future become excessive for the available export markets the Mauritian Government might be tempted to introduce a licensing system within Mauritius which limited the quantity of sugar canes which each planter could produce. This might happen either because of the existence of a revived International Sugar Agreement by which the permitted quantity of sugar exports from Mauritius was limited in quantity or else because the world price received for the marginal quantities of Mauritian sugar was so low that it was considered expedient to restrict Mauritian exports so that the average return (from world price and Commonwealth Sugar Agreement Negotiated Price) was maintained at a more 'reasonable' level. This would, in my opinion, be a most undesirable development. Just as in the United Kingdom it is important nowadays to be born not with a silver spoon but with a licence to grow hops in one's mouth, so Mauritian society would be divided between the 'haves' and the 'have-nots' of licences to grow sugar. There are enough potential group conflicts in Mauritius without introducing this one, which in Mauritius would be a basic division into privileged and unprivileged. Those unfotunate persons in this country like myself who have not inherited a right to grow hops have a number of alternative occupations to turn to; but the unfortunate Mauritian who had no right to plant sugar canes would indeed be lost. If it ever became necessary to discourage sugar output in Mauritius this should be done by heavier taxation of sugar production, the proceeds from which could be used to subsidise new labour-intensive activities. A new potential source of social conflict between the 'haves' and the "have nots' of sugar licences should certainly be avoided.

pace of structural change will be very rapid for a rather conventional, multi-racial community such as Mauritius.

I have spoken of these problems in terms of matching a 50% increase in the Mauritian population with a 50% increase in real income, i.e. in terms only of preventing a fall in the standard of living. But even so, Mauritius would be still faced with two formidable problems.

First, the formidable effort of economic development so far outlined would do nothing to absorb the Mauritian unemployed. On the contrary, the large existing volume of unemployment in Mauritius would grow considerably, by 50% because we are assuming that all the demographic classes will be 50% greater and by something more because there is unlikely to be any significant expansion (certainly not a 50% expansion) of the labour force in the sugar industry.

Secondly, as can be seen from Table VI, in the developed countries real income per head is rising – by 2.1 per cent per annum in the United Kingdom, for example. The formidable effort so far outlined for Mauritius would thus not prevent the gap in real standards between herself and the rich countries from growing rather rapidly still greater. The Mauritian programme would have to be a good deal more ambitious to prevent the gap widening, to say nothing about beginning actually to close it.

The implication of these two problems is obvious. It would be desirable in Mauritius to achieve a still more rapid rate of growth of production over the next fifteen years in order to absorb some of the unemployed and to achieve some modest rise in standards of living. Any such more ambitious programme of development would merely intensify the problems which I have already examined. A higher proportion of current income would have to be saved to supply the additional capital equipment required; the threatened strain on the balance of payments would be increased; and the pace of structural change would have to be still quicker.

This last problem which I have illustrated from the experience of Mauritius – namely, the increasing gap between the standards of living in the rich and in the poor countries of the world – is of very great and very

Table VI    *Growth of income and of population – average annual percentage growth rates*

|  | *Developed countries* | *Less developed countries* |
|---|---|---|
| Total income | 4·4 | 4·0 |
| Population | 1·3 | 2·6 |
| Income per head | 3·1 | 1·5 |

*Source:* Ministry of Overseas Development, *Overseas Development – The Work of the New Ministry*, Cmnd 2736 (London: HMSO, 1965), p. 9.

general importance, as the figures in Table VI show. Total income is growing almost as quickly in the less developed as in the developed territories. But population is growing much more rapidly in the former than in the latter countries. Income per head is thus growing almost twice as rapidly for the rich as it is for the poorer citizens of the world. If the arguments of this paper are correct the rapid rate of growth of population is itself a major cause of the slow rate of growth of income per head in the less developed countries. If these trends continue in a world in which communications become easier and easier and citizens of one land become more and more aware of the way in which citizens of other lands are living, international envy and jealousy will grow. I am no sociologist and no expert on international relations; but may this not prove an important factor in causing international tension?

Apart from these possible dangers of social conflict between countries, there are two implications – one demographic and one economic – of this state of affairs to which, in conclusion, I would like to draw your attention.

First, if the world is made up of two populations, a poor one which is growing at a high rate and a rich one which is growing at a low rate, and if these two growth rates continue, then as the years pass by the former population will, of course, become a larger and larger proportion of the total. The ratio of the number of poverty-stricken people to the number of rich people in the world will grow larger and larger; and this is perhaps a cause for disquiet additional to the fact which I have already discussed that the ratio of the standard of living of each individual poor citizen to that of each individual rich citizen will be falling.[8]

Second, there will be – and indeed there already are – important repercussions on world trade and financial relations. As the relatively poor population-explosion countries become and more and more densely populated they may well find it harder to produce all their own foodstuffs and may have to rely more and more on foreign aid and the export of labour-intensive manufactures not only to finance the import of the elaborate capital goods needed for their economic development but also to finance the import of their foodstuffs, which may well come to be increasingly produced in the prosperous less densely populated countries. Already this is happening. Before the Second World War there were five important areas of the world which were net exporters of grains – North America, Latin America, East Europe and the USSR, Asia and Australia – exporting a total of some 24,000 metric tons a year. In 1965/66 there were only two such areas – Australia, with an export of 7,000, and North America, with an export of no less than 60,000 metric tons. In North America both Canada and the United States are important exporters; but only the United States could readily further expand its output. In 1964 one-fifth of the total United States crop was given in aid to India, and this represented about 5 per cent of India's total consumption

---

[8] Divergences of growth rates of the kind mentioned above mean that the growth rate of the total world population will tend to rise. The growth rate of the total is some weighted average (at present 1.7) of the 2.6 per cent per annum of the less developed, and the 1.3 per cent per annum of the more developed countries. But as the former population becomes larger relatively to the latter, the growth rate of the world's population will tend to rise from 1.7 to 2.6 per cent per annum. The demographic figures for the world's population are already revealing this effect; and even if fertility rates are quite considerably reduced in the poorer countries, the growth rate of the world's total population may still rise rather than decline.

of food grains. This year India's requirements of aid in grains from the United States may represent some 15 per cent of India's total consumption. North American wheat is now being sold both to the USSR and to China. Is it desirable that the North American continent should be feeding the rest of the world? Will the Americans reverse the whole of their existing domestic agricultural policies, which are designed to limit output, in order to meet by unrequited gifts the needs of increased populations in the rest of the world? Will the Americans and the other developed countries be ready to expand their aid to the necessary extent? Will they lower their duties and other import barriers on such imports as cheap cotton textiles sufficiently to enable the Indias of this world to pay for their food – quite apart from their need for capital goods?

How much easier we could feel about the future of international relations if these questions did not arise.

# Index

T - #0002 - 230425 - C0 - 234/156/26 [28] - CB - 9780415350518 - Gloss Lamination